The Middle East

NEWS IN PRINT SERIES

The Middle East: Issues and Events of 1978
from The New York Times Information Bank

Focus on Health: Issues and Events of 1978
from The New York Times Information Bank

Key Issues: Issues and Events of 1978
from The New York Times Information Bank

The Middle East

Issues and events of 1978
from 𝕿𝖍𝖊 𝕹𝖊𝖜 𝖄𝖔𝖗𝖐 𝕿𝖎𝖒𝖊𝖘 Information Bank

Edited by David Chaffetz

Arno Press Inc.
A New York Times Company
New York, 1980

UPSALA COLLEGE LIBRARY
WIRTHS CAMPUS

DS
63.1
.N5
1980

Copyright © 1978 by The New York Times Company
Copyright © 1980 by Arno Press Inc.
All rights reserved

Published by Arno Press Inc., A New York Times Company
Three Park Avenue, New York, N.Y. 10016

Editorial supervision: Mitchell Rapoport, Janet Byrne
Book design by David Rollert

Library of Congress Cataloging in Publication Data
New York Times Information Bank(Firm)
   The Middle East.
   (News in print)
   Bibliography: p.
   Includes Index.
   SUMMARY: Abstracts from major newspapers
and magazines, topically and chronologically
arranged, deal with the leading issues and events
of 1978 that occurred in the Middle East.
   1. Near East—Politics and government—
1978—Abstracts. [1. Near East—Politics
and government—1978—Abstracts]
I. Title. II. Series.
DS63.1.N5 1979   956'.046   78-32140
ISBN 0-405-12875-4

Manufactured in the United States of America

Contents

Preface

This volume of news summaries on events in the Middle East during 1978 is the third title in the News in Print Series, a current affairs reference service that makes accessible in conventional reference book form a wealth of information mainly derived from an unconventional information source, The Information Bank.®

News in Print summarizes a vast amount of periodical and newspaper literature, arranges it in a logical manner, provides subject access to it, and significantly reduces the time and effort of the research process.

The Information Bank

The Information Bank is an on-line computerized bibliographic information retrieval system, operated by The New York Times Company and used by subscribing companies, government agencies, libraries and research institutions in the United States, Europe and Japan. Stored in The Information Bank's memory are more than 1,500,000 paragraph-sized abstracts (summaries) of published articles and analyses from the 63 newspapers and magazines of international significance listed on page xii of this book. Each year more than 160,000 abstracts are added to The Information Bank.

News in Print

The content of News in Print derives mainly from The Information Bank. The student, teacher, librarian or researcher may use it as an annotated index to the events and issues that are the subject of each single-topic chapter. The introductory essays and the full-text articles provide a background for and perspectives of the topic. Abstracts within a chapter are presented in chronological order to facilitate tracing the origin, development and consequences of an issue. A bibliography and index complete each volume.

News in Print was not designed to replace the sources it abstracts, but, rather, to enable more efficient use of them by eliminating the hours ordinarily required to identify, collect and order facts and themes for a research project.

Organization of
The Middle East

Each chapter in this book is devoted to a single issue as indicated in the table of contents.

Essay

At the beginning of each chapter is an essay, written by the volume editor, which summarizes the issues and events detailed in the abstracts that follow and provides a background that sets the episode in context.

Abstracts

In each chapter there are between 75 and 100 abstracts, selected from The Information Bank. Each abstract is clearly identified by a caption (headline) and concludes with full bibliographic information. Abstracts summarize both narrative accounts and analyses of a given issue in 1978. (For further discussion of abstracts, see What Is an Abstract on page ix.)

Reprinted Full-Text Articles

At the end of each chapter, there is a selection of full-text articles, reprinted from the *New York Times*. These articles were chosen either for archival value or for the special insight or detail presented.

Bibliography

At the back of the volume is a bibliography of approximately 2,500 newspaper and magazine articles and books on Middle East subjects, including all articles abstracted in this volume. The bibliography is arranged by chapter and chapter subdivision with the publication sources listed alphabetically.

Index

An index of subjects and names found in the abstracts and full-text reprints completes the book.

What Is an Abstract

Elements of an Abstract

Below is a sample of an abstract, with the key elements of headline, abstract text and bibliographic citation indicated.

Headline

PRIME MINISTER SHARIF-EMAMI RESIGNS

Abstract text

Iranian Prime Minister Jaafar Sharif-Emami, 69, appointed August 27 as part of Shah Mohammad Reza Pahlavi's effort to stem Moslem opposition to his rule, resigns after anti-Shah demonstrators rampage through streets of Teheran; resignation is not unexpected, but this is no indication whether it has been accepted by Shah, whose efforts to form provisional government that includes opposition figures are again rebuffed; Shah is expected to name new government with military men in key posts; orders armed forces to restore order as rioters set fire to British embassy and other buildings

Bibliographic citation

(NEW YORK TIMES, November 6, 1978, P1)

The Headline

The first element in an abstract is its headline. The headline quickly summarizes the abstract and, hence, the corresponding original article. Headlines were written by the editor of this volume and may differ from the headlines or titles of the corresponding original articles.

The Abstract Text

The second element of an abstract is its text. An abstract conveys in as few words as possible the essential information supplied by the original article. It contains all of the current developments reported in a news story and the main points of an analysis. Omitted is the recapitulation of past events—a major portion of most news articles and commentaries—since each significant development along the way is summarized by an abstract of its own. Every abstract is, of course, a reduction of material that is considerably longer than the abstract itself. Just as there are discrepancies of facts between articles, there are occasional discrepancies of fact between abstracts.

Writing Style of the Text

The text of an abstract in this volume is composed of short declarative "sentences" (separated by semicolons) with the theme or focus indicated in the first two lines. When two or more sequential sentences share the same subject, the subject is usually dropped from the second sentence rather than restated. Articles (*a, an* and *the*) are often omitted for a brisker reading. In passive sentences, the verb "to be" is often eliminated. Like the article from which it derives, an abstract is generally written in present tense.

Author

Some abstracts identify the author of the article by such terms as "commentator," "byliner" or "columnist." These reflect an opinion or particular perspective of the incident being reported. The names of reporters of non-analytic or narrative news accounts are not indicated.

The Bibliographic Citation

The third and final element of an abstract is its bibliographic citation. This includes the name of the newspaper or magazine from which the abstract derives; the month, day and year of publication; the section (S) number (when applicable); and beginning page (P) number.

Some newspapers are divided into sections, each of which starts with page 1. To identify *which* page 1 an abstract refers to, section numbers are included (when applicable) in the bibliographic citations. These section numbers correspond to the numbers *or* letters assigned to sections by the newspaper; S4 then, denotes either Section 4 or Section D, depending on the system a newspaper uses. If an article appears in the first section, no section reference appears in the bibliographic citation. Similarly, no section is noted if a newspaper contains only one section. Since magazines are all in one section, there is no section reference in the bibliographic citation for periodicals.

New York Times Citation

Sections 11, 21, 22 and 23 of the *New York Times* are regional supplements included only in Sunday editions distributed to limited parts of the New York metropolitan area, but all four supplements are included in the *New York Times* on microfilm.

Between August 10 and November 5, 1978, the *New York Times* suspended publication because of a strike by employees. Abstracts from this period ascribed to the *Times* come from reports carried either by the *New York Times* wire service or the Associated Press news service. The full text for each of these articles can be found in the *New York Times* on microfilm on the frame corresponding to the date and page cited at the end of the abstract.

The Process of Abstracting

How does the identification and compilation of a year's worth of news proceed? The process begins at The Information Bank. There a team of 12 editors scans more than 60 leading newspapers and magazines, choosing the most significant articles among them. Almost all stories appearing in the *New York Times* are included in The Information Bank; the coverage of other magazines and newspapers is selective. If there is a duplication of coverage between a *New York Times* article and another source's article, only the *Times* article is included. The *Times* maintains the most extensive international and domestic news-gathering operation among American newspapers and in this volume, especially regarding international coverage, there is a preponderance of *Times* articles.

After an article has been selected by the Information Bank editor, one of 40 indexer/abstracters summarizes its basic themes and facts into what is called an "abstract," and, working on a video display console (similar to a television screen) connected to a computer, writes the abstract. As it is typed, it appears on the screen. The abstract is next assigned as many as 25 index terms, corresponding to subjects, locations and names of organizations and persons. These terms become the access points by which Information Bank subscribers retrieve the abstracts they seek from the data base.

The indexer/abstracter checks the abstract and index terms assigned to it. The editor examines the indexer's work for accuracy, clarity and conciseness, makes any needed changes and then presses a button which admits the abstract into The Information Bank's memory to join the over one million abstracts similarly entered. Through the Bank's retrieval system, and, now, through News in Print, information contained in an original news story is permanently on file for quick and efficient research.

Guide to Use and Research

If you are researching one of the issues in this volume, it may be helpful to focus on one aspect of the issue. Then use the *index* to locate *abstracts* on these specific aspects of the issue.

After reading the abstracts within a chapter, you may wish (need) to read the full text of some articles for fuller, more detailed treatment. Copy the *bibliographic citations*, as described on page x in the section What Is an Abstract, on index cards. Arrange them by title of the periodical or newspaper. Then go to the *Bibliography*, which is arranged by issue, in the same order as the chapters, and look for other articles from that same periodical or newspaper titles that concern the issue but were not abstracted in this volume. Especially if you will be using microfilm, it will take only a little extra time to read other articles from that same year's title.

Use the Bibliography to identify articles from periodicals and newspapers that represent different political and geographical perspectives. The list of *Periodicals and Newspapers Included in News in Print* gives a fuller title citation than in the Bibliography, if you are unfamiliar with some titles. The Bibliography lists titles of magazines in alphabetical order so that all citations from one title will be together. Remember that the Bibliography also includes citations that are not in the abstracts or Index of this volume.

Many events and issues have associated with them significant primary documents, such as Supreme Court decisions and speeches. They are sometimes included as *full-text reprints* at the end of each chapter.

Book titles will also be found in the Bibliography. These titles were referred to (or cited in) a periodical or newspaper article.

If you are unfamiliar with how to obtain periodical and newspaper articles whose full text is not in this volume, read the section *Periodicals and Newspapers Included in News in Print* on page xii.

Periodicals and Newspapers Included in News in Print

How to Locate Full Texts of Abstracts and Other Articles Listed in the Bibliography

The following are suggestions for obtaining the full text for articles found in the abstracts and bibliography section of this book.

Go to the reference/information desk of your local school or public library and ask if there is a printed list of the library's periodical and newspaper holdings. Then you can see if the library subscribes to the magazine or newspaper you want and if the library retains a back file of it. You may be directed to a Periodical and Newspaper Room; non-current issues are often kept in a separate area.

Many periodicals and newspapers are available on microfilm. The "Holdings List" should indicate this. Microfilm is viewed on a microfilm reader. Your library may also have a microfilm reader/printer that will allow you to photocopy the article at a nominal cost.

If the library does not own the title, ask if there is a "Union List" for you area, which indicates the periodical holdings of a group of libraries. If you go first to your public library, ask if another branch or the central library might own it.

If you are still unable to locate it, go to a nearby university library. Most college libraries will allow the public to use their reference materials within the library without any charge and may even provide periodical holdings information over the telephone. If you do telephone first, ask for the "Serials" department, which is the librarian's technical word for periodicals. If none of the above results in locating the article, request the article from another library on "Inter-Library Loan." There may be a small fee for this service. You may be asked to locate a specific library that owns and either lends or will photocopy articles. There is a national directory of the periodical holdings of libraries called *The Union List of Serials* and *New Serial Titles*. These are found in large public and university libraries. After locating your periodical, note the nearest library that owns and lends its copies through inter-library loans.

*Abstracts appearing in News in Print volumes derive from the following periodicals and newspapers. The subscription address, which often differs from the editorial address, is provided beside each title, along with the frequency of publication. All publications are available on microform except those identified by an asterisk (*).*

Advertising Age; the national newspaper of marketing. 740 N. Rush Street, Chicago, IL 60611. Weekly

American Banker. 525 W. 42nd Street, New York, NY 10036. Daily

American Scholar; a quarterly for the independent thinker. United Chapters of Phi Beta Kappa, 1811 Q Street, NW, Washington, DC 20009. Quarterly

Astronautics and Aeronautics. 1290 Avenue of The Americas, New York, NY 10019. Monthly

Atlanta Constitution. 72 Marietta Street, Atlanta, GA 30303. Daily

Atlantic Monthly. Box 1857, Greenwich, CT 06830. Monthly

Atlas World Press Review. P.O. Box 2550, Boulder, CO 80302. Monthly

Automotive News; weekly newspaper of the industry. 965 E. Jefferson Avenue, Detroit, MI 48207. Weekly

Aviation Week and Space Technology. Box 503, Hightstown, NJ 08520. Weekly

Barron's National Finance and Business Weekly. 200 Burnett Road, Chicopee, MA 01021. Weekly

Black Scholar; journal of black studies and research. P.O. Box 908, Sausalito, CA 94965. Monthly

Bulletin of the Atomic Scientists; the magazine of science and public affairs. 1020-24 E. 58th Street, Chicago, IL 60637. Monthly

Business Week (Industrial Edition). Box 506, Hightstown, NJ 08520. Weekly

Chicago Tribune. Tribune Square, Chicago, IL 60611. Daily

Christian Science Monitor. 1 Norway Street, Boston, MA 02115. Daily

Commentary; journal of significant thought and opinion on contemporary issues. American Jewish Committee, 165 E. 56th Street, New York, NY 10022. Monthly

Consumer Reports. P.O. Box 1000, Orangeburg, NY 10962. Monthly

*Current Biography. 950 University Avenue, Bronx, NY 10452. Monthly

Economist (London). 75 Rockefeller Plaza, Room 2102, New York, NY 10019. Weekly

Editor and Publisher, the Fourth Estate. 575 Lexington Avenue, New York, NY 10022. Weekly

Edmonton Journal. 10006 101st Street, Edmonton, Alberta, T5J 2S6, Canada. Daily

Far Eastern Economic Review. P.O. Box 160, Hong Kong. Weekly

Financial Times (London). 75 Rockefeller Plaza, Room 2101, New York, NY 10019. Daily

Financial Times of Canada. 1885 Leslie Street, Don Mills, Ontario, M3B 3J4, Canada. Weekly

Forbes. 60 Fifth Avenue, New York, NY 10011. Bi-weekly

Foreign Affairs; an American quarterly review. Council on Foreign Relations, 58 E. 68th Street, New York, NY 10021. Quarterly

Foreign Policy. P.O. Box 984, Farmingdale, NY 11737. Quarterly

Fortune. 541 N. Fairbanks Court, Chicago, IL 60611. Monthly.

Harper's Magazine. 1255 Portland Place, Boulder, CO 80323. Monthly

Harvard Business Review. Harvard Graduate School of Business Administration, Soldiers Field, Boston, MA 02163. Bi-monthly

Houston Chronicle. 801 Texas Avenue, Houston, TX 77002. Daily

Industrial Research. 1301 S. Grove Avenue, Barrington, IL 60010. Monthly

Journal of Commerce. 110 Wall Street, New York, NY 10005. Daily

*Latin America Economic Report. 29-01 8th Street, NW, Washington, DC 20009. Weekly

*Latin America Political Report. 29-01 8th Street, NW, Washington, DC 20009. Weekly

Los Angeles Times. Times Mirror Square, Los Angeles, CA 90053. Daily

Manchester Guardian Weekly. 20 E. 53rd Street, New York, NY 10022. Weekly

Miami Herald. 1 Herald Plaza, Miami, FL 33132. Daily

*Middle East. 63 Long Acre, London WC2 (JH, England. Monthly

Nation. 333 Avenue of the Americas, New York, NY 10014. Weekly

National Journal; the weekly on politics and government. 1730 M Street, NW, Washington, DC 20036. Weekly

National Review; a journal of fact and opinion. 150 E. 35th Street, New York, NY 10016. Bi-weekly

New Republic; a journal of opinion. 1220 19th Street, NW, Washington, DC 20036. Weekly

New York Magazine. Box 2979, Boulder, CO 80302. Weekly

New York Review of Books. P.O. Box 940, Farmingdale, NY 11737. 22 issues yearly

New York Times. 229 W. 43rd Street, New York, NY 10036. Daily

New Yorker. 25 W. 43rd Street, New York, NY 10036. Weekly

Newsweek. Newsweek Building, Livingston, NJ 07039. Weekly

San Francisco Chronicle. 110 Mission Street, San Francisco, CA 94119. Daily

Saturday Review; a review of ideas, creative arts and human conditions. P.O. Box 10010, Des Moines, IA 50340. Bi-weekly

Science. 1515 Massachusetts Avenue, NW, Washington, DC 20005. Weekly

Scientific American. 415 Madison Avenue, New York, NY 10017. Monthly

Sports Illustrated. 541 N. Fairbanks Court, Chicago, IL 60611. Weekly

Time; the weekly newsmagazine. 541 N. Fairbanks Court, Chicago, IL 60611. Weekly

Times (London). 201 E. 42nd Street, New York, NY 10017. Daily

Toronto Star. 1 Yonge Street, Toronto, Ontario, M5E 1E6, Canada. Daily

U.S. News and World Report. P.O. Box 2629, Boulder, CO 80322. Weekly

Variety. 154 W. 46th Street, New York, NY 10036. Weekly

Village Voice. 643 Ryan Way, Marion, OH 43302. Weekly

Wall Street Journal. 22 Cortlandt Street, New York, NY 10007. Daily

Washington Monthly. 1028 Connecticut Avenue, NW, Washington, DC 20036. Monthly

Washington Post. 1515 L Street, NW, Washington, DC 20005. Daily

Women's Wear Daily; the retailer's daily newspaper. 7 E. 12th Street, New York, NY 10003. Daily

Introduction

During the 1970s a region of the globe long regarded by the West as peripheral has assumed major importance on the world scene. This region preoccupies the strategic consideration of the super powers, dictates economic policies to the industrial nations and leads an ideological confrontation of the have-not countries against the haves. The new role of the Middle East in Western perception is an anomaly that is difficult to explain. But to the peoples of the Middle East it is the centuries of life on the periphery of world events which seem anomalous. It is not the recent emergence of the Middle East that needs explaining, but the interim of colonial domination.

The Middle East considers itself the center of the world, a position once accorded to it in earlier Western traditions. The Ptolomaic schema of geography taught that the Middle East was the "Middle Climate" of the world. For the ancient Greeks as well as the crusading knights, the Middle East was the source of civilization, the home of the sciences, astronomy, astrology, codified laws and the art of government. Archaeologists confirm this traditional view of the Middle East, crediting the prehistoric inhabitants of the region with the discovery of cultivated grains, building with brick and domesticating animals. On stones in the Syrian desert one can still read the scratchings which prefigure every alphabet in the world. And although the names of the ancient civilizations of Babylon, Assyria, Petra and Palmyra were all forgotten in the Middle East before the advent of the archaeologist's spade, legends of the ancient kings and the huge barrows of tomb and temple served to remind the peoples of the Middle East of their long and rich past, confirming them in their self-centric view of the world.

Judaism, Mandaeism, Gnosticism, Manichaism, Christianity and Islam all flourished in this Middle Climate, endowing the region with relics of saints and places of pilgrimage. Islam is now the dominant religion, yet as an eclectic faith it venerates over 70 major prophets and enrolls in its own ranks the holy places and holy individuals of the ancient Middle East. Islam's most sacred city, Mecca, is said to be the site of Adam's first dwelling, rebuilt by Father Abraham under divine direction.

The land of prophets, patriarchs and holy mountains has undergone a traumatic confrontation with the West. From the eighteenth century onward the military might of Europe eroded the borders of the Middle East. One by one the sheikhs of the Persian Gulf, the Bey of Tunis, the Pasha of Egypt and the Sharif of Morocco either lost their thrones to the colonial powers or became puppets in a European protectorate. By 1923 there were only three sovereign Middle Eastern states—Turkey, Iran and the Kingdom of Najd (now Saudi Arabia). The experience under colonial administration varied with the nature of European rule: the French annexed Algeria directly into metropolitan France, without, however, extending citizenship to practicing Muslims. The British ruled the Persian Gulf states through discreet, almost invisible political agents. Egypt endured a military occupation, as the British made it the strategic base for their Middle East empire. Obvious or invisible, heavyhanded or subtle, the colonial administrations inevitably provoked nationalist opposition among their subjects. The mere presence of foreign troops, foreign flags, banks and agencies struck Middle Easterners as an affront to their own identity, their own talents and national traditions. A period of great economic hardship caused by World War II provided the mass dissatisfaction required to resist colonial rule. Massacres in Algeria in 1945 and bloody strikes in Egypt in 1951 signaled the beginning of the end of colonialism.

Since World War II, decolonialization has given rise to 18 new and unsteady sovereign entities. With the British withdrawal from the Persian Gulf in 1971 the UAE (United Arab Emirates) became the last European protectorate in the region to assume full independence. Although colonialism is thus a matter of history to the West, it is still recalled by the peoples of the Middle East. In a spirit of determination the Middle East has set on its path of development. Technological and social changes which an earlier, atavistic generation of Middle Easterners scorned now provide the unique chance to catch up with the industrial nations and wipe out the past humiliations of colonialism. The unanimity of the Middle East about the need for development is a striking fact. The last holdout against the tide of development and technology was Oman's sovereign Sultan Said ibn Taymur, whose vision of an orderly, traditional world excluded schools, hospitals or even exploitation of the Sultanate's oil revenues. His son Qabus seized power in a palace coup in 1970, leading Oman headlong into the race for development.

The rush to development in the Middle East has aroused uncertainty in the West. Iran or Saudi Arabia's ostensible bid for "super-power" status gives rise to concern for the balance of power, the stability of the world political order, based on the long pre-eminence of the Soviet Union, the United States, Europe and Japan. When radical, rhetorically strident regimes in Tripoli and Baghdad assert their intentions to obtain nuclear weapons, world peace seems to face an imminent danger.

The rhetoric in the Middle East is loud and the saber-rattling is disquieting, but in this part of the world words often have their own reality and leaders are given to voicing their wishful thinking aloud. Iraq's President Saddam al-Bakr, for example, declares "Iraq has oil reserves second to none in the world," while in fact the country's reserves are a fifth of Saudi Arabia's (US Department of Interior estimates). The asserted ambitions of the Iraqi government (they expect a 30% rise in industrial productivity in their current five year plan) contrast perhaps with easily obtainable objectives. For the country to reach the economic level of poorer European countries like Spain or Greece, let alone become highly industrialized as Iraq's leaders intend, the country will have to sustain an annual growth rate of 6% until the end of the century. To reach such a high rate of growth (cf. current USA rate of 4% a year) Iraq must seek the cooperation and support of the world community, that is, loans from international banks, technical cooperation from private Western enterprises and advisory expertise from groups like the UN. In short, the Middle East's orientation towards development is contingent on a process of cooperation and interdependence.

The road to parity with the West is a long one. Yet Middle Easterners have an advantage: resources of oil. The first Saudi monarch, Ibn Saud, did not question the providential nature of the region's oil in its struggle for self-assertion. "God provided us with oil in order to restore the faith." Saudi Oil Minister Sheikh Yamani is more sanguine. "Without oil," he has said, "the Middle East would be one of the poorest regions in the world." What oil means to the Middle East can be seen in figures which, though often cited, never seem to lose their impact. Iraq—whose development forecasts have been outlined—possesses estimated reserves of 30 billion barrels of oil. At 1978 prices those reserves are worth $381 billion, although the buying power of oil is sure to rise as world reserves are depleted. Iraq currently invests 50% of its oil revenue in development projects including irrigation schemes, industrial plants, communications and education. It expects to increase its gross national product (GNP) by one dollar for every three dollars of investment. With a projected investment of 200 billion, Iraq's GNP could jump from $17 billion a year to $80 billion before reserves are exhausted. Saudi Arabia, with estimated reserves of 129 billion barrels, has prospects all the more remarkable.

Unlike many regions in the developing world, the Middle East could benefit from increased population. This may seem confusing to the West, with its awareness of overpopulation in developing regions. Nevertheless several countries in the Middle East have a population lower than the optimum required to utilize natural resources, or lower than the population of earlier historical periods. Archaeologists have documented the much greater extent of habitation in the Middle East during ancient times, as compared with the present, while economists cite the growing shortage of labor both in the expanding petroleum industry and in the agricultural sectors of the region. Iran, for example, had a population estimated at 60 million in the sixteenth century. In 1978, with slightly smaller territory, Iran's some 35 million inhabitants have acres of wasteland to reclaim, forests to replant and waterways to excavate afresh. While one million families left the rural economy for the industrial sector in the period 1963–1978, Iran still imports Afghan, Baluch, Pakistani and Indian labor for its booming Persian Gulf ports and petroleum complexes.

While the population of the Middle East is currently below a theoretical optimum, nevertheless the short-term population growth poses a problem to regional economies. Economic growth (a rise in GNP) must at least equal the rate of population increase, in order to provide higher standards of living.

Before World War II the Middle East had an estimated 1.5% annual growth in population. In the postwar explosion in birth rates which occurred worldwide, Syria, Jordan and Iraq saw that prewar average rate more than double, while Egypt's surpassed four percent, among the highest in the world. Postwar economic growth in these same countries had a mixed record, rising in the fifties and slowing in the sixties. As a result, standards of living in the sixties steadily declined.

Egypt is the most sobering example of this reverse development. Having emerged successfully from an intensive land and water reclamation scheme in the nineteenth century, Egypt has been robbed of economic well-being by an explosive birth rate. Among both the masses of poor and the governing elite the spectre of population disaster seems unavoidably closer each year. Slim progress towards family planning has been made to avert disaster. But many observers feel that only as Egypt's population becomes intensively urbanized and industrialized will the country's population growth rates fall to levels which characterize developed countries.

Some Middle East countries have managed to avoid either stagnation or regression, yet their success has brought in its wake a host of pitfalls and problems. Dynamic economies, founded on transit trade, oil or communications have provided a number of selective "economic miracles," notably in Lebanon and Iran. Yet the facts of these economic miracles are not as tangible as the disorder which they have produced in their respective societies. A fractional percent increase in the GNP per capita is not in itself a guarantee against social unrest or even violence, as politicians of the Middle East have learned.

A typical vicious cycle of social unrest runs as follows: a government eager to spend excess revenues improves the capital city and subsidizes services for its inhabitants. Rural dwellers, attracted by the boom conditions in the city (and the prospect of employment in construction) uproot themselves from the countryside and immigrate. At first the subsidies hold out the promise of the "easy life"; the new immigrants receive certain concrete benefits in the urban setting, including access to education, water, electricity and medical care. Yet the urban slums of the poor lack the rich and human fabric of social life in the village. The new city dweller seeks to replace his loss of cultural and traditional life with material acquisitions. What seemed like an adequate living to a villager is now considered poverty by the urban consumer. The poor demand more services, straining the city's resources. The higher the subsidies go, however, the greater the influx of immigrants from the countryside. The vicious cycle of "rural flight" has left Cairo (population eight million) and Teheran (six million) bloated cities.

The masses of dissatified urban poor behave as a praetorian guard in the capital city, ready to resort to violence whenever the government moves to cut spending on consumers. They present a ready resource to radical politicians who promise to improve their lot, thus leading to a merry-go-round of regimes, each more radical and ambitious for social welfare than the next. The strongest regimes, with their security apparatus and their control of the armed forces, have had to give way to mob violence in the streets, as Iran's experience in 1978 has demonstrated. Iran's instability is only the most current expression of a pattern which has overthrown regimes in the Middle East at a high rate. Since 1958 there have been four coups d'etat in Pakistan, two in Afghanistan, eight in Iraq, four in Turkey, one in Lebanon, six in Syria, three in North Yemen and two in South Yemen.

The intense dissatisfaction of the masses of the poor in the Middle East is the background for understanding the political currents in the region. As a legacy of colonialism most of the new states inherited parliamentary legislative structure and an independent legal system rooted in the traditions of the Western democracies. These institutions did not long survive the storm of political crises that burst upon them. The establishment of the state of Israel in 1948, the Suez Canal crisis of 1956, along with the massive social changes of the postwar period affected and led to the abolition of political parties in Egypt (1953) and military rule in Syria (1948) and Iraq (1958). In the wake of revolution and coups d'etat, intellectuals and politicians in the Middle East sought a basis for a popular, nationalist ideology upon which to build their political institutions. For the most part they have eschewed communism, with its emphasis on class struggle and scientific (pious Muslims would say "atheistic") historicism. Instead they have put forward ideologies which emphasize the collegial, humanistic aspect of mankind. "There is no class struggle in Arab Socialism," declared Egyptian Gamal Abdul Nasser, outlining the founding principles of the Arab Socialist Union party. Michel Aflaq, leading theorist of the Baath party of Syria and Iraq, speaks of the idealistic aspirations of the Arab people and their traditions of consensus-oriented, communalistic society. They reject the European view of society as a nexus for conflict and competition, which they see at the heart of both liberal capitalism and communism. In this respect, the Middle East has been at the ideological forefront of the Third World's rejection of both Western and communist influences.

As stimulating and as promising as the political dialogue in the Middle East may be, its ideologies are still new and untried. They have not yet taken hold among the masses, nor have their theoreticians organized popular political parties in order to represent these views. As a result, the volatile urban masses are inarticulate and under-represented in the political process. A crisis of legitimacy plagues the regimes of the region, as the governing elites cannot be sure they are ruling in the name of the popular masses. The Shah of Iran fell victim to this failing in 1978, after ruling in an absolutist manner for 15 years, unwilling and unable to gauge popular opinion.

A further aspect of the crisis of legitimacy which underlies the instability of Middle East politics is the persistence of communal loyalties at odds with the framework of the nation-state. The terms "Arab" and "Muslim" themselves give rise to oversimplification. In this book "Arab" is used in a political sense, referring to those countries which belong to the Arab League. Among them are members like Somalia and Mauritania, whose Arabic-speaking communities are culturally dominant but in a minority. Elsewhere in the Middle East, Arabic-speaking groups have a specific identity which is often more influential in their political orientation. Such are the Druze of Lebanon, Syria and Israel, the Christian Copts of Egypt, the Shiites of Iraq and the Bedouin tribes of Sinai and Arabia. Beyond the "Arab States," in Iran and Afghanistan Persian-speaking elites overlie an ethnic and tribal patchwork of Kurds, Lurs, Turkmen, Uzbegs, Arabs, Mongols, Baluch, Pashtoons, in addition to smaller groups little known within the countries themselves. Pakistan's ethnic population is also heavily fragmented.

The effect of this patchwork has often been violent: Iraq underwent civil war (1960-1975) duing the Kurdish rebellion. Ethnic and religious sentiments moved Lebanon into a 1975 civil war which continued to smoulder in 1978. At the end of 1978 communal violence forced martial law on Turkey, a country whose ethnic tensions have been little studied until now. Syria, which has not yet experienced open communal conflict, is concerned that its volatile mixture of Orthodox Muslims, Heterodox Alwaites, Kurds, Greek Orthodox Christians and smaller tribal groups may erupt into civil war. The conflict between the Arabs and the Israelis tends to obscure the great ethnic diversity within the Arab world itself, although this conflict between two closely related faiths serves to underscore the nature of communal conflict elsewhere in the Middle East.

Internal instability, endemic in every Middle East state, gives rise inevitably to external aggression. Afghanistan, in the wake of its 1978 coup, resumed its aggressive verbal campaign against Pakistan. King Hassan of Morocco sought to unite national feeling behind him in his 1976 move into Spanish Sahara, an expansionist move in the opinions of his neighbors. While much aggressive activity in the Middle East remains verbal, time and again words have led to war.

The instability of the region has fueled an arms race. In 1978 Egypt spent over a billion dollars on defense, while servicing an undisclosed, crippling debt for Soviet equipment. Israel, Syria and Jordan each spends over 25% of their budgets on defense. Tensions in the Persian Gulf have cost Iran, Iraq, Saudi Arabia and the smaller states seven billion dollars. The arms race brings in its train renewed penetration of outside influences. Having expelled the British and French colonial powers in 20 years of struggle, the Middle East now faces the situation of inviting the foreigners back. They come not as viceroys and governor-generals but as "technical advisers," economists and sellers of arms. Opponents of Western influence in Iran claimed that the kingdom seemed as encumbered by foreign obligations in 1978 as it had under Russian-British condominium before World War I.

Symptomatic of the communal hostilities threatening the Middle East and the vital element in the region's instability is the 30-year-old Arab-Israeli conflict. The course of that conflict is, in many ways, the mirror of the history of the postwar Middle East. That the conflict remains unsettled in 1978 reflects the continuity of the basic regional problems discussed above. The increasing urgency with which leaders in the Middle East and abroad have sought a solution to the conflict reflects the new role of the Middle East in the world.

The story starts with two nationalisms, Zionist and Pan Arab. Zionism was the response of European Jewry to the breakdown of traditional communal barriers. The ghetto walls had preserved Jewish culture and community, which now had no defense against the mass, nationalist, popular culture of modern, industrial Europe. In order to preserve their continued existence as a unique and vital culture and to escape persecution, a movement began among European Jews to establish a homeland where the attributes of nation-state and sovereignty would provide for the survival of the Jews in an increasingly nation-oriented world. The spiritual aspiration of the Jews to return to the Holy Land (the Promised Land after 2000 years) became the practical focus of the Zionists. At the turn of the century Jewish settlement in Palestine was already of significant proportion.

The national movement of the Arabs runs parallel to that of the Zionists. The steamboat and telegraph ended the isolation of the Middle East and allowed European penetration into the region. European colonialization, with its attendant nationalist propaganda, threatened the values and institutions of the Middle Easterners. They turned first to a Pan-Islamic reaction, and by the end of the nineteenth century to a Pan-Arabic reaction which was more strictly comparable to the national ideologies of the Europeans. Zionism, though also a reaction to European nationalism, came to be seen by the Arabs as another threat to Arabism. Even at the turn of the century Arab intellectuals criticized the growing Jewish immigration to Palestine.

After World War I the British administered Palestine under international mandate. Having made wartime pledges to both the Arab nationalists and the Zionists (the former pledge embodied in the famous Balfour Declaration of 1917), Britain found itself unsuccessfully playing the role of arbitrator in the rivalry between the twin national movements. The Zionists urged Britain to allow widescale Jewish settlement. In deference to the Arabs, the British greatly restricted Jewish immigration. Yet even this limited immigration, tied in their minds to the presence of the imperialist occupation inflamed Arab sentiment against the Zionists and led to the Arab Revolt of 1936-1939. Bowing to Arab pressures, the British prohibited further immigration, just at the moment when anti-Jewish movements in Europe were about to destroy Europe's Jewry. In response to Britain's ban on immigration and then in the aftermath of Hitler's genocide, Zionism gained strength. At the war's end the necessity of giving Europe's devastated Jewry a homeland coincided with the Zionists' long frustrated and now intense desire to establish a sovereign Jewish state in Palestine. Palestine's Arabs were adamantly against the idea, and had widespread support among nationalist political groups in neighboring Arab states. Thus, when the British mandate ended in 1948, the Zionists proclaimed the state of Israel, and Egypt, Lebanon, Syria and Jordan attacked Israel. The first Arab-Israeli war ended in Arab defeat. Peace was immediately proposed by outside mediators as well as moderates on both sides. Certain issues, including Israeli navigation of the straits of Tiran, the repatriation of refugees, etc., were mooted.

The Arab leaders, who had committed their forces to the war in face of strong popular pressure, were strongly censured by the nationalists for their failure. In the wake of military defeat, Syria's regime fell. King Talal of Jordan, father of Hussein, was assassinated by nationalists fearful of the king's rapprochement with Israel. Egypt's failure in the first war brought about revolution in 1952 and Gamal Abdul Nasser's subsequent rise to power. It was President Nasser who galvanized the nationalist sentiment of the Arabs, and fixated that nationalism into confrontation with Israel.

Nasser's policies dominated the Arab world down to his death in 1970. Unity among the Arab states, opportunistic use of aid from the Soviet Union, opposition to the West, all were Nasserist policies focused on the goal of defeating Israel.

Israel initially sought a tacit *modus vivendi* with the Arabs based on a recognition of the status quo. But the growing stridency of Arabism on radio Cairo strengthened the conviction of militant Zionists that no accommodation, other than a balance of terror, was possible between Israel and her neighbors. The Arab-Israeli war of 1956, provoked on one side by terrorist raids into Israel and on the other by Egypt's closing the Suez Canal to Israeli shipping, set the seal on this pattern of confrontation.

International mediation in the fifties and sixties was persistent but low-key. It is not hard to see why at this stage of the conflict Europe's leaders did not urgently seek a peace settlement. The international repercussions of the Arab-Israeli conflict were minimal. The Middle East was peripheral, a backwater. The strategic value of the region's oil was diminished by extensive finds elsewhere in the world and a sinking price for the product. The UN contented itself with the role of preventing another outburst of armed hostilities by posting peacekeeping observers on the contested borders of the combatants.

Mutual suspicions and provocation again led to war in 1967, which this time resulted in the crushing defeat of Egypt, Jordan and Syria. With the occupation of the Sinai desert, the closing of the Suez Canal and the destruction of the Egyptian army, Nasser's military capability was reduced to zero; his policy of total confrontation with Israel was bankrupted. Moreover, the deficiencies of modernism among the Arabs, their technical and societal shortcomings were made public in the defeat. Through the aftermath of the war, the death of Nasser in 1970 and the launching of the fourth Arab-Israeli war in 1973, the Arab world awakened to the need to develop its human and economic potential. In consequence, the policy of confrontation with Israel was reduced. Moderate Arab leaders began to redefine the Arab world's posture towards Israel. Egypt's Sadat and Jordan's King Hussein discarded the rhetoric of confrontation and began seeking a diplomatic settlement based on recognition of the sovereignty and security of Israel as a basis for lasting peace in the region. "Rejectionist" Syria has recently expressed willingness to acknowledge Israel's security, though it continues to reject diplomatic recognition of the Israeli state. Even Palestinian Liberation Organization leader Yasir Arafat has occasionally indicated a willingness to live in peace with Israel, despite the group's official commitment to total confrontation. (See Chapters 8 & 9 for details.)

In Israel 30 years of conflict have made many eager for peace, but left a significant group of Israelis wary of the Arabs' willingness to make a lasting peace. The key question Israel faces in making peace with the Arabs is the disposition of territories overrun by Israel during the 1967 war, including the Egyptian Sinai desert, the Syrian Golan heights and the West Bank of Jordan. The Israelis now militarily administer these territories, and some are reluctant to return them to Arab sovereignty.

The urgency of peace in the Middle East became most apparent during the 1973 war, when the Arab oil producers embargoed industrial nations viewed as sympathetic towards Israel. The effect was disquieting in an America increasingly dependent on Arab oil, and serious difficulty for Japan and Western Europe as well. The oil weapon, in addition to the campaign of sensational terrorism committed by Palestinian groups, made the issue of peace in the Middle East a burning one, and nowhere more so than in Washington. Jimmy Carter made his 1976 Presidential campaign commitment to seek peace in the Middle East in the same vein as candidate Nixon had announced his secret plan to end the war in Vietnam.

The stage was set for the 1978 attempt to end the Arab-Israeli conflict and bring to a close a period of violence, political instability and frustrated material progress. Though at the Camp David summit conference Egypt and Israel signed the most comprehensive accord ever between the two enemies, the momentum generated by this event failed to produce a settlement by year's end.

The events of the Middle East provide ground for both hopeful and pessimistic prognostications. Some will see in the Middle East a better future arising, pointing to the massive development of the desert fueled by oil revenues. In the growing voice of cooperation and pragmatism in the petroleum producers' organizations, they will hear the Middle East taking a responsible, indeed, all-important role in world affairs, becoming the flywheel between economic expansion in the developed countries and in the developing countries. In the political dialogues in Khartoum, Damascus, Cairo and Riyadh, they will hear an increasing voice of pragmatism and common sense, as the gains and risks in the future of the Middle East take on more serious proportions. In the signing of the accords between Egypt and Israel, they will see a 30-year era between two nations give way to regional cooperation and a new, cosmopolitan spirit of humanity.

But pessimists will only have to look at the daily bombardment of Beirut, to conclude that in the Middle East, "*plus ca change, plus c'est la même chose.*" The mob violence in the streets of Iran was a terrible reminder of the dissatisfaction and frustration which the masses of people in the Middle East still feel towards their political institutions. Coups d'etat in Yemen and Afghanistan with the casual, inevitable purges and executions recall the merry-go-round governments of the last decade in the Middle East. Guerrilla wars in the Sahara and in South Arabia, together with the persistence of terrorism as a means of political expression throughout the Middle East is a grim reminder that the region's political problems are far from being solved. Finally, in the salvo of recriminations and countercharges which erupted in the aftermath of the Camp David accords, Israel and Egypt revealed the still fundamental and intractable contentions which divide the Middle East.

1

The Impact of Oil

Like a story out of a thousand nights was the Middle East's sudden
accumulation of wealth, following the hike in petroleum prices in 1973.
Successive price rises in that year raised the cost of a barrel of Persian Gulf
oil from an average of $2 to $11—just when analysts were predicting an
"earthshaking" rise to $5 per barrel (*New York Times*, October 7, 1973).
The unprecedented 470% increase in the price of oil filled the coffers of
the Organization of Petroleum Exporting Countries's (OPEC's) Middle
Eastern members—Algeria, Iran, Iraq, Kuwait, Libya, Saudi Arabia and the
United Arab Emirates (UAE)—with a greater inflow of revenue than had
ever changed hands before, and this in a space of a few months. Few
Cassandras had been prepared to foretell a price rise of this magnitude and
fewer now would accurately predict the results.

   Pessimists in the international financial community predicted the
imminent collapse of the world monetary system, with the industrial
countries facing an unforeseen trade deficit of $30 billion. Japan alone had
a whopping deficit of $9 billion, after several years of a modest surplus. A
worldwide liquidity crisis was narrowly avoided by the international banks,
who adroitly pursued Middle East oil revenues for deposits and then
recycled these "petrodollars" in loans to oil consuming nations. The system
strained without buckling.

   Some went on to predict that the Arabs, having amassed their
petrodollars, would use this source of power to disrupt the world economy.
With the memory of the 1973 oil embargo fresh in the minds of Western
policymakers, the danger of political blackmail at the hands of OPEC's more
radical members, Libya and Iraq, seemed particularly real. Several
economists, notably Hendrick Houthacker, suggested that the oil embargo
had taught an important lesson to the oil producers of the region, who had
suffered revenue loss and economic dislocation during the embargo.
Observers of Mid-East politics, for example, political scientist George
Lenczowski, asked the economists how they could be certain that the

radical oil states would act as rational economic agents. The answer to that important question has become increasingly clear since 1973. With larger rewards in the form of higher revenues and the promise of unlimited economic growth, Middle East oil producers now have a great deal at stake. Few could repeat the remark of a Libyan negotiator in 1971 that the oil companies could pack up and leave: "We were bedouins for a thousand years before; we could very well become bedouins again." Since 1973, a watershed has been crossed in the relations of oil producers and consumers. Iranian Shah Mohammad Reza Pahlavi summed up the new view in a December of 1973 conference. "We don't want to hurt the industrial world. We will be one with them soon."

Throughout 1973 and 1974, the glut of petrodollars found its way back to the industrial nations. The OPEC members' surplus ran as high as $60 billion, which could neither be invested within the producers' countries nor be spent on commodities. A scramble ensued among money managers from London, Zurich and New York to share in the repatriation of this "windfall." The scramble had an unknown quality about it. At first, it was unlcear where $60 billion could be spent.

Following the line of least resistance, Middle East investors proceeded to the money markets of London and New York, buying government bonds and prestige real estate. Property prices in the luxury Mayfair district of London and in Beverly Hills, California skyrocketed. When the mighty German Krupp Company announced a 25% sellout to the Iranian government and the Daimler Benz Company relinquished 14% to Kuwait, some analysts concluded that petrodollars would indeed take over the world.

The acquisitions of petrodollar spenders has prompted criticism that Middle Easterners would do better to spend their national wealth at home. Arab purchases of luxury hotels in London could be seen as an ironic contrast to the low standard of living in most OPEC countries. Yet this criticism underestimates a crucial factor in Arab spending abroad. Faced with a huge surplus in revenues, the oil producers have had to find the quickest and most risk-free investments just to be able to stash their wealth away until they could learn how to use it most effectively in their own countries.

Conspicuous consumption of Middle Easterners in Europe and the U.S. provided another instance of criticism. But with double digit inflation and housing shortages facts of life in oil capitals such as Teheran and Kuwait, luxury housing in New York, Palm Beach and London strikes Mid-East investors as a bargain. The sum of $300,000 fetches a modest house in Teheran's wealthy suburbs; one can do better than that in Malibu.

Ultimately, the Middle East must call its investments home to roost. Expanding domestic capacity to absorb investments generated by the oil money is an arduous process, which means for many Middle Eastern states hauling their economies, deeply rooted in the Middle Ages, into the twenty-first century. For the states of the UAE, this means transforming fishing villages and pastoralized back-land into the sight of energy intensive foundries, refineries, aluminum rolling and construction. This requires huge outlays of petrodollars, but ultimately only such investments will assure the people of the Middle East any lasting legacy from their oil.

Investing in the Middle East requires the accumulation not of money but of fixed capital within the Middle East. This, in turn, entails expenditures on the infrastructure of these sparsely inhabited, resource-poor (other than oil) countries. Desert states of the Persian Gulf must expand their port capacity by 100% to 150% in order to receive the flow of capital goods from abroad. Roads must be pushed through the desert and mountains to diffuse industrialization throughout the countryside. Local services must eventually arise to maintain the imported industrial plants. At present, Saudi Arabia imports a burdensome duplicate of every mechanical part in its import inventory because of the difficulty of servicing its purchases when sited in the desert.

Industrialization must be linked to progress in the agricultural and pastoral sectors of Middle East economies. The flight of labor from herding and cultivating occupations into industrial roles has lowered food outputs throughout the region and leaves Middle Eastern states unsatisfactorily dependent on imports for foodstuffs. The rise of food imports to 14% has become a key issue in Iran. Investment in agriculture, particularly in large agribusinesses, such as in Ahwaz in Iran or in the Sudan, has become an important goal in the development of the region.

The critical shortage in almost every sector of industrialization and development has proved to be trained manpower. The scenario above, for example, requires port pilots, container handlers, surveyors, mechanics, warehouse inventory persons, engineers, not to mention government planners, budget control officers and economists. It is no wonder that Saudi Arabia, falling far behind in spending its allocated $144 billion five-year-plan, decided to devote 40% of its expenditures in 1978 to education.

Much of the 1973 windfall of oil money went to expenditures on arms. The result has been a spiraling arms race in the Persian Gulf, with Iran, Iraq and Saudi Arabia seeking access to the sophisticated arsenals of the North Atlantic Treaty Organization (NATO) powers. Iran's spending totaled $17 billion, including a single $4 billion contract with France. Saudi Arabia stirred controversy with its intent to purchase F-15 fighter planes from the U.S.

The limited ability of OPEC members to absorb their post-1973 surpluses raised high hopes for financial assistance among the non-oil producers in the region; Egypt, linked to the oil states through Arab nationality, was the recipient of a fund of $2 billion in 1978, which enabled it to avoid bankruptcy in its international payments. Muslim Pakistan has had limited success in calling for "Islamic solidarity" and a commitment for petrodollars to aid its development. The oil states responded by giving Pakistan $34 million in disaster relief during 1975.

But, so far, the call for Islamic or Arabic cooperation has produced more single shot grants like the aid to Pakistan and Egypt rather than a coordinated flow of aid to the developing world. The United Nations Conference on Trade and Development (UNCTAD) criticized the capricious and uncertain nature of Arab aid to the Third World. At the same time, the large surpluses of the past five years have decreased: $50 billion in 1973, $5 billion in 1978. The OPEC surplus continued to fall in 1978 so that almost all the excess petrodollars have been returned to the industrial nations. Except for Iran, Kuwait, Saudi Arabia and the UAE, Mid-East OPEC members have had to borrow to finance their development. As spending slowed even in Kuwait by 15% in 1978, the pace of development, both at home and in the region, was on the decline.

The Changing Face of the Middle East

EUROPEANS SEEKING ALGERIAN CONTRACTS

French companies bidding for contracts in Algeria remain optimistic about prospects, despite virtual embargo that Algerian government has declared on new import contracts with France; important contracts at stake include Berliet's order to double productive capacity of Algerian truck plant at Poueba, Renault's possible contract to supply a 100,000 unit per year automobile plant; meanwhile Italians are making solid advances as suppliers of know-how and equipment to Algerian petrocarbon industry   (FINANCIAL TIMES,   January 12, 1978,   P2)

IRAQI ATOM SALE DISCLOSED

Jack Anderson reveals French President Valery Giscard d'Estaing has secretly decided to sell controversial nuclear materials to Iraq; notes intelligence sources consider Iraq one of most militant nations in Arab bloc; reports Iraq is closely aligned with Libyan leader Muammar Qaddafi who is seeking to purchase nuclear weapons to use against Israel   (WASHINGTON POST,   January 12, 1978,   P7)

MIDDLE EAST DEVELOPMENT SLOWING

Washington Post Business Outlook reviews major Middle East economic developments; observes cutbacks in development programs, reshuffling of cabinets and reassessment of long-term spending goals in response to "cooled down" world oil market and inflation; notes domestic turmoil during 1977 in many Middle East countries with little or no oil; notes oil producing countries remain optimistic about their economic future; notes establishment of Arab Monetary Fund through which oil-producing nations will extend credit to their impoverished neighbors and allies   (WASHINGTON POST,   January 15, 1978, S8 P2)

SAUDIS FACING CULTURAL CONFLICT

Commentator Richard Harwood discovers conflicting cultures in Saudi Arabia; notes Muzak and Swiss beer in Riyadh restaurants, General Motors trucks, modern office buildings and Kentucky Fried Chicken; notes government is concerned about loss of culture and tradition; reports medical care and education are free; notes families wanting to build houses are given interest-free loans and up to $80,000 for construction; reports government allowances for aged and disabled are more generous than in US; reports average wage of $7,200 per year; adds there is no taxation   (WASHINGTON POST,   January 15, 1978,   S2   P1)

INSURANCE RISKS IN MIDEAST NOTED

Financial Times survey on Middle East insurance finds that local conditions often lead to high risk business and awkward operation conditions; new challenge has been posed in Gulf region by magnitude of projects' values and vulnerability of oil and petrochemical installations; discusses many hazards which construction contractors must consider; names lack of national and regional capacity as number one problem; explains Middle East industry is still at stage of handling relatively few large potential catastrophe risks; comments on need for reinsurance facilities which has been increased by explosion of Umm Saled gas liquefaction plant at Qatar; remarks that Iran remains vastly uninsured, both in private and commercial life; holds that overall lack of sufficient expert manpower has serious consequences in areas where nationalist pride insists insurance is placed with local market   (FINANCIAL TIMES,   January 19, 1978,   P9)

Smaller oil-producing nations like Qatar flaunt their new economic advantage.

SAUDI G.N.P. RISING

Middle East Economic Survey reports that Saudi Arabia's current 5-year plan has achieved a 15.4% growth in the country's gross national product over the last two years, which is 4.2% higher than planned; quotes Saudi Planning Minister Hisham al-Nazer as saying that growth in non-petroleum private sector amounted to 18% as against target of 13.4%, during 1975–77; Minister appeared to refute allegations that $142 billion plan was running into bottlenecks, with planners unable to spend allocated sums   (FINANCIAL TIMES, January 24, 1978, P6)

ARABS BACK SUDAN FARMING

Plans by Arab states to turn Sudan into major food supplier for Middle East provide feeling of euphoria for first International Trade Fair in Khartoum, where tractors and agricultural machinery dominate the fair; problems do exist, however, particularly concerns about availability of foreign exchange and alarmingly wide range of estimates on size of Sudanese tractor market; nevertheless, all major agricultural machinery companies are represented (FINANCIAL TIMES, January 26, 1978, P4)

PETRODOLLARS AID EGYPT'S ECONOMY

Egypt has received considerable financial aid from Persian Gulf oil producing nations and from the US but has yet to tap some $4 billion in additional aid offers; has also been slow in producing priority list of aid projects and has been unwilling to improve deficit budget by cutting back consumer subsidies; despite plight, Egypt is relatively solvent as result of Arab aid; 4 oil producers—Saudi Arabia, Kuwait, Qatar and United Arab Emirates—formed consortium in 1976 capitalized at $2 billion to organize aid effort; at least $850 million was used to pay interest on Egypt's debts and Western experts estimate that $450 million is yet undrawn; US aid program is now running at nearly $1 billion a year   (NEW YORK TIMES, January 29, 1978, S4 P3)

SAUDI GROWTH CONTINUES

Saudi Arabian business community reports improvement in pace of country's economy; increased business activity is reportedly fueled by acceleration of government purchasing, and marked by awarding of some major contracts; present business pickup contrasts with slowdown which began late in 1976 and continued through spring 1977; slowdown was partly caused by government restraining and retrenchment measures; government's current $30-billion budget has been held to same size as those of previous 2 years, while government continues to fight inflation in other ways; anxiety about US taxing money earned abroad is hindering growth of country's US community   (NEW YORK TIMES, February 11, 1978, P27)

SAUDIS BUILDING INDUSTRIAL SITE

Bechtel Corporation is directing construction of new Saudi Arabian industrial center near Jubail; Bechtel field manager Alden Yates indicates firm's task is to map out entire infrastructure for industrial complex and city, supervise granting of contracts after evaluating bids, and oversee actual construction; firms from around world are participating in $45-billion project; Bechtel executives assert most serious obstacle was finding skilled labor force, while lack of infrastructure also cost time; linchpin of new industrial complex is cheap natural gas, which will be used to fuel new complex in Jubail and in other parts of country   (NEW YORK TIMES, February, 13, 1978, S4 P3)

JUBAIL COMPLEX DETAILED

Transformation of Jubail, tiny Saudi Arabian fishing village, into multibillion-dollar industrial center is described as largest single construction project in history; smaller industrial center is planned for Red Sea port Yenbo; Jubail and Yenbo complexes will include oil refineries, petrochemical plants, other industrial installations and extensive permanent housing; Jubail site will also have aluminum smelter, steel mill, international airport, 2 deepwater ports, several power generating plants, extensive telecommunications system and world's largest desalination complex; Saudi Arabian industrialization strategy aims at diversifying kingdom's industrial base; Saudi Arabian Bechtel Corporation, arm of US construction firm Bechtel Corporation, is providing overall assistance to Saudi commission developing Jubail center   (NEW YORK TIMES, February 13, 1978, S4 P1)

SUDAN DEVELOPMENT REVIEWED

Sudan announces 180 million pounds sterling farming development project; 800,000 acres at Rahad will be brought under cultivation and will provide work for at least 100,000 people; more than 3,600 miles of canals and drainage systems have been excavated to expedite project; authorities are having severe problems in coping with cotton crop that is already in need of cultivation; 17,000 workers are needed to cultivate initial 300,000 acres but authorities are unable to induce that many workers to come to Rahad; Sudan's 17 million persons spread over 1.6 million square miles makes it very difficult to accomplish any large-scale project without mechanization; power is in short supply for Rahad; Rahad now has 800 houses, 18 workshops, schools and clinics and 100 miles of internal roads   (FINANCIAL TIMES, February 16, 1978, P3)

SAUDI WEAPONS FACILITY PLANNED

Saudi Arabia plans to create city of 100,000 people that will be designed as modern military center for production of weapons, according to US business and government sources; Edward Durrell Stone Associates confirms that it has been commissioned to prepare master plan for city by Saudi Ministry of Defense and Aviation; company spokesman reveals that new community will be at Al Kharj, 60 miles southeast of Riyadh; cost is estimated at $10 billion   (NEW YORK TIMES, February 18, 1978, P1)

MIDEAST FACING DEVELOPMENT SETBACKS

Shortage of skilled personnel and bottlenecks at ports, on roads and in telecommunications are escalating development costs in Middle East; Algeria hopes to be industrialized by 1982, when present 5-year plan ends; Saudi Arabia is falling far behind in its ambitious $144-billion, 5-year development plan; limited populations in certain Arab countries viewed as impediment to rapid industrial and economic development; Chase World Information Corporation spokesman Jack Kramer suggests Algeria needs labor and management expertise; development problems cause Middle East oil producing countries to scale down projects   (NEW YORK TIMES,   February 20, 1978,   S4   P1)

OIL MONEY DEVELOPS SUDAN

Sudan's huge sugar-producing project hopes to start full operations by March 1979; the cost of the Kenana sugar operation is over $600 million, well over the estimate of $125 million projected by the Lonrho Company of Britain in October 1973; the operation has been depicted as the first major model of cooperation between Western technology, Arab money and an African natural resource   (CHRISTIAN SCIENCE MONITOR,   February 24, 1978,   P13)

SAUDI ECONOMIC DEVELOPMENT PROFILED

Survey on Saudi Arabia assesses country's economic development and related effects on its politics and social affairs; notes that traditional political structure is capable of withstanding strains imposed by rapid economic development, but internal confidence could be shaken if its moderating role in Middle East and Organization of Petroleum Exporting Countries does not receive US support; notes that foreign aid goes to areas where country has major policy interests, such as Middle East and Horn of Africa; describes protective role of Saudi defense forces, which is supported by a current defense budget of 26.96 billion Saudi riyals, but crippled by shortages in manpower; discusses country's lack of basic infrastructure, including such elements as a stock exchange, required to create a capital market; comments on decision by Saudi Arabian Monetary Agency that all commercial banks be taken over by 60% to 65% Saudi interests; observes that country has developed a substantial insurance market, but lacks nationally sponsored insurance industry to serve it; describes government plans to build up mining and manufacturing sectors to broaden economy in anticipation of falling oil income by the next century; reviews plans to increase port capacity by 150% to prevent any check to its industrial construction and development program and outlines possible revival of massive expansion plans for its shipping industry   (FINANCIAL TIMES,   March 20, 1978,   P13)

FRENCH JETS TO MIDEAST

French figures indicate that arms exports, led by Mirage jet fighter, increased by almost half last year to 27 billion francs; notes that military aircraft, helicopters and missiles account for about 2/3 of the total; says that Dassault-Breguet aircraft company heads the arms exporters with export orders worth 8.2 billion francs; points out that the signing of a cooperation and arms production pact between France and the Arab Industries Organization will further increase Middle East orders   (FINANCIAL TIMES, March 23, 1978,   P6)

WEST FINDS WELCOME IN ALGERIA

Western businessmen in Algeria carefully avoid references to Algeria's left-wing politics, and Algerian officials reciprocate by refraining from any criticism of Western politics; separation of business and politics is reflected in Hotel Al Aurassi, Algiers, which was originally intended to be proud symbol of Algeria's revolutionary struggle against France, but now houses Western businessmen and has distinctly Western atmosphere; foreign companies, recognizing high profits available in Algeria, are willing to tolerate difficulties such as customs delays, poor telephone systems and contracts which sometimes require purchase of equipment from Algerian state companies; Algeria's economic development and modernization goals, based on abundant gas reserves and human resources, discussed   (BUSINESS WEEK,   March 27, 1978,   P36)

BAHRAIN'S ECONOMY PROFILED

Survey of Bahrain discusses slackening pace of country's economic and construction boom that followed 1973–1974 oil price explosion; notes that economy is being geared towards development of service industries, which are likely to complement rather than compete with economies of other Gulf states; also notes overall economic conditions, highlighted by a fall in inflation, as cost-of-living for average Bahraini family decreased to about 13% in 1977 and by a balanced budget for 1978; details declining business of Bahrain's commercial banks, citing a fall in growth of bank lending to 27% at end of 1st quarter 1977, compared to a high of about 66% in 1976; describes causes behind recent growth of Bahrain-based Saudi riyal market, noting that at end of March 1978, Saudi riyals accounted for some $2 billion of Bahrain offshore banks' assets; also focuses on country's high aluminum output level, slowdown of imports, depletion of oil reserves, possible construction of $800 million Bahrain-Saudi Arabia causeway, manpower problems, expansion of Gulf Air and Bahrain International Airport, declining orders for Arab Shipbuilding and Repair Yard and slowdown in hotel and housing development construction   (FINANCIAL TIMES,   April 3, 1978,   P15)

SAUDI ECONOMIC DEVELOPMENT SURVEYED

Second of a 2-part survey of Saudi Arabia details country's long-term economic goals and strategies; 1980-1985 economic development plan emphasizes manufacturing capability, major industrial projects and agricultural development; refineries, petrochemical, cement, aluminum, fertilizer plants and an iron and steel foundry are already under construction; electricity generating network has been expanded to keep pace with demand; road building program has been designed to spread industrial and agricultural development to all regions of country; trend towards establishing joint Saudi-foreign companies for new industrial projects noted   (FINANCIAL TIMES,   April 17, 1978,   P15)

GULF STATES DIVERSIFY INDUSTRY

Commentator Michael Field discusses efforts by Saudi Arabia and Gulf states to substitute energy-intensive heavy industry for oil as a major earner of foreign exchange income and tax revenue; says most of proposed plants would run off locally produced low-cost gas; notes industries under consideration are petrochemicals and fertilizers, export oil refineries, steel and aluminum smelters, natural gas liquid plants and liquefied natural gas plants; observes that most heavy industries now operating in Arabian Peninsula are highly unsuccessful; says this is due largely to poor world market conditions and technical difficulties arising from severe environmental conditions   (FINANCIAL TIMES,   April 17, 1978,   P14)

BRITISH-IRANIAN ARMS COMPLEX PLANNED

Following 20 months of difficult negotiations, an agreement between Iranian and British officials has been approved for construction of the Isfahan ordnance complex which will produce a wide range of ammunition and military hardware; some work is expected to go to other European and US contractors, but most of the 700 million pound sterling project will go to the Wimpey-Laing consortium, working through Millbank Technical Services, the British government's defense sales agency; means of payment have not yet been worked out, but payment in oil is expected to be a likely possibility; agreement is considered Great Britain's largest single contract in the Middle East   (FINANCIAL TIMES,   May 11, 1978,   P1)

ARABS DEVELOP ARMS INDUSTRY

Arab Organization for Industrialization (AOI) plans program of training, marketing and production activities aimed at developing military and civil industrial base in Arab territory; hopes to establish economic independence from other industrialized nations for production of military equipment; present emphasis is placed on advanced training for existing management and technical personnel in Egypt, Saudi Arabia, Qatar and United Arab Emirates; program eventually will be expanded to provide advanced technical and management education for students entering AOI after completing their standard education
(AVIATION WEEK AND SPACE TECHNOLOGY,   May 15, 1978,   P14)
1978,   P14)

NEW ARCHITECTURE IN MIDEAST

Western architects have developed innovative new structures in Middle East; projects such as the 1,200 acres set aside for Teheran's new urban center Shahestan Pahlevi, at estimated cost of more than $5 billion, are biggest feats of architectural construction in history; Saudi Arabia's new airport at Jidda, designed by US firm of Skidmore Owings and Merrill, will be opened in the 1980's and will be world's biggest airport; new Saudi town of Assad, designed by Edward Durell Stone, will have computerized mass transit system   (NEWSWEEK,   June 5, 1978,   P65)

SAUDIS TAP NATURAL GAS

Saudi Arabia is beginning to cap its oil wells, capturing some of the estimated $16 billion worth of natural gas that is burned daily as waste; captured gas is expected to be foundation for country's industrialization and source for

much of world natural gas liquids supply by early 1980's; about 75% of Saudi gas is now burned up in oil fields, since large-scale collection was previously considered uneconomic; main elements in first phase of gas program are three major plants located in east central part of country at Berri, Shedgum and Uthmaniyah; US company Fluor Corporation is involved in construction of natural gas liquid fractionation center at Juaymah   (NEW YORK TIMES,   June 13, 1978,   P25)

PETRODOLLARS SUPPORT EGYPT'S DEBT

Egypt wins sufficient financial support to stave off defaulting on its huge $78 billion foreign debt; Saudi Arabia and other Arab oil nations pledge $650 million, while Japan and International Monetary Fund promise to contribute to necessary $1 billion fund; however, insist that Egypt borrow $750 billion from IMF and carry out its mandated 3-year domestic austerity program in return; Dr. Munir Benjenck, vice president of International Bank for Reconstruction and Development, expresses optimism over Egypt's ability to repay its debts, but warns that ready cash may be depleted soon if lending nations fail to reduce interest rate charges and extend repayment terms   (NEW YORK TIMES,   June 17, 1978,   P28)

Construction scaffolding surrounds a natural gas sweetening unit above a bank of air coolers in Berri.

Aramco Photo

KOREANS BUILD IN MIDEAST

South Korean construction companies have some 50,000 workers in Mideast and about $6 billion worth of contracts in Saudi Arabia, Iran, Bahrain, Kuwait, Iraq and United Arab Emirates where they are building schools, ports, military bases, civilian housing and roads; hold that secret of their successful business in Mideast is that they are better-organized and more productive than their competitors; Hyundai Construction Co is the most active among 6 Korean contractors working in Mideast; has nearly $3 billion worth of contracts in Saudi Arabia   (NEW YORK TIMES,   June 19, 1978,   S4 P5)

EGYPTIAN SUGAR PROJECT LAUNCHED

International Financial Corporation will invest $23 million in a beet-sugar project in Egypt; venture, called Delta Sugar Company, will cost a total of about $126 million and is being sponsored by Societe des Sucreries; other financing for project will be provided by Egyptian investors, French government and several Arab financial institutions, including Arab banks and Cairo branch of Citibank; company will be located in northern Nile Delta   (WALL STREET JOURNAL,   July 18, 1978,   P37)

SAUDIS SEEK SOCIAL BALANCE

Saudi Arabia tries to strike balance between sensible spending for Western-style industry and preservation of its traditional way of life; settles down to more sensible and deliberate approach to economic development; awareness of need for some financial discipline exists; Saudi Arabia elects to invest large amounts of capital and small amounts of manpower in few key industries; concentrates on 2 heavy-process industries: basic metals and petrochemicals; preservation of Islamic values and traditions overrides everything else in national planning; objectives and courses of action are defined with eye to their effect on family, community and Islamic tenets; Saudis' fundamental aim is to develop domestic productive capacity that does not rely on fluctuations of energy market and uncertain future of fuel oil; Saudi planning also concerns itself with defense   (FORTUNE,   July 31, 1978,   P114)

GULF STATES AID EGYPT

Gulf Organization for the Development of Egypt (GODE) agrees to provide sufficient support to allow Egypt to cover estimated $250 million current account deficit for 1978; GODE's $2 billion capital and interest accrued on it will remain with Egypt for the remaining 23 years of GODE's life; the fund will also underwrite short term loans to the value of next year's interest payments, which total $150 million   (FINANCIAL TIMES,   August 15, 1978,   P3)

CONCERN VOICED ON MIDEAST ARMS

World concern is felt over ultimate effect that delivery of advanced weapons systems to and military improvements in Arab states will have on precarious Middle East situation; Carter Aministration officials, while not sharing rising fears of Israeli government, concede that there is a calculated risk inherent in the transfer of weapons into areas of tension where revolutions and coups, such as that recently carried out in South Yemen, can have serious international repercussions; contrary to President Carter's 1977 promise that US would use arms transfer only in exceptional circumstances, Brookings Institution study discloses that three-quarters of US arms sales in fiscal 1977 were to Iran, Saudi Arabia and Israel   (NEW YORK TIMES,   September 6, 1978,   P114)

YEMENI BOOM TIED TO OIL

James Buxton analyzes reasons why Yemen Arab Republic (North Yemen) is Britain's fastest growing export market, noting country is undergoing consumer boom despite fact it is not oil producer; consumer boom is attributed to fact that about 1 million North Yemenis work in Saudi Arabia and other Arabian oil states and spend about $1.4 billion per year to acquire whatever goods are available before country's 30% inflation erodes value of their money; main source of spending is private sector, but government has development plan involving expenditure of about $3.6 billion over 5-year period to develop resource industries; British exports to Yemen rose from 9.2 million pounds sterling in 1975 to 28.4 million pounds in 1977 and 26.1 million pounds for first half of 1978   (FINANCIAL TIMES,   September 25, 1978,   P3)

Dubai Harbor, a seaport in northeast Trucial Oman, could one day have a larger harbor than New York City.

American Petroleum Institute

There is a reduction in construction of such public places as airports in Saudi Arabia due to the recession following the rapid growth of 1973-76.

MIDEAST CONSTRUCTION DECLINES

Michael Cassell analyzes diminishing construction market in Middle East and its effect on British contractors, who have for past several years used Gulf area as cushion against recession in Britain's domestic construction; major cause of slowdown in Middle East is substantial reduction in public sector expenditures due to recession that followed rapid growth of 1973-1976; other problems include dwindling need for "jumbo" development projects, growing overcapacity at existing complexes such as airports and dry docks, and growing competition from local contractors; in addition, competition from other foreign contractors, especially South Koreans, is also making Middle East much more difficult market for the British (FINANCIAL TIMES, September 27, 1978, P29)

SYRIA SEEKS DIVERSIFICATION FROM OIL

Syrian Minister of Petroleum Isa Darwish believes his country has relied too much on oil as energy source; Syrian long-range planners are paying new attention to development of gas, uranium extraction, phosphates and iron ore; country continues to expand and modernize its oil refinery operation even as it seeks to diversify its energy base; government is conducting feasibility study on upgrading facilities at Homs oil refinery and Rumania is constructing new refinery at Baniyas which will have annual capacity of six million tons (JOURNAL OF COMMERCE, September 29, 1978, P9)

EGYPT COPES WITH ASWAN PROBLEMS

Commentator Thomas Lippman reports Egyptians are spending millions of dollars on subsidiary projects aimed at coping with side effects of Aswan Dam; notes Egyptians are building Toshka Canal to channel off excess water at same time that Sudanese are building their own canal that would increase flow of Nile River northward into Egypt; reports water from Lake Nasser is threatening to spill over Aswan Dam; reports erosion might occur if large quantities of water were allowed to flow through spillway to Mediterranean (WASHINGTON POST, November 12, 1978, S2 P2)

ARAB DEVELOPMENT PROJECTS PROFILED

Arab states have turned to lavish development projects, with $50 billion per year in oil revenues to invest; sheikdoms along Persian Gulf tended at outset to give priority to projects that they felt symbolized modern state; Dubai and Sharjah, for instance, both built airports capable of handling jumbo jets; both airports are closer together than Washington's National is to Dulles; Dubai also contracted to build more than 70 shipping berths that would give it larger port capacity than New York City; shift toward more conservative view of development has begun, however, coinciding with easing of world demand for oil (WASHINGTON POST, November 23, 1978, S5 P10)

MIDEAST FOOD CRISIS FORESEEN

Arab League and Arab Authority for Agricultural Investment and Development issue report warning Arab World that it may face major food crisis by 2000 AD, despite its oil wealth; forecasts Arab population increase from present estimated 140 million to 240 million; notes oil-rich countries will be forced to spend large portion of oil money on food imports, and poorer countries will have to rely on aid from richer countries; appeals for cooperative agricultural planning include exploitation of arable land and massive training of agronomists, which experts believe could cut food imports by 70% within next 20 years; also suggested is creation of an Arab "wheat belt" which would include Iraq, Syria, Morocco and Algeria; most Arab governments are preoccupied by more immediate political problems, and long-term agricultural planning has little support (LOS ANGELES TIMES, November 26, 1978, S5 P8)

The Middle East in World Economy

ARAB AID CRITICIZED

UN Conference on Trade and Development (UNCTAD) report on OPEC and to developing world annoys OPEC's Arab members; report implies OPEC Arabs tend to help other Arabs and attach strings to bilateral aid they give to non-Arab states; notes aid is haphazardly handled and needs better fact finding and policy coordination; suggests establishing central data bank on projects and faster dispersement of funds; suggests marshaling high credit standing of OPEC nations to guarantee development funds; OPEC Secretary-General Ali Jaidah was the only Arab to attend UNCTAD meeting   (MIDDLE EAST,   January 1978,   P66)

WORLD ECONOMY WORRIES SAUDIS

Sources attending European Management Forum say that Saudi Arabia is concerned that continued economic sluggishness and rising unemployment expected in 1978 will encourage protectionist pressures in Western Europe and eventually frustrate Arab world's desire to diversify its exports into a variety of manufactured goods; Abdulhady H. Taher, governor of Saudi state oil company Petromin, in speech to business leaders, calls for "urgent" domestic-policy changes to "support and sustain expansion of consumer and investment demand"; notes his government would like to invest a much larger proportion of its reserves in currencies other than US dollar, but that Western Europe, Japan and other developing countries offer only "very limited" opportunities for investment   (WALL STREET JOURNAL,   February 1, 1978,   P16)

O.P.E.C. DEBT GROWS

OPEC members turn net borrowers of new funds from international banking system during 1977 3d quarter for first time since 1973; Bank of International Settlements reports OPEC members, which need funds to finance ambitious development plans, borrowed $2.2 billion and made net deposits of only $400 million; OPEC, however, still continues to be major source of funds for international lending; deposits as of September 30, 1977, totaled $73.1 billion and borrowings were $31.9 billion, meaning surplus in OPEC's favor of $41.2 billion   (WALL STREET JOURNAL, February 9, 1978,   P16)

BAHRAIN'S BANKING HITS $15 BILLION

Arabian and European financial institutions are demonstrating increased interest in Bahrain's offshore banking market; total assets of market increased from $6.2 billion in 1976 to $15.7 billion in 1977; 33 offshore banking units were in operation in 1977 and 7 more are planned for 1978; liabilities to Arab countries increased from $2.6 billion in 1976 to $8.2 billion in 1977 and loans were up from $2.5 billion in 1976 to $7 billion in 1977; liabilities to European markets increased from $2.3 billion to $5 billion from 1976 to 1977, and assets rose from $1.1 billion to $3.9 billion   (FINANCIAL TIMES,   February 9, 1978,   P27)

PETRODOLLARS IN LONDON MARKETS

Arab money continues to find its way into Great Britain; $500 million of $4,500 million brought in 1976 was invested in stocks while the rest went into banks and other short-term monetary assets; a small portion was spent on property; Kuwait Investment Office became one of Great Britain's largest institutional investors with investments of 400 million pounds sterling in British corporate assets; it has significant stakes in 5%-10% of British companies; Arab money is also playing an active part in the British financial sector where Arabs, linked with Nigerians and Barclays Bank, rescued Edward Bates merchant bank when losses wiped out shareholders' funds in 1976; Arabs own up to 9% of Hill Samuel merchant bank; Dorchester Hotel (London) was bought by Arabs in 1976 for 9 million pounds sterling with hope of making it "the best hotel in the world"; wealthy Arab investors are forming their own international financial organizations   (TIMES OF LONDON,   March 7, 1978,   S2   P1)

Saudi Oil Minister Sheikh Ahmed Zaki Yamani (right) talks with Iranian Oil Minister Dr. Mohamed Eghani (left) and Iranian Ambassador to Saudi Arabia Ga'afar Ra'ed (at Eghani's left) during the second session of a conference of OPEC countries. Both Saudi Arabia and Iran opposed a proposal to shift OPEC pricing from the dollar to "a basket of various world currencies."

United Press International

ARAB INVESTMENT GROUP FORMED

A group of businessmen from the ruling family of Kuwait and merchant families in Saudi Arabia and United Arab Emirates join US executives to form Petra Capital Corporation; company is investment banking venture in US designed to recycle petrodollars into investments in US and abroad; Petra Capital chairman Peter Tanous identifies three majority shareholders as Sheikh Ali al-Salem al-Sabah, son of former Kuwait ruler and chairman of Kuwait Financial Center, Sheikh Abdelaziz al-Sulaiman, wealthy Saudi businessman, and Abdelwaha Galadari, leading businessman from Dubai; William Hannah and Kenneth Dolan are also part of new firm's management; Hannah indicates Petra would not seek industries which are sensitive to criticisms, such as communications, transportation and broadcasting   (NEW YORK TIMES, March 20, 1978, S4 P1)

ARAB AID PROJECTS GROW

Arab oil producing nations increase foreign aid to developing countries; Arab aid program has been institutionalized in seven funds with potential lending power of $25 billion, and with access to government loans to augment their capital; Saudi Arabia, United Arab Emirates and Kuwait provide most of foreign aid; Arab foreign aid constitutes high percentage of donor countries' GNP; Arab aid, unlike Western aid, does not flow back to donor countries, but is recycled to West; Chase World Information Corporation official John Law points out Africa is growth area for Arab lending; largest and oldest Arab aid vehicle is Kuwait Fund for Arab Economic Development   (NEW YORK TIMES, April 10, 1978, S4 P1)

ARAB BANKING REVIEWED

Special Report on banking in the Arab world notes that only four of the 13 members of OPEC will see a significant increase in their external wealth; says that Saudi Arabia, Kuwait, the United Arab Emirates and Iran will see a net growth but most other OPEC members have already become large net borrowers in the international banking markets; points out that in 1977 OPEC's borrowing is estimated to have risen from $4 billion to $7.35 billion; contemplates what countries like Kuwait can do with a revenue surplus of $35 billion, considered the "wrong" kind of money because of its liquidity; observes the historical connection between British banking and the Middle East; says the strongest bonds were forged by the overseas banks including the British Bank of the Middle East, Standard Chartered group and Grindlays Holdings; claims that Arab underwriters are becoming established in the international capital markets with Arab banks and investment companies taking leading roles in the management of Eurocredits and Eurobonds; cites priority of foreign aid given by the Arab states is to rectify years of neglect and underdevelopment by spending lavishly on their own economies, then the rest of the Arab world, then other Moslem countries and finally other developing nations; notes that the bulk of Arab aid has gone to Egypt, Syria and Jordan; points out that investment in property, equities, paper securities and establishing banks are popular with Arabs; notes Arab-Malaysian Development Bank, the Bank of Bahrain and Kuwait, the Allied Arab Bank in London, the International Resources and Development Bank in Luxembourg and the European Arab Banking Group are some banking interests of Arabs   (TIMES OF LONDON, April 10, 1978, S2 P1)

PETRODOLLARS RECYCLED IN U.S.

Commerce Department reports that almost all money paid by US to oil exporting countries from 1974 to 1977 returned to US in bank accounts and investments; US imported $108 billion in goods and services from OPEC countries during period, sold those countries $70 billion in goods, for net outflow of $36 billion; OPEC countries channeled $38 billion into US in form of Treasury securities, stocks and bonds, private investments and advance payments for military equipment; much of money returned to US was loaned to other countries that have trade deficits because of their heavy importation of foreign oil   (NEW YORK TIMES, April 29, 1978, P29)

SAUDI BUYS FRENCH BANK

French-based Saudi Arabian businessman Akram Ojjeh becomes one of leading shareholders in Credit Commercial of France, which ranks among the main French private commercial banks; Ojjeh, who made headlines last year with his purchase of the luxury liner S.S. France, has bought about 5% of Credit Commercial stock on Paris Bourse; the shares are unofficially estimated to have cost Ojjeh 50 million French francs   (FINANCIAL TIMES, May 6, 1978, P25)

INVESTOR FOR THE ARABS

Profile of David H. Sambar, executive vice president in charge of international investments for Sharjah group, an investment-advisory firm headquartered in Sharjah, one of the United Arab Emirates; 66 founding partners are all Arab millionaires, including ruler of Sharjah and 16 members of Kuwait ruling family; Sambar is a petrodollar manager who tailors his investment decisions to special financial needs of Arab businessmen and governments; petrodollar management has become an important force in international finance because of Arabs' general inclination to leave investment decisions to their advisers; Sambar indicates that his clients expect him to be ultra-conservative with their money; he knows that for investment to be sound in the eyes of an Arab, it must not only make money, but also must demonstrate investor's concern and interest in doing something for his country   (WALL STREET JOURNAL, May 9, 1978, P1)

O.P.E.C. INVESTMENTS TERMED MODEST

American Banker editorial comments on study by Christopher Bach of Commerce Department's bureau of economic analysis; study estimates international transactions between US and OPEC members from 1972 to 1977; finds that OPEC members' direct investments in US have been modest, running to $111 million in 1974 and mere $12 million in 1977   (AMERICAN BANKER, May 12, 1978, P4)

ARABS ARE INVESTING CAUTIOUSLY

Arab investments in US tend toward safe vehicles such as certificates of deposit and US government securities; most Arab investments in US come from government, rather than private, sources; Arab governments are moving slowly to diversify interests, venturing into the stock market, making private placements or acquiring real estate and equity in valuable assets; Arab and US bankers note most Arab surplus money for investments comes from oil revenues to Arab governments that view them as reserve assets for future domestic development plans; shortage of experienced Arab money managers and Arab investment firms inhibits greater diversification of Arab surplus funds; Saudis are the most conservative investors, while Kuwaitis are the most innovative; US economy remains principal investment attraction for Arab surplus money   (NEW YORK TIMES,   June 15, 1978,   S4   P1)

ARAB AID STUDIED

Organization for Economic Cooperation and Development study shows Arab nations give more than 5% of their gross national product as aid to poor countries, while average for industrialized nations is 0.39% of their GNP and US figure is 0.25%; observers say Arab foreign aid may benefit Western industrial nations by generating orders for technology that would not have been possible without Arab aid money   (CHRISTIAN SCIENCE MONITOR,   June 15, 1978,   P1)

PETRODOLLARS FAVOR U.S. BANKS

US Government and banking sources contend Arab countries with surplus money favor US banks over Arab banks; experts say principal reason is that most new Arab banks are pan-Arab enterprises, leaving little room for control by individual partners; new banking ventures are young and need time to mature before they can effectively handle billion-dollar deposits; Citibank, Chase Manhattan, Morgan Guaranty Trust and Bank of America are prominently involved in managing Arab funds   (NEW YORK TIMES,   June 15, 1978,   S4   P4)

GREEK-ARAB BANK FORMED

Greece, Kuwait and Libya sign agreement establishing an Arab-Greek bank in Athens; bank is seen as primary vehicle for future Arab investment in Greece; Angelos Angelopoulos, governor of National Bank of Greece, notes bank is first established in Greece as distinct from branches of foreign banks, in which majority participation is not Greek; it is hoped that other Arab countries will eventually participate in the bank   (JOURNAL OF COMMERCE,   June 29, 1978,   P1)

SAUDIS SEEKING INFLUENCE IN U.S.

Commentator Jack Anderson discusses Saudi Arabian investments in US; raises possibility that Saudis believe Jewish financial power is key to Jewish political influence and so are trying to equalize it; reports sources close to Treasury Secretary W. Michael Blumenthal place Saudi investments in US at $50 billion to $70 billion; notes that Saudis may be largest single shareholder of Federal Home Loan Mortgage Corp. bonds; reports Saudis have made $300 million in loans to American Telephone & Telegraph Co. and three of its operating companies; asserts US Steel and Pacific Gas & Electric Company have also received multi-million dollar loans   (WASHINGTON POST,   July 23, 1978,   S3   P7)

SAUDIS DEBATE CORPORATE TAKEOVERS

The Saudi Arabian government's inner circle is debating whether it should begin to acquire strategic stakes in selected Western companies; objective is to attract much-needed industrial technology; Saudi investment would mean injection of perhaps $1 billion to $2 billion into stock markets and corporate treasuries; Saudi Arabia currently makes only modest portfolio investments in corporate stocks, up to ceiling of 5% of company's capital; more conservative faction in Saudi leadership opposes greater equity investment and holds that minimum-risk portfolio approach is sounder in long run   (BUSINESS WEEK,   July 30, 1978,   P38)

KUWAIT SLOWS SPENDING

Kuwait plans to cut public expenditures for fiscal 1978-1979 to Kuwaiti dinars 1,950 million, down 1.9% from year-earlier KD1,988 million; real spending will be sharply curtailed through current estimated 15% annual inflation; revenue for 1978-1979 is estimated at KD2,301 million, compared with KD2,272 million in 1977-1978, with oil revenues expected to retain 95% share; projected surplus is placed at KD352 million against KD285 million expected for 1977-1978; revenue losses resulting from US dollar's decline since the end of 1976 are estimated at $500 million   (FINANCIAL TIMES,   August 3, 1978,   P3)

DROOPING DOLLAR DRAWS ARAB INVESTORS

Commentator Ed Blanche detects relocation in investment focus by wealthy Arabs from Britain to Western Europe and especially US; quotes Abdul Ghani al-Dalli, economist for Arab and International Bank for Investment, as seeing same depressed prices and currency in US that drew Arabs to Britain in 1973; prestige real estate and industry are cited as main investment objectives of Arabs in Britain; instances of overcharging of Arabs in Britain are cited as indicative of reasons why Arabs are turning elsewhere for travel and investment   (NEW YORK TIMES,   August 22, 1978,   P18)

RIYAL SHUNS RESERVE CURRENCY ROLE

Saudi Arabia is seeking to prevent its currency, the Saudi riyal, from becoming an international reserve currency; fears that such a development would cause Saudi Arabia to lose control over its domestic economy; growing number of investors are trying to buy Saudi riyals to protect the value of their capital, in response to falling value of US dollar; Saudi Arabian Monetary Agency's recent success in blocking a Citicorp loan to Morocco which was to be denominated in riyals cited as an example of Saudi Arabia's opposition to the riyal's becoming an international reserve currency   (BUSINESS WEEK,   September 11, 1978,   P126)

O.P.E.C. SHOWS PAYMENTS DEFICIT

International Monetary Fund finds that 13 members of OPEC registered combined deficit of $1.7 billion in their international payments in first quarter of 1978; deficit is largest of 3 quarterly deficits OPEC reported since 1973–1974 price hike, leading analysts to forecast swing back toward pattern of international payments that prevailed before price hike, and long-term trend to reduce oil surpluses in consumer countries   (NEW YORK TIMES,   September 13, 1978,   P31)

MONTEDISON GETS PETRODOLLAR INVESTMENT

A consortium of private Arab investors from Saudi Arabia, Kuwait and the United Arab Emirates plans to invest $42.5 million in Italian chemical company Montedison's $239 million new share issue, according to unidentified financial sources in New York City; investment would equal 10% of outstanding Montedison shares   (BUSINESS WEEK,   October 2, 1978,   P48)

Saudis Grow Polished in a More Assertive Role Abroad

By ERIC PACE

Special to The New York Times

RIYADH, Saudi Arabia—The leaders of this enormously wealthy oil state are growing increasingly practiced and confident in the more assertive role they have assumed in Middle Eastern and world affairs in the last few years.

The Saudi royal family has become more assured about its dominance of the Arabian Peninsula, according to Arab and Western sources, and in recent months it has quietly taken a more intense interest in the Horn of Africa, where it has smoothly engineered an end to the Soviet military role in Somalia.

"The Saudis have gotten more used to playing the power game," said one high United States official who was involved in President Carter's visit this month.

The interests of King Khalid, Crown Prince Fahd and other senior members of the Saudi ruling family, as perceived here in the Saudi royal capital, include protecting their rule, safeguarding the Saudi oil industry, nurturing a favorable political environment in the region, furthering Islam, and combating Communism, radicalism and Zionism.

Style Is Decorous and Discreet

Unlike such Arab nations as Syria, Libya and Iraq, the Saudis' style is deliberate, decorous and discreet, exercised in courtly letters, low-keyed visits, unannounced payments and meetings behind closed doors.

This calm style may in part reflect the fact that Saudi Arabia did not undergo the painful experience of rule by Western powers shared by other Arab nations, some diplomats here suggest. It also fits the Saudi leaders' conception of themselves as mediators and stabilizers in the area.

Despite Saudi Arabia's oil wealth—now coming in at the rate of $40 billion a year—and its strategic position between the Red Sea and the Persian Gulf, the kingdom long remained relatively uninvolved in world affairs. It was held back by conservatism and its consciousness of the vulnerability of its oil wells and the small size of its population, which numbers well under 10 million despite an influx of foreign workers.

That cautious role was maintained by the late King Faisal, a cautious conservative who was denounced and opposed by Gamal Abdel Nasser, Egypt's President in the 1950's and 1960's, and by others in the radical Arab camp.

Assertiveness Grows Under Khalid

Assassinated by an obscure relative, King Faisal was succeeded in 1975 by his brother Khalid, whose regime has been generally more assertive outside Saudi Arabia's borders while avoiding the extremes of oil embargo and war.

Striving for a favorable political climate in the Horn of Africa, across the Red Sea from its western coastline, Saudi Arabia has backed Somalia against Ethiopia, which has become increasingly dependent on Soviet military support.

In the past six months, the Saudi Government has poured aid into Somalia in an effort to wean it away from reliance on the Soviet Union, which had provided almost all of Somalia's military support in recent years. By some accounts, recent Saudi assistance to Somalia has totaled more than $150 million. The Saudi effort was successful last year when the Somali

Gamma

King Khalid

Government ordered Soviet technicians out of the country.

Saudi officials have also expressed approval privately of the rebellion being carried out in Ethiopia's northern coastal region of Eritrea.

Underwriting the new activism has been Saudi Arabia's burgeoning wealth. The Saudi Government's reserves, largely in overseas investments and convertible foreign currencies, have been authoritatively estimated at $60 billion.

However, certain factors operate to limit the power conferred by this great wealth. For example, the real value of Saudi Arabia's oil revenues and of its reserves have diminished with worldwide inflation and with the decline of the dollar in recent months.

Nonetheless, Saudi Arabia's wealth is expected to continue to increase, making possible increases in Saudi foreign aid, through which Egypt alone has received more than $5 billion within the past four years.

The ruling family has been putting the growing Saudi wealth to work to buttress its position within the kingdom. For example, oil revenues finance an extensive security apparatus which keeps watch on, among other things, the arrival of Arabs of suspect political backgrounds in Jidda, the commercial center, and even on the presence of foreigners in their rooms in Riyadh's crowded hotels.

Oil wealth is also being used to finance a buildup of Saudi Arabia's regular armed forces and the National Guard, an independent force commanded by the third-ranking member of the royal family, Prince Abdullah.

All told, Saudi military expenditures last year were about $10 billion out of a total budget of $30 billion, according to well-placed members of the foreign community.

Among the difficulties facing the Saudi military, in addition to the small size of its forces, are the Saudi soldiers' lack of familiarity with modern warfare, their high degree of individualism, which makes them reluctant to accept strict discipline, their lack of discipline in firing weapons, their relative lack of concern about the maintenance of equipment, and excessive reliance on American instructors, technicians and equipment.

Economic Aid Programs

The Saudis have also been influential in the Arab-Israeli conflict, which is important to Saudi Arabia for reasons of Arab patriotism and because it is felt here that another Arab-Israeli war might strengthen radical forces in the area, possibly posing a threat to the Saudi regime.

The Government of King Khalid has

been continuing King Faisal's policy of financial support for Egypt's moderate President, Anwar el-Sadat, but it is widely expected that this support would be cut back if Mr. Sadat reached a separate peace agreement with Israel. The Saudis, as fervent advocates of Arab unity, strongly oppose such a move.

The Saudis have also been giving smaller amounts of assistance to other Arab nations bordering Israel, and to the Palestine Liberation Organization. Saudi officials assert, however, that their Government withholds support from radical Palestinian groups.

A high Saudi Foreign Ministry official indicated recently that Saudi Arabia would provide financial support to a Palestinian entity if one is created in a peace settlement. Such support is widely expected in the Arab world and frequent predictions are heard that a Palestinian entity might become very largely dependent on Saudi aid.

It has become known that President Sadat did not consult Riyadh before deciding to make his visit to Jerusalem in November, and that he gave no immediate answer when King Khalid wrote him a letter asking what he hoped the visit would achieve.

All the available evidence indicates that the Saudi Government has stayed out of the detailed maneuvering toward a settlement. It has given its approval in private to President Sadat's diplomacy, while publicly reaffirming its support for what it calls the rights of the Palestinians, the establishment of a Palestinian state and the restoration of Arab control over East Jerusalem.

Under King Khalid, Saudi Arabia has achieved amicable relations with Iran, which loudly opposed Saudi Arabia's policy on oil pricing at the conference of the Organization of Petroleum Exporting Countries in Qatar in late 1976.

There is a long history of mistrust between the Arab world and Iran, which is not an Arab nation, and Saudi officials express uneasiness in private about Iran's growing military might, as well as concern about what sort of government will eventually succeed that of the present Shah. But Iran and Saudi Arabia share a common desire that their oil exports proceed unhindered, and a common opposition to radicalism and Soviet influence —notably Moscow's stepped-up role in Ethiopia.

Saudi Arabia has also worked for smooth relations with Syria's President, Hafez al-Assad, despite his relatively radical political philosophy. The Saudis consider Mr. Assad a reasonable man with whom they can deal.

NEW YORK TIMES, January 24, 1978, P8

Mideast: Aging Boom, Oil Cutback, Costly Arms

By MARVINE HOWE

BEIRUT, LEBANON

Boom times in the Middle East, with all the phenomenal construction projects that followed the quadrupling of the price of oil in 1973, have begun to ease off to a slower rate of growth, according to Arab economists. Rapid development has run into problems.

The United Arab Emirates and Qatar actually suffered something of a recession last year. The crisis became public with the closing of two banks for lack of liquidity. Inflation soared at about 35 percent. Real-estate speculation was frantic and merchants panicked as their stocks piled up.

But, as a Lebanese banker put it, "Recession in the Gulf doesn't really mean decline, just fewer big projects and a slowdown in government spending."

"Our generation was lucky," Jamshid Amouzegar, Prime Minister of Iran, said. "Our grandfathers didn't have oil and our grandchildren won't have any either, so it is our duty to spend our oil revenue wisely."

But growth has been marred, particularly in the small newly rich countries of the Persian Gulf, which seem persuaded that national sovereignty implies the most extravagant international airports, hotels, steel mills and petrochemical complexes.

Rivalry among nations appears to be the main cause for the spending. Each is trying to outdo the other with luxury hotels, cement factories, petrochemical industries and fertilizer plants. The United Arab Emirates, with a population of 700,000, has eight international airports completed or under construction. The tiny

states of Sharjah and Ras al Khaima opened their huge airports this year. Qatar recently built a magnificent sports city and now Abu Dhabi is building one that will probably hold its entire population.

The oil wealth is spilling over and filtering down and, as a result, the living standard of the average Arab has improved. A whole new class—grocers, clerks, low-ranking officials—has appeared. They are venturing abroad to see the wonders of Cairo and Damascus and buy pleasures unavailable in their own puritanical societies.

But in view of an oversupply of oil with Alaskan, North Sea and Mexican production, there are certain to be cutbacks in Middle East output this year. Iran and Abu Dhabi have already indicated about a 15 percent cut in production. The Saudis too are expected to cut their output by 10 to 15 percent and Kuwait has said it would vary monthly production.

Saudi Arabia has accumulated reserves estimated to surpass $50 billion. Revenue for 1977 was said to be in the neighborhood of $41.4 billion while expenditures ran at $31.5 billion. The Saudis earmarked 68 percent of the expenditures for social and economic development but the largest single allocation, or $9 billion, went to defense and the National Guard.

Saudi Arabia's main constraint is shortage of skilled manpower. The short-term answer is foreign labor. For the next five years, planners estimate it will be necessary to import 500,000 workers, or two-thirds of the labor supply, which could mean social problems as well as high costs.

"The trouble is that the Saudis now have an aversion to manual labor—which means continued dependence on immigrant workers and more problems of social discontent and new ideologies," a Syrian consultant who deals with the Saudis said.

King Khalid recently inaugurated what is said to be the world's largest industrial complex at Jubail on the Gulf coast. It will include three refineries, four petrochemical plants, two fertilizer plants, two methanol plants, an aluminum smelter and a steel mill. Progress on these projects is reportedly slow because of high costs and the skilled labor shortage.

Iran ran into a capital shortage last year despite an estimated oil income of around $23 billion and had to lean heavily on foreign loans. Prices for imports and wage increases outran production, hampered by shortages of cement, electricity and inadequate port facilities.

Consequently there was a slowdown in growth from the target of 13 percent to about 10 percent, which was a significant drop from the heady 40 percent of 1974. Shah Mohammed Riza Pahlevi ordered his Government to slow down its expansion to a rate "which can be digested." He also named a new Prime Minister, the former oil negotiator, Mr. Amouzegar, who favors restraint in spending.

Nevertheless, the Government is pursuing its ambitious nuclear-power program. It has obtained a $1.6 billion credit from six French banks for two nuclear plants and is holding talks with West German banks for an $8 billion credit for the construction of four more nuclear plants.

Kuwait enjoys one of the world's highest per capita incomes but is heavily dependent on oil, a depleting resource. Highest priority is being given to diversification in petrochemical projects, petroleum refining, natural and liquefied gas and other petroleum derivatives. But there is fear that too many of these industries are being built in the Gulf.

Because of its limited outlets for domestic investment, Kuwait is an important exporter of capital. It led the Arab aid effort and since 1973 has been joined by Saudi Arabia and Abu Dhabi. The largest disbursements go to the Arab "front line" nations—Egypt, Syria and Jordan—and the Palestine Liberation Organization.

Continuation of tensions has meant high expenditures for national defense, particularly by Egypt, Syria and Jordan. Tensions have also meant little or no foreign investment for these countries. "Who's going to put money into an area where you could have war next week?" an American said here. The nations that don't expect oil, including Syria, Jordan, Lebanon, Yemen, Southern Yemen and Bahrain, suffer from shortages of capital and foreign exchange despite assistance from the Gulf states.

Egypt became a net oil exporter in 1975 and aims to earn $1 billion from its oil by 1980. At present, however, its exports are modest and developments problems so enormous that it is generally grouped with the nonoil countries.

The most populous country of the Middle East, with 40 million inhabitants, Egypt has an annual 2.3 percent population increase and that erodes economic growth. Because of political uncertainties, no major foreign industrial investments have come in. To encourage foreign investments, Cairo signed agreements with the Coca-Cola Company and the Ford Motor Company a few months ago on the understanding that it would get them off the Arab black list, or failing that, at least off the Egyptian list. President Anwar el-Sadat's peace drive was intended to resolve economic problems by improving the investment climate and decreasing costly military expenditures.

Syria and Jordan are also heavily dependent on the Gulf states. Foreign aid accounts for about 60 percent of Jordan's budget, mainly from the Arab nations. Jordan has increased investment in mining and agriculture to avoid dependency on outside financing. Jordan's development, however, could be hurt by the departure of 150,000 Jordanians—engineers, agricultural technicians, doctors, nurses, teachers—for jobs mainly in the Gulf.

Lebanon, the darkest spot on the horizon a year ago, has shown remarkable recovery. Prime Minister Selim al Hoss estimates direct material losses from the 19-month civil war at $4 billion and indirect losses to the national income up to 1980 of as much as $7.3 billion. The city's center, which was virtually destroyed, still resembles Berlin in 1945.

Shopkeepers have reopened their enterprises in the ruins, on sidewalks and in the periphery of Beirut and are flourishing. Banks have a surplus liquidity of about $600 million and the central bank's gold and foreign exchange reserves are put at $750 million; in reality they exceed $1 billion because they are quoted at the old gold rate of $42 an ounce.

NEW YORK TIMES, February 5, 1978, S12 P69

Relaxation of Spending Curbs Spurs the Saudi Arabian Economy

By ERIC PACE
Special to The New York Times

RIYADH, Saudi Arabia—The pace of Saudi Arabia's economy has been picking up again after lagging early last year, members of the business community here and in Jidda report.

Fueled by $40 billion a year in oil revenues and $30 billion a year in Government spending, business activity has resumed markedly in the last six months, although at a less feverish rate than in past years, which were marked by steep inflation and severe bottlenecks.

The Government has been pushing ahead with development expenditures, but at an uneven pace, and it claims to have surpassed its ambitious schedule in school construction.

United States exports to Saudi Arabia have been increasing, although anxiety about United States income taxing of money earned abroad has been a brake on the growth of the American community here.

"My goodness, it is a busy time now," Ghaleb Abu al-Faraj, president of the Saudi International Company for Trading, Industry and Agencies, recently told a traveler in Jidda, the kingdom's commercial capital.

The business pickup contrasts with the slowdown that began late in 1976 and continued through last spring. The slowdown was caused in large part by government restraining and retrenchment measures, and included a slowdown in the real estate sector and cutbacks on imports by merchants who had earlier overordered and overstocked.

Now the flow of goods through Saudi

ports has increased—and is especially visible in Jidda—and there are fresh goods in many stores.

With business proceeding at a more measured rate than in the first years after oil prices began skyrocketing in late 1973, no severe shortages have materialized lately, business sources say, and no notable bottlenecks have appeared except for the long-standing shortage of labor, which continues despite the presence of an estimated 1.5 million nonwage-earners here in a total population of between six and eight million.

The pickup began last summer with a surge in business activity before the beginning of the Moslem holy month of Ramadan, which began in August. It has been fueled, sources report, by a reacceleration of Government purchasing, which had been held back in the early summer, and has been marked by the awarding of some major contracts. These have included a $3 billion contract, awarded last month to three concerns: Phillips, the Dutch electronic concern; Bell of Canada, and the L. M. Erickson Company, a Swedish concern. The contract is for telephone equipment that is to be installed throughout the country.

Easing Port Congestion

The Government's current $30 billion budget has been held to the same size

as those for the previous two years, and the Government is continuing in other ways to combat inflation, which is expected in the near future to be roughly half the unofficially estimated rate of 35 to 45 percent that had jolted Saudi business life before the lag.

Although firm statistics are often hard to come by here, Saudi Government officials say that the inflation rate fell to below 10 percent last year, after the Government had taken such anti-inflation measures as easing port congestion and reducing the rate of growth of the nation's money supply—considered a major determinant of inflation—in addition to postponing some development projects.

"I think things are under control now," Ghazi al-Qusaibi, the Saudi Minister of Industry and Electricity, told reporters last year.

Implementation of the country's spectacular $142 billion plan for industry has been continuing although numerous goals are not expected to be met. Mr. Qusaibi has estimated that targets of the plan will be only 80 percent fulfilled by the end of 1980, the period set for the completion of the plan.

"People were accusing us of dreaming" when the plan for industry first was made public in 1975, Faisal al-Bashir, the undersecretary in the planning ministry said in a recent interview,

while computers whirred on the ground floor of the ministry building here.

"But rest assured that we can spend the money," he continued.

Mr. Bashir noted that part of the Government's recent fiscal retrenchment had occurred through a series of project postponements that arose when officials here concluded that foreign construction companies had been submitting bids that were far higher than was justified.

"These companies were trying to take us for a ride," Mr. Bashir said. Accordingly, he reported, in the winter of 1975-76 bids were rejected on large-scale desalination and rural electrification projects, among others.

After months of postponements, contracts for most of those projects have now been awarded and the second round of bids was substantially lower than the first, he said, adding, "I believe we have saved Saudi Arabia billions" of Saudi Riyals.

"Saving the money was well worth the headache," Mr. Bashir observed, asserting that some foreign concerns had engaged in collusion in originally submitting bids that were unduly high.

NEW YORK TIMES, February 11, 1978, P27

Industry to Transform Saudi Village

By ERIC PACE
Special to The New York Times

RIYADH, Saudi Arabia—The roads in eastern Saudi Arabia have grown crowded with trucks carrying construction equipment. Dredging is churning the coastal waters of the Persian Gulf. Work is under way on housing to shelter more than 30,000 workers.

The oil-rich Saudi Government is pressing ahead with work on a vast, multibillion-dollar industrial center beside the coastal town of Jubail, 55 miles northwest of Dhahran, the capital of the Saudi oil industry. The decision to transform the tiny fishing village of 4,000 in a decade has been described as the largest single construction project in history.

"We are going at a fast rate to modernize the country," a traveler was told here in the Saudi capital recently by Farouk Mohammed Akdar, the secretary general of the Saudi Government commission that is overseeing the development of Jubail and of Yenbo, a port on the Saudi Red Sea coast, where another, smaller industrial center is planned.

Fuel for Industry

The natural gas extracted along with the oceans of crude oil in Saudi

Arabia's huge oilfields is to be exploited to fuel the Jubail and Yenbo complexes, which are to include oil refineries, petrochemical plants, lesser industrial installations and extensive permanent housing.

The Jubail site, where construction is scheduled to continue into the 1980's and perhaps beyond, is also to include an aluminum smelter, a steel mill, an international airport, two deepwater ports, several power generating plants,

The New York Times/Feb. 13, 1978

an extensive telecommunications system and the world's largest water desalination complex.

Interviewed at the commission's headquarters building here, Dr. Akdar, whose doctorate in economics is from the University of California at Riverside, declined to predict what the costs of the complexes would be.

Unofficially, Saudi officials have been saying that infrastructure and basic industrial facilities at the two centers would cost a total of $30 billion, but other estimates run much higher. The Saudi press has estimated recently that the figure will be between $20 billion and $30 billion for Jubail alone. By industry estimates, Jubail carries an ultimate price tag of $45 billion.

Such enormous outlays are within the financial means of Saudi Arabia, which has oil revenues of $40 billion a year and reserves of $60 billion or so.

The long-term rationale for the projects was put forth in these words in the commission's annual report for last year:

"To continue exporting our oil wealth in its crude form, to the point of total depletion, would have adverse economic effects in the not-too-distant future. For then the kingdom would find itself with no economic basis to rely on.

"Thus our industrialization strategy aims at the long-term objective of diversifying the kingdom's industrial base, thus enabling Saudi Arabia to realize a greater measure of economic self-sufficiency and allowing it to reap the benefits of local production."

A first big step at the Jubail site has been the dredging of the harbor and the construction of port facilities. These are to be completed by the spring of 1979—which will ease the burden on the kingdom's highway system and its existing ports.

Overall assistance to the Saudi commission in developing the Jubail center is being provided by the Saudi Arabian Bechtel Company, an arm of the Bechtel Corporation, the giant American construction company.

The commission says it is keenly concerned about avoiding duplication between Jubail's industrial facilities and those that have been erected in other oil states adjoining the Persian Gulf.

In the interview, Dr. Akdar said the problem had been complicated by duplicity on the part of would-be contractors.

"Large multinational companies have come to us with feasibility studies for certain projects, based on the assumption that no other countries in the region are doing such projects," he said.

"But then they take the same feasibility studies and suggest the ideas to each one of our neighbors. They want to sell their equipment and services" wherever they can, he went on. Saudi planning officials have been in touch with their counterparts in neighboring states to minimize overlapping in their respective development plans.

Two fertilizer plants are also to be built at Jubail, along with half a dozen petrochemical and related plants, the steel mill and the aluminum smelter. These installations are to be owned by the Saudi Government jointly with non-Saudi concerns.

In addition, the ancillary installations are to include a steel-rolling mill to make steel reinforcing rods for the construction that is under way all around the Gulf region.

These ancillary plants are expected to be owned by the Saudi private sector largely in joint ventures with Western and Japanese concerns. Joint ventures to operate in the industrial centers have already been negotiated by such major United States concerns as Dow, Exxon, Grace and Mobil.

One of the tasks of the commission is to approve additional companies to be invited to bid for contracts.

More than a score of contracts have been let already by the commission to contractors ranging from various Arab concerns to the mammoth and versatile Arabian American Oil Company, which has become increasingly involved in construction in recent years.

Work at Yenbo, which began early in 1976, is about two years behind the development at Jubail. Yenbo's existing port facilities have been expanded, and a work camp was set up last year for construction crews.

At this stage, the Saudis are evaluating construction bids for a $1.06 billion pipeline that would bring crude oil to Yenbo from the eastern Saudi oilfields 750 miles away. Spanning the entire peninsula, the pipeline would link the Red Sea port with the oilfields at Abgaig, close by the Persian Gulf. Scheduled for completion in mid-1981, the pipeline would spare tankers the long trip around the peninsula and up into the gulf.

The choice of the site at Yenbo "means that we'll have another access to the world market, through the Red Sea and the Suez Canal, which will make us closer to the European market," Dr. Akdar said, noting that the Jubail site "is closer to the Asian consumer."

Furthermore, Saudi officials say that having the centers divided by the width of the Arabian peninsula will make Saudi industry less vulnerable to outside attack.

NEW YORK TIMES, February 13, 1978, S4 P1

Bechtel Orchestrates Building of New Saudi City

By YOUSSEF M. IBRAHIM

It has become a global undertaking. From San Francisco to Boston and from London to Seoul, an army of draftsmen, architects, engineers, urbanologists, lawyers and laborers has enlisted in creating the huge Saudi industrial center at Jubail, at a cost as high as $45 billion.

"In dollar volume, the project is the largest we have had. In magnitude, it is simply incomparable," said Alden Yates, vice president of the Bechtel Corporation, hired overseers for the project. "We are building the whole thing from scratch."

In June 1976, Bechtel received a 20-year contract to manage the implementation of the master plan it had submitted to the Saudi Royal Commission on Jubail and Yenbo, the policy-making body for the project. Mr. Yates, who was interviewed during a recent visit to Bechtel's San Francisco headquarters, is Bechtel's field manager.

Bechtel's task, he said, was to map out the entire infrastructure for the industrial complex and the city, supervise the granting of contracts after evaluating bids, and oversee the actual construction.

"We make sure all the pieces fit together," says Charles G. Wolfe, engineering manager in the Bechtel's San Francisco support office, where some 20 technicians spent all of last year preparing "requests for proposals" to go out to hundreds of contractors this year.

Already more than 100 contracts have been awarded and nearly $2 billion spent.

The Hyundai Group, a South Korean construction venture, already has a $1 billion contract to dredge and build Jubail's industrial port. It is putting 2,500 Koreans to work in around-the-clock shifts seven day a week, racing to meet a 1979 deadline.

Area's Ecology Is Assured

Another commercial port is being built by a consortium of Dutch, Lebanese and Greek companies. Together, the two ports will handle 5 million tons of general cargo, 5 million tons of bulk cargo and 26 million tons of liquid cargo, a year.

The New York-based firm of Sanderson & Porter Inc., is supervising the engineering and construction of a $5 billion water desalination plant, the world's largest, at Jubail to provide drinking water and power to the city. It says the first phase of the station will be finished in mid-1980. It is to provide 30 million gallons of water a day and generate 300,000 kilowatts of power.

In Jubail, employees of Tetra Inc., a Pasadena, Calif., company, are winding their way through a $6 million assessment of the impact of the industrial plan on the area's ecology.

In Boston, the Architects Collaboratives Inc. are working on community design for the future city, while in London, Colin Buchanan & Partners Ltd. is preparing an urban blueprint for Jubail—including studies on the social, economic and demographic distribution of the multinational population that will fill out the city.

By 1995, Bechtel estimates, Jubail will have about 300,000 people, a great many of them expatriates working and living in Saudi Arabia.

In West Germany, engineers of the Karf-Stahl Company are laying out final plans for an 800,000-ton steel mill to be built in joint venture with the Saudis.

The Saudis have also contracted with the New York law firm of Sherman & Sterling, one of the nation's largest, to review all contracts signed with the Royal Commission. Frederick R. Harris Inc., a consulting engineering firm, is working out financial controls guidelines for the projects to come on stream.

When Bechtel started mapping out its plans back in 1976 it began to realize the awesome dimensions of the project. Jubail had no major road connections, no labor force, no power supply, no housing, and no sweet water, save for a few wells. Construction material had to be trucked in from Dammam, farther south, on a narrow two-lane highway already choked with traffic.

The most serious obstacle, however, was finding the labor force, Bechtel executives say. When construction gets into full swing—sometime in 1983— nearly 40,000 workers must be on the site, Bechtel estimates. Virtually all of them will be foreigners brought in to work under special contracts because Saudi Arabia, with a native population of around 5 million, already has nearly 2 million aliens in the labor force.

Six thousand of these workers must arrive by this year-end, Bechtel said.

Work is under way on two labor camps to house them. The workers, Bechtel said, will be recruited from the Philippines, Pakistan, and India.

Lack of Housing Felt

The lack of infrastructure has also cost time. The initial team of 200 Bechtel managers—mostly Americans and Europeans—was forced into Al Khobar, a city 35 miles north of Jubail, early last year for lack of housing on the construction site itself. Only a few weeks ago did they move to newly-built quarters.

"Wives and families only started to come in six months after we moved into Saudi Arabia," said Mr. Yates. "We had to start with trailers and beach camps at first." He will have 300 staff members on the site soon, and by 1985, he expects to draw a thousand managers to Jubail from the various affiliates of Bechtel around the world.

The linchpin of the industrial complex is cheap natural gas, which has been abundant in Saudi Arabia.

Under a 1975 agreement between the Saudis and the Arabian American Oil Company, Aramco, a total of 5 billion cubic feet a day of ethane and methane, as well as 10 million tons a year of petroleum gas liquids, will be gathered, processed and distributed as feedstock to fuel the new industries in Jubail and other regions in Saudi Arabia.

Part of the project is being carried out by subsidiaries of the Fluor Engineers and Constructors Inc. of Los Angeles under contract to Aramco.

The Saudis have yet to decide the final shape of the complex. One reason is the bulging cost of the gas gathering project, which in 1975 was estimated at $4.5 billion. It had nearly tripled by the end of 1977. The steep rise forced another look into the economics of the industrial projects, which were based on the premise of cheap energy supplies.

Another problem is that all the petrochemical projects scheduled for Jubail will be 50-50 joint ventures with Exxon, Mobil Oil, Dow Chemical and Shell Oil, with investment outlays of $1 billion per plant or more.

Industry sources say the foreign partners, and the Saudis, are reluctant to commit the large investments in money, equipment and technicians at a time when demand for petrochemicals around the world is soft and is forecast to remain so in the near future.

NEW YORK TIMES, February 13, 1978, P3

2

A Durable OPEC

When a five member Organization of Petroleum Exporting Countries (OPEC) constituted itself in 1960, long-time observers of the oil industry pointed to the inherent strains and conflicts in the nascent cartel and predicted it would never last. At that time Iraq, Iran, Kuwait and Saudi Arabia tried unsuccessfuly to keep oil prices from falling in a decade-long buyers' market for their product. When a sellers' market took shape in the seventies the cartel, expanding to include Algeria, Libya, Qatar, the United Arab Emirates (UAE), Nigeria, Ecuador, Venezuela, Indonesia and Gabon, scored a notable success by raising the price of oil about 25% in 1971. Two years later they increased the price of a barrel of oil from around 1.80 to 11.5 dollars. In the process, oil revenues rose such that while OPEC earned 5.8 billion dollars in 1970, by 1974 Saudi Arabia alone was earning $7 billion. Yet in face of this success, the same critics of the cartel continue to predict its collapse. And indeed, in 1978 there were many indications that the cartel would break apart. The threat of breakup hung over the OPEC ministers' meetings in Geneva and Taif, Saudi Arabia, yet they ended the year by announcing a 14% price, effective January, 1979. It was the largest price rise in five years.

The issues threatening OPEC with dissolution, and which resulted in the year's price increase, are complex yet basic to the understanding of how the cartel operates. It has taken OPEC members five years to master the implications of their 1973 decision. In that year OPEC suddenly increased their prices by 470%. The consuming nations said this was "too high." The Shah of Iran defended the move by saying that during the 1960s the price of oil had sunk "too low." What the price of oil should be is difficult to determine, for there is in the oil industry no market mechanism like the London Metal's market or the Chicago Grain Exchange, where the demand and supply for a commodity is constantly spotted. With oil, the producers fix a price without knowing whether that price will increase or decrease demand. If demand should increase, the producers' cartel will encourage larger production schedules to its members. If demand falls, then the cartel must impose unpopular cutbacks among its members. The latitude for making mistakes in this delicate process became only too apparent in 1973.

As a result of the price hike oil consumption, which had been expanding at a rate of 11% a year, now fell by 6%. A glut materialized on the market, which the recession-racked industrial nations could now no longer afford to buy. The accusation that OPEC had brought on this recession particularly rankled the oil sovereigns. The Shah of Iran argued that the world demand for oil could never take into account the replacement value for oil·(that is, the cost of the next economic fuel to be used to replace oil when reserves are exhausted). The Shah wanted a higher price than the world was willing to pay because he knew (and the world presumably did not) that oil was an exhaustible resource. Nevertheless, to unload the growing glut of oil, Iran resorted to cut-rate sales and barters, to the chagrin of its fellow OPEC members. Price cutting by one member, of course, is one of the pitfalls facing a cartel.

As OPEC members argued about what price they were actually selling their oil for, they faced a rift over the need to reduce allocation. While demand shrunk, particularly needy members pleaded not to have their production cut back. Indonesia, for example, argued successfully that its output was already such a small fraction of OPEC's production and its revenue needs so great that it should continue to produce at full capacity. But conflict developed between Iraq and the cartel over the same issue. Looking forward to annual oil revenues of $10 billion in the coming years, Iraq's 1975–1980 development plan called for spending 5.5 billion petrodollars. Now, with the slump, the country was rapidly going into debt. Cutbacks would have increased the deficit even further, so Baghdad bitterly resisted the notion of holding back production.

Coming to the rescue of the cartel, Saudi Arabia and Kuwait, with nearly half of the production of the cartel, voluntarily agreed to keep down production. This action by two of the largest producers helped to reduce the glut to a manageable size. From 1975 to 1977 OPEC restricted its production so that it was operating at only 70% capacity. This policy began to pay off as the market responded to the shortfalls in oil by seeking out higher prices.

Besides pricing and allocation, a third issue arose out of the 1973 price rise which in 1978 became the most bitterly debated issue at OPEC meetings. With the decline in the value of the dollar triggered by the price rise, the value of oil denominated in the dollar fell precipitously against hard currencies. Moreover, the vast petrodollar holdings of the oil states, by simply sitting in banks, cost OPEC $14 billion in 1977. The oil states possessed so many dollars that any attempt to sell them would further bring down their value, perhaps catastrophically. Finally, every time OPEC discussed the possibility of denominating oil in some other currency, which would greatly increase the price of oil for the many consumers paying in dollars, the threat to the dollar's convertibility sent the dollar plummeting lower and lower. The OPEC members were in a quandary; the mere mention of their dollar-denominating problems exacerbated the same problems.

Saudi Arabia, OPEC's leading producer, has been decisive in resolving these three issues facing the cartel. By taking the lead in reducing production, the kingdom has been able to impose on the cartel the 1975–1978 freeze of prices. This, Saudi oil analysts felt, would enable the West to adjust to the higher price of oil and to bring their economies out of recession. Because of their cartel-saving sacrifice of production, the Saudis were in a position to argue against the revaluing of oil from the dollar to another currency or a combination of other currencies; OPEC survived its own success in 1973 because Saudi Arabia was willing to act as a bumper for the organization's rougher driving.

In 1978 oil prices firmed in response to the self-imposed cutbacks in OPEC and members of OPEC felt the time was ripe for another increase in the price. Saudi Arabia disagreed, and industry observers again predicted the cartel's demise. The combination of a plummeting dollar, a firmer price of oil and the decline of OPEC-produced oil (from 70% of the world market in 1973 to 50% in 1978) stimulated enough unity among OPEC members for them to insist on Saudi cooperation with a price hike. If Saudi Arabia had cooperated, the cartel would have ended in 1978. That kingdom continued to play its role of regional moderate and maker of compromises, by going along with the highest price hike in five years, which is 14.5%.

YAMANI EMPHASIZES INDEPENDENT POSTURE

Saudi Arabian Oil Minister, Sheikh Yamani, denies US pressured OPEC on decision to freeze oil prices until mid-1978; Yamani says freeze will give industrial countries of Europe and Asia time to adjust their energy policies in accordance with expected rationing by oil producing countries   (TIMES OF LONDON,   January 3, 1978,   S2   P1)

REPORT URGES HARD LINE

Controversial General Accounting Office report suggests that US government should take a more activist role in dealings between multinational oil companies and oil exporting nations; does not advocate specific approaches but lists number of alternatives, such as reconsideration of favorable trade terms, that could be used as levers to encourage oil prices; also urges greater government involvement in companies' crude oil acquisition and in development of foreign energy sources outside OPEC nations; report is "confrontational" in tone and has generated opposition both within GAO and within other Federal departments   (NEW YORK TIMES,   January 4, 1978,   S4   P1)

BASKET PRICING URGED

Commentator Samuel Brittan urges Saudi Arabian Oil Minister Yamani to shift oil price from dollar basis to basket of currencies; argues switch would benefit world economy, oil producers and, eventually, US; holds change would lessen jerky movement of oil prices; observes dollar pricing has been based on assumption of dollar stability, which has declined markedly; argues struggle to maintain artificial parities brings crises and forces governments to impose trade and payments restrictions in attempt to preserve exchange rate structure   (FINANCIAL TIMES, January 16, 1978,   P8)

KUWAIT ADJUSTS HEAVY CRUDE

Kuwait announces 10-cent reduction in price of heavy crude oil, to $12.27 per barrel; gives no reason for reduction, which is retroactive to January; other OPEC members have also reduced prices slightly since December meeting in Caracas, Venezuela, and Nigeria has announced plans for 5% price reduction   (NEW YORK TIMES,   January 18, 1978,   S4   P2)

O.P.E.C. PONDERS DOLLAR SLIDE

OPEC Secretary-general Ali Jaidah reports that oil exporting nations are concerned over effect of falling value of US dollar on oil prices; holds OPEC countries have not discussed measures to combat dollar's slide   (NEW YORK TIMES,   February 2, 1978,   S4   P10)

O.P.E.C.-U.S. COOPERATION SOUGHT

Discussion of conciliation strategy used by Department of Energy officials towards members of OPEC finds that energy officials have been stressing importance of working with major oil producers particularly to increase exchange of information and obtain greater knowledge of producers' plans, intentions and capabilities which can help US improve its own energy planning; Secretary James R. Schlesinger and his top aides have in the last year visited key nations to try to implement strategy; another aspect of current international orientation involves identifying potential major new producers so that diplomatic efforts can begin as soon as possible   (NEW YORK TIMES,   March 2, 1978,   S4   P13)

DOLLAR SLIDE THREATENS O.P.E.C. RIFT

OPEC fears its members may split in face of weakening US dollar; Saudi Arabia has indicated willingness to act in favor of members, but rejects proposals to stop using dollar as basis for oil prices; OPEC Secretary-General Ali Jaidah estimates decline of dollar is costing members $14 billion per year   (NEW YORK TIMES,   March 7, 1978,   P53)

MEETING ON DOLLAR SLIDE

Iraq news agency reports OPEC will hold informal Geneva meeting on April 3; US dollar's decline on foreign exchange markets and its effect on oil revenues will likely be subject of discussion; OPEC's Arab members have called for new system of calculating oil prices, following dollar's decline during week beginning February 26   (NEW YORK TIMES,   March 9, 1978,   S4   P7)

OIL PRICING CHANGES CONSIDERED

Continuing decline in value of US dollar revives discussion among oil producing nations over raising oil prices or abandoning dollar as price basis; OPEC members will meet in Geneva during April to discuss problem; paying dollars but pegging oil prices to range of currencies poses technical difficulties and financial risk for OPEC; oil exporting nations tend to lose in trade with countries whose currency has strengthened against dollar; oil analysts and industry executives contend price increase now is highly unlikely; OPEC may consider pricing oil on basis of Special Drawing Rights established by International Monetary Fund; OPEC nations would get fewer dollars for oil priced in SDR's if dollar begins to recover   (NEW YORK TIMES,   March 17, 1978,   S4   P1)

An oil rig. Oil pricing remained an issue throughout the year as OPEC members continued to debate use of the dollar as a basis for buying.

Oil exploration continues in the OPEC nations. Here, a desert vehicle sets out from an exploration camp in the Rub' al-Khali.

OIL WEAPON PONDERED

S. Fred Singer of University of Virginia holds US should not base its foreign policy on misconceptions about the strength of Arab oil power; claims Saudi Arabia will oppose too-rapid price increases on economic and political grounds; believes if US appears convinced that it will be hurt, another oil embargo will be more probable; says terrorist raid on oil supply is more likely than embargo; believes strategic oil stockpile and growing interdependence between US and Saudi Arabia make embargo less likely; indicates Arabs could not create havoc within Western banking system by withholding petrodollars because Arabs must invest in or purchase from oil-consuming nations with those petrodollars; believes there is not much point in bargaining with, cajoling or threatening OPEC, even for benefit of less developed countries; concludes US should be aware that "oil power" will not protect Saudi Arabia's oil reserves from radicals and ambitious politicians, both Arab and non-Arab   (FOREIGN POLICY,   April 1978,   P53)

STABLE OIL PRICES FORESEEN

Robert S. Pindyck of Massachusetts Institute of Technology believes oil shortage caused by short supply will not occur because of impact of past and future energy price changes on supply and demand; holds oil embargo or OPEC production cutback is more likely, and needs more attention in design of US energy policy; reviews way OPEC sets world oil prices, claiming OPEC's main considerations are economic; predicts OPEC will raise oil prices slowly, unless political events dictate otherwise; says most important measure for US is development of strategic oil reserve; reports OPEC's price hikes have made world a little poorer; concludes US and other industrial nations must respond to any future oil embargoes with expansionary macroeconomic policies to counteract adverse short-run effects of embargo on unemployment and gross national product   (FOREIGN POLICY,   April 1978,   P36)

O.P.E.C. PRICING SCORED

Economist editorial attacks OPEC ministers for having created complex pricing structure for oil which even they now have no control over; notes that they are now incapable of fixing prices because they have lost control to world stagnation and rising oil production in non-OPEC countries   (ECONOMIST,   April 1, 1978,   P65)

OIL PRICE INCREASE LOOMS

Dollar closes mostly lower in foreign exchange trading in Western Europe and Tokyo, and drops sharply in New York after announcement that Saudi Arabia might agree to raise price of oil; Saudi oil minister Sheikh Ahmed Zaki Yamani states that if Western economies recovered and demand of oil increased, OPEC would raise its price   (NEW YORK TIMES,   April 7, 1978,   S4 P2)

MONETARY SYSTEM REVISIONS SCORED

Editorial sees grave threat to international monetary system and world trade and prices if International Monetary Fund staff-plan, offered by fund's managing director H. Johannes Witteveen, of substituting Special Drawing Rights (SDR's) for dollars held by foreign governments is implemented; urges Treasury Secretary W. Michael Blumenthal to strongly oppose plan at IMF Mexico City meeting; concedes general long-term merit of plan in that it would help stabilize world trade and prices; warns that espousal of plan by Europe and Japan may convince OPEC members to change pricing of oil from dollars to SDR's resulting in sharply higher oil prices for everyone and creating another source of instability for exchange rates   (NEW YORK TIMES,   April 28, 1978,   P26)

SAUDIS CITE TRADE FIGURES

Saudi Arabian Sheikh Abdullah Tariki visits seminar for US executives in Houston; tells businessmen that

Organization of Petroleum Exporting Countries has $140 billion to invest annually in US services and machinery; trade with Arab countries in 1977 ran two to one against US with $8 billion in exports vs $16 billion in imports; Carter Administration sends Treasury Secretary Michael Blumenthal and Commerce Secretary Juanita Kreps to calm Arabs' fears about dollar and new US regulations which prohibit US companies from participating in Arab boycotts by blacklisting subcontractors who do business with Israel   (NEWSWEEK, May 8, 1978, P77)

O.P.E.C. SEEKS STABLE ECONOMY

OPEC oil ministers stress need for internal harmony and increased oil field security as they open informal 2-day meeting at Taif, Saudi Arabia; Iranian Minister Mohammed Yeganeh says organization does not want to do anything that would disturb world economy; says question of whether to price oil in something other than dollars was discussed, but indicates there will be no change so long as dollar does not suffer further large declines; says recent recovery of dollar supports Iranian view that dollar has been undervalued   (NEW YORK TIMES, May 7, 1978, P6)

OIL HIKE SPLITS MINISTERS

OPEC oil ministers remain divided over prospect of raising oil prices; recently met in Taif, Saudi Arabia, to review issues passed over in OPEC's semiannual price-setting discussions; ministers agree to continue pricing oil in US dollars; Saudi Arabian Oil Minister Ahmed Zaki Yamani does not expect price increase in 1978; predicts current world glut of oil will end by late 1979, followed by period of supply-and-demand balance for "something like seven years"   (NEW YORK TIMES, May 8, 1978, S4 P1)

SAUDI OIL EXPORTS SLIP

Saudi Arabian oil exports in April declined to 6.2 million barrels per day, 30% lower than 1977 average; experts believe that decline diminishes surplus in world oil markets; exports from other OPEC states have also been declining, but by much smaller proportions   (NEW YORK TIMES, May 11, 1978, S4 P9)

PRODUCTION LEVELS DISPUTED

OPEC spokesmen deny reports that there is OPEC-wide program to reduce production because of world oil glut; reports were sparked by Kuwait's oil minister, who said all members of OPEC cartel were participating in program to reduce total OPEC crude oil output 20%   (WALL STREET JOURNAL, May 18, 1978, P29)

OIL GLUT COOLS PRICE RISE

United Arab Emirates Oil Minister Maneh Said al-Otaiba expects no oil-price increase at June's Geneva meeting of Organization of Petroleum Exporting Countries, according to Middle East Economic Survey; cites surplus of more than 2 million barrels per day as major factor in keeping prices down   (NEW YORK TIMES, May 23, 1978, S4 P11)

O.P.E.C. COHESION ASSESSED

Organization of Petroleum Exporting Countries is seen as facing serious internal strains because of current glut of oil on world market, but analysts note OPEC is aware of importance of working together; divisions are thought to reflect economic problems that member countries face; Saudi Arabia's indication that it may agree to price increase in December 1978 seen as support for OPEC; International Energy Agency's (IEA) monthly report on oil trends notes OPEC members operated at barely 70% of capacity during 1st quarter of 1978; IEA analyst attributes decline to competition from non-OPEC crudes; Petroleum Industry Research Foundation, Inc. director John Lichtblau predicts that by 1990, OPEC's share of market will decline to about 50%; OPEC supplied about two thirds of world oil consumption in 1976   (BUSINESS WEEK, June 12, 1978, P60)

O.P.E.C. SPLIT FORESEEN

Saudi Arabia and Iran are reportedly blocking efforts by other OPEC members to raise oil price in 2d half of 1978 and fix it in currency more stable than US dollar; Saudi Sheikh Yamani and Iranian Minister Mohammed Yeganeh are said to argue that Western world cannot afford to pay more when it is struggling to break out of economic recession; desire to maintain US good will at time of tensions in Middle East is also seen as factor   (NEW YORK TIMES, June 18, 1978, S5 P1)

SAUDI SHORES SINKING DOLLAR

Saudi Arabian Oil Minister Sheikh Ahmed Zaki Yamani explains that his country's stand in favor of oil price freeze stems from concern that any price increase will help in deterioration of dollar; contends that Saudi Arabia has huge investment in the dollar and therefore would not want anything to happen to their interests; remarks were made at news conference after OPEC's ministerial conference in Geneva   (NEW YORK TIMES, June 20, 1978, S4 P1)

King Khalid (far left) and Yamani (middle) of Saudi Arabia.

Pipe sections await installation in the 750-mile Abqaiq-Yanbu pipeline to the Red Sea.

American Petroleum Institute

DEADLOCK OVER OIL PRICES

Ministers of OPEC nations remain deadlocked in Geneva over plans for new pricing system that could raise cost of oil if US dollar declines in value; arrival of Saudi Arabia's chief oil policymaker Crown Prince Fahd raises speculation that world's biggest oil exporter may be prepared to compromise; Saudi Arabia previously opposed change in pricing arrangements; adoption of plan could lead to disguised increases in cost of oil; Saudi Arabia made concession in May to pressure for higher prices by agreeing to join six-member OPEC committee to plan long-term pricing strategy   (NEW YORK TIMES, June 19, 1978, S4 P1)

O.P.E.C. TO MAINTAIN PRICES

Organization of Petroleum Exporting Countries, concluding 3-day meeting in Geneva, decides to maintain present world oil price for rest of 1978; also decides to form committee to study ways of protecting its revenues, paid in dollars, against declining value of US currency, with one possible approach being to set up an official oil price in terms of a "basket" of more stable currencies; OPEC decision to maintain price leaves much dissatisfaction among more militant OPEC delegates, who charge major oil producers Iran and Saudi Arabia with acting as agents of US and other Western countries in effort to assist their economic recovery, strengthen dollar and solidify political ties with them   (NEW YORK TIMES, June 20, 1978, P1)

O.P.E.C. DECISION ASSESSED

Financial Times editorial comments on OPEC's decision to defer an increase in oil prices at its recent conference in Geneva, Switzerland; notes that current market surplus, due largely to North Sea and Alaskan oil, has made it easier for Saudi Arabia and Iran to push for price stability; contends, however, that some sort of price rise is inevitable by early 1979; cites argument by Saudi Oil Minister Sheik Ahmed Zaki Yamani that a progressive price increase is needed to encourage development of alternative energy resources   (FINANCIAL TIMES, June 21, 1978, P18)

O.P.E.C. CAUTION ANALYZED

Journal of Commerce editorial maintains that it is not surprising that Organization of Petroleum Exporting Countries has again decided to delay any further oil price increase until at least end of 1978; contends OPEC must proceed very cautiously before posting increases that would force US to adopt economic measures that could further damage dollar's position against other major currencies; asserts threatened increase stems from impression that Carter Administration either cannot or will not do anything to halt dollar's decline; contends dollar's position as world's principal reserve currency is threatened by inability of US government to keep its affairs in reasonable order   (JOURNAL OF COMMERCE, June 23, 1978, P4)

IRANIAN WARNS OF PRICE RISE

Iranian Finance Minister Mohammed Yeganeh asserts dollar cost of oil can go up within month or so despite OPEC's 1978 price freeze; committee set up by OPEC to protect producers' effective revenue is working out formula to provide for adjustments in quoted price according to dollar's value; Yeganeh notes measures taken at July economic summit meeting in Bonn would effect OPEC position; indicates Iran believes oil is selling at 50% of what price should be   (NEW YORK TIMES, June 30, 1978, S4 P1)

FUTURE OF O.P.E.C. CONSIDERED

Commentators Roy Eales and Robert Magnuson hold that OPEC committee that is scheduled to meet late in summer of 1978 deserves close attention by West's oil-consuming nations; note group represents OPEC's first formal attempt to devise medium- and long-term strategies, including oil pricing, based on interests of oil-consuming nations as well as those of oil-producing countries; note that majority of OPEC members agrees that OPEC should broaden its role from that of price fixer; point out that majority thinks that OPEC should evolve into international body that considers such issues as OPEC's future relations with Organization of Economic Cooperation & Development and with developing countries   (BUSINESS WEEK, July 10, 1978, P27)

END OF OIL GLUT PREDICTED

Iranian Economic Affairs and Finance Minister Mohammed Yeganeh predicts increased oil demand in 2d half of 1978 and higher oil prices in 1979; anticipates rise in oil revenues in current fiscal year to $22 billion from $21 billion in 1978, despite lagging production and exports; production is averaging 5.6 million barrels per day, down 2.7% from year-ago period; exports are down to 5 million barrels a day or 4%; Yeganeh predicts price increase accord at December OPEC meeting; Iran does not want to abandon dollar, but wants to index dollar fluctuations and tie oil price increases to fluctuations   (WALL STREET JOURNAL,   July 13, 1978,   P12)

O.P.E.C. DISCUSSES DOLLAR

OPEC Committee of Experts on Fluctuation of Exchange Rates fails to reach decision during 3-day meeting discussing continued use of US dollar as medium of exchange for oil transactions; suggestion favored by Saudi Arabia was that oil price be measured by mixed basket of Arab-dominated currencies, but disagreements evolved on basket's makeup; delegates also considered further undercutting of dollar and consequent additional OPEC losses with prospect of dropping dollar standard   (NEW YORK TIMES,   July 18, 1978, S4   P1)

DOLLAR SLIDES IN RENOMINATION FEARS

US dollar suffers widespread decline following report that OPEC had moved closer to dropping dollar as reference for setting oil prices   (NEW YORK TIMES,   July 22, 1978,   P32)

O.P.E.C. PRESIDENT SABAH INTERVIEWED

OPEC president Sheikh Ali Khalifa Al-Sabah interview discusses recommendations which will be brought forth at OPEC's new "Committee of Experts" meeting in London; notes committee was set up to make recommendations on "adjusting" oil prices to compensate for fluctuations in dollar; sees series of smaller oil price increases, instead of one large increase; notes OPEC is seeking to add "aura of statemanship"; notes OPEC plans to play more direct role in financing industrialization of developing world (BUSINESS WEEK,   July 24, 1978,   P136)

OIL PRICING DISCUSSED

Journal of Commerce editorial comments on latest proposal that Organization of Petroleum Exporting Countries stop pricing their oil in depreciating dollars; contends any such switch away from dollar should be seen as attempt to raise prices at time of weak demand and excess supply; cites impact on confidence in dollar and inflationary implications of any further increase in price of oil as two major dangers of switch; hopes Saudi Arabia can once again persuade its OPEC partners to abandon idea; asserts mere existence of proposal should prompt Carter Administration to take action on economic fundamentals which have undermined confidence in dollar   (JOURNAL OF COMMERCE,   July 31, 1978,   P4)

PRICE RISE RUMORS NOTED

OPEC officials refuse to confirm reports that OPEC will raise oil prices by 5% to 15% at special meeting in September; industry observers expect price rise to be ordered at OPEC's next scheduled meeting in December, with increase to become effective in January; estimate that price rise would raise US gas and heating oil prices by 1 cent to 3 cents per gallon   (NEW YORK TIMES,   August 12, 1978,   P24)

O.P.E.C. FINANCIAL NEED CITED

OPEC Secretary-General Ali M. Jaidah declares that OPEC members want oil prices increased because real value of barrel of oil has been "more than halved" in terms of 1973 dollars; speaks before Scandinavian-Arab oil seminar in Oslo, Norway; asserts that several members have become net borrowers in international credit market, and that members are in race against time to bring their economies to levels of sustainable growth while oil era lasts   (NEW YORK TIMES,   September 30, 1978,   P54)

OIL DEMAND ON RISE

Oil brokers report that oil prices, for both light and heavy crude, have firmed dramatically in last six weeks on spot market centered in Rotterdam, Netherlands; attribute tightening of market for light crudes to increased demand for gasoline in Europe, Japan and US and cutback in production by Saudi Arabia; also note oil companies are stockpiling as much oil as possible in anticipation of expected OPEC oil price increase on January 1, 1979; point out that tanker charterers have benefitted from increased activity in oil market   (BUSINESS WEEK,   October 9, 1978,   P46)

DOWNSTREAM EXPANSION SOUGHT

OPEC Secretary-General Ali Jaidah tells OPEC seminar on "downstream operations"—producing and selling refined petroleum products—that OPEC countries can no longer be simply suppliers of raw petroleum but must get into downstream operations; seminar chairman Ali Khalifa al-Sabah warns industrialized nations that OPEC will cut back oil supplies unless they make it easier for oil producing nations to get into such operations; EEC energy commissioner Guido Brunner tells seminar that Western Europe cannot now absorb more refined oil products; Chemical Systems Incorporated marketing analyst Peter H. Spitz tells seminar that studies show that OPEC countries should build up their refining and petrochemical industries   (NEW YORK TIMES,   October 10, 1978,   P1)

O.P.E.C. CHIEF SEES SUBSTANTIAL RISE

OPEC chief Sheikh Ali Khalifa al-Sabah declares in *Der Spiegel* interview that oil producers' loss in purchasing power has been 30%, and hence next oil price increase is likely to be over 5%; declares that demand is quickly catching up with supply   (NEW YORK TIMES,   October 10, 1978,   P6)

OIL INDUSTRY DIVERSIFICATION SOUGHT

Kuwaiti Oil Minister Ali Khalifa al-Sabah asks industrial countries for help to OPEC nations to develop own petroleum refining industries in speech at OPEC seminar in Vienna; asserts that efforts by OPEC countries to diversify into refineries and petrochemicals are being discouraged, and even obstructed, by developed nations; Western oil firms have maintained at seminar that economic stagnation and sub-par utilization of existing refineries would be aggravated by such competition, while small domestic markets, lack of skilled labor, inadequate infrastructure and high transportation costs would make OPEC-member endeavors unprofitable   (NEW YORK TIMES,   October 12, 1978,   P4)

SPLIT IN O.P.E.C. THREATENED

Iraqi Oil Minister Tayeh Abdul-Karim warns of potential split in Organization of Petroleum Exporting Countries if it fails to adopt price increase in December 1978; adds that Iraq will reject any proposal to freeze oil prices or for "symbolic hike"; predicts that anti-Camp David Arab summit scheduled for November 2, 1978, in Baghdad will result in unanimous decision "on the correction of oil prices in a rewarding percentage"; contends that current $12.70 price for barrel of crude oil equals $4 in real terms because of inflationary losses and US dollar devaluation   (NEW YORK TIMES,   October 16, 1978,   P24)

SAUDIS WILL SEEK FREEZE

Saudi Oil Minister Sheikh Ahmed Zaki Yamani declares that Saudi Arabia intends to ask for oil price freeze for 3d straight year at December OPEC meeting, but hints strongly that it does not expect its position to prevail; speaks in Jidda to journalists accompanying Treas Secretary W. Michael Blumenthal on Middle East tour; later tells Blumenthal, according to sources, that Saudi Arabia is unwilling to break ranks and threaten cartel as it did in its refusal to raise prices in 1976; Iraq is asking for 25% increase; Blumenthal acknowledges that it will be difficult to prevent oil price increase but says he is "encouraged" by Saudis "great understanding" of need for caution in raising prices   (NEW YORK TIMES,   November 20, 1978,   P1)

14.5% HIKE, HIGHEST IN 5 YEARS

OPEC, at general meeting in Abu Dhabi, United Arab Emirates, announces 14.5% oil price increase in various stages through 1979; dollar is retained as pricing unit; price will rise from $12.70 per barrel to $13.33 on January 1, 1979, with quarterly increases until reaching $14.54 in October; size of increase is greater than expected; Saudi Arabian Oil Min Sheikh Ahmed Zaki Yamani cites shortage caused by Iranian situation as decisive factor in size of increase; expresses confidence that world economy will be able to deal with increase   (NEW YORK TIMES,   December 18, 1978,   P1)

U.S. DEPLORES HIKE

Carter Administration statement deplores 14.5% oil price increase by OPEC and asks members to reconsider, warning that rise could endanger world economic recovery and hinder efforts to slow inflation; Administration is seen as resigned to increases; anti-inflation adviser Alfred E. Kahn predicts inflation in US will rise by "a couple of tenths of a point" as result of price rise; Energy Secretary James Schlesinger predicts 1/2 of 1% inflation increase, and estimates that retail gasoline prices may rise up to 5 cents per gallon   (NEW YORK TIMES,   December 18, 1978,   P1)

The New York Times/Cathy Hull

For Oil Pricing, a Basket Of Currencies in Offing?

By YOUSSEF M. IBRAHIM

The continuing slide of the dollar has revived talk among oil-producing nations of raising their prices or abandoning the buffeted American currency as the basis for pricing oil.

But according to economists and oil specialists, when the members of the Organization of Petroleum Exporting Countries meet next month in Geneva, they will be hard put to devise an alternative to pricing oil in dollars, or to agree on any new solution to their problem.

The informal OPEC session—tentatively set for April 3—was called to discuss what many members of the 13-nation oil cartel consider an alarming erosion of their oil revenues because of the dollar's depreciation and to consider what, if anything, they can do about it.

Pricing of Crude Oil

"Although we sell the barrel of crude oil for $13, its effective purchasing power is no more than $5," Tayeh Abdul-Karim, Iraq's oil minister, told a gathering of students in Baghdad earlier this week. He urged OPEC to find a new basis for the price of oil.

That is no simple matter. The dollar is so dominant in world finances

that no other single currency is seriously discussed as a substitute.

Paying in dollars but pegging oil prices to a whole range of currencies — a "currency basket" — has more support, but poses both technical problems and great financial risk for OPEC. And at present, it is unlikely that any price increase for oil — whether imposed by fiat or derived from a currency index— would stick.

Because American dollars are the accepted standard for oil transactions, the exporting nations tend to lose out in their trade with countries whose currency has strengthened against the dollar. The goods they buy from Germany and Japan, for example, become more expensive as the West German mark and the Japanese yen have greatly appreciated against the dollar.

Although the loudest complaints about the dollar comes from such countries as Iraq and Libya, which trade more with Europe than they do with the United States, economists say all OPEC countries have been hurt since the dollar's slide began last year.

John Mugno, a Citibank oil economist, estimated that over the last six months OPEC members sustained loss-

es of about $5 billion because of the dollar's plight.

Earlier this month, Kuwait's oil minister, Sheikh Ali Khalifa al-Sabah, asserted that the only way to make up for these losses was to raise the prices of oil. But oil analysts and industry executives contend that a price rise now would be highly unlikely.

"An oil price increase would further weaken the dollar—and that's not in the interest of many OPEC countries as Saudi Arabia, Iran and members," said Marcus Namui, an oil analyst with American Middle East Research, a Wall Street firm.

In keeping with other analysts and economists, Mr. Namuj said that such OPEC countries as Saudi Arabia, Iran and the United Arab Emirates, all with huge dollar holdings and investments in the United States, would not have the dollar weaken and further depreciate their holdings.

Although no comprehensive official estimates exist, the Treasury Department and banking sources say members of the OPEC cartel have $35 to 45 billion invested in the United States, most of it in such instruments as short-term bank deposits and long-term Treasury securities.

According to Chase Manhattan Bank, at least half of the money is owned by Saudi Arabia, the largest of the OPEC's so-called "surplus" countries, which earn more oil revenues than they can spend.

Saudi Arabia, OPEC's most influential member and the world's largest oil exporter, has opposed increasing the price of oil or moving away from the dollar in pricing oil.

A Buyer's Oil Market

Oil industry executives also generally rule out an oil price increase because of the current glut of oil in world markets.

As a substitute for the dollar, the OPEC gathering next month will almost certainly consider pricing oil on the basis of the Special Drawing Rights, medium of monetary exchange established by the International Monetary Fund. S.D.R.'s are based on an assortment of 16 currencies, including the dollar, the West German mark, the French and Swiss francs and the British pound, among others.

Using such a "basket" of currencies to price oil would allow OPEC to move away from sole reliance on the dollar, although when oil changed hands, it would continue to be paid for in dollars. The amount would vary according to fluctuations in the S.D.R. yardstick.

According to the I.M.F., an S.D.R. is now valued at about $1.22. Last September, before the dollar started to drop substantially in value, an S.D.R. was valued at only $1.16. As the dollar weakens, S.D.R.'s command more dollars.

Adopting S.D.R.'s in pricing oil would mean larger dollar payments to oil exporters—assuming the dollar slips further—and higher prices to American consumers for imported oil. West Germans, on the other hand, would not be adversely affected unless the mark also slipped against the S.D.R. To the contrary, their marks would buy more dollars.

But, an I.M.F. economist said, using a basket to price oil now would be bad timing.

In addition, the S.D.R.'s "are not very popular with OPEC these days," another source said, because they give too much weight to the dollar itself. One third of its value is derived from the dollar. By contrast, the mark is given a weight of 12.5 percent, and the yen and the French franc 7.5 percent each. All these currencies have gained against the dollar—a gain not fully reflected in the S.D.R.'s value.

The Oil Minister of the United Arab Emirates, Manei al-Otaibah, last week floated his own version of an "OPEC dollar" to be used as an oil pricing unit. According to press reports, it would give the dollar less weight— only 15 percent—and other Western currencies greater weight. It would also be based in part on gold and on the currencies of Saudi Arabia, Kuwait and the United Arab Emirates.

Making up such baskets of currencies would be a headache, however. "Each OPEC member is likely to come up with his own basket—one that favors his currency," an economist said. There was little likelihood, he predicted, that the various OPEC members could come to an agreement on that anytime soon.

NEW YORK TIMES, March 17, 1978, S4 P1

OPEC OIL MINISTERS CONTINUE UNDECIDED ABOUT RAISING PRICE

DOLLAR'S ROLE IS KEPT INTACT

Major Change at Geneva Meeting in June Appears Unlikely—Saudi Sees End of Glut After 1979

By ROBERT D. HERSHEY Jr.
Special to The New York Times

TAIF, Saudi Arabia, May 7—Oil ministers of 13 major petroleum-producing nations closed their weekend meeting tonight, still divided over whether to raise oil prices when they reconvene formally in Geneva next month.

They met in this mountain resort in western Saudi Arabia primarily to discuss issues that have been pushed aside in the Organization of Petroleum Exporting Countries' semiannual price-setting discussions. On one such issue, whether to continue pricing oil in dollars, they agreed to make no change. But it was clear that the price question was on everyone's mind.

Late tonight Ahmed Zaki Yamani, the Saudi Oil Minister, predicted that the current world glut of oil would end by the end of next year and that a period of supply-and-demand balance would then begin, lasting "something like seven years."

Outlook for Pricing

"We don't think there will be a price increase in 1978," he added. "Some members are asking for that, and they will probably keep asking for that when we meet in Geneva. But this won't change the reality of the situation."

There seemed little doubt that Iran's Oil Minister, Mohammed Yeganeh, was referring to price increases when he told two other ministers this afternoon, "So now the question is how to narrow the gap before Geneva." Indonesia's Deputy Oil Minister, when asked how big the gap was, declared: "It is not yet quantified. Nobody's talking about figures."

After this morning's session the ministers left the Massarrah Intercontinental Hotel, heavily guarded by Saudi soldiers carrying submachine guns, and drove about 40 miles through the desert to a breezy mountaintop retreat.

There they admired the view while Sheik Yamani, the host, posed for pictures. Then the group went inside to feast on lamb, rice, fruit and special Saudi delicacies. Sheik Yamani, wearing a red-and-white checked bernoose, joked with the other ministers. After the meal there were a few informal huddles, and then he drove his silver Rolls-Royce back to the hotel.

Despite the pressures within OPEC to raise prices or to change the pricing mechanism to reflect the dollar's yearlong decline in foreign-exchange markets, it still appeared probable that no major change would be made at the Geneva meeting.

Modifying Position

Ezzudin al-Mabrouk of Libya, which has been one of OPEC's most militant members, said this morning that "we are trying to soften our position" so as to be "reasonable, logical and fair." And Mohamed Ghozali, the Oil Minister of Algeria, usually another tough-line nation, said, "I would prefer to do nothing now," presumably referring to prices.

After the final session tonight it was announced by OPEC's Secretary General, Ali M. Jaidah of Qatar, that a committee of six member nations had been formed to deal with unresolved issues. These include the pricing mechanism and the present world oversupply of oil. The members of the committee are Saudi Arabia, Algeria, Iran, Iraq, Kuwait and Venezuela. The other OPEC nations are Ecuador, Gabon, Indonesia, Libya, Nigeria, Qatar and the United Arab Emirates.

When asked at a brief news conference whether the dollar had been discussed at any length, Mr. Jaidah said it had not, adding, "When something is not discussed, there won't be any alternative for it."

NEW YORK TIMES. May 8, 1978, S4 P1

OPEC WILL MAINTAIN PRESENT OIL PRICE FOR THE REST OF '78

Saudi Arabia and Iran, Accounting for 40% of Production, Force Decision on Other Members

By PAUL LEWIS
Special to The New York Times

GENEVA, June 19—The world price of oil will remain frozen at its present level for the rest of this year, the Organization of Petroleum Exporting Countries announced today.

But OPEC is forming a committee to study ways of protecting its revenues, paid in dollars, against the declining value of the American currency. Some delegates predict this will lead to higher oil prices next year.

The decision to hold oil prices steady for the rest of 1978 was imposed on the 13-member organization by its pro-Western conservative faction, headed by Saudi Arabia and Iran. Together, these two countries account for more than 40 percent of total OPEC production. The decision was announced by OPEC's Secretary General, Ali M. Jaidah of Kuwait. It came after three days of sometimes bitter wrangling and left delegates still deeply split on the pricing issue.

Militant Delegates Angry

Although Sheik Ahmed Zaki Yamani, Saudi Arabia's Oil Minister, pronounced himself "very satisfied" with the outcome of the meeting, some of the more militant OPEC delegates did not disguise their anger or their conviction that Saudi Arabia and Iran were acting as agents of the United States and other Western nations.

"When some countries have a free political will, we'll have a stronger OPEC," fumed Ezzedin Ali Mabruk, Libya's Oil Minister.

"We are very dissatisfied," said Noudine Ait-Laoussine, the delegate from Algeria. "All the elements are already present for a decision to increase prices."

Today's announcement means the con-

tinuation for six more months of the 18-month-old freeze that has held the price of oil at about $12.70 a barrel since the beginning of 1977.

Weaker Purchasing Power

Most OPEC members wanted a price increase to compensate for the declining purchasing power of their oil revenues—a result of world inflation and the falling value of the United States dollar, the currency in which they are paid.

But after the three days of talks (extended from an originally scheduled two days) the more militant among the oil producers failed to budge Saudi Arabia and Iran from their commitment to hold prices steady this year—a commitment designed to assist Western economic recovery, strengthen the dollar and cement their political ties with the United States and Western Europe, which buy most of their oil.

Without the support of these two major oil producers, the other OPEC members would face the nearly impossible task of trying to raise their own prices at a time when more oil is being produced than the world can consume.

A Meeting With Saudi Ruler

Before the meeting finally broke up this morning, Sheik Yamani conferred here with Crown Prince Fahd, the effective ruler of Saudi Arabia. . The Crown Prince was said to have instructed Sheik Yamani to stand firm. Prince Fahd was passing through Geneva on his way to West Germany for an official visit.

In an effort to paper over the acrimonious split on pricing, the OPEC oil ministers agreed to set up the committee to recommend how to protect their oil revenues against the falling value of the United States dollar, perhaps by setting the official oil price in terms of a "basket" of more stable currencies.

Report Expected This Year

The committee, which will be examining a problem that has already been analyzed exhaustively by the OPEC secretariat, is to report during the second half of the year, perhaps as early as July.

Mr. Jaidah, the OPEC Secretary General, said today that an extraordinary meeting may be called to consider the committee's recommendations in advance of the next regular OPEC meeting, scheduled in Abu Dhabi on Dec. 16.

Iran's Oil Minister, Muhammed Yeganeh, predicted that the new committee's report could well lead to a decision to increase oil prices at least nominally next year to compensate for the dollar's fall.

Whether any price rise is feasible while the world is glutted with oil remains a matter of dispute. Saudi Arabia and Iran say it is impossible. But others argue that Saudi Arabia, which is already earning more from its oil exports than it needs to pay for its imports, could afford to reduce production to make higher prices stick.

Long-Range Policy Studied

The moderates in OPEC have already been forced by the militants (at a meeting in Taif last month) to set up another committee to consider long-range pricing policy, including possible cutbacks in production.

The general view among delegates and observers here is that the moderates are now certain to come under massive pressure to make price concessions at December's meeting, if the United States still has not acted 'to strengthen the dollar by reducing its oil imports.

OPEC's heavily populated developing countries, such as Algeria and Venezuela, have been badly hurt by the long price freeze and the decline in their purchasing power it has brought.

Many of these countries embarked on ambitious development plans shortly after the first big oil price increase of 1974. Now they are being forced to cut back on development. And their commitment to more expensive oil is sometimes reinforced by a radical ideology, which holds that higher oil prices are a way of redistributing the world's wealth from the haves to the have-nots.

However, higher oil prices would hurt other developing countries, the ones that do not produce oil. They are spending more than $10 billion a year on imported oil at a time when the true (inflation-adjusted) prices of most of the raw materials they export have declined even more sharply than the true price of oil.

Iran also needs all the money it can earn from oil for its development program. But as an emerging Middle Eastern power, observers here say, the Shah has adopted a moderate position on oil prices, essentially to reinforce his links with the West.

By contrast, Saudi Arabia and the small Persian Gulf producers are already major holders of dollars and have an interest in keeping the United States currency strong. And they are sensitive to the argument that higher oil prices would just swell America's trade deficit by increasing its oil bill and weaken the dollar still more.

NEW YORK TIMES, June 20, 1978, P1

OPEC RAISING PRICES OF OIL 5% ON JAN. 1, 14.5% BY END OF 1979

AN AVERAGE OF 10%

U.S. Faces Rise of Penny a Gallon for Fuel Now and 3 Cents Total

By YOUSSEF M. IBRAHIM
Special to The New York Times

ABU DHABI, United Arab Emirates, Dec. 17 — The world's leading oil exporters today decided to raise the price of petroleum by 14.5 percent in stages by the end of next year, thus ending an 18-month price freeze.

The size of the increase took many by surprise. The price rise will take effect in quarterly stages, making the average increase during 1979 10 percent — a compromise that was reached at the insistence of Saudi Arabia, which was said to be eager to keep the price increase below 10 percent.

[In the United States, the rise is expected to add about a penny a gallon immediately to prices of oil products ranging from fuel oil to gasoline, and to result in a 3-cent rise over the full year, American experts said. Utilities and industries, paying higher prices for their fuel, are expected to pass along their cost increases as well. Page D6.]

First Increase Next Month

The 13 members of the Organization of Petroleum Exporting Countries ended two days of meetings here, with the announcement that the price increase would be applied to their oil exports in four stages, starting with an increase of 5 percent on Jan. 1

Further increases in April, July and October will take the international price of a barrel of oil up to $14.54 on Oct. 1 from its present level of $12.70, OPEC said.

The move marked the first time the oil cartel has tried a staggered price-rise policy, and several sources here speculated that this new approach might establish a precedent that would lead to continuing quarterly increases.

"This is a trap we were hoping to avoid," a senior Western diplomat here said. "The graduated-increase approach is extremely difficult to stop and we may find that the price of crude will get very expensive within a very short time."

Smaller Increase Was Forecast

Many observers in this seaside capital of the United Arab Emirates expressed a measure of surprise at the cumulative size of the increase. Most sources had predicted that the rise would fall within a range of 5 to 10 percent, chiefly because of repeated warnings from Saudi Arabia, the world's largest oil exporter, and OPEC's most powerful member, that it would not settle for more.

When asked why the Saudis went along with the 14.5 percent price rise, Sheik Ahmed Zaki Yamani, Saudi Arabia's influential Oil Minister, said at a news conference that "it was a medium solution representing the best we could do under the circumstances."

"I wanted something lower than that," he added. "I was hoping for 5 percent in fact, but when you look at what happens in the market, and particularly at the shortage caused by the Iranian situation, it is very difficult to hold the prices down under such circumstances."

Iran's Output Down

Iran's oil output has fallen far below its average daily production of six million barrels, which the country produced before a wave of civil disobedience and strikes. Last week, it averaged a million barrels a day.

Sheik Yamani did have some promises for importers in the future, however. "You can bet that we will have a freeze for the price of oil in December next year," he said, referring to the group's annual price-setting session. And he said there would be no added increase in June, when another regular OPEC meeting takes place. Other delegates were not so sure, however.

Despite today's unanimous agreement, there were some profound differences among the OPEC members, and many of the 13 oil producers were siding with the hawks, who demanded much higher oil prices. They want to compensate for the erosion in revenues because of worldwide inflation and the slide of the dollar in international markets over the last two years.

Last night it became clear to the Saudis that they could no longer hold out for anything under 10 percent. Their resistance would have meant risking a split in OPEC similar to the one that occurred in 1976, when the hawks voted for a 15 percent increase, while the Saudis and their staunch allies in the United Arab Emirates held to 5 percent. That bitter pricing split was not resolved until the following July, when the members compromised on a 10 percent increase.

The latest compromise was agreed to last night at a dinner given by Sheik Zayed bin Sultan al-Nahiyan, President of the United Arab Emirates. The details of the gradual price increase were hammered out this morning in a meeting limited to the oil ministers and called by Sheik Manae Said al-Oteiba, the newly elected President of OPEC and the United Arab Emirates' Minister of Oil.

It was agreed that the price increase would be 5 percent in January, 3.809 percent on the first of April, 2.294 percent on the first of July and 2.691 percent on the first of October. In dollar terms, it would mean that the price of a barrel of oil would rise from $12.70 now to $13.33 next January, and $13.84 in April, to $14.16 in July and $14.54 in October.

"We believe this to be a reasonable increase that the world economy can absorb without problems," Sheik Manae said. "We believe the increase represents the minimum we should get to compensate for some of our losses over the last two years."

Revenues Have Dwindled

He reiterated what many other OPEC members have said for days — that their revenues have dwindled by nearly 40 percent of what they were two years ago when the price of oil was frozen at $12.70. "We lost some 20 percent to worldwide inflation, and another 20 percent because of the slide in the dollar on world money markets," the official said, speaking before a large crowd of reporters and television crews.

But even as the conference ended in unanimous agreement on a new price for oil, there was still a visible split among the members about the future outlook. The OPEC communiqué warned that "should inflation and currency instability continue, thus ad-

Complex OPEC Pricing

The new Organization of Petroleum Exporting Countries pricing schedule is the most complex in the cartel's history. It also appears to embody some very exacting — and politically telling — mathematics.

The price of Arabian light oil, the so-called benchmark crude, will rise exactly 5 percent on Jan. 1. That means it will go from the present level of $12.70 to $13.335, or $13.34, rounded off to the nearest penny.

A second increase of 3.809 percent will come on top of that higher price on April 1. The price for the following three months will then be $13.84 (plus a fraction). A third increase of 2.294 percent will be posted on July 1, once again on top of the first two. Arabian light oil will then sell during July, August and September for $14.16 (rounded down ever so slightly).

Finally, a 2.691 percent increase will be added on Oct. 1, bringing the rounded price to $14.54 (actually $14.541544 and then some).

The final figure, before rounding, is almost exactly 14.5 percent higher than the current price of OPEC's benchmark crude. But since the increase becomes effective only gradually, the average percent increase that customers will incur during 1979 is less.

That average, with appropriate compounding, works out to about 9.998 percent — just a shade below the absolute maximum of 10 percent that the Saudis said they would tolerate.

And in dollar figures, the average price for 1979, rounded off to the nearest penny, happens to work out to $13.97 — or exactly 10 percent more than the current price of $12.70.

---

versely affecting the oil revenues of the member countries and encouraging the wasteful use of this important, but depletable, resource, the conference will find it imperative to adjust fully for the effects of such inflation and dollar depreciation." The warning was added at the insistence of the price hawks, sources said.

Both Sheik Yamani and Sheik Manae rejected the abandonment of the dollar as a means of payment for oil. The adoption of a basket of currencies — in other words, a grouping of different currencies, each having varying importance in setting the overall price — as a way of pricing oil was rejected by OPEC because of strong Saudi pressures, sources reported.

"Resorting to a basket while the market is fluctuating would hurt the dollar even more," Sheik Yamani said. He said he expected the dollar to experience "a little decline in 1979" because of continuous high inflation in the United States, but that it would pick up greater strength toward the end of next year with President Carter's anti-inflation measures.

Sheik Yamani also expressed confidence that the world economy would be able to override the oil price increase, pointing out that the Iranian shortfall in production had caused crude prices to rise on the spot market for oil.

But even as he spoke there was a negative worldwide reaction to the 14.5 percent rise in oil prices. Spokesmen for the nine-member European Economic Community said the increase would severely test its new monetary system and would add considerably to its oil bill. In Japan, which imports 99 percent of its oil, Trade and Industry Minister Masumi Esaki said that "such

a sharp increase" could delay world economic recovery.

For the United States, which will import nearly $41 billion worth of oil this year, the new price tag, plus the higher volume of imports projected for next year, will mean an increase in the overall cost of 26 to 30 percent, according to an oil economist for a major American investment house who attended the conference here today.

The price increase will be even higher than the 14.5 percent on lighter crude, which represents 30 percent of OPEC's output of 30 million barrels of oil a day, and which is in high demand all over the world. All OPEC members said they were imposing higher premiums on their lighter crude.

The technique of gradual increases culminates two years of study and research and it serves many purposes, according to the oil ministers.

"It will help us fight speculation at the end of the year, when certain oil companies resort to over lifting," Sheik Yamani said. Oil companies tend to buy more oil before the prices go up and then sell it at the new higher prices. With increases staggered throughout the year, it will be more difficult for the companies to do so.

Sheik Yamani also said that the gradual approach avoids "sizable" sudden increases, which send shocks through the world economy. Valentin Hernandez-Acosta, Venezuela's Minister of Oil, said the gradual increases might be "a permanent pattern if they succeed."

Despite the larger-than-expected increase, several ministers left Abu Dhabi clearly disappointed with its size.

Libya's Oil Minister, Ezzedin Mabrouck, called it "pitiful." Libya, Algeria and Iraq have been demanding an increase of over 20 percent in oil prices.

CARTER DISAPPOINTED

Fearing Spur to Inflation, the White House Bids OPEC 'Reconsider'

By B. DRUMMOND AYRES Jr.
Special to The New York Times

WASHINGTON, Dec. 17 — The Carter Administration called upon the Organization of Petroleum Exporting Countries today to "reconsider" its 14.5 percent increase in crude oil prices, declaring that the rise would endanger world economic recovery and impede efforts to slow inflation.

A statement issued by the White House declared that market conditions did not warrant such an increase.

"We regret OPEC's decision and hope that it will be reconsidered before the next steps take effect," the statement said. "This large price hike will impede the programs to maintain world economic recovery and to reduce inflation."

The oil-exporting countries, the statement added, "share the responsibility" for keeping the world's economy on an even keel.

The Administration seemed resigned to some increase in oil prices. But the size of the one approved today by the 13-nation cartel caused shock and disappointment.

There were predictions from Administration officials and members of Congress that even the economies of the oil-exporting countries themselves would be adversely affected in time.

There also were warnings that American relations with some of the exporting nations might become strained, particularly with those countries that depend on the United States for security assistance.

Alfred E. Kahn, the director of President Carter's anti-inflation effort, said that the OPEC decision had left him "profoundly unhappy and terribly disappointed." He predicted that inflation in this country would increase by "a couple of tenths of a point" next year as a result of the price rise. "This will make the fight against inflation so much harder. It'll be more difficult to get people to stay within the guidelines," he added, referring to the Administration's wage and price guidelines.

"You don't help yourself by impoverishing your customers," he said of the OPEC nations.

"If the OPEC countries say they had to do this because of past inflation, well, there's no question that they, in turn, are creating still more inflation. It's kind of a vicious circle," he concluded.

Secretary of Energy James R. Schlesinger said that the United States had hoped for a "minimal" price rise by OPEC. "This is hardly a minimal increase," he added. "It is substantially larger than we had hoped."

Estimates of Effect Made

Mr. Schlesinger estimated that inflation in the United States probably would increase by about half a percentage point as a result of the OPEC price increase.

On the question of what effect that increase would have on gasoline at the pump in this country, he said it would depend on what happened on the domestic price front, but estimated that overall, gasoline prices might rise next year by upwards of 5 cents a gallon.

Asked on ABC's "Issues and Answers" whether the 14.5 percent increase represented a failure on the part of Secretary of the Treasury Michael W. Blumenthal and others who recently toured the Middle East in an effort to persuade OPEC to hold down the price of crude, Mr. Schlesinger said, "one does not know how much the increase would have been in the absence of the attempt."

"The second point that must be kept in mind," Mr. Schlesinger added, "is that the developments in Iran have had a major impact on world oil markets. Spot prices have gone up, the market for crude is far tighter than we would have anticipated in the absence of the short fall in Iranian productions. This has had an impact on the psychology of the members of OPEC."

Mr. Schlesinger, asked if his estimates of increases in the cost of oil and gasoline were based on imports remaining at the same level as last year, answered, "No, we would expect the imports to rise."

He added that they could rise by 10 percent or "probably a little bit less." Imports are now running at about 8 million barrels a day, accounting for about 45 percent of consumption.

The full text of the White House statement was as follows:

"We regret OPEC's decision and hope that it will be reconsidered before the next steps take effect. Market conditions do not warrant price increases of this magnitude, since the current tightness in the world oil market is a temporary situation that does not reflect underlying demand forces. This large price hike will impede the programs to maintain world economic recovery and to reduce inflation. Responsibility for the success of these programs is shared by the oil producing countries."

NEW YORK TIMES, December 18, 1978, P1

ECONOMISTS EXPECT OPEC RISE TO WIDEN U.S. RECESSION RISK

SOME LAG ABROAD FORECAST

Worse Inflation Predicted — Gold Gains as the Dollar Falls and Stocks Plunge by 17.84

By CLYDE H. FARNSWORTH
Special to The New York Times

WASHINGTON, Dec. 18 — The price increase set by the Organization of Petroleum Exporting Countries widens the risk of a recession in the American economy next year and will probably result in somewhat slower growth abroad, according to Government and private economists.

But Carter Administration economists and the chairman of the Federal Reserve Board said that a recession could be avoided even though the rise announced yesterday was higher than expected.

The economists agreed that the increase would probably make inflation in 1979 worse than it might have been and

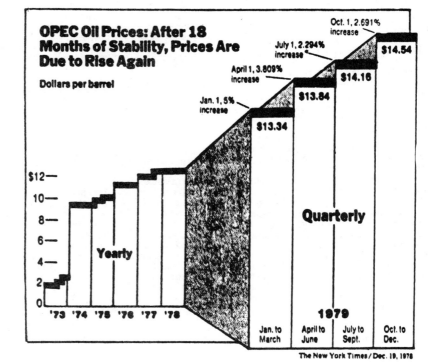

OPEC Oil Prices: After 18 Months of Stability, Prices Are Due to Rise Again

Dollars per barrel

Jan. 1, 5% increase
April 1, 3.809% increase
July 1, 2.294% increase
Oct. 1, 2.691% increase

$13.34
$13.84
$14.16
$14.54

Yearly
'73 '74 '75 '76 '77 '78

Quarterly
1979
Jan. to March | April to June | July to Sept. | Oct. to Dec.

The New York Times/Dec. 19, 1978

growth slower than it might have been, in effect leaving the United States a poorer country. "It's not a disaster, but it means we all have to work harder just to stay where we are," said a top-level Treasury official who asked not to be identified.

Deregulation to Be Reassessed

One result the inflationary impact of the OPEC increases may have is to delay deregulation gasoline and crude oil, according to Administration officials. President Carter had been expected to move to deregulate motor fuel in January and crude oil next May. His press spokesman, Jody Powell, said today that a reassessment of policies was under way, with the OPEC move a factor in it.

A monetary reaction may come tomorrow when the Federal Reserve System's policy-making Open Market Committee holds its regular monthly meeting to consider higher short-term interest rates.

The announcement of the oil-price rise set off ripples worldwide today, with the following among the major effects:

¶The dollar plunged on the foreign-exchange markets, falling 2.65 yen in Tokyo, while the price of gold soared more than $6 an ounce in London and more than $7 in Zurich. On Wall Street, the Dow Jones industrial average fell 17.84 points, and interest rates rose.

¶West European economists and Government officials said the oil-price rise could be absorbed without undue strain because it was partly offset by the savings Europe had enjoyed as the value of the dollar fell over the last two years. American business leaders took a similarly positive view, but in Japan, officials said the rise would further delay economic recovery. [Pages D1, D6 and D15.]

The dollar's weakness late last week and today, combined with greater inflationary expectations, points in the direction of higher interest rates, many analysts said.

"We made a commitment on Nov.1 to hold" the value of the dollar "and we may have to tighten the monetary screws a lot tighter with a greater risk of recession," said Walter W. Heller, chairman of the Council of Economic Advisers in the Administration of President Kennedy. Mr. Heller is now a Minneapolis consultant.

"In my view the hawks will have it tomorrow," said David Jones, vice president of Aubrey Lanston & Company, Government bond traders in New York who forecast a rise in the Federal funds target rate to 10¼ percent from the present 9⅞ percent. This key rate is what banks short of reserves pay to borrow money from other institutions with excess reserves. It has a chain-reaction effect on other interest rates.

While he did not comment on tomorrow's meeting, G. William Miller, the Reserve's chairman, cautioned against the interpretation that the OPEC rise would mean higher interest rates. "I don't see it affecting us in the short term," he said. About 10 days ago he said in an interview that he believed the present degree of restraint was about right.

Some other economists in the private sector, such as Charles Reeder, chief economist for E. I. du Pont de Nemours & Company, agreed that the present restraint was strong enough.

Mr. Miller said he thought today's foreign-exchange market reaction, in which the dollar dropped about 1½ to 2 percentage points against the Japanese yen and the West German mark, showed a "general emotionalism about the subject" that was not justified by economic analysis. His main point was that both Japan and Germany would be hit even harder than the United States by higher oil prices because they are much more dependent on foreign energy sources than is the United States.

The OPEC increases will raise the American import bill by about $4 billion at an annual rate by the end of next year, said Mr. Miller, but the import bills of other industrial countries — of which West Germany's and Japan's are a large factor — will rise by $8 billion.

"When you compare it with the 400 percent increase five years ago that the world was able to absorb without falling apart, then you get a better perspective."

Projections Are Reviewed

The leading economic forecasting services began reviewing their projections for next year on the basis of the OPEC decision. Some made some changes. Some did not. Here is a partial breakdown:

¶ Chase Econometrics, partly owned by the Chase Manhattan Bank, had seen a decline in economic activity to 1½ percent growth in next year's third quarter, and a rebound in activity in the fourth quarter. Now it sees no recovery. "The recession will deepen," says Michael Evans, the president of Chase Econometrics. The inflation forecast had been 8 percent. Now it has been raised to 8½ percent.

¶ Data Resources Inc. had seen a recession in the second and third quarters next year with overall growth for 1979 as a whole, compared with this year, at 2 percent. Robert Gough, associate director for national forecasting, said the recession would now come in the third and fourth quarters and be a "little deeper." He estimated that inflation would run a little over 8 percent, compared with the 7.9 percent that had been envisaged.

¶ Townsend Greenspan Inc. of New York is making no changes in its forecast, noting that it had factored in an 8 percent OPEC price increase and that the average OPEC rise for the year works out to 10 percent, which is not enough to make that much of a difference. Kathryn Eickhoff, vice president, said the concern still looked for a recession in the second half, and real growth for the year as a whole at 2½ percent.

There was a much wider variation in the thinking of bank economists. George McKinney, senior vice president of the Irving Trust Company, emphasizing the current strength of the economy, says he still expects a 4 percent growth next year — which is more optimistic even than the Administration.

"I think there has been an overreaction to the OPEC business," he stated.

Milton Hudson, senior vice president of the Morgan Guaranty Trust Company, said the OPEC move means "somewhat greater probability that short-term rates will move up, which makes relatively little difference in the early part of the year, but will accentuate the emergence of recession in the winter of 1979."

The Carter Administration is counting on inflation next year slowing to the 6½ to 7 percent range, but the cluster of private forecasts is now at a much higher level. Even Mr. Miller thinks this year's expected increase of greater than 8 percent will be reduced by not much more than three-quarters' to one percentage point. Should the private forecasters and the Reserve's chief prove correct, it could make the Administration's "real wage insurance" program a costly proposition.

Under the Administration's wage and price guidelines, Congress is to be asked to approve tax rebates to groups of workers accepting the Administration's 7 percent wage guidelines if the inflation rate exceeds 7 percent.

Employment, retail sales, housing, industrial production and other statistics all point to an exceptionally strong fourth quarter, and most forecasters now expect momentum to continue into the new year. But high interest rates are expected to cause sluggishness later in the year. Mr. Miller said economic growth in the current quarter was running at greater than 4 percent.

NEW YORK TIMES, December 19, 1978, P1

3

A Fragile Mosaic

Leadership in the Arab world is a role in search of a hero. This was the dictum of former Egyptian President Gamal Abdul Nasser. When Nasser surveyed the political topography of the Middle East in the 1950s, he saw shaky regimes, threatened by military coups, tribal revolts or simply a lack of any aura of legitimacy attending their rule. Violence and frequency of violent change characterized the governments of the region at that time. Nasser's arch rival, Abdul-Karim Qasim's regime in Baghdad (Iraq), witnessed almost daily demonstrations by the Communists, then against the Communists, a pogrom against the Turkmen of northern Iraq, followed by an insurrection in 1961 of the Kurds, which was to continue for 14 years. Coups d'etat rocked Baghdad in 1963, deposing Qasim, and again in 1967, ousting Qasim's opponents. Now, Baghdad has been under steady rule for a decade. Syria, after three revolutions in 20 years likewise has had an interval of stability. Yet, throughout the Middle East the search for leadership and legitimacy continues in a turbulent pattern, while even within the "stable" states of Egypt, Iraq, Sudan and Syria threats of violence and division persist.

Arab regimes in the Middle East can be characterized by the importance of tribal, confessional or ethnic communities, the highly personalized nature of political bonds, and the tension of transition between traditional power bases and modern ones. Each factor is significant in explaining the violence on the political scene of the Middle East in 1978 and in explaining the strains underlying the eventful months in the region.

Tribal, ethnic and confessional divisions splinter the Middle East into a mosaic of communities (the image is Carleton S. Coon's in his work, *Caravan: The Story of the Middle East*, Krieger, 1958). Each has a long memory for injustices suffered at the hands of neighbors. Frontier arbitrating has proven unsuccessful in shielding these communities from one another, since they are not articulated into homogeneous territories. There is no parallel to the Basque provinces of Spain or the Sudetan Germans. Commissions have tried and failed to solve by partition the ethnic complexities of a state like Iraq, where living side by side, village by village are bedouin Arabs, Turkmen, Soleymaniyye Kurds, Circassians, Mandeans, Lurs, Yazidis, Nestorian Christians, Armenians, and an almost even proportion of Shiite and Sunni Muslims (who form the majority of Iraqis).

In order to survive in dispersed groups, individuals maintain strong loyalty to cliques and clans. The more cohesive the group, the better it can protect its members, and the greater role it can play in the politics of a wider society. It is for this reason that the smallest sects often show influence far out of proportion to their numbers. The non-Muslim Druze of Lebanon are also leaders of that nation's Socialist Party, while the Baath Party of Syria is dominated by members of the schismatic Muslim Alawite sect. Within small, cohesive groups, political loyalties and family loyalties are congruent. Especially within a dynasty, clan or tribe, family ties are political ties. Even in nationwide political parties and in revolutionary fronts, the image of family ties predominates. The sheikh, party boss or cell chairman resembles more the figure of the Mafia godfather than a Western politician.

This personalized politics often accounts for the volatility of conflicts in the Middle East. Perhaps it accounts for the bitterness with which conflicts are waged, the abruptness with which they are broken off, and the lack of finality of each settlement. The Middle East is a political society where personal grievances can spark a general conflict. Such was the break between Libyan head of state Colonel Muammar Qaddafi and Egyptian President Anwar el-Sadat, which erupted in a miniature war in 1977. Yet, because of the personal level of conflicts enemies can also bury the hatchet after a brief *tête à tête*. For example, at a 1975 Organization of Petroleum Exporting Countries (OPEC) conference, Algerian President Houari Boumedienne engineered a meeting between Iran's Shah Mohammad Reza Pahlavi and President Saddam al-Bakr of Iraq which resulted in those two countries ending a clandestine war and a four-year rift in relations. In 1978, just before Boumedienne's death, King Muhammad Hassan II of Morocco had been trying to meet with him to discuss ending Algeria's and Morocco's war over Spanish Sahara. This kind of personalized politics and flexibility has prevented perennial minor conflicts among the Arabs from developing into formal hostilities.

The instability, though, is chronic, as a glance at the region in 1978 makes clear. On the Atlantic seaboard, the Popular Front for Liberation of the Sahara (Polisario Front) is battling to achieve independence from Morocco and Mauritania, which annexed the former Spanish possession (Sahara) in 1976. To the east, Libya provides support for "national liberation" of the wandering tribes that make up the heartland of the Sahara, partly on principle and partly to weaken more conservative regimes along Libya's borders. Sudan has ended a 10-year civil war with non-Muslims in the Sud and now faces threats from Libyan-backed guerrillas on its desert frontier. Across the Red Sea, the Sultan of Oman has been battling a rebellion in Dhofar since 1972, supported by 30,000 Iranian troops until 1978. Since the collapse of their rebellion in 1975, the Kurds of Iraq have been resentfully administered by Baghdad. The restiveness of Baluchi tribes in Afghanistan, Pakistan and Iran provokes fears, both in Islamabad and Teheran, that a separatist movement—activated in 1972—will try to readjust old borders along the Persian Gulf.

This flexibility of personalized politics and the role of charisma and clannishness have been instrumental in shaping Arab policy. These characteristics of the region's politics are part of the fabric of traditional Arab society and, as the region changes, modern mass-based politics begin to take shape. Mass politics offer a chance for participation of economic interest groups, rather than personality cliques, and promise less ephemeral attention to concrete issues. Regimes like Syrian President Hafez al-Assad's Baath in Damascus and Bakr's rival faction in Baghdad allow a limited amount of local participation among the new classes of urban dwellers, civil servants, industrial workers, newly propertied peasants and settled tribes, all converts from traditional to modern society. In meeting the needs of these classes, the two Baath regimes have experienced some stability. And in the Middle East this reliance on the new classes has provided stable support for regimes like Sadat's Egypt, Boumedienne's Algeria, and President Gaafar al-Numeiri's Sudan.

But as the new classes mount pressure for political and economic issues in a society not yet transformed from the traditional model discussed earlier, tensions arise which cannot be dealt with through "flexibility." Politicians who continue to wheel and deal in the old, personal style often face an alienated constituency that is indifferent to the survival of the government. Such was the nature of events in Afghanistan's 1978 coup d'etat, in which general disaffection for President Mohammad Daud allowed a small group of leftists to overthrow his regime. In South Yemen the unpredictable behavior of President Robaye Ali called out a challenge within the national revolutionary committee, which resulted in his death. Thus, while in the long run the hardening of issues and the consolidation of popular participation promise some stability for the region, in the short run many regimes are unable to cope with the growing social tensions and loss of maneuvering room created by the new classes. For that reason, even the stable governments of Algeria, Egypt, Iraq, Jordan, Sudan and Syria face an uncertain future—the lesson of Yemen and Afghanistan before them. With Baghdad executing 12 Communists in 1978 and Syria's President Assad retaining key military posts in the hands of his own family, stability in the Middle East may yet be a mirage. Further discussion of Middle Eastern political transition is found in each of the chapters that follow.

Politics in Transition

TRILATERAL ORDER OBSERVED

Fouad Ajami, assistant professor of politics at Princeton University, examines new trilateral order in Arab politics; explains that new order is comprised of Egypt, Saudi Arabia and Syria; discusses differences between new order and original trilateralism, which linked US, Japan and Western Europe; notes that new trilateral order inherited problems of how to secure harmony in Arab ranks, how to modernize Arab societies and how to produce settlement with Israelis; examines differences among members of Arab triangle in regards to their regional roles and relationships, their conflicts of ideology and their attempts at modernization; contends that two major issues that will test American role and strength of Arab trilateralism are future of Lebanon and choice of Palestinian representations at future Middle East negotiations   (FOREIGN POLICY,   January 1978,   P90)

Gaafar Mohammed Numeiri, Sudanese President.

United Press International

POLISARIO FRONT PROFILED

Commentator Judith Perera compares Polisario Front to Palestinian resistance movement; notes Polisario Front is tightly knit, with mass organizations and a detailed long-term national program; notes Polisario has backing of Algeria and, to some extent, Libya while Palestinians are involved in inter-Arab rivalry and disunity; suggests Polisario's military cunning, cohesion, freedom from inter-Arab rivalry and weakness of its opponents create strength; Polisario Political Bureau member Al-Aini Sayed discusses military successes, tribalism and need for food and medical supplies, Sayed says guerrilla tactics are highly successful and denounces Morocco's ambitions (MIDDLE EAST,   January 1978,   P31)

ALGERIA, FRANCE CLASH ON POLISARIO

President Boumedienne of Algeria instructs Algerian ministries and state companies to stop ordering imports from France; action is believed to have been triggered by recent French intervention in support of Mauritania against Algerian-backed Polisario Front which is struggling to establish an independent state in former Spanish Sahara; steel products and pharmaceuticals, which account for 11% and 6% respectively of French sales in Algeria, are likely to be affected   (FINANCIAL TIMES,   January 11, 1978,   P1)

PAKISTAN TRIBES FAVOR SEPARATISM

Commentator Simon Henderson examines Baluchistan tribes' adherence to their ancient freedoms; reports that there have been no violent incidents since overthrow of Zulfikar Ali Bhutto in July 1977, but notes that normality has still to return to province; finds that several hundred tribesmen and their families prefer security of hills or neighboring Afghanistan; states that National Awami Party (NAP) is still banned, and local political leaders have failed to follow North-West Frontier NAP leader, Khan Abdul Wali Khan, who has joined National Democratic Party; concludes that it will take 10–15 years for younger elements to gain control   (FINANCIAL TIMES,   February 11, 1978,   P10)

SUDAN IS FOLLOWING MODERATE COURSE

Sudan's preoccupations with reconciliation with its neighbors are examined; Sudanese government, now pro-Western after having killed off its Communists in 1971, is trying to reconcile itself with Libya, Ethiopia and Egypt in the dream of realizing a dazzling future as the "granary of the Arab world"; Sudan is also concerned about internal unity, after a ghastly civil war that cost 600,000 lives and left still precarious peace in southern Sudan (MANCHESTER GUARDIAN,   February 26, 1978,   P11)

MOROCCAN JET SALE SHELVED

The Carter Administration has bowed to some strong Congressional opposition and deferred indefinitely a plan to sell aircraft to Morocco for use in Western Sahara against Polisario Front; reason for deferment was opposition voiced by several influential Congressional members and concern about having to defend the controversial sale to Morocco at a time when the Administration is facing

United Press International

Kurdish troops. Iraqi crackdown on Kurdish dissidents resulted in hundreds of thousands being deported from Kurdish districts of Iraq to Arab ones.

severe criticism of a $4.8 billion package of sales of fighter aircraft to Egypt, Saudi Arabia and Israel   (NEW YORK TIMES,   February 28, 1978,   P6)

SUDAN SEEKS RECONCILIATION

Analysis of Sudan's new political alignment asserts national reconciliation is reflected in President Gaafar Mohammed Numeiri's appointments to the Central Committee of the Sudanese Socialist Union (SSU), the country's only legal political organization; reports among Numeiri's appointments is Sadiq Abdul Rahman, better known as Sadiq al-Mahdi, who is one of the men Numeiri sentenced to death in absentia for his involvement in the Libyan-backed coup attempt three months earlier (FINANCIAL TIMES,   March 21, 1978,   P4)

GREEK COMMUNITY IS EMBATTLED

Greek Orthodox Church in Turkey is troubled by diminishing membership and official discrimination; the number of Christian Greeks, or Rumlar, in Turkey has fallen from 1.5 million in 1914 to 7,000 in 1978; pressure from Eastern Orthodox and Roman Catholic prelates in US and US State Department has prompted Turkish Prime Minister Bulent Ecevit to review plight of Rumlar; Ecevit promises reform in treatment of Rumlar, including freedom to repair buildings, possible reopening of press and seminary, end to new church tax and removal of travel restrictions on clergy; Demetrios I, who is Patriach of Greek Orthodox Church and Ecumenical Patriarch of all Eastern Orthodox Churches, has considered relocating out of Turkey, but fears departure from Istanbul could cause him to lose recognition as Ecumenical Patriarch (TIME,   April 3, 1978,   P44)

CONFESSIONAL RIVALRY PLAGUES SYRIA

Report on political turmoil in Syria notes killing of President Hafez Assad's cousin, Dr. Mohammed Naama, brings to at least 13 the number of Alawite sect members killed in past year; reports killings have provoked Alawite community,

a minority sect that comprises 11% of total population but whose members dominate Syria's military and internal security organizations; notes government blamed rival Arab Baath Socialist Party government in neighboring Iraq for terrorism at first; adds informed sources report Alawites now tend to blame extremists of orthodox Islam, perhaps the Moslem Brotherhood; reports Assad fears that factional or sectarian strife could fragment Syria (WASHINGTON POST,   April 7, 1978,   P20)

LIBYAN ARMS THREAT CITED

Commentator Smith Hempstone examines threat to Egypt by Libya's Colonel Muammar Qaddafi who is supported by large supply of Russian arms; comments that Qaddafi is dedicated to Israel's destruction and views himself as champion of Moslems and bitter foe of Western "imperialism"; adds that he has supplied training, guns, and financial support for Palestinian, Irish, African and Philippine guerrillas; claims Qaddafi has amassed $2 billion arms inventory since 1974; mentions theory that Libya's arsenal is strategic reserve for USSR for use in future African conflict or against Europe in event of conflict with Atlantic Alliance   (US NEWS AND WORLD REPORT,   April 10, 1978,   P39)

SUDAN ACHIEVES RECONCILIATION

The Sudanese government and leaders of the opposition announce in London a reconciliation agreement formally ending 9 years of intermittent conflict; official statement declares that the opposition has agreed to disband training guerrilla camps, mainly in Libya, and turn its arms over to Sudanese armed forces; reports dissolution of National Front Party, coalition of exiled parties banned by President Numeiri; at news conference announcing agreement, former Finance Minister Sharif Husein al-Hindi expresses hope for new era of understanding; Hindi, together with former Prime Minister Sadiq al Mahdi, had been tried in absentia and sentenced to death on charges of planning 1976 coup that failed; Mahdi had returned to Sudan in 1977 after Pres Numeiri had sought reconciliation   (NEW YORK TIMES,   April 13, 1978,   P6)

KURDS AND IRAQIS IN CONFLICT

Prisoners of Conscience series describes plight of Hafza Mulla Hassan, grandmother of a Kurd who is being sought by authorities for his alleged part in guerrilla war between Kurds and Iraqis; Hassan has been held by Iraqis since 1976 without trial; Kurdish sources report that 300,000 Kurds have been deported from Kurdish districts of Iraq to Arab ones in effort to subdue them; arrest of family members contravenes Iraq's constitution   (TIMES OF LONDON,   April 24, 1978,   P6)

WESTERN SAHARA FIGHTING CONTINUES

Mauritania, Morocco and Algeria continue 2-year-old war over Western Sahara; some observers believe there can be no military solution to the war; Western Sahara is former Spanish colony which was divided between Mauritania and Morroco in 1976, giving two nations administrative control but no sovereignty; Algeria supports guerrilla army group Polisario, which is fighting for independence for Western Sahara; US, USSR and Cuba have maintained a cautious, low-key attitude toward conflict   (LOS ANGELES TIMES,   May 8, 1978,   P1)

POLITICAL VIOLENCE DISRUPTING TURKEY

Commentator Nicholas Gage blames epidemic proportions of political violence in Turkey on ineffectiveness of authorities, who are sometimes sympathetic to extremists and seemingly resistant to reform; notes that in 1977 262 people died and more than 1,500 were wounded in political violence, and that 1978 death toll thus far is 157, nine times the highly publicized toll in Italy; notes ethnic and religious differences have also become factors in violence which has spread to include Islamic traditionalist Kurds and non-Kurds, and Moslems in eastern Turkey, where existing strong hostilities have been fueled by spreading political factionalism; says that, although Ecevit Government discounts threat of civil strife in east and is optimistic that it can control violence, optimism is not widely shared   (NEW YORK TIMES, May 17, 1978, S4 P6)

IRAN FEARS SEPARATIST THREAT

Iran fears USSR will stir up separatist movements in Baluchistan and Pushtunistan; Shah Mohammad Reza Pahlavi reportedly warns Pakistan not to execute former Prime Minister Zulfikar Ali Bhutto, or Iran will cut off $300 million in annual aid   (NEW YORK TIMES, May 20, 1978, S4 P3)

NUMEIRI RETURNS EXILES

Sudanese President Gaafar al-Numeiri's program for "national reconcilation" with political enemies outlined; Numeiri has been luring prominent exiles back into political life by means of agreement which allows them to compete for influence within government if they forsake violence and end plotting; government sources indicate that between 600 and 800 political prisoners have been released; return to prominence of religious leaders Sadiq al-Mahdi and Hassan al-Turabi outlined   (NEW YORK TIMES, June 2, 1978, P4)

QADDAFI SUPPORTS POLISARIO

Libyan Col. Muammar Qaddafi, addressing Algerian legislature, rejects any prospect of negotiated settlement in Algerian-supported Polisario Front's war against Mauritania, Morocco and Western Sahara; Qaddafi's change in attitude is seen as diplomatic victory for Algerian President Houari Boumedienne   (TIMES OF LONDON, June 5, 1978, P7)

BALUCHI INSURGENCY FORESEEN

Examination of Iranian concern about Soviet expansion following Afghanistan coup which produced pro-Communist government tells of movement by Baluchis to claim large area of Iran and Pakistan as national homeland; cites Iranian analysts who believe execution of former Prime Minister Zulfikar Ali Bhutto by current Pakistani regime could cause unrest in Pakistan that might signal or trigger Baluchi insurgency, especially if USSR helps it along   (CHRISTIAN SCIENCE MONITOR, June 9, 1978, P4)

His Majesty King Hassan II, President of Morocco.

KURDISH UNREST CONTINUES

Discussion of Iraqi crackdown on its domestic Communists and Kurdish dissidents reports 1,000 arrests of Communists in Iraq, of which 40 were executed; says official Iraqi newspaper Al-Thawra has warned that attempts to seize power within Iraqi armed forces, as well as politics contrary to ruling Baath Party, will incur death penalty; cites report that dissident Kurds have been attacking Iraqi forces   (CHRISTIAN SCIENCE MONITOR, June 13, 1978, P4)

LIBYAN ATTACK REPORTED

Chad President Malloum says thousands of Libyan troops, backed by Cubans, are thrusting southward into Chad in support of National Liberation Front guerrillas   (NEW YORK TIMES, June 24, 1978, P4)

POLISARIO IN CEASE-FIRE

Popular Front for Liberation of Sahara (Polisario) announces July 12 cease-fire as good will gesture toward Mauritania's new military junta; new Mauritanian leader Lieutenant Colonel Mustapha Ould Mohammed Salek implies that his country will cooperate with Morocco and continue fighting Polarisario's attempt to create independent state in Western Sahara   (NEW YORK TIMES, July 13, 1978, P2)

FOREIGNERS UNDER CONSTRAINT IN ARABIA

New Saudi Arabian law stating that all foreigners without Saudi sponsors must leave the country or face deportation causes serious disruption for many construction companies; vast majority of Saudi Arabia's Moslem work force are pilgrims to the holy land and success of the new law depends on supervising the Pilgrimage to Mecca and returning pilgrims to their point of entry; among the reasons for the clampdown is the fear that foreign workers could be politically subversive   (FINANCIAL TIMES, July 25, 1978, P16)

SAUDI INSECURITY DESCRIBED

Princeton University Assistant Professor Fouad Ajami comments that Saudi Arabia's oil wealth is source of political, psychological and cultural problems, concealed by apparent calm; notes that Saudi Arabia remains an underpopulated, insecure society, uneasy in its new efforts at industrialization; reports fear of return to "more socially conservative theocratic politics" (NEW YORK TIMES, July 30, 1978, S4 P23)

PAKISTAN INSURGENCY REVIEWED

Selig S. Harrison of International Fact-Finding Center of Carnegie Foundation examines scope and implications of political crisis in Pakistan which pits Baluch and Pushtun tribesmen, who live in borderlands of Afghanistan, Pakistan and Iran, against Pakistani government; contends real underlying issue of crisis now confronting Pakistan is how to define its national identity; notes question is whether USSR's influence over new regime in Afghanistan will be used to restrain or encourage Afghanistan's support for separatism in Pakistan; asserts critical factor affecting Soviet and Afghan policy is evolution of intense leadership struggle within Baluch and Pushtun tribes between committed separatists and old guard tribal politicians who are wary of becoming dependent on Communist aid and willing to settle for greater autonomy within existing Pakistani and Iranian political structures; asserts Pakistan has no choice but to move toward a looser federalism, while failure to do so would result in further breakup of Pakistan regardless of Soviet and Afghan actions (FOREIGN POLICY, October 1978, P136)

MOROCCO AND ALGERIA CLASH

The Moroccan government reports its troops fought tank battle with Algerian army units that crossed border and ambushed Moroccan supply convoy; reports unspecified number of men on both sides were killed and wounded in battle, which is 2nd serious border clash in 5 weeks and first battle in 3 years to involve use of tanks; Moroccan King Hassan II sends message to Algerian President Houari Boumedienne warning of dangers which could result from outbreak of hostilities and hinting at reprisals (NEW YORK TIMES, October 3, 1978, P56)

SYRIA, IRAQ RECONCILING DIFFERENCES

Syrian officials report Pres Hafez Assad plans to visit Iraq to discuss dangers of Camp David greements; sources reveal Assad and Iraqi Pres Ahmed Hassan el-Bakr also hope to reconcile differences between their rival Baathist Party regimes; note meeting represents first summit between Syria and Iraq in 15 years, and signifies most concrete move thus far to end bitter political feud between countries (NEW YORK TIMES, October 22, 1978, P24)

RELIGIOUS UPHEAVAL THREATENS REGION

James Reston interprets Iranian turmoil as symbol of fundamentalist religious counterrevolution that is influencing politics and diplomacy throughout Middle East, from Turkey and Lebanon through Syria, Iraq and Saudi Arabia; sees potential peril in confusion arising from new financial wealth amid traditional religious values; warns that widespread political destabilization resulting from religious counterrevolution could paralyze Arab countries and prevent them from achieving peace or compromise with Israel; argues that threat of Middle East destabilization must now be key topic of Israeli-Arab negotiations (NEW YORK TIMES, November 19, 1978, S4 P19)

UNCERTAINTY IN ALGERIA

Grave illness of President Houari Boumedienne places Algeria in period of uncertainty, since successor cannot be chosen unless he dies; Boumedienne is being attended by doctors from 6 nations; reportedly stands small chance of full recovery; frequently mentioned successors are National Liberation Front leader Colonel Mohammed Salah Yahiaoui, Foreign Minister Abdelaziz Bouteflika, Irrigation Minister Colonel Ahmed Bencherif, and Transport Minister Colonel Ahmed Draia; National Assembly president Rabah Bitat is believed likely to preside over a transitional period (NEW YORK TIMES, November 24, 1978, P5)

RELIGIOUS MINORITIES IMPERILED IN IRAN

Iran's religious minorities, including 230,000 Christians, 100,000 Jews and 25,000 Zoroastrians, reportedly fear advent of new Moslem order in Iran; wonder whether their lives will be altered if revolt against Shah Mohammad Reza Pahlavi is successful, despite fact that Iran's 36 million Shiite Moslems have shown great tolerance toward religious minorities for decades; Bahai sect is most alarmed of all minority groups, since Moslems have made no pledges to protect this group, and Bahais are viewed as illegal sect (NEW YORK TIMES, December 10, 1978, P1)

ETHNIC STRIFE IN TURKEY

Turkish Prime Minister Bulent Ecevit reports troops have restored order in southeastern city of Kahramanmaras, where 93 people were killed in sectarian fighting; asserts

Former Algerian President Houari Boumedienne (left) greets Kuwait's Chief of State, Sheikh Babah al-Salim al-Sabah, at Algiers Airport.

United Press International

fighting between rightist Moslem sect Sunni and leftist Moslem sect Alevi, also known as Shiite, has ended; Interior Minister Irfan Ozaydinli reports 25 persons were arrested in connection with riots, which began when rightists allegedly tried to disrupt funeral for 2 slain leftist teachers, and Anatolia News Agency reports 1,052 persons were injured; universities in Istanbul, Ankara and Izmir are closed as students continue to stage protests and boycott classes   (NEW YORK TIMES,   December 26, 1978,   P1)

BOUMEDIENNE'S DEATH ANNOUNCED

Algerian President Houari Boumedienne dies after being in coma for several weeks   (NEW YORK TIMES,   December 27, 1978,   P1)

Afghanistan

AFGHAN REGIME OVERTHROWN

Afghanistan military insurgents overthrow Government of President Mohammad Daud in fierce fighting; official radio announces that a military revolutionary council headed by Lt. General Abdul Qadir has assumed power; Daud's

This newsmap pinpoints Afghanistan in relation to its neighbors.

United Press International

whereabouts are unknown; diplomatic sources believe immediate provocation was Government's arrest of several Communist leaders who led demonstrations protesting murder of Communist leader Amir Akbar Khyber, and announcement of search order for others involved in agitation; report that Presidential Palace and French Embassy, where Daud's family sought refuge, have been badly damaged; battle involved tanks and strafing by MIG fighters; insurgents' radio broadcasts pledge friendship with all countries, and pledge to institute domestic policies that are based on Islamic democracy (NEW YORK TIMES,   April 28, 1978,   P1)

FIGHTING IN KABUL CONTINUES

Sporadic fighting erupts between rival political factions in Kabul, Afghanistan, following military coup in which President Mohammad Daud was killed; a new military revolutionary council is reported in control; Daud reportedly was shot at the Presidential Palace after refusing to surrender to leaders of the coup; Kabul radio warns against political demonstrations or other signs of resistance to new regime; says Constitution has been abolished; urges officers of old regime to surrender; announcements made in name of Col. Abdul Qadir; nation's borders and airport remain closed   (NEW YORK TIMES,   April 29, 1978,   P3)

AFGHAN RADIO DETAILS KILLINGS

Afghan government radio, in first details of April 27 coup, says 4 senior members of Daud government were killed with President Daud and chief adviser Mohammad Naim; dead are Defense Minister Lieutenant General Ghulam Rasuli, Vice President Syed Abdullah Illahi, Interior Minister Abdul Karim and Defense Chief Commissioner Lieutenant General Mohammad Musa   (NEW YORK TIMES,   April 30, 1978,   P10)

NEW AFGHAN LEADER EMERGES

Afghanistan junta proclaims new "Revolutionary Council" to rule by martial law; names civilian Nur Mohammad Taraki Prime Minister; Afghanistan radio announces that USSR has extended recognition to new regime; although USSR has not officially confirmed recognition, Tass quotes full text of new regime's announcement; other reports say President Daud, his brother, his wife, 3 sons, their wives and some of his grandchildren were killed by machine gun fire in presidential palace; new Government has reportedly killed over 100 police officers and other officials   (NEW YORK TIMES,   May 1, 1978,   P1)

NEW REGIME IN FIRM SEAT

Conditions in Afghanistan are returning to normal in wake of violent coup; Prime Minister Nur Mohammad Taraki is named head of Revolutionary Council; Council names Shah Mohammad Dost and Abdul Hadi Mokamel to share post of Foreign Minister; new government is recognized by USSR, Bulgaria, India and, reportedly, by Cuba and Iraq; diplomats and analysts in New Delhi speculate on relationship of new Govt with USSR; Taraki is a leader of Afghan Communist Party   (NEW YORK TIMES,   May 2, 1978,   P5)

Nur Mohammad Taraki, new Afghanistan Prime Minister.

U.S. TAKEN BY SURPRISE

Coup that installed what appears to be pro-Soviet government in Afghanistan came as surprise to US; State Department spokesman Hodding Carter 3d says diplomatic relations, not recognition, are at stake; says new government's policies are not yet clear, except that Communist Party secretary general Nur Mohammad Taraki has emerged as Prime Minister and head of Revolutionary Council   (NEW YORK TIMES,   May 2, 1978,   P4)

KHALQ PARTY DESCRIBED

Afghanistan's new ruling Revolutionary Council appoints 2 dozen Cabinet ministers, most reportedly members of small pro-Soviet Communist party known as Khalq; has reportedly not used word Communist or Socialist to describe itself in radio broadcasts which have stressed commitment to nationalism, nonalignment and Islamic religion; USSR and several other countries extend diplomatic recognition; Revolutionary Council chairman and new Prime Minister Mohammad Taraki and deputy chairman Barbak Kamal are known leaders of Communist party; many tanks, decorated with flowers and streamers, and patrolling soldiers are in Kabul in wake of coup; estimated thousands were killed in previous week's fighting, including members of deposed Daud government cabinet   (NEW YORK TIMES,   May 3, 1978,   P1)

NEW REGIME LISTS POLICIES

Official radio of Afghanistan reports policy of new government will be based on Islam, promotion of human values, peaceful coexistence and nonaligment; say coup was not foreign-inspired, and could not be called Communist takeover; reports casualties during fighting last week totaled less than 100   (NEW YORK TIMES,   May 4, 1978,   P11)

PRIME MINISTER OUTLINES DIPLOMACY

Afghan Prime Minister Nur Mohammad Taraki, head of new government that assumed power after coup d'etat 9 days earlier, declares that he does not intend to move Afghanistan into USSR bloc, but intends that country remain nonaligned and independent to prevent any "justification" of outside forces to intervene in Afghan affairs; speaking at first news conference, appeals for friendship and aid of all of world's nations, singling out US; describes and explains in fluent English overthrow of President Mohammad Daud, attributing his death and that of some of his family's members to refusal to surrender; calls change of government "our revolution," but is noncommittal on future domestic policies; seeks to reassure anti-Communist neighbors Pakistan and Iran that Afghanistan will remain dedicated to Moslem principles, shared by all 3 nations   (NEW YORK TIMES, May 7, 1978,   P1)

AFGHAN TO SEEK NON-ALIGNMENT

Commentator Simon Winchester believes new Afghan Government under Nur Mohammad Taraki genuinely seeks non-alignment; contends Taraki's angry denials of initial Western press reports about Afghan coup are not indications of pro-Soviet and anti-capitalist outlook; points out press coverage of coup was considerably exaggerated and encouraged Taraki's view of Western press as purveyor of propaganda; discusses Afghanistan's importance as buffer state; calls on West to understand that Afghanistan wants and needs financial, economic and moral help and support   (WASHINGTON POST,   May 8, 1978,   P16)

NEW REGIME PROFILED

Commentator Richard Wigg examines the new realignment of political forces in Afghanistan following the coup in April which removed the Muslim League from power and installed the communist People's Democratic Party; cites the new intelligentsia and the armed forces as the main pillars of support for the new government   (TIMES OF LONDON,   May 9, 1978,   P18)

SOVIET ROLE IN AFGHANISTAN EXAMINED

Presence of Soviet transport planes and advisers in Afghanistan generate speculation in US government circles; State Department officials are unwilling to accept statements from Pakistan and Iran that Afghanistan has become communist state; new Afghanistan government headed by Nur Mohammad Taraki sprung from People's Democratic Party, which reportedly was not recognized by Moscow; USSR reportedly played no role in April 17 coup in which government of Mohammed Daud was overthrown   (WASHINGTON POST, May 29, 1978,   P12)

REGIME'S PROGRAMS ANALYZED

London Times editorial discusses confusing situation in Afghanistan created by successful coup of Mohammad Taraki in April 1978 and his as yet unannounced program to reconcile country's conflicting and overlapping secular modernization, Islamic traditionalism and imported left-wing revolutionary ideas; points out that Taraki speaks in terms of communist ideas but still insists that country is democratic republic; expresses concern over Taraki's overtures to Cuba and questions weight of their influence in terms of Afghanistan's much affirmed attachment to non-alignment   (TIMES OF LONDON,   May 30, 1978,   P15)

AFGHAN-SOVIET TIES STRENGTHENED

New Afghanistan government has reportedly taken significant steps to strengthen relationship with USSR; has arrested many supporters of former government and purged civil service of reactionary elements; Prime Minister Nur Mohammad Taraki stresses that his domestic program is designed "in the interest of the toiling masses"; program includes land reforms, price controls, limits on private profits and strengthening of public sector; since taking over, Taraki regime, run by known Communists, has announced many agreements with USSR in such areas as highway construction, mining technology and insect control; national press agency Bakhter has signed agreement with Tass for news exchange and technical cooperation; USSR is Afghanistan's largest trading partner and has trained military; Pakistan fears new threats from Afghanistan and worsening of border dispute over Pushtunistan; Iran fears threats to oil-passage routes and possible Soviet-inspired Afghan support for Iranian rebels; India is concerned that US may step up arms sales to Pakistanis; US is concerned that its longterm half-billion-dollar aid program to Afghanistan may now be lost   (NEW YORK TIMES,   June 16, 1978,   P1)

CIVIL WAR IN AFGHANISTAN SEEN

Spokesman for National Rescue Front that opposes left-wing regime in Afghanistan; speaking in Islamabad, Pakistan, says its backers are fighting guerrilla war; says Front was formed by 8 right-wing parties, is headed by law prof at Kabul University named Rabbani, and has support of more than 100 of 374 members of Afghanistan's last Parliament before coup   (NEW YORK TIMES,   July 1, 1978,   P4)

U.S.-AFGHAN TIES DISCUSSED

State Dept official reveals Afghanistan's 3-month-old leftist Government asked US for increase in foreign aid during recent talks between Undersecretary of State David D. Newson and President Nur Mohammad Taraki; notes Carter Administration is considering request, which followed 30 aid and cooperation agreements between Afghanistan and USSR, but that US will not compete with USSR in providing aid; request is seen as sign Afghanistan intends to remain nonaligned and to preserve good relations with US   (NEW YORK TIMES,   August 14, 1978,   P4)

COUNTER-COUP QUASHED

Major General Shah Pur, chief of staff of Afghanistan's army, is arrested for attempting to overthrow country's new government; Defense Minister Brigadier General Abdul Qadir is also arrested   (NEW YORK TIMES,   August 19, 1978,   P161)

INDIA TO HELP AFGHANISTAN

India and the new pro-USSR government of Afghanistan conclude their first high-level consultations with joint pledge to reinforce their friendship and to consolidate and expand the areas of cooperation between them; India promises to give new development assistance to Afghanistan, but does not say how much; new Afghan government attaches great deal of importance to Indian good will because of India's dominance in region and because India has so far proved to be its best friend among non-communist nations; review of politics in Afghanistan since April coup discusses massive influx of USSR advisers, struggles within ruling People's Democratic Party and disappearances of persons suspected of sympathies with former regime   (NEW YORK TIMES,   September 22, 1978,   P113)

AFGHAN RADICALS CAUTIOUS

Leftists who seized power in Afghanistan in April continue to improve ties with USSR, but are moving slowly in imposing Marxist policies on their backward and deeply religious nation; diplomats says that new government's foreign policy fits Soviet-bloc mold, but new leaders appear to be taking care not to antagonize conservative governments in neighboring Iran and Pakistan; Deputy Premier Hafizullah Amin recently reported that Afghanistan is thinking of joining COMECON; meanwhile, revolutionary government continues to insist that it seeks friendly relations with Western nations, including US, especially if they provide foreign aid   (NEW YORK TIMES,   September 24, 1978,   P14)

AFGHANISTAN SLOWLY MOVES LEFT

Leftists who seized power in Afghanistan in April continue to improve ties with USSR, but are moving slowly in imposing Marxist policies on their backward and deeply religious nation; diplomats say that new government's foreign policy fits Soviet-bloc mold, but new leaders appear to be taking care not to antagonize conservative governments in neighboring Iran and Pakistan; Deputy Premier Hafizullah Amin recently reported that Afghanistan is thinking of joining Council for Mutual Economic Assistance (COMECON); meanwhile, revolutionary government continues to insist that it seeks friendly relations with Western nations, including US, especially if they provide foreign aid   (NEW YORK TIMES,   September 24, 1978,   P14)

FIVE-YEAR PLAN ADOPTED

Afghanistan's six-month-old Khalq government, headed by Prime Minister Nur Mohammad Taraki, intensifies relations with USSR and pledges itself to abolish feudalism; USSR model of development based on industrialization is accepted by the government as the most valid approach for Afghanistan's future development; 5-year plan now being prepared is intended to introduce the first serious industrialization in Afghanistan's history;

intention is for share of industry to increase with each subsequent 5-year plan, agriculture to be collectivized on a voluntary basis and private enterprise will eventually be abolished   (FINANCIAL TIMES,   October 31, 1978,   P31)

WEST SUPPORTS NEW GOVERNMENT

US and Western governments support Afghanistan's revolution despite reservations about its pro-USSR outlook; world's least-controlled opium production occurs in tribal areas along Afghan-Pakistan border; annual production is estimated at 300 tons in Afghanistan and 400 to 600 tons in Pakistan; biggest problem for Afghan government is establishing its authority in areas traditionally outside central control; foreign specialists assert government will not move forcefully against opium trade until financing of crop substitution plan is agreed upon   (WASHINGTON POST,   November 2, 1978,   P30)

POPULATION 'APATHETIC' TO TAKEOVER

Afghanistan's estimated 15 million people are apathetic to recent leftist takeover; estimated 80% of people are illiterate and live on or close to subsistence level, hoping only for enough food and work in future; leftist takeover is blamed on greed and poverty of Afghanistan's past governments, and country's long-standing dependence on USSR for military supplies and officer training, which helped leftist leader Hafizullah Amin to successfully penetrate army ranks with Masses Party doctrine
(LOS ANGELES TIMES, November 4, 1978, P1)

GOVERNMENT FACES OPPOSITION

Commentator Jonathan C. Randal examines political tensions in Afghanistan; notes Afghanistan's new pro-Soviet government faces armed uprisings by insurgents in mountains east of Kabul, resistance to social reforms and repercussions from military and civil service elite over repeated purges; observes Soviet presence in Afghanistan is resented by Afghanistan public; notes USSR seeks Afghanistan for its geographical position offering bridge to Persian Gulf   (WASHINGTON POST, November 7, 1978, P17)

AFGHANISTAN IN SOVIET ORBIT

Afghanistan has moved clearly into USSR orbit; Prime Minister Nur Mohammad Taraki stresses friendship with USSR, and most important jobs in government and military have been given to members of his party, People's Democratic Party, regarded as Communist; in ongoing political purge, many have been executed and hundreds jailed; Afghan national flag has been changed to resemble that of USSR; Taraki claims government has support of populace, but there is strict curfew, military checkpoints on highways, and government installations are heavily guarded; presence of many Soviet political and military advisers noted   (NEW YORK TIMES,   November 18, 1978,   P1)

TREATY SIGNED WITH U.S.S.R.

Afghanistan and USSR sign 20-year friendship and cooperation treaty; pledge economic and military cooperation, following 2 days of discussion in Moscow between Soviet leader Brezhnev and Afghanistan Prime Minister Nur Mohammad Taraki; Afghanistan government vows to remain officially nonaligned   (NEW YORK TIMES, December 6, 1978, P1)

MOSLEMS OPPOSE NEW REGIME

US has strategic interest in emerging opposition of Afghanistan's Moslem population to President Nur Mohammad Taraki's pro-Soviet regime; conflict adds to turmoil that has engulfed neighboring Iran and Pakistan, which, along with Afghanistan, have barred Soviet hopes of dominating Persian Gulf's vast oil riches and Indian Ocean; experts believe Taraki's planned reform of Afghanistan's feudal landholding system could touch off civil war, which opens possibility of Islamic nationalism and conservatism ousting Marxist regime and returning Afghanistan to its traditional non-alignment; Afghan people's resentment of 5,000 Soviet military advisers in country and Taraki regime's strong ties with USSR detailed   (US NEWS AND WORLD REPORT,   December 11, 1978,   P55)

FRENCH FIRM WINS CONTRACT

Fives-Caille Babcock, French engineering firm, wins contract to supply machinery and expertise for $53 million sugar beet processing plant in Afghanistan; deal, to be financed under grant-in-aid from Kuwait government, is Afghanistan's first major industrial project involving a Western company since April 1978 coup d'etat; French firm beat a Polish company in competition for contract   (FINANCIAL TIMES,   December 18, 1978,   P3)

U.S. INTERESTS SEEN ENDANGERED

Commentators Rowland Evans and Robert Novak criticize Carter Administration for failing to protest Soviet-Cuban operations in Middle East; charge new Soviet-Afghanistan treaty brings USSR close to converting Afghanistan into base for subversive operations in Iran and Pakistan; note eyewitnesses report small numbers of Cuban troops are now in Afghanistan; point to warnings about Soviet-Cuban subversion in Iran; charge movement of "larger" Middle East (Turkey, Iran, Afghanistan and Pakistan) out of US orbit threatens success of Egyptian-Israel peace agreement   (WASHINGTON POST, December 20, 1978, P19)

Yemen

NORTH YEMEN DEVELOPMENT PROFILED

Yemen Arab Repub Pres Ahmad Hussein al-Ghashmi, in interview, focuses on Yemen Conference to discuss 5-year development plan and relations with South Yemen; says Yemen plans to implement policy discussed at conference, emphasizing electricity, water and other urgent needs; says unifying 2 Yemens is most important national objective; comments on desire for US, USSR and European investment as well as Arab investment in 5-year plan   (MIDDLE EAST,   January 1978,   P30)

YEMENIS NATIONALIZE BRITISH INTEREST

South Yemen minister of communications announces its Marxist government has nationalized the communications system there of Cable & Wireless Ltd, says new national Yemeni communications company will be operated by Yemeni workers; does not disclose whether any agreement had been concluded with Cable & Wireless, which has operated only communications system in area; British company could not be reached for comment   (WALL STREET JOURNAL,   March 27, 1978,   P7)

NORTH YEMEN LEADER PROFILED

Commentator Scyld Berry says that North Yemen President Ahmad al-Ghashmi has established himself as a slow but thorough leader; says North Yemen people compare him unfavorably with the late President Ibrahim al-Hamdi; points out that North Yemenis believe Saudi Arabia is the power behind Ghashmi; notes that Ghashmi has placated the northern tribesmen and ended any

Street scene in Sana, capital of the Yemen Arab Republic.

United Nations/FAO/F. Mattioli

possibility of unification with South Yemen   (TIMES OF LONDON,   May 10, 1978,   P18)

GHASHMI ASSASSINATED

Iraqi press agency reports President Ahmad Hussein al-Ghashmi of (North) Yemen was assassinated in explosion of bomb hidden in visiting Southern Yemen envoy's bag; says Yemen later severed diplomatic relations with Southern Yemen; slaying, if confirmed, would be second assassination of Yemeni President in last 6 months   (NEW YORK TIMES,   June 15, 1978,   P1)

SOUTHERN YEMEN DENIES INVOLVEMENT

Southern Yemen issues statement denying any involvement in June 24 assassination of Yemen Pres Lt. Col. Ahmad Hussein al-Ghashmi, noting government has sent message of condolence of Ghashmi's family condemning treacherous act; Yemen claims Ghashmi, 39, was killed by bomb carried into his office by unidentified special envoy of Southern Yemen President Salem Robayya Ali, reporting envoy was also killed; Arab diplomatic sources believe Yemeni exiles in Aden, led by Major Abdullah Abdel Aalem who defected to Aden 4 weeks ago after declaring mutiny against Ghashmi, are responsible for assassination   (NEW YORK TIMES,   June 26, 1978,   P5)

ROBAYYA ALI OUSTED

State-controlled Aden (People's Democratic Republic of Yemen) radio reports that President of South Yemen Salem Robayya Ali has been deposed after day of heavy fighting and has been put to death; fighting broke out after President of Yemen Arab Republic, Col. Ahmad Hussein al-Ghashmi, was assassinated; radio reports say that Robayya Ali and two members of governing National Liberation Front Jasem Saleh and Salem Awar were shot by firing squad after having been found guilty by revolutionary court for their part in attempted coup to oust pro-Soviet government   (NEW YORK TIMES,   June 27, 1978,   P1)

YEMEN: FEUD REVIEWED

Times of London editorial reviews background events leading up overthrow of South Yemen President Salem Robayya Ali in military coup; notes long-standing feud between Robayya and pro-Soviet National Front leader Abd al-Fattah Isma'il, which paralleled growing strength of pro-Soviet forces within National Front; links overthrow to assassination of North Yemen President Ahmad Hussein al-Ghashmi   (TIMES OF LONDON,   June 27, 1978,   P17)

U.S. MISSION THWARTED

Mission headed by State Department official Joseph Twinam to improve Southern Yemen ties with US, and lessen its dependence on USSR bloc, appears aborted by overthrow of South Yemen Pres Salem Robayya Ali; Twinam is blocked from entering South Yemen and instructed to proceed instead to Yemen   (NEW YORK TIMES,   June 27, 1978,   P2)

MARXISTS SEIZE POWER

Three Southern Yemeni Marxists, Ali Nasser Mohammed Hasani, Abdel Fattah Ismail and Lieutenant Colonel Ali Antar, reportedly share power following ouster and death of Pres Salem Robayya Ali on June 26; Robayya Ali's death apparently leaves Southern Yemen even more closely allied with USSR; diplomatic sources report governing National Liberation Front decided to depose Robayya Ali on charges that he had part in June 24 assassination of Yemen Pres Ahmad Hussein al-Ghashmi; however, Yemeni newspaper Al Thawra has apparently absolved Robayya Ali of Ghashmi's death on June 27 (NEW YORK TIMES, June 28, 1978, P7)

SOUTH YEMENI MODERATES PURGED

Abdul Fattah Ismail, secretary-general of National Front ruling party in Southern Yemen, announces purge of moderates in army and in National Front; purge comes after victory of pro-Soviet militants in power struggle against President Salem Robayya Ali; Ismail notes front's 3 constituent parties would unite during July in new Communist grouping known as Vanguard Party (NEW YORK TIMES, June 30, 1978, P7)

SOUTH YEMEN COMPLICITY CHARGED

Yemen Foreign Minister Abdullah al-Asnag appeals to Arab League to expel Southern Yemen from 22-nation group, at emergency session of Arab League Council; holds he will produce documents showing that Southern Yemen planned assassination of Yemen President Ahmed Hussein al-Ghashmi; Southern Yemen denies charge (NEW YORK TIMES, July 2, 1978, P8)

TWO YEMENS SKIRMISH

North Yemeni forces reportedly shell and occupy two South Yemeni villages, but are then routed and expelled by South Yemeni forces aided by Popular Democratic Front for Liberation of Palestine (PDFLP); report, announced by South Yemen and PDFLP, follows Arab League vote to suspend political and diplomatic relations with South Yemen (CHICAGO TRIBUNE, July 4, 1978, P10)

U.S. YEMEN POLICY SCORED

Representative Paul Findley scores US State Department for its delay in accepting friendship offered by South Yemen's late President Salem Robayya Ali; points out South Yemen, with its port at Aden, is vital to US security; suggests prompt US response to Ali's offer of friendship could have averted violence that led to Ali's death; urges US to seek good diplomatic relations with South Yemen (WASHINGTON POST, July 7, 1978, P19)

RECENT COUPS ANALYZED

Editorial on series of coups in Yemen, Ghana and Mauritania holds it is better to try to understand events than to attempt to connect upheavals, since such exercise, while tempting, is often unrealistic; describes recent "bizarre" events in Yemen and South Yemen, but believes coups will not affect strategic balance in Red Sea; holds reconciliation between Yemens would be significant,

South Yemen President Salem Robayya (left) is shown here with National Liberation Front Party leader Abdul Fattah Ismail (center) and Premier Nasser Mohammed during a celebration marking the tenth anniversary of independence November 30, 1977 in Aden, South Yemen. Robayya Ali was executed June 26 by the pro-Moscow ruling political party following a coup in which Nasser Mohammed was named the new President.

and claims it is possible that deposers of South Yemeni President Salem Robayya Ali, who supported reconciliation, will follow same course (NEW YORK TIMES, July 12, 1978, P18)

SOUTHERN YEMEN ANNOUNCES ELECTION

Southern Yemen announces first election since 1967 independence from Britain; also states that parliament will replace 101-member council appointed by overthrown regime of executed President Salem Robayya Ali (NEW YORK TIMES, July 31, 1978, P3)

U.S. DROPS DIPLOMATIC EXCHANGE

State Department reports Carter Administration has decided there is no point in pursuing efforts, begun in June, to open diplomatic exchanges with Southern Yemen, due to recent coup that led to execution of President Salem Robayya Ali; US officials acknowledge concern over possibility that South Yemen, under leadership of Abdel Fattah Ismail, may grant naval base rights to USSR, but believe South Yemeni leaders are too rooted in nationalist tradition to agree to establishment of such bases (NEW YORK TIMES, August 6, 1978, P11)

ADEN SUFFERS ECONOMIC DECLINE

Description of conditions in Aden (South Yemen) in months since political victory of Abdul Fatah Ismail notes decline of once-rich commercial port; points out that British Petroleum operation in Aden now services 100,000 tons annually compared to 2.5 million in 1967; indicates that citizens are prohibited from talking to foreigners except in line of business (WASHINGTON POST, August 15, 1978, P8)

POLITICAL OPPONENTS EXECUTED

Yemen Arab Republic executes 12 persons for participating in October 1978 attempt to overthrow

President Ali Abdullah Saleh; among those executed are Labor, Youth and Social Affairs Minister Abdul Salam Muqbil, Salem al-Saqqaf, deputy director of President Saleh's office and Mohammad Ahmed Ibrahim, director of cultural exchange at Education Ministry   (NEW YORK TIMES,   November 6, 1978,   P25)

CHINA TO BUILD CONFERENCE HALL

China's Council of Ministers approves plan to extend technical aid to Yemen to build $20 million international conference hall outside Sana   (NEW YORK TIMES,   December 22, 1978,   P7)

LEFTIST PRESIDENT ELECTED

Southern Yemen radio announces that Abdul Fatah Ismail, 40, has been elected President; Ismail is also secretary general of Yemeni Socialist Party, which was formed in October by merger of ruling National Front and 2 smaller factions; party has adopted Marxist-Leninist platform drafted largely by Ismail   (NEW YORK TIMES,   December 29, 1978,   P7)

Afghans, Reporting Soviet Backing, Proclaim 'Revolutionary Council'

By WILLIAM BORDERS
Special to The New York Times

NEW DELHI, April 30—The military junta that seized power in Afghanistan Thursday in a bloody coup proclaimed a new "Revolutionary Council" tonight, headed by a civilian, Nur Mohammad Tarakki, the Afghan radio announced.

Mr. Tarakki, who was described by informed sources here as a prominent member of the Afghan Communist Party, was named President of the country, succeeding President Mohammad Daud, who was killed in the coup. He was also named Prime Minister. Proclaiming a new "Democratic Republic of Afghanistan," the Government radio, monitored in India, described Mr. Tarakki as "the outstanding national revolutionary" of the country.

The Soviet Union, which is on Afghanistan's northern border, immediately extended diplomatic recognition to the new Government, according to the radio. The report heightened the initial impression that the new Afghan regime was sympathetic to the Soviet Union. [However, there was no confirmation from the Soviet Union that it had recognized the new regime.]

Described as a Political Activist

Diplomatic sources outside Afghanistan described Mr. Tarakki as a political activist in his late 50's who had not recently held any political office. The radio said that Mr. Tarakki was head of a newly constituted Revolutionary Council that would rule the country under martial law.

The council, it said, held its first meeting this afternoon. There was no indication of who else might be a member, and the broadcasts today made no mention of Col. Abdul Khadir, the young air force officer who had appeared to be leading the coup.

Meanwhile, other authoritative reports reaching India today said that President Daud's wife, his three sons, their wives and some of his grandchildren had been executed in the coup last week.

The reports also gave the first independent confirmation that President Daud and his politically influential brother, Mohammad Maim, had been killed in the coup. They depicted a bloody scene at the presidential palace as about 25 members of the President's family and inner circle were slain in burst after burst of machine-gun fire.

According to one interpretation, attributed to a witness, the family members were killed in an unsuccessful attempt to apply pressure on Mr. Daud into pledging allegiance to the new military junta. When he remained unpersuaded, he was shot as well.

Since those killings, which were said to have taken place either Thursday night or Friday morning, troops loyal to the new Government have slain more than 100 police officers and other officials loyal to the Daud Government, according to reliable reports. Those deaths are in addition to the dozens of people said to have been killed in heavy street fighting that raged through Kabul for much of Thursday and Friday.

With Afghanistan still virtually sealed off, it was not possble to confirm the killings. But all reports from Kabul today said that the city was once again calm, three days after tanks began rumbling through its old and narrow streets.

"Complete peace has been restored in Afghanistan," the Government radio said, in an assessment generally confirmed by diplomats on the scene. "The situation has returned to normal."

The radio said that several generals, ministers and top officials had been arrested, and that the "necessary decision" would be made about what to do with them. Other sources identified two of the leading figures under arrest as Abdul Rahim, the Governor of Kabul Province, and Lieut. Gen. Mohammad Ismail Farman, who was President Daud's security chief.

The new Government, which calls itself a revolutionary military council, announced yesterday the names of four other top aides who were slain during the coup. But the fate of other leaders in the Daud Government was still unknown.

NEW YORK TIMES, May 1, 1978, P1

Afghan Press Indicates Direction of New Regime

By WILLIAM BORDERS
Special to The New York Times

KABUL, Afghanistan, May 5—The army pulled many of its tanks off the torn streets of this city today and more and more soldiers returned to their barracks as the routine of Afghan life returned following last week's coup.

As the new Government, which is led by Communists, intensified its efforts to stress that it does not intend to become a Soviet satellite, the official newspaper came out for the first time since the coup, giving many Afghans their first look at photographs of the new leaders

"The true democratic and national revolution has begun," declared a proclamation in the paper reporting the killing of President Mohammad Daud last week.

"The defense of this revolution in the sacred responsibility of every individual of the fatherland."

No Party Called 'Communist'

Diplomatic observers familiar with this intensely Islamic country of 13 million people saw significance in the fact that many of the articles in the paper began "In the name of Allah," reinforcing a stress on religion that they thought was intended to counter the charges that the Government was pro-Moscow.

Noor Mohammad Taraki, the new Prime Minister and chairman of the ruling Revolutionary Council, is also general secretary of the Khalq Party, which knowledgeable people here, foreigners and Afghans, regard as the country's

Communist party. But in radio broadcasts, he has denied that his Government was Communist and pointed out that technically "there has never been a party under the name of the Communist Party" in Afghanistan.

Mr. Taraki's irritation at the "false propaganda" that he said the Western press was spreading about his Government was presumably the reason for the almost complete communications blackout of the country following the first news reports early in the week.

The telex and telegraph office here has been refusing since Wednesday to accept news dispatches from Western reporters, who also have been told in most cases that the international telephone lines were out of order. Most reports from here have been carried out of Afghanistan by travelers and filed from other countries.

Mr. Taraki and others in the new Government, both in their public statements and their private conversations, have also sharply disputed the estimates of the number of people killed in the 24 hours of intense fighting between rival military units during the coup.

Not More Than 100 Dead

"Not more than a hundred people were killed because of resisting the revolutionaries," Mr. Taraki said.

According to other, independent sources here, some of the men in the units that remained loyal to President Daud fled into the steep brown hills that surround Kabul, leading to excessive initial estimates of the number of dead. Authoritative estimates of those killed, nevertheless, still ranged from several hundred to a few thousand.

The new Government is being prompt about repairing damage left by the fighting, with masons hard at work all over town repairing the gaping holes left by tank and artillery fire.

Soldiers who distributed the Government newspaper from army buses were besieged at every corner by crowds of eager buyers Even people who are illiterate—as nine out of ten Afghans are—seemed eager to study the photographs, which showed the extensive damage done during the coup and scenes of "citizens welcoming the elimination of the despotic sultanate" of President Daud.

The paper also carried accounts or photographs of "citizens happily welcoming the revolution" in every other region of the country, presumbly to show that there was no significant resistance in the provinces.

The photographs of the new Cabinet reflected the Government's degree of ethnic diversity. Most or perhaps all of the 21 ministers are thought to be members of the Khalq Party, but ethnically they are said to represent this land's different tribes, such as the Pathans, the Tajiks and the Uzbeks, better than the Daud Government, which tended to be dominated by upper-class Pathans related to the old royal family.

NEW YORK TIMES, May 6, 1978, P5

New Afghan Leader Denies Aim Is to Move Closer to Soviet Union

At First News Parley, Taraki Asks Aid— U.S. Reaffirms Ties

By WILLIAM BORDERS
Special to The New York Times

KABUL, Afghanistan, May 6—The head of the new Government said today that he had no intention of moving the country into the orbit of the Soviet Union.

"We are not a satellite of anyone, as some say," said Prime Minister Noor Mohammad Taraki, who came to power in a coup d'état nine days ago. "We are nonaligned and independent and no country will have justification to interfere in our internal affairs."

At his first news conference, with soldiers standing behind him holding rifles with fixed bayonets Mr. Taraki appealed for the friendship and aid of "all the world's nations, including the United States." [In Washington, the State Department said it had informed the new Afghan Government that it would maintain diplomatic relations.]

Taraki Rules Out Military Pacts

The Prime Minister said, in answer to a question, that "we will not take part in any military pact" with the Soviet Union, Afghanistan's northern neighbor, or with any other country.

Although Mr. Taraki's political party, which he referred to today as the People's Democratic Party of Afghanistan, has been regarded as a pro-Moscow Com-

Associated Press
Prime Minister Noor Mohammad Taraki of Afghanistan in official Government photograph.

munist party, he disputed suggestions that it was Communist or Marxist or part of any international movement.

"Ours is the party of all the people," he said. "Our main objective is to secure the welfare of the workers and the peasants right here in Afghanistan."

Mr. Taraki, a 61-year-old former journalist who says he has written "10 or 12" novels, spoke softly with an occasional twinkle in his eyes, and a calm, profes-

sorial demeanor that contrasted with the security at the news conference.

As the two dozen foreign reporters entered the old yellow stone building that houses the Prime Minister's office behind a high wall, they were checked with metal detectors. The new Prime Minister was preceded and followed into the ornate conference room by armed guards, including one who stood directly behind him holding a pistol.

Mr. Taraki, who was press attaché at the Afghan Embassy in Washington in the mid-1950's, spoke in fluent English, as he described and explained the overthrow of President Mohammad Daud, who was killed during the fighting that rocked Kabul on April 28.

"He and some of his family members were destroyed" because they refused to surrender, Mr. Taraki said. Disputing estimates that thousands had been killed in the coup, he put the total number of dead on both sides at 72 or 73.

He said 20 to 25 officials of the Daud Government, including a number of ministers, had been arrested, but that some had subsequently been released on condition that they remained politically inactive.

"The intelligentsia is the main force of the country and every effort will be made to attract them," he declared. "But we want to re-educate them in such a manner that they should think about the people, and not, as previously, just about themselves—to have a good house and a nice car, and yet other people die of hunger."

With evident pride, Mr. Taraki described the change of government as "our revolution," pointing out that it had brought an end to the rule of the upper-class Mohammadzia clan, which has been running this country since the early 19th century.

"We are not aristocrats," declared Mr. Taraki, who wore a gray suit, white shirt and blue necktie. "We are not from the high families. We came out from among the people."

Remains Vague on Domestic Policies

When asked about his domestic policies, the Prime Minister was not specific. He said the Government, which has already seized the property of the former ruling family, would carry out land reform and reduce consumer prices. He hinted at nationalization, but conceded that there was little to nationalize in this underdeveloped land.

Afghanistan has been receiving foreign aid from both the United States and the Soviet Union, and Mr. Taraki asked that the aid continue.

"Our relationship with all the countries will be based on the amount of their support to our Government in political and economic terms," he said, specifically mentioning American aid projects. "We have lots of problems and we appreciate very much those countries who give us aid without conditions."

Taraki Assures Pakistan and Iran

Referring to both Pakistan and Iran, two anti-Communist neighbors that have been distressed at the change in Afghanistan, as "brothers," Mr. Tarki reiterated his Government's dedication to Islam, which is the common religion of all three countries.

He said the ruling Revolutionary Council, of which he is chairman, has about 35 members, only five or six of whom are military officers. According to other sources, all its known members are members of the political party known as the Khalq, which means "Masses." Mr. Taraki is secretary general of the party, he said, and the chairman of its Central Committee It is presumably the same party that he referred to today as the People's Democratic Party.

"This revolution was not done by a handful of soldiers, but by the party, which has been opposing the oppressors for years." he said. Then he chuckled and added, with a gesture toward the reporters, most of whom were British or American, "When I say words like that our oppressors or workers, then you say, 'You're a Communist.'"

NEW YORK TIMES, May 7, 1978, P1

How Afghans Fit Into Soviet Global Strategy

By DREW MIDDLETON

The establishment of a powerful Soviet military and political influence in Afghanistan is regarded by experienced analysts as more valuable strategically to Moscow than any of the Kremlin's gains in Africa.

Military Analysis — "The Great Game is over and the Russians have won it," said one of the United States' most experienced students of Soviet policies during a high-level symposium conducted by the North Atlantic Treaty Organization's Atlantic Command.

He referred to the long duel, fought by espionage and diplomacy, between Russia and Britain in the last century for control of Afghanistan. Rudyard Kipling named it "the Great Game."

The installation of a pro-Soviet Government in Kabul and the impact of this on Iran, other Persian Gulf States and Pakistan is part of the rapid change in the strategic environment.

270 Attend 3-Day Seminar

This change and its implications for America and its allies in NATO was studied by the symposium, which met for three days at Annapolis, Md. Called Sea Link, it attracted more than 270 senior generals, admirals, diplomats, scholars and officials.

The revolution in Afghanistan was one of many problems discussed.

The strategic result of the revolution is that Iran, the United States' closest ally in the area, now faces the possibility of an eastern neighbor that is not only armed with Soviet weapons—as Afghanistan has been for years—but that is also advised by Soviet officers.

Five years ago, one participant pointed out, the danger might have seemed remote. But Soviet expansionism, he argued, is moving faster today.

Impact on the Gulf

Pakistan, in the throes of an internal political struggle, must expect Afghan hostility to continue. The difference is that the Afghans may now have a claim on more advanced Soviet arms, which could conceivably be used should Afghanistan decide to help the dissident Baluchi tribesmen or reopen their territorial claims in the Khyber Pass area.

For over a decade, the Afghans have been using Russian financial and technological help to build a multilane highway from the Soviet Union south to Kabul, Kandahar and Pakistan's northern frontier.

Three years ago the Shah of Iran and his military leaders were acutely concerned by the possible strategic impact of this program.

"If Pakistan should fall apart," one of the generals said, "the Russians would have a clear road to the Arabian Sea and the capability to build bases near the exit from the Persian Gulf through the Strait of Hormuz."

NATO military leaders, studying the impact of events in Afghanistan, Soviet progress in the Horn of Africa and the establishment of naval anchorages and facilities and air bases along the oil route around the Cape of Good Hope to Europe and North America, perceive a new and troubling element in the global strategic situation.

The long-term improvements in NATO's military stance in Central Europe, authorized at the alliance's Washinton meeting in May, will not solve the problems raised by Russian penetration outside the NATO sphere, which is bounded on the south by the Tropic of Cancer.

A NATO senior official said it was "self-delusion" to believe that reinforcement in Europe would compensate for the implications of Soviet actions elsewhere.

The consensus at Sea Link was that the West can no longer afford to concentrate on scenarios for fighting a war in Europe but must find more effective means to cope with global Soviet power in the years ahead.

Effect on Naval Strength

One example of the rapid changes in the strategic environment was the disclosure, by a highly placed source, that Moscow apparently has made a new attempt to obtain base rights at Cam Ranh Bay in Vietnam.

A Soviet fleet operating from the base built by the United States during the Vietnam War would more than balance Chinese naval power to the north and, possibly, pose a threat to the Navy's base at Subic Bay in the Philippines.

Considering the scope and speed of Soviet military-political operations, European participants argued against any further reduction of American and allied naval strength. New cuts, they thought, would involve unacceptable risks.

Most naval leaders present could understand a flexible American naval building program if flexibility involved only a delay in construction to take advantage of new technologies. But flexibility that denies the Navy sufficient ships to deal with the Soviet submarine fleet and modern surface combatants was regarded as unacceptable.

Soviet military and political policies and their supporting weaponry were discussed with special attention to what a participant called the "relentless" rise in arms levels.

One Kremlinologist said he thought the Central Intelligence Agency estimated too low in saying the Soviet Union spends 15 percent of its gross national product on defense.

The pattern of Soviet military and political expansion laid before the conference included two complimentary strategies.

The first is to besiege Europe by severing its ties with the United States through submarine and air warfare, challenging NATO's capability to move reinforcements and supplies by sea across the North Atlantic. The second deals with the development of nuclear strategy.

One student of the Soviet Union said he believed that the Russians intended to create a strategic nuclear force that in a first strike would destroy so large a part of the American strategic force in position that the United States would not be tempted to launch a retaliatory strike.

United States strategy, he said, would be influenced in that situation by the knowledge that even if the second strike was launched, the Soviets would retain enough nuclear weapons to deliver a third nuclear attack.

NEW YORK TIMES, June 24, 1978, P5

President of Yemen Reported Murdered

By The Associated Press

BEIRUT, Lebanon, June 24—President Ahmed Hussein al-Ghashmi of Yemen was assassinated today in the explosion of a bomb hidden in a visiting diplomatic envoy's bag, the Iraqi press agency said.

The Yemeni leader was killed as the envoy, from adjoining Southern Yemen, was about to hand him a message, the press agency said. The envoy was also killed in the blast, the report said, quoting information from the Yemen radio broadcasting from Sana, the country's capital.

The bomb exploded when the envoy opened the bag to produce a letter for President Ghashmi from the Southern Yemen leader, President Salem Robaye Ali, the agency said. It was not clear from the report whether the envoy was believed to have been aware of the bomb's presence.

The Yemen broadcast was quoted as having said that President Ghashmi "was killed from a quarter known for its perfidy against the nation and Allah." This was an apparent allusion to the Marxist regime in Southern Yemen. Yemen later severed diplomatic relations with Southern Yemen, the Iraqi press agency said.

The slaying, if confirmed, would be the second assassination of a Yemeni President in the last six months. President Ibrahim al-Hamdi was murdered in October. His assassins were never identified.

The Hamdi Government had followed a policy of close alignment with Saudi Arabia and of cooperation with the United States. President Ghashmi, who was the commander of the armed forces, assumed office two months ago after having served as chairman of a three-member command council that took over after the assassination of President Hamdi's assassination.

U.S. Government Lacks Details

WASHINGTON, June 24 (AP)—A State Department spokesman issued a statement today that said in part:

"We have had a report from our embassy in Sana that a bomb exploded Saturday morning in the Yemen Arab Republic's military headquarters and we are, of course, aware of reports saying that President Ghashmi was killed. However, we do not yet have a detailed account of the incident. As of last report, Sana was calm and the small American community was safe."

Yemen Arab Republic Set Up In 1962

Yemen, which has a population of about 6 million, was established as the Yemen Arab Republic in 1962 when a group of army officers overthrew the country's imam, who was both king and spiritual leader.

The new regime formed close ties with Egypt and was recognized by the United States and other nations. Civil war, however, broke out between the government and rival royalist groups and continued until 1969.

In 1970, under an informal compromise, royalist elements were incorporated into the government. A new constitution was drawn up and elections were held in 1971 stabilizing the power of Prime Minister Hassan al-Amri and his successor, Muhsin al-Aini.

A seven-man military command council headed by President Ibrahim al-Hamdi seized power in 1974.

Camera Press

Ahmed Hussein al-Ghashmi

Southern Yemen, officially known as the People's Democratic Republic of Yemen, is the former Aden Protectorate, a group of sultanates and sheikdoms that was controlled by Britain. It gained independence in 1967, and acquired its present name in 1970.

Border clashes with Yemen, to the north, led to an agreement in 1972 calling for eventual merger of the two countries, but the accord has not been carried out.

NEW YORK TIMES, June 25, 1978, P1

South Yemen Chief Reported Slain, But Pro-Red Group Stays in Power

BEIRUT, Lebanon, June 26—The President of Southern Yemen, an ally of the Soviet Union on the Arabian Peninsula, was deposed today after a day of heavy fighting and was reported to have been put to death.

The fighting in Aden, the capital of what is known formally as the People's Democratic Republic of Yemen, broke out two days after the President of its northern neighbor, Yemen, a country oriented to Saudi Arabia, was assassinated.

The state-controlled Aden radio said President Salem Robaye Ali, head of the Southern Yemen Presidency Council, which also included the Prime Minister and the secretary general of the governing National Liberation Front, had been ousted because he had tried to seize complete power.

Loyal Troops Were Defeated

The radio said later that he and two other members of the Liberation Front's leadership, identified as Jasem Saleh and Salem Awar, were put to death by firing squad after having been tried by a revolutionary court for their part in the attempted coup.

[The Prime Minister, Ali Nasser Mohammed Hasani, has been named council chairman, Agence France-Presse reported from Beirut, quoting the Aden radio.]

A pro-Soviet "people's militia," led by Abdel Fattah Ismail, the Liberation Front's secretary general, defeated troops loyal to the President in fighting that involved planes, artillery and mortars. According to diplomatic sources, the militia had been trained by East German and Soviet military advisers. As an ally, the Soviet Union uses the port of Aden and an air base outside the capital.

Mr. Robaye Ali, although a leftist like other Southern Yemeni leaders, wanted to follow a balanced policy in relations with his country's three neighbors, Saudi Arabia, Yemen and the sultanate of Oman. He reportedly opposed involvement earlier this year on the side of Ethiopia in the fighting against Somali-backed insurgents in the Ogaden region of Ethiopia. Southern Yemen sent a battalion to support the Marxist Ethiopian Government of Lieut. Col. Mengistu Haile Mariam.

Last week it was reported that the conflict in the Southern Yemeni Government had worsened. Arab diplomatic sources said the dispute came to a climax over the assassination Saturday of Lieut. Col. Ahmed Hussein al-Ghashmi, the President of Yemen, known officially as the Yemen Arab Republic.

A Charge and a Denial

The authorities in Sana, the Yemeni capital, said their President was killed by the explosion of a booby-trapped parcel carried to his office by a special envoy of the Southern Yemeni President. Yesterday the Southern Yemeni Government denied the charge.

According to the Yemeni radio, President Ghashmi was buried today after a state funeral.

According to diplomatic sources, the fighting in Aden once the center of a British territory, broke out at dawn after an all-night session by the eight-man Politburo of the front, at which the Ghashmi assassination was discussed. The Iraqi press agency said the meeting ended inconclusively, with several members calling for the dissolution of the presidency council, to which Mr. Ismail and Prime Minister Hasani belonged.

The account by the diplomats said Mr. Robaye Ali left the meeting and joined loyal troops at army barracks near Bab al Mandab, the point that commands the southern entrance to the Red Sea while the other leaders remained at the presidential palace. At dawn three Soviet-built MIG's bombed and strafed the palace. Then troops supporting Mr. Robaye Ali tried to march on the capital but were stopped by the militia, the sources added.

Abdel Fattah Ismail led the people's militia in Aden takeover.

Camera Press

Southern Yemen's President, Salem Robaye Ali, was ousted yesterday.

Front Won a Power Struggle

Southern Yemen with a population of perhaps two million, has an army of 21,000 men and an air force of 32 combat planes mostly MIG's. The strength of the militia is not known.

As the fighting went on in Aden, communications with the outside world were cut and the airport was closed. The Aden radio interrupted its regular programs and for several hours broadcast only readings from the Koran. At first it made no mention of the fate of the 43-year-old Mr. Robaye Ali who took office at the head of the Presidency council nine years ago.

Southern Yemen gained independence from the British in November 1967, and the Liberation Front won a power struggle against other nationalist factions shortly thereafter. The front's Marxist ideology has its origins in the Arab nationalist movement founded 28 years ago by Dr. George Habash, who is now leader of the militant Popular Front for the Liberation of Palestine and has maintained close ties with the Southern Yemeni leaders, especially Mr. Ismail.

Aden's Soviet ties and support for rebel forces in the Arab world have been a cause of anxiety for neighboring conservative regimes, especially those in Saudi Arabia, Iran and Oman, a bloc to which Yemen inclined. A year ago President Robaye Ali succeeded in improving relations with the Saudis, but strain recurred over Southern Yemeni involvement in Ethiopia, with the Saudis backing Moslem Somalia.

Though the Southern Yemenis are overwhelmingly Moslem, opponents of the regime in Aden have accused it of atheism.

NEW YORK TIMES, June 27, 1978, P1

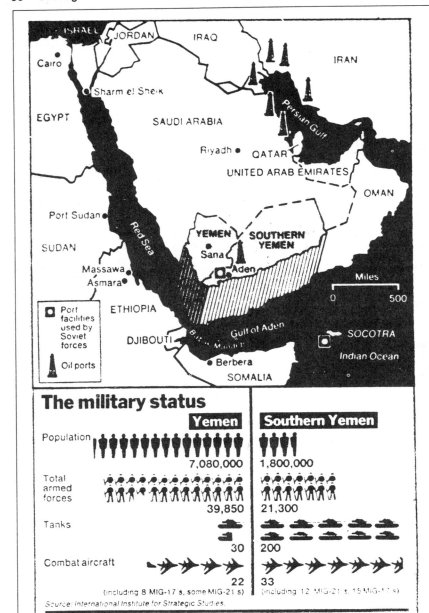

The military status

	Yemen	Southern Yemen
Population	7,080,000	1,800,000
Total armed forces	39,850	21,300
Tanks	30	200
Combat aircraft	22 (including 8 MIG-17 s, some MIG-21 s)	33 (including 12 MIG-21 s, 15 MIG-17 s)

Source: International Institute for Strategic Studies.

Shifts of power in the Yemens

SOUTHERN YEMEN

The Sultanates of the Federation of South Arabia were overthrown by the National Liberation Front in November, 1967; the rulers were deposed or fled. Their successors:

Qahtan al-Shaabi; November 30, 1967—June 22, 1969: resigned; later, placed under detention by the new three-man council, where he remains today.

Salem Rubaye Ali; June 22, 1969—June 26, 1978: executed after military coup.

YEMEN

Imam Ahmad; March 14, 1948—Sept. 18, 1962: died from chronic ailments and old wounds. His successors:

Col. Abdullah al-Salal; Sept. 28, 1962—Nov. 5, 1967: deposed in a military coup led by dissident republicans released from detention in Egypt.

Abdul Rahman al-Iryani; Nov. 5, 1967—June 13, 1974: deposed in a bloodless coup, then deported to Syria.

Col. Ibrahim al-Hamdi; June 13, 1974—Oct. 10, 1977: killed when his car was machine-gunned.

Ahmed al-Ghasmi; Oct. 10, 1977—June 24, 1978: killed by a bomb contained in a briefcase carried by a visiting diplomat from S. Yemen.

NEW YORK TIMES, July 2, 1978, S4 P3

Yemens Imparting Red Sea Troubles

The arid, impoverished states of Yemen and South Yemen on the southwest corner of the Arabian peninsula have few natural resources other than their strategic location and limitless mutual suspicion. The former gives them potential control of vital oil routes through the Red Sea and the Suez Canal, and the latter is enough to make the rest of the world concerned.

The first act in new violence that embroiled the area last week was the assassination of north Yemen's President Ahmed Hussein al-Ghashmi by a bomb planted in the briefcase of an envoy from President Salem Robaye Ali of South Yemen. The murder was first blamed on President Ali and was cited as a factor in his overthrow and execution two days later by colleagues in South Yemen's pro-Soviet National Front. But even as the new regime was being announced in Aden, the South's capital, sources in north Yemen said the bomb had been planted by persons unknown in a secret switch of briefcases, shifting suspicion to northern Yemeni rebels now in the south or to members of the new southern Government.

Whoever was responsible, the upheavals in both Yemens added volatility to the political situation in southern Arabia and across the Red Sea in the Horn of Africa. South Yemen has already been involved in Africa by helping Ethiopia in its war with Somalia. In South Yemen itself, President Ali, who was once regarded as more pro-Chinese than pro-Soviet, had been trying to establish ties with conservative Saudi Arabia, Oman and northern Yemen as well as China and the United States. His elimination has put the leadership into the hands of a troika headed by Abdul Fattah Ismail, a pro-Soviet Marxist ideologue.

The Soviet Union already has a naval base at Aden. It lost a base at Berbera in Somalia, but if Ethiopia, with Russian help, can subdue an insurrection in Eritrea, the Russians could get a new base there and cement their control of the trade routes of the Red Sea and Suez, if not of other sea lanes over which much of the West's oil passes. Last week this possibility seemed heightened when Eritrean Marxist guerrilla leaders offered to negotiate peace with Ethiopia.

The upheavals in the Yemens could add to existing tensions in Oman, where a Marxist National Liberation Front aided by South Yemen nearly seized power in 1976. Iranian troops helped Oman put down the 1976 rebellion but this month Oman moved to get further outside help by sending a delegation to China.

4

Anarchy in Lebanon

1978 did not bring peace to Lebanon, plunged into civil war since April 1975. Though Lebanon's violence is viewed in the West through the prism of the Arab-Israeli conflict, the tiny, ethnically plural nation's problems have a deeper significance for the Middle East. The problems of ethnic and confessional rivalry experiences in other countries once sought their model solution in the stable Lebanese republic. Now, in wake of civil war, the same problems have reached their most destructive proportions. The impact of the Lebanese tragedy on the Middle East is magnified by the special position of Lebanon. Long the most dynamic of the Arab states, Lebanon's banks, shipping services and clerical facilities provided the Arab world with the nervous system of its growing business world. Equally important, the country's democratic politics, free press and lively intellectual life gave the Arab world its freest forum for debate and introspection.

Lebanon embodies many of the contradictions characterizing the region's politics. It is a country at once modern and traditional, where a highly urbanized population still retains grim loyalty to rural warlords and where technically complex business operations are run as the private fief of a clan. With their television and free press the Lebanese are the Middle East's best informed and politically acute citizens, yet ancient attitudes toward faith and tribe persist. Observers of Lebanese history credit this persistent traditionalism to the National Pact, an unwritten agreement forged in 1943 between Christian and Muslim leaders of the then French mandate. The pact guaranteed a six-to-five predominance of Christian to Muslim legislatures in the national assembly, while otherwise the balance between the communities making up Lebanon were preserved through a set of delicate formulas arrived at through painstaking flexibility and compromise. As a result, Lebanon was not only dominated by cabalistically pervasive multiples of 11, but labored under a fossilized governmental status quo that could not be tampered with. The suspicious jealousy of the small ethnic and religious groups prevented that.

The pact was a solid one. The republican regime of Lebanon, independent since 1945, has persisted without any change in its constitution since that year. Of all the Arab governments to intervene against the Zionists in Palestine in 1945, Lebanon was the only government not to suffer overthrow in wake of the Arab defeat. Although a coup d'etat threatened in 1958, prompt compromise by Lebanese leaders made the subsequent intervention by American troops virtually unnecessary. As revolutions racked the rest of the Middle East in the turbulent fifties and sixties and as land reform, genocide and partition changed the society of the "Old Orient" elsewhere, in Lebanon a regime of warlords, clan leaders and religious community heads continued to back the National Pact.

The very conservatism of Lebanon turned out to be an agent of change. Lured by the stability of the political scene, Arab and Western capital turned Beirut into the hub of the Middle East, the center of advertising, publishing, banking, marketing and tourism. The most conspicuous sign of Lebanon's economic "miracle" was the rising skyline of Beirut—big hotels, corporate offices and casinos.

Two Lebanons existed side by side. Great economic development had created an outward looking, businesslike society which held aloof from most of the quarrels within the Arab world, including the feud with Israel. Political conservatism and the National Pact preserved the clannish, confessional nature of politics in a glacially static form. The two sides of Lebanon can be seen in the figure of Camille Chamoun, president of the republic (1952–1958), business-suited statesman, francophile and autocratic *za'im* with a 5,000-man private army.

Some Lebanese were willing to live with these contradictions. They vented a good deal of their frustration with the medieval mentality of confessional politics in a free press and in sophisticated humor. While they realized they had outgrown the strictures of the National Pact, they saw in it at least a known quality which promised them security and economic growth. Yet a few Lebanese were willing to tamper with the status quo for the sake of issues and principles. The Nasserites, local supporters of Nasser's Arab-wide policies, urged Lebanon to sacrifice its "parasitic" role as service and banking agent for "Western imperialism" in the Middle East and follow Egypt down the road to socialism. They also urged greater participation in the confrontation with Israel. Branches of the Syrian Baath and the Communist party were likewise active in Lebanon throughout the sixties and seventies.

Yet these were a small minority and could never have had the revolutionary impact on traditional Lebanese society they sought had it not been for the presence of 400,000 Palestinians in Lebanon. The Palestinians, augmented by radical factions expelled from Jordan in 1970, ran a state within a state, complete with a government, gendarmerie and "borders," the undefined vicinity of the many Palestinian refugee campus. To the conservatives, especially the Catholic Maronite leaders, the presence of the Palestinians was a threat to the National Pact. To the leftists, the Palestinians were a godsent opportunity to create a revolution from within to Arabicize and radicalize the fossilized Lebanese polity.

Tensions among the conservative Lebanese against the Palestinians led to the massacre of a busload of Palestinians on April 15, 1975, sparking the subsequent civil war. Leftist Lebanese joined Palestinians against the conservatives. Religious communities took sides, the Druze behind Socialist Party leader Kemal Jumblatt, the Maronites backing Suleiman Franjieh's Phalangists. The Palestinians, long armed and equipped for their operations against Israel, overcame the rightists and were on their way to a clear-cut victory.

Syria's President Hafez al-Assad intervened on the side of the underdogs in 1976 and prevented a leftist victory. 30,000 Syrian troops, with the financing of the Arab League, occupied Lebanon in an attempt to impose peace on the combatants. The Arab world hoped to restore to Beirut the important service and commercial functions which had fled during the war, as well as restore the much-heralded confessional peace which had once made tolerant Lebanon the showpiece of what the Middle East hoped to become. But as the leftists and Palestinians grudgingly acceded to the Syrian mandate, the rightists, always suspicious of Syrian ambitions in Lebanon, broke with their allies. A second phase of war began in February with Syrian troops pounding the Christrian ghettos of Beirut while the Phalangist leaders spoke of virtual succession from Lebanon.

Through its involvement in the problem of the Palestinians, Lebanon had been an indirect victim of the Arab-Israeli conflict; now in 1978 it became a direct one. Israel saw in the presence of Syria's 30,000 troops in Lebanon the chance to tie down its opponent on the Eastern Front with minimal effort, simply by arming the Christians opposing them. Israel's intervention in the Spring, though triggered by a terrorist raid near Tel Aviv, was part of Israeli policy to strengthen the position of the Christians against Syria and create a "Vietnam" situation for Hafex al-Assad. The Israelis hoped to tie down large numbers of Syrian troops in a no-win holding operation against the rightists.

In the aftermath of Israeli intervention the combatants of Lebanon are further polarized than before. The left accuses the right of being agents of Israel, a view which leaves little room for compromise or forgiveness. The right sees a Muslim conspiracy to eliminate the Maronite community altogether. And although Lebanon's traditional leadership of *za'ims* and *muftis* parleys and pledges and speaks sweet reason, in the streets, violence is the initiative of gangs and gunmen, beyond the leaders' control.

President Elias Sarkis, elected by a shotgun legislature in 1977, is a well-regarded technocrat who has taken the right steps toward saving the country from further civil war. He has formed an above-politics cabinet without ties to the traditional leaders, although he has the support of many of them. He has cooperated with the Syrian occupation troops and pragmatically bargained with Assad for returning control to the reconstituted Lebanese army. But the involvement of Lebanon in the wider conflict between Syrians, Israelis and Palestinians makes it impossible for Sarkis to seek a solution outside the framework of general Middle East peace.

The country whose open, complex politics were a mirror of the Arab world, showing the currents and trends of political thought and social change, is thus in a state of suspended animation. Until a wider peace comes to the Middle East, the Arab world will have lost an important window into itself.

Israel Crosses the Border

HOUSING PROBLEMS REVIEWED

Lebanese government hesitates over the building of houses because of tense political situation, de facto segregation and limited capital; the government is temporarily allowing squatters to remain, assuming property owners have other places to live; the UN has plans for 5,000 housing units and for refugee camps providing for 10,000–15,000 people   (MIDDLE EAST, January 1978,   P74)

LEBANESE FACTIONS DESCRIBED

Lebanon's Christians are divided into different groups, providing the country with varied political views; the Maronites, the largest Christian community, have provided most of the leaders for the militant pro-Christian right-wing movements; the Eastern Orthodox Church has produced spokesmen for left-wing and Arab nationalist groups; each of the Lebanese churches regulate all affairs of marriage, divorce, adoption and guardianship within their own congregations; the churches have built schools and hospitals where the government has not   (CHRISTIAN SCIENCE MONITOR,   January 6, 1978,   P16)

P.L.O. BUILDUP WORRIES RIGHTISTS

Lebanese Christian leaders say arms for Palestinian guerrillas are pouring into Tyre; situation is reportedly discussed between Lebanese Front leader Camille Chamoun and President Elias Sarkis; guerrillas, backed by Lebanese leftists and Christians, reportedly supported by Israel, exchange gunfire after battle to control village of Blat; village has been recaptured by Palestinians   (NEW YORK TIMES,   January 26, 1978,   P10)

ANTI-PALESTINIAN FEELING RISING

Rising anti-Palestinian feelings in Lebanon are believed caused by long war, continued conflicts among splinter guerrilla groups, Palestinians' sometimes abusive behavior toward Lebanese and what many see as diminishing prospects of Mideast peace settlement; notes Palestinian leader Yasir Arafat, under pressure of irate citizens, called meeting of chiefs of all guerrilla organizations and political council of Lebanese National Movement earlier in week; says official statement announced that meeting reviewed measures adopted by Palestinian command to safeguard relations between revolution and southern masses; PLO sources say agreement was reached to close all Palestinian offices in towns and villages in south except in certain strategic areas; also notes there would be crackdown on undisciplined elements; all offices of Palestinian guerrilla groups have been closed in Saida and armed Palestinians no longer are seen in streets; pressure has also been brought by leaders of orthodox Sunni Moslem community   (NEW YORK TIMES,   February 6, 1978,   P8)

SYRIANS AND LEBANESE CLASH

Lebanese soldiers clash with members of Syrian peacekeeping force as Syrians seek to set up new checkpoint near Lebanese Army barracks; at least 2 are reported dead; Lebanese Army and Arab peacekeeping force issue joint statement attributing outbreak of violence to "personal reasons" and pledging "prompt disciplinary measures"; general mood of tension is heightened by reports that 2 Christians had been kidnapped and murdered in Naameh; Syrian peacekeeping forces surrounded village and detained a number of suspects   (NEW YORK TIMES,   February 8, 1978,   P9)

RIGHT-WING MILITIA ATTACKED

Fighting between Syrians and Lebanese spreads from suburbs to East Beirut, predominantly Christian section, on February 8; is most serious flare-up since end of civil war 15 months ago; Syrian troops of Arab peacekeeping force attacks headquarters of National Liberal Party, Lebanese right-wing organization, in Ain al-Rummaneh section and Lebanese Army barracks in Christian suburb of Fayadiyeh; unofficial death toll put at 12; Syrian forces in other Christian sections put on alert; occupy strategic sites in downtown Beirut   (NEW YORK TIMES,   February 9, 1978,   P5)

SYRIAN AIMS ANALYZED

Negotiations intensify in Beirut as Syrian and Lebanese officials meet to resolve conflict between Syrian peacekeeping force and Lebanese Christian militia forces, who were allies during civil war; Syria seen having 2 aims, to prevent Israeli intervention and to preserve Lebanese unity against Christian moves for partition   (NEW YORK TIMES,   February 12, 1978,   P3)

SARKIS AND SYRIA IN ACCORD

Lebanese President Elias Sarkis and Syrian Foreign Minister Abdel-Halim Khaddam agree on measures to end confrontation between Syrian peacekeeping forces and Lebanese Army and Christian militiamen; state radio reports that total calm has been restored to Beirut   (NEW YORK TIMES,   February 13, 1978,   P4)

PALESTINIANS, RIGHTISTS CLASH

Palestinian guerrillas in southern Lebanon report heavy artillery exchanges with Christian forces supported by Israel; Israel denies involvement; Lebanese military spokesman confirms that 150 people were killed and 339 wounded in 4 days of fighting between Syrians and Lebanese Christians last week; cease-fire remains in effect for 3d day   (NEW YORK TIMES,   February 14, 1978,   P11)

MILITARY TRIBUNAL ESTABLISHED

Lebanese Parliament votes, 72-1, to set up Syrian-Lebanese military tribunal to try those responsible for 4-

day outbreak of hostilities; casualties put at about 100 Syrians and 50 Lebanese   (NEW YORK TIMES, February 15, 1978, P3)

ISRAELI COLLUSION CHARGED

Palestinian press agency WAFA charges Israeli troops and Christian militia forces with attack on 7 Lebanese border villages; Israeli military spokesman refuses comment on report but says there is no activity on Israel's northern border   (NEW YORK TIMES, February 19, 1978, P14)

LEBANESE MOSLEMS FLEE ISRAELIS

Mufti Abdel Amir Kabalan, spiritual leader of Shia Moslem community, says Israelis have failed to win cooperation of 7 Moslem villages on Lebanon's southeastern border; says villagers have begun to flee because they fear Israeli retaliation   (NEW YORK TIMES, February 26, 1978, P11)

NEW OUTBREAK OF FIGHTING REPORTED

Marvine Howe reports on outbreak of fighting in Marun Al-Ras, Lebanon, between leftist-Palestinian coalition and Israeli-supported right-wing Christians; reports coalition in control after heavy losses by Christian militiamen, and villagers fleeing; 300 civilians reportedly remain of 4,000 population; leftists display Israeli and American made armaments used by rightists   (NEW YORK TIMES, March 4, 1978, P3)

TERRORISTS ATTACK ISRAELIS

Thirteen Palestinian terrorists, landing by boat, attack a bus on outskirts of Tel Aviv and, in ensuing gun battle, 20–30 Israelis are killed and an estimated 70 are wounded; Israeli police report no evidence that any of terrorists escaped; PLO guerrilla group Al Fatah claims responsibility for attack; names operation after Kamal Adwan, killed in 1973 Israeli raid; PLO statement declares action was aimed at "escalation of our armed struggle against the Zionist enemy"; Israeli Defense Minister Ezer Weizman cuts short US visit to return to Israel, presumably to discuss possible military retaliation against Palestinians   (NEW YORK TIMES, March 12. 1978. P1)

RAID COINCIDES WITH BEGIN'S VISIT

PLO sources claim Al Fatah attack on Israel was designed to show there can be no Middle East peace settlement without Palestinians; say raid was planned to coincide with visit of Israeli Prime Minister Begin to US; also link timing to Yasir Arafat's visit to USSR last week; claim he received firm commitments of diplomatic support and advanced arms; say they expect Israeli reprisals   (NEW YORK TIMES, March 13, 1978, P10)

BEGIN HINTS REPRISAL

Israeli Prime Minister Begin hints strongly that Israel will stage military reprisal for terrorist bus attack in Tel Aviv which ended in death of 37 Israelis and 9 terrorists; says terrorists came from Lebanon; expresses grief and verbally attacks PLO, al-Fatah and USSR for supplying arms; says Israel remains ready to resume peace negotiations with Egypt   (NEW YORK TIMES, March 13, 1978, P1)

ISRAEL CROSSES INTO LEBANON

Israeli military command reports Israeli forces have crossed into Lebanon "to root out terrorist bases"; claims intention is not to harm population, Lebanese Army or inter-Arab force, and is not retaliatory; says aim is to protect Israel from attacks by al-Fatah and PLO; map indicates Israeli landing areas in southern Lebanon; US intelligence sources estimate Israelis sent 10,000 men, plus armor, artillery and planes, on raid   (NEW YORK TIMES, March 15, 1978, P1)

P.L.O. REPORTS INVASION

PLO announces that Israeli land, sea and air forces have attacked key bases of Palestinians and Lebanese leftists in southern Lebanon along border; says Israelis landed troops near Tyre and are operating from areas controlled by right-wing Christian militiamen; reports 12,000 Israeli ground forces were supported by jets that bombed several Palestinian strongholds; reports artillery shelling from border   (NEW YORK TIMES, March 15, 1978, P1)

ISRAELI LINE ADVANCES

Israeli forces overwhelm Palestinian guerrillas in at least 7 strongholds in southern Lebanon with land, sea and air operations from Mediterranean to Mount Hermon, occupying 4½-to-6-mile-wide security belt along Israel's 60-mile northern border; Israeli Chief of Staff Lieutenant General Mordechai Gur reports major fighting is over, but Prime Minister Begin holds troops will remain until agreement is reached which will insure area is never again used for raids on Israel; Gur and Israeli Defense Minister Ezer Weizman are careful to point out that action is limited to southern Lebanon, and that there is no intention to involve Syria; Israeli planes were reptdly fired on by Syrian unit during raid at Damur, 20 miles south of Beirut, but Israelis did not return fire, and no Syrian ground force activity was detected; Israel refuses to disclose number of troops involved, noting only that 100 Palestinian guerrillas

The Israeli army drove into Lebanon along the entire length of the border late March 14 in a "purifying act" against Palestinian guerrillas who massacred 32 Israelis in an attack on a tourist bus March 11.

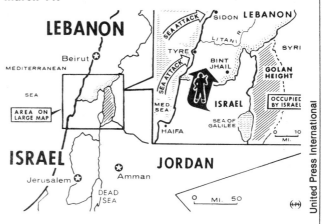

are known dead, but foreign press reports estimate forces total 20,000 Israelis and 5,000 Palestinian guerrillas   (NEW YORK TIMES,   March 16, 1978,   P1)

ISRAELI AIMS ANALYZED

Drew Middleton analyzes Israel's military strategy in raid on southern Lebanon; notes that US military analysts feel Israelis will probably not occupy entire area between Litani River and Israeli border but will patrol area with tanks to discourage Syrian retaliation; reports that Syria's 30,000 peacekeeping troops in Lebanon are inferior to Israeli forces in training, heavy weapons and experience; says Israelis' main objectives were to wipe out hilltop Palestinian forts and to neutralize PLO camps in area of Tyre; cites Israeli military source who notes that PLO is trained and equipped for guerrilla warfare but not for fighting trained forces of greater quantity and quality (NEW YORK TIMES,   March 16, 1978,   P17)

P.L.O., REFUGEES MOVE NORTH

Palestinian and Lebanese families flee from southern Lebanon population centers as Palestinian military spokesman concedes that leftist forces have lost their key border positions of Khiam, Ibl al-Saqi and Taibe in east, Bint Jbail and Marun al-Ras in center, and Alma al-Chaab in southwest, to Israeli forces; young Lebanese and Palestinian guerrillas hold they will maintain "fierce resistance," despite evidence of widespread retreat, while PLO member contends PLO will not allow annihilation, and will make tactical retreat after inflicting as many casualties as possible   (NEW YORK TIMES,   March 16, 1978,   P1)

SYRIAN DILEMMA NOTED

Commentator Jonathan C. Randal observes Syria's unwillingness to intervene on behalf of Lebanon and Palestinians following Israeli reprisal raid in southern Lebanon was humiliating for Lebanese and Palestinians; points out Israeli raid should have triggered automatic aid for guerrillas as part of mutual defense pact that Lebanon signed in December 1977 with Algerians, Libyans, Syrians and South Yemenis; observes Syria's caution reflects fears of being sucked into full-scale war with Israel; notes Israel has apparently achieved its goal of excluding both Palestinians and Syrians from border area   (WASHINGTON POST,   March 16, 1978,   P14)

RETALIATORY RAID APPRAISED

Commentator Richard Johns discusses Israel's March 11, 1978, retaliatory raid against PLO in southern Lebanon; says action will likely inflame Palestinian issue, with possibility of pushing Syria into counterattack that could spark off a 5th Arab-Israeli war; notes that Israeli action will also sour Prime Minister Begin's upcoming meeting with Pres Carter in Washington, DC   (FINANCIAL TIMES, March 16, 1978,   P20)

LEBANESE SCORE INCURSION

Port city of Saida fears it will be next target of Israel's military operation in southern Lebanon, noting gunboats were seen off coast and airplanes are circling area; PLO orders Palestinian refugees to evacuate Ain al-Hilweh camp and other refugee camps, since Israeli raids have been aimed at camps and civilians, but Lebanese refugees continue to arrive in Saida by thousands; Lebanese, most of whom are critical of Palestinian raid which provoked attack, are outraged by extent of Israel's reprisals, and Nasserist Popular Front leader Mustafa Saad holds Israelis are trying to deepen animosity between Lebanese and Palestinians   (NEW YORK TIMES,   March 17, 1978,   P10)

LEBANESE BATTLEFIELD ANALYZED

US officials familiar with area of southern Lebanon in which Palestinian and Israeli forces battled describe it as "no man's land" consisting of villages and market towns abandoned during fighting in 1972 and 1973; claim area is now largely occupied by Palestinian guerrillas, and assert that it would be an "exaggeration" to describe villages as Palestinian strongholds; 1 official who witnessed recent Israeli raid on few straw huts near mouth of Litani River states that Israeli radio broadcast subsequently described raid as attempt to destroy "a fedayeen naval base"   (NEW YORK TIMES,   March 17, 1978,   P10)

ARAB INACTION OBSERVED

Commentator Jonathan C. Randal asserts that Israel's recent attack on southern Lebanon reveals weaknesses of those Arab states who have often taken toughest line against Israel; points out that Syria, who once criticized Lebanese Army for not taking action to protect Palestinian guerrillas in Beirut, has avoided taking any action against Israel; discusses Israeli proposal to have joint force of Christian allies and elements of new Lebanese Army patrol southern border   (WASHINGTON POST,   March 17, 1978,   P21)

ISRAELI POLICY SCORED

Christian Science Monitor editorial asks if Israel wants peace or more land; says Israel is perhaps justified in its attacks on southern Lebanon after recent Palestinian terrorism, but it is not justified in inflicting heavy civilian casualties; hopes for UN peacekeeping force in Lebanon; wonders if negotiators will be soon asking Israel to pull back from its March 1978 borders; says PLO actions have made concept of Palestinian state in West Bank virtually out of the question   (CHRISTIAN SCIENCE MONITOR,   March 17, 1978,   P28)

REFUGEES FLOOD BEIRUT

Beirut is reportedly trying to cope with flood of refugees fleeing advance of Israeli troops; official Beirut radio claims guerrilla stronghold at Tibnine, 1½ miles beyond 6-mile Israeli security zone, has been taken by Israelis; Israeli Defense Minister Ezer Weizman contends Israeli ground forces have not moved north of Litani River; Red Cross reports shortage of personnel, supplies and money to deal with refugee influx; estimates over 250 Palestinians and Lebanese have been killed and 350 wounded; 15 civilians were reportedly killed and 57 wounded Mar 16 in predawn raid on Aadlun, including a senior Palestinian officer; Israeli command reports 1 civilian was killed by guerrilla rocket attacks on Israel's northern settlements; reports Palestinians fired rockets across border into Israeli towns of Metulla and Qiryat Shemona; Lebanese

United Press International

A Lebanese boy waves to Israeli troops in an armored personnel carrier as they drive through Israeli-held Lebanon on the second day of invasion.

government calls for urgent meeting of UN Security Council to obtain Israeli withdrawal; estimates 100,000 refugees have fled northward; reports some 60,000 Palestinians have fled refugee camps shelled by Israelis   (NEW YORK TIMES,   March 18, 1978,   P1)

LEBANESE DEMAND WITHDRAWAL

Lebanese Government asks Security Council to demand that Israel immediately withdraw its troops from 6-mile strip of Lebanon occupied in recent raids; indicates preference to have Lebanese Army control area with support of UN; Israeli delegate Chaim Herzog states that Israel has no wish to retain Lebanese territory but wants assurance that Palestinian guerrillas will not re-establish bases in area; supports idea of Lebanese Army controlling area; claims USSR probably will not agree to UN forces in area since it supplies arms to guerrillas; US continues to seek support for its proposal to have UN forces man area on Lebanese side of border; Arab delegates want immediate withdrawal unlinked to proviso requiring UN forces to control area; experts believe Lebanese Army is inadequate to control area   (NEW YORK TIMES,   March 18, 1978,   P6)

ISRAEL SEEKS SECURITY ZONE

Israeli drive into southern Lebanon continues for third day and Israelis make no response to US demands for withdrawal or to US suggestion that UN international peace force replace Israeli army in southern Lebanon; Israeli Government spokesman indicates that Prime Minister Begin and Foreign Minister Dayan will discuss idea of UN peace force in upcoming visit to US; meanwhile, Palestinian guerrillas continue firing rockets and mortars into northern Israel, making Israeli analysts

skeptical about effectiveness of so-called "security zone"; Israeli army spokesman claims 200 Palestinian guerrillas have been killed in raids; some analysts believe likelihood of clashes with Syrian forces has increased since Israeli forces have advanced so close to Litani River   (NEW YORK TIMES,   March 18, 1978,   P6)

OBSERVERS SKEPTICAL ON U.S. PLAN

Reporter James Markham reports that observers in southern Lebanon are pessimistic about success of US plan to establish UN or Lebanese peacekeeping forces; notes that existence of many different kinds of military forces already in area may be deterrent to creation of peacekeeping forces; notes that Israel insists that it will not withdraw its forces without guarantee that guerrillas will not return and that UN force would not have guarantee of Palestinian cooperation   (NEW YORK TIMES,   March 18, 1978,   P6)

REFUGEES, CASUALTIES SWELL

Refugees entering Beirut, Lebanon, occupy public buildings and vacant apartments, often by force, as government reports growing inability to cope with problem; Red Cross reports total of 700 casualties in 4th day of Israeli offensive, including over 300 deaths; police report 52 civilians killed and 100 wounded March 17; Lebanese government source holds that UN peace force would not be able to control Palestinian guerrillas if Syrian peacekeeping troops did not cooperate; in Damascus, Syrian Foreign Minister Abdel Halim Khaddam meets with US and USSR ambassadors; elsewhere, Palestinian sources say guerrillas would comply with agreement for international peacekeeping force but that fight would go on; reporter Marvine Howe reports Israeli seized main Palestinian-leftist strongholds along border but that guerrillas have regrouped into small units to carry out hit-and-run operations; reports heavy air attacks and artillery fire on Tyre, Nabatiye and Tebnine; Israelis reportedly now control Litani River   (NEW YORK TIMES, March 19, 1978,   P1)

SYRIA ENCOURAGES MILITARY RESPONSE

Syrian President Hafez al-Assad declares that land and skies of Syria are open to all Arabs who want to pass through to fight against Israeli forces in southern Lebanon, and to movement of military equipment; asserts that invasion of Lebanon will not insure Israel's security   (NEW YORK TIMES, March 19, 1978,   P10)

WAR IN LEBANON CONTINUES

Most residents of Tyre, Lebanon, have abandoned area to join refugees fleeing Israeli advance; James Markham describes exchange of fire between highly visible Israeli weaponry and dug-in Palestinians; says Palestinians are able and eager to drag war out for a long time; suggests that if Israeli army actually came into Tyre and Saida, Palestinians would be likely to crumple   (NEW YORK TIMES,   March 19, 1978,   P10)

ISRAEL CONSOLIDATES POSITION

Israeli Army takes control of almost all of Lebanon south of Litani River, moving beyond 6-mile "security belt"; Israeli soldiers are reportedly within machine gun range of Litani River; Israeli Chief of Staff Mordechai Gur indicates that concept of 6-mile security belt was abandoned after UN entered picture; Israeli spokesman reports 7 more villages captured; Defense Minister Ezer Weizman assures that there will be no further advances; sources say Israel did not advance on Eastern flank because it wanted to avoid confrontation with Syrians; Weizman and Gur claim many Lebanese villages invited Israelis; however, Israeli TV shows armored forces shooting their way through villages; Gur suggests Israel will not withdraw without understanding, involving Lebanese government and Christian community and Arab peacekeeping force, that terrorist activity will be stopped; maintains Israel has no intention of remaining in Lebanon   (NEW YORK TIMES, March 20, 1978,　P1)

U.N. CALLS FOR WITHDRAWAL

Security Council approves, by 12–0 vote, US resolution calling on Israel to withdraw forces immediately from Lebanon and setting up UN peace force; approves 6-month mandate for international force of 4,000 men; UN officials say advance contingent of several hundred Austrian, Finnish and Swedish troops would be in border area within 24 hours; USSR and Czechoslovakia abstain from voting; China does not participate because it does not approve of UN peacekeeping; Israeli delegates complained to US privately before mandate about last-minute changes they charged were made under Arab pressure; contend that substitution of new vague language at Arab states' insistence makes it less clear that force has power to prevent return of Palestinian guerrillas to border area; protest that US did not consult with Israel on late changes; American official denies this and scores Israelis for not informing US of their intentions; Israeli Ambassador Chaim Herzog comments that withdrawal is matter to be

Yasir Arafat makes a statement to the press on March 28 following his acceptance of Kurt Waldheim's call for a general cease-fire in southern Lebanon. He is flanked by Major-General Emmanuel Erskine of Ghana (left) and James O.C. Jonah of the Secretary-General's office.

United Nations/J. K. Issac

negotiated by parties involved; USSR insists that $68 million cost of operations for proposed 6-month period should be paid by Israel   (NEW YORK TIMES, March 20, 1978,　P1)

ISRAELI TACTICS ASSESSED

Military analysts see Israeli victory in southern Lebanon as missed opportunity to wipe out Palestinian guerrillas; claim that by blocking 2 main exits from southern Lebanon and seizing bridges over Litani River, guerrillas could have been contained in area instead of being allowed to flee; speculate that limited initial drive aimed at capturing guerrilla bases may have been prompted by fear of arousing conflict with Syrian force in Lebanon, as well as desire to limit number of casualties in fighting; Arab sources claim 10,000 guerrillas escaped into central Lebanon; American sources estimate that more than 8,500 guerrillas were based in southern Lebanon   (NEW YORK TIMES,　March 21, 1978,　P16)

PROBLEMS FOR U.N. FORCE FORESEEN

Commentator John R. Walker warns Lebanese army must be made able to function in territory it has been unable to control for 3 years; notes UN peacekeeping force could not withdraw until it was evident Lebanese army could handle area and fears peacekeeping force will be mired there for more than the 6 months projected by UN (EDMONTON JOURNAL,　March 21, 1978,　P15)

ISRAEL CONSIDERS RESOLUTION

Israeli Foreign Ministry spokesman says Israel has not rejected UN Security Council resolution calling for withdrawal from occupied Lebanon; notes that Israel is waiting for a clarification before announcing acceptance; meanwhile, Israeli forces take over most of southern Lebanon up to Litani River; Mordechai Gur and Defense Minister Ezer Weizman explain that they did not take Tyre because it has large population, and bridge was allowed to remain open for refugee traffic; Gur reports 18 Israeli soldiers and 250-450 guerrillas killed so far; says Israel has taken about 20 prisoners; Lebanese officials claim 1,168 Lebanese and Palestinians have been killed; Israel reportedly has advanced to 15 miles beyond 6-mile "security belt"; Weizman meets with UN forces head Major General Ensio Siilasvuo of Finland to discuss Security Council resolution; Israeli officials criticize speed with which Security Council acted while Prime Minister Begin and Foreign Minister Dayan were on way to US   (NEW YORK TIMES,　March 21, 1978,　P1)

ISRAEL ORDERS CEASE-FIRE

Israel issues cease-fire order in Lebanon; shows little confidence in ability of UN peacekeeping mission to protect Israel from terrorists; will expect guarantees in exchange for withdrawal; in related news, Israel reports it removed right-wing Lebanese Phalangist forces from battle, who were cooperating with Israelis, because Phalangists massacred about 40 Moslems, including women and children at Marun al-Ras and Bint Jbail; casualty reports for week differ greatly; Israel reports 20 deaths among its forces and estimates total Palestinian dead at 400; Lebanon reports 1,168 Lebanese and Palestinians killed; PLO reports 144 of its forces dead and claims 450 Israelis killed or wounded   (NEW YORK TIMES,   March 22, 1978,   P1)

U.N. TROOPS ARRIVE

Lebanese authorities welcome arrival of advance UN troops in southern Lebanon, while French Ambassador Hubert Argod meets with PLO leader Yasir Arafat to discuss arrival of 212 French soldiers March 23; some Palestinian guerrilla chiefs have declared they will not obey Israeli cease-fire, but PLO indicates its forces will not fire unless fired upon; PLO notes fighting has continued for 8th consecutive day, although on reduced scale; Foreign Minister Fuad Butros holds cease-fire must be observed to protect unity, future and interests of Lebanon   (NEW YORK TIMES,   March 23, 1978,   P16)

FIGHTING ABATES

The Lebanese government and Syrian-dominated Arab peacekeeping force in Lebanon announce total ban on entry of military assistance for Palestinian guerrillas into southern Lebanon; announcement comes as 200 Iraqis arrive in Lebanon to aid guerrillas and 200 Libyans are reported enroute to Lebanon; announcement points to arrival of UN troops and need to effect speedy Israeli withdrawal from southern Lebanon; meanwhile, PLO appeals for money and volunteers through its Abu Dhabi office in effort to reinforce guerrillas in southern Lebanon; in Lebanon, presence of Arab volunteers had drawn strong protest from former President Camille Chamoun, right-wing Christian leader   (NEW YORK TIMES,   March 25, 1978,   P1)

SYRIA'S LEBANON ROLE REVIEWED

Discussion of Syria's role in Lebanon; Syria is cautious not to provoke war with Israel in dealing with Palestinians; Syrian President Hafez al-Assad has eliminated any truly independent guerrilla presence inside Syria, stopped Palestinian forays into Israeli-occupied Golan Heights and subjected smaller Palestinian groups to his dictates; Israel suggests that Syria police Palestinian units north of Litani River; hopes, along with US, that Syria will become responsible for Palestinian comportment in northern Lebanon; however, Syria is reluctant to comply and draw criticism from allies Libya and Algeria   (NEW YORK TIMES,   March 26, 1978,   S4 P2)

ISRAELI AIMS ANALYZED

Dial Torgerson holds that recent Israel offensive into Lebanon was not, primarily, revenge for killing of 13 children by Palestinian terrorists but was long-planned defensive strategy; contends that large number of Israeli forces employed in offensive could not have been mobilized in short amount of time and that Israel needed "security belt" in southern Lebanon as well as relief for its Christian Phalangist allies there   (LOS ANGELES TIMES, March 26, 1978,   S6 P2)

P.L.O., ISRAEL CONTINUE BATTLE

PLO officials report that clashes between guerrillas and Israelis in southern Lebanon took place near Kawkaba-

Hasbani bridge over Litani River, and in Qlaia and Marj 'Uyun areas in east and Bazuriye in west; claim that guerrillas destroyed two Israeli vehicles and killed or wounded 15 soldiers; UN peacekeeping forces, which are outmanned and outgunned, appear caught in middle of continued fighting; Lebanese authorities are reported to be worried over buildup of Palestinian forces in Tyre area and are concerned over Israel's refusal to withdraw its forces until Palestinians are out of area and stop firing on Israeli positions; UN commander Major General Emmanuel Erskine is to meet with PLO leader Yasir Arafat to discuss security of UN forces and withdrawal of Palestinians from Tyre; UN forces' fruitless efforts to dislodge Palestinians from their position at bridge over Litani River noted   (NEW YORK TIMES,   March 28, 1978,   P3)

ARAFAT ACCEPTS CEASE-FIRE

PLO leader Yasir Arafat says that guerrilla movement would provide all facilities to help UN peacekeeping forces carry out their task; announcement comes during meeting between Arafat, Lebanese President Elias Sarkis and UN commander in Lebanon Major General Emmanuel Erskine; Arafat, however, does not say whether PLO would comply with cease-fire proclaimed week ago; Lebanese authorities are putting pressure on PLO to pull its guerrillas out of border area and to freeze all military activity; UN troops are finally able to gain control of Khardali Bridge on Litani River without interference from guerrillas   (NEW YORK TIMES,   March 29, 1978,   P3)

AL-FATAH TO HOLD FIRE

Saleh Khalef, second-in-command of PLO's al-Fatah group, reports that guerrillas will hold their fire in some parts of southern Lebanon so as not to provide "pretext to perpetuate Israeli occupation"; notes that troops have been instructed not to shoot from positions north of Litani river; asserts there can be no peace as long as Israeli forces remain in southern Lebanon; praises resistance against Israeli invasion and vows that PLO will fight to preserve its position in Lebanon as recognized by 1969 Cairo accords   (NEW YORK TIMES,   March 30, 1978,   P11)

PEACE RETURNS TO LEBANON

Fragile peace returns to southern Lebanon as UN troops take up new positions between Israeli and PLO forces; there are no reports of shooting, for first time since Israeli forces invaded country two weeks ago   (NEW YORK TIMES,   March 31, 1978,   P3)

P.L.O. OBSERVES CEASE-FIRE

Palestine Liberation Organization spokesman Mahmoud Labadi confirms that PLO forces are observing cease-fire as they regroup and review strategy against Israeli occupation troops in southern Lebanon; PLO leader Yasir Arafat has pledged to cooperate with UN peacekeeping force in its supervision of Israeli withdrawal; indicates that cease-fire will be for a reasonable time to allow for Israeli withdrawal; PLO sources put their total casualties from first eight days of fighting at 71 dead and 131 wounded   (NEW YORK TIMES,   April 1, 1978,   P2)

COMBATANTS, U.N. FORCES FORTIFY POSITIONS

Israeli occupation troops, Palestinian guerrillas and UN peacekeeping forces fortify positions in Sakra, Lebanon, strategic area overlooking Litani River; although truce in southern Lebanon held for 4th day, Israeli bulldozers begin making earthen ramparts to secure their positions and Palestinian and Lebanese leftist guerrillas digging foxholes and trenches on roads leading to Israeli posts; French soldiers with UN peacekeeping forces observed building bunkers on hilltop about 2 miles southeast of Qasimiye Bridge on main coastal highway to Tyre   (NEW YORK TIMES,   April 3, 1978,   P4)

P.L.O., ISRAEL IN DEADLOCK

Sporadic gunfire breaks out between Israeli troops and Palestinian guerrillas as Lieutenant General Ensio Siilasvuo, commander of UN peacekeeping forces, meets with Lebanese authorities to discuss problems facing UN troops; chief problem is deadlock arising from refusal of both Israelis and Palestinians to leave southern Lebanon before departure of the other; Gen. Erskine also encountered problem resulting from guerrillas' refusal to relinquish control over coastal highway bridge crossing Litani River; Lebanese authorities insist that Israelis and Palestinians simultaneously withdraw from territory and demand that UN peacekeeping troops adopt strike tactics and discontinue defensive role; meanwhile, Lebanese rightists are fighting Palestinian presence in nation   (NEW YORK TIMES,   April 5, 1978,   P10)

ISRAEL BEGINS WITHDRAWAL

Israeli soldiers begin first phase of withdrawal from southern Lebanon, leaving eastern village of Rasheiye al-Fukhar and 6 others stretching to vicinity of Ibl as-Saqi; second stage of withdrawal, called by UN Security Council, is expected to begin April 14, when troops will leave central section near village of Taibe; withdrawal is conducted without incident, despite continued Israeli skepticism that UN Interim Force in Lebanon will prevent return of PLO members to southern Lebanon; Lebanese government reports it began sending convoys of refugees back to villages in south, estimating 2,700 people returned to villages they had fled; Ghanaian Major General Erskine, commander of UN forces, notes 1,800 UN troops are in place, but questions whether even full force of 4,000 will be adequate to police area; holds that it is difficult to identify Palestinians, but reports forces would fire back if fired upon, and that forces have fired on parties on 3 occasions   (NEW YORK TIMES,   April 12, 1978,   P1)

SYRIAN POSITION EXAMINED

Commentator Robert Fisk examines problems facing Syrian President Hafez al-Assad in fighting between Israel and Lebanon in southern Lebanon; notes that Syrians are lending their presence to fighting Lebanese forces but are not willing to join fighting; says that Assad hopes that guerrilla fighting will continue between Israel and Lebanon and that it will develop into Vietnam type situation where no one actually wins; maintains that Assad is aware that Israel would fare better in all-out war and wants to avoid it;

notes precarious position of Palestinians   (TIMES OF LONDON,   April 14, 1978,   P14)

REFUGEES FLEE TO BEIRUT

Lebanon's civil war and invasion of southern Lebanon by Israeli troops have spawned hundreds of thousands of refugees, with perhaps 100,000 taking up residence in Beirut, in abandoned or bomb-damaged apartment buildings, schools, Government offices and hotels; Government efforts to persuade refugees to return to their villages discussed   (WALL STREET JOURNAL,   May 10, 1978,   P1)

ARAFAT REJECTS CEASE-FIRE

Palestinian leader Yasir Arafat asserts Palestinian guerrillas have not agreed to cease-fire in southern Lebanon; says PLO has not and will not accept Security Council Resolution 425 authorizing the UN peace force's activity in the area, asserting that Palestinian guerrillas are in the south under an agreement with Lebanese authorities, and no UN force has the right to interfere   (NEW YORK TIMES,   May 12, 1978,   P7)

U.N.-P.L.O. CLASHES TERMED INEVITABLE

UN Interim Force in Lebanon (UNIFIL) Commander Major General Emmanuel Erskine says that clashes between UNIFIL and armed Palestinian groups are inevitable until PLO alters its interpretation of key agreement reached with Lebanese government in 1969; Erskine conveys that PLO leader Yasir Arafat believes that 1969 Cairo agreement permits Palestinian guerrillas to maintain armed presence in south Lebanon; says that UNIFIL purpose and Arafat belief puts two parties in direct confrontation   (TIMES OF LONDON,   May 17, 1978,   P6)

P.L.O. PLEDGES COOPERATION

Yasir Arafat, head of Palestine Liberation Organization, meets with Lebanese Prime Minister Selim al-Hoss, and pledges to end presence of armed guerrillas in southern Lebanon, to withdraw non-Palestinian "volunteers" from area and to cooperate with UN peacekeeping forces; 3-member military committee will be formed to oversee application of agreement; committee will be made up of representatives of PLO, Lebanese security forces and Syrian-dominated Arab League peace forces policing area   (NEW YORK TIMES,   May 26, 1978,   P4)

P.L.O. TO RESTRAIN GUERRILLAS

PLO military leader Zuheir Mohsen reports PLO has pledged to end shelling of Israel from Lebanese territory and will try to curb guerrilla infiltration in area, at least until the Israeli withdrawal; stresses that guerrilla movement will maintain forces in positions stipulated by the Cairo 1969 agreement, which allowed limited guerrilla presence in Lebanon under Lebanese supervision; confirms reports that PLO is seeking new political image; asserts that PLO needs a "military presence" to assure its political presence; al-Fatah meanwhile issues orders against guerrilla infiltration into Lebanese territory now under control of UN forces; in related news, Palestinian, Lebanese and Arab peacekeeping force officers reportedly meet to plan means for ending visible Palestinian presence   (NEW YORK TIMES, May 28, 1978, P3)

SARKIS, ASSAD IN PARLEY

Lebanese President Elias Sarkis and Syrian President Hafez al-Assad agree on measures to restore Lebanese authority in south, which was occupied by Israel in March and is to be evacuated by Israel by June 13; in related development, United Nations peacekeeping forces in Lebanon report activities in violation of their mandate; report clashes between Israeli-supported Christian militia forces in Qlaia area and Palestinian-Lebanese leftists at Beaufort Castle   (NEW YORK TIMES, June 2, 1978, P6)

ISRAELI EVACUATION UNDER WAY

Israel has reportedly evacuated most of its forces from southern Lebanon preparatory to total evacuation on June 13; turns its positions over to Lebanese Christian right-wing militia units led by Major Saad Haddad rather than to UN forces; UN officers meet with Lebanese officials to discuss issue; leftist newspaper *al-Safir* reports Israelis have turned over military equipment to Haddad; claims Israeli officers threatened Lebanese villagers in Bint Jbail with punishment if they aided Palestinian guerrillas   (NEW YORK TIMES, June 13, 1978, P3)

Armies and Factions

CLASHES BREAK OUT IN BEIRUT

Intensifying armed hostilities between Lebanese right-wing Christian neighborhoods and leftists force Syrian-dominated Arab peacekeeping troops to use heavy weapons to halt fighting; intervening troops bombard southeastern Christian district of Ain al-Rummaneh with rocket and artillery fire after heavy exchanges of fire between Christians and Moslem district of Chiyah; Lebanese Prime Minister Selim al-Hoss appeals for calm; Interior Minister Dr. Salah Salman links hostilities with March 1978 Israeli drive against Palestinians in southern Lebanon; leaders of Christian groups conversely blame Palestinians for latest round of fighting; PLO denies involvement in conflict   (NEW YORK TIMES, April 13, 1978, P3)

BEIRUT CEASE-FIRE ANNOUNCED

Syrian peacekeeping forces in Beirut and Lebanese Christian rightists announce cease-fire and truce in fighting that has erupted between Ain al-Rummaneh Christian sector of Beirut and Moslem Chiyah sector after 5 days of intense fighting; hospital and police sources report that 102 persons had been killed and 294 wounded in clashes; most of casualties are reported to be civilians trapped in apartments or basement shelters during shelling and sniping; rightists claim that over 200 apartments have been destroyed in clashes   (NEW YORK TIMES, April 14, 1978, P9)

SYRIA SHELLS CHRISTIANS

Widespread bitterness is reported among residents of the affluent Christian Beirut suburb, Badaro, over heavy shelling inflicted on neighborhood by Syrian peacekeeping force; neighborhood had escaped widespread destruction of 1975–78 civil war, and residents assert that no paramilitary groups or offices of political parties operate in district; residents cannot explain origins of fighting but feel that it could have remained local incident without intervention of outside force   (NEW YORK TIMES, April 18, 1978, P5)

MUSLIMS, CHRISTIANS PARLEY

Lebanon's Christian and Moslem political leaders hold conference in attempt to reach agreement on program of national unity as first step toward formation of new government; nonpolitical cabinet of Prime Minister Selim al-Hoss had resigned following 2 weeks of fighting between Christians and Moslems; resignation was aimed at compelling traditional political leaders to share responsibility for governing Lebanon   (NEW YORK TIMES, April 21, 1978, P9)

P.L.O. TO RETAIN ROLE

Palestine Liberation Organization declares that it will not disarm its guerrilla groups in Lebanon, despite joint call by Lebanese Christian and Moslem leaders for ban against any armed presence other than Lebanon's legal forces; PLO stand is taken after emergency meeting presided over by PLO chairman Yasir Arafat; Lebanese National Movement, which groups main leftist parties, declares its support for continued armed Palestinian presence   (NEW YORK TIMES, April 26, 1978, P8)

BAN ON MILITIAS SOUGHT

Lebanese Parliament approves ban on all private militia forces and all Palestinian guerrilla activity in Lebanon; action is part of political platform intended to provide basis for new government; platform, 6-point program of "national accord" that includes declaration of principles, had been presented by committee of 13 Christian and Moslem leaders on April 21, 1978, and has broad support from nation's political and religious factions, including right-wing Christians, conservative Moslems and part of leftist National Front; officials concede that enforcing ban will be difficult   (NEW YORK TIMES, April 28, 1978, P6)

SARKIS CALLS ON TECHNOCRATS

Lebanese President Elias Sarkis reinstates Cabinet of technocrats after failing in his efforts to form government of national union; states that he will continue his efforts to establish coalition between Christian and Moslem politicians; Prime Minister Selim al-Hoss announces that he withdrew resignation he submitted 28 days ago   (NEW YORK TIMES, May 16, 1978, P8)

LEBANON TO REDEPLOY ARMY

Lebanese Government's plans to send units of reorganized Lebanese Army to south to assist UN peacekeeping forces are opposed by Christian rightists, Moslem leftists and Palestinian guerrillas; about 2,000 Lebanese soldiers are awaiting orders to move south; Christian rightist leader Camille Chamoun warns President Elias Sarkas against sending army before its supply and communications lines are secure from threat of Palestinian guerrillas; National Movement, coalition of Moslem and leftist factions, is demanding restructuring of ranks to insure balance of Moslems and Christians   (NEW YORK TIMES, June 6, 1978, P12)

Army tank rolling through the streets of Beirut.

CRIME ON RISE IN LEBANON

Lebanon is suffering rise in crime and violence in wake of 1975-76 war; Beirut has had large increase in crimes of violence in past 6 months; protection racket is flourishing, as militiamen demand "contributions"; among reasons for crime rise is release of some 10,000 prisoners from jails opened during war; also, government did not disarm warring factions after civil war; new generation of youths has grown up in time of lapse of order and law; jobs are scarce, salaries are low and costs high   (NEW YORK TIMES, June 7, 1978, P3)

P.L.O. DISARMAMENT SOUGHT

Right-wing Christian leaders of Lebanese Front issue declaration calling for immediate disarmament of Palestinian guerrillas in Lebanon, and ask Lebanese Government to cancel all agreements with Palestine Liberation Organization; reject idea that relationship between Lebanon and guerrillas should protect Palestinian resistance movement's interests along with Lebanese sovereignty; urge strengthening of Lebanese army in preparation for eventual departure from Lebanon of Syrian-dominated Arab peacekeeping force   (NEW YORK TIMES, June 8, 1978, P9)

SON OF EX-PRESIDENT KILLED

Tony Franjieh, son of former Lebanese President Suleiman Franjieh, his family and at least 25 other people are killed in clash between Phalangist Party, largest Christian group in Lebanon, and Christian supporters of former President Franjieh; Phalangists attacked rivals while Israelis were withdrawing their troops from southern Lebanon, and political sources speculate that attack was so timed because Syrian troops and Lebanese Government troops were busy with withdrawal; participants in clash have no connection with Christian militia force taking over positions in southern Lebanon as Israelis withdraw   (NEW YORK TIMES,. June 14, 1978, P12)

FRANJIEH VOWS VENGEANCE

Former Lebanese President Suleiman Franjieh leads 20,000 mourners at funeral of his son Tony Franjieh, slain by militia members of Phalangist Party; swears vengeance; meanwhile, Syrian troops of Arab League's peacekeeping force storm Deir al-Ahmar in search of killers; reportedly seize 15 suspects after killing a Lebanese corporal and wounding 6 militia members; in Beirut, Phalangist leader Bashir Gemayel claims raid that killed Franjieh, his wife, daughter and 42 supporters, had not been authorized   (NEW YORK TIMES, June 15, 1978, P14)

TRADITIONAL VIOLENCE HAUNTS LEBANON

Lebanon awaits more violence as armed factions multiply; bloody vendetta begins among feudal chieftains of important Maronite Catholic community in mountainous heart of country; Christians, Palestinians, Israelis and UN peacekeeping force are maneuvering for positions in south; 30,000-man Syrian-dominated Arab peacekeeping force has helped maintain balance between Palestinian guerrillas and Christian militias; Phalangist Party militiamen recently killed Tony Franjieh and family, and now former Lebanese President Suleiman Franjieh is expected to attempt to avenge son's death; Lebanese President Elias Sarkis has been rebuilding Lebanese Army, but no one is sure of its reliability in battle   (NEW YORK TIMES, June 26, 1978, P8)

FRANJIEH VENDETTA CONTINUES

Gunman raid four Christian villages near Baalbek, Lebanon, on June 28, reportedly leaving at least 22 people dead; victims were believed to have taken part in killing of 34 people during week beginning June 11 in town of Ehden; former Lebanese President Suleiman Franjieh's son Tony Franjieh was among 34 killed; Suleiman Franjieh set June 30 deadline for reprisals against Phalangists, but it is not known if June 28 killings were carried out by Franjieh's followers   (NEW YORK TIMES, June 29, 1978, P7)

SARKIS STRUGGLES WITH FEUDS

Lebanon's President Elias Sarkis holds emergency meetings with Cabinet ministers and security chiefs on June 29 as result of June 28 raids in eastern part of country by unidentified gunmen who killed 36 Christian militants; Interior Minister Salah Salman asserts that responsibility for killings has not been established; sources close to Government link violence to feud between rival Christian leaders Pierre Gemayel and former President Suleiman Franjieh (NEW YORK TIMES, June 30, 1978, P7)

SYRIANS, CHRISTIANS IN COMBAT

Heavy fighting breaks out between Lebanese Christian militia groups and Syrian-dominated Arab peacekeeping forces after assault on Beirut's Christian suburb of Ain al-Rummaneh; at least 22 persons are reported killed; fighting spreads to Ashrafiyeh in eastern Beirut after brief lull; Lebanese President Elias Sarkis telephones Syrian President Hafez al-Assad in effort to end battle, while Lebanese and Syrian Army officers, as well as Christian militia leader Bashir Gemayel, meet to discuss cease-fire; new violence follows strong Syrian warning, after 2 mass killings in Christian villages in June, that it would not tolerate deterioration of order; also fulfills prediction by Lebanese political leaders of showdown between Syrians and Phalangist Party, most dominant right-wing Christian faction (NEW YORK TIMES, July 2, 1978, P1)

CHRISTIAN DIVISIONS ANALYZED

Commentator Marvine Howe examines vendetta traditions that characterize divided Christian minority in Lebanon; 2 main factions are Phalangist Party, which favors close cooperation with Israel and wants Lebanon divided into Moslem and Christian sectors, and Zghartawi faction, which favors close cooperation with Moslem leftists and Arab world and rejects close ties with Israel; massacre of Zghartawis, including former President Suleiman Franjieh's son Tony, allegedly by Phalangists, is latest incident (NEW YORK TIMES, July 4, 1978, P2)

TRADITIONAL VIOLENCE REVIEWED

Financial Times editorial discusses recent clashes between the two largest Christian militias in Lebanon and the Syrian peacekeeping forces; says the clashes are a symptom of blood-feuding and anarchical tendencies within the Maronite community and their paramilitary groups, and notes that this militia, under orders from Maronite leaders in alliance with Israel, is a grave embarrassment and irritation to the Syrians (FINANCIAL TIMES, July 5, 1978, P16)

ISRAEL WARNS SYRIA

Low-flying Israeli fighter planes are sent over Beirut to underscore warnings to Syria to end its shelling of Christian sectors of Beirut; warnings follow intense bombardment of Christian villages by Syrian-dominated Arab peacekeeping forces in past 6 days; President Carter appeals to all parties to attempt to immediately end

fighting, while Lebanese President Elias Sarkis threatens to resign in attempt to pressure Syrians to halt fighting; threat causes alarm in political circles, and Sarkis decides to retain post after receiving pleas from Lebanese Christian and Moslem leaders and US, British and Saudi Ambassadors (NEW YORK TIMES, July 7, 1978, P1)

SARKIS RESIGNS

Lebanese President Elias Sarkis is letting his resignation stand despite pleas from US, Britain, France, West Germany, Saudi Arabia and most recently Foreign Minister Sheikh Sabah al-Ahmed al-Sabah of Kuwait in personal visit; Sarkis is reported to be working behind scenes for compromise in role of Arab peacekeeping forces; meanwhile Syrian-dominated force reports 2 Syrian soldiers killed, and 4 others, including 2 Lebanese policemen, wounded (NEW YORK TIMES, July 10, 1978, P5)

SYRIAN-CHRISTIAN BREAK ANALYZED

Commentator Marvine Howe analyzes deterioration of relations between Syria and 2 main right-wing Christian Lebanese parties, Phalangists and National Liberation Party; notes that Syrian-Lebanese Christian alliance in 1975–1976 war was fragile one; notes that erosion of relations began with Egyptian President Sadat's journey to Israel, which upset traditional Middle East alliances; contends that Syria and PLO become allies because they were both opposed to Sadat's peace drive; sees murder of Tony Franjieh as breaking point between Lebanese Front and Syria (NEW YORK TIMES, July 12, 1978, P6)

SARKIS TO STAY

Lebanese President Elias Sarkis has withdrawn his resignation, according to Prime Min Selim al-Hoss; Sarkis will make radio-TV address at undisclosed date to outline future plans (NEW YORK TIMES, July 16, 1978, P4)

REALIGNMENT OF FACTIONS SEEN

Commentator Ihsan Hijazi attributes Syria's new friendship with Lebanese Moslems to fear of growing cooperation between Israelis and Christians; notes that assassination of Tony Franjieh divided Christians, causing Christian leader Suleiman Franjieh to renew his friendship with Moslem leader Rashid Karami; discusses political system in Lebanon that has placed power in hands of Maronite Christians; notes that inequities have led Moslems to seek a common ground with Palestinians (NEW YORK TIMES, July 30, 1978, S4 P2)

PROXY WAR SEEN

Commentator Marvine Howe foresees that sniping exchanges between Lebanese Christian militiamen and Syrian peacekeeping troops are "dangerous showdown" with risk of direct Syrian-Israeli confrontation; reports that Phalangist Party and National Liberal Party, Syrian opponents, do not represent most of Lebanese; describes the 2 parties as nationalist, anti-Communist, anti-Palestinian, and essentially anti-Arab; finds Phalangists have a standing militia force of 5,000 men "and can easily muster 15,000," while Liberals reportedly have a permanent force of 2,000 and ability to mobilize 5,000 (NEW YORK TIMES, August 8, 1978, P3)

TRUCE FOR BEIRUT SOUGHT

Sources report Lebanon is proposing to make Beirut "open city" in attempt to end fighting between Syrian peacekeeping forces and rightist Christian guerrillas; proposal calls for demilitarizing financial and commercial center of city and removing barriers hampering movements between Christians and Moslems (WASHINGTON POST, August 10, 1978, P31)

SYRIANS FIRE ON CHRISTIANS

Syrian peacekeeping forces break 48-hour cease-fire and resume firing heavy artillery against Christian militia forces in East Beirut, after threatening strong retaliation for continued sniping in Christian suburbs; accuses small militias of starting shooting in Ashrafiyeh section, but Voice of Lebanon, radio of Christian Phalange party, accuses Syrians of renewing fighting for no apparent reason, noting fighting spread to southeastern suburbs of Tahwita, Furn al-Chebback and Ain al-Rumanneh (NEW YORK TIMES, August 12, 1978, P111)

SYRIAN WITHDRAWAL URGED

Lebanese Ambassador to US Charles Malik asserts Lebanon cannot return to stable self-government as long as Syrian forces remain in country; urges Senate subcommittee on Middle East to again probe dominance of Syrian element in Lebanon, maintaining Lebanese cannot accept anything imposed on them under duress (NEW YORK TIMES, August 17, 1978, P45)

KIDNAPPINGS ON THE RISE

Political kidnappings in Lebanon are on the rise, with new outbreak coinciding with eruption of fighting between Christian militias and Syrian-dominated Arab peacekeeping force; newspapers daily carry pictures of missing people and pleas for their return; a 19-year-old American youth who disappeared August 27, son of a professor at American University at Beirut who has asked that the family not be identified, is still missing despite concern shown by Government, US embassy and main political party leaders (NEW YORK TIMES, September 8, 1978, P105)

SARKIS SEEKS SOLUTION

Lebanese President Elias Sarkis, in speech broadcast to Lebanese people, announces he will form a new government and introduce security plan within 10 days to try to resolve national crisis; speech follows weekend of worst shelling of Beirut in long civil strife, which had resumed October 2 with no end in sight; former President Camille Chamoun, leader of coalition of rightist parties known as Lebanese Front, calls for Sarkis's resignation, rejects new government and asserts that Syrians have already turned down security plan; leftist Voice of Arab Lebanon also denounces Sarkis's speech as "biased" in

favor of Christian militias and recalls earlier failure to form political cabinet; Pierre Gemayel, leader of main Christian party Phalange, hardens his position, declaring there can be no security or peace with Syrian presence in Lebanon (NEW YORK TIMES, October 3, 1978, P14)

BEIRUT SUFFERS URBAN BREAKDOWN

Beirut suffers shortages, breakdown in communications and flight of foreigners as clashes between Syrian peacekeeping forces and Christian militia continue for 5th straight day; President Elias Sarkis, at shell-scarred presidential palace in Baabda, discusses deteriorating situation with British and French ambassadors and at emergency cabinet meeting; government is reportedly divided over French proposal for cease-fire, with Lebanese army forming buffer force; critics hold newly created army would be ineffective, noting army was recently unable to impose order in southern border area (NEW YORK TIMES, October 5, 1978, P10)

MARONITE STRATEGY REVIEWED

Jonathan C. Randal asserts Lebanese Maronites may have made another in long series of foreign policy errors by contracting alliance with Israel in recent Lebanese conflict; points out that Israel's failure to aid Maronites in current round of fighting illustrates Israel's unwillingness to sacrifice Camp David accords for sake of foreign ally (WASHINGTON POST, October 8, 1978, P23)

CEASE-FIRE HOLDING

Syrian peacekeeping troops and Lebanon's Christian militia units generally observe cease-fire agreed to October 7 by Syrian President Hafez al-Assad and Lebanese President Elias Sarkis; Assad and Sarkis continue meeting for 3rd day in Damascus in determined effort to stop fighting and reach political solution to crisis; Christian militia commander Bashir Gemayel predicts talks will resolve nothing, and believes fighting may resume at any time, noting his men have orders to respond if attacked (NEW YORK TIMES, October 9, 1978, P10)

ARAB SUMMIT ON LEBANON

Foreign ministers of Syria, Saudi Arabia, Kuwait, United Arab Emirates, Qatar and Sudan will meet at Lebanese presidential summer palce of Beituddin in effort to arrive at peace plan for Lebanon; meeting was called by Lebanese President Elias Sarkis; reports that 3 main points in plan to be discussed by Arab foreign ministers are replacement of Syrian troops by Saudi Arabians, removal of Syrian troops from sensitive areas in Beirut to outskirts, and introduction of Lebanese army and police units to some Christian areas (NEW YORK TIMES, October 15, 1978, P54)

FRENCH MINISTER SCORES ISRAEL

French Foreign Minister Louis de Guiringaud blames Israel and former Lebanese President Camille Chamoun for battle of Beirut; charges they are fostering "wild dream" of partition; asserts that Israelis sent 10 times more arms to Christian militias than they had surrendered during cease-fire; correspondent Flora Lewis reports related rumor in France that US and France have decided to abandon Lebanon to Syria; notes that US is being accused of seeking to compensate Syria, at Lebanon's expense, for its failure to regain Golan Heights in Camp David talks   (NEW YORK TIMES, October 17, 1978, P21)

ARABS END LEBANON SUMMIT

Lebanon, Syria, Saudi Arabia, United Arab Emirates, Sudan, Kuwait and Qatar end 3-day summit meeting called by Lebanese President Elias Sarkis to restore peace to Lebanon; pledge to neutralize right-wing Christian militias that have been fighting against Syrian peacekeeping forces, and issue 8-point statement threatening to use force to end collaboration between Christian militiamen and Israel; Sarkis also reportedly presented security plan to conference which envisages replacement of Syrian troops with enlarged Saudi Arabian contingent   (NEW YORK TIMES, October 18, 1978, P8)

SYRIAN TROOPS TO WITHDRAW

Christian-rightist "Voice of Lebanon" radio claims that 10,000 Syrian troops located in Beirut will be withdrawn and replaced by peacekeeping soldiers from other Arab nations, including Jordan; indicates that this is part of 8-point secret security plan which was worked out at Beiteddin conference on future of Lebanon called by Lebanese President Elias Sarkis and attended by 7 Arab nations; says withdrawal will begin to consolidate cease-fire between Syrians and Israeli-backed Christian militia; there has been no independent confirmation of radio report   (NEW YORK TIMES, October 19, 1978, P50)

SECURITY PLAN IMPLEMENTED

Arab Deterrent Force attempts to implement security plan intended to calm tense situation in Lebanon; troops regroup but last minute obstacles prevent actual disengagement of Syrian peace-keepers and right-wing Christian militias; main problem is refusal by Sudan to reconsider earlier decision to withdraw troops from Arab Force; new security plan stipulates that Sudanese troops should replace Syrians at 2 strategic bridges at Beirut's northeastern approaches; Lebanese government sources say Sudanese move might delay full implementation of security plan, but would not block it   (NEW YORK TIMES, October 20, 1978, P13)

SYRIAN TROOPS BEGIN WITHDRAWAL

Discussion of reaction of inhabitants of Christian section of Beirut to withdrawal of Syrian troops from two strategic bridges, ending a 22-day blockade; immediately after the withdrawal, thousands of jubiliant inhabitants began streaming through the bridges bringing badly needed food, medicine and other supplies; partial withdrawal of Syrian forces from Christian east Beirut and their replacement by Saudi Arabian troops was first step taken in a plan designed to strengthen the 12-day-old cease-fire   (NEW YORK TIMES, October 21, 1978, P14)

HADDAD AND CHIDIAC ON TRIAL

Lebanese military court will try Major Saad Haddad and his former 2d in command, Sami Chidiac, probably in absentia, for "collaboration with Israel" and "inducement to mutiny"; byliner Marvine Howe notes general opinion that Haddad and Chidiac are scapegoats in attempt to reach settlement between right-wing Christian Lebanese Front and Syrian peacekeeping forces; notes that Lebanese Front Leader, President Camille Chamoun, is known to have close relations with Israel but that no one expects Chamoun to be brought before courts; notes that Haddad and Chamoun both perceive Lebanon as not belonging to Arab world but as identified with Europe; recounts details of resistance to UN peacekeeping forces by Haddad's militias   (NEW YORK TIMES, October 23, 1978, P31)

NEW PLAN TO END CONFLICT

Lebanese government announces program to pave way for solution to country's prolonged conflict; emergency Cabinet meeting approves 7-point program, which includes ban on unauthorized military manifestations of any kind; tour of Beirut on October 25 reveals varying reactions to government's peace plan and possible difficulties in implementing it; only instrument that government has to enforce law and order is Arab Deterrent Force, which is largely Syrian   (NEW YORK TIMES, October 26, 1978, P23)

PALESTINIANS OFFER TRUCE

Palestinian guerrillas in Lebanon, fearing confrontation with Israel in event of Israel-Egypt peace treaty, have reportedly offered to end conflict with Lebanese Christians on condition that Christians terminate their cooperation with Israelis; offer is reportedly carried by 2 professors unattached to guerrilla movement, Dr. Walid Khalidi and Dr. Hassib Sabbagh, to Lebanon's top Christian leaders Pierre Gemayel, of Phalange party, and former President Camille Chamoun; offer is publicly endorsed at news conference by Salah Khalef, PLO's 2d in command   (NEW YORK TIMES, November 14, 1978, P2)

ARMENIANS SUFFER CASUALTIES

Armenian refugees in Beirut begin returning to their devastated neighborhood of Burj Hammud, one of hardest hit areas of fighting between Lebanese Christian militiamen and Syrian peacekeeping forces; Armenians had been caught in crossfire between 2 sides and had steadfastly refused to participate; some Armenian political leaders claim that militiamen deliberately shelled Armenian neighborhoods to provoke a reaction; Armenian casualties in 10-day period of fighting are 60 dead and over 200 wounded   (NEW YORK TIMES, November 14, 1978, P2)

SECURITY PLAN THWARTED

Lebanese Cabinet fails to reach agreement on new security plan to stabilize 6-week-old ceasefire; meanwhile, clashes between Christian militia forces and Syrian peacekeeping forces intensify in Beirut, with police reporting 6 persons were killed and 18 wounded   (NEW YORK TIMES, November 16, 1978, P6)

United Press International

A group of village elders outside a house in the town of Abaseeyeh, southern Lebanon, after their return from refugee camps in Beirut.

LEBANON DEVASTATED BY WAR

Beirut residents ponder dilemma of rebuilding devastated homes and property or leaving; fears are widespread that new Arab-Israeli war will erupt following Israel-Egypt peace and will be fought in Lebanon; at same time, business is reported at standstill, with only 100 of 450 industrial enterprises resuming activity, according to official report, and 90,000 workers unemployed; most foreign companies have left; only 10 US firms remain in country, while before 1975–1976 civil war there were 250; government tries to reassert authority by reforming army, redefining role of Syrian peacekeeping force and banning carrying of arms as well as illegal publications and radio stations run by militant Moslems and Christians   (NEW YORK TIMES,   December 6, 1978,   P2)

Israel Plans to Pull Back Farther in South Lebanon

Special to The New York Times

TEL AVIV, April 18—Israeli and United Nations military commanders agreed today to schedule Israeli withdrawals from southern Lebanon by early next month to a line some six miles from the international frontier.

Lieut. Gen. Rafael Eytan, the new Israeli Chief of Staff, and Lieut. Gen. Ensio Siilasvuo of Finland, coordinator of United Nations peacekeeping forces in the Middle East, negotiated the agreement this morning while Secretary General Kurt Waldheim of the United Nations was conferring in Jerusalem with Prime Minister Menachem Begin and Foreign Minister Moshe Dayan.

Mr. Waldheim, who had complained of the slow pace of Israel's compliance with the Security Council resolution of March 19, told the Israeli leaders that he planned to report this week to the General Assembly on the pullout. He noted that the resolution had called for the Israelis to withdraw "forthwith" and said there was some concern in the United Nations.

Bigger U.N. Force Sought

Mr. Begin assured the Secretary General that Israel had no claim to Lebanese territory and he noted that his Government had announced its intention to withdraw even before the Security Council convened. However, he said the Israelis first wanted to be sure the United Nations interim force was sufficiently organized to prevent southern Lebanon from again becoming a staging area for attacks on Israel.

According to United Nations data, only 2,500 of the planned force of 4,000 have been deployed. Mr. Waldheim said the force would reach its planned strength in two weeks. A participant in the meeting said the Secretary General informed Mr. Begin that he planned to seek approval for the enlargement of the force to 6,000. He said France, Iran, Ireland, Senegal and Nigeria had agreed to send additional men.

Mr. Waldheim said the force was taking

The New York Times/April 19, 1978

Next Israeli position reportedly will extend from Ras Bayada along a line to Merj 'Uyun.

its mandate to control movement in the area very seriously.

But the commander of the French contingent was quoted tonight on Israeli television as having said that his men were permitting refugees to return to the area without checking their identities and some could very well be guerrillas. The officer said three men were intercepted this week trying to bring arms and grenades into the area. The weapons were confiscated but the men released.

Israeli officers said that there were still secret arms caches in cellars and bunkers all over the area and that returning guerrillas could easily re-equip themselves. Yesterday, the Israelis found a truck with a large supply of weapons including a rocket launcher in a citrus orchard near Tyre.

The new Israeli line after the withdrawals early next month will run from Ras Bayada on the Mediterranean coast to Merj 'Uyun, according to a military source. The Israelis will thus give up their strategic heights overlooking Tyre, the guerrilla supply port.

The Israelis will control the area they had originally intended to purge of guerrillas when they crossed the border on March 14. They advanced to the Litani River after the Security Council decided to post a peacekeeping force in the occupied area.

The area remaining under Israeli control will include the enclaves with Christian villages friendly to Israel whose inhabitants have requested continued Israeli protection.

P.L.O. Pledge Reported

BEIRUT, April 18 (AP)—Yasir Arafat, the Palestinian guerrilla leader, has pledged a moratorium on attacks into Israel to speed the Israeli withdrawal from southern Lebanon, the independent Beirut newspaper An Nahar said today. The paper said Mr. Arafat made the promise during a 70-minute meeting in Beirut yesterday with Secretary General Waldheim. A spokesman for the Palestine Liberation Organization declined comment.

NEW YORK TIMES, April 19, 1978, P3

7 Weeks Later, the Israelis Debate Benefits and Losses From the Invasion of Lebanon

By WILLIAM E. FARRELL
Special to The New York Times

JERUSALEM, May 6—Seven weeks after Israel's land, air and sea invasion of southern Lebanon, the pluses and minuses and the ambiguities of the attack, along with the extent of the impact on Palestinian guerrilla strongholds, are still being debated and analyzed here.

The examination of the attack, the largest Israel has mounted against the Palestinians, touches on the political and the military aspects and on Israel's always-precarious image abroad.

Israel has withdrawn from about two-thirds of the lands it captured, originally running from its northern border to the Litani River. Israeli soldiers have been replaced by a United Nations peacekeeping force that includes Senegalese, Swedish, Norwegian, Iranian, Nepalese and French troops. Increasingly the international contingents are experiencing first hand the tangled web of animosities and violence that has turned the farmland and hills of southern Lebanon into a killing ground.

A Terrorist Rampage in March

The invasion was prompted by a Palestinian terrorist rampage in Israel in

March conducted by 11 guerrillas who landed by sea and commandeered a bus filled with Israeli tourists. The attack left 35 Israelis and an American and 9 of the attackers dead. More than 70 people were wounded.

There was little doubt in Israel or anywhere else that the carnage would prompt retaliation, but few envisioned the dimensions of the Israeli assault on southern Lebanon, from which many Palestinian guerrillas had fled in anticipation.

There are nearly 100 villages in the region, some of them depopulated many months ago by protracted civil strife. The powerful Israeli Army struck dozens of them; some were hit to a lesser extent but others known to be Palestine Liberation Organization strongholds were demolished by bombs and artillery and fire by the troops.

A spokesman for the Israeli armed forces said there was no official figure publicly available on how many villages were hit, nor one for how many were severely damaged or destroyed. A military analyst, not a member of the regular army, said 10 communities had been leveled and an undetermined number, probably about a quarter of the total, subjected to shelling.

Intense Destruction Encountered

On a recent trip in the region this reporter was in the following communities in which the destruction was intense: Sreifa, Joya, Bint Jbail, Rasheiye al-Fukhar, Ghanduriye, Taibe and Qantara. Khiam, which was largely deserted and leveled, was viewed from a distance through binoculars.

According to a Government spokesman, the Israeli forces have no reliable estimate of civilian casualties, which Lebanese sources put as high as 1,200. The Israelis say that 350 Palestinian guerrillas were killed and that 34 Israeli soldiers died—23 in action, 4 during a prohibited tour after an Israeli cease-fire went into effect and 7 in military accidents.

The scope of the incursion, much of it involving the use of the most sophisticated weapons, has been a source of domestic controversy.

On the one hand, some defend its intensity as necessary to keep Israeli casualties to a minimum and as a vivid reminder to hostile Arab neighbors of the Israeli Army's strength.

Among the defenders, some analysts view the failure of Syria, Egypt and other Arab nations to do more for the Palestinians than mere statements as evidence that declarations about Arab unity are not much more than a flimsy, facade that ill conceals simmering rivalries and animosities as well as rather limited sympathy for the Palestinians. They point to the fact that while Israel was occupying southern Lebanon, the Israeli Defense Minister, Ezer Weizman, was welcomed in Cairo by President Anwar el-Sadat for talks aimed at renewing the still-stalled peace negotiations.

Mr. Weizman commented on this recently in an interview with the news-

paper Yediot Ahronot, saying: "The Syrians did not lift a finger, which is today causing great debate in the Arab world. They are arguing over the question of who did not. I don't want to say that we will achieve something because of conflicts within the Arab world, but it is certainly interesting."

There is also a view here that Mr. Sadat's relatively subdued response to the invasion of Lebanon should be noted by those still in doubt about the sincerity of his peace moves, which began when he visited Jerusalem last November.

The opposite assessment of the Israeli attack is that the military engaged in overkill in places where the Palestinian guerrillas had fled after the attack on the bus, that the magnitude of the incursion erased the sympathy engendered by the bus incident and that Israel's image was tarnished abroad.

New Lease on Life Seen for P.L.O.

Some critics of the intensity of the reprisal—hardly anyone here argues that Israel should not have made some retaliatory response—say that it did not thwart the P.L.O. and may even have given the organization, which some regard as having lost important ground in the international political sphere in recent months, a new lease on life. This stems from assertions by its members that it withstood a seven-day attack against overwhelming military odds and that, all in all, it fared better than did the Arab nations that fought Israel and lost in the 1967 six-day war.

Still other Israelis, among them sup-

The New York Times/May 7, 1978
Destruction was intense in communities with names underlined.

porters of the invasion, are angered that the Israeli media, particularly television, played down its impact. While foreign newspaper and television reporters filed vivid accounts that were read and seen by millions, Israelis got a more sanitized version that tended to emphasize the aftermath, when Israeli medical teams and emergency crews attempted to aid villagers who remained and, later, refugees who began to return home.

"Why shouldn't I have found out in detail what happened in the beginning of the attack?" an Israeli who supported the scope of the invasion remarked to a foreign friend. "I shouldn't have had to read foreign magazines and papers to know."

There are also some, admittedly a minority, who feel that Prime Minister Menachem Begin lost a chance to make a big stride toward peace by not retaliating at all, not out of weakness but out of strength. There is hindsight in this, however, for the mood of the country after the bus attack was overwhelmingly for revenge.

Focus on the New U.N. Force

A main focus of interest now is the United Nations peacekeeping force, which was hurriedly created shortly after the Israelis moved across their northern border.

On the basis of a decade of distrust of United Nations troop missions, Mr. Begin's Government was not pleased at the dispatch with which the Security Council with the urging of the United States, adopted the resolution creating the United Nations Interim Force in Lebanon. The major concern, as enunciated by Israeli leaders, is whether the force will be able to prevent a reconcentration of Palestinian guerrillas in southern Lebanon. Nonetheless, the Israelis acceded to the action, and they have been accused by Secretary General Kurt Waldheim of withdrawing too slowly.

The most recent withdrawal—the third phased retrenchment so far—took place last Sunday in the extremely volatile western section in the vicinity of the Litani River. Israeli troops are now at a distance averaging a little over six miles from their border, or roughly where Israeli leaders said they intended to advance when the attack started.

Another question being debated is why Israel went so deep into Lebanon. Defense Minister Weizman answered that bluntly in the Yediot Ahronot interview when he alluded to the speed with which the United States pushed the Security Council resolution to passage. "We set short-term goals for ourselves," he said. "But then something happened. The U.S. Government got involved, mistakenly to my mind, like a bulldozer."

How Far Should They Go?

When it was clear that a United Nations presence was imminent, he added, "we had to decide where it would be best for the U.N. force to be stationed—on the banks of the Litani or someplace else, perhaps closer to our border." He continued: "Yours truly went with the Chief of Staff to present the matter to the Prime Minister, and we met, discussed and decided. I have heard it said that the political echelon was pulled along in this by the military. What rubbish! It was decided that it is better for a U.N. force to be stationed on the Litani, and that's how we got there, so that U.N. soldiers would be situated there."

One view of the United Nations presence is rather positive from Israel's perspective. An analyst, referring to recent confrontations involving United Nations soldiers and Palestinians, said: "It means the P.L.O. is now an international problem. Before it was just Israel and Lebanon."

There have been fatalities in the international force in its brief assignment, most recently among the French contingent, which has exchanged fire with Palestinian guerrillas. While Israeli officials express regret over the attacks, they maintain that they bear out Israel's initial resistance to a speedy total withdrawal, as required by the Security Council resolution. "There seems to be a war going on between the Palestine Liberation Organization and the U.N. at this time," a Foreign Ministry spokesman said.

So far no timetable has been made public for the next phase of Israeli retrenchment, with officials here apparently waiting to see whether the guerrillas are able to regroup near the frontier.

A De Facto Role for the P.L.O.

Mordechai Gur, the recently retired Israeli Chief of Staff, who was in charge of the operation in Lebanon, has said that one result of the invasion is that the P.L.O. is inescapably a de facto partner to any accord in southern Lebanon.

Some here are focusing on a more nebulous possibility revolving around the role of the United Nations in Lebanon: If it succeeds in maintaining calm in the south, then a precedent might be set that could apply to the problems of the Israeli-occupied West Bank of the Jordan River and the Gaza Strip, on the Mediterranean. The idea of a United Nations presence in those territories, at least as a temporary way out of a situation that has resisted resolution for over a decade, had been offered before, but the Israelis have scorned it. A United Nations success in Lebanon would do much to change the Israeli attitude; on the other hand, if the force proves ineffectual, Israeli skepticism will be strengthened.

The pluses and minuses of the Israeli incursion do not yield a neat answer. For some it was warranted, although there are regrets at the devastation of villages whose civilian populations had already been victimized by more than two years of fighting between right-wing Lebanese Christians and Palestinians, the latter aided by Moslem leftists.

For others the military response was an overreaction for which Israel may pay a high price diplomatically. For still others—those whose sorrow at the bus attack was transmuted into a cry for revenge—there is a desire, perhaps a need, to see the bloody episode recede into memory.

NEW YORK TIMES, May 7, 1978, P3

A DELICATE STANDOFF IN SOUTHERN LEBANON

U.N. Force, Blocked by Christians, Avoids Confrontation, but Threat of New Civil Strife Remains

By JAMES M. MARKHAM
Special to The New York Times

NAQURA, Lebanon, June 20—The Christian irregulars lounge near their American-made Sherman tank, a gift of the departed Israeli Army, under two Lebanese flags. Soldiers of the 6,000-strong United Nations peacekeeping force go about their business. A Norwegian-piloted helicopter chatters to a landing near the Mediterranean.

This is a Wild West-style standoff between the lightly armed representatives of the Security Council and about 1,500 heavily armed Lebanese stretched along the length of the Israeli border, but today there is little tension. With Levantine resourcefulness, one of the Christian irregulars, leaving his Soviet-designed assault rifle near the tank, runs a makeshift soft-drink stand patronized by the French, Senegalese, Norwegians, Nepalese, Irish, Iranians, Nigerians, Canadians and Fiji islanders who pass through Naqura.

So far, the United Nations seems to be relying on diplomacy, rather than force, to complete its takeover of the main roads that run through the gnarled hills south of the Litani River. Several hundred Palestinian guerrillas are believed to have filtered into the region, but they and the United Nations troops have avoided confrontations. The Palestinians have left their artillery and other heavy weapons north of the river.

The Christian militiamen are now running things in the border zone, and they have promised to "fight to the last drop of blood" if the United Nations tries to enter it—a threat the United Nations, which cannot afford to either inflict or suffer heavy casualties—i staking seriously. The only solution, many United forces have recently been bolstered, according to reliable Western diplomats, by Christian volunteers brought by ship from central Lebanon to Israel and trucked up to the frontier zone.

U.N. Troops Seem Popular

If the United Nations force fails to move into the Christian-held zone, which is three to four miles deep, the promising semblance of peace that has begun to settle over the villages south of the Litani could unravel. There is concern in Beirut that the sterile shelling war that flared up sporadically between Christians and Palestinians in the south before the Israeli invasion could easily resume.

But, now at least, the bulk of the Lebanese and Palestinian refugees who fled the Israeli invasion have returned to their villages and camps, or what remains of them. And the United Nations troops seem genuinely popular as a sign of the stability and security that have long been absent here in the south.

One of the first children born in the south after the peacekeeping force arrived—to a pregnant woman from the village of Tibnine who was rushed to the field hospital here—was gratefully named Unifil, for the initials for United Nations Interim Force in Lebanon, the peacekeeping force's official name.

Among the most popular are the soldiers from the Fiji islands, a remote former British colony in the Pacific that has contributed 500 men from its 650-man army. "Yes, they like us," agreed one genial Fiji sergeant at a checkpoint south of Tyre, "because we smile, and we pick up their children." He patted an imaginary Lebanese child. "It's very much like Fiji here, but we're working hard, only four hours' sleep a night."

The French Foreign Legionnaires seem upset that things are quieting down in southern Lebanon after last month's tense confrontations with Palestinian gunmen that left a number of people dead and wounded. A sign in French put up by the leftist Popular Front for the Liberation of Palestine seemed designed to rub salt in old wounds—"Remember Vietnam and Algeria," it said.

"At the beginning it was interesting," said one legionnaire, browsing in the bazaar outside the Tyre barracks, "but now it's boring. I would have rather gone to Zaire. That was a success, don't you think?"

NEW YORK TIMES, June 21, 1978, P3

Faction in Lebanon Trying To End Vendetta Traditions

By MARVINE HOWE
Special to The New York Times

ZGHARTA, Lebanon, July 1 — "We have finished with the eye-for-an-eye business," said Selim Bey Karam, chief of one of the five ruling families in this feudal stronghold in northern Lebanon. "We are tired of fighting and killing each other — tired of old women wearing black."

The leaders of this traditionalist Maronite Catholic community are trying to avert a vendetta by opting for political revenge for the massacre last month in which their chieftain's heir apparent, Tony Franjieh, his wife and 3-year-old daughter and 31 partisans were slain. Suleiman Franjieh, former President of Lebanon and partron of the Zgharta clans, has accused the right-wing Phalangist Party, a rival Christian group, of the crime and ordered all Phalangists in the region to resign from the party or leave by yesterday, or face the consequences.

Challenges Angered Syrians

The massacre was the last straw for the Syrian-led Arab peacekeeping forces, charged with security in Lebanon since the end of the civil war in November 1976. The Syrians have been increasingly angered by the right-wing Christians' challenges to their authority as well as by their open cooperation with Israel and, according to authoritative Damascus sources, have decided to teach the group a lesson. The result is the current Syrian offensive against the right-wing Christian parties and militias in Beirut. The Syrians are said to have chosen this time to crack down on the Phalangists and their allies of the National Liberal Party because of the open split in Christian ranks since the killing of Tony Franjieh.

The violence among the Christians, which appears to be much more than the usual struggle for power and influence, reflects the two political options open to Lebanon's Christians, who make up a bit less than 50 percent of its three million inhabitants.

The Phalangists and the Franjieh people fought side by side during the civil war against the Palestinians and Moslem leftists but are now at odds on basic issues. The Phalangists openly favor cooperation with Israel and want the country divided by cantonization or even partition, with the Christians and Moslems each running their own affairs. While the Phalangists accepted Syrian help to end the civil war and curb the

Palestinians, they now want the Syrians to leave and suspect Damascus of "greater Syria" ambitions. On the other hand, the Zghartawis, as the members of the Franjieh faction are known, believe in reconciliation with the Moslem leftists and close cooperation with the Syrians and the rest of the Arab world, and they reject cooperation with Israel.

Ultimatum Is Termed Success

The Zgharta ultimatum has succeeded, according to Samir Franjieh, nephew of the head of the clan and said by some to be his possible successor. There have been no bloody reprisals, the younger man said, and at the expiration of the deadline 40 of 450 Phalangists from the 52 villages in the Zgharta district had turned in their party cards and the others had left the region, which is near Tripoli.

Today repentant Phalangists continued to arrive from the neighboring district of Koura and turned in their cards at an improvised office on the ground floor of Samir Franjieh's newly built stone mansion on the Zgharta plateau.

For many Zghartawis, however, the blood debt has not been paid. The old town is adorned with black flags and idealized photographs of Tony Franjieh, and people vow that he will not be forgotten. "I will get the man responsible for the massacre if it takes me 20 years, or my son will get him," a distant relative of the former President said, explaining that he had lost his brother, sister-in-law and nephew in the incident.

This country, so used to violence, was shocked by the brutality of what is now known as the Ehden massacre, named for the mountain resort where the Franjiehs have a summer residence. On the night of June 13, 800 Phalangist militiamen attacked Ehden with rockets and heavy machine guns. Their main target was the Franjieh residence, where everyone was killed.

The Zgharta leadership, which has been struggling to curb its militants' longings for vengeance, was enraged by reports of another mass killing on the Bekaa Plain north of the ancient city of Baalbeck. Unidentified gunmen kidnapped and killed 32 young men, said to be Phalangists, last Wednesday.

Role In Massacre Denied

Chief Karam, firmly denying that the

Zgharta people had anything to do with the Bekaa killings, said, "Since we condemn the violence of our enemies, we will not use their methods." Showing visitors lists of Phalangist defectors, he said that the civil war had turned people in the region against violent revenge.

The chief, who is 33 years old, is a graduate of the American University of Beirut in business administration and is involved in development projects in Lebanon and other Arab countries. Other members of the younger generation in Zgharta join him in strong opposition to the tradition of vendetta.

Some political analysts describe the conflict between the Zghartawis and the Phalangists as a struggle between the traditional feudal clan and the modern political party. In reality, behind Lebanon's trapping of liberal democracy and a modern, aggressive economy, political life remains dominated by clans and families, with chieftains acquiring power through force and charisma and protecting their constituents in return for political and financial support.

"Lebanon is a republic of petty kingdoms," Clovis Maksoud, former roving ambassador for the Arab League, commented in Beirut the other day. "During the civil war these petty kingdoms took on the attributes of sovereignty when the central authority broke down, and now they are reluctant to relinquish their autonomy."

Invading the Franjieh Fief

The trouble began in Zgharta a few months ago with reports that the Phalangists were beginning to move into what was regarded as the Franjieh family's fief.

The Phalangist Party, which presents itself as an alternative to feudalism and clannish politics, was founded in 1936 by a Maronite, Pierre Gemayel, as an apolitical youth movement in 1936, but it soon acquired a political and paramilitary structure influenced by the prewar National Socialism of Germany and Italy. The Phalangist Party gained its present strength as the main Lebanese political force during the civil war because it was able to mobilize the largest number of fighters against the Palestinians and leftists.

The party does not give its membership figures; a recent survey in the independent Middle East Reporter estimates 100,000 members, with a well-armed militia of 10,000 plus a reserve force of 15,000. Although it has a broad base, the Phalange is still very much a family concern, dominated by its founder, known as Sheik Pierre, and his two sons, Amin and Bashir, with various cousins holding key posts.

Though the Zghartawis have never set up an organized party, essentially because the elder Franjieh believed that the family system had worked for a thousand years and should not be changed, the main political families have formed a joint directorate and are said to be establishing the basis of a political party or movement.

The Franjieh people believe that it was their chief's decision to break with his erstwhile allies in the right-wing Christian Lebanese Front that led to the Ehden massacre. The break was consummated on May 12 when the former President, a Maronite, met in a public reconciliation with former Prime Minister Rashid Karami, a Moslem, for the first time since the civil war. For the Phalangists that was tantamount to treason; for the Zgharta clans it could be the basis for a new nonsectarian front leading the way to national reconciliation.

NEW YORK TIMES, July 4, 1978, P2

5

Iran in Revolution

Revolution in Iran came as a surprise to many regional observers who considered the most enduring regime in the Middle East to be among the most stable. Yet when demonstrations broke out in March 1978, a classic pattern was already in the making. The country's economic growth had slowed from 10% to 4% under premier Amouzegar's austerity government. Industrial workers, although among the highest paid sectors of the work force, felt the slow-down in the rate of pay increases and began to strike sporadically across the country. Anti-government sentiment was fed by the 22% inflation rate, military spending totaling $18 billion and an unresponsive bureaucracy which promised more of the same. Life did not improve at as fast a rate as Iranians had become accustomed to and the autocracy of the Shah no longer had its justification.

Shah Mohammad Reza used to tell foreign visitors to his country that he hoped to make Iran "*une petite Suisse contente.*" His peacock throne was far from steady after a coup d'etat in 1952, an assassination attempt and several bloody demonstrations against his regime. The second monarch of a dynasty founded in 1926, the King of Kings resided in a tiny, unheated palace, entertaining family friends on the floor. The Shah's optimism paid off in 1971 when the oil price increase endowed Iran with a billion dollar revenue and an explosive economic growth rate of 11% a year. Riding on this boom the monarch staged a gala celebration at ancient Persepolis to commemorate 2,500 years of royal Iran. Flushed with the success of his domestic social reforms which had transferred land to peasant ownership and an aggressive foreign policy designed to make Iran the "gendarme of the Persian Gulf," the Shah began to talk about Iran's becoming a "great power" by the end of the century.

To many Iranians the Shah's goal seemed both attractive and plausible. Iran, like China, has a tradition of being the middle, culturally dominant kingdom in the region. Nationalists had smarted under the scaling down of self-importance when Britain and Russia divided the country in 1907, occupied it forcibly during both world wars and interfered with its internal affairs up to 1953. These nationalists supported their monarch's goal of making Iran the premier power in the region and revelled when the Shah began to lecture the British during their 1973 fiscal crisis on how to set their house in order. It was a revenge for a century of colonialism.

The small, progressive elite which identified its interests with the monarch's aggressive nationalism lived in a bubble of prosperity the existence of which was nothing short of miraculous. They believed that Iran could overtake Britain by 1990, having seen Teheran, the capital, grow from a sleepy, walled village to a metropolis of six million. Here the Shah's great society had an elusive tangibility. Thanks to generous subsidies, meat was three times cheaper than elsewhere in the nation. Fresh fruits and fish were brought from the Caspian and abroad, while favorable currency policies flooded boutiques on fashionable boulevards with luxury items unheard of in the rest of the Middle East.

And in the rest of the country—the realities. In the villages, money lenders had replaced feudal landlords in the wake of the land reform. Soaring inflation cut into the income of the farmers, while massive imports of food held down their profits. They fled agricultural work to swell the urban slums, leading to a fall in agricultural output. In a bureaucracy centralized to the point of strangulation, little could be done in the remotest villages without intervention on the highest levels. Few, spectacular agribusinesses in the Ahwaz region contrasted with the depressed conditions of thousands of small farms. Dependent on imports for 30% of its foodstuffs, tied to oil for its source of foreign earnings, with an industrial base straining to assimilate thousands of unskilled former peasants, Iran was far from being the potential great power Iranians and many foreign observers imagined.

The stability of the country during the booming seventies was less a sign of general satisfaction as a sign of the weakness of the groups opposed to the Shah's rule. Politicians, surviving from the period of active parliamentary life (1941–1953) differed from the Shah more in style than substance. They opposed close ties with the USA, military spending and government inefficiency. Some hated the Shah personally and questioned his ability to rule. The monarch used a velvet fist against this opposition, jailing them occasionally, other times coopting them with a diplomatic post. Among politicians and the public a cynical disrespect of the parliamentary opposition developed.

The clergy of the Shiite faith, a sect of Islam to which millions of Persians in the country belong, had a traditional enmity against the throne, based on a rivalry for temporal power. While it is true that the clergy opposed the Shah's outlawing of the veil and granting certain rights to women, they saw their power more directly threatened in the government's confiscation of religious endowments, the abolition of the tithe and the tightening political controls on the kingdom's bazaars, once the exclusive domain of religious judicial control. They had led revolts against the Shah's rule in 1961 and 1963, but since then, the growing erosion of their economic and judicial prerogatives had greatly weakened their power.

The third component of opposition to the monarch was the radical left. Since the CIA-supported counter-coup in 1953 against the communist-supported government of Mohammad Mosaddeq, the Shah had relentlessly pursued members of the Iranian Communist party (the Tudeh) and created the infamous security apparatus Savak in order to root out the leftist currents in the country. By the middle of the seventies the Savak had succeeded, at the cost of driving hundreds of young Iranians abroad and bringing the intellectual life of the country to a standstill.

The Shah's expressed confidence at the beginning of 1978 can be understood in light of the weaknesses of his three traditional opponents. Moreover, his "White Revolution" had created that now familiar new class of civil servants, soldiers, technocrats and industrial workers which the monarch believed to be more significant politically than religious scruples or intellectual or political freedom. While the Shah spoke of "social discipline" and the need to mobilize the new class into participation in politics, this was one of his signal failures. The much touted free election in 1975 met with such indifference that the government had to make voting mandatory, rather than risk mass absence from the polls. This should have been a clue that the new class might not support the throne in a crisis.

The economic slowdown of 1977-1978 was just such a crisis. With a flexibility characteristic of Middle East politics, the Shah's opponents ignored their mutual differences and united to overthrow him. The new class stood by indifferently, or joined the mass demonstrations against the monarchy. The Shah was reported surprised, even bitter about the "ingratitude" of his subjects. After 36 years of rule which earned him the reputation of being one of the canniest political actors in the region, the Shah seemed to be at a loss before the unexpected defection of the public. In the Middle East within 36 years nations had changed faster than individuals.

IRAN'S MILITARY PROFILED

Profile of Iranian military notes Iran is strongest nation in Persian Gulf region possessing some $17 billion worth of arms purchased from US, Great Britain and USSR; US advisers numbering around 30,000 help train Iranian military but many advisers fear it will be another decade before Iran can effectively use purchased weapons, planes and other equipment   (CHICAGO TRIBUNE, January 9, 1978, P1)

IRAN RELAXES REPRESSION

Charges that secret police use torture on political prisoners reviewed; Shah estimates political prisoners number 2,200 but opponents of Shah claim many more exist; former prisoners and opponents charge secret police called SAVAK still use torture and offer evidence that it is still occurring even though Shah says torture has been banned; SAVAK's repressive policies against written and oral statements against Shah have been easing with over 15,000 people attending 10 "poetry nights" where censorship was discussed and no one was arrested CHICAGO TRIBUNE, January 10, 1978, P1)

IRAN'S ECONOMIC INEQUITIES

Economic and social problems in Iran are attributed to rapid expansion; more than half of Iran's 35 million people live in poverty without electricity, sewage and paved roads; 37% of people work in agriculture producing only 70% of food demands; conspicuous consumption reigns in larger cities and inflation runs at 22% yearly; Shah's attempt to cool economy has so far had little effect   (CHICAGO TRIBUNE, January 11, 1978, P1)

SCANDAL TAINTS ARMS SALES

New charges emerge concerning questionable activities in payment of agents' fees in Grumman Corporation's sale of F-14 fighters to Iran; new disclosures show that Grumman executive Peter Oran wrote memo in April 1974 claiming would-be agent Albert J. Fuge offered him

View of petroleum refinery at Abadan.

United Press International

"unspecified sum of money" to insure that fees in F-14 sale would be distributed "in accordance with his wishes"; Fuge categorically denies charge; Oran denies that he accepted the offer, yet Grumman reached agreement with Fuge and others just over a month later on contract under which Fuge's company would receive 65% of fees on transaction; case was originally brought by Houshang Lavi, claiming that Grumman, Fuge and top-rank Iranian generals joined in "conspiracy" to "unlawfully persuade" him to sign away his rights to F-14 commissions; Lavi's 3 brothers, also involved in original sale, retain their right to the 35% of fees that were not given to Fuge's company; reorganization of fee outlays was apparently prompted by objections from Iranian authorities   (NEW YORK TIMES, January 11, 1978, S4 P1)

EMPRESS DESCRIBES IRAN'S TURMOIL

Empress Farah Pahlavi says Iran is faced with tension between its traditional values and demands of Western science and technology as well as with environmental, urban and even energy problems in January 12 speech to Asia Society in New York; Shah's supporters and opponents stage demonstrations outside hotel   (NEW YORK TIMES, January 13, 1978, S2 P3)

CLASHES IN HOLY CITY

Iran's Moslem faithful conduct demonstrations and strikes throughout country provoked by anger over police shooting into crowd of worshippers killing many, in city of Qom on January 9, 1978; shopkeepers in city of Teheran defy police threat to revoke licenses; the Ayatollah Sayed Qasem Shariatmadari, Iran's highest Moslem leader, claims that "holy city" of Qom is effectively under martial law; denies government version of shootings that says crowd of worshippers attacked police; writes open letter to "believers" condemning shooting as "un-Islamic and inhumane"; Shah Mohammad Reza Pahlavi orders busing of thousands of Teheran factory workers and low-level government employees to Qom to stage pro-Shah demonstrations as part of massive campaign to counter public outrage over shootings   (WASHINGTON POST, January 20, 1978, P31)

EMPRESS LAUDS WOMEN'S ADVANCE

Iranian Empress Farah Pahlavi says that the Shah of Iran has given women in Iran equal rights to vote, run for office, and has lifted employment restrictions in all fields (CHRISTIAN SCIENCE MONITOR, February 8, 1978, P22)

OIL BARTER COMPOUNDS TRADE DIFFICULTIES

Iran's practice of shaving oil prices through series of barter or "parallel" deals with Western companies could irk other OPEC members during weak market for crude and also make business harder for American companies in Iran; deals generally are based on discounted oil traded against military equipment or entire industrial projects; supplier gets paid in cash generated by sale of crude to an oil company, generally of National Iranian Oil Company choice; Iranian contracting agencies are now finding it easier to get official approval of projects if they have

The Shah of Iran, Mohammad Reza Pahlavi.

United Press International

arranged parallel deals; also enables agencies to circumvent Iran's bureaucratic budgeting system; parallel sale system was designed to augment NIOC's direct exports   (BUSINESS WEEK,   February 20, 1978,   P40)

DEMONSTRATIONS IN TABRIZ

Iranian army takes over Tabriz as death toll from rioting reportedly rises to at least 9; repairs begin in city; government blames riots on "Islamic Marxists" opposed to its land-reform program, which involves expropriation of mosque lands, and to emancipation of women   (NEW YORK TIMES,   February 22, 1978,   P9)

LEGAL PROCEEDINGS SCORED

Amnesty International charges Iranian government with denying terrorist defendants possibility of a fair trial; claims accused were denied legal advice during pretrial detention, security police conducted secret investigations, and appeal procedures were unsatisfactory; discloses that British lawyer Brian Wrobel had made these charges before Congressional subcommittee on international relations   (NEW YORK TIMES,   March 1, 1978,   P20)

SHAH REPORTED LOOSENING GRIP

Foreigners visiting the Shah report him troubled and disillusioned by recent events in Iran; telltale signs are that the Shah's long-held iron grip on Iran is ever-so-slightly, but steadily, coming loose; after years of apparently affluent indifference to the Shah's harsh regime, the county's politically articulate intellectuals are beginning to speak out; passive resistance appears to be giving way to ever more vocal protests; the Shah's secret police SAVAK fear there will soon be too many dissidents to monitor;

political hardliners in the regime urge a crack down on students and Islamic religious leaders, who they feel are the source of the troubles; the Shah's tightly controlled press has begun to label key trouble-makers as "Islamic Marxists"   (ECONOMIST OF LONDON,   March 4, 1978,   P59)

WIDESPREAD DISCONTENT REPORTED

Commentator Paul Hofmann discerns broad pattern of discontent in February 1978 rioting in Iran extending beyond official government charge that "Islamic Marxism" was responsible for apparently well-coordinated violence; holds that political opposition to what is regarded as Shah's paternalistic efforts to modernize country, as well as religious conservatism and Moslem anger at emancipation of women, are as responsible for disturbances as Marxists; cites eyewitness account by American scientist that women not wearing traditional head covering and wearing Western clothes had been pulled out of taxis and beaten; finds province of Eastern Azerbaijan still sullen and tense; points out that Shah's quick political action, dismissing provincial governor and shaking up Tabriz police, also suggests that government is aware of broader discontent   (NEW YORK TIMES,   March 5, 1978,   P7)

STRIKES HIT GOVERNMENT, BUSINESS

Wildcat strikes have hit Iranian industry in recent weeks, with foreign joint venture companies the chief targets; although pay and conditions appear to be main grievances, company managements do not discount possibility of political motivation as well; 3 US companies affected are General Motors, Union Carbide and Fluor Corporation; no news of the strikes, which are also reported to have affected certain government institutions such as the Post Office, have been mentioned in local press; strikes are technically illegal in Iran, but have grown to worrying proportions over past 2 to 3 years; managements are generally reluctant to discuss terms under which strikes have been ended, but it is generally thought they have given in; private sector employers are virtually ignoring Iranian government's call for voluntary wage freeze   (FINANCIAL TIMES,   March 14, 1978,   P4)

IRAN'S TRANSFORMATION PROFILED

Commentator Andrew Whitley says that Iran faces increase in problems as Shah of Iran achieves height of power during 37 year reign; attributes adoption of liberal policy as gesture of good intentions to US for its supply of weapons to Iran and as means of recognizing President Carter's strong belief in human rights; also says it is indicative of Shah's recognition of need for revitalized society as precondition for dynamic development; says Iran is facing international, economic and domestic tensions; cites abrupt breaking off of relations with Kenya over petty quarrel, lack of confidence in economy including $3 billion outflow of funds from country, traumatic change from rural life to technological development in countryside and unhealthy reliance on oil revenues as examples of Iran's problems; says acceptable balance between lower imports and external borrowings hides underlying weakness in domestic economy including below-capacity industrial production and drop in non-oil exports; says decline in traditional exports such as hand-made carpets and new manufactured goods and low prices of Iran's alternate exports such as copper and natural gas compound its problems (FINANCIAL TIMES, March 15, 1978, P4)

SAVAK REBUKED OVER TABRIZ

Commentator Paul Hofmann's impressions on Iranian public's opinion of their national intelligence agency SAVAK find Iranians astonished that government has publicly chastised Tabriz branch of SAVAK and announced shakeup for not developing intelligence on growing strains that resulted in rioting there (NEW YORK TIMES, March 16, 1978, P14)

USE OF FORCE PROTESTED

Iranian legislator Ahmad Baniahmad introduces Parliamentary motion censuring Iranian government's handling of recent riots in Tabriz; Baniahmad asks why security forces had not used tear gas against rioters "instead of shooting and killing people"; 12 persons died and more than 100 were injured in riots, which, according to officials, were instigated by political insurgents (NEW YORK TIMES, March 17, 1978, P2)

POLITICAL OPPOSITION CONTINUES

Commentator Paul Hofmann discusses opposition to the rule of Shah Mohammad Reza Pahlavi of Iran; asserts that social tensions and political groundswells are probably the cause of illegal dissent and intermittent terrorism in Iran, rather than Islamic Marxists as the Shah claims; cites recent outbreaks marking end of 40-day Moslem mourning period for victims of February riots in Tabriz, which in turn marked end of mourning for victims of January demonstration in holy city of Qom; notes that unrest continues to build at universities with fresh anti-Shah slogans on campus walls; asserts that although Shah is secure at present, recent events indicate Iranians are dissatisfied with his rule (NEW YORK TIMES, April 2, 1978, S4 P5)

BALANCE OF TRADE WORSENS

Iran registers 24% increase in volume of imports to 17.1 million tons for 1977-1978; increase in value is recorded at only 14% because cost of bulk commodities rose considerably; total imports for 12 months ending March 31, 1978, are reported at $1.835 billion; non-oil exports rose 8.3% in volume and 7.3% in value; exports of "traditional" goods totaled 1.13 million tons in 1977-1978 as compared to 2.3 million tons in 1972; real value of exports fell 19.1% in 1977-1978 because of 25% inflation rate (FINANCIAL TIMES, April 14, 1978, P3)

RELIGIOUS DISSIDENTS IN CLASH

Reports by Iranian official press agency and Teheran newspaper *Ettelat* indicate that 3 students were killed and scores of people injured during past 2 days of clashes between religious dissidents, pro-government groups and police; clashes took place in several Iranian cities where religious dissidents, orthodox Moslems, oppose government liberalization of Iran's traditional Islamic society, and are demanding end to sex integration in universities and restoration of traditional requirement for women to wear veils in public (NEW YORK TIMES, May 10, 1978, P6)

RIOTING IN QOM

New anti-government rioting in Iran breaks out in holy city of Qom, in 3d day of political violence across Iran that has caused death of at least 12 persons; dissidents burn shops, set up barricades, fight policemen, halt trains and smash buses, roughing up passengers; reports indicate 9 people are killed and hundreds injured, including 10 policemen and 300 bus passengers; one Iranian newspaper reports that rioting has spread to 23 cities, but worst violence appears to be in Qom; Iranian government blames riots on "unholy alliance of Communist subversives and Moslem extremists," and hints at forthcoming crackdown on dissidents (NEW YORK TIMES, May 11, 1978, P11)

SHAH TAKES PRECAUTIONS

Shah of Iran postpones a trip to Eastern Europe and takes command of troops acting to break up demonstrations by thousands of Iranians demanding the ouster of the Shah and a return to strict Islamic principles of rule; troops fire into the air and hurl tear-gas grenades at demonstrators marching down the main street of the capital, Teheran, shouting "Down with the Shah!"; there are no reports of casualties in the latest clash in Teheran, but at least 9 people have been killed in riots in Qom, Tabriz and 32 other cities and towns since the outbreak of the protests on May 9 (NEW YORK TIMES, May 12, 1978, P4)

GOVERNMENT ISSUES WARNING

Warning by Iranian government that it will tolerate no further disorders causes lull in outbreaks throughout nation by anti-government religious and leftist groups (NEW YORK TIMES, May 14, 1978, P12)

SHAH'S PROBLEMS ANALYZED

Commentators Anthony McDermott and Andrew Whitley analyze the problems facing the Shah of Iran; say that in the last 6 months unrest has manifested itself in demonstrations and strikes by university students; point out that opposition to the Shah has become more obviously rooted in the religious community of the Shites, a branch of Islam, who constitute about 90% of the population; note that rapid modernization and Westernization has raised concern about the conservative elements of the country; note the role of the Rastakhiz, the Government party, and its failure to dispel the apathy and cynicism of the masses or to win acknowledgement of the progress the Government has made in some areas; point out that the Shah seems unwilling to recognize that the disturbances arise from genuine grievances among a large number of Iranians, not from a small minority of anti-nationalists (FINANCIAL TIMES, May 15, 1978, P23)

ECONOMIC LAG CITED

Times of London editorial holds that the source of the current unrest in Iran could be that the economic surge of 1974–1976 has been followed by advances not quite as great; says the nature of the Shah's autocratic rule makes him the target of all political opposition; claims what is needed is a national consensus for moderate political change   (TIMES OF LONDON,   May 16, 1978,   P15)

SHAH'S OPPOSITION PROFILED

Shah of Iran does not appear worried despite strongest opposition in 15 years, marked by 4 days of bloody riots in major cities recently; improved organization and boldness of opponents is seen as stemming from Shah's loosening of reins, partly impelled by pressure from West and partly because he wants to decentralize government that has become too complex for him to manage alone; principal opponents include: Moslem traditionalists loyal to exiled religious leader Ayatollah Ruhollah Khomeini, the most powerful opponent; bazaris, powerful merchants who have close links to Moslem clergy; liberal politicians who belong to National Front of late Mohammad Mossadegh who almost ousted Shah in 1953, and students, writers, intellectuals and professionals, who have been persistent critics of regime and of security police   (NEW YORK TIMES,   May 18, 1978,   P1)

PRISON CONDITIONS SCORED

Iranian torture of prisoners exists in prisons where conditions do not meet standards set by the International Red Cross; representatives of 7 families of political prisoners met with a correspondent of the *The Times of London* and told that the Iranian authorities have deceived both the International Red Cross and Amnesty International in their efforts to find out the conditions under which political prisoners are held   (TIMES OF LONDON, May 19, 1978,   P8)

IRAN'S COURSE DEBATED

Iranian Ambassador to Britain Parviz Radji responds to *Times of London* article of May 16 entitled "Disturbances in Iran"; says *London Times'* call for "a real national consensus for moderate political change" is more hopeful than realistic; asserts Iran's policy of "political liberalization" will continue as in the past with a firm stand against lawlessness and violence   (TIMES OF LONDON, May 20, 1978,   P15)

TROOPS PATROL TEHERAN STREETS

Iranian government troops and antiriot police patrol streets of Teheran after government opponents ordered stores to close and motorists and pedestrians to stay off streets; most shops remain open, but it is estimated that more than half city's million motorists heeded order; small groups of dissidents attack stores and traffic in 2 outlying areas of city, but flee when police arrive; no casualties are reported   (NEW YORK TIMES,   May 26, 1978,   P2)

ROOT OF DISCONTENT TRACED

Commentator David Watts examines efforts being made by Shah of Iran to industrialize country before oil runs out; notes that outwardly grandiose development scheme is main attraction for outsiders but that development of vocational training, low rewards for teachers, high inflation, poorly developed agricultural scheme, strict cultural and news censorship and government-dictated nomination of candidates for election remain major problems for residents   (TIMES OF LONDON,   May 26, 1978,   P18)

CAUSES OF QOM VIOLENCE TRACED

Commentator Jonathan Randal notes turmoil between Shah of Iran and mollas centers on mollas' demand for return to the liberal 1906 constitution and their opposition to land reforms; adds government denunciations of exiled Ayatollah Ruhollah Khomeini led to protest demonstrations and violence in Qom   (WASHINGTON POST,   May 26, 1978, P23)

UNEASINESS ABOUT FUTURE DISCERNED

Byliner Jonathan Randal, commenting on civil disturbances in Iran, reports relatively little has happened except for 2 outbreaks of violence in Qom and Tabriz; finds uneasy feeling in Teheran because no one knows where crisis is heading; asserts government does not acknowledge that many Iranians have grievances, which range from quality of life to corruption in high places (WASHINGTON POST,   May 29, 1978,   P23)

ROLE OF PRESS OUTLINED

Discussion of press freedom in Iran cites Information Minister Darius Homayoun who says Iran thinks of newspapers as corrective channel between people and government; Hamayoun says material against Shah Mohammad Reza Pahlavi and the government is regularly broadcast by powerful Persian-language Communist station; close watchers of Iranian news media say newspapers and Pars, official news agency, now report anti-government demonstrations and violence in some detail, though generally terming protesters as hooligans   (CHRISTIAN SCIENCE MONITOR,   May 30, 1978,   P5)

TEHERAN UNIVERSITY CLOSED

Teheran University closes dormitories following clashes between police and student demonstrators; students are demanding immediate removal of police guards at campuses across Iran and greater representation in administration of campus libraries and restaurants (NEW YORK TIMES,   June 4, 1978,   P10)

OPPOSITION'S GRIEVANCES ANALYZED

Commentator Nicholas Gage reports movement against Shah is led by clergy of conservative Moslem Shiite sect, whom Shah has deprived of property and powers, and who resent his drive toward modernism and dictatorial methods; aligned with clergy are intellectuals, merchants, Marxists and students; faced with worst crisis since 1963 riots, Shah is backed by armed forces, workers, upper middle class, and US; despite continued uprisings, he is believed strong enough to retain his throne; highly effective and feared secret police, SAVAK, known to use torture, has successfully infiltrated dissident groups; government is blamed for galloping inflation, corruption and waste of public funds; religious differences are another source of turbulence as conservative Moslems express hatred of Bahai sect, Armenians and Jews; Pepsi-cola plants, controlled by a family of Bahai faith, have been violently attacked; bazaar merchants are angry over repression of freedom   (NEW YORK TIMES,   June 4, 1978,   P1)

SHAH'S GOALS OUTLINED

Discussion of problems Shah Mohammad Reza Pahlavi is having in meeting 2 goals of reform in Iran; says first goal is to make society and economy independent of oil revenues, which will cease with exhaustion of the resource in 30 years; reports second goal is to provide peaceful transition to less absolute and more constitutional monarchy by time his son, Crown Prince Reza, is ready to rule   (CHRISTIAN SCIENCE MONITOR, June 6, 1978,   P7)

NEW SECURITY CHIEF NAMED

Shah of Iran appoints General Naser Mogaddam as head of SAVAK, Iran's security organization, reputed to be one of the world's toughest and most efficient internal security forces; Mogaddam was the country's military intelligence chief and will replace General Nematollah Nasiri, who was dismissed as SAVAK head and appointed ambassador to Pakistan; no official reason was given for Nasiri's dismissal; Mogaddam, as SAVAK chief, will hold rank of assistant prime minister   (NEW YORK TIMES,   June 8, 1978,   P22)

CONFLICT WITH CLERGY TRACED

Shah of Iran is threatened by Shiite mollas, Islamic religious leaders who want Iran to be governed by Islamic law; mollas' conflict with Shah dates back to 1963, when they were divested of vast religious endowments under land-reform program; clergy has joined student activists in opposing Shah; 40 people have been killed in riots staged by clergy in several cities in 1978; shooting death of theological student by government troops at Qom, Shiite center, has inflamed clergy to point of revolution; few believe Shah is in any danger of being overthrown; government indicates it is trying to make concessions to sect   (TIME,   June 15, 1978,   P39)

PROTESTS PEACEFUL ACROSS IRAN

Conservative Moslems protest peacefully in Iranian holy city Qom; Shiite Moslem leaders asked residents to slow down Qom's activity to protest May killing of a theology student by government troops; similar peaceful protests are reported in cities of Isfahan, Tabriz, Ahwaz, Khorramshahr, Yezd and Zenjan   (NEW YORK TIMES,   June 18, 1978,   P8)

The western business suit and the mosque form a paradox in Iran's future.

AUTHOR CRITICIZES REGIME

Dr. Gholam-Hosein Sa'edi, prominent Iranian author and playwright, is on brief US visit to arrange for publication of his works, some of which are banned in Iran, and to disclose facts about Iranian censorship; charges, at news conference, that Iranian government's repression and censorship have destroyed all forms of freedom of expression, but believes international pressure for human rights can be effective in Iran; Sa'edi spent one year in Iranian prison, and his recent visit was allowed after pressure from human rights groups and writers' organizations   (NEW YORK TIMES,   June 18, 1978,   P28)

SHAH PRESENTS VIEWS

Shah of Iran, in interview, asserts he does not view Iranian communist and Moslem opposition to his regime as serious threat; maintains he is too powerful to be overthrown; attributes upsurge in leftist and rightist opposition to gradual liberalization taking place in Iran; maintains leftist opposition is more dangerous than rightist; asserts leftist rebels are supported by foreign groups; plans to encourage political debate and discussion, but does not aim for establishment of 2-party system; vows liberalization will continue even if political demonstrations and acts of violence persist; views law and order as separate issue from liberalization; asserts Iran observes human rights more so than do many other countries; reiterates national goal of building industrial system which can eventually replace oil as major source of revenue; indicates Crown Prince Reza's official preparation for the throne will begin in about a year   (U.S. NEWS AND WORLD REPORT,   June 26, 1978,   P37)

CONDUCT CODE PROMULGATED

Shah Mohammad Reza Pahlavi of Iran issues orders barring members of his royal family from business deals in which they stand to benefit; reports "code of conduct" is being drawn up for royal family; orders ministers and key government officials to report directly to Shah's office any request they receive from member of royal family that could involve business interest; move extends earlier edict barring members of government from becoming involved with companies doing business with state (NEW YORK TIMES, July 4, 1978, P1)

U.S. MILITARY TIES STRONG

US ties with Iran are reportedly much stronger than with any other developing country due to 20-year arrangement which has been mutually profitable; US has sold over $18 billion worth of arms to Iran and has helped organize and equip security system that gives ruler Shah Mohammad Reza Pahlavi absolute control of country, while Shah has agreed to protect vital Persian Gulf routes that carry oil used by Western countries; relationship, however, has been criticized both by domestic opponents of Shah and by Americans who condemn Shah's autocratic rule and who fear Iran's growing military strength will lead to aggressive actions in which US would become involved; US diplomats reportedly hope some criticism will cease as result of Iran's current liberalization program, but changes have not appeased Shah's opponents (NEW YORK TIMES, July 9, 1978, P1)

SHAH CHARGES COMMUNIST INTERFERENCE

Shah of Iran, in interview, discusses outlook for Iran in wake of recent violent anti-government protests; attributes major blame for protests to "subversive penetration of international communism"; contends Iran does not face real danger from communists since it has improved its economy and has taken steps toward opening up its one-party government; holds that West must "put its own house in order" before interfering in East Asia and Middle East (NEWSWEEK, July 24, 1978, P56)

DRASTIC RENT LAWS IMPOSED

Teheran's landlords are agitated by Iran's drastic new laws to control rents and land speculation; new laws include a rent freeze, forced rental of empty units, heavily subsidized construction of housing units and use of government's right of eminent domain as a sword over every speculative real estate transaction (WALL STREET JOURNAL, July 25, 1978, P8)

VIOLENCE IN MASHHAD

Iranian government sources indicate one policeman was killed and 24 people were injured in riots in Mashhad during week beginning July 16; Iranian press agency reports trouble began when rioters shouting anti-government slogans attacked a crowd gathered for a funeral at mausoleum of Shiite Moslem saint; rioting was apparently linked to religious opposition to authorities (NEW YORK TIMES, July 26, 1975, P7)

OPPOSITION TO LIBERALIZATION BROAD

Commentator Ray Vicker discusses political opposition to Shah of Iran Mohammad Reza Pahlavi's aim to continue country's program of political liberalization; holds that most opposition stems from dissatisfaction with Shah's leadership and course of economics in Iran; notes that Prime Minister Jamshid Amouzegar and other diplomats declare that opposition to Shah ranges from far-right religious leaders, who want modernization trend slowed, to far leftists who seek overthrow of Shah and substitution of a Marxist regime (WALL STREET JOURNAL, August 3, 1978, P12)

CURFEW IMPOSED IN ISFAHAN

Iran imposes dusk-to-dawn curfew in Isfahan following 18 hours of anti-Shah rioting and arson; US consulate asks 12,000 Americans in Isfahan to remain indoors until further notice; government officials in Teheran report 4 demonstrators were killed and 7 wounded; rioting appears to be biggest wave of protest yet against Shah in 1978 (WASHINGTON POST, August 12, 1978, P15)

CLASHES IN SHIRAZ REPORTED

Press reports indicate demonstrators and police clashed August 13 in Iranian city of Shiraz in 4th day of religious and anti-government disturbances; government spokesmen contend Shiraz disturbance was touched off by religious extremists opposed to annual arts festival held in city; disturbance is also reported in Isfahan; conservative Moslem militants are protesting reforms ordered by Shah of Iran; most of disputed reforms deal with women's liberation and redistribution of church lands (NEW YORK TIMES, August 13, 1978, P63)

CONSERVATIVES GROW MILITANT

Islamic conservatives grow increasingly militant; Western civilization and moral laxity seem to be primary targets of their revival; Moslem leaders in Iran feel Shah Mohammad Reza Pahlavi is too progressive; oppose reforms that have advanced women's rights, placing women in jobs alongside men and easing dress restrictions; advocate slowdown of development that might conflict with religious traditions; attack banks, theaters and television stores, which they feel are symbols of Western intrusion (WALL STREET JOURNAL, August 15, 1978, P1)

SHAH PROMISES FREE ELECTIONS

Shah of Iran Mohammad Reza Pahlavi, in broadcast marking anniversary of 1906 establishment of constitutional monarchy, declares his personal commitment to free elections; confirms that laws governing freedom of political meetings and of press will be enacted, as previously announced, but adds that limits to political freedom will be fixed, as they are in democratic countries (NEW YORK TIMES, August 16, 1978, P5)

ECONOMY DARKENS CELEBRATIONS

Shah of Iran celebrates 25th anniversary of his return to power amid signs of growing dissatisfaction with his

A street in Abadan. During August a fire, apparently set by Islamic extremists, destroyed a theater in the working-class district of Abadan, killing more than 400 persons.

leadership and present economic conditions; government-organized pro-Shah rallies in most major cities are characterized by lack of public enthusiasm; recent political unrest in nation is attributed to citizens lashing out against inflation, unemployment, unequal distribution of wealth and government corruption   (WASHINGTON POST,   August 20, 1978,   P29)

THEATER BURNS IN ABADAN

Fire apparently set by Islamic extremists burns down theater in working class district of Abadan killing at least 377 persons, mostly youths; police say that theater's only exits had been locked as anti-terrorist measure, trapping crowd inside theater; police say that 20–40 patrons escaped; survivor says many people were trampled to death; police arrest theater attendant Hamid Payan and owner Ali Naderi without announcing charges; investigators say they suspect arsonists are Moslems opposed to state-ordered religious reforms and to attendance at movies during religious month of Ramadan; Shah of Iran, in message to victims' families, vows severe punishment for arsonists   (NEW YORK TIMES,   August 21, 1978,   P20)

CRACKDOWN IN FIRE AFTERMATH

Police in Abadan report arrests of 10 persons in connection with weekend theater fire that killed at least 377; say arrested include 2 employees of theater and owner, as well as 3 individuals arrested with explosives in their possession; Police Chief General Reza Razmi blames fire on "anti-reform radicals"; press reports say only 200 of badly burned bodies have been identified and unconfirmed reports put death toll at 430; all businesses are closed in Abadan in mourning   (NEW YORK TIMES, August 22, 1978,   P45)

'WHITE REVOLUTION' REFORMS ANALYZED

Analysis of conflict between Iran religious leaders and Shah Mohammad Reza Pahlavi attributes conflict to series of reforms, known as "White Revolution," which Shah initiated 15 years ago; reports reforms stripped leaders of predominant sect Shia Moslems of control over vast land holdings and gave equal rights to women; claims that while some factions seek creation of pure Islamic state, others believe coexistence with secular government is possible; asserts religious leaders, however, object to Western influences, and think Western permissiveness will erode Islamic traditions   (NEW YORK TIMES,   August 23, 1978,   P15)

FIRE INVESTIGATION CONTINUES

Teheran newspaper reports workmen searching through debris of Cinema Rex Theater in Abadan have found 45 more bodies from August 19 firebombing of theater; 5 persons described as Islamic Marxists have confessed to setting off bombs, but police chief Brigadier General Reza Razmi reports they are among 10 suspects arrested, several of whom admitted they were assigned to set off bombs in other parts of Abadan; Razmi refutes earlier reports that arsonists poured gasoline on building, claiming fire was caused by bombs placed at corners of building   (NEW YORK TIMES,   August 23, 1978,   P79)

DEMONSTRATORS PROTEST ARSON

Police in Abadan clash with grieving, angry demonstrators demanding punishment for those who set previous weekend fire in theater; related developments: Shah of Iran declares on French TV that recent disturbances in Iran are part of "coordinated effort" by elements seeking to impose foreign domination of Iran; does not identify foreign country, but says it is Marxist-inspired; in New York City, International League for Human Rights declares its Iran affiliate wants international investigation of Abadan fire   (NEW YORK TIMES,   August 24, 1978,   P77)

SHARIF-EMAMI NAMED PRIME MINISTER

Iran's Shah Mohammad Reza Pahlavi, in apparent effort to appease Moslem opposition, appoints Jaafar Sharif-Emami as Prime Minister, replacing the recently resigned Jamshid Amouzegar; Sharif-Emami, grandson of noted religious leader, announces that all legal political parties will be allowed to participate in government; opposition leader Karim Sanjabi welcomes pledge, but says he must wait to see if commitments will be fulfilled   (NEW YORK TIMES,   August 28, 1978,   P9)

'FRANTIC' MODERNIZATION SCORED

Commentator Joseph Kraft suggests protests in Iran by Islamic fundamentalists underline necessity of Shah of Iran's regime; points out protesters contend Shah has driven Iran toward modernization at too frantic a pace; observes fundamentalists are incapable of managing modernization process that has now gone too far to be reversed; contends overthrow of monarchy in Iran would probably result in initial chaos followed by despotic rule   (WASHINGTON POST,   August 29, 1978,   P15)

APPOINTMENT DISCUSSED

Financial Times editorial notes that the Shah of Iran's appointment of Jaafar Sharif-Emami to replace Jamshid Amouzegar as prime minister came as a surprise because it occurred soon after the Abadan cinema fire and just before the visit of Chinese Chairman Hua Kuo-feng; says appointment of Sharif-Emami is symptomatic of the Shah's recent displays of apparent flexibility and liberalism (FINANCIAL TIMES,   August 30, 1978,   P14)

OPPOSITION LEADERS RELEASED

New Iranian Prime Minister Jaafar Sharif-Emami agrees to release 7 opposition leaders from internal exile in effort to end months of anti-government demonstrations by religious groups   (NEW YORK TIMES,   September 1, 1978,   P28)

SHAH'S QUANDARY EXPLORED

Commentator George A. Krimsky analyzes religious and political protests in Iran; finds Shah Mohammad Reza Pahlavi is being forced to choose between dictatorship more repressive than that already attributed to him by his critics, or turning over substantial power to people; believes source of turmoil is Shah's rush into 20th century, using revenue from nationalized petroleum industry for industrial development and for arsenal of modern weapons unequalled in Persian Gulf; thinks modernization has collided with ancient social and religious traditions (NEW YORK TIMES,   September 5, 1978,   P37)

UNFULFILLED EXPECTATIONS PERVASIVE

Commentator Jay Ross analyzes political demonstrations in Iran; asserts Shah's plans for Westernizing Iran have left unfulfilled expectations of better living conditions among middle class and students; reports mollas oppose Westernization on religious grounds; asserts many policies of religious leaders are anathema to students, adding diverse dissident elements are held together by their opposition to Shah; asserts Shah is in no danger of being overthrown as long as military remains secure (WASHINGTON POST, September 9, 1978, P14)

MASS PROTEST IN CAPITAL

Commentator George Krimsky analyzes Iranian religious and political unrest; notes Iranian government declared martial law September 7 after 100,000 demonstrators massed in Teheran to demand Shah's resignation; points out Iranian troops fired into crowd, and as many as 100 were killed   (NEW YORK TIMES,   September 9, 1978,   P14)

TANKS ARE CALLED OUT

Iranian troops backed by tanks fan out to enforce martial law decree in Teheran where at least 86 persons died September 8 as troops fought anti-government rioters; Shah of Iran postpones trip to Romania and East Germany to deal with violence; much of rioting stems from demonstrations called by Moslem religious extremists

Protesters in Teheran made bonfires using smashed kiosks and road signs in an attempt to blockade army patrols during anti-Shah violence that erupted December 22.

United Press International

opposed to Shah's attempt to Westernize country; numerous anti-government groups join religious leaders in demanding return to Islamic law   (NEW YORK TIMES, September 10, 1978, P82)

CROWN PRINCE PROFILED

Commentator George A. Krimsky profiles 18-year-old Crown Prince Mohammad Reza Pahlavi as speculation mounts over his ability to succeed to Iranian throne if his father should step aside in favor of his son in order to stifle national revolt and salvage monarchy; Krimsky describes Prince Reza as "exuberant, intelligent, insatiably curious and talented in athletics and technical matters"; reports that he is taking pilot training at Reese Air Force Base, Texas, and will return to Iran in June, 1978   (NEW YORK TIMES,   September 10, 1978,   P127)

SHAH OUTLINES STRATEGY

Iran's Shah Mohammad Reza Pahlavi, in interview broadcast by ABC-TV, claims that recent anti-government protests have had major impact but have not critically threatened his regime; asserts he is still working to bring reform to country; unidentified government official declares that Shah would "rather be deposed" than abandon attempts to democratize Iran; also contends that members of Shah's family, excluding his wife and children, will soon be asked to leave Iran because of expected allegations of corruption; feels that former Prime Minister Amir Abbas Hoveida, who resigned as minister of court last week, may face charges, along with other ministers, of abuses of government; predicts that Iranian Ambassador to US Ardeshir Zahedi might become prime minister or minister of court; in related development, Shah reports that Egyptian President Sadat had offered support to Shah in recent telephone call   (NEW YORK TIMES,   September 12, 1978,   P97)

NEW CRACKDOWN, ARRESTS REPORTED

Hardline Moslem leader Sheikh Yahya Nasiri Nuri and several journalists are among scores of persons arrested September 12 in sweeping crackdown on opposition groups ordered in Iran by Shah Mohammad Reza Pahlavi; action was taken under provisions of martial law decreed after more than 100 persons were killed during new anti-government protests that erupted September 8 in Teheran and other cities   (NEW YORK TIMES,   September 13, 1978,   P108)

MOLLA SUSPECTED KIDNAPPED

Iman Mousa Sadr, spiritual leader of Lebanon's Shiite Moslems, has not been heard from for nearly 3 weeks and leftist newspaper, *al-Safir*, speculates that Iran's secret service may have kidnapped him because of his opposition to Iranian government and support of Moslem foes of Shah Mohammad Reza Pahlavi   (NEW YORK TIMES,   September 13, 1978,   P78)

IRANIAN SOCIETY 'OPENING UP'

Kendall Dudley, former Peace Corps volunteer in Iran, says developments in Iran are opening up society there, allowing chance for discussions to take place; holds Iranians are beginning to look beyond family welfare to that of society; believes problems are not simply those caused by Marxist and religious extremists, as reported in Western press; tells how oil wealth has enormously magnified weaknesses in Iranian society which stem from widening gap between wealthy and poor; notes riots and demonstrations are seen as caused by religious differences because the only place Iranians can assemble legally is the mosque   (CHRISTIAN SCIENCE MONITOR, September 15, 1978,   P27)

NONCOOPERATION VOWED

Shariatmadari, one of the spiritual leaders of Iran's 32 million Shiite Moslems, vows "no cooperation" with new government of Prime Minister Jaafar Sharif-Emami; says that recent killings of dissidents by troops makes him unfit to govern; predicts more violence or revolution if Shah Pahlavi's political and social liberalization policies are not modified   (NEW YORK TIMES,   September 16, 1978,   P66)

EMAMI SEEKS LEGISLATIVE BACKING

Prime Minister Jaafar Sharif-Emami's government wins vote of confidence from Iran's lower house of Parliament; must gain vote of confidence in Senate, which is virtually assured; promises continued social and political reforms and new reconciliation efforts with conservative Moslems who have rioted against reforms; devout Moslem Sharif-Emami was recently chosen prime minister in attempt by Shah Mohammad Pahlavi to appease conservative Moslem clergy   (NEW YORK TIMES,   September 17, 1978,   P10)

'PAPER' REFORMS SCORED

Iranian Shiite Moslem leader Shariatmadari asserts he lost confidence in government of Prime Minister Jaafar Sharif-Emami on September 8 when government troops killed about 100 demonstrators in Teheran; contends reforms announced by Sharif-Emami only exist on paper; would like to see greater political rights, free speech, more equitable distribution of wealth and closer adherence to Islam   (NEW YORK TIMES,   September 17, 1978,   P18)

FOREIGN EXCHANGE OUTFLOW UP

Outflow of foreign exchange from Iran is reported to have increased from average of $10 million per day to $50 million per day as result of recent civil unrest; foreign bankers in Iran suggest that as much as $700 million may have left country since martial law was declared in major urban areas 16 days ago, although no exact figures are available   (FINANCIAL TIMES,   September 25, 1978,   P42)

YOUTHS DEMONSTRATE AGAINST SHAH

Several hundred school-aged demonstrators protest against Iranian Shah Mohammad Reza Pahlavi in Jan-Abad cemetery, one of few places in Iran where crowds can gather legally; protestors drown out taped prayers broadcast by several hundred mourners of 377 persons who died in Rex Cinema fire August 19   (NEW YORK TIMES,   September 29, 1978,   P90)

KHOMEINI IN PARIS

Ayatollah Khomeini, spiritual leader of Shiite Moslem community in Iran and major opponent of Shah, arrives in Paris October 6 after being expelled from Iraq where he has lived in exile since 1963; Ayatollah has wide support among conservative Moslems who have been at center of protest movement against Shah of Iran; the Ayatollah's expulsion from Iraq is an indication of continuing rapprochement between Iraq and Iran; relations between the 2 countries have improved during last 3 years after Shah withdrew support from Kurdish secessionist rebels in northern Iraq   (NEW YORK TIMES,   October 7, 1978,   P44)

WOMEN'S RIGHTS THREATENED

Feminist leaders voice concern that Iranian women may be heading for period of regression because of recent Iranian religious and political disorders; are concerned because Shah Mohammad Reza Pahlavi made concessions to religious leaders who demanded stricter adherence to Islamic social principles, which sometimes conflict with concepts of women's liberation; the government under Prime Minister Jaafar Sharif-Emami has dropped post of Minister for Women's Affairs created in 1975, and headed by Mahnaz Afkhami; Afkhami is also secretary-general of influential Woman's Organization of Iran; emphasizes Iran cannot return to past regarding women's rights   (NEW YORK TIMES,   October 7, 1978,   P24)

KHOMEINI INTERVIEWED

Shiite Moslem community spiritual leader the Ayatollah Khomeini, in interview with French newspaper *Le Figaro*, holds he is prepared to urge his followers toward armed insurrection against Shah of Iran; holds aim of demonstrations is to overthrow Shah and replace his regime with Islamic republic permitting total liberty; denies Marxists and left-wing extremists are influencing protest movement; the Ayatollah has been living in France since October 6, after being expelled from Iraq, where he was living in exile since 1963   (NEW YORK TIMES,   October 19, 1978,   P14)

OIL STRIKE TAKES TOLL

Oil workers' strike in Iran substantially slows down oil industry, cutting shipments from 6 million barrels a day to rate below one million barrels a day; workers demand end to martial law, release of political prisoners, and immediate trials of oil industry officials accused of corruption; US, whose Iranian oil imports make up 10% of total crude oil imports, appears to be well protected against cutbacks in Iranian production for short term, but may have problem if Iran's labor problems are not solved; crude oil prices are currently rising, and if strike continues, prices may increase further   (JOURNAL OF COMMERCE,   November 1, 1978,   P1)

Ayatollah Khomeini, Iranian Moslem religious leader, in his temporary place of exile at Pontchartrain, France, near Paris. Khomeini was expelled from Iraq early in October when Iraqi authorities prevented him from having contact with representatives of Iranian opposition groups seeking the overthrow of the Shah of Iran.

United Press International

PRIME MINISTER SHARIF-EMAMI RESIGNS

Iranian Prime Minister Jafar Sharif-Emami, 69, appointed August 27 as part of Shah Mohammad Reza Pahlavi's effort to stem Moslem opposition to his rule, resigns after anti-Shah demonstrators rampage through streets of Teheran; resignation is not unexpected, but there is no indication whether it has been accepted by Shah, whose efforts to form provisional government that includes opposition figures are again rebuffed; Shah is expected to name new government with military men in key posts; orders armed forces to restore order as rioters set fire to British embassy and other buildings   (NEW YORK TIMES,   November 6, 1978,   P1)

OPPOSITION LEADERS DENOUNCE SHAH

Ayatollah Khomeini, Moslem religious leader exiled from Iran, and Karim Sanjabi, who heads opposition National Front, issue statement in Paris calling for end to Shah of Iran's "illegal monarchy" and for nationwide vote for new government based on "Islamic principles"; Shah meets with former Prime Minister Ali Amini in first effort to form provisional government with opposition leaders; also asks to see Sanjabi, who declines in view of Khomeini's objections to provisional government as long as Shah is in power; anti-Shah demonstrators are reportedly not guided by any leaders, but by their goal to oust Shah; pro-Shah groups in countryside are increasingly challenging anti-Shah demonstrators   (NEW YORK TIMES, November 6, 1978, p18)

IRAN'S STRATEGIC IMPORTANCE NOTED

Commentator Drew Middleton discusses Iran as "pivotal state in global balance of power"; notes that Strait of Hormuz, between Persian Gulf and Indian Ocean, is considered of great importance to West; observes alarm among military planners over turmoil within Shah of Iran's government, which controls Strait of Hormuz; adds that planners fear Iran, in its state of conflict, is susceptible to subversion and external pressure by USSR; holds that Western military authorities agree that interruption of oil traffic through Strait of Hormuz would have serious repercussions on Western Europe; asserts that Iran has most advanced arms of any Asian country east of Israel, noting that Shah has spent $14 billion on weapons during past decade   (NEW YORK TIMES, November 6, 1978, P18)

MILITARY RULE DECLARED

Iranian Shah Mohammad Reza Pahlavi places Iran under military rule, but maintains move is only temporary measure to restore order; names 11-member Cabinet, headed by armed forces chief of staff General Gholam Reza Azhari and including 6 military leaders and 4 civilians, to end violent demonstrations that have continued for 10 months and left more than 1,000 dead; pledges to rectify past mistakes, fight corruption and injustice and form national government to carry out free elections; Teheran is relatively calm as opposition leaders urge followers to avoid clashes with troops   (NEW YORK TIMES, November 7, 1978, P1)

STUDENTS AND MERCHANTS UNITE

Activist Teheran University students form unlikely alliance with conservative street merchants against Shah Mohammad Reza Pahlavi of Iran; military government closes bazaar and university in attempt to sever bond between students and merchants; government maintains that both students and merchants have received satisfactory benefits from oil boom; university enrollment has doubled since 1971 to over 150,000 students and higher education budget is $4.3 billion; merchants control two-thirds of wholesale trade and larger share of retail business; bazaar merchants rely on Moslem clergy for support   (NEW YORK TIMES, November 7, 1978, P15)

KHOMEINI CALLS FOR DETHRONEMENT

Reporter Flora Lewis interviews exiled Iranian religious leader the Ayatollah Khomeini, who indicates he will call for civil war in Iran if current strategy, using political methods, fails to depose Shah Mohammad Reza Pahlavi; reveals he has candidate in mind to lead new regime, that Americans who intereferein internal affairs would be asked to leave, and that Iran's oil policy is totally unacceptable and would be changed to benefit interests of poor people in Iran; also holds religious minorities would be protected under his Islamic republic, but fails to provide specifics on rule he is trying to establish   (NEW YORK TIMES, November 7, 1978, P1)

ANTI-SHAH POSITIONS EXAMINED

Commentator Nicholas Gage analyzes political position of Iranian opposition groups following imposition of military rule by Shah Mohammad Reza Pahlavi; says groups can either challenge military rule, risking suppression of their movement, or accept Shah's offer of coalition government; notes that Western diplomats in Iran believe that prospects for coalition government have increased since military rule has forestalled and possibly blocked opposition's efforts to destroy the monarchy; reveals that prominent figures in principal opposition group National Front favor compromising with Shah, although National Front leader Karim Sanjabi refuses to support coalition government; notes than stands taken by Moslem conservatives, powerful opponents of Shah, and by national liberation movement, which can influence religious and political camps, will influence Iran's future political arrangements; reports that Sanjabi is currently meeting with most popular Moslem leader Ayatollah Khomeini to discuss issue   (NEW YORK TIMES, November 8, 1978, P14)

UNCERTAIN FUTURE SEEN FOR IRAN

Editorial questions whether Iranian Shah Mohammad Reza Pahlavi's response to his people's unrest has come in time; points out that wealth has not satisfied Iranians, noting that per capita income, at $2,000 per year, is 10 times that of 1968; adds that literacy has doubled in 15 years and average life expectancy has risen from 32 to 52 years; attributes riots and strikes of past year to inflation, shortages of food and electric power, corruption and mismanagement, and increasing gap between rich and poor; observes that press criticism of the government has been halted by revived censorship; fears that military suppression may provide illusion of stability   (NEW YORK TIMES, November 8, 1978, P26)

IRANIAN GOVERNMENT CRACKS DOWN

Iran's military government arrests 14 prominent officials and businessmen on corruption charges and issues arrest warrants for 52 others; action follows Shah Mohammad Reza Pahlavi's November 6 speech pledging to deal harshly with corrupt officials, and is seen as important gesture toward Shah's political opponents; former SAVAK head General Nematollah Nasiri and 6 former Cabinet members are among those arrested; in related developments in Iran, only incidents reported in Teheran are scattered warning shots fired by troops; students are kept away from Teheran University, a center of previous confrontations; government continues its suspension of newspaper publication and control over radio and TV broadcasts   (NEW YORK TIMES, November 8, 1978, P1)

FORMER PRIME MINISTER ARRESTED

Iranian Shah Mohammad Reza Pahlavi orders arrest of former Prime Minister Amir Abbas Hoveida, who headed Cabinet and served as Pahlavi's closest adviser from 1965 to 1977; also orders investigation of all investments and business dealings of imperial family, since it has been rumored for years that Shah's brothers and sisters received vast payoffs from local and foreign companies;

Shah's military government reports 54 former officials and businessmen have been indicted on charges of corruption and abuse of power; show of force by Shah and government has reportedly calmed Teheran and countryside, where demonstrations have raged for 10 months (NEW YORK TIMES, November 9, 1978, P1)

OPPOSITION PARTY URGES STRIKES

Iranian National Front, largest opposition party in Iran, calls for continuation of all strikes until a civilian government is formed; vows to use strikes as main weapon against new military rule of Shah; National Front leader Karim Sanjabi is due for return from 2 weeks of talks in Paris with exiled Iranian Moslem leader, the Ayatollah Khomeini, noted as religious figure with most influence over conservative Moslem strikers; in related development, Shah calls for review of Pahlavi Foundation, which controls Shah's personal funds for benefit of poor; oil strike noted as having so far cost Iran over $500 million in oil revenues (NEW YORK TIMES, November 10, 1978, P11)

FOREIGNERS LEAVING IRAN

Iranian strikers, who have crippled oil production, are demanding that military government expel all foreigners from petroleum industry; express increasing hostility to more than 40,000 Americans and 70,000 other aliens who live and work in Iran, mainly because they are closely identified with rule of Shah Mohammad Reza Pahlavi; about 4,000 Americans have left Iran, but US officials maintain there is no reason for panic; oil analysts claim move to expel foreigners could upset production and undermine plans to develop new oil fields (NEW YORK TIMES, November 11, 1978, P1)

NATIONAL FRONT LEADER ARRESTED

Iranian military government arrests National Front leader Karim Sanjabi, 73, as he attempts to hold his first news conference since returning from consultation with Shah's religious opponent Ayatollah Khomeini in Paris, France; Sanjabi distributes statement to journalists attacking Shah's continuing rule and rejecting all possibility of cooperating with Shah's military government; National Front spokesman Darius Forehar is arrested along with Sanjabi, with arrests expected to worsen unrest in Iran (NEW YORK TIMES, November 12, 1978, P1)

STRIKERS RETURNING TO WORK

More than 60% of Iran's striking oil workers return to work as troops carry out Shah Mohammad Reza Pahlavi's threat to arrest strike leaders and oust workers who refuse to end walkout; National Iranian Oil Company reports production reached 2.7 million barrels November 13, up from low of 1.1 million, and predicts production will be back to normal level of about 6 million barrels per day within 4 or 5 days; Shah and his supporters hope return of oil workers resumption of business in Teheran and absence of large-scale demonstrations will weaken resolve of opposition leaders (NEW YORK TIMES, November 14, 1978, P1)

U.S.-IRAN TIES ASSESSED

Article examines United States' unconditional support for Shah of Iran and discusses Carter Administration's policy reviews spurred by Iranian situation; notes closer attention is now being given to countries like Saudi Arabia, Brazil and Nigeria, all regarded as regionally influential and all embarking on similar ambitious development programs and liberalization; blames breakdown in US intelligence regarding its ability to predict situation in Iran and long-standing US-Iranian ties as major reasons for rapid and unconditional US backing of Shah; reports that crisis is spurring US officials to reassess US support for human rights, political use of arms sales and US intelligence priorities; points out danger of anti-American regime gaining power with US-supplied, modern-arms arsenal; mentions that National Security Council has decided to stop relying on local powers to protect US interests and is accelerating programs for training and equipping special American combat units for combat in Persian Gulf; use of such forces in Iran is deemed unlikely to succeed, because of social turmoil (NEW YORK TIMES, November 15, 1978, P3)

OIL INDUSTRY STRUCK

Iranian oil centers report almost all striking workers have returned to job at Abadan refinery and 4 offshore installations, but indicate some workers in Ahwaz oilfields continue to resist government's back-to-work order; note that despite break in strike, discontent among workers is widespread, and some are engaging in slowdown; reports from oil centers indicate break in strike apparently came when representatives of workers met with local military governor, General Bokhari Jaafarian, who agreed to their demands for higher wages and allowances; nation's oil production increases, reaching 3.3 million barrels on November 14 after 2.7 million barrels on November 13 and low of 1.1 million barrels on November 7; meanwhile, demonstrators clash with troops in Teheran for first time since military rule was imposed November 6, but no deaths or injuries are reported; demonstrations also continue in provinces, where 6 people are killed and 41 are injured in 2 separate incidents (NEW YORK TIMES, November 15, 1978, P1)

RELIGIOUS FUNDAMENTALISM ASSESSED

Princeton University Assistant Professor of Politics Fouad Ajami assesses religious aspect of dispute between Shah of Iran and his people; sees lesson that masses must be persuaded of purpose and integrity of their government if split between official government culture and popular culture is to be avoided; holds that religious fundamentalism taking hold in Iran is alternative channel to express socio-economic political grievances; considers establishment of "Islamic republic" unrealistic; warns against interpreting Iranian civil strife as Communism-anti-Communism confrontation (NEW YORK TIMES, November 15, 1978, P29)

RURAL-URBAN SHIFT CITED

Commentator Jonathan Kandell outlines rural exodus and urban industrial expansion in Iran; reports that in past 15

Demonstrators march in Teheran in support of the Ayatollah.

United Press International

years, Iran's rural population dropped from 75% to 52%, with only one-third of labor force working in countryside; notes both supporters and opponents of Shah blame violent political upheaval on modernization process, but holds there are many other factors causing unrest, such as Shah's iron rule, charges of political corruption, history of torture, imprisonment and censorship, expectations created by oil riches, and religious discontent (NEW YORK TIMES, November 16, 1978, P11)

SHAH'S BEHAVIOR ASSESSED

Diplomats who have recently seen Shah of Iran reportedly believe Shah is on his way out as absolute ruler; diplomats portray him as broken individual, given to periods of depression brought on by bitter feeling of having been betrayed by his people; some supporters assert Shah is on verge of becoming constitutional monarch, move they feel could allow him to retain his throne; by agreeing to share power, Shah would pave way for coalition government (WASHINGTON POST, November 17, 1978, S1 P22)

LACK OF SUPPORT NOTED

Reporter Jonathan Kandell reports that Shah of Iran is receiving little support from middle and upper classes who owe him most; notes that thousands of wealthy Iranians have fled country, taking with them savings estimated at $1.5 billion to $3 billion; reports that well-to-do blame Shah for not having dealt more firmly with opposition and believe that mild reforms have halted business momentum; notes that with bribery a common practice, businessmen fear Shah's drive against corruption; reports resentment against widening of public education and inadequacies of universities; notes that estimated 325,000 students went overseas to study since 1969 and less than 22,000 have returned; notes that businessmen also complain that labor reforms have cut sharply into profits (NEW YORK TIMES, November 18, 1978, P1)

SHAH'S ACUMEN DOUBTED

Harvard Professor Richard N. Frye, in letter, rebuts news media's portrayal of Shah of Iran as shrewd and tough leader; reports Shah's leadership capacity diminished when his 2 most valuable advisers died in 1977; asserts Shah is out of touch with events and cannot comprehend movement against him   (WASHINGTON POST,   November 19, 1978, S3 P6)

SHAH DECLARES DETERMINATION

Shah of Iran declares that he will not allow any friendly country, even Moslem nations, to intervene in Iran to help retain monarchy; concedes that he has weighed many possibilities in last 10 months, including leaving throne, but has decided to stand firm; will make changes in distribution of power, especially in drive toward modernization, in order to give people more of sense of shared power; intends to free more than 400 political prisoners, but 300 whom he calls "terrorists" will remain in custody; will continue efforts to form coalition government to prepare for free elections despite response from opposition, but will not hold elections while military government is in power; expects military rule to last only few months unless there is major uprising; sees possibility of major offensive by opponents on December 11 religious holiday; concedes that force of rebellion that erupted early in 1978 caught him by surprise; expresses reliance on religion and mysticism   (NEW YORK TIMES,   November 19, 1978, P1)

POLITICAL PRISONERS FREED

Iran frees 210 political prisoners as Shah renews pledge made 2 weeks earlier to hold free elections in June 1979 and bring end to military government he has installed to end widespread rioting; Shah's statement also reminds Minister of Justice to diligently prosecute former officials accused of corruption charges, including former Prime and Court Minister Amir Abbas Hoveida and former SAVAK security police head General Nematollah Nasiri; Empress Farah, on state visit to Iraq, visits religious shrine in Najaf, Iraq, in what is interpreted as move to mollify Moslem opposition; effects of intermittent strikes include growing gas shortage as pipeline that feeds major cities and goes into USSR remains idle; telephone and telecommunications services are reported deteriorating (NEW YORK TIMES,   November 20, 1978,   P1)

AZHARI RECEIVES CONFIDENCE VOTE

Iranian government under Prime Minister General Gholam Reza Azhari receives unexpected strong vote of confidence in Parliament November 22, while Shah's opponents mount pressure on him to resign; lower house of Iranian Parliament approves government's program to restore order after its presentation by General Azhari; Teheran was without electricity as workers in National Power Company staged slowdown while vote of confidence was being taken; demonstrations of protest against Shah are reported in several cities over 48-hour period   (NEW YORK TIMES,   November 23, 1978,   P2)

ANGUISH FOR MODERATES

Commentator Jonathan C. Randal observes middle class Iranians feel trapped between mobs' excesses and vague

political demands and Shah's systematic repression of middle class intellectuals and political aspirations; notes many middle class Iranians admit that for sake of security they want Shah to remain as figurehead constitutional monarch; notes many foreigners are disappointed at middle class' reluctance to defend its interests; sees no sign that middle class will come out openly in Shah's favor   (WASHINGTON POST,   November 26, 1978,   P25)

ECONOMY IN PARALYSIS

Six-month-old civil revolt is bringing Iran's economy to brink of paralysis; banks are barely functioning because of sporadic strikes and slowdowns and damage caused by demonstrations at individual branch offices; thousands of tons of imported food, raw materials and industrial goods are sitting in ports because customs officials refuse to clear them; productivity in all government and private industries has been severely curtailed by power failures and scarcity of natural gas; government assertions to the contrary, oil production has not returned to its normal level of 6 million barrels per day; work slowdown continues among 67,000 workers who produce Iran's oil, which accounts for almost all of nation's annual revenues of $22 billion; many projects, including proposed construction of nuclear power plant and building of a subway in Teheran, are either being cancelled or reduced; other changes in economic policies noted   (NEW YORK TIMES,   November 28, 1978,   S4   P1)

AYATOLLAH CALLS STRIKE

Exiled Moslem leader Ayatollah Khomeini calls for indefinite general strike in Iran December 2; asks oil workers to stage walkout and disrupt Iran's oil production; action suggests Ayatollah plans to intensify his struggle against Shah Mohammad Reza Pahlavi during Moslem holy period Moharram, which begins December 2; Iran's military government attempts to avoid violence by banning public religious processions   (NEW YORK TIMES,   December 1, 1978,   P6)

TEHERAN REPORTED QUIETER

Iranian soldiers again fire on anti-government protesters, but overall Teheran is calmer in wake of 2 nights and 1 day of bloodshed; Iranian Prime Minister General Gholam Reza Azhari, blames Communist Tudeh Party for inciting demonstrations; Western diplomatic and intelligence sources believe Tudeh's involvement is slight; hospital reports of deaths indicate that government claim that 12 died in rioting is drastically understated; reporters note large-scale digging of graves; Teheran airport resumes full operations, but most banks and shops remain closed; in related development, Carter Administration officials note unsubstantiated report that Shah's Moslem opponents are secretly receiving funds from foreign sources, notably USSR and Libya; in Paris the Ayatollah Khomeini calls upon members of Iran's armed forces to desert if ordered to fire on demonstrators, and urges resumption of strike by oil workers   (NEW YORK TIMES,   December 4, 1978, P1)

SHAH ALLOWS PARADES

Iranian Prime Minister Gholam Reza Azhari lifts ban on parades for 48-hour Moslem period of mourning known as Ashura; reportedly received assurances that protests would be peaceful; decision to allow parades is reportedly solely Shah's; meanwhile, anti-American feeling reportedly rises in provinces; protesters fire-bomb Grumman Aircraft Corporation which has contract to train Iranian fighter pilots; about 1,500 wives and children of US military men leave following Defense Department decision to pay for transportation of dependents   (NEW YORK TIMES, December 9, 1978,   P1)

FOREIGNERS LEAVE IRAN

Exodus of Americans from strife-torn Iran intensifies after US decision to fly military and civilian dependents out of Iran at expense of US government; latest count shows 1,200 wives and children of US servicemen and embassy employees leaving; move has set up wave of departures by dependents of US company employees stationed in Iran; at least 1,000 non-government US employees have left Iran; at least 7 US companies have sponsored departure of many of their dependents by specially chartered planes or scheduled commercial fights; business sources and Iran-American Chamber of Commerce estimate that 8,000–10,000 American expatriates have left Iran over previous 2 months, excluding present exodus; other expatriate communities are also reported sending people home, including Japan, which is in process of sending 300 home   (NEW YORK TIMES,   December 10, 1978,   P1)

ASHURA PROTEST DRAWS THOUSANDS

Hundreds of thousands of Iranians stage powerful protest against rule of Shah Mohammad Reza Pahlavi in Teheran, but not a single violent incident is reported during demonstration; in theory, demonstration is religious procession marking eve of Moslem holy day Ashura; opponents of regime act as marshals, controlling traffic and calming demonstrators; police and military had been withdrawn from area, but were guarding roads leading to Shah's palace; protest is seen as impressive show of strength for Shah's opponents, but also as victory for Shah, who took considerable risk in permitting procession without military supervision   (NEW YORK TIMES,   December 11, 1978,   P1)

OPPOSITION TO SHAH GROWS

Several million anti-Shah protestors fill Iranian streets during celebration of Ashura, high point of Shiite Moslem month of mourning; at least 5 men die during clash with Iranian troops in Isfahan as large group of demonstrators set fire to buildings; estimated half million demonstrators march through central Teheran, shouting "Death to the Shah!" and "The Shah and his family must be killed!"; Iranian religious leader Ayatollah Shariatmadari contends size of protests indicates opposition's demands are supported by entire nation; sources close to Shah report efforts to persuade major opposition leaders to join in coalition to ease crisis are at impasse   (NEW YORK TIMES,   December 12, 1978,   P1)

SHAH MEETS WITH OPPOSITION

Shah of Iran meets with opposition leaders Ali Amini and Karim Sanjabi in apparently unproductive effort to form coalition government; meanwhile, violent demonstrations erupt in a dozen Iranian cities; National Front party sources suggest Front wants to lead government even with Shah in power, provided he meets its terms   (NEW YORK TIMES,   December 15, 1978,   P1)

IRAN ARMY UNDER STRESS

R.W. Apple Jr. reports growing signs of stress among lower ranks in Iranian armed forces, as troops at Tabriz refuse to fire on demonstrators; notes reported desertions by hundreds of soldiers in Mashhad and Qom; notes vast difference in pay and benefits between officers and enlisted men; observes close ties between Shah and military; reports that Prime Minister, General Gholam Reza Azhari, has indicated that he is uncomfortable in role of civil leader and wishes to return to primary job as Chief of General Staff; notes analysts' opinion that new military strongman would come from ranks of younger generals, although some see political hard-liners General Gholam Ali Ovassi and General Amir Hossein Rabii in role   (NEW YORK TIMES,   December 19, 1978,   P1)

U.S. INTELLIGENCE CRITICIZED

State Department and CIA officials respond to White House complaints about failure of intelligence community to perceive weakening of Iranian government; note policy established in mid-'60's prohibits them from contacting Iranian opposition groups; also charge that key Presidential aides refused to accept State Department analyses suggesting Shah Mohammad Reza Pahlavi was facing growing military, social and economic problems due to his multi-billion-dollar arms purchases; assert security adviser Brzezinski refused to permit State Department review of Iran to be placed on agenda for Cabinet meeting on Iranian arms sales; disclose their intelligence activities in Iran because of anger and concern that CIA will become scapegoat for not adequately warning President Carter of impending crisis   (NEW YORK TIMES,   December 21, 1978,   P1)

CRISIS CAUSES ECONOMIC UPHEAVAL

Political crisis in Iran has reportedly caused economic upheaval for about 300 US companies operating in Iran; has resulted in loss of billions of dollars in military orders, property damage, and delayed payments, as well as concern about loans made by US banks; companies that have been hurt most are large defense contractors who benefited most from Shah's rule in past; Textron Inc. subsidiary Bell Operations Corporation has announced suspension of $575 million contract, while 2 arms sales, involving General Dynamics Corporation, Pratt & Whitney Corporation, McDonnell Douglas Corporation and Texas Instruments Corporation have also been cancelled; Boeing Company and Lockheed Corporation report there have been no delinquent payments on their contracts, but $1.2 billion order of AWAC surveillance planes from Boeing is considered vulnerable; heavy-equipment

Premier Shahpur Bakhtiar,

suppliers and construction companies are also suffering major losses, with Bechtel Corporation, Westinghouse Electric Corporation, AT&T, General Telephone and Electronics Corporation and General Electric Company cited as having lost sales or suspending work; firms whose buildings have been firebombed or damaged include Pepsico Inc., Grumman Corporation, Pan American Airways, IBM and several banks and hotels, including Teheran's Intercontinental Hotel   (NEW YORK TIMES, December 22, 1978, P1)

OIL STRIKE PRECIPITATES CRISIS

Iran's political crisis appears to reach decisive stage after day of violence, marked by wild shooting, use of tear gas and shutdown of all schools, airline, rail and bus services,

and virtual stoppage of country's oil production; National Iranian Oil Company announces that oil rationing will begin December 29; Western analysts say Iranian fuel crisis could have greater effect in forcing Shah out of power than have street demonstrations   (NEW YORK TIMES, December 28, 1978, P1)

U.S. NAVY ON ALERT

US orders carrier task force to leave Philippines for South China Sea for possible movement to Persian Gulf area if Iranian political crisis warrants it; State Department spokesman declares that Iranian situation is not deemed serious enough to warrant evacuation of US nationals; naval task force includes carrier Constellation with 80-90 fighter airplanes and escort ships, including destroyers and tankers; 2 special groups have been set up within Administration to monitor Iranian developments: Zbigniew Brzezinski aide David L. Aaron heads White House group and State Department Undersecretary for Political Affairs David Newsom heads larger interagency group   (NEW YORK TIMES, December 30, 1978, P1)

NEW GOVERNMENT CONFLICT

Royal palace spokesman discloses that Shah of Iran has named opposition leader Shahpur Bakhtiar to head new civilian government, succeeding military government of General Gholam Reza Azhari; declares that Shah has no intention of relinquishing power or leaving country; statement contradicts that of Bakhtiar, who had said that Shah would leave country temporarily and hand power to emergency regency council; spokesman also denies that Shah's mother and Shah's 3 youngest children have left country, but US State Department asserts that Shah's mother has arrived in US; economy is at standstill, with central bank closed, no public transportation and few businesses operating; announcement is made that all electric power to factories will be cut off   (NEW YORK TIMES, December 30, 1978, P1)

OIL SHORTAGE AFFECTS COUNTRY

Iran's daily oil production falls to new low of 250,000 bbl., compared with 350,000 bbl. previous day and normal daily production of 6.5 million bbl. according to independent oil industry official; report indicates that Iran is producing only ½ enough oil to meet own needs, with no surplus for export; accord is reported between National Front negotiators and government that would return enough workers to oil fields to meet Iran's domestic requirements in exchange for withdrawal of troops deployed at oil installations and commitment not to resume exports; oil shortages in Teheran bring 50% increase in some taxi fares and restriction of bread sales because of fuel shortage at bakeries; Army is said to have plenty of fuel for its vehicles; motorists wait in long lines for gasoline   (NEW YORK TIMES, December 31, 1978, P1)

SHAH OF IRAN FACING GROWING OPPOSITION

By NICHOLAS GAGE
Special to The New York Times

TEHERAN, Iran, May 16—After four days of bloody riots in major Iranian cities last week, Shah Mohammed Riza Pahlevi is facing the strongest opposition to his rule in 15 years.

The Shah, however, does not appear particularly worried. He said at a news conference last week that he intended to continue his present policies and, as rumors spread through the country that even more violent demonstrations were imminent, he flew to Bulgaria yesterday for a state visit.

The Shah seems confident that his opponents are not strong enough to mount a serious assault against his power, which is backed by a well-equipped army and security forces.

Many of the Shah's supporters do not share his confidence. They recall that during riots in Tabriz in February, local policemen let the demonstrators roam through the streets, apparently unwilling to fire on people protesting violations of Islamic traditions, a protest that the policemen believed in.

The army had to be brought into Tabriz and scores of deaths were reported. Riots in three other cities, including Teheran, resulted in more deaths and extensive property damage.

Unrest has continued across the country since the February disturbances, with the worst demonstrations having occurred last week in Tabriz, the holy city of Qum and the capital, in which more than a dozen people were reportedly killed and hundreds injured. The protests subsided after the Government said it would not tolerate further outbursts.

The continuing demonstrations have convinced many Iranians that the forces gathering against the Shah are rapidly growing and will produce a major explosion if he does not find a way to defuse them.

The Shah's followers believe that his best option is to try to divide the opposition by opening discussions with its strongest group—traditionalist Moslems.

So far he has not tried to open such discussions, some of his supporters feel, because it goes against his convictions. "But he's got to do it," said one supporter. "He knows that in Iran power has been taken and lost in the streets and the bazaars."

The most powerful group opposing the Shah is made up of Moslem traditionalists loyal to Ayatollah Mohammed Khomeini, the religious leader who has been in exile in Iraq since 1963 when he launched a nationwide drive against the Shah following the introduction of land reform and other modernization measures he opposed.

The second major group is the Bazaris, powerful merchants who have close ties to the Moslem clergy, usually contributing 20 percent of their profits to the clergy to distribute to the poor.

Politicians Oppose Shah

A third group are liberal politicians who belong to the National Front of the late Mohammed Mossadegh, the former Prime Minister who came close to ousting the Shah in 1953.

Finally, there are the students, writers, intellectuals, and professionals who have been persistent critics of the Shah's autocratic regime, particularly its security police.

Each group has its own grievances. The Moslem clergy object to the modernization measures that have reduced their power and the land reform plan that took away most of their holdings.

The merchants are upset because the Shah has slowed the economic boom that followed the tripling of oil prices five years ago. They have criticized him for submitting to American pressure to keep the lid on oil prices.

The politicians want an end to the single-party system the Shah has established so that they can share power. The students and intellectuals want reforms in the economic system, and would make Iran less dependent on the United States.

United Behind Single Objective

These groups, however, have submerged their individual goals, which kept them divided in the past, to unite behind a single objective—the establishment of a democratic government. "What we want is the return of our rights, to be free to elect our own representatives and to have power vested in the people," said Ayatollah Kazem Shareatmadary, leader of the Moslem opposition inside Iran. "Whether the Shah stays as the head of state or not does not concern us."

The followers of the dissident Moslem leaders are the key to the opposition's hopes to change the political system. As a result, even students and intellectuals who once scorned Moslem believers as reactionary, have come to espouse their causes, such as the right of women to wear the chador, a veil covering the whole body, a right that the Shah has tried to discourage.

The improved organization and the new boldness of the Shah's opponents are seen as a result of the Shah's loosening of his hold on Iran, partly because of pressure from the West and partly because he wants to decentralize a Government that has become too large for him to direct alone.

To some degree the opposition appears to be trying to find out how far the Shah will allow himself to go under his new policy. They justify the risk that the Shah may strike back at them on the ground that they would still gain through the international repercussions such an action would bring.

NEW YORK TIMES, May 18, 1978, P1

Shah of Iran Faces Challenge Headed by Moslem Clergy

By NICHOLAS GAGE
Special to The New York Times

TEHERAN, Iran—A battle line is being drawn across this tumultuous land of vast oil wealth, enormous military power and mounting social unrest.

At first glance the two camps seem dramatically unmatched. On one side is the autocratic monarch, Shah Mohammed Riza Pahlevi, with his oil money, American support and the army behind him

On the other side is a weak federation of unlikely bedfellows, including intellectuals, merchants, Marxists and students who have allied themselves with the mullahs, or clergy, of the conservative Moslem sect that dominates Iran.

This alliance presents the Shah with the worst crisis he has faced since mass riots against his rule broke out in 1963.

Nevertheless, most analysts do not believe that the Shah will be forced from his throne. He is too powerful, not only because he has the backing of the armed forces and the United States, but also because he enjoys support from large numbers of peasants and workers, the traditional bases for successful revolutions.

But riots against the Government will continue and probably get worse unless the Shah finds some way to make peace with the Moslem leadership. Most Western analysts feel that he cannot back away from his two-year-old policy of liberalization. "Without liberalization he won't be able to attract the kind of people into the system who are crucial to his dream of turning Iran into a powerful industrial state," said an American diplomat.

For the last six months the two forces have periodically engaged in a series of bloody skirmishes in several major cities. The casualties are difficult to estimate because both sides misrepresent the figures, but scores have died, hundreds have been injured and millions of dollars worth of property has been destroyed.

So far the Shah has managed to quell the uprisings using only a small part of the power at his command. "This trouble will play itself out," Prime Minister Jamshid Amuzegar said in an interview. "It poses no threat."

Many Iranians are not so sure, however, and some are hurrying to sell property in a declining market in order to send cash abroad. They know that when reformist elements put their liberal, revolutionary and even heretical ideas aside and ally themselves with the mullahs, it means trouble, because only the mullahs have the power and influence to threaten the Government.

Suspicion of Authority

The leadership of the Shiite sect, to which 90 percent of the Iranian people profess allegiance. has joined the opposition movement for several reasons. The sect is traditionally suspicious of the authorities. "Unlike Sunni Moslems, the majority in Islam, Shiites never have close ties with authorities," said Karim Sanjabi, a longtime political opponent of the monarchy.

The disenchantment of the mullahs with the Shah, however, goes beyond this general suspicion of authority. It is focused on the Shahs 15-year-old modernization drive, in which he has taken away much of their property and power. His land reform program stripped the Shiite religious establishment, the second largest landowner in the country, of its holdings, and other measures ended their jurisdiction over marriage and divorce and their control of education.

These moves led to the widespread demonstrations in 1963, which he put down forcefully, ordering his troops to fire on rioters. He also exiled Ayatollah Mohammed Khomeini, a religious leader who was the most vigorous opponent of the modernization drive, to Iraq.

The New York Times/June 4, 1978

Protests erupted recently in Tabriz, Qum and Teheran.

Shah Strengthened Grip

The Shah also took longer-range measures to strengthen his grip on the country. He developed a highly effective and feared secret police called Savak, prosecuted political crimes in military courts and had great success in infiltrating the clergy, student groups and nearly every level of society with spies. Dissidents were frequently tortured and given long prison sentences.

Then, in the early 1970's, a number of factors began to erode the Shah's power. In 1973 he quadrupled oil prices, bringing a flood of wealth into the country, making many Italians rich overnight. The Shah poured much of the new wealth into development, but with progress came galloping inflation, extensive corruption and waste of public funds.

As economic difficulties set in, creating growing discontent, the Shah came under sharp criticism for his violations of human rights from groups abroad, including the International Association of Jurists and Amnesty International. Later President Carter's emphasis on human rights added to the pressures on the Shah to make some gesture toward liberalization.

Religious Leader Criticized

As repressive measures were eased, dissidents increased their activities, but with little success. Effective opposition to the Shah was sparked, as in the past, by a religious issue: criticism of Ayatollah Khomeini, the exiled religious leader, in an Iranian newspaper early this year. His supporters felt that the attack was the work of the Government, and rioting broke out in May in the holy city of Qum, causing several deaths.

Forty days later, at the end of the traditional mourning period for the dead, a memorial service took place in the city of Tabriz for those slain in Qum and erupted into riots involving close to 25,000 Moslems. The resulting casualties were officially reported as 9 dead and 125 injured, but unofficial reports put the death toll at about 100.

Ever since the riots in Tabriz, demonstrations have broken out regularly at 40-day intervals, with the last incidents occuring in several cities, including Teheran and Qum, during the second week in May.

"Despite what the Government says, our people do not demonstrate against modernization but against dictatorship," said Ayatollah Kazem Shareatmadary, a small, turbaned man of 72 who is considered the most important Shiite religious leader in Iran. "The land reform program has not worked because of the way it was imposed. We have to import almost all of our food today."

Two Killed in Raid

The frail, gray-bearded religious leader was speaking while seated on the floor of a room illuminated by a single bare bulb and empty except for cushions. The home where he usually received visitors had been peppered with bullets in an army raid during the previous week, during which two people waiting to see him were killed, reportedly because they had refused to shout "Long live the Shah." Bloodstains on the carpet of the shattered waiting room and the bloody turban of one of the dead still marked the spot.

Ayatollah Shareatmadary's home and headquarters are in Qum, about 90 miles south of Teheran, on the edge of the bleak salt deserts of the interior. At the time he was interviewed, Qum was filled with 32 tanks, a reminder of the military might available to the Shah if disturbances should break out again. Two of the tanks had their guns trained on the theological school near the religious leader's house. "The tanks are proof of our power," the old man said.

Among the devout Moslems who follow the mullahs, the strongest support comes from two groups: the merchants in the bazaars and the young, unskilled workers who have been moving from the villages into the cities without the training necessary to secure work there.

The merchants, or "bazaaris," have lent financial support to the movement and have strongly opposed the Shah even though some of them became very wealthy as a result of the prosperity brought about by the increase in oil prices.

'A Golden Cage'

During an interview, a group of bazaaris said that the main reason they opposed the Shah was his dictatorial rule. "We Shiites are different from other Moslems—we respect freedom," one said. "A sound society must have freedom, or what good is material progress? We don't want to live in a golden cage."

The young, unskilled laborers who have been in the forefront of the demonstrations are disturbed by what they consider the decadence they see in the cities when they arrive from the villages, a state of affairs for which they blame the Shah.

Committed Moslems in the universities are also playing a major role in the movement against the monarchy, in many instances supplanting leftist student leaders who have stepped aside for the moment in the hope that the Moslem-dominated popular movement will be more successful than they were. Demonstrations at the universities have followed those in cities such as Tabriz and Qum and have been put down forcefully by the authorities. In protest, most students in several of the larger universities have refused to go to classes.

Support for the Shah

For his part, the Shah enjoys strong support among several powerful segments of Iranian society. During the interview in his office, Prime Minister Amuzegar pointed out that the peasants and workers had not joined the opposition. The reason is that the Shah has taken great care to build both elements into pillars of support for his regime. He has been generous to both, starting with the first phase of the land reform program in 1962 when he gave 600,000 peasant families the land they had been working for large landholders. Later two million more peasants received land under the program.

For the workers, the Shah has instituted a profit-sharing plan requiring employers to pay them annual bonuses. Last year the Shah also initiated a program to offer up to 49 percent of the stock in many industries to workers and farmers. In addition, the Government has permitted large wage increases for industrial workers despite its worry over inflation, a concern that has led to the cutting back of some development projects.

The Shah also enjoys considerable support among the upper middle class, which has earned vast profits in recent years. It is not clear, however, how many members of this group would stay to fight for the monarchy rather than take their money and flee abroad if the situation became desperate.

The new Moslem-led alliance is well aware that it will have to attract large numbers of workers and peasants if it is going to shake the Shah's regime. Therefore it is concentrating its propaganda drive on ridiculing his policies, charging, for instance, that the land redistribution program has been poorly administered and that the peasants have not been given the support necessary to make their land productive and profitable.

Bigots and Reactionaries

The Government has attempted to discredit the Moslem dissidents by painting them as bigots and reactionaries who oppose all modernization and who attack women seen on the streeet without the traditional chardor, a veil that covers the entire body.

Ayatollah Shareatmadary insists that the wearing of the chardor is not a principle of his religion but merely a custom "We do not force women to wear the veil." he said, "But on the other hand, nobody has the right to order them not to."

Nevertheless, this custom seems to be much more closely observed in Qum, where nearly every woman seen on the street was covered from head to toe, than in Teheran, where only about one woman in five wore the veil.

Although the religious leaders disavow extremist tactics, there is abundant evidence that many conservative Moslems harbor violent hatred against certain religious and ethnic groups. One of their targets is the Bahai religious sect, which numbers many prominent Iranians among its members. The family that controls the Pepsi-Cola concession in Iran is Bahai, and Pepsi-Cola plants, trucks and distribution centers are a favorite target of rioters. In Qum, not a single store could be found that sold Pepsi-Cola.

Other groups that are unpopular with the conservative Moslems include Armenians and Jews, many of whom had their businesses destroyed during the recent troubles. Ayatollah Shareatmadary said that such acts were the deeds of an uneducated extremist minority and did not reflect the beliefs of his movement.

On the Government side, spokesmen took offense at the frequent charges that only businessmen opposed to the Shah are arrested for profiteering and have their stores closed, while other businessmen are allowed to charge above the permitted prices for their products and to smooth their business dealings with bribes.

"Everybody does it," said a cheese wholesaler in Teheran, "but only those opposed to the Government are arrested. Corrupt people are prosecuted only when they do something else wrong."

'We Can't Win'

The Minister of Information, Dariush Homayun, bristled at the suggestion that arrests were made selectively. "We are accused of tolerating corruption and when we fight it they say it's for political reasons," he complained. "We can't win."

The Shah has taken a strong public stand against corruption, jailing many officials, including high military officers, on bribery charges.

But prosecution is said not to reach as high as the corruption itself. "Ministers and people close to the palace are not prosecuted when they have been found taking payoffs," a high Government official confided privately. "Ministers have been dismissed quietly, but they have not been prosecuted."

Corruption pervades every aspect of public and business life in Iran. "I have to count on 15 percent of profits going to payoffs," said a successful electronics dealer here. "I pay purchasing agents, tax officials, inspectors, telephone installers, everybody."

Charges of Torture Denied

Dr. Amuzegar is also sensitive to charges that political opponents are tortured or given severe jail sentences. He insisted that torture of prisoners did not exist in Iran and said that only about 2,100 political prisoners were currently being held, adding: "They will probably be released within a short time." Others put the figure at closer to 10,000.

Dr. Amuzegar said, however, that the Government plans to use tough measures against rioters and will bring those charged with trying to disrupt public order before military tribunals. Such trials are held in secret and the accused are required to choose their counsel from a list of military men who need not be lawyers.

Opponents of the Shah concede that officially sanctioned torture has apparently been ended. But Abdulkarim Lahidji, a lawyer who has been active in the movement to expand civil rights in Iran, charged that other types of intimidation continue. He said that several weeks ago he was seized and severely beaten by a group of men. Some time later a bomb exploded outside his office, damaging walls and windows in the building.

"Many others have been beaten and have had bombs explode outside their homes." Mr. Lahidji said. "The Government says this is the work of unknown extremists, but obviously Savak is behind it."

'Total Free Expression'

The Government is most sensitive to suggestions from the West that the Shah should institute a Western-style democracy. "I remember that in 1940 an American judge banned 'Lady Chatterley's Lover'" said Dr. Amuzegar, "and yet Americans want us to have total free expression in a country that was 95 percent illiterate 15 years ago." He said that such a degree of freedom would make it impossible for the monarch to achieve his goal of transforming the country from a feudal state to a leading industrial nation within his lifetime.

No one envisions Iran moving toward a constitutional monarchy as long as the Shah stays on the throne. People who know the Shah say he will leave to his son, Crown Prince Riza, 17, the choice of whether or not to allow democracy in Iran after he has modernized it.

At a recent news conference the Shah made clear what he thought of Western systems of government. Referring to the terrorism and disruption that are taking place in many European countries, he asked: "Which of the Western models is beautiful enough to justify our copying it?"

NEW YORK TIMES, June 4, 1978, P1

U.S.-Iran Links Still Strong

By NICHOLAS GAGE
Special to The New York Times

TEHERAN, Iran — During the last 20 years the United States has sold more than $18 billion worth of arms to Iran and has helped organize and equip a vast security system that gives its ruler, Shah Mohammed Riza Pahlevi, absolute control of the country.

In exchange for that support the Shah has committed his country to protect the vital routes out of the Persian Gulf that carry more than half the oil used by Western countries. Furthermore, the income from his arms purchases plus the American technology he buys to help develop

his country return to the United States almost $2 annually for every $1 the United States spends on Iranian oil.

Move Toward Libereralization

The mutually profitable arrangement has forged bonds that are much stronger than American ties to any other developing country. At the same time the relationship has been sharply criticized, both by domestic opponents of the Shah and by Americans, some of them in Congress, who condemn his autocratic rule and are fearful that growing Iranian military strength will tempt him into aggressive actions that might drag the United States along.

During three visits to Iran totaling more than five weeks, the depth and implications of the United States' involvement were examined in dozens of interviews with American and European diplomats, military and intelligence experts, high Iranian officials and Americans and Europeans working here, as well as with Iranian students, intellectuals, merchants and Moslem religious leaders who have joined the mounting opposition to the 58-year-old sovereign.

The American diplomats hope that some of the criticism will be deflected by the current liberalization program, which is said to include cessation of the torture — long officially denied — of political prisoners, curtailment of the use of military courts and improved prison conditions. Recently the Shah replaced Gen. Nematollah Nassiri, for 12 years the iron-fisted leader of Savak, the secret police force, who built it into the largest force of its kind outside the Communist bloc.

These changes have not appeased the Shah's opponents, who have organized huge demonstrations that have caused the loss of more than 100 lives since the beginning of the year in Teheran, Tabriz and the holy city of Qum. Explaining the demonstrations, Medhi Barzegan, an opposition leader, said, "When you see a little light, you can't stand the darkness any more."

The opposition credits President Carter's human rights campaign with the light that has been shed, but it blames Washington as much as the Shah for the darkness that persists. "The Shah can't remain a dictator without American support," said E. K. Lahidji, a lawyer who is an opposition leader. American officials deny culpability, saying that they are trying to encourage further liberalization and are not involved in internal security.

Their response is accurate as far as it goes. American officials are trying to promote liberalization, but not if it conflicts with the Shah's objectives. "Iran is too important for us to risk that," a diplomat acknowledged. Furthermore, while the contention that Americans are not directly involved as advisers in internal security is generally accepted even by leading members of the opposition, it is also known that American advisers helped organize the security forces, particularly Savak, trained their ranking officers and provided them with the latest police equipment. Among American supplies that helped the security forces quell the demonstrations were 50,000 tear-gas grenades, 356,000 gas masks and 4,300 handguns.

Savak is reported to have more than 4,000 career agents and more than 50,000 paid informants, who, according to Government sources, have infiltrated not only opposition groups but also all ministries and most foreign missions, including the United States Embassy. "There are little shadows everywhere," an Iranian minister remarked.

Set up in 1957 by the Central Intelligence Agency and later assisted by Mossad, the Israeli intelligence service, Savak was managed at its inception by 20 officers retired from the Iranian military who, intelligence sources say, received special training at the Marine base in Quantico, Va., and attended orientation programs at C.I.A. headquarters at Langley, Va. More Savak agents received American training under police programs financed by the Agency for International Development, which spent more than $2 million on "public safety."

Torture of Political Prisoners

In the late 1960's criticism of Savak's methods, including torture of political prisoners, moved American officials to end their assistance to the police and to curtail the number of Iranian security officers going to the United States for training. Since 1973 the only policemen known to have received training are some 20 narcotics officers who attended special Drug Enforcement Administration courses.

However, more than 250 military officers are trained in the United States every year, and it is believed that some, particularly those attending counterinsurgency courses, are affiliated with Savak. The new head of the agency, Gen. Nasser Moghadam, came to the job from the command of the intelligence branch of the armed forces.

Moreover, while American officials no longer advise or train the security forces, they exchange information with them. The Americans insist that this is restricted to the subjects of drug traffickers and of terrorists whose targets may be Americans, several of whom have been killed by guerrillas. Well-placed Iranian sources say the information also deals with opposition movements and their leaders.

The C.I.A. maintains the closest contact with Savak, often undertaking joint operations with it involving third countries, particularly the Soviet Union, Iraq and Afghanistan. Despite such contacts, or perhaps because of them, American intelligence experts have a low opinion of Savak, describing it as big, clumsy and not particularly effective, and recalling that it did not foresee the riots in Tabriz last February that involved 25,000 people and obviously required a good deal of planning. (Savak did predict the Communist coup in neighboring Afghanistan last April, which the C.I.A. did not.)

Just How Retired Are They?

Fifty agents are in the C.I.A. station here. At least 100 retired intelligence specialists work for private American companies hired by Iran to set up and operate a sophisticated monitoring network. How retired some of these specialists are is questioned, even by Western diplomats. "What civilian would spend a year in a monitoring station high up in the moun-

tains seven miles from the Russian border without friends, without women?" a European attaché asked rhetorically.

Since Turkey, retaliating for the Congressional arms embargo after the Turkish invasion of Cyprus in 1974, shut down American bases used to monitor the Soviet Union, Iran has become a center for intelligence-gathering on the Soviet Union. It also serves as the main listening post for countries such as Iraq and Afghanistan, where Soviet influence has been strong, and even for friendly nations in the Middle East such as Saudi Arabia that sometimes pursue policies that diverge from those of the United States.

Within Iran the C.I.A.'s main goal is to monitor the loyalty of the armed forces, on whose support the Shah's power rests. It has concluded that the higher levels of the officer corps are solidly behind the Shah, who scrutinizes the records of anyone to be promoted above the rank of major, but they are less certain about younger officers, many of whom come out of the universities, where hostility to the Shah from both leftist and Moslem students has been intense.

Perhaps overshadowing the intelligence and security operations is the matter of arms supplies. For many years the United States was Iran's primary source, but as criticism of the sales has intensified in the United States, the Shah has turned increasingly to European countries, particularly West Germany (for submarines), Britain (tanks) and the Netherlands (frigates). The United States now accounts for only 20 percent of arms sales to Iran, but it remains the principal supplier to the air force, which has bought the most advanced jet fighters, including 141 F-4E's, 40 F-14A's and 20 F-14's; on order are 20 F-14's and 160 F-16's, the latter to be delivered over the next seven years.

Active and Former Military Men

Some 1,100 American military men are teaching Iranians how to use and maintain the sophisticated arms they have purchased. The large number of retired American military officers working for private companies that have sold military equipment here brings the total providing military training close to 8,000, or a fifth of the Americans in Iran.

Rather than purchasing equipment designed to perform best with particular tanks, planes and ships, the Iranians often buy accessories for them from companies or countries other than the originators. This happens, according to intelligence sources, because the payoffs that accompany such sales, amounting to 10 percent of the price, must be spread among a number of generals, ministers and palace contacts, each supporting a different interest.

As for the apprehensions that Iran might undertake a military adventure that would drag the United States along with it, the Shah, in interviews, has scoffed at them. Iran, he said, has enough mineral wealth — not just oil but vast deposits of gas and copper — so that it does not need to tap its oil-rich neighbors to the south, and any move to the east would only bring in hordes of hungry and uneducated people who would drain Iranian resources. He has made it clear, however, that he would intervene if he perceived a threat to Iran in a change in the area, such as "the further disintegration of Pakistan," which he views as a buffer against the Soviet Union.

Such talk causes anxiety in the Western diplomatic community but is quickly rationalized when the strategic importance of Iran is considered. "After the Vietnam disaster the United States would find it difficult to get involved in direct fighting, even to protect oil, resources and transportation routes in this area," a high American official said. "Iran has accepted that role for us."

Joint Control of Vital Strait

So far Iran has been called upon to play the role only once, in Oman, where, over several years, it sent 35,000 troops to crush a Communist-supported rebellion in the southern region of Dhofar. Last December Iran and Oman declared that they would be jointly responsible for protecting the Strait of Hormuz, the 20-mile channel through which two-thirds of the oil for the non-Communist world passes. Although Iran has not engaged in any fighting in Iraq, it has helped counter the efforts of that country, long backed by the Russians, to export revolution to the United Arab Emirates, Bahrain, Kuwait and Qatar—all lying on the Persian Gulf.

Iran has carried out American policy objectives in the Red Sea area as well, supplying arms to Somalia after that country ordered the Russians out, economic aid to Ethiopia before it warmed up to Moscow and material and diplomatic support to both the Sudan and Egypt, and the Shah enthusiastically supported President Anwar el-Sadat's Middle Eastern peace initiative from the start. In the view of American diplomats, the developments in Afghanistan, where a Communist-supported faction has seized power, add even more to the need of the United States to stand solidly with the Shah.

The Shah's pragmatic attitude toward Israel is another reason given by American diplomats for maintaining such a close relationship with him; they point out that he continued supplying oil to Israel during the 1973 Arab-Israeli war and to the United States during the Arab oil

embargo that followed. "We sell oil to anyone who wants to buy it," the Iranian Prime Minister, Jamshid Amouzegar, has said in explaining Iranian policy. "We don't mix politics with oil."

The usefulness of the Shah as a surrogate policeman for Washington depends on the effectiveness of his armed forces. In Oman, the only place where Iranian troops have been battle-tested, their performance has not been rated high. American military experts say that the armed forces are improving, not least at using the sophisticated armaments the Shah buys them. But others feel that the air force, on which victory against a formidable foe like Iraq would depend, could not operate without direct American support. "Without Americans to maintain balance and load our fighters, we would be grounded within two days in a war situation," an Iranian general confided. "Unfortunately our own people do not have the technical skills to keep us in the air."

Clear Economic Benefit to U.S.

Not only strategic but economic considerations figure in Iran's value to the United States, and on that score the benefits are clear. Added together, the military purchases, the products and services imported for the industrialization of the country and the money Iranians spend on investment, education and travel in the United States tally up to a tidy profit. Last year the United States took in about $6 billion from Iran and paid out $3.5 billion, mostly for oil.

Furthermore, whenever the Americans sell anything to Iran, they also sell the services of experts who can teach Iranians to operate and repair the product. When Bell sold the Iranians 491 helicopters for $500 million, it signed a contract to teach the operation and service of the craft, which brought in another $500 million.

Despite the heavy economic and military interest of the United States in Iran, Mohammed Riza Pahlevi does not feel secure about its support. Like the Russian exile Aleksandr I. Solzhenitsyn, he has doubts about the will of the West to oppose Soviet aggression. In recent conversations he has expressed fears that the Americans would allow the Russians to

take over some of Iran's northern provinces if they guaranteed that they would stay out of the southern areas where most of the oil reserves are.

To avoid exacerbating those fears, American diplomats have been extremely cautious about establishing substantive contacts with the opposition, many of whom express pro-American sentiments because they credit the liberalization in Iran to President Carter's emphasis on human rights, although, in fact, it started before he won office.

Contacts 'Very Low Key'

"We maintain some contacts — very informal, very low key — but it's just not worthwhile to go beyond that," an American diplomat said. "The strength of the opposition and its future are both limited."

Illustrating the small importance given the opposition is that the United States Embassy's only contact with the Moslem leaders who have led the anti-Shah demonstrations is carried out by a second secretary who makes infrequent visits to their stronghold in Qum, which is 90 miles from Teheran.

Many critics of the Shah feel that it would be in the American interest to encourage the development of a responsible opposition. "It is the only way for the United States to prevent eventual revolution in this country," said Hedayat Matine-Daftary, a lawyer and grandson of Mohammed Mossadegh, who almost succeeded in driving the Shah from the throne in 1953.

Mr. Barzegan, a leader of what remains of the Mossadegh movement, said that the Shah's opponents were disappointed but not disheartened by the strong support that President Carter expressed for the Shah when he visited Teheran on New Year's Day.

"President Carter's words on human rights were what originally raised the people's hopes and gave them courage to defy the dictatorship," he said. "Now, no matter what Mr. Carter says, the people will not become silent again. They're not afraid any more."

NEW YORK TIMES, July 9, 1978, P1

U.S., Short on Intelligence and Tied to the Shah, Decided It Had to Support Him

Special to The New York Times

WASHINGTON, Nov. 14—Early this month, as the political turmoil in Iran appeared to be getting out of control, a high-level group of Carter Administration aides met to determine what, if anything, the United States could do to help stabilize the situation.

Several alternatives for American action were considered at the meeting at the White House, which occurred on Nov. 2, including State Department suggestions that Shah Mohammed Riza Pahlevi be asked to bring his opponents into a coalition government or even that pres-

sure be put upon him to abdicate. In the end, however, it was decided that the United States had no real alternative but to offer unconditional support for the Shah.

The next day, Zbigniew Brzezinski, President Carter's adviser on national security, telephoned the Shah, telling him that the White House would give full backing to any effort he took to restore order. Two days later, with the apparent support of the United States, the Shah formed a military Government which, for the time being at least, has served to halt the spiral of riots and strikes.

Frustration Amid Little Information

The episode reflects the frustration expressed by many officials involved in the Iranian crisis. Several factors, including the inadequacy of intelligence information, are said to have narrowed American choices, forcing the White House to adopt a policy described by one Presidential aide as "voicing support for the Shah, but doing little more than watching, waiting and hoping."

The United States, despite its long history of involvement in Iranian politics and fully aware of Iran's strategic importance to the West, has nonetheless found itself unable to influence events there.

Strangely, in view of the United States' limited choices, giving the Shah a free hand appears to have paid off. But few believe that military rule offers a long-term solution to the Shah's problems.

Several State Department officials believe that with more warning, the Administration could have assumed a more active role early in the crisis, pressing the Shah to enter discussions with his opponents. But the disorder is widely acknowledged to have caught the Administration off guard. "In hindsight," one specialist remarked, "we should have seen it coming and been prepared. But the threat of an internal revolt was seen as the least likely contingency."

Politics of Oil and Reform

The Administration's policy now is to continue to offer full support for the Shah's efforts to quell the riots and strikes that have led to a cutback in oil production and thus endangered the economy. American officials also expressed hope that once the situation was under control, the Shah would be able to reinstate the program of gradual liberalization that he embarked on two years ago.

At the same time, the crisis is said to have spurred a review of some basic aspects of Administration foreign policy, ranging from its support for human rights, to its use of arms sales, to its priorities for intelligence collection.

One of the most controversial questions still confronting officials is whether the White House should have accepted the advice of State Department regional specialists who argued for some type of coalition rule for Iran. While some officials argued that such an arrangement was yet possible, a majority believed that the decision to refrain from pushing the Shah in this direction was correct.

Shah Didn't Solicit U.S. Advice

The majority noted that the Shah's own efforts to form a coalition had ended in failure, and they cited other factors that limited the Administration's options.

One of the most important limitations was said to have been that the Shah did not appear receptive to American advice. Despite reports that the monarch often seemed overwhelmed by the disorders, American officials insist that he never sought advice on specific decisions.

The United States Ambassador in Teheran, William H. Sullivan, and others kept in close touch with the Shah, but officials here said that the Americans, not the Shah, had prompted contacts. "The Shah's a big boy," a White House aide said. "He knows his country better than we do and he's not exactly the kind of person who is used to following orders."

Officials also said the Administration's stance on the Iranian crisis was based on a strong desire not to reinforce an argument used by the Shah's opponents — that Iran is an "American puppet."

"We haven't wanted to appear to be running the show," a State Department official said.

Several officials said that a critical limit on American involvement was the lack of hard intelligence data. They said that when when widespread rioting broke out last summer, practically nothing was known about the makeup and aims of the various factions arrayed against the Shah, especially the Moslem fundamentalists who appeared to have the best organization and the largest following.

C.I.A. Estimate of Danger Disputed

"The C.I.A. simply missed the whole thing," said one high-ranking official, adding that when the rioting began, the agency was putting the final touches on an intelligence estimate that said the Shah faced no significant internal threats.

Intelligence officers contend that the failure to predict the revolt and to identify the main elements of the Shah's opposition stemmed from the lack of interest of Administration policymakers in Iranian politics. State Department and White House officials disputed this, and one said that more than a year ago, the C.I.A. was asked to prepare a study on the impact of Moslem traditionalists on the stability of such countries as Iran, Turkey and Pakistan. The agency was said by this aide to have reported that it could not find anyone to do it.

One immediate result of the Iranian crisis is a review of the policy governing arms sales to Iran and to other allies.

Although the acceleration of American arms deliveries to Iran and the Middle East stemmed from the dramatic increase in the price of oil after 1973, it also reflected the view that Iran was a pillar of stability in the area and a bulwark against the expansion of Soviet influence into regions surrounding the Indian Ocean.

Iranian Arms Were Not Cut Back

In the Nixon-Ford years, with the United States cutting back on its global military commitments, the Shah was sold more than $10 billion in advanced weapons. The Carter Administration, despite its goal of reducing arms sales, has continued this practice, agreeing to deals exceeding $5 billion during 1977-78.

But these sales are acknowledged to have created a new and serious security risk. "The worst contingency," a Pentagon official said, "is the possibility of an anti-American regime coming to power and having those weapons arrayed against us. But even a neutralist Iran, or one weakened by continuing strife, would pose huge new problems in the Gulf."

As a result, National Security Council aides have begun to question the strategy of relying heavily on local powers to protect American interests and, according to one, the Administration is accelerating programs for training and equipping special American combat units for combat in the Persian Gulf.

Officials agree, however, that forces for intervening in the area would be of little use in dealing with crises like the one in Iran, which is largely a case of social turmoil growing out of the tensions of rapid modernization.

In the short run, they said, better intelligence would be necessary to enable the Administration to anticipate domestic problems in critical countries.

'Regional Influentials' Get Priority

But in the longer term, they maintained, Iran should not be seen as an isolated case, but perhaps indicative of the problems that countries such as Saudi Arabia, Brazil or Nigeria might soon face. Like Iran, these "regional influentials," as Mr. Brzezinski has termed them, have been accorded high priority in Administration policy, and all have embarked on ambitious development programs and tentative moves toward liberalization.

In part these steps toward liberalization stemmed from the Administration's emphasis on human rights, and some officials acknowledged that the policy may have added to Iranian political strains. At the same time, they argued that the reforms initiated in Iran in recent years were not stimulated only by American pressure, but rather reflected the Shah's recognition that continued political stability required a gradual move toward democracy.

As a result, officials contend the Administration's human rights policy played a minimal role in the current crisis.

Whether Iran and other key third world nations can make an orderly transition and what role the United States can play in the process have become dominant questions for the Administration.

"The problem of assisting these countries through modernization and liberalization is probably the biggest challenge we face," one high-ranking official said, "because for all our talk, we really don't know how to do it."

NEW YORK TIMES, November 15, 1978, P3

Strife Cripples Iran's Economy

Cutbacks in Iran's Economic Development Program

	Program	Description	Approximate value of cutback
CANCELLED			
1.	Shahestan Pahlavi Project	Huge housing development on the northern outskirts of Teheran where all government officers were to be relocated; a sort of Brasilia in the Middle East.	Several billion dollars
2.	Teheran Metro	Iran's first subway, which was to be built by a French company.	$5 billion
3.	Isfahan Aryamehr Iron and Steel Complex	Expansion of this industrial plant to a capacity of 10 million tons a year from current capacity of 600,000 tons by 1980.	Not available
4.	Astara-Gorgan Highway	A 470-mile, six-lane highway running along the Caspian Seacoast.	$2 billion
5.	Abadan Lube Oil Plant	A joint venture between the National Iranian Oil Company and the Shell Oil Company	$300 million
6.	Peugeot-Citroën Plant	A joint venture with the Iran National Car Company, Peugeot-Citroën, expected to produce 100,000 Peugeot 305 sedans a year at the facility.	$450 million
7.	Volkswagen Plant	Another joint venture with the Iran National Car Company, the plant that would have produced 300,000 Rabbits a year.	Not available
8.	Shah Reza Industrial Park	A complex to be built south of Isfahan as a joint venture between West Germany's Krupp and Iran's Industrial and Development Renovation Organization.	$3.1 billion
9.	AWAC Airplanes	The planned purchase of seven sophisticated air surveillance Boeing airplanes.	$1.7 billion

In addition, other projects have been curtailed. see Page D6.

The New York Times / Nov. 28, 1978

Amid Chaos, Planners Alter Goals Sharply

By YOUSSEF M. IBRAHIM

Special to The New York Times

TEHERAN, Iran, Nov. 27 — The six-month-old civil revolt that continues to grip Iran has brought the nation's economy to the brink of paralysis.

Banks are barely functioning because of sporadic strikes and slow-downs and the damage done by demonstrators at thousands of bank branches. As bills go unpaid and new letters of credit go unissued, a severe liquidity crisis has developed.

Thousands of tons of imported food, raw materials and industrial goods are sitting in the ports, blocked by rebellious customs officials. At least 60,000 factory workers have been laid off. Productivity in all Government and private industries has been severely curtailed by power failures and a scarcity of natural gas.

More Convulsions Ahead

In addition, despite Government assertions that oil production has returned to its normal level of six million barrels a day, there are daily reports of trouble in the oilfields. Work slow-downs continue among the 67,000 workers who produce Iran's oil, which accounts for almost all of the country's annual revenues of $22 billion.

These problems have become a nightmare for Iran's economic planners, who already forecast a major cutback in economic development and more serious convulsions for the economy over the next two years. The planners are waiting for order to be restored before assessing the damage.

"We are running around like a chicken without a head," said a senior official at the Ministry of Finance, one of the few officials who would consent to an interview.

Even as he sat talking in his office, he was interrupted by several telephone calls — all bad news. The employees of Iran's central bank had struck to protest the arrest of a banker. Several hundred white-collar employees of the National Iranian Oil Company, which oversees Iran's oil production, were staging a sit-in at company headquarters. And a call for a general strike was issued by the mullahs to protest the army's violent crushing of a demonstration in the holy city of Mashad.

Despite all the chaos, however, a few things are beginning to grow clear to the economic planners:

¶Iran will have to forget its ambition of becoming a modern industrial society by the mid-1980's.

¶A change in development strategy, already being worked out, will divert funds away from lavish defense and industry programs and toward the long-neglected agricultural sector, social services and labor-intensive domestic industries that meet basic needs such as food and housing.

¶These shifts in spending patterns will mean a sharp reduction in imports from the West and thus a loss of several billion dollars in sales for the American, European and Japanese multinational companies that have accounted for nearly 85 percent of Iran's imports (which last year totaled $16 billion).

"What is going to happen here is major surgery," the senior official in the Ministry of Finance said. "By next February, assuming things have calmed down, we will have an entirely new outlook on our economic future."

Among other things, the economic planners of Iran must cope with a loss of oil revenues. This loss is expected to be $1.5 billion to $2 billion by the end of Iran's fiscal year, March 31. In addition, the huge raises granted to all employees by the Government, ranging from 40 percent to as much as 100 percent, will add about $2 billion in expenses through March, and more than $4 billion in the next fiscal year.

There is still no way to estimate what the production slowdown will cost the Government in reduced tax revenues and other losses. But a conservative estimate places the total at close to $4 billion over the six months of civil strife.

Bankers here also estimate that a total of $3 billion has been taken out of the country since June by private entrepreneurs who were frightened by the violence and fled with their money.

Economists, both inside and outside the Government, estimate that the Iranian Government will have to slash $10 billion from this year's $47 billion budget. The Government has various options, however, to make up for this deficit. Apart from cutting military and other purchases, the Iranian Government plans to go into debt.

Surge of Inflation Expected

"The Government's attitude is that if we can't find a political solution we don't care if we print money for a while," a well-placed United States official said here.

Apparently there are no plans for coping with the surge of inflation that is sure to follow the sharp salary increases and the shortages of some commodities that are already appearing. The inflation rate, which slowed to 14 percent from 30 percent in 1976 and 1977, seems destined to shoot back up to 30 percent early next year, economic analysts agree.

Unemployment is also all but certain to return ne : year. With the flight of private capital and a crippling of demand and supply, the private sector (which accounts for one-third of Iran's gross national product of about $70 billion) has been deeply hurt.

Iran's credit rating in international money markets is a casualty of the nation's upheaval. Economists here say that Iran may need to borrow up to $4 billion next year, and they say the money will be hard to find until political stability returns.

Setbacks for Corporations

The foreign companies that do business with Iran have also encountered bad news.

E. I. du Pont de Nemours & Company, which has a 40 percent stake in a large polyester plant that started production this year, reportedly took a big loss on its operation. To help the plant compete in world markets, the Iranian Government had promised Du Pont and its partner in the venture (a wealthy Iranian investor) several protective measures, including freedom from import duties on raw materials. But when the factory started production this year, none of the promises materialized.

"It would be unconscionable to extend such protection to this venture, which favors some wealthy people, and to take the money away from basic needs at home now," a Government official said.

France's Régie Autonomes des Transports de Paris, which hoped to receive a $5 billion contract to build Teheran's first subway, was told the deal had been canceled. "How can we spend that kind of money on a subway when we still have slums around the city and no housing for most of the middle class?" an Iranian deputy minister said.

More Projects Deteriorate

The cancellation of the Iranian nuclear program, announced a few weeks ago, will cost three Western companies — France's Creusot-Loire, West Germany's Kraftwerk Union and America's Westinghouse Electric Corporation — a total of more than $30 billion in potential sales to Iran.

An American steel company expects its sales in Iran to slump next year. "I forecast a 50 percent reduction in my sales next year and a 30 percent increase in expenses because of the huge raises the Iranian employees are demanding," the American manager of the company's Teheran office said.

Iranian officials remain unclear on how much extra spending will go to agriculture next year, but a significant increase in subsidies to farmers is expected. Prices paid to farmers for wheat have already gone up 20 percent this year and are due for a 50 percent increase next year. Subsidies are planned for cotton, barley, eggs and poultry. The budget outlay for agriculture is to rise far above this year's $2 billion.

The move was prompted by a drastic drop in agricultural production in Iran over the last few years and a huge flight of farmers to the industrialized urban centers, where high wages were being paid. This year wheat production dropped 10 percent to 5.5 million tons from last year's output. Barley output fell 18 percent, and rice 10 percent. Iran, which was a net exporter of food a decade ago, today imports $2 billion worth of food a year.

NEW YORK TIMES,
November 28, 1978, S4 P1

SHAH NAMES AN OPPOSITION LEADER TO HEAD CIVILIAN CABINET IN IRAN

SAYS HE WON'T LEAVE

New Nominee a Respected Opponent — Regency System Ruled Out

By JOHN VINOCUR
Special to The New York Times

TEHERAN, Iran, Saturday, Dec. 30 — An opposition leader was chosen yesterday by Shah Mohammed Riza Pahlevi to form a civilian government. Later yesterday, he said the Shah had agreed to leave Iran temporarily and turn over power to a regency council, but this was denied by the imperial palace.

A spokesman at the palace said last night that "the Shah has no intention" of leaving or of turning over power. A regency council can be created, under the Iranian Constitution, only if the Shah dies or leaves the country, the spokesman said, reiterating that leaving was not the Shah's intention.

Shahpur Bakhtiar, the 62-year-old opposition leader chosen by the Shah, reported the monarch's plans to the National Front, the organization grouping the major Iranian opposition parties.

Shah's Request to Form Government

Mr. Bakhtiar told an official of the front that the Shah had asked him Thursday night to form a civilian government to replace the military regime set up to bring Iran's revolt against the monarchy under control. It was in this context that Mr. Bakhtiar informed the front of what he said was the Shah's decision, according to a spokesman for the group.

Several American reporters were given substantially the same information by Mr. Bakhtiar when he was reached here last night and asked about the report.

However, in an atmosphere thick with confusion that appeared to mirror the chaotic conditions in the capital, an adviser to Mr. Bakhtiar who is expected to be in his cabinet said early this morning that he thought there would not be a regency council, which would require the Shah to leave the country, but an advisory council that would assume some of the powers of the Shah and act as a buffer between the palace and the Government.

He also said that there had been discussions about the Shah taking "a very short trip," but probably within Iran, possibly to Kish Island, which is one of the Shah's favorite resorts.

General's Resignation Denied

The National Front spokesman said that Mr. Bakhtiar had told some of the front's members that the chief of the military Government, Gen. Gholam Riza Azhari, intended to resign last night. The Iranian Ambassador to the United States, Ardeshir Zahedi, who has been serving as a go-between in attempts to form a civilian government, is in Teheran now and denied in a telephone conversation with reporters that a resignation had been offered.

But Mr. Zahedi said it was hoped that Mr. Bakhtiar could form a government quickly.

A palace spokesman denied reports that the Shah's mother and his three youngest children had left Iran. [In Washington, the State Department said, however, that the Shah's mother had arrived at McGuire Air Force Base, in New Jersey, Friday afternoon, and United Press International reported later from Los Angeles that her plane had arrived there.]

The spokesman said the Shah would quickly appoint Mr. Bakhtiar to head a new government as soon as he succeeded in forming one. If that happened today, for example, the spokesman added, the Shah would act immediately.

He said that the Shah and Mr. Bakhtiar could have discussed the creation of an advisory council to assume some of the Shah's powers, but with the ruler remaining in the country.

Mr. Zahedi indicated that the Shah would probably meet this morning with the leaders of the two houses of the Iranian Parliament. He declined to give details of the meeting.

Last night, the official press agency, Pars, distributed a dispatch that it restricted until today for release, saying that the Shah had said he would "step aside and allow a regency council to be formed to run affairs in his absence."

The dispatch was in the form of a mimeographed release distributed to subscribers to the agency in Teheran. But Mr. Zahedi said that Mr. Bakhtiar had been misquoted and that the agency had withdrawn its dispatch as erroneous.

The National Front reported that its leadership would meet this morning to discuss the new developments.

During the day the country tried, on the Moslem sabbath, to cope with the now daily dose of rioting, shooting and economic disintegration. Oil production and refinery activity, a central factor in the struggle for power, was reported by an industry source at about 350,000 barrels, well under the country's minimum needs for heating oil and fuel.

But a foreign oil expert with an authoritative knowledge of the industry here said that the heating-oil and gas shortages "can get only marginally worse, and if refinery activity continues at present pace, there should be no total shortage of oil."

Explaining his political assignment, Mr. Bakhtiar said early yesterday that consultations would take several days and involve "politicians outside the front, who have not been involved in the corruption of the past 25 years," and religious leaders "with whom I have good relations."

Progress in Talk With Shah

In a brief interview, he said that he had seen the Shah Thursday night and "had the impression that we made progress in finding his role. He has his conditions, and the front has its own. I'm going to try and see if we can work something out."

Last week, anticipating his present problem, Mr. Bakhtiar said: "If the Shah agrees publicly to a reduced role and the United States declares that it would not support him if he goes back on his commitment, then I believe many opposition leaders would end their insistence that he abdicate, or join a coalition government and even accept that he remain as commander in chief of the armed forces."

Most Western leaders gave Mr. Bakhtiar a somewhat better chance to form a cabinet than Gholam Hussein Sadighi, a former Interior Minister active in the early 1950's, whom the Shah asked almost two weeks ago to try to set up a cabinet.

In Mr. Bakhtiar's favor were his credentials as an opponent of the Shah, his refusal over the years to cooperate with the imperial house in any way, his leadership of the Bakhtiar clan, which includes many Iranian oil workers, and support for his effort from Ardeshir Zahedi, the Iranian Ambassador to the United States, who has close ties with the military leadership.

Operating against Mr. Bakhtiar was the momentum of the opposition to the Shah in the streets and the likelihood that his initiative would be rejected by the influential Moslem leader, Ayatollah Ruhollah Khomeini.

Electricity to Factories to Be Cut

Meanwhile, a state of near paralysis of the economy continued. With the central bank closed, almost all public transportation suspended and few businesses functioning, electrical-power officials in Teheran announced that all current to factories would be cut off. The state radio and television networks each limited their broadcasting to a single station.

The effectiveness of the general strike was expected to be heightened today, which is normally a business day, because the Ayatollah Khomeini has called for a national day of mourning in honor of those killed in clashes with the army.

National Front spokesmen described the situation as "the start of the period of chaos," but declined to suggest that a decisive moment would come over the weekend.

Thurday night, protesters challenged the 9 P.M. military curfew in the capital for the first time. Troops opened fire at many locations at opponents of the Shah, who shouted "Allah Is Great" from rooftops. A reporter at the city mortuary said today that he counted 14 bodies with fresh bullet wounds.

There was shooting and car burning in Teheran, and the state radio said that mobs had burned banks in the city of Ahwaz. There were four dead in rioting in the provinces, the radio reported.

U.S. MOVING CARRIER

Hopes Civilian Government Will End Recent Chaos That Cut Oil Output

---

By BERNARD GWERTZMAN
Special to The New York Times

WASHINGTON, Dec. 29 — The United States ordered a carrier task force to depart from the Philippines today for possible movement to the Persian Gulf area if the situation in Iran warranted it, Administration officials said.

With the report from Iran that Shah Mohammed Riza Pahlevi had asked a leading opposition figure to head a civilian government to replace the current military regime, the Administration was taking steps to prepare for major trouble in Iran, including possible Soviet moves to take advantage of changes.

But officials were also hoping that a civilian government might bring stability to Iran and end the chaos that has halted oil production.

Shah's Future Unclear

The future of the Shah, the American officials said, was unclear. What was crucial was whether his opponents would agree to a new civilian government, with the Shah remaining in power.

United Press International reported that the Shah would temporarily leave Iran, but a senior State Department official said tonight after speaking with the American Embassy in Teheran, "We have no reason to believe that the Shah is leaving."

There was particular concern at the White House, officials said, over what they have repeatedly described as steppped-up Soviet propaganda broadcasts to Iran, backing efforts to topple the Shah. Officials also said that some Soviet planes had recently flown over Iranian territory near the border, but that there were no signs of Soviet units going on any special alert status in that area.

Concern, but No Air of Crisis

But there was no air of crisis in the Administration. President Carter remained at Camp David, where he has been mixing pleasure with work all week, and Secretary of Defense Harold Brown flew to California for a holiday. Zbigniew Brzezinski, the adviser on national security, was also not at work today.

Yesterday, officials said that consideration was being given to the sending of a carrier task force into the Persian Gulf if the Soviet Union showed signs of becoming directly involved in Iranian affairs.

This afternoon, in response to questions, officials said that the carrier Constellation, with 80 to 90 fighter planes, and escort ships, including destroyers and tankers, were ordered to leave Subic Bay in the Philippines, and proceed to the South China Sea, where the task force was to await further orders. It will take about two days for the force to reach its destination at the entrance to the Strait of Malacca, the passage that leads to the Indian Ocean.

Officials said that no orders had been given to proceed further at this time.

As the task force's orders were made public, the consensus of key American policymakers continued to be that the Shah's troubles were still primarily internal and that there was little the United States could do to restore stability in Iran.

For that reason, there was interest in reports from Teheran that the Shah had asked a leading opposition figure, Shah-

pur Bakhtiar, to form a civilian government.

Mr. Bakhtiar, a member of the National Front, the major political opposition group, might insist that the Shah leave the country at least temporarily to allow order to be restored. But officials here said that, as of late this afternoon, they had no confirmation of reports that the Shah had in fact decided to leave Iran temporarily.

This has always been seen as a possibility, but as recently as noon today, the State Department spokesman, Hodding Carter 3d, was expressing support for the Shah and confidence that he could remain in Iran as part of a transition to a new government of national reconciliation.

The State Department telephoned the United States Embassy in Teheran to check on the report from the United Press International bureau there that the Shah had agreed to leave the country. The embassy, in the early morning hours of Saturday, Teheran time, said that it could confirm that Mr. Bakhtiar had been asked to form a government but that it knew of nothing to back the report of the Shah's departure.

Two special groups have been set up here to monitor developments in Iran. One at the White House is headed by David L. Aaron, deputy to Zbigniew Brzezinski, the President's adviser on national security. It has been involved in such decisions as the movement of the carrier task force.

A larger interagency group headed by David D. Newsom, Under Secretary for Political Affairs, has been meeting at the State Department to discuss contingency problems dealing with such subjects as the possible evacuation of the 35,000 Americans in Iran and the removal of sensitive military equipment if the country was thrown into total disorder.

No U.S. Evacuation Planned

But the department spokesman, Mr. Carter, stressed today that "we are not planning any evacuation. We don't consider the situation to warrant an evacuation program."

Mr. Carter was asked about the American view of Soviet broadcasts to Iran, and he said that "what we seek is action by all parties to help stability in Iran."

"We've had a number of conversations with the Soviet Union, about this," he said.

In particular, the Administration was concerned by an article in the Soviet party daily, *Pravda*, yesterday that accused the United States of "inadmissible interference" in Iranian affairs.

Reporters were told that there were broadcasts in at least two languages to Iran that "we don't find helpful."

Shah's Mother Reported in U.S.

LOS ANGELES, Dec. 29 (UPI) — The mother of Shah Mohammed Riza Pahlevi of Iran, several Iranian Government officials and other members of the Shah's family arrived in Los Angeles tonight aboard an Iranian air force jet. [State Department officials confirmed earlier today that the Shah's mother had arrived at at McGuire Air Force Base in N.J.]

The white Boeing 747 jumbo jet touched down at Los Angeles International Airport at 8:55 P.M. (11:55 P.M. New York time) and taxied to a remote area of the airport.

Robert Joyce, a Pan American Airways spokesman, said the Shah's mother, who is in her 90's, was aboard the plane as well as "several Government staff members and other members of the Shah's immediate family."

The spokesman said the entire entourage will stay in Beverly Hills at the home of the Shah's sister, Princess Ashraf.

The plane was hidden from view by a Pan Am maintenance hangar and dozens of armed security guards, and the police kept reporters and photographers far from the area.

"At no time will any reporters be allowed to see the plane," an airport official said.

The jet flew to Los Angeles, reportedly from Teheran. It made a brief refueling stop at McGuire Air Force Base in New Jersey.

The 18-year-old Crown Prince, Riza Pahlevi, who has been training as a jet pilot at Reese Air Force Base in Lubbock, Tex., was reported to be "on vacation" in the United States.

NEW YORK TIMES, December 30, 1978, P1

6

The Palestinians

When the Arabs of Haifa were urged by their communal leaders to get out of the way of the fighting in 1948 they were assured, "You will return soon." Elsewhere in Palestine the rapid departure of British police and municipal servants left the Arab residents fearful and disorganized. They fled on their own initiative. One and a half million Palestinian Arabs left the scene of the first Arab-Israeli war, and have been waiting 30 years to return to their homes. Of these, 500,000 live in refugee campus in Jordan and Lebanon, while another million are scattered throughout the Arab world, with 200,000 in the Gulf and 100,000 in Egypt.

The Palestinians have remained unassimilated in the midst of the Arab states which have harbored them since 1948. The reasons for the non-assimilation of the Palestinians are many and complex: the poorest refugees represented a great financial burden to the host countries, which could only get UN aid for them so long as they remained in displaced persons camps. Of the educated elite of the Palestinians, many did find careers for themselves in Egypt, the Fertile Crescent and the Gulf, but in the highly particularized, clique-structured politics of the Arab states, the Palestinians would always be made to feel the outsiders. In Jordan the refugee elite did come to dominate the politics of the Hashimite throne, in alliance with the million and a half Palestinians annexed to the Kingdom of Transjordan in 1948. In Lebanon, Christians opposed the assimilation of the Palestinians on the grounds that it would upset the balance between Christians and Muslims. Nevertheless, Christian Palestinians were issued Lebanese passports at the insistence of the Maronite leaders in a display of realpolitik.

But above all the factor which prevented the Palestinians themselves from seeking assimilation was their desire to return home. It is a desire which has experienced an ebb and flow of hope and disappointment in the last 30 years. The prospect of peace in the Middle East in 1978 being now closer than ever, the prospect of some form of return is tantalizingly real. At the same time, the closeness of peace gives rise to tough questions about the nature of the Palestinian return.

The most radical Palestinians and their Libyan and Iraqi supporters urge the destruction of Zionism in Palestine. Colonel Muammar Qaddafi of Libya insists that all post-1948 immigrants to Israel return to their country of origin, while Iraq has widely publicized an invitation to Iraqi Jews to return. Other positions suggest that the original mandated area of Palestine pass under secular control, ruled without distinction between Arab, Christian and Jew. They demand that Israel give up its law of return, which extends privileges of citizenship to any Jew wishing to immigrate. Additionally, more radical Palestinian representatives call for Israel to make reparations to the million and a half refugees.

More moderate Palestinians call for Israel to relinquish the West Bank and the Gaza region, occupied in 1967, and accept the formation of a Palestinian state there. This position assumes that the million and a half refugees will return in large numbers and join the residents of Gaza and the former Jordanian citizens on the West Bank. There is some question whether the territory, which is smaller than Israel and lacking the contiguous boundaries of Israel, could support the same population as that in Israel, of three million. This plan, though, is backed by Israel's neighbors, Syria, Jordan and Egypt. The Arab states authorized the Palestinians to negotiate for "any piece of Arab land relinquished by Israel" at the Rabat (Morocco) conference in 1974.

The consensus of moderate Arabs on this position poses a quandary for Israel, which prefers to see the Gaza returned to Egyptian control and the West Bank to Jordan. Israel's two old enemies represent at least a known factor. Israel has often expressed the fear that a Palestinian entity on its borders would be an unstable haven for terrorists. Spokesmen for Israeli views have long asserted that the events of the 1948 war made Jordan the *de facto* Palestinian state, in which Palestinians outnumbered residents of Transjordan two to one.

Undermining the chances for a settlement favorable to the Israeli position is the almost total rift between the West Bankers and their former monarch King Hussein. Having renounced sovereignty over the West Bank at Rabat in 1974, Hussein insists he will not speak for the West Bankers unless they ask him to do so. There is little chance of that now, as in the wake of Israeli municipal elections on the West Bank in 1976 the pro-Hashimite leadership lost power to radical, Palestinian nationalists. Further, if Hussein were to resume sovereignty over the West Bank as a Palestinian entity he would have to invite the return of all Palestinians, including the guerrilla groups who tried to overthrow him in September of 1970. The king's suppression of the guerrilla groups is bitterly remembered as "Black September" in radical leftist Palestinian circles. The king's subsequent close ties to the US army is another obstacle for reconciliation with the militant leftists.

Israel claims that if the West Bank is to have autonomy, it cannot do much better than its existing municipal autonomy, under which the West Bankers enjoy municipal self-government. Israeli defense minister Moshe Dayan concedes, however, that the scope and visibility of the Israeli military government on the West Bank would have to be reduced. The present Israeli government of Menachem Begin adamantly opposes relinquishing its military presence on the West Bank or extending sovereignty to the West Bankers.

The most moderate Arabs, however, insist on the rights of the Palestinians on the West Bank to self-determination, almost certainly a step toward establishment of a sovereign state with full control of its security and foreign alliances. President Anwar Sadat is firmly committed to this view, though he envisions it taking place gradually, over a transition period during which the Israelis would become convinced of the counterproductive nature of their occupation. Syria and Jordan insist on the principle of sovereign rights for the Palestinians.

What do the Palestinians want? Without a government, with a host of spokesmen and a range of political ideologies that spans the spectrum of the Arab world, the Palestinians have had a difficult time making themselves heard in the world forums. In 1974 at Rabat the Arab states recognized Yasir Arafat's Palestinian Liberation Organization (PLO) as the "sole legitimate representative of the Palestinian People." The same year the PLO won observer status in the United Nations. These two events seemed to seal the authority of Arafat, who had contended with other Palestinian groups for the position. The results of the West Bank municipal elections in 1976, in which the key mayoralties went to PLO supporters, was a further mandate for the PLO's leadership of the Palestinian movement.

Yet the events of 1978 have partly eroded the PLO's preeminent position. The Sadat peace initiative caught Arafat in between moderate members of the PLO who sought conciliation with Israel and radicals who hoped to scuttle the peace initiative. Arafat, whose approach had proved effective earlier in avoiding statements of principles and ideologies, was unable to commit himself either to or against Sadat's move. Disappointment in both camps resulted. A PLO terrorist raid into Israel shocked sympathizers of the PLO abroad, who hoped to see the organization act as a government in exile now that it had won UN status. Arafat's denunciation of a terrorist attack on Egyptian officials in Cypress angered radical Palestinians. The Israeli raid in Southern Lebanon weakened the organization's autonomy and left it more dependent on Syrian goodwill. The rival factions of Palestinians, Abu-Nidal and the Democratic Front, both backed by Iraq, have engaged the PLO in a bloody series of vendettas.

As peace draws nearer, the cohesion of the Palestinian movement becomes all the more important. The PLO finds peace raising more questions than answers. While the Arab states insist on the PLO being brought into peace negotiations, the PLO itself may not survive the burden of being the sole representative of the Palestinian people.

The Homeland Issue

SAUDIS SUPPORT PALESTINIAN STATE

King Khalid and other Saudi leaders will reportedly press President Carter on Palestinian question during Carter's visit; officials are dismayed over recent Carter statement indicating opposition to establishment of independent Palestinian state   (NEW YORK TIMES,   January 2, 1978,   P3)

CARTER DISCLOSES REFERENDUM PLAN

President Carter discloses, during a meeting with reporters on flight to US, his plan for Palestinian referendum, which was proposed privately to Middle East leaders he saw during foreign trip; declares US would endorse limited-choice referendum for Palestinians living on West Bank of Jordan River and on Gaza Strip on their political future, but choices would not include independent Palestinian nation; plan calls for choice of Palestinian alignment with Jordan or for plan of international administration of 2 regions; holds that Palestinian problem can be resolved through an interim solution for joint administration of areas by Israel, Jordan, Palestinians and perhaps UN; Carter reveals that King Hussein has not been urged to participate at this point in Egypt-Israel negotiations; claims support for negotiations from Iran, Jordan and Saudi Arabia; holds that Syria, Iraq, Libya and "more radical Arabs" continue to seek destruction of Israel and are opposed to peace initiatives   (NEW YORK TIMES,   January 8, 1978,   P1)

SADAT CALLS FOR TRANSITION

President Sadat says he could accept President Carter's proposal calling for 5-year transition period leading to self-determination for Palestinians with West Bank and Gaza Strip administered by Israel, Jordan, Palestinians and perhaps the UN   (NEW YORK TIMES,   January 9, 1978,   P7)

HOMELAND ESTABLISHMENT SEEN ESSENTIAL

Commentator Ray Vicker sees establishment of Palestinian homeland as prerequisite to Middle East peace settlement, and issue which will ultimately determine success or failure of current round of negotiations initiated by President Anwar Sadat; maintains that peace negotiators will be making grave error if they try to circumvent question of Palestinian self-determination, and instead attempt diplomatic subterfuge which would create appearance of independent Palestinian state which would in reality be dominated by Israel; suggests that key to compromise may lie in mutual wish of Israel and most Arab nations that moderation, rather than radicalism, will prevail among Palestinians; asserts that Israeli armed forces and settlements in occupied areas should be phased out; concludes that if Israel refuses to make concessions, result could be another war which would jeopardize Israel far more than would a neighboring Palestinian state   (WALL STREET JOURNAL,   January 13, 1978,   P12)

SELF-DETERMINATION PLAN PROPOSED

Professor Stanley Hoffmann holds durable Middle East settlement hinges mainly on solution to Palestinian problem; suggests only practical solution would be creation of international trusteeship in Gaza Strip and West Bank during transition period; supervisors' role would be to see that Palestinians in both areas freely elected delegates who would then negotiate with Israel and Jordan the terms of self-determination referendum   (NEW YORK TIMES,   January 22, 1978,   S4   P19)

DIVERGENT VIEWS NOTED

Commentator Felix Kessler examines Egyptian-Israeli deadlock over Palestinian issue and what constitutes peace and security; notes some observers think that Israel's spurned proposals for Palestinian home rule and Israeli military control in occupied territories probably go further toward eventual creation of Palestinian state than Arabs and even Israelis might realize; diplomat points out that once any area is given some form of self-rule, historical predecent without exception has gone in direction of independence; Palestinians claim Prime Minister Menachem Begin's offer of Israeli citizenship would actually submerge their own nationalism within enlarged Israel; Begin's Israeli critics claim opposite; hold their Zionist nation would develop into secular binational state, official goal of Palestine Liberation Organization   (WALL STREET JOURNAL,   January 25, 1978,   P1)

PALESTINE SUMMIT SOUGHT

Former Egyptian Foreign Minister Ismail Fahmy, who resigned his post when President Sadat said he would visit Israel, calls for summit conference of Arab leaders and formation of Palestinian government in exile   (NEW YORK TIMES,   February 4, 1979,   P3)

KUWAIT HOME TO PALESTINIANS

Series on Palestinian communities in Middle East notes 250,000 Palestinians reside in Kuwait—accounting for nearly one-quarter of sheikdom's population; finds Palestinians are recognized as aliens and are regarded with some suspicion; finds widespread feeling of alienation among them   (NEW YORK TIMES,   February 19, 1978,   P16)

PALESTINIANS DIVIDED ON AIMS

First in series of articles on Palestinians cites comments of several prominent Palestinians, noting there is wide difference of opinion among 3.5 million Palestinians scattered throughout Middle East; reports poorest and most desperate still dream of returning to land that is now Israel, while others, particularly those living in Jordan and occupied territories, take more moderate stand toward Israel; holds Egyptian President Sadat's peace initiatives came at time when Palestinian cause seemed to be at low point, and notes that while some Palestinians initially expressed hope that Sadat would be successful in achieving breakthrough they now feel his efforts have failed and that Palestine Liberation Organization (PLO) is "framework of Palestinian peoplehood"; reports that most Palestinians feel their relationship with host country is uneasy, while others simply want an identity rather than residence   (NEW YORK TIMES,   February 19, 1978,   P1)

PROBLEMS OF 'HOMELAND' EXAMINED

Second in series of articles on Palestinians describes problems involved in creating Palestinian homeland; notes there is increasing international agreement to create homeland or some other "entity" on West Bank of Jordan River and Gaza Strip; reports solution, however, raises several unresolved questions, such as whether homeland should be independent or placed under control of Jordan; notes there is widespread support for Palestine Liberation Organization (PLO) although not necessarily for leadership of Yasir Arafat, and that most Palestinians say they would accept Jordan over Israel; holds very few Palestinians support Israeli Prime Minister Begin's proposal, allowing self-determination but giving Israel right to retain troops in area, holding Begin's plan is worse than continued occupation or annexation   (NEW YORK TIMES, February 20, 1978,   P1)

TERRORIST IMPACT QUESTIONED

Washington Post editorial chides Israeli Prime Minister Begin's suggestion that Palestinian state would be governed by terrorists; notes remark was made after Palestinian radicals killed Egyptian editor Youseff el-Sebai in Cyprus; notes Egyptian President Sadat and other Arab moderates hope for Palestinian government based on stability and growth; claims Begin's comments rekindled old Israeli fears   (WASHINGTON POST,   February 21, 1978,   P16)

PALESTINIAN AIMS ANALYZED

Commentator Anthony Lewis cites recent *Times* series on Palestinians as example of presenting picture of group of people not well understood; notes most Palestinians seek homeland and envision it co-existing with Israel; discusses possible dangers arising from President Sadat's peace initiative with Israel, namely growing extremism if initiative fails; also notes that while people differ on Palestine Liberation Organization leadership, they see the

organization as embodiment of Palestinian identity and nationalism   (NEW YORK TIMES,   February 23, 1978,   P21)

EGYPT'S NEW MOOD ANALYZED

News analysis of anti-Palestinian feeling among Egyptians, following assassination of *Al Ahram* editor-in-chief Youssef el-Sebai by terrorists in Cyprus and by reports that Palestine Liberation Organization representatives who were sent to seize terrorists aided Cypriot troops in battle against Egyptian commandos at Larnaca Airport; holds Egyptians feel they are recipients of Palestinian ingratitude, despite loss of 100,000 Egyptian lives in struggles against Israel; finds Egypt has lost patience with bickering among Palestinian factions and are beginning to question where their best interests lie   (NEW YORK TIMES,   February 28, 1978,   P3)

P.L.O. SCORES EGYPTIAN ACTIONS

Palestine Liberation Organization (PLO) news agency editorial accuses Egypt of imposing "mass punishment" on Palestinians in move to disengage itself from Palestinian cause and Arab world; declares that decision to withdraw special rights of Palestinians living in Egypt reflects President Sadat's willingness to abase himself to reach a settlement; PLO sources say they fear Sadat's next move may be to expel Palestinians, estimated as numbering 30,000 in Egypt   (NEW YORK TIMES,   March 1, 1978,   P12)

SYRIAN COMMENTS ON U.S. STANCE

Syrian Ambassador to US Sabah Kabbani reminds US that President Carter, speaking in Clinton, Massachusetts, in March 1977, publicly acknowledged that Palestinians have a right to a homeland; contends that Palestinians inevitably will fight until they have homeland; asserts that Israelis have pattern of occupying increasing amounts of Arab lands under pretext of military security needs, and recent Israeli reprisal for guerrilla raid means more land will be occupied; accuses Prime Minister Begin and his supporters in US of deflecting confrontation on Palestine issue by creating debate over aircraft offered to Egypt by US; contends that creation of Palestinian homeland is essential to peace in Middle East; urges US, as major world power and arms supplier to Israel, to act to bring Israel back to its international border with Lebanon lest new occupied territory be created   (NEW YORK TIMES, March 17, 1978,   P29)

HOMELAND PLANS REVIEWED

Author James Michener discusses proposal to combine West Bank of Jordan River and Gaza Strip with Israel in joint Israeli-Palestinian occupation; reviews 5 similar joint-occupation models on islands of Cyprus, Hispaniola, Ireland, New Guinea and Fiji; concludes that to expect Arabs and Jews to occupy territory jointly is unrealistic; claims aligning West Bank and Gaza Strip with Jordan to be governed by Arabs including Palestinians makes sense   (WASHINGTON POST,   April 26, 1978,   P27)

Courtesy of PLO

PLO Leader Yasir Arafat.

ARAFAT STRESSES GUARANTEES

Palestine Liberation Organization leader Yasir Arafat declares, in interview, that only possible solution to Middle East problem is for US and USSR to provide guarantees for Israel and a Palestinian state; contends Israel would have nothing to fear from a new Palestinian state preoccupied with its own problems, cites USSR-US declaration of October 1, 1977, as basis for a settlement; stresses that Palestinians have more need than Israel for peace guarantees; Arafat's military chief of staff Abu-Walid interjects that Palestinians are now a revolution but as a state will have a different outlook   (NEW YORK TIMES,   May 2, 1978,   P1)

PALESTINIAN OUTLOOK PROFILED

Commentator Anthony Lewis offers impressions of Palestinian consciousness based on meetings with Palestinians in Syria and in Beirut and on interview with Palestine Liberation Organization (PLO) leader Yasir Arafat; concludes that, with all its faults, most Palestinians seem to regard PLO as their collective voice; reports that feelings of pride and sensitivity seem universal among Palestinians, adding Arafat's claim that, although

Palestinians number less than 4 million, they have 112,000 students at universities throughout world; Arafat states that only "possible solution" of Israeli-Arab conflict is for independent Palestinian state and Israel to live under joint guarantee of US and USSR   (NEW YORK TIMES,   May 4, 1978,   P22)

WEST BANK ARABS DISSATISFIED

Discussion of complaints of citizens of Nablus in Israeli-occupied land on Jordan River's West Bank tells how Mayor Bassam Shakaa has not been given permission by Israeli military government to build three new power plants and drill new water wells for Nablus; says he received $10 million in pledges for projects from several Arab oil states; reports Israel wants to tie Nablus into Israeli electric grid; tells of rough raids and searches by occupation forces; says the more than 100,000 Palestinians in Nablus are independent and do not "collaborate" with Israeli occupiers   (CHRISTIAN SCIENCE MONITOR,   June 8, 1978,   P20)

JORDANIAN ROLE EXAMINED

Commentator Christopher Wren reports that Jordan appears unwilling to take on proposed role as guarantor of future of occupied West Bank and Gaza Strip; Jordanian officials say there is no point in discussing a Jordanian role so long as Israel refuses to work out some transition for self-determination for Palestinians; also note that Jordan surrendered its claim to speak for Palestinians at Arab League summit meeting in Rabat, Morocco, in 1974; Jordanian foreign policy strategist Sherif Abdul-Hamid el-Sharaf observes that Jordan is not ready to step in unless specifically asked to do so by Palestinians in occupied areas   (NEW YORK TIMES,   June 21, 1978,   P3)

EIGHT PROFESSORS BARRED

Israeli government denies 8 foreign professors, including 4 Americans, the right to teach at Bir Zeit University on West Bank; Bir Zeit, Palestinian national college, has been site of frequent political protests; University President Gabi Baramki scores decision, charging Israelis are attempting to ruin university; military official claims status of all temporary residents is subject to periodic review and denies harassment   (WASHINGTON POST,   June 24, 1978,   P21)

BETHLEHEM MAYOR ASKS AID

Mayor of Bethlehem Elias Freij appeals to Congress to approve direct aid to Jordan West Bank and Gaza Strip as means of helping bolster moderate Palestinian forces in those areas; both houses of Congress are considering legislation that would provide modest aid to promote Arab-Israeli economic cooperation, but far less than the $50 million per year sought by Freij; Freij assails Prime Minister Menachem Begin's Middle East peace proposal   (NEW YORK TIMES,   July 20, 1978,   P8)

WEST BANK RESENTMENT NOTED

Commentator Christopher Wren, sampling public opinion in calm town of Ramallah (Israeli-occupied West Bank), finds simmering resentment after 10 years of Israeli rule; chief causes are Israeli security forces' actions against Palestinian guerrillas, stern vigilance over population and fear of permanent land takeover by Israeli settlers; Mayor Karim Khalaf, a Palestine Liberation Organization (PLO) supporter, says that 400–500 town residents are in jail for alleged underground activity (NEW YORK TIMES, July 25, 1978, P2)

ZIONIST PROPOSES PALESTINIAN STATE

Professor Raanan Weitz, head of World Zionist Organization's Settlement Department distributes to Israeli Cabinet and Parliament members a plan calling for halt to Jewish settlement in nearly all Arab territory and eventual creation of independent Palestinian state; plan also calls for demilitarization of evacuated territories, which would be guaranteed by buffer zones of Jewish villages in northern Sinai and along Jordan River Valley; World Zionist Organization chairman Arieh Dulzin says Weitz has no authority to recommend proposals calling for Palestinian statehood; Shimon Peres, leader of opposition Labor Party, disassociates his party from Weitz plan; Begin government does not respond to Weitz's proposal, but observers note there is a competing plan suggested by hawkish Israeli Agricultural Minister Ariel Sharon which would concentrate permanent Israeli settlements in densely-populated areas of West Bank (NEW YORK TIMES, August 26, 1978, P97)

DAYAN ASSESSES WEST BANK

Israeli Foreign Minister Moshe Dayan surveys Palestinian Arab opinion in West Bank of Jordan River to assess what Palestinians feel about Israeli peace proposals that will be taken to Camp David summit; *Jerusalem Post* reports Dayan is considering dropping demand that Israeli troops handle security on West Bank and in Gaza if self-rule plan is accepted by Egypt at summit (NEW YORK TIMES, September 2, 1978, P7)

WEST BANK ARABS PROTEST

Two dozen West Bank Arab landowners appeal to Israeli Supreme Court to return land taken from them by Israeli military occupation; claim land is being "fraudulently" used for Israeli settlement after they were assured it would be used only for military purposes; case involves Toubas, near Nablus, and Beth El, near Ramallah; in related development Jewish settlers have reportedly moved into buildings still under construction on disputed site in Beth El (NEW YORK TIMES, September 15, 1978, P135)

P.L.O.'S DIPLOMATIC GAINS NOTED

Kathleen Teltsch finds PLO has made impressive gains in support from UN General Assembly members during current session; notes that while Arab countries have been able to round up majorities for anti-Israel resolutions, PLO is now enhancing its political status in its demands for inclusion on equal footing in Middle East negotiations; cites as indication of trend the naming of PLO to be sole recipient of Palestinian aid from UN Development Program; sees little likelihood of reversal in Congressional cut of $27 million in technical aid to UN (NEW YORK TIMES, December 25, 1978, P8)

The PLO

PALESTINIANS RALLY FOR P.L.O.

Some 10,000 Palestinians from all rival factions, in attempt to show that they will not be easily excluded from Middle East peace process, join in largest PLO rally to mark 13th year of their guerrilla activity; Yasir Arafat warns that there will be no stability in region without creation of independent Palestinian state; denounces US; Popular Front for Liberation of Palestine leader George Habash and Marxist Democratic Front for Liberation of Palestine leader Nayef Hawatmeh attend rally (NEW YORK TIMES, January 2, 1978, P3)

PALESTINIAN SOLUTION SOUGHT

Carter Administration officials report compromise between Israel and Egypt over Palestinian issue may be possible despite current deadlock, noting compromise would involve modifying Israeli Prime Minister Menachem Begin's peace plan to include eventual full self-determination for Palestinians in West Bank and Gaza Strip; hold issue is delicate one, since self-determination could lead to domination by Palestine Liberation Organization (PLO) radicals, but Israel, Egypt, Jordan and US reportedly oppose such domination, leading to speculation that acceptable agreement can be reached (NEW YORK TIMES, January 3, 1978, P1)

P.L.O. WARNS CARTER

Palestine Liberation Organization (PLO) spokesman Mahmoud Labadi says President Carter is vague and uncertain when he voices support for "legitimate rights" of Palestinians; says PLO demands sovereign, independent state (NEW YORK TIMES, January 5, 1978, P3)

United Nations

Palestinian refugees are scattered in several Middle East countries. This camp is located in Damascus.

P.L.O. REPRESENTATIVE KILLED

Said Hammami, chief Palestine Liberation Organization representative in Britain, is shot dead in Mayfair office on January 4; his moderate positions and antiterrorist speeches in Britain are said to have upset Palestinian militants   (NEW YORK TIMES,   January 5, 1978,   P3)

ARAFAT AFFIRMS P.L.O.'S PRIMACY

Palestine Liberation Organization (PLO) leader Yasir Arafat, interviewed by David Hirst, asserts that PLO remains the basic factor in the Middle East equation and predicts that the US will one day regret its hostile policy of "Bye-bye, PLO" expounded by Zbigniew Brzezinski (MANCHESTER GUARDIAN WEEKLY,   January 8, 1978, P1)

SADAT AIDE ASSASSINATED

Two terrorists believed to be Palestinians shoot and kill Youseff el-Sebai, chairman and chief executive of official Egyptian newspaper *Al Ahram*, in lobby of Nicosia Hilton Hotel; and then take 30 hostages to airport to bargain for airliner to fly them out of country; after several hours, they release more than half of hostages and take off in Cyprus Airways jet for unknown destination; plane is refused landing by Kuwait and Libya and later reports have plane flying for Aden (South Yemen) and over Athens; one of hostages freed, Cypriot Socialist Party leader Dr. Vassos Lyssarides, had carried messages between terrorists and Cypriot officials at airport; Moustapha Amin, columnist for Egyptian daily *Al Akhbar*, discloses that Sebai had been warned by friends not to attend Nicosia meeting because of threats made in Baghdad by radical Palestinian group that anyone who had accompanied Egyptian President Anwar el-Sadat to Israel would be shot   (NEW YORK TIMES,   February 19, 1978,   P1)

EGYPTIAN COMMANDOS STORM JETLINER

Egyptian commandos fly to Cyprus and storm jetliner at Nicosia airport in attempt to rescue 15 hostages held by 2 Palestinian terrorists who had assassinated Egyptian publisher Youssef el-Sebai; battle between Egyptians and Cypriot National Guard ensues in which 15 Egyptians are reported to have been killed; raid sets off angry exchange between governments of Cyprus and Egypt; Cyprus claims Egyptians had landed without permission and attack had caused needless bloodshed, because terrorists had already agreed to give up and had been preparing to free hostages at time of attack; Cypriot government spokesman Miltiades Christodoulou asserts that Egyptians had landed under "false pretenses" and had led Cypriots to believe that Egyptian ministers were arriving to participate in negotiations; charges that, disregarding Cypriot instructions, Egyptians had charged out of plane shooting indiscriminately and hitting control tower where Cypriot President Spyros Kyprianou had to take cover to avoid being hit; President was in tower overseeing negotiations with terrorists; after hour-long gunfight, Cypriots disarmed Egyptians and marched them away to undisclosed destination   (NEW YORK TIMES, February 20, 1978, P1)

EGYPT DEFENDS RAID

Egypt contends that it had given Cyprus advanced notification that its commandos were going into action against plane held by Palestinian terrorists at Larnaca Airport (Nicosia), and asks that commandos be allowed to return home; statement by Culture and Information Minister Moneim el-Sawi also asks that 2 Palestinian assassins of Egyptian publisher Youssef el-Sebai be handed over to Egypt for trial; claims that Egyptian commando force was taken by surprise when Cypriot National Guard opened fire against it and shelled and destroyed commando transport plane; denies that commandos had sought to violate Cypriot sovereignty by its action; meanwhile Sebai receives military funeral in Cairo; in another development, Egyptian President Anwar el-Sadat has told delegation of American Jews that he expects more Egyptians to become targets of assassins and terrorists as result of his overtures to Israel, but pledges to continue peace efforts   (NEW YORK TIMES, February 20, 1978, P1)

CYPRUS, EGYPT WITHDRAW MISSIONS

Cyprus agrees to free Egyptian commandos who survived airport battle with Cypriot troops but demands recall of Egyptian Military Attache Colonel Suleiman Hadad in protest over incident; Egypt counters by withdrawing its diplomatic mission and ordering Cypriot diplomats to leave Egypt; states move is not break in relations but attempt to review relations between 2 countries; Cyprus refuses to extradite 2 Palestinian terrorists accused of assassinating Egyptian publisher Youssef el-Sebai on February 18; Cyprus also issues announcement on behalf of terrorists stating that they do not belong to any Palestinian organization; Cypriot President Spyros Kyprianou meets with Egyptian Foreign Affairs Minister Butros Ghali in Nicosia to arrange for return of commandos   (NEW YORK TIMES, February 21, 1978, P1)

ARAFAT SCORES CYPRUS ATTACK

Palestine Liberation Organization (PLO) head Yasir Arafat scores Cyprus attack and pledges guerrillas will strike at

those responsible; Palestinian sources believe 2 gunmen belonged to radical Iraqi-backed Palestinian group led by Abu Nidal   (NEW YORK TIMES, February 22, 1978, P7)

EGYPT BREAKS CYPRUS TIES

Egypt breaks diplomatic ties with Cyprus after Cairo funeral for 15 commandos killed at Larnaca airport by Cypriot forces turns into demonstration against Palestinians and Cypriots; Deputy Foreign Minister Butros Ghali says break follows President Anwar el-Sadat's decision that he will not recognize Spyros Kyprianou as Cypriot President; orders Ambassador Antis Soteriades to leave Egypt; outpouring of anti-Palestinian sentiment reflects Egyptian disenchantment with Palestinian cause in view of PLO's criticism of Sadat's peace overtures to Israel; Sadat later scores Palestinians, in speech to commandos; says his forces will continue to strike back at extremists who threaten Egyptians abroad; lauds commando leader Brigadier General Nabil Shukry; says he attacked plane held by terrorists when he learned Cyprus prepared passports for assassins to leave Cyprus; sees no justification for Cypriot attack   (NEW YORK TIMES, February 23, 1978, P3)

EGYPT RESCINDS PALESTINIAN PRIVILEGES

Egyptian Prime Minister Mamdouh Salem says special privileges granted Palestinians over past 2 decades will be withdrawn and that they will be treated as other Arab aliens, in speech to Parliament; move is in response to slaying of *Al Ahram* editor-in-chief Youssef el-Sebai by Palestinian terrorists and criticisms of President Sadat by Palestinians; Salem says Egypt will deal firmly with Palestinian terrorists; War Minister General Mohammad Abdel-Ghany el-Ghamasy defends commando raid; reiterates with Salem criticisms of Cyprus's handling of affair; Egyptian officials say assassination was part of larger plot to kill Egyptian journalists who accompanied Sadat to Jerusalem; Palestinians have, since 1956 war with Israel, been on virtual par with Egyptian citizens and have lacked only right to vote and run for political office   (NEW YORK TIMES, February 28, 1978, P1)

IMPROVED JORDAN TIES SOUGHT

Palestine Liberation Organization (PLO) delegation will reportedly arrive in Jordan shortly in attempt to improve PLO-Jordan relations and ask King Hussein to join "confrontation front" of Arab nations opposed to Egyptian President Sadat's efforts to negotiate with Israel; Amman daily newspaper *Al Destour* sharply criticizes Sadat   (NEW YORK TIMES, March 3, 1978, P3)

TERRORISTS ATTACK BUS

Palestinian guerrilla organization Al Fatah claims responsibility for attack on bus in Israel that had been timed to precede Israeli Prime Minister Menachem Begin's visit to US; claims that 39 Israeli soldiers died in attack   (NEW YORK TIMES, March 12, 1978, P14)

TERRORIST RAID DETAILED

Commentator Moshe Brilliant reports detailed account of guerrilla terrorist raid on Israel; according to Prime Minister Begin, information from 2 guerrillas who survived reveals terrorists were on mission to seize luxury hotel in Tel Aviv; they carried leaflets spelling out demands, including one that British and Rumanian ambassadors and UN representative in Israel give themselves up as hostages to guarantee safe conduct to Damascus of raiders and freed guerrilla prisoners' Begin says raiders apparently made day landing because they ran out of fuel; says they murdered young girl who gave them directions, stopped a taxi and killed its passengers and then went on rampage of shooting and killing involving the tourist bus they captured   (NEW YORK TIMES,   March 13, 1978,   P10)

SAUDIS CRITICAL OF RAID

Saudi Arabian officials are publicly silent on issue of recent Palestinian guerrilla raid into Israel, but privately they are quite critical of raid   (NEW YORK TIMES,   March 15, 1978,   P10)

AIM OF RAID EXPLAINED

PLO spokesman, Ghasi Hussain, at news conference in Vienna, states that recent Palestinian raid into Israel did not proceed as planned; claims raid was aimed at military targets; calls killing of women and children in raid "regrettable"   (NEW YORK TIMES,   March 17, 1978,   P7)

ARAFAT'S STAND ON TERROR

Commentator Jack Anderson reveals Palestine Liberation Organization (PLO) leader Yasir Arafat plainly and repeatedly denied that PLO condoned terrorism in January 1978 discussion with US Representatives Paul Findley, Helen Meyner, Leo Ryan and Larry Winn; notes Arafat acknowledged only that some acts of terrorism had been committed by individuals whom PLO could not control; suggests Arafat's statements indicate either that Arafat is flagrant liar who could not be trusted to keep any Palestinian agreement, or that Arafat has lost control over PLO and can no longer speak with authority   (WASHINGTON POST,   March 24, 1978,   S2 P17)

ARAFAT STRENGTHENS SOVIET TIES

Commentator Paul Wohl thinks Palestine Liberation Organization (PLO) leader Yasir Arafat's visits to Moscow and East Berlin around the time of the PLO incursion into Israel March 11 points to tightened coordination between communists and PLO; suggests that Leonid Brezhnev may have had a hand in PLO's strategy in hopes that it would increase Middle East tension; says another purpose of Arafat's visits was to move PLO closer to Arab communists, including leftist Progressive Party of Egypt   (CHRISTIAN SCIENCE MONITOR,   March 31, 1978,   P27)

EGYPT HUNTS TERRORISTS

Cairo newspaper *Al Ahram* reports that Egyptian authorities have broken up terrorist ring that had allegedly planned campaign of assassinations and sabotage in Egypt; authorities are trying to determine whether ring had links with other terrorist organizations; 20 people arrested are not identified in *Al Ahram*, but new reports from Switzerland indicate 3 Swiss and 2 West German citizens were arrested in Cairo, possibly because of contacts with Palestinian groups; Egyptian authorities are known to fear reprisals against prominent Egyptians who supported President Sadat's peace initiative in November 1977; Palestian extremists say they have list of prominent Egyptians marked for death   (NEW YORK TIMES,   April 12, 1978,   P13)

SENATOR SCORES P.L.O.

Senator Jacob K. Javits urges Arabs to face up to Palestinian question and stand up against Palestine Liberation Organization (PLO), which he calls single greatest obstacle to peace; holds that Arabs who seek peace demand of Palestinian people leaders who are prepared to accept achievement of peace with Israel if they are not to forfeit claim of voice in settlement concerning West Bank and Gaza Strip   (NEW YORK TIMES,   April 14, 1978,   P7)

ATTACK PREPARATIONS ALLEGED

Egyptian prosecutor general Ibrahim al-Kalyubi charges that terrorist group with international connections, 24 of whom are under Egyptian custody, had plotted attack against Egyptian and Israeli peace negotiators; Mena House, site of December 1977 preliminary peace talks, was to have been target; Kalyubi links group to splinter Palestinian terrorist group headed by late Wadi Haddad, recently dead of cancer; also links group to Italy's Red Brigades   (NEW YORK TIMES,   April 27, 1978,   P3)

TERRORIST TARGETS ALLEGED

Egyptian newspaper *Al Akhbar* reports that band of 24 suspected terrorists arrested earlier in April 1978 in Cairo had planned to assassinate Jordanian Prime Minister Mudar Badran on trip to Switzerland; Badran had reportedly been chosen as target because of reports that he had met with Israeli Foreign Minister Moshe Dayan; Egypt's prosecutor general Ibrahim Kalyubi had announced earlier in week that suspects included Europeans, Palestinian Arabs, Egyptians and Jordanians   (NEW YORK TIMES,   April 30, 1978,   P40)

SPLITS IN P.L.O. REPORTED

Democratic Front for the Liberation of Palestine and 4 other Arab groups opposed to negotiated settlement with Israel, known as "rejection front", challenge Yasir Arafat's leadership of Palestinian guerrilla movement; complain that Arafat's Al Fatah has been making decisions on its own and presenting them in name of all Palestinian guerrillas; Al Fatah reportedly now has support of only 2 guerrilla organizations, al-Saiqua and Popular Front for the Liberation of Palestine-General Command, both aligned with Syria; is said to control about 75% of total guerrilla strength, estimated at 12,000 troops; "rejectionists" are calling for elimination of Israel as an independent state;

Courtesy of PLO

The Palestine Liberation Organization seeks membership in the United Nations.

have criticized Arafat's decision against large-scale guerrilla infiltration of UN-occupied southern Lebanon (NEW YORK TIMES, May 25, 1978, P14)

TERRORISTS BOMB BUS

Bus traveling from Arab section in East Jerusalem to Jewish section in west explodes near Mount Herzl in primarily Orthodox neighborhood of Bayit Vegan, killing 4 children and one American, and injuring at least 20 others; Beirut news agencies report Palestinian guerrillas calling themselves General Command of the Palestinian Revolution's Forces claimed responsibility; Jerusalem Mayor Teddy Kollek thinks explosion may have been linked to plans for June 5 celebrations commemorating 11th anniversary of reunification of Jerusalem, but opposes changing plans (NEW YORK TIMES, June 3, 1978, P2)

JORDAN VALLEY SETTLEMENT RAIDED

Arab guerrillas raid Israeli settlement in Jordan Valley village of Mehola; troops reportedly arrived after villagers repelled invaders, killing 1; raiders reportedly crossed to Jordan; analysts speculate that raid may have been signal from King Hussein that he is factor to be considered (NEW YORK TIMES, June 13, 1978, P3)

'MODERATE' PALESTINIAN KILLED

Palestine Liberation Organization representative Ali Yasin, regarded as "moderate" in Palestinian movement, is shot to death at his home in Kuwait; Al Fatah, guerrilla organization in which Yasin was a member, accuses extremist elements in Iraq of having instigated murder; Yasin came to Kuwait 13 years ago after receiving his law degree from Cairo University (NEW YORK TIMES, June 16, 1978, P4)

P.L.O. GAIN IN LEBANON SEEN

Correspondent James M. Markham reports that the Israeli invasion of southern Lebanon seems to have increased stature and morale of Palestine Liberation Organization (PLO); notes Palestinian contention that guerrillas stood and fought Israelis, beating an orderly retreat, that they did not have very high casualties, and that weapons captured or destroyed have been replaced by Arab suppliers; observes that in wrangle over positioning of UN forces, PLO is seen to have emerged with enhanced diplomatic standing; notes that Syrian Arab peacekeeping forces, concerned with possible confrontation with Christian militiamen, have avoided clash with Palestinians; observes that continuing anti-Palestinian feeling among Lebanese Christians and Moslems has failed to coalesce because of their own differences (NEW YORK TIMES, June 25, 1978, P10)

U.S. STANCE ON P.L.O. ASSAILED

Commentator Norman Podhoretz assails US for its alleged support of establishment of PLO-dominated Palestinian state on Jordan West Bank and Gaza Strip; contends US is sponsoring formation of another totalitarian regime; suggests alleged US policy is being pursued at direct expense of Israel, only remaining democratic country in Middle East; cites other examples of alleged US support of totalitarian political forces in Rhodesia and Angola (NEW YORK TIMES, June 28, 1978, P23)

BOMB ROCKS JERUSALEM MARKET

Two persons are killed and at least 35 are injured when bomb explodes in Jerusalem's central market; news agencies in Beirut report that a Palestinian group has taken responsibility for bombing; Palestinian agency WAFA attributes attack to unit named after deceased PLO leader Ali Yasin; bombing takes place day before arrival of Vice President Mondale in Israel   (NEW YORK TIMES,   June 30, 1978,   P4)

FATAH, IRAQ IN CLASH

Al Fatah discloses that Iraqi Government seized its arms plant and facility for making naval vessels in Iraq; confiscation was allegedly result of feud between Al Fatah and Iraq; Al Fatah accuses Iraqi Government of using diplomatic pouches, embassies and state-run airline for promoting terrorism abroad; charges Iraqis confiscated shipment of arms from Communist China valued at $50 million and medical and other supplies for Palestinian guerrillas worth $30 million   (NEW YORK TIMES,   July 18, 1978,   P2)

IRAQI MISSION HIT

Terrorist attack in Paris on Iraqi Embassy which resulted in death of a French police inspector and an Iraqi security agent has been attributed to feud between hard-line Iraqis and Palestine Liberation Organization (PLO) factions which take more moderate stance toward Israel; Iraqi press agency confirms that terrorist is brother of a PLO representative, Said Hammami, murdered in London; press agency charges that assault on embassy was carried out at order of PLO "in coordination with Syrian intelligence"; in related news, about 200 police inspectors demonstrate to protest any moves by French government to free the Iraqi security agents who had killed a French policeman while attempting to shoot terrorist who was being led away by police; French officials have not yet indicated what action will be taken regarding the Iraqis   (NEW YORK TIMES,   August 2, 1978,   P3)

P.L.O.-IRAQ FEUD CONTINUES

Two terrorists with possible Iraqi links murder Palestine Liberation Organization (PLO) chief Ezzedine Kalak and aide Hammad Adnan in PLO headquarters in Paris; August 3 assault seems to be response to a Palestinian's July 31 takeover of Iraqi Embassy in Paris and is apparently part of intensifying Iraqi-PLO feud; terrorists are identified as Hatem Abdul-Qadir, Palestinian with Jordanian citizenship, and Ishem Mustapha, who was carrying Algerian passport; history of enmity between PLO and Iraq noted   (NEW YORK TIMES,   August 4, 1978,   P1)

IRAQI TIES REPORTED

French police sources reveal that 2 Jordanian terrorists who murdered Palestine Liberation Organization (PLO) representatives Ezzedine Kalak and Hammad Adnan on August 4 have admitted membership in radical PLO offshoot now largely controlled by Iraqi intelligence agents; assailants are identified as Hatem Abdul-Qadir and Qayed Assad   (NEW YORK TIMES,   August 5, 1978,   P24)

FUNERAL FOR P.L.O. OFFICIAL

Hundreds of mourning Palestinians and other Arabs cry for vengeance as Palestinian flag-draped coffins of 2 PLO officials are carried out of Paris to be flown to Middle East for burial; Hatem Abdul-Qadir, 25, and Qayed Assad, 21, are charged with murder, and face possible death penalty; inform French investigators their orders came from Palestinian extremist leader Abu-Nidal; PLO leaders accuse Iraq of instigating killings, with UNESCO head of PLO mission Ibrahim Souss maintaining Iraq is responsible for acts of Abu-Nidal gang   (NEW YORK TIMES,   August 6, 1978,   P10)

P.L.O. POLICY CHANGE FORESEEN

Commentator Ihsan Hijazi holds Palestine Liberation Organization (PLO) is on brink of instituting significant changes to deal with increasing pressure from Israel, disunity within its own ranks and its exclusion from Middle East peace negotiations; cites recent violence in Israel and Palestinian guerrilla war with Iraqi agents as evidence of shifts and strains within PLO, noting Popular Front for Liberation of Palestine spokesman Bassam Abu-Sharif warned fighting could lead to Palestinian civil war; details friction between various factions within PLO, but claims PLO leader Yasir Arafat, despite criticism, remains most widely-accepted leader   (NEW YORK TIMES,   August 6, 1978,   S4 P1)

IRAQ CONDEMNS FEUDING

Iraq warns Palestinians not to be drawn into conflict with guerrilla forces or participating in attacks against Iraqi missions abroad; governing Baath Socialist Party condemns attacks on diplomatic missions in London, Paris, Karachi and Beirut   (NEW YORK TIMES,   August 7, 1978,   P3)

COUNCIL TO MEDIATE

Fifty-five-member Palestinian Central Council will meet in Damascus August 22 to seek ways to mediate feud between factions of Palestinian guerrillas; Al Fatah group says its central committee has approved plan for Palestinian unity and will submit it to council conference   (NEW YORK TIMES,   August 18, 1978,   P11)

FEUD RESULTS IN 80 DEATHS

Powerful explosion in western district of Beirut destroys 8-story apartment house that headquarters pro-Iraqi Palestinian Liberation Front (PLO); informed Palestinian sources put number of dead at 80 and similar number of wounded; most casualties are Palestinian families living in building; PLO, which has been involved in feud with the Front, denies involvement, cancels mass commemorative rally on August 13 and calls emergency meeting of PLO executive committee, where it is announced that security measures have been taken and committee formed to investigate blast   (NEW YORK TIMES,   August 14, 1978,   P69)

10,000 Palestinians Rally in Beirut; Arafat Hardens Anti-U.S. Position

By MARVINE HOWE
Special to The New York Times

BEIRUT, Lebanon, Jan. 1—The Palestine Liberation Organization put on a demonstration of strength and unity here today in an attempt to show that it will not be easily excluded from the Middle East peace process.

Some 10,000 Palestinians from all the rival factions joined in the largest P.L.O. rally anyone could recall to mark the 13th year of their guerrilla activity.

Yasir Arafat, who appeared as the uncontested leader of the P.L.O., warned that there would be no stability in the Middle East without the creation of an independent Palestinian state.

Weeklong celebrations, which opened yesterday in the refugee town of Damur, mark the first military action by Al Fatah, the main guerrilla organization led by Mr. Arafat. On Jan. 1, 1965, members of Al Fatah blew up an Israeli pumping station said to be diverting the waters of the Jordan River.

The Palestinian activities this year showed a strong anti-American trend as a result of what is seen as an American attempt to bypass the P.L.O. in moves toward a Middle East peace settlement.

Significantly, the P.L.O. is now concentrating its attacks on President Carter and has reduced its criticism of President Anwar el-Sadat. The Egyptian leader was denounced as a traitor to the Palestinian cause after his trip to Israel, but now he is more often portrayed as the instrument of an alleged American-Israeli plot against the Palestinians.

Mr. Arafat, who heads the main line of the P.L.O. and approved of Mr. Sadat's peace drive until the Jerusalem visit, has now adopted a hard line.

In his regular New Year's Eve message to the Palestinians and Arabs, Mr. Arafat repeatedly accused President Carter and the United States of leading a "conspiracy" against the Palestinians.

Today's demonstration was an unusual display of Palestinian unity both because of the principal leaders who were present and because of the units from different guerrilla groups that marched in the parade.

George Habash, leader of the Popular Front for the Liberation of Palestine, which rejects any negotiated settlement in the Middle East, sat near Mr. Arafat in the reviewing stand. Nayef Hawatmeh, leader of the Marxist Democratic Front for the Liberation of Palestine, who has recently criticized the P.L.O. for following too soft a line, also appeared to be satisfied with Mr. Arafat's words.

Mr. Arafat, the only leader to speak, said, "Say firmly to Carter and all his agents in the Arab world, if you think you can force anything on the Palestinian revolution, you're wrong."

"When Carter says no to an independent Palestinian state, I answer there will be no stability," he said.

Mr. Arafat said, "We're not calling for war but we are finding out that the late President Gamal Abdel Nasser was right when he said: What was taken by force must be got back by force."

NEW YORK TIMES, January 2, 1978, P3

Sadat Says 'Great Effort' Is Needed To Sort Out the Palestinian Issue

By CHRISTOPHER S. WREN
Special to The New York Times

CAIRO, Jan. 1—President Anwar el-Sadat said in an interview published today that "great efforts" would be required to overcome the problems created by President Carter's recent statement that he opposed creation of a Palestinian state. But Mr. Sadat said that he remained optimistic about the outcome.

Mr. Sadat also disclosed to October Magazine that some Palestinians publicly opposed to his negotiations with Israel had tried to meet with him secretly, but he said that he had turned them down. He said that the Palestinians made a similar overture to Foreign Minister Moshe Dayan of Israel, but he said they were rebuffed by him, too.

The Egyptian leader arrived today in Aswan in Upper Egypt after a boat trip up the Nile from Luxor with Chancellor Helmut Schmidt of West Germany. Mr. Sadat will remain in Aswan, where he will receive President Carter on Wednesday for talks aimed in part at resolving their public clash of views over the Palestinian issue.

A meeting with Mr. Sadat was added to President Carter's current foreign tour

in a bid by Washington to sooth Egyptian feelings ruffled by Mr. Carter's statement last Wednesday in a television interview. Mr. Carter said that he did not favor the establishment of a "fairly radical new independent" Palestinian state. President Sadat said that he was disappointed and embarrassed by the remark, which in his view undercut Cairo's negotiating position with Israel.

Expanding on this theme, Mr. Sadat told October Magazine, a weekly, that if the statement truly reflected President Carter's position, "Then this will create severe difficulties in the negotiations. If it is true, then he has created for me an obstacle that will need great efforts to overcome."

But Mr. Sadat added: "We must expect many differences over this Palestinian issue, but I am still optimistic on the outcome of the dialogue that has started with Israel."

Mr. Sadat said, "I have reasons to justify my optimism," but he did not explain what they were.

President Carter is expected to fly into Aswan from Saudi Arabia at about noon

Wednesday and spend several hours with Mr. Sadat before flying to Paris. It will be the first time that Mr. Carter has seen Mr. Sadat since the Egyptian leader undertook his dramatic new peace policy by visiting Israel in November.

While Washington sought to discount the friction created by Mr. Carter's statement on the Palestinian issue, Egyptians still appear piqued by what they see as an uncomfortable tilt toward Israel's position that a Palestinian state would threaten Israel's survival. Officials acknowledge that Mr. Carter has expressed his opinion before, but they say that the timing last week was particularly awkward.

The authoritative newspaper al-Ahram, continuing the sniping at the Carter Administration that has developed in Egyptian press commentary, said today that, "It is strange that Mr. Carter made his statements before the start of the delicate and crucial negotiating process which will be resumed in Jerusalem through the political committee."

In their meeting at Ismailia, Mr. Sadat and Prime Minister Menahem Begin of Israel agreed to set up political and military committees at the ministerial level to continue the work begun at the Cairo preparatory conference last month. When the Jerusalem meeting starts in two weeks, the Egyptians will present their counterproposal to the peace plan offered by Mr. Begin at Ismailia.

NEW YORK TIMES, January 2, 1978, P3

Saudis to Press Carter on Palestine

By ERIC PACE
Special to The New York Times

RIYADH, Saudi Arabia, Jan. 1—Well-placed Saudi officials said today that King Khalid and other Saudi leaders would press President Carter on the Palestinian question when Mr. Carter arrived here Tuesday for an overnight visit.

Speaking privately, the officials expressed dismay over a recent statement by President Carter indicating opposition to the establishment of an independent Palestinian state, and the Government-subsidized Saudi press published mild criticism of the President's view. The newspaper al-Madina said the statement "does not seem to be an effective step on the road to a just and lasting peace in the Arab world."

Saudi Arabia, which has annual oil revenues of $40 billion, and Kuwait, which has oil revenues of more than $10 billion, are both widely expected to provide extensive financial support for a Palestinian state if one should be formed.

A senior Saudi Foreign Ministry official, Sheik Abdel Rahman al-Mansouri, declared in an interview in Jiddah last week that Saudi Arabia wanted Israel to affirm Israeli recognition of "the legitimate rights of the Palestinian people, including their right for self-determination and their right to establish their own independent state," but he did not mention the Palestine Liberation Organization.

Saudi officials have been questioning United States officials and private citizens here in the isolated Saudi capital in an effort to get clarification of President Carter's views about the Palestinians, and the subject is expected to take up much of the time scheduled for talks during Mr. Carter's brief visit here. Some of the informants say that the Saudi royal family evidently wants to hear at least an affirmation that President Carter favors self-determination for the Palestinians.

There has been no official reaction here to a statement reported to have been made by Zbigniew Brzezinski, Mr. Carter's national security adviser, suggesting that Saudi Arabia and moderate Palestinians as well as Jordan might become active participants in the current Middle East peace efforts—a possibility that King Hussein of Jordan has since ruled out for the present—nor has there been any public discussion of it.

NEW YORK TIMES, January 2, 1978, P3

Palestinians, People in Crisis, Are Scattered and Divided

This article, written by James M. Markham, is based on his own reporting and that of John Darnton, Marvine Howe and Eric Pace.

Special to The New York Times

BEIRUT, Lebanon—"I imagine it as a land . . ." said Ismail Abdullah, hesitating as he reached for the right word. "I imagine it as a paradise." A 17-year-old Palestinian in a refugee camp near the Lebanese port of Tyre, he spoke with the yearning on which he had been nurtured for a village he had never seen—the village where his father was born, 25 miles down the coast near the Israeli city of Acre.

In a luxury apartment in Beirut, Mohammed Othman, speaking Arabic in a distinctive accent of rural Palestine, voiced the fear that his land might be "liberated" before he was old enough to fight in a war. Mohammed Othman is 9½ years old.

His father, Ali Othman, a prominent educator here who comes from a village near Jerusalem, commented, "To be in a place where you say: 'This is my home, this is my home'—this is something that is more important to the Palestinian than any material thing. No matter how successful he may be outside, the Palestinian is still in transit."

The question of whether there will be wars to be fought in the Middle East when Mohammed Othman is old enough to fight them turns in part on the question of whether the cause of Palestinian nationalism will have found a measure of fulfillment for at least some of the roughly 3.5 million Palestinians scattered throughout the Middle East and beyond.

Not all Palestinians are raised to fight, of course. Deadly acts of international terrorism—and vicious civil wars in Jordan and Lebanon—created the idea that Palestinians were a desperate people prone to violence. But there is another reality.

It is the reality of a thriving middle class in exile, with the highest levels of literacy and academic achievement in the Arab world, dominating the economy of Jordan, filling key positions in the Syrian bureaucracy, forming the professional backbone of oil states like Kuwait, reporting and editing for a disproportionate number of periodicals that mold Arab opinion.

Further down the class ladder, there is a vast Palestinian proletariat—sometimes defiant, sometimes resigned—that provides a pool of cheap labor not only for Jordan, Lebanon and Syria but also for Israel. These are the mercurial constituencies of Palestinian nationalism, which found themselves in intense emotional conflict when President Anwar el-Sadat of Egypt made his stunning visit to Jerusalem on Nov. 19.

The Sadat initiative came at a time when the Palestinian cause — battered militarily in the Lebanese civil war and tarnished in the eyes of many Arabs— seemed to be at its lowest ebb. As they surveyed their losses after Lebanon, a majority of Palestinians scaled down their once-passionate hope of destroying Israel by force.

However incoherently and conditionally, leaders of the Palestine Liberation Organization and most of their followers came to accept the idea of a miniature Palestine that would be built on the Israeli-occupied West Bank of the Jordan River and the Gaza Strip. This state—which could not physically accommodate all Palestinian Arabs any more than Israel can accommodate all Jews—would be born of diplomacy, not war.

But this consensus is unstable, a team of New York Times reporters found. Some Palestinians, especially those in Jordan and the occupied territories where two-thirds of all Palestinians live, incline to a moderation that comes from confronting the reality of Israel. But many others, often the poorest and most desperate, still harbor the dream of returning to the land that is now Israel.

Viewed from the perspective of the Palestinians, the paradox of the Sadat initiative is this: Although it came at a time when the moderate view that compromise with Israel is possible seemed to be prevailing, it may end by giving Palestinian extremism a new lease on life.

Moderates and Extremists Divided

At bottom, Palestinian moderates and extremists have divided on the question of what they might expect to receive in a settlement with the Israelis. The extremists argue that Israel would never accept any Palestinian demands unless forced to do so. Now, with the Sadat initiative nearly grounded, they can claim to have been right all along.

Other Palestinians, whose hopes were initially stirred by the prospect of a negotiating breakthrough, now tend to see the Egyptian President as yet another Arab leader who speaks in their name but puts his own interests first. Still others, more charitably, see Mr. Sadat as a desperate or generous man doomed to failure.

"I think he will fail," said Dr. Hatem Abu Ghazaleh, a member of the Municipal Council of Nablus on the West Bank. "We must take in a new phase of the struggle. We think from month to month they will withdraw," he said of the Israelis. "Now we know they won't. Sadat's visit unified us. Those who thought there will be peace will now understand."

Strongly felt throughout the Palestinian diaspora—which has striking parallels with the Jewish diaspora of an earlier age—Palestinian nationalism would most likely splinter along geographic and political lines if self-determination in the Israeli-occupied territories seemed genuinely to be in the offing.

Key Aim Is to End Occupation

"If the Israelis had any brains they could neutralize Palestinian irredentism just by giving back the West Bank," asserted Rashid Khalidy, an American-educated Palestinian who teaches political science at the American University of Beirut and also works for the P.L.O. "It would split us."

West Bank Palestinians want, above all, to throw off the Israeli occupation—even if that means a generally undesired federation with King Hussein's Jordan. Significant numbers of Palestinian professionals, dispersed now throughout the Middle East, want a passport—an identity—more than actual residence in a state known as Palestine. Many poorer refugees say they would return instantly to a new state, no matter how small, but those holding decent jobs might in fact stay where they are.

The various guerrilla groups, which would not be so easily satisfied, are already embryonic, disputatious political parties. Should a Palestinian homeland fall under some form of international supervision, there would be little place in it for their Kalishnikov-wielding guerrillas who are now in Lebanon.

'P.L.O. Is the Framework'

In Jordan and the occupied territories a fine shading of opinion was found, a willingness to make potentially important distinctions between the P.L.O's Beirut-based leadership and the organization itself as the embodiment of Palestinian identity and nationalism.

Yet a fundamental strength of the organization is its very ampleness, its amorphousness. "The P.L.O. is the framework of Palestinian peoplehood," said Clovis Maksoud, an Arab nationalist close to Yasir Arafat, the leader of the P.L.O.

"We are speaking about aims, not names," said Jahed al-Quawasmi, the mayor of the West Bank town of Hebron, who was overwhelmingly elected in April 1976 on a pro-P.L.O. slate. "The names will change over time."

Across the Jordan River in Amman, the Rev. Elia Khoury, a Palestinian activist, said, "If I am to choose between the land and persons, I'd rather choose the land."

But many Palestinians bristle when it is suggested that they should abandon the P.L.O. "Whoever is telling us to find someone else than the P.L.O. is asking us to find someone who will turn his back on us and sell us more cheaply to the Jordanians and the Israelis," said an intense young professor at Bir Zeit University on the West Bank.

Artificial Solidarity

The currently dim prospects for any kind of self-determination produce an artificial solidarity in the Palestinian ranks, drawing together the rich and poor, radicals and moderates, those on the "inside" and those on the "outside," those who fled Palestine as Israel came into being in 1948, those who fled in 1967 when the Israelis captured the West Bank from Jordan and the Gaza Strip from Egypt and even those born after these searing experiences.

This veneer of unity masks differing priorities and needs among Palestinians in different places. With his potential adherents dispersed "in transit," Mr. Arafat finds himself speaking in many voices to reach a subtly varied constituency—Palestinians who, perhaps like himself, would like to believe that a negotiated settlement is possible and many who, in the failing light of the Sadat initiative, now fear, or are convinced, one is not possible.

An Uneasy Relationship

Wherever they live, Palestinians find their relationship with the host country uneasy—and often taut.

Al Fatah, Mr. Arafat's own group within the P.L.O. and by far the largest within the organization, has said that it would accept the creation of a state on the West Bank and Gaza. This stance has put special strains on the 650,000 Palestinians in Lebanon and Syria, who are from or trace their heritage to places now part of Israel. These people stand little chance of living in their "homes" under proposals now being talked about by peace negotiators, although the P.L.O. regularly insists on "the right of return" for at least some refugees and compensation for lost property.

Following is a rundown of the situation of Palestinians in the Middle East:

Lebanon

Although Palestinians in Jordan and the occupied territories will probably have the decisive say in a settlement, extremists in Lebanon constitute Mr. Arafat's immediate environment, which sharply restricts his ability, for example, to acknowledge Israel's right to exist.

Extremist sentiment is strong in the gutted coastal town of Damur, which two years ago in the civil war was sacked and burned by Palestinian-led forces and is now a makeshift home for 10,000 Palestinian and 4,000 Lebanese refugees. Most of them are survivors of the Christian siege and capture in 1976 of the Tell Zaatar refugee camp in east Beirut.

Fatima Najamy recalls fleeing her village near Haifa in 1948 at the age of 16. Twenty-eight years later she survived the nightmarish, 52-day encirclement of Tell Zaatar, during which her husband, daughter and son-in-law were killed.

She expresses approval of Mr. Arafat, known widely by his nom de guerre, Abu Amar, but when asked what would happen if he were to accept a West Bank-Gaza state, she answered, "If Abu Amar said this, it would mean his life was finished and we will have to kill him. Then we will get another Abu Amar who will demand all of Palestine."

Such sentiments perhaps help explain Mr. Arafat's somewhat blurred positions. "Maybe Sadat has gained a lot from Western public opinion," conceded Salah Khalaf, the number two man in Al Fatah.

But even at the extremist end of the Palestinian spectrum, positions have been softening, largely as a result of the Lebanese civil war. Mahmoud Darwish, a leftist Palestinian poet, argued that the traumatic war brought many extremists to accept the idea of a ministate, if only to get out of Lebanon.

"You know, before the war a Palestinian state was condemned," said Mr. Darwish, who left Haifa for Moscow and Beirut in 1970 after being put under house arrest by the Israelis. "It was a crime to call for a Palestinian state."

But the building consensus in favor of a state in the West Bank and Gaza rests, in the minds of many extremists and others, on the unvoiced premise that it would be only a stage—the end of "armed struggle," maybe, but the beginning of a period in which the sheer force of demographics would be on the side of the new state and against Israel.

Statistics on the actual number of Palestinians are a matter of dispute, but in Lebanon there are thought to be roughly 400,000. Half of them are registered with the United Nations Relief and Works Agency for Palestine refugees, and of those a little under half live in camps. Between 60,000 and 100,000 Palestinians, mostly Christians, obtained Lebanese

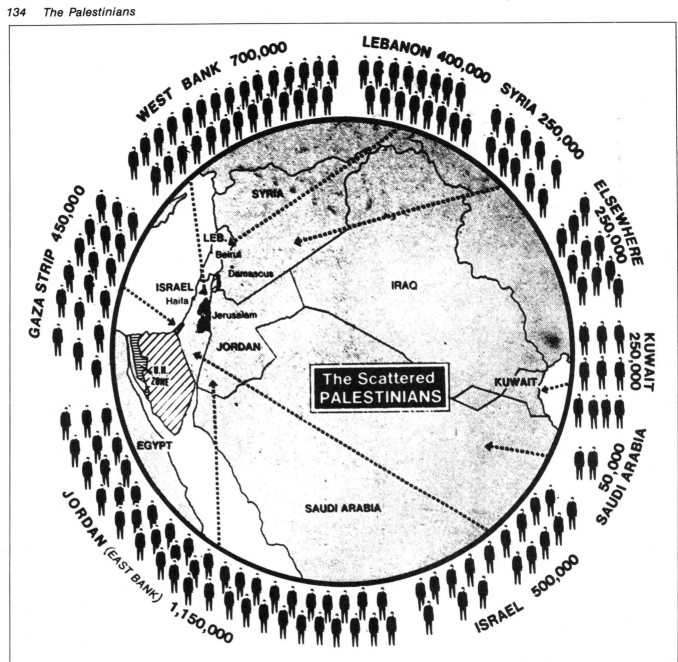

WEST BANK 700,000
LEBANON 400,000
SYRIA 250,000
ELSEWHERE 250,000
GAZA STRIP 450,000
KUWAIT 250,000
SAUDI ARABIA 50,000
ISRAEL 500,000
JORDAN (EAST BANK) 1,150,000

The Scattered
PALESTINIANS

The New York Times/Feb. 19, 1978

Since Palestinian population figures are estimates subject to disputes, those used on chart are low ones on which some agreement may be possible. There also can be disputes over who is a Palestinian, as in the case of 500,000 Arabs listed by Israel as citizens but by the P.L.O. as Palestinians. The 250,000 shown on chart as living "elsewhere" include 80,000 in Egypt, Iraq, Libya and Algeria, 50,000 in Europe and 70,000 in the Americas.

passports in the years after Israel gained independence, since local Christian politicians wanted to expand their own religious ranks.

The United Nations agency, established in 1950 to cope with the Palestinian refugees, lists 1.7 million people as qualifying for some sort of assistance. Of this total, only 35 percent live in "camps," which typically are anonymous lanes of cinderblock dwellings. Half of the people on the agency's rolls are 20 years old or younger.

Although individual Palestinians have prospered in Lebanon—Assad Nasir, chairman of Middle East Airlines is a Palestinian—the community is perhaps the least assimilated in the Arab world. "I've been a Lebanese citizen for exactly 20 years and 6 months," said a successful journalist born in Jaffa, "and I don't feel Lebanese and the Lebanese don't feel I'm Lebanese. The Lebanese, and I don't entirely blame them, have gotten fed up with us."

In the 19-month civil war, which ruined the Lebanese economy and took possibly 60,000 lives, Palestinian guerrillas formed the spine of a heavily Moslem coalition that battled Christian forces, armed in the latter stages of the conflict by Israel. In the summer of 1976, Syrian troops and tanks intervened against the Palestinian-led forces when it appeared they might triumph, install a radical state and incite a war with Israel.

Now, many Lebanese Moslems have turned on their one-time Palestinian allies, particularly in southern Lebanon, where leaders of the Shiite Moslem community blame the guerrillas for huge population shifts caused by the guerrillas' clashes along the border with Israeli-supported Christian forces.

Syria

A more hospitable climate prevails in Syria, where some 250,000 Palestinians live, but President Hafez al-Assad's decision to intervene in Lebanon in 1976 embittered many Palestinians. During the war, two Palestinian pilots serving in the Syrian Air Force defected to Iraq with their planes, and several others were said to have been executed. Syrian-based units of the Palestine Liberation Army threw off Syrian control when they were sent to Lebanon and joined Mr. Arafat's forces. Damascus closed guerrilla training camps and bases on the Golan Heights, and scores of Palestinians were jailed. Most have been released.

Now that President Assad and Mr. Arafat have mended what has been rather implausibly termed a "a family quarrel," the situation has eased. "We don't feel like foreigners here," said Khaled al-Fahoum, the Damascus-based head of the P.L.O.'s Central Council, who is married to a Syrian. Successive Syrian governments have absorbed many Palestinians into the bureaucracy, military establishment and economy. Assad Elias, the President's Christian-Palestinian translator and constant companion, gently reminds visitors that at the turn of the century Palestine was considered a southern province of Syria.

Among Palestinian militants, though, mistrust persists and it is reciprocated by an edgy Assad Government. The suspicion lingers in Al Fatah that Syria would like to control the guerrillas in Lebanon as a step toward having a major voice in whatever Palestinian "entity" one day emerges. "All the Arab states want to have a finger in this Palestinian state," said Shafiq al-Hout, a journalist and envoy for the P.L.O.

Saudi Arabia and Persian Gulf

Unlike Syria, which must constantly worry about the guerrillas embroiling it in an untimely war, Saudi Arabia and the oil states of the Persian Gulf are far enough away from the "confrontation" with Israel to have slightly more relaxed relations with their sizable Palestinian population.

In the shifting politics of the Arab Middle East, Mr. Arafat and his closest aides at times set important and wealthy Palestinians in the Gulf area against radicals who have their strongest followings in Lebanon, Libya and Iraq.

About 250,000 Palestinians make up nearly a quarter of the population of Kuwait; another 50,000 work in Saudi Arabia and roughly 50,000 live in other states on the Arabian peninsula. Many have family ties to the West Bank and, as one P.L.O. militant put it, it is in this area that the "illusion" that a negotiated settlement is possible is strongest.

"There is a silent tension between the Palestinians and those states," said a Palestinian consultant who work throughout the Gulf area, "because those states are always afraid that the Palestinians will do something mischievous."

In the rest of the peninsula the pattern is mixed. The Sultan of Oman is highly suspicious of Palestinians and lets few into his sultanate; in Abu Dhabi, a Palestinian is a key advisor to the ruler, but, generally, Palestinians are kept out of the armed forces and the police.

Jordan

While the Arabian peninsula is the source of the P.L.O.'s money, the largest single concentration of Palestinians is beyond the reach of the organization—in Jordan, where Palestinians comprise more than half of the East Bank's population of two million. Some 364,000 refugees on the East Bank arrived or are descended from those who fled in 1948; 473,000 others arrived at the time of the June 1967 war.

The P.L.O. has been effectively banned from Jordan since September 1970, when King Hussein's army, goaded by the guerrillas' open flouting of Jordanian authority, suppressed them and later drove them from the kingdom. After the 1974 meeting of Arab leaders at Rabat, Morocco, proclaimed the organization "the sole legitimate representative" of the Palestinian people and gave it responsibility for the West Bank, King Hussein has accelerated a process of "Jordanization" in sensitive areas of the armed forces and the bureaucracy.

Before the Rabat meeting, Palestinians traditionally held half the cabinet posts in Jordan; today they hold a fifth. Palestinians are excluded from divisional and some lesser commands in Jordanian infantry, artillery, tank or special-forces units. Palestinians, however, make up a part of the technical and support services of the Jordanian Army and Air Force—although they cannot be pilots.

Yet Jordan is the one Arab country that systematically offers its Palestinians nationality—passports—and an economic boom has eased the militancy of many middle-class Palestinians, who find good things to say about the King.

"We admire the man as a leader; we disagree with him, but we admire him," said Sari Nasir, an Illinois-educated Palestinian who is chairman of the sociology department at the University of Jordan in Amman.

Mr. Nasir said he was delighted that "this madman Sadat did such a great thing" by going to Jerusalem and, he maintained, showing that the Israelis did not want peace.

"The more I watch Sadat's initiative, the more I am drawn toward George Habash," he said, referring to the radical Palestinian leader who rejects a negotiated settlement. "Seeing the attitude of the Israelis is definitely driving me toward the extreme, toward George Habash's camp. This is true of Palestinians across the board."

Paradoxically, it is also true that Palestinian opinion, a fluid commodity, would be moving away from Mr. Habash and toward the so-called "moderates" like Mr. Arafat had Mr. Sadat wrested significant concessions from the Israelis.

Palestinians still constitute Jordan's intellectual and business elite and have a strong foothold in the state-controlled press. While top government posts often elude them, the governor of the central bank is a Palestinian, the head of the National Planning Council is a Palestinian, and so is the director of the national television network.

Moreover, the distinction between Palestinians and Jordanians is somewhat artificial, since many of the "best" Jordanian families are only a few generations removed from the West Bank and still have relatives there. "There is and have been so many relations between the Jordanians and the Palestinians," said a Palestinian executive from Bethany. "that it is going to be difficult to separate them, whether the King likes it or not, or whether Arafat likes it or not."

Anti-Jordanian, pro-P.L.O. sentiment runs high in Palestinian refugee camps in Jordan, which the United Nations refugee agency says have a population of 298,000, and among poor Palestinians outside the camps, but it has mellowed since September 1970 when the King's soldiers battled guerrillas in the streets of the capital.

In his office overlooking Amman's rooftops, which bristle with television antennas, Mahmoud el-Sherif, who was born in El Arish in Sinai and now publishes the daily Ad Dustur, said he believed many Palestinians in Jordan "still follow the P.L.O. to a degree" but had begun to realize that the organization was being excluded from the Middle East negotiating process.

No Other Organized Representative

"After all," he said, "what they want is the land, and if King Hussein can get it back for them, that's all right with them."

Even so, no "alternate" or "moderate" leadership has emerged within Jordan to counter the P.L.O. "There is no other organized body to represent the Palestinians," said Anwar Nashashibi, a member of a prominent Palestinian family who has served as an ambassador for King Hussein. "The P.L.O. revived the Palestinian question when it was almost dead, and they sacrificed their young men by the thousands, whereas other people like me were just talking. How can the non-P.L.O. people deny them a say?"

It is far too soon to say that the Palestinians will have the chance to have a say in deciding their future. But if a building international consensus prevails, it would probably not be in Beirut, Damascus, Kuwait or Amman that "self-determination" would be gauged.

Most likely it would be on the other side of the Jordan River, where 1,150,000 Palestinians, living under Israeli control in the West Bank and the Gaza Strip, would, by proxy, cast their ballots for the rest of their scattered brethren.

NEW YORK TIMES, February 19, 1978, P1

Palestinians Cling to Vision of a Homeland

By JOHN DARNTON
Special to The New York Times

RAMALLAH, Israeli-occupied West Bank — If there is to be a Palestinian homeland, it will most likely come about on the West Bank of the Jordan River and in the Gaza Strip, along the rocky slopes that step down to the Dead Sea and on the sands of the Mediterranean coast.

An international consensus—including the United States, most Arab countries and the Palestine Liberation Organization—is developing around the idea of creating a "homeland" or some other "entity" in these two noncontiguous territories conquered by Israel in June, 1967.

Suc an entity, its proponents argue, would satisfy the Arab demand for return of the land lost in the six-day war of 1967 and at the same time, perhaps, pacify the troublesome Palestinian refugees whose presence has so destabilized the Arab world and whose terrorism has outraged and puzzled the West.

The West Bank-Gaza solution, however, seems to raise as many questions as it resolves. A key one, in the minds of American negotiators, is whether such an entity should in fact be independent. Making-up only 23 per cent of the area of the British Palestine mandate, would it be radical and harbor designs on its neighbors' territory?

Should it be placed under the control of Jordan, a country that has a predominantly Palestinian population but is ruled by a conservative monarch despised by the exiled Palestinian left wing and disliked by many on the West Bank as well?

Some day, the 1,150,000 Palestinians in the West Bank and the Gaza Strip may be asked to express their political sentiments in a referendum. In a sense, those "inside" would be casting a proxy for the more than 2 million Palestinians "outside"—a minority speaking for a majority. Although the two groups now share a sense of history, family ties and a fervent nationalism, at some point their views may diverge.

"How can I speak for my brother carrying a gun in a camp in southern Lebanon?" asked a pensive, 30-year-old professor at Bir Zeit University, a cauldron of nationalist thinking on the West Bank. "Our desires, our hopes are identical. But the fact that he is there and I am here makes us different."

Slogans of solidarity with those in the Palestinian "diaspora" are proclaimed, but distinctions are drawn.

"We are desperate," said a shopkeeper here, pouring a cup of tea in a back room. "Even more desperate than those on the outside. We have a saying in Arabic: 'It is not the same for the man who gets the whipping as for the one who counts the strokes.' "

The peace initiative of President Anwar el-Sadat of Egypt, and especially his visit to Jerusalem last November 19, sent ripples of confusion through the West Bank. It stirred a stronger response here than among Palestinians elsewhere.

The fears of being "betrayed," in an agreement that would return the Sinai Peninsula to Egypt in exchange for thinly disguised Israeli sovereignty over the West Bank and the Gaza Strip, clashed against hopes, often unexpressed, that a proven ally would bargain a viable settlement.

"It was all so confusing," said Raymonda Tawil, a staunch P.L.O. supporter whose outspokenness has meant arrest in the past. "I feared a sell-out, but at the same time, I felt this man is taking a courageous step. His speech at the Knesset was good — it was thrilling to hear Arabic spoken there—but he did not mention the P.L.O.

"That he should pray at the mosque under Israeli protection, this was like a shot to us. It was humiliating. But at the same time, he had a kind of forgiveness, almost divine. Here is the hero of the October war! Such humiliation! Such greatness! It was confusing."

Outwardly, the Palestinians present a united front, engendered no doubt by their anger over the 48 Israeli settlements that have sprung up inside the two territories, the annexation of East Jerusalem,

and the daily humiliations and outright injustices that are inevitable under a military occupation.

Indeed, some regard Israeli tax levies, land confiscation and security arrests not as administrative measures but as a plot to drive out the Arab population—an "occupation of elimination" in the words of a prominent Palestinian who once served in the Jordanian Cabinet.

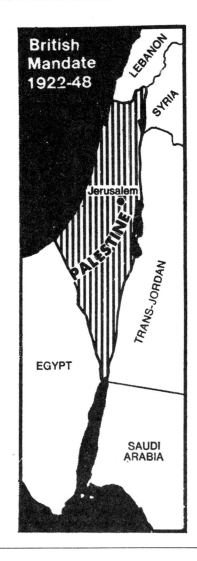

British Mandate 1922-48

LEBANON

SYRIA

Jerusalem

PALESTINE

TRANS-JORDAN

EGYPT

SAUDI ARABIA

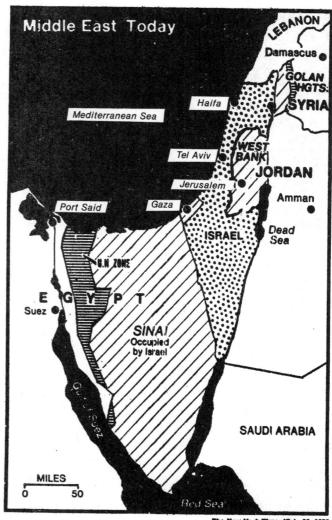

The New York Times/Feb. 20, 1978

Support for the P.L.O. is widespread. From the northern town of Nablus, ringed with terraced hills and olive trees, to the ancient biblical city of Hebron in the south, scores of people interviewed said that the Palestine Liberation Organization was the only voice that represented them.

Slogans on the Walls

P.L.O. slogans are painted on village walls. The Voice of Palestine blares out of radios in Arab-populated East Jerusalem. Anti-Israeli literature circulates underground.

One explanation for the P.L.O.'s popularity is its character as an all-embracing assembly with representatives from almost every West Bank town, leading family and political view. Another is an almost visceral identification with the symbolism of the organization; the facts that the organization has been recognized by Arab states and has achieved observer status at the United Nations are cited frequently here, almost as a surrogate for statehood.

When other nations attempt to cast doubt on the status of the P.L.O., said the Rev. Audeh G. Rantisi, an Episcopal clergyman in the heavily Christian town, they are trying "to make us lose our identity, our nationality, to make us less than ourselves."

A waitress here declared, with a trace of anger: "For years journalists used to ask, 'do you have anyone to represent you?' And we always used to hesitate because in fact there was no one. Now circumstances have changed and we do have someone. Now the journalists say: 'But these people are extremists, they can't really represent you.'"

Support for the P.L.O. does not necessarily mean support for the leadership based in Beirut, Lebanon. No, said Ali Keishe, city manager of Al Bireh, shaking his head slowly, there is no special allegiance to Yasir Arafat. "Most of us are not concerned about persons, but about the symbol of representation," he explained.

If there was any doubt about the P.L.O.'s hold on the West Bank, it was

dispelled in April, 1976, when the Israeli Government held elections and watched as every town but tourist-oriented Bethlehem voted in mayors and councilmen who supported, or were supported by, the P.L.O.

Mostly teachers, lawyers and engineers, the new mayors replaced older, more conservative members of the aristocratic land-owning families that had risen during the period of Jordanian rule from 1948 to 1967. Their campaigns were conducted in a kind of code. "We didn't speak for the P.L.O. out loud," said Mayor Jahed al-Quawasmi of Hebron, sitting back in his drafty office. "A small town like this, they all know how you feel."

Once installed, the mayors openly proclaimed their support of the P.L.O. They became embroiled with the military administration in innumerable disputes over electric power lines and water pipes because they attempted, usually without success, to remain independent of Israeli supply systems. They have not forged strong constituencies of their own.

The Israeli authorities and media, exasperated at the mayors, have tried to bolster "alternate leaders." Some of them receive frequent exposure on television and others are able to help people out in special ways, such as by obtaining travel permits. But these leaders, less than half a dozen in number, seem to be generally regarded as opportunists and do not wield great popular influence.

Israeli commentators often assert that the P.L.O. maintains a grip upon the West Bank through terror and intimidation.

Since December, there has been a series of political assassinations on the West Bank. At least two people, and possibly as many as five, have been killed. In two instances, responsibility has been taken by the P.L.O., apparently operating through a sub-group called the "November 19th Organization" after the date of President Sadat's visit.

The surprising thing about the killings is how few people condemn them. "There is some thought on the West Bank that the P.L.O. doesn't engage in enough intimidation," remarked Hanna Nasir, the Purdue-educated president of Bir Zeit University who was deported in 1974 and now lives in Amman, Jordan.

A handful of moderates on the West Bank have proposed a period of United Nations supervision for the territories, coupled with guarantees of self-determination. Very few can be found who will voice support for the autonomy plan presented by the Israeli Prime Minister, Menachem Begin, to the Israeli Parliament on December 28.

The plan, under which Israelis could buy land here and Israel would retain the right to station troops on the West Bank and veto the repatriation of Palestinians from the outside, has aroused deep-seated fears that the Likud Government has no intention of relinquishing the land it calls Judea and Samaria, Biblical names that suggest the West Bank belongs to "Eretz Israel," the land of Israel.

Worse Than Annexation

"His plan was much worse than the continuance of the occupation," said Tayseer Kanaan, "or even outright annexation. If they annexed the West Bank, it means they have about 2 million Arabs in Israel. It means the color of Israel is changed and in a decade it becomes a secular state. This was a plan to annex the land without the people."

For the moment, what is perceived by West Bank residents as intransigence on the part of the Begin Government has undercut the moderates and strengthened the hand of the few radicals who still maintain that the 1967 lines are not enough for a Palestinian state.

West Bank residents have always tended toward the moderate end of the Palestinian political spectrum. Rejectionism, the political current that dismisses the idea of negotiating with Israel, exists, particularly among the young; it gains and loses strength as the situation changes but it is clearly a minority view.

Unlike Palestinians in exile or in the Gaza Strip, a densely populated, 140-square-mile ribbon along the Mediterranean coast, most people in the West Bank have never had to flee their homes. Their primary objective is to throw off the occupation.

In the Gaza Strip, about 300,000 of the area's 450,000 people are refugees from the fighting of 1948 and almost two-thirds of them live in teeming and squalid camps.

On the West Bank, according to the United Nations Relief and Works Agency, there are a little more than 300,000 refugees out of about 700,000 people. One quarter of them live in camps that are more like villages, substandard but not altogether destitute or unassimilated into the surrounding society.

In early 1974, a group of professionals on the West Bank with links to the Communist Party in Jordan came together to form the West Bank Palestine National Front. The movement advocated accepting a state in the occupied territories—an idea that implicitly recognized Israel's existence—and provided the impetus for the Palestine National Council, the Palestinian parliament-in-exile, to move toward this more moderate position later that year.

'We Have to Face the Facts'

"We have given up the idea of realizing our dream by force," said Zuhair el-Rayess, chairman of the board of the leftist Arabic daily Al Fajr, "We have to face facts. The facts are that there's now a Jewish people living here, and we can't ask them to go back or kick them into the sea."

Aziz Shehade, a lawyer from Al Bireh who faced Israeli negotiators across a table in Europe 30 years ago, said: "There was a time, after the war in '67, when I called for a Palestinian state in the West Bank and Gaza and I was called a traitor. Now, easily 80 percent of the people support it."

Mr. Shehade, noted, however, that the Israeli Government's response to the Sadat initiative so far may radicalize Palestinians.

"I heard Begin speak at the Knesset and I was furious. What are we? Are we just beasts living here hundreds of years? He is from Poland and he thinks he has more right to live here than me. I'm supposed to be one of the more moderate Palestinians. Begin is not making me any more moderate."

On the West Bank, tensions flare from time to time, causing localized disturbances, but there have been no widespread strikes or demonstrations for 18 months. In part, this may stem from tighter, and in some ways more sophisticated, control by the Israeli forces.

Many Palestinian leaders have been put out of action. Between 1967 and 1976, according to a study by a foreign religious organization active in the area, over 1,100 people were deported, in a few cases simply by being blindfolded and carried over the border.

Last February the Israeli prisons service commissioner stated that there were 3,227 people in prison on security charges. The number being held without charge in short-term detention can only be guessed at, but is believed to be high.

Schools are still arenas for confrontation, but when problems erupt they are rarely reported in the heavily censored Arab press. Whereas two years ago Israeli soldiers used to break up demonstrations with a show of force, the authorities now try to head them off; parents are warned that they face heavy fines if trouble occurs and students are called in for interrogation in twos and threes.

The Gaza Strip has been peaceful for years. In 1972 the Israeli authorities completed a project to crisscross the camps with wide roads, demolishing structures that housed 16,000 people as a security measure to cut the camps into segments that could be effectively patrolled. It has been effective.

There is an impressive array of statistics to show that West Bank and Gaza residents have benefited economically from Israeli occupation, chiefly by finding employment in Israel. In 1973, when employment of Arabs from the occupied territories in Israel peaked, about 60,000 people worked there. Most commuted daily and worked in construction and other low-salaried jobs.

In recent years, however, these workers have seen their gains eroded by taxes and inflation. Capital investment inside the occupied territories has been meager, and some view the economic relationship as exploitative.

Among many residents of the occupied territories, there is a deepening mood of resignation and apathy.

Faiz Abdinnour, a member of the Arab Chamber of Commerce who runs a tourist agency in East Jerusalem, said he could not bear the thought that his taxes went to buy American planes that might be used for reprisal raids across the border and "hit my brothers in Lebanon." But he said he no longer believed in antitax strikes.

"We tried it," he shrugged. "You know what was the result? The army came and broke the lock on our stores. When we put the locks back, we were brought into the police station and threatened with deportation if we did not reopen the shops. What's the good?"

Ibrahim al-Tawil, the mayor of Al Bireh looked through his window to the bare summit of a mountain called Jebel Tawil. The Minister of Defense had just requisitioned it, he said, indicating that some time soon an Israeli settlement will appear, the first in his town. "We will not oppose it," he added. "What can we do?"

Certainly some of the Palestinians' despondency comes from having witnessed the fate of fellow Palestinians at the hands of nominal allies, the Arab regimes. Especially traumatic was the Lebanese civil war, in which Syrian troops intervened to defeat the Palestinian guerrillas and their Lebanese leftist allies in their struggle against right-wing Christians.

'Look What Happened!'

"We were brought up all our lives to believe that Syria is the beating heart of Arab nationalism, and look what happened!" exclaimed a student at Bir Zeit.

The response has been a decline in pan-Arab sentiment and a sense that in order to be secure once and for all, the Palestinians need a country of their own as a first priority.

Paradoxically, for some this has led to rejection of an option that would make such a state more acceptable to the West —union with Jordan—because then the Palestinians' haven would fall under the dominion of another foreign Arab leader.

In fact, the deepest divisions among Palestinian Arabs on the West Bank have little to do with Israel. They center upon attitudes toward Jordan, which annexed the West Bank and ruled it for 19 years until the 1967 war.

To some, King Hussein of Jordan is a fellow Arab and patron. To others he is remembered as the perpetrator of "Black September" in 1970, when his army suppressed and later expelled the Palestinian guerrillas.

The division could come to the surface were a moment of decision ever to arise. If, as seems likely, a possible settlement is in the air that offers something less than total independence, complete Israeli military withdrawal, the return of East Jerusalem to Arab control and unrestricted rights of repatriation or compensation for those in exile, many—possibly most—on the West Bank would be tempted.

King Hussein's influence on the West Bank is difficult to gauge. He still pays the salaries of about 5,000 people who are hold-overs from his administration. Most people carry Jordanian passports. The Jordanian currency, the dinar, circulates together with the Israeli pound.

Under the "open bridges" policy initiated by Israel, there is a steady movement of goods and people between Jordan and the West Bank. In 1976, $35 million in exports and 348,000 people crossed the bridges to Jordan.

At Israel's insistence, much of the economic aid from the Arab world to the West Bank is funneled through a bank in Amman, thus insuring that it will get to the P.L.O. The sums are substantial, since each town on the West Bank has been "adopted" by a sister city in one of the countries belonging to the Arab League.

Against this economic leverage, there are still harsh memories of Jordanian rule, when the East Bank of the Jordan was favored over the west for investment, when radicals and nationalists were rounded up and jailed, and curfews were imposed to block demonstrations against Israeli border incursions.

"In 1967, the Jordanian troops withdrew two days before the Israelis got here," said Father Rantisi bitterly. "Imagine how you feel if you hire a guard to protect your house and he turns you over to your enemy."

Point of Division Shifts

But such memories have faded, and now are overshadowed by the daily reminders of Israeli rule. When pressed, most will say they would accept Jordan over Israel.

Eight years ago, the defining issue between moderates and militants on the West Bank was whether or not Israel should be absorbed into secular Palestinian state. Four years ago it was whether or not to have an independent Palestinian state in the occupied territories. Now it is whether or not such a state can be absorbed into a union with Jordan.

This is a change that has not been followed by Palestinians in the "diaspora"—especially in Lebanon and Syria— where Palestinian radicalism has been kept alive in clashes with Arab states.

The political complexion of the Palestinian "entity," if it comes into being, will depend to a certain degree on how many of the "outsiders" will chose—or be allowed—to return to the West Bank and Gaza.

"The process that brings independence will determine the nature of the state," observed the 30-year-old Bir Zeit professor.

"If the world presses for any plan that falls short of true self-determination on the part of Palestinians, if they press it we are too weak to resist. We would sulk for a while and accept it. And the seeds of future conflict would be sown.

"But if it comes as a result of a prevailing good will toward us, from an understanding of our grievances, if it is not imposed on us, then we are inclined to be a little ashamed of our troublesomeness. You know, if you look back into history, we haven't always been a troublesome people."

NEW YORK TIMES, February 20, 1978, P1

Despite Diplomatic and Battle Scars, P.L.O. Is the Palestinians' Only Voice

By JAMES M. MARKHAM
Special to The New York Times

AMMAN, Jordan—Since Yasir Arafat addressed the United Nations General Assembly on Nov. 13, 1974, the Palestine Liberation Organization he heads has attained an impressive degree of international recognition and has put the Palestinian question high on the agenda for a Middle East settlement.

But since President Anwar el-Sadat of Egypt went to Jerusalem on Nov. 19, 1977, the P.L.O. and many Palestinians who give the organization allegiance feel caught in a pincers between Israel and Arab countries, notably Egypt and Jordan, that might be tempted into a Middle East settlement that would shelve or muffle Palestinian aspirations for a state.

For, while it has established itself on the international scene, the P.L.O. has suffered disastrous setbacks in the field. By carrying out its doctrine of armed struggle not inside Israel or the Israeli-occupied West Bank of the Jordan River and the Gaza Strip, but in Lebanon, the organization became bogged down in a devastating, 19-month civil war that brought its guerrillas into open conflict with one of their chief allies and arms suppliers, Syria.

The result is that Palestinian guerrillas in Lebanon are now under the supervision of 27,000 Syrian peacekeeping troops. Weapons continue to pour into Lebanon, and lately bombings, kidnappings and shootings have markedly increased.

Mounting hostility among Lebanese Moslems and Christians has put the Palestinians even more on the defensive. In southern Lebanon Palestinian fighters face a small Christian force supported by Israel, which could mount an operation of its own to wipe out the guerrillas.

The apparent failure of "armed struggle," which for the Palestinians began in 1970 in the streets of Amman when King Hussein began a drive that forced the guerrillas from his country, has obliged Mr. Arafat and his colleagues to try to advance their cause in the field of Arab and international diplomacy.

Diplomatic Frustrations

But here, too, they have been frustrated. Many Palestinians perceive President Sadat's peace initiative as an effort to outflank the P.L.O. and eventually deliver its constituency to King Hussein. But so unsure is Mr. Arafat of his support in other Arab capitals that he is unwilling to break openly with Mr. Sadat, who he hopes will be forced by Israeli inflexibility to return to a united Arab front.

Last month, the guerrilla leader even went so far as to make a plaintive appeal to President Carter, taking issue with the President's contention that the P.L.O's "negative" attitude had removed it from serious consideration in the negotiating process. "We are trying to stress positive views," Mr. Arafat said in a message relayed by a Congressman. "I most sincerely hope that you will not further push me into a corner because I would like to maintain my moderate balance."

However, for his immediate audience in the Middle East, Mr. Arafat must maintain a posture of steadfastness and defiance in the face of what he usually calls "American and Zionist schemes."

There is a foreboding in the higher ranks of the P.L.O. that Mr. Sadat's diplomacy has ushered in a new and dangerous phase in which the Palestinian militants could be the losers. In Lebanon, the guerrillas feel that they have their backs to the sea; there is talk of a revival of international terrorism should Mr. Sadat strike a peace accord that altogether excludes them.

Even so, despite its serious setbacks, the unruly coalition called the Palestine Liberation Organization has managed to survive and, for the moment, has managed to retain the loyalty of enough Palestinians, notably in the Israeli-occupied territories, to prevent the emergence of any alternative "moderate" leadership. What a young Palestinian said about the Lebanese civil war applies elsewhere: "the big win we got from this war is that we still exist."

Scores of interviews over a two-week period with Palestinians and others in the Middle East indicate that the current absence of challengers to the P.L.O. leadership does not mean that they will never emerge, perhaps within the organization itself. What does seem clear, however, is that significant numbers of Palestinians see no one else capable of delivering what they consider minimal demands: self-determination and a state or "entity" of their own on the West Bank and Gaza Strip, possibly linked to Jordan.

Should someone else emerge who could make these things possible—King Hussein, Mr. Sadat or Mr. Carter—there seems little doubt that the surface unity of the Palestinians would begin to break up. Said one East Jerusalem Palestinian of Mr. Arafat: "Look, if there is a settlement, and he does not adapt himself to a settlement, he will not come back."

Talk of International Plots

The Sadat visit to Jerusalem provided a glimpse of the potential rifts among Palestinians, who are torn between eagerness for a negotiated settlement and the conviction that one is not possible.

"President Sadat would have been praised as a hero by almost all Arab states if, after his unprecedented feat, he had returned with an Israeli commitment to withdraw from the occupied areas or to recognize the rights of the Palestinians," Isam Sartawi, a P.L.O moderate, reportedly said Dec. 12 at a private gathering in Vienna that was attended by Austria's Chancellor, Bruno Kreisky. "As it was, President Sadat returned from Israel with the pit of the olive and not the branch."

Three weeks after Mr. Sartawi's speech, Said Hammami, the P.L.O.'s London representative, who had openly advocated coexistence with Israel and had initiated a dialogue with leftist Israelis, was assassinated. After receiving death threats himself, Mr. Sartawi, the organization's representative in Vienna, has gone underground.

One of Mr. Hammami's closest Israeli friends was Uri Avneri, a maverick Israeli politician who at the age of 15 joined the Irgun terrorist group—later led by Mr. Begin—but who now calls for the creation of a Palestinian state alongside Israel.

In his Tel Aviv apartment, Mr. Avneri mused on what he saw as ironies of the Palestinian question:

"As a former terrorist, I can tell you they're not very good terrorists—the P.L.O. really doesn't have practical roots on the West Bank and Gaza. It is a guerrilla movement based on the outside. If the Israelis had allowed the West Bank Palestinians freedom, the P.L.O. would have been undercut. Fortunately for the P.L.O., Mr. Begin seems determined not to see the P.L.O. undercut."

For the present, the Sadat initiative has led to increased solidarity between Mr. Arafat's dominant Al Fatah group, which espouses a nonideological brand of Palestinian nationalism with a faint Islamic tinge, and avowedly Marxist organizations like George Habash's Popular Front for the Liberation of Palestine, which formally adhere to the "rejectionist" position, opposing any negotiated settlement with Israel. Mr. Habash's group, which most Arab regimes consider subversive, also maintains that they must be toppled and replaced by "revolutionary" ones before Palestine can be "liberated."

In private, Mr. Arafat and his group are said to have persuaded Mr. Habash to accept the idea of a Palestinian state on the West Bank and in Gaza, in return for agreement by Al Fatah to reject the idea of Middle East peace negotiations—talks to which they are not about to be invited.

'A Very Strong Front Indeed'

In Jerusalem, Anwar Nuseibeh, an urbane former Jordanian defense minister and ambassador to London, observed: "Even Habash, if he were told today, 'All right, you're getting Gaza, the West Bank and East Jerusalem—for God's sake, shut up,' he would. But a rejectionist front in the face of an initiative which offered the Palestinians nothing, would be a very strong front indeed."

Overshadowing all other guerrilla groups, Al Fatah's cardinal tenet is aloofness from inter-Arab quarrels, a position that enables it to receive substantial financial support from conservative regimes such as those of Saudi Arabia, Kuwait and Morocco as well as radical governments like that of Algeria. But within Al Fatah's diverse ranks runs a strong current of "rejectionism" that rises and falls with the prospects of negotiations. It is now rising fast.

Mr. Arafat, who believes that without the support of Egypt and Syria his cause cannot be seriously advanced, has studiously avoided personal criticism of Mr. Sadat. This makes his own position within the P.L.O. increasingly uncomfortable. In the words of one Damascus-based Palestinian leader, Mr. Arafat "is now a political captive of the more radical tendencies."

In a shabby office in Beirut's heavily Palestinian Tarik el Jdeideh quarter, Saleh Khalef, the second-ranking Fatah leader, warned that the Sadat initiative had strengthened "radical" forces in the P.L.O. and the Arab world, had helped Soviet influence and could spark "a wave of anti-Americanism."

Mr. Khalef predicted failure for Mr. Sadat and spoke of international "plots" to provoke a resumption of the Lebanese civil war. "But the green light has not been given yet," he continued. "After the success, or failure, of Sadat, things will start up in Lebanon."

Palestinians in Lebanon recall edgily that the divisions within the Arab world

THE PALESTINIAN GUERRILLAS

PALESTINE LIBERATION ORGANIZATION

Serves as umbrella organization for eight guerrilla groups, including four small ones that oppose any negotiated settlement of Middle East conflict. Formed in 1964. Came under control of Al Fatah, the main guerrilla organization, in 1969. Governed by 15-member Executive Committee dominated by Fatah and headed by Fatah leader, Yasir Arafat. Based officially in Damascus but actually in Beirut. Proclaimed by leaders of Arab countries at 1974 conference in Rabat, Morocco, as the only legitimate representative of the Palestinian people.

Yasir Arafat

EXECUTIVE COMMITTEE

Elected by P.L.O.'s legislative arm, the Palestine Liberation Council, with two of committee's 15 members from Al Fatah, one each from four other guerrilla groups including one of those that oppose peaceful Middle East settlement, and nine independents, most of whom back Mr. Arafat.

PALESTINE LIBERATION ARMY

Organization's regular army, numbering about 12,000 men, with units stationed in Syria, Egypt and Jordan. Headed by Yasir Arafat as "commander in chief of forces of the Palestinian Revolution."

PALESTINE NATIONAL COUNCIL

Palestinians' 295-member "Parliament in exile." Selected, not elected, for three-year term by Executive Committee from nominations made by Al Fatah and other member organizations. Roughly one-third from Fatah, one-third from other groups and one-third independents, most of whom back Mr. Arafat. Meets periodically in various Arab capitals.

PALESTINE ARMED STRUGGLE COMMAND

P.L.O.'s security or police organization, dominated by Al Fatah.

PALESTINE CENTRAL COUNCIL

A 55-member policy-making body selected by National Council to function while it is in recess. Based in Damascus.

P.L.O. GUERRILLA GROUPS

AL FATAH

About 10,000 members. Operates as fighting organization in Lebanon under name Al Asifah. Represented on P.L.O. Executive Committee by Yasir Arafat and Farouk Kaddoumi, the "foreign minister" of the P.L.O.

Farouk Kaddoumi

AS SAIQA

Perhaps 3,000 to 5,000 members, many of them Syrians. Represented on P.L.O.'s Executive Committee by its leader, Zuheir Mohsen, head of P.L.O.'s military department. Sponsored by Syria's governing Baath Party.

Zuheir Mohsen

DEMOCRATIC FRONT FOR THE LIBERATION OF PALESTINE

About 1,500 men. Led by Jordanian, Nayef Hawatmeh. Marxist oriented, pro-Soviet and close to Syria. Represented on P.L.O's Executive Committee.

POPULAR FRONT FOR LIBERATION OF PALESTINE — GENERAL COMMAND

About 500 men. Led by Ahmed Jabreel. Pro-Syrian. Represented on P.L.O.'s Executive Committee.

ARAB LIBERATION FRONT

Several hundred men. Led by Abdel Rahim Ahmed. Controlled by Iraq's governing Baath Party. Rejects peaceful Middle East settlement. Represented on P.L.O.'s Executive Committee.

POPULAR FRONT FOR THE LIBERATION OF PALESTINE

1,000 to 1,500 men. Led by Dr. George Habash. Rejects peaceful Middle East settlement. Quit P.L.O.'s Executive Committee in 1974.

Dr. George Habash

PALESTINE LIBERATION FRONT

About 150 men. Led by Abul Abbas. Backed by Iraq. Rejects peaceful settlement of Middle East conflict. Not represented on P.L.O.'s Executive Committee.

PALESTINIAN POPULAR FRONT

About 300 men. Led by Dr. Samir Ghosheh. Not represented on P.L.O.'s Executive Committee.

The New York Times/Feb. 21, 1978

There are two groups outside P.L.O. and based in Iraq that approve officially of hijacking. One, headed by Waddi Haddad, has about 150 men; the other, led by Abu Nidal, has several hundred.

caused by Mr. Sadat's second Sinai disengagement agreement with Israel in 1975 ultimately turned the Lebanese civil war into a Middle East war by proxy, with Israeli-supported Christian rightists battling a coalition of Palestinians and Moslem leftists armed by various Arab states.

Palestinians watch the complex undercurrents of inter-Arab politics closely because their own organizations mirror the divisions among the Arab states and have tended to get swept up in them—disastrously, so far.

"It's a race between the ability of the regimes to put down the Palestinians and the internal risks they face in doing so," said Constantine Zurayk, a thoughtful scholar at Beirut's Institute for Palestine Studies. "This is why the Palestinians are in some kind of fix. What does the West Bank and Gaza represent out of the original area of Palestine? Some 23 percent. If the Palestinians are ready to accept 23 percent of their original homeland, how much farther can they go without losing everything?"

In the vision of many American and some Israeli policymakers, the preferable alternative to the P.L.O. is King Hussein, a tested conservative and anti-Communist who has brought a degree of prosperity and contentment to his discreetly authoritarian kingdom.

Among the Palestinians who make up more than half of his two million subjects on the East Bank, many aspire to see some sort of Palestinian "entity" created on the other side of the Jordan River. On the West Bank, which has been under Israeli occupation for almost 11 years, sentiment is openly favorable to the P.L.O. and, at times, extremely hostile to King Hussein. But, on both banks of the Jordan, Palestinians would prefer a federation with Jordan to continued Israeli occupation of the West Bank.

The King is known to believe that in an election free from intimidation, West Bank Palestinians would produce a leadership that would displace the P.L.O. He dreams of reuniting the West Bank, which he ruled from 1948 to 1967, with the rest of his kingdom, although within the royal family and his own military establishment there is resistance to the idea of absorbing and policing 700,000 troublesome West Bank Palestinians.

Whether a kingdom so overwhelmingly Palestinian would survive, more than one East Bank resident has asked privately.

In dealing with the Sadat initiative, King Hussein is no freer of the pressures of Arab politics than is Mr. Arafat. Should he join the Egyptian President's peace initiative, the King would open himself to the wrath of neighboring Syria, not to speak of the P.L.O. The pressures on President Hafez al-Assad of Syria either to stop King Hussein or join him would mount. Should Syria also join, it could face a rebellion from Palestinians in Lebanon, in addition to the violent sniping it already receives from its neighbor Iraq.

'Holding Bag for Separate Peace'

Over the years, King Hussein has held secret talks with several Israeli leaders, and he has an idea of what Israel would yield and what it would not. He feels strongly about recovering East Jerusalem, which Mr. Begin says he will never surrender, and, in the words of one who knows the King well, he is reluctant to enter talks that would "leave him holding the bag for a separate peace."

According to foreign and Jordanian sources in Amman, the King would not want to try to speak for the Palestinians, thus openly repudiating the decision of the 1974 Arab summit meeting in Morocco, which declared the P.L.O. their sole legitimate representative, unless he thought that he stood a good chance of recovering the West Bank. At present, that chance does not look strong.

Who does speak for the Palestinians, then? So far, only the battered, weakened P.L.O., which finds itself diplomatically isolated, physically removed from its constituency in Jordan and the West Bank, and thoroughly on the defensive. The dynamics of the Middle East situation might throw up other contenders, but could this happen without more violence?

As for Mr. Avneri, the former Irgun member, said of the Palestinians: "They've got nothing in their favor, except that they're there. And any peace without the Palestinians will be nonsense and won't last."

NEW YORK TIMES, February 21, 1978, P14

ARAFAT HINTS EASING OF P. L. O.'S ATTITUDE

Suggests Guarantees by U.S. and Soviet for Israel and Palestinians

By ANTHONY LEWIS
Special to The New York Times

BEIRUT, Lebanon, May 1—Yasir Arafat said today that "the only possible solution" to the Middle East problem was for the United States and the Soviet Union to provide guarantees for Israel and a Palestinian state.

The chairman of the Palestine Liberation Organization, in an interview, declared that Israel would have nothing to fear from a new Palestinian state. Such a state would have to "start from zero" and would be preoccupied with its own problems, he said.

The Soviet-American declaration of last Oct. 1 could be "a fundamental basis for a realistic settlement," Mr. Arafat said. In that declaration, which aroused sharp criticism in the United States, the two powers said among other things that they wanted to insure "the legitimate rights of the Palestinian people" and would help guarantee "the security of the borders between Israel and the neighboring Arab states."

Shift of Position Suggested

These and other comments appeared to go beyond anything the P.L.O. leader had said previously about the possibility of coexisting with Israel—that is, accepting Israel as a nation.

The interview, lasting something over an hour, took place in what seemed to be Mr. Arafat's office. There were six telephones behind his desk, and from time to time he received a call.

Mr. Arafat's manner was relaxed and he broke into laughter a number of times. He wore his usual checked kefiyeh headgear, with one end tucked into an olive-colored sweater.

The building looked like an ordinary Beirut apartment house, and children's voices indicated that families lived on other floors. But sandbags were piled up at the building entrance and P.L.O. soldiers with Kalashnikov rifles stood guard there and on the stairs.

Stress on 'Recovered' Territory

The Palestine Liberation Organization originally took the position that all of what was Palestine before the establishment of Israel in 1948 should become a secular democratic state. Then, in 1974, the Palestinian National Council called for establishment of a Palestinian state on any territory "recovered" from Israel, presumably in the West Bank of the Jordan River and Gaza.

Today Mr. Arafat referred pointedly to the 1974 proposal. He spoke in Arabic, with the Palestine Liberation Organization's representative in Lebanon, Shafik el-Hout, acting as translator.

When Mr. Hout spoke at one point of "the establishment of a Palestinian state on any piece of territory liberated from our homeland," Mr. Arafat, correcting him, said in English: "Liberated or from which the Israelis have withdrawn." He evidently wanted to make clear the possibility of a peaceful settlement.

Mr. Arafat was asked whether he would state directly that a Palestinian state could live in peace with Israel. He leaned forward on his desk and said with emphasis:

"Taking into consideration the aggressiveness Israel has shown against Syria, Lebanon, Jordan and Egypt, as a matter of fact this question must be posed by us—because it is us, the Palestinians, who need the guarantees for peace.

Need for Soviet-American Guarantee

"That is why I have referred to the American-Soviet declaration, because I feel the necessity of these two powers' guarantee to have such a new situation left in peace."

Does that mean, he was asked, he envisages "a situation in which Israel and a Palestinian state could live under the mutual guarantee of the Soviet Union and the United States." He replied:

"I think this is the only possible solution. And this is why I said that the Soviet-American declaration could be considered a fundamental basis for a realistic settlement in the Middle East."

At one point in the interview Mr. Arafat disclosed that he had made a videotape, from Israeli television, of the visit of President Anwar el-Sadat of Egypt to Jerusalem. Then, laughing, he added: "It is one of our records."

The central question of a Palestinian state's coexisting with Israel came up when he was asked about the fear—in Israel and among its friends—that such a state would pose a mortal threat to Israel's survival.

"That is a big lie," Mr. Arafat said. He said such a fear was shown to be groundless by, among other things, "our participation in the activities of the United Nations and our approval of the U.N. resolutions."

At this point Mr. Hout turned to the interviewer and said he wanted to add an interpretation of his own, for clarification. It was that the United Nations resolutions "recognize Israel's existence." Mr. Arafat made no comment.

Last year the Carter Administration tried to get the Palestine Liberation Organization to abandon language in its covenant indicating that Israel should be replaced by a secular state, and to endorse Resolution 242 adopted by the United Nations Security Council in 1967. The resolution calls on Israel to withdraw from occupied territory but also speaks of assuring "secure and recognized borders."

The P.L.O. refused in the end to make such statements. Privately, its officials have said that recognition of Israel was a vital card for them, to be played only when and if Israel is willing to deal with the Liberation Organization as the representative of Palestinians.

Today Mr. Arafat drew attention to the fact that Resolution 242 did not mention Palestinians except in a reference to "refugees." He suggested that it had to be taken along with other United Nations resolutions recognizing Palestinian rights.

On the question of Israeli fears, Mr. Arafat continued his answer with a series of questions.

"Would you believe," he asked, "that Israel, which scares all the Arab states around it, is afraid of the Palestinian resistance movement? This state armed to the teeth, including nuclear weapons?

"Assume that a Palestinian state has been founded. Would you believe that a state which is going to start from zero for the establishment of its institutions, its economy, culture, social problems— would such a state be able to form any serious threat against Israel?"

Then he was asked about guerrilla actions, such as rocket attacks. Would such attacks be directed against Israel from a new Palestinian state? Again he answered with questions.

"Assuming that the fear exists," he said, "why are the Israelis refusing to withdraw from the Sinai despite the fact that President Sadat has gone to Israel and offered a peace treaty, and there are no commandos in the Sinai? Which do you think will endanger peace more: having the Palestinians as they are, deprived of their national rights, their human rights, scattered here and there, having ill treatment everywhere, or having the Palestinians settled as normal civilians with their national pride restored and with a flag of their own."

Gen. Abu Walid, Mr. Arafat's military chief of staff, entered the room during the interview. He is a graduate of the United States Army Staff College at Fort Leavenworth, Kan., which he attended as a Jordanian Army officer. At this point he intervened.

"We have to differentiate between a state and a revolution," the general said.

"Now we are a revolution," he said. "But once we become a state, we'll be taking a different form and different restrictions and a different outlook. From the president of that state to a small citizen, everyone will be very keen and careful and worried about the safety of his establishment and the institutions that form the state.

"In addition to that fact, a guerrilla war could never emerge from a small young state just coming into existence.

"And with such a state's abilities, and with the balance of power, it's crazy to think of waging a classical war against the huge power of Israel. The blah-blah about fear is nothing but justification for the permanent Zionist strategy of expansion and denying Palestinians their national rights.

Asked whether he agreed with General Walid's comments, Mr. Arafat said he did.

The Soviet-American declaration of last October blew up a storm among American supporters of Israel, who said the Carter Administration had unnecessarily and unwisely brought the Soviet Union back into Middle East politics. As a result, United States officials have scarcely mentioned the declaration in recent months.

President Carter has said on many occasions that he did not want an independent Palestinian state. He said it again in an interview published yesterday, adding that he thought the proposal by Prime Minister Menachem Begin of Israel for municipal "self-rule" by Arabs on the West Bank and Gaza should be the basis of further negotiation.

Mr. Carter's comment drew criticism today from Mr. Arafat, who said he was "surprised" and "disappointed" by it. "He is trying to form the future of people the way he likes it," the Palestinian leader said. "Of course we as Palestinians just simply reject that."

Pessimistic View Taken

Asked whether he had hopes of a reasonable relationship with Israel, Mr. Arafat said he was "sorry to say" that he had "no hope" so long as the present Israeli policy stood.

"One would require a real change in the mentality ruling Israel nowadays," he said. "Without this mental change, there will be neither stability nor peace."

He was particularly critical of a resolution passed by Israel's Parliament on March 13. It gave Prime Minister Begin a free hand to retaliate for the Palestinian raid that had caused the death of 37 Israelis two days earlier.

Mr. Arafat called it "a barbarian resolution." He said it asserted that "they have the right to annihilate the P.L.O., its military troops, its representatives."

As for Mr. Begin's proposal for "self-rule" in the West Bank and Gaza, Mr. Arafat dismissed the offer as "less than a Bantustan," a reference to the South African Government's policy of setting up so-called tribal homelands for blacks.

He spoke with confidence of the performance of Palestinian fighters in southern Lebanon against Israel's invasion last month. He said his forces, "outnumbered 12 to 1," had been able to fight on "for eight days and nights."

Would he be more optimistic over prospects for Israeli-Palestinian relations, Mr. Arafat was asked, if Egypt and Israel reached an agreement and Israel withdrew from Sinai?

"When Sadat started his initiative," Mr. Arafat said, "he expected withdrawal in a month's time. They did not withdraw. The problem has not been solved. And another war has occurred in the south of Lebanon. Do you expect me to forget these realistic facts and speak about a hypothetical future?

"If they ever come to such an agreement, you are welcome for another interview!"

NEW YORK TIMES, May 2, 1978, P1

7
Egypt on Its Own Course

Anwar Sadat succeeded to the presidency of Egypt on Nasser's death in 1970. He was not expected to succeed to Nasser's unofficial role as first statesman of the Arab world. But partly because of Egypt's position as the most populous and central of the Arab states, and partly because of the Egyptian public's expectation that their president must be premier of the rest of the Arabs, Sadat had a mandate to transform Egypt, speak with a voice of authority in the Arab world and seek a solution to the 22-year deadlock with Israel.

While inheriting Nasser's tasks Sadat radically changed his methods. Nasserism had failed by 1970. The five-year plan of 1965-1970 had stagnated because of defense spending. Society had grown increasingly closed as political and military elites struggled with one another and the security apparatus began a series of unpopular purges and investigations. 20,000 Russian military advisers formed a state within a state while Egypt's dependence on the Soviet Union made a mockery of its "anti-imperialism." Russian support notwithstanding, the Israelis had occupied the Suez Canal since the 1967 war.

To untie the gordian knot of difficulties which faced Egypt in 1970, Sadat started with the problem of Israel. He sent out peace feelers to Israel which came to nought. Among other reasons for the failure of Sadat's tentative initiative was the conviction of many Israeli and US analysts that Sadat was a Soviet puppet. But Sadat was to surprise these observers as well as the Arab world when he expelled the Soviet advisers from Egypt in July of 1972 and ended Egypt's unilateral dependence on Soviet aid by seeking support from Saudi Arabia and other oil states. Pro-Soviet figures in the government were ousted and the "power circles" of Nasser's regime were eliminated. Censorship was relaxed, political prisoners were released, summary confiscations of property were restored. Though these moves won Sadat widespread popularity, they did not strike at the heart of the problem, a stagnant economy, huge defense debts and Israeli occupation of the canal.

Pressures within Egypt and in the Arab world for decisive actions led Sadat to try a war option. He launched his surprise attack in October 1973 in concert with Syria and, overturning all expectations, gained initial success in crossing the Suez Canal. With the aid of US Secretary of State Kissinger's shuttle diplomacy he managed to engineer an Israeli pull-back and open the canal to traffic for the first time in six years. Sadat's prestige in the Arab world as a result of this military cooperation against Israel and his diplomatic maneuvering with the United States, creating an outcome favorable to the Arabs, confirmed him in his role as successor to Nasser, not only in Egypt but in the Arab world.

The 1973 war did not bring peace, however; nor did it bring the solution to the problems besetting Egypt. In hopes of heading off Egypt's economic disaster, Sadat pressed for an "opening" of the economy similar to his "opening" of the Suez Canal. In 1976 and 1977 free-zones of trade were established in the canal zone, while industrial bases throughout the country were offered up to foreign investment on favorable terms. Aspiring to the support of the old commercial classes which had been dispossesed by Nasser's 1960 socialist turn, Sadat restored nationalized businesses and banks. As a further concession to old elites, he promised a return to liberal democracy.

Sadat's "opening" was only a qualified success. Though some foreign businesses, including Coca Cola, returned to Egypt in 1978 after an 18-year absence, most foreign capital stayed clear of Egypt, which was still in a state of war with Israel. An octopus-like bureaucracy further discouraged ventures, both foreign and Egyptian, by tangling business initiative in red tape. Even the denationalization scheme advanced at a snail's pace because the state apparatus struggled to hold on to its privileged position as the nation's biggest businessman. Only the massive, $2-billion worth of aid from the Gulf oil states and international aid for Egypt's debt-servicing staved off the country's economic collapse.

The problems Sadat faced were those of a country which had been in a state of war since 1948. When the Zionists declared their partitioned part of Palestine to be the Jewish homeland, a wave of sentiment swept the Arab world which was anti-Zionist and anti-British, since the Arabs believed Britain had engineered the Jewish state. Bloody riots broke out against British and foreign interests in Cairo, forcing the Egyptian government, otherwise lukewarm to the idea, to send troops to put down Zionism in Palestine. Its failure to do so brought about a change of regime and a hero of the Palestine defeat. Gamal Abdul Nasser came to power in 1951. Five years later the joint Anglo-French and Israeli attack on the Suez Canal confirmed for Nasser an identification of Zionism with imperialism and hardened the country into a permanent war stance against Israel.

Breaking Egypt out of that attitude has been one of the chief accomplishments of Sadat's rule. Deadlocked still in his social and economic reforms, Sadat again tackled the heart of the problem. In 1973 his solution had been a surprise attack. In November 1977 his solution was an equally surprising peace initiative. His speech at the Israeli parliament affirmed, as much for home consumptiom as for an Israeli audience, that Egypt was prepared to live in peace with the Zionists and that Egypt was committed to seeking lasting peace in the Middle East.

In the aftermath of Sadat's trip to Jerusalem, Egypt and Israel began a diplomatic dialogue which lasted to the year's end. Although the dialogue often threatened to break off, high-level and low-level meetings quickly convened to keep the momentum going. The spring impasse was ended by a ministerial-level conference in Leeds, England in July 1978. When that ended on a less than satisfactory note, Egypt declared the United States would have to take a major role in the discussions.

All of Sadat's moves have greatly affected his position as leader of the Arab world. His liberalization was hailed by moderates in the region as a constructive step forward for the Arab people, while leftists condemned his rapproachment with Egypt's commercial elite as a sellout to capitalism. As for Sadat's trip to Jerusalem, all Arab states were disturbed by the unilateral action on Sadat's part which eroded the carefully composed front of Arab political cooperation which proved so fruitful to Sadat in 1973. While moderate Arab states with sympathy for Sadat's initiative, like Morocco, Saudi Arabia and Sudan have muffled criticism of the "rejectionist front" of Libya, Syria and Iraq, Sadat's position in the Arab world is increasingly one of isolation. Moreover, his almost total reliance on American support has forced the rejectionists to strengthen their ties with the Soviet Union. The prospect of the Arab world divided into rival, superpower camps, so inimical to Arab ideals, may be a result of Sadat's diplomacy. On the other hand, the prospect of peace with Israel is crucial to Egypt itself and vital to the Arab world at large. Those are Sadat's risks and his rewards.

The Political Backdrop

EGYPT'S DEVELOPMENT PORTRAYED

First of 2 articles by Jean-Pierre Peroncel-Hugoz on Egypt's economic development describes signs of shabbiness in Cairo; discusses problems of overflowing sewers of Greater Cairo, housing crisis, unemployment and bureaucracy; wonders at optimism of Egyptian people despite their poor economic conditions; suggests that temporary emigration, moonlighting, baksheesh (bribery), state subsidies and a stable rural structure are major factors in Egypt's survival   (MANCHESTER GUARDIAN, January 15. 1978,   P13)

EGYPT'S FUTURE TERMED BLEAK

Second of 2 articles on Egypt stresses the zest for life that Egyptians have even in face of adversity; describes endless frustrations consumers have to put up with; criticizes waste of precious currency on foreign imports such as high-powered cars; describes economic picture as "climate of unreality, chaos and stagnation" which critics call "an economy of the absurd"; hope in drop in population growth; describes government optimism on development after peace comes; says peace in Middle East will psychologically liberate Egypt   (MANCHESTER GUARDIAN,   January 22, 1978,   P13)

WORLD BANK HOPEFUL

World Bank economists are optimistic about Egypt's long-run economic outlook despite severe population pressures, high unemployment and a $2.6 billion trade deficit; optimism stems in part from Egyptian progress over last 5 years on basic projects financed and coordinated by World Bank and its affiliate International Development Association believe country's development depends on willingness of lending nations and agencies to continue high level of economic aid and on ability of President Anwar el-Sadat's government to make tough decisions necessary to move from wartime to peacetime economy and to move away from Nasserite socialism   (NEW YORK TIMES,   January 30, 1978,   P6)

WAFD PARTY REVIVED

Egyptian government spokesman says that Wafd Party, outlawed in 1952, has been officially revived as part of President Sadat's political liberalization   (NEW YORK TIMES,   February 5, 1978,   P13)

WAFD LEADER CHOSEN

Faud Seraguddin, first chairman of Egypt's New Wafd political party, is elected on pledge of support for President Sadat's peace efforts; the party, formed 13 days ago, has 24 supporters in 360-seat People's Assembly   (NEW YORK TIMES,   February 18, 1978,   P4)

U.S. SEEN CRUCIAL TO SADAT

Commentator Max Lerner indicates that Egyptian President Anwar Sadat's actual target in his quest for Middle East settlement is US favor; maintains Sadat needs sophisticated American weapons, US investment in Egypt's industries and hard pressure which US can employ with Israel   (HOUSTON CHRONICLE,   February 26, 1978,   S3   P27)

FREE PORT DESCRIBED

Port Said, strategically located between Suez Canal, Mediterranean Sea and Lake Manzala, appears destined to attract an increasing number of foreign investors; Egyptian President Anwar Sadat designated Port Said a duty free area in 1976; the 422,000-square-meter area has been set aside in Port Said for cold storage, warehousing and factory projects; 118 industrial projects have thus far been approved for the city; Mohamed el-Harizy, director of public relations for the free zone, reports 98 of the 118 projects are either under construction or have been completed; also reports that 43 of the 98 projects are completely foreign-owned, while 32 have only Egyptian investors and 23 are joint ventures   (JOURNAL OF COMMERCE,   March 27, 1978,   P1)

U.S. INVESTMENT MAY INCREASE

US private investment in Egypt may increase significantly in near future; major impediments to investment, discounting the threat of war, are legal, financial psychological and cultural, but these impediments are far less formidable today than they were when US and Egypt normalized relations in 1974; Jim Roberts of US Agency for International Development (AID) contends major impediment to US investment in Egypt is the fact that US business persons are a good deal more conservative in investing than they were 10 years ago   (JOURNAL OF COMMERCE,   March 29, 1978,   P1)

INCREASED U.S. ROLE SEEN

Commentator William J. Lanouette discusses steadily increasing commerce between US and Egypt; points out Egyptian government expects foreign investment to play

United Nations

Visitors to Cairo, Egypt's capital, are struck by the contrast between its modern architecture and busy bazaars. Here, the entrance to the Mowsky, one of the city's celebrated bazaars.

important role in Egypt's industrial development; discusses growing need in Egypt for US technology in such sectors as construction, harbor facilities, freight handling and city planning; notes US banking operations are doing booming business in Egypt; observes difficulties faced by companies doing business in Egypt include acute shortage of commercial and residential space in Cairo, sky-high rents, unreliable telephone and Telex connections and fluctuating tax policies   (NATIONAL JOURNAL,   April 8, 1978,   P564)

PORT SAID BOOMING

Reporter Christopher Wren assesses impact on economy of Port Said of designation after 1973 war as duty-free zone; holds that new prosperity has been fostered more by smugglers and shoppers from other parts of Egypt who flock to Port Said and attempt to sneak imported goods, usually subject to stiff taxation, into other areas of Egypt; area has also attracted foreign investments, including 4 plants and 33 planned new ones, spurred by low electricity, fuel and labor and absence of strikes   (NEW YORK TIMES,   April 19, 1978,   P3)

GOALS OF NEO-WAFD NOTED

Commentator David Watts describes the emergence of the Neo-Wafd Party in Egypt, led by Faud Seraguddin; says for students Seraguddin represents an alternative to the present government and a chance for real political expression; outlines the objectives of the Party as increased encouragement of foreign investment, reduction in military budget, development of tourism and agriculture and incentives to attract skilled people who have left Egypt for better jobs in Europe and the US to come back   (TIMES OF LONDON,   April 20, 1978,   P18)

SPENDING PROGRAM OUTLINED

Egypt's Minister of Economy Hamed el-Sayeh reports Egyptian government will spend between $3.1 billion and $3.5 billion on economic development in 1978; notes medium-term goal is to reduce budget deficit and push investment to highest possible level; cites government's efforts to get foreign investors, Arab investors and private Egyptian investors to undertake a much larger share in development; reports government intends to spend 8%–9% of investment funds through 1982 on agriculture and 27% on industrial development; attributes Egypt's current inflationary spiral to high level of government spending on subsidies, investment and defense, but notes it is politically difficult to make reductions in subsidies and defense　(JOURNAL OF COMMERCE,　May 1, 1978,　P10)

SADAT TIGHTENS GRIP

Egyptian President Anwar el-Sadat announces he will reorganize his Cabinet to make it more dynamic, warns critics they risk confrontation if they continue to criticize government's performance, and charges leftist and rightist opponents in Parliament and press with stirring up social unrest; calls on People's Assembly to draft legislation to control slander against government officials, but promises not to dissolve Parliament without required plebiscite and pledges to uphold democratic reforms he instituted; observers believe lack of more stringent responses to critics indicate Sadat feels he is still in control of situation　(NEW YORK TIMES,　May 3, 1978,　P16)

WAFDIST PROFILED

Profile of Faud Seraguddin, leader of Egypt's Neo-Wafd Party, discusses formation of first genuinely independent legal political party in Egypt since 1953; observes Seraguddin supports Egyptian President Anwar Sadat's foreign policy, while seeking domestic, social and economic changes; notes Seraguddin claims party is national organization that represents all classes and political views; observes changes Seraguddin is seeking include parliamentary style democracy, direct Presidential elections, elimination of obstacles to economic liberalization, end to guaranteed government jobs for university graduates and increased productivity (WASHINGTON POST,　May 6, 1978,　P14)

SUEZ PLANNING FOR BOOM

City of Suez is in the middle of a massive rebuilding program designed to make it one of Egypt's major industrial centers; Suez's governor, Major General Mahrous Abu-Hussein, reports work has recently begun on 2 multimillion dollar industrial projects in Suez, a cement plant financed with US aid funds and a joint Egyptian-Iranian textile factory; notes factories in Suez have been badly damaged in wars with Israel, but asserts city is making progress toward recovery; notes city is emphasizing trade and industrial development first and agricultural development second; reports Suez will be able to supply all its electric power needs by end of 1978; notes projects are under way to widen and deepen Suez sweet water canal and to build a new water plant　(JOURNAL OF COMMERCE,　May 8, 1978,　P1)

CABINET SHUFFLE PURGES ECONOMIST

Egyptian Cabinet reshuffle resulting in removal of Egypt's top economic strategist, Dr. Abdul el-Kaissouny, has caused concern about effect on Egyptian Government's ability to attract foreign aid and to retain international business confidence; strong-willed Dr. Kaissouny was widely credited with having helped pull Egyptian economy back from brink of collapse by persuading Arab oil-producing states to pay Egypt's huge debts on assurance that Egypt would institute financial reforms; now, Cabinet shuffle has left Prime Minister Mamdouh Salem in control; Salem is opposed to Kaissouny's planned cutbacks in huge consumer subsidies to help balance budget; government's silence thus far on successor for Kaissouny has left some Western economic specialists wondering whether Cairo will remain committed to Kaissouny's planned reforms　(NEW YORK TIMES,　May 10, 1978,　P4)

SADAT FACES HARDSHIPS

Egyptian President Anwar el-Sadat is coming under heavy pressure to improve Egypt's economic system; exports climbed from $1 billion in 1973 to $1.6 billion in 1976 while imports tripled to over $4.2 billion creating huge balance of payments deficit; despite improved performances of such invisibles as tourism and the Suez Canal, an annual deficit on current account of around $2 billion is expected until the 1980's; Egypt is the biggest Arab recipient of US aid, but unless the economy improves, Sadat will soon encounter increasing popular pressure to step down　(FINANCIAL TIMES,　May 13, 1978,　P2)

SADAT CALLS FOR REFERENDUM

Egyptian President Anwar el-Sadat, responding to growing criticism of his domestic policies, calls for national referendum next week giving him vote of confidence and asking Egyptians whether Communists, certain pro-USSR leaders and pre-revolutionary politicians should be allowed to retain positions of influence; announcement follows Sadat's second complaint in less than 2 weeks about "campaign of doubt" being spread by his opponents in Parliament, particularly leftists and members of Neo-Wafd Party, and press; referendum is expected to run heavily in Sadat's favor, giving him leverage to move against opponents as he sees fit, and is seen as step backward from controlled democracy he has been espousing　(NEW YORK TIMES,　May 15, 1978,　P1)

CLAMPDOWN ACCOMPANIES REFERENDUM

Reporter Christopher Wren discusses effects of Sadat's forthcoming referendum asking approval of ban on activity by "atheists" and "corrupters" of political life; reports that leftist Progressive Unionist Party weekly *Al Ahaly* edition urging readers to say "no" to referendum was confiscated while going to press, although a few issues reached street; reports that leftist leader Khalid Mohieddin has told news conference that confiscation was illegal and that Sadat is bent upon "liquidating all opponents"　(NEW YORK TIMES,　May 19, 1978,　P7)

REFERENDUM'S AIMS ANALYZED

Egyptian referendum that would give President Anwar el-Sadat mandate to crack down on his political critics and limit expression in the press is expected to run overwhelmingly in Sadat's favor; is generally assumed to be aimed at undercutting 2 of Egypt's 4 legal political parties, Unionist Progressive Party and Neo-Wafd Party; members of both parties have assailed Sadat's handling of economy but not his peace initiative with Israel; critics of referendum complain that definitions are so imprecise that

Sadat and his adherents in Parliament could apply proposed sanctions as they choose   (NEW YORK TIMES, May 22, 1978, P6)

SADAT RECEIVES ENDORSEMENT

Egyptian Minister of Interior Ismail Nabawi reports final results of national referendum show 98.29% of voters endorse Sadat's proposals to curtail political dissent and criticism in press; asserts over 85% of 11 million eligible voters participated in referendum; principles of referendum, to be enacted into law by People's Assembly, would exclude Communists from public posts and journalism, prohibit political activity for anyone who held office before 1952 revolution, and compel press to adhere to Sadat's precepts of democratic socialism, national unity and social peace   (NEW YORK TIMES, May 23, 1978, P2)

SADAT DENOUNCES OPPOSITION

Egypt's President Sadat denounces opposition leftist Progressive Unionist Party and rightist Neo-Wafd Party at press conference following his victory in referendum to curb dissent; avers that he is still dedicated to "democratic experiment" but opposes "anyone who tries to exploit democracy for his own ends"; in related development leftist party issues statement urging avoidance of "futile confrontation with the government" but says it will continue struggle   (NEW YORK TIMES, May 24, 1978, P11)

SADAT CLASHES WITH CRITICS

Egyptian authorities seize latest issue of *Al Ahaly*, weekly newspaper of leftist Progressive Union Party, because it allegedly contains "sensational and hostile articles"; in related news, Sadat tells editors and journalists he erred in allowing "rotten elements" created and supported by USSR to enter Egyptian politics   (NEW YORK TIMES, May 25, 1978, P7)

CRACKDOWN POINTS UP UNCERTAINTY

Reporter Christopher Wren discusses Sadat's political difficulties; notes that Sadat's crackdown on dissent appears to show that while he espouses democracy he cannot tolerate political opposition; observes that his peace initiative is at standstill, his attempts to attract foreign capital have benefited only a few, and that average Egyptian is economically worse off than before; notes annual inflation rate of about 25%; reports deterioration of life in Cairo, with periodic food shortages, power and equipment breakdowns and decaying buildings; observes that this has provided ammunition for opponents; leftist weekly *Al Ahaly* has reportedly increased circulation from 50,000 to 135,000, with sharp attacks on government (NEW YORK TIMES, May 29, 1978, P2)

PRESS HIT IN CRACKDOWN

Five leading Egyptian journalists and writers, including Mohammed Hassanein Heykal, former editor of *Al Ahram*, have been forbidden to travel abroad pending investigation into materials published or broadcast abroad that authorities contend are slanderous to Egypt; other journalists under investigation are Mohammed Sidi-Ahmed, Ahmed Fuad Negm, Sheikh Imam, Ahmed Hamroush and Salah Eissa; according to press reports, Interior Minister Ismail Nabawi sent names of 5 to socialist prosecutor, Ahmed Habib, who is empowered to investigate political offenses   (NEW YORK TIMES, May 29, 1978, P2)

I.M.F. VOTE OF CONFIDENCE

Egypt reaches agreement in principle with International Monetary Fund in its effort to obtain a 3-year loan for up to $720 million; agreement is seen as significant achievement because few nations qualify for more than 1-year standby credit; Egypt's economy faces close scrutiny by aid donors at June 14–16 meeting in Paris between Egyptian officials and representatives of several international financial agencies, including World Bank, US Agency for International Development and fund for OPEC; Egypt will be seeking financial assistance to implement its $20 billion 5-year plan drawn up in 1977   (NEW YORK TIMES, June 2, 1978, S4 P9)

WAFD DISBANDS IN PROTEST

Egypt's conservative opposition Neo-Wafd Party disbands rather than submitting to new political restrictions imposed by President Sadat; new legislation would have purged at least 3 top Neo-Wafd members, deputy chairman Faud Seraguddin, secretary general Ibrahim Farag and deputy chairman Abdel-Fattah Hasan; party statement charges laws "swept away all political freedom gained by the people" and aims at destroying Neo-Wafd Party; Neo-Wafd Party reportedly has 20 members of Parliament; 3 political groups remain, representing right, left and center   (NEW YORK TIMES, June 3, 1978, P1)

LEFTISTS SUSPEND ACTIVITY

Egypt's leftist Progressive Unionist Party announces it is suspending "mass political activity" in protest against newly imposed restrictions on political dissent; says constituent assembly will meet to decide party's future; announces it will study legal action to challenge constitutionality of new curb on political groups; says its weekly newspaper, *Al Ahaly*, will stop publication June 14   (NEW YORK TIMES, June 6, 1978, P3)

COURT UPHOLDS LEFTISTS

Egyptian judge overturns government order that resulted in confiscation of latest issue of leftist party paper, *Al Ahaly*, which has become primary target of President Sadat's drive to silence his critics   (NEW YORK TIMES, June 8, 1978, P10)

SADAT'S IMAGE DAMAGED

Reporter Christopher S. Wren reports that criticism of Sadat's crackdown on political opposition "has left him visibly defensive"; observes that harsh measures have eroded Sadat's image as a statesman above petty politics;

reports he has antagonized educated Egyptians by claiming democracy remains unaffected; notes that Sadat has warned foreign correspondents of expulsion if they are too critical, accused Egyptian journalists of denigrating Egypt abroad for handsome fees, and lashed out at university professors who asked him to reconsider his referendum; holds that Parliament is left with only the majority centrist party and "a small sycophantic rightist party"; claims that Sadat has insured popular support by describing his critics as atheists, corrupt reactionaries or Soviet agents   (NEW YORK TIMES,   June 12, 1978,   P1)

TIGHT STRINGS ON I.M.F. LOAN

International Monetary Fund agrees to lend Egypt $750 million over next 3 years to supplement Egypt's 3-year economic program, which is aimed at producing annual growth rate of 8%, reducing inflation to less than 10% per year and improving its balance of payments with other nations   (NEW YORK TIMES,   August 1, 1978,   P4)

EGYPTIAN PARTIES MERGE

Ruling Egyptian Arab Socialist Party, headed by Prime Minister Mamdouh Salem, announces it will merge with President Anwar el-Sadat's new National Democratic Party which is now being formed; new party will base power on 308 seats out of 360 it currently has in Parliament   (NEW YORK TIMES,   August 14, 1978,   P61)

SADAT LAUNCHES NEW PARTY

Egypt's President Sadat pledges to seek peace with Israel but says he will not seek "separate solution" at Camp David summit, in speech marking 5th anniversary of 1973 Middle East war; devotes most of speech to launching his new National Democratic Party; suggests he is thinking of outlawing leftist National Progressive Unionist coalition; Government has reportedly filed suit to ban leftist paper, *Al Ahaly*   (NEW YORK TIMES, August 15, 1978,   P94)

PREMIER JOURNALIST SUSPENDED

Egyptian authorities suspend journalist Mustapha Amin after he criticized Parliament members who joined President Anwar Sadat's new political party; authorities act under 2-month-old law that allows them to suspend any journalist whose writings or broadcasts threaten social peace or national unity; Amin is co-founder of mass-circulation newspaper *Al Akhbar*   (NEW YORK TIMES, August 20, 1978,   P83)

PRIME MINISTER'S RESIGNATION HINTED

Report by Egyptian newspaper *Al Ahram* that Prime Minister Mamdouh Salem has resigned cannot be confirmed; Information and Culture Minister Abdel-Moneim el-Sawi denies report; other high-level Egyptians also discount resignation report; Salem has submitted resignation 3 times in last 20 months, but President Anwar el-Sadat has refused to accept it   (NEW YORK TIMES, August 23, 1978, P121)

SALEM RESIGNS

Egyptian Prime Minister Mamdouh Salem resigns as head of Misr Party, nation's ruling party, signaling end to his political career and probably to his government service as well; is expected to resign as Prime Minister when President Anwar el-Sadat returns from summit conference at Camp David; Sadat rearranged political system after many sessions of Parliament were delayed due to squabbling among members of Misr Party; Sadat has disbanded party and will lead new National Democratic Party; high Egyptian official says Salem's biggest problem was failure to control party establishment   (NEW YORK TIMES,   September 2, 1978,   P32)

DEMOBILIZATION DIFFICULTIES ANALYZED

Egyptian Planning Minister Razak Abdel-Neguib proposes plan to demobilize thousands of soldiers and put them to work in public works construction and farming; details of secret report are being studied by top military and government leaders; economists fear demobilization may place added burden on struggling economy at time when unemployment is at 12% and under-employment is widespread   (NEW YORK TIMES,   September 29, 1978,   P96)

NEW CABINET FORMED

Egyptian President Sadat carries out major cabinet shakeup in consultation with new Prime Minister Mustapha Khalil; cabinet is reduced from 31 to 28 members, 2 ministries are abolished and 2 others are divided in 2; Major General Hassan Kamal Ali is named new minister of defense and commander-in-chief of Egypt's armed forces, replacing General Mohammed Abdel-Ghany al-Gamasy, who has become a Presidential adviser; Major General Ahmed Badawy replaces armed forces chief of staff Lieutenant General Mohammed Ali Fahmy, who is named a Presidential adviser; departure of Gamasy and Fahmy is viewed with surprise by political observers, who are speculating on possible disaffection within military over Camp David peace accords; position of foreign minister is left vacant for time being; Butros Ghali has been acting as foreign minister; ministers of finance, irrigation and transportation and communications are also replaced; Ministry of Information and Culture is abolished, with responsibilities for culture grouped under Ministry of Education; State Information Service, Cairo Radio and Television and semi-official Middle East News Agency are reportedly becoming independent; Ministry of Local Government is eliminated and Ministry of Cabinet Affairs is entrusted with transferring its authority to nation's governors   (NEW YORK TIMES,   October 5, 1978,   P14)

NEW EGYPTIAN ARMY IN MAKING

Commentator Thomas W. Lippman speculates that new role is being envisioned for Egyptian military in future; describes Egypt's recent annual display of military power showing Egypt remains most powerful military machine in Arab world while indicating changes in way forces are being equipped; points out Egypt's newest military acquisitions would be more useful in context of war in Africa than in war with Israel   (WASHINGTON POST, October 7, 1978,   P16)

Diplomacy after Jerusalem

HUSSEIN REJECTS CURRENT NEGOTIATIONS

King Hussein says President Carter has failed to persuade him to change his stand and join current negotiations in

Jordan's King Hussein.

Cairo; Hussein's refusal leads US sources to conclude that main theme of Arab leaders in their coming talks with Carter will be insistence that US put increased pressure on Israel to offer more sweeping concessions on Palestinian issue; Carter notes that he sees no reason for Jordan to join talks directly, in speech at airport in Teheran; Cairo is expected to maintain without change its demand for total withdrawal from occupied territory and full self-determination for Palestinian Arabs   (NEW YORK TIMES,   January 2, 1978,   P3)

Jimmy Carter and Anwar Sadat embrace following forty-five minutes of talks at the Aswan Airport January 4. Carter spent only an hour in Egypt on a tour that took him to Europe, Asia and North Africa.

SADAT TO TAKE 'FLEXIBLE' STAND

Official Egyptian sources report that President Anwar el-Sadat would take "moderate and flexible approach" to problem of Palestinian state in meeting with US President Carter in Aswan, Egypt; Egyptian position is said to be inflexible only on basic principle that Palestinians on West Bank of Jordan River and in Gaza Strip must be given chance to exercise right to determine status of their territory whether independence or federation with Jordan; Egyptians contend that once principles are enunciated, including principle of ultimate Israeli withdrawal from Arab lands, specifics can be worked out to satisfaction of both Arabs and Israelis; Egypt is believed ready to accept transition of several years leading up to self-determination, and hoping that more radical elements of Palestine Liberation Organization would lose influence over West Bank population over transition period   (NEW YORK TIMES,   January 4, 1978,   P1)

CARTER, SADAT MEET AT ASWAN

President Carter meets with Egyptian President Anwar el-Sadat at Aswan, Egypt, for talks lasting about 50 minutes and then flies on to France; after meeting Carter reads prepared statement in which he says that Palestinians should have opportunity to "participate" in "determination" of their future; repeats view, shared with Egyptians, that basic principles of "fundamentals" should be agreed on before comprehensive Middle East peace can be achieved; lists Palestinian role in determining own future as one of principles; mentions 2 other principles including Israeli withdrawal from Arab territories occupied in 1967 and agreement that peace between Arabs and Israel must bring "normal relations" and not just nonbelligerency; President Sadat, expressing satisfaction over talks, calls Carter's views "identical" to his own   (NEW YORK TIMES,   January 5, 1978,   P1)

BEGIN REJECTS SELF-DETERMINATION

Israeli Prime Minister Menachem Begin expresses satisfaction that President Carter and Egyptian President Sadat did not use term "Palestinian state" in statements they made after meeting in Aswan; says self-determination for Palestinian Arabs urged by Sadat is tantamount to Palestinian state and is unacceptable to Israel; speaks with Carter by telephone; Foreign Minister Dayan says talks with Egypt could end in separate treaty between Egypt and Israel; forecasts active role in talks for US   (NEW YORK TIMES,   January 5, 1978,   P3)

U.S. ADVANCES PEACE PLAN

US plans to propose temporary arrangement in which Israel and Egypt would agree to principles governing further negotiations on Palestinian issue and overall Arab-Israeli settlement; hopes principles will appeal to Jordan and "moderate" Palestinians, and that they will join in negotiations regarding West Bank and Gaza Strip; plan will be discussed at January 16 Jerusalem meeting of Israeli and Egyptian foreign ministers, where Secretary of State Cyrus Vance is expected to take more active role in mediating Israeli-Egyptian differences; plan reportedly calls for postponement of determination of Palestinian society, which is subject of controversy since Israel advocates "self-rule" for Palestinians and Egypt demands "self-determination"; also proposes interim 5-year plan in which Israeli military government would end, while Jordanians and Palestinians join in negotiating security agreements for West Bank and Gaza Strip   (NEW YORK TIMES,   January 14, 1978,   P1)

SADAT DISCOURAGED

President Sadat sees "absolutely no hope" that Israeli-Egyptian Political Commission will be able to achieve agreement on principles of Middle East peace settlement; cites Israeli "intransigence" regarding terms for returning occupied areas, particularly the future of Israeli settlements in Sinai; says he offered Israel everything and received nothing in return   (NEW YORK TIMES,   January 15, 1978,   P6)

VANCE DELAYS VISIT

State Department announces that Secretary of State Cyrus Vance postponed his departure for Jerusalem 90 minutes before scheduled flight time, because Israeli and Egyptian officials were unable to reach agreement on how to describe Palestinian issue in agenda for January 16 meeting of foreign ministers; US reportedly informed both Israel and Egypt that Vance would delay trip if there

was no agreement, since he wanted to discuss only "substantive" issues; delay, which came as surprise to reporters accompanying Vance, is expected to be at least 24 hours, with State Department noting Vance is prepared to leave January 16 if agreement is reached; controversy centers around wording of West Bank-Gaza Strip-Palestinian issue, with Egypt favoring term "Palestinian question" and Israel demanding reference to "Palestinian Arabs of Judea, Samaria and the Gaza district"   (NEW YORK TIMES,   January 15, 1978,   P1)

KAMEL, DAYAN AND VANCE CONFER

Egyptian Foreign Minister Mohammed Ibrahim Kamel and Israeli Foreign Minister Moshe Dayan, joined by Secretary of State Cyrus Vance, open Jerusalem talks on principles for overall Middle East settlement; officials report that both Kamel and Dayan publicly stressed their differences, but were privately beginning to discuss possible compromises; note Israeli Prime Minister Begin surprised 700 guests at elaborate Jerusalem Hilton dinner honoring Kamel and Vance, by lecturing Kamel rather than toasting new peace efforts; it is believed that Begin was irritated by Kamel's reiteration of Egypt's demands for total Israeli withdrawal from occupied Arab lands, and "self-determination" for Palestinians; note Begin also told Kamel, who appeared shocked by Begin's comments, that he was "a young man" who was unaware that "self-determination" was misused in Europe and contributed to World War II   (NEW YORK TIMES,   January 18, 1978,   P1)

FOREIGN MINISTER KAMEL RECALLED

Egyptian President Anwar el-Sadat orders Foreign Minister Mohammed Ibrahim Kamel to return to Cairo from Jerusalem, informing President Carter that talks on Middle East peace settlement will resume if Israel changes its position; receives telephone call from Carter, asking that he reconsider his stand, and agrees to allow continuation of military talks, scheduled to take place in Cairo January 21; action has caused speculation that Sadat will announce "some fresh surprises" in his address to Parliament, noting Sadat had stated he would resign if his peace efforts failed; resignation is not considered likely to be accepted, however, since peace efforts have been strongly supported in Egypt   (NEW YORK TIMES,   January 19, 1978,   P1)

TALKS BREAK-OFF ANALYZED

Commentator H.D.S. Greenway's analysis of unexpected termination of Jerusalem talks between Israel and Egypt notes misperceptions on both sides; reports Israel envisioned long negotiating process while Egypt hoped to avoid prolonged bargaining; notes Egyptians grew impatient with Israeli Prime Minister Begin's adamant opposition to Palestinian self-determination; adds Egyptian President Sadat's recall of delegation was viewed as mercurial by Israelis and Americans; reports US probably will be relied upon to rescue peace initiative   (WASHINGTON POST,   January 19, 1978,   P20)

EGYPTIAN-ISRAELI CONVERGENCE SEEN

Aides to Secretary of State Cyrus Vance contend that despite sharp exchanges between Israel and Egypt, both sides are moving closer on terms of statement of principles on peace, noting main controversy centers around which Palestinians would be allowed to participate in negotiations; report that when negotiations broke off January 18, Israel had objected to paragraph stating Palestinian resolution "must recognize the legitimate rights of the Palestinian people and enable the Palestinians to participate in the determination of their own future"; note Israel interprets term Palestinians to mean those already living in Israeli occupied zones, and excluding those in Lebanon, Syria, US and elsewhere, and also refuses to recognize "legitimate rights" of Palestinians; claim Egyptians, who do not object to language of compromise, have been angered by Israel's insistence on keeping and defending Sinai settlements, while also promising to return sovereignty of area to Egypt (NEW YORK TIMES, January 22, 1978, P1)

SADAT EXPLAINS POSITION

Egyptian President Anwar el-Sadat addresses Egyptian Parliament, pledging to continue with peace effort and blaming Israeli "negotiating tactics" for breakdown in political committee talks January 18; holds peace initiative is no longer simply an Egyptian affair but international matter which world will not allow to fail; speech, termed "surprisingly moderate" by observers, does not reveal any new plan of action and implies that solving of impasse is now up to others, including Israeli people; also claims that Israeli Prime Minister Begin's tough stand on issues is result of US "arsenal which was given to Israel"; reveals that Israeli Cabinet ministers had privately apologized for Begin's dinner toast to Egyptian Foreign Minister Mohammed Ibrahim Kamel, and that Sadat asked Secretary of State Cyrus Vance to inform Carter that Egypt wants to be equipped with "every armament" that was sent to Israel (NEW YORK TIMES, January 22, 1978, P1)

ISRAEL CONTINUES TALKS

Israeli Cabinet votes unanimously to resume participation in joint Egyptian-Israeli Military Commission in Cairo, following recommendation by Prime Minister Begin; Defense Minister Ezer Weizman and aides are expected to leave for Cairo within a few days to resume contacts with Egypt's Defense Minister General Mohammed Abdel Ghany el-Gamasy; Cabinet spokesman Aryeh Naor observes that decision to resume political talks is up to Egyptians (NEW YORK TIMES, January 30, 1978, P1)

U.S. ROLE SEEN PIVOTAL

Commentator Thomas W. Lippman sees US entering critical period in relations with Arab governments; notes most urgent question likely to be raised by visiting Egyptian President Sadat concerns US participation in securing Israeli concessions on occupied territory and Palestinian rights; reports US will not be moved by threats that intransigence may jeopardize oil supplies and Arab moderation; adds US will not threaten Israel with aid cutoff; questions whether US can hold together fragile relationships with Saudi Arabia, Egypt, Sudan, Jordan and Syria; reports one reason Sadat broke off direct negotiations with Israel was his displeasure at finding US assuming middle ground rather than advocating Egypt's interests (WASHINGTON POST, February 3, 1978, P21)

SADAT AND CARTER MEET

President Carter and Egypt's President Sadat begin talks at Camp David, Maryland, meeting alone and later with aides; source reports Carter agrees with Egypt that Israel should withdraw forces from Sinai, Golan Heights and West Bank, but disagrees that Israel must return all land; says Carter believes Israel should not retain settlements in Sinai Peninsula and opposes self-determination for Palestinians if this means creation of Palestinian state on Israel's borders; Sadat reportedly wishes to discuss expanded American economic investment in Egypt and purchase of military equipment (NEW YORK TIMES, February 5, 1978, P1)

SUMMIT MEETING CONCLUDES

President Carter and Egypt's President Sadat return from "extraordinarily warm and relaxed" weekend at Camp David; they agreed there to try to get Middle East peace talks started again and to broaden negotiations to include Jordan; in later NBC-TV interview with David Brinkley, Sadat says Carter did not give him a definite answer on his request to buy US arms; explains that his sudden decision to break off Israeli-Arab talks in Jerusalem was related to Israeli decision to "thicken" existing settlements (NEW YORK TIMES, February 6, 1978, P1)

SADAT SCORES BEGIN

Egypt's President Sadat, in speech to National Press Club, accuses Israeli Prime Minister Begin of "damaging the spirit" of peace talks by insisting on retention of Sinai Peninsula settlements; maintains he himself has wanted to establish broad negotiating principles while Begin has been exact and detailed; suggests he might quit office if peace talks collapse; asserts that his proposal that Israel evacuate Sinai airfields and plow them under to insure they would not be used by Egyptians was distorted by Begin, who accused Sadat of saying he would burn Israeli settlements "as Nero had burned Rome"; repeats that Israel has to reciprocate to his peace initiative by withdrawing from all Arab lands occupied since 1967, granting Palestinians self-determination and providing guarantee for mutual security; calls on Israel to give up control over East Jerusalem; supports internationalization of both sides of city; asks US to treat Egypt and Israel equally in supplying arms; says he would support demilitarization of area; during later talk with press, says he would accept interim arrangement for control over West Bank and Gaza Strip shared by Palestinians, Israelis, Jordanians, Egyptians and UN, so long as end was independent Palestinian state; also meets with Cabinet members, Henry Kissinger, Defense Secretary Brown on arms issue, and Agriculture Secretary Bergland on food-for-peace shipments and purchase of US cotton (NEW YORK TIMES, February 7, 1978, P1)

SADAT, CARTER CONCLUDE TALKS

President Carter and Egypt's President Sadat end talks in Washington; Sadat says talks will make him persevere for peace; Carter Administration statement stresses US will remain faithful to its commitment to Israel but will also adhere to UN Resolution 242, thus indirectly reminding Israel that US expects it to withdraw from substantial portions of West Bank, Golan Heights and Sinai; indirectly criticizes Israel for settlements in occupied territory; reaffirms US commitment to Aswan formula calling for Palestinian self-determination; Administration officials note that Assistant State Secretary Alfred L. Atherton Jr. will return to Middle East to work out declaration of principles; express hope that Jordan will join talks; Defense Department officials report they expect Carter to approve sale to Egypt of F-5E planes; Sadat has stressed he wants planes to offset USSR threat in Ethiopia and Libya   (NEW YORK TIMES,   February 9, 1978,   P1)

CONFLICT ON U.N. RESOLUTION

Israel informs US that it does not accept US interpretation of UN Security Council Resolution 242 requiring Israel to withdraw occupation forces from parts of West Bank and Gaza Strip, causing major behind-the-scenes dispute between Israel and US; Carter Administration has avoided public discussion of issue since Prime Minister Begin, Foreign Minister Moshe Dayan, and Defense Minister Ezer Weizman are scheduled to visit US shortly, but Administration sources hold issue could upset hopes for overall Middle East settlement; issue has also become domestic political issue in Israel, with Labor Party leaders, including former Prime Ministers Golda Meir and Yitzhak Rabin, pointing out Israel was committed to UN resolution under their governments; Israeli officials, who have privately accused Carter Administration of creating new issue because of its inability to pressure Egypt and other Arabs in negotiations, contend they still accept Resolution 242, but hold their interpretation differs from that of preceding Labor Party government   (NEW YORK TIMES,   March 5, 1978,   P1)

BEGIN, SADAT EXCHANGE NOTES

Israeli Prime Minister Menachem Begin sends secret message to Egyptian President Anwar el-Sadat, to be hand-delivered by US Assistant State Secretary Alfred L. Atherton, which urges resumption of direct negotiations between the 2 countries; responds to earlier message received from Sadat; exchange itself is regarded in Jerusalem as renewal of direct contact between Egypt and Israel   (NEW YORK TIMES,   March 6, 1978,   P1)

EGYPTIAN, ISRAELI POSITIONS ANALYZED

Editorial criticizes Israeli Prime Minister Menachem Begin's "dream" of permanent Israeli rule over West Bank of Jordan River and warns of eventual US disenchantment with Israel that could flow from Begin's current stance; urges Begin to accept territory-for-peace formula contained in UN Resolution 242 adopted after 1967 Arab-Israeli war, pointing out that all previous Israeli governments had accepted it and that there is good

reason to believe that Egyptian President Anwar el-Sadat is ready to accept; affirms that no one expects Israeli withdrawal in foreseeable future from West Bank and recalls that even President Sadat favors 5-year interim agreement; concedes that Israel has made great efforts to reciprocate Sadat's recognition of Israel's legitimacy in Middle East, including acceptance of Egyptian sovereignty over all of Sinai and pledge to return it in stages and agreement to let Palestinians in territory have voice if not actual self-determination in their future; points out, however, that Sadat wants and probably needs more concessions before he can conclude peace treaty and gain minimum of respect from more conservative Arab allies   (NEW YORK TIMES,   March 7, 1978,   P34)

EGYPT'S MOOD ANALYZED

Commentator Thomas W. Lippman discusses mood of Egypt in wake of faltering Middle East peace initiative by President Anwar Sadat; asserts that nation's hopes for quick settlement and instant prosperity have faded as have its fears of disastrous consequences arising from settlement; holds that Egyptians are not angry with Sadat but rather resent Israel's diplomatic intransigence; reports that many informed Egyptians feel Sadat has succeeded in driving significant wedge between Carter Administration and Israel   (WASHINGTON POST,   March 9, 1978,   P1)

BEGIN'S PERSPECTIVE EXAMINED

Harvard scholar on Jewish history Leon Wieseltier holds Israeli Prime Minister Begin is negotiating with Egyptians not only as an Israeli, but also as a Jew, and that as consequence Begin bases his politics on grim history of Jews in exile; claims Begin feels accountable to Auschwitz and other Nazi death camps, producing instincts of distrust, self-reliance and unslackening vigilance; maintains Arabs and other nations must realize that emotional scars of Jews inhibits them from entrusting their safety simply to words of others, but holds that real sin against Auschwitz would be to let present opportunity for peace slip away   (NEW YORK TIMES,   March 10, 1978,   P29)

EFFECT OF INCURSION ANALYZED

Commentator Ray Vicker indicates Egypt's desire for continued peace negotiations with Israel does not appear to have been deterred by recent Israeli invasion of Lebanon; notes there is widespread hope in Egypt that world opinion will react against invasion, that Israelis will begin to question leadership of Prime Minister Menachem Begin and that US will take firmer stance toward Israel, thereby enhancing Egypt's negotiating position; indicates many Egyptians believe Israel's invasion of Lebanon has demonstrated Egyptian President Anwar Sadat is correct in seeking broad-based settlement which will resolve Palestinian question; adds Egypt's position has also been bolstered by refusal of "rejectionist" Arab nations, which have professed support of Palestine Liberation Organization, to attempt to counter Israeli action thereby undermining integrity of rejectionist bloc; suggests Palestinians may consequently begin to perceive Egypt as their true defender   (WALL STREET JOURNAL,   March 23, 1978,   P20)

CARTER, BEGIN TALKS WIND UP

President Carter and Israeli Prime Minister Begin end 2 days of intensive talks in Washington with little evidence that their differences over issues on Middle East peace have been narrowed; national security adviser Zbigniew Brzezinski agrees with reporter's assessment that talks appear to be grim, while Secretary of State Vance emerges from working lunch with Begin by conceding differences have not been reduced; US and Israeli officials have been unsuccessful in drafting mutually acceptable statement to summarize talks, although Press Secretary Jody Powell holds such a statement will probably be issued March 23; sources note that neither side had expected to resolve differences at this meeting, but US now hopes Begin will discuss disputed points with members of his government to seek compromise which will allow negotiations to resume; issues under discussion included interpretation of UN Resolution 242, Israeli settlements in occupied areas, and proposed US sale of military aircraft to Israel, Egypt and Saudi Arabia (NEW YORK TIMES, March 23, 1978, P1)

BEGIN APPEALS FOR SUPPORT

Israel's Prime Minister Begin makes several public appearances appealing for support of Americans following impasse in talks with President Carter; claims his 3 days in Washington were most difficult in his life; tells National Press Club Israel has learned that Saudi Arabia has agreed to give F-15 planes, which it plans to buy from US, to another Arab country, presumably Egypt; a news agency report, attributed to those close to Begin, claims Carter is hoping to drive Begin from office by emphasizing differences between US and Israeli positions; President Carter, in meeting with Senate Foreign Relations Committee, asks committee for its help in reactivating diplomatic processes, but proposes no new formulas (NEW YORK TIMES, March 24, 1978, P1)

BEGIN DESCRIBES TALKS WITH CARTER

Israeli Prime Minister Menachem Begin declares on returning home that his talks in US were "difficult" and calls some US demands "unacceptable," in news conference at Ben-Gurion International Airport; again pushes own peace plan, defends unwillingness to bend on positions that put him in conflict with Carter Administration and asserts his meetings with US have not set back stalled talks with Egypt; several Israeli newspapers call for reassessing Israel's positions in light of talks with US, while Labor Party newspaper *Davar* calls for new elections; poll conducted by Pori Public Research Institute finds that 69.8% of respondents had chosen peace behind secure borders over right to settle on West Bank or Gaza, while 60.9% said that policy on settlements was harmful to Israel's image abroad; earlier in day, newspaper *Maariv* had published interview with Defense Minister Ezer Weizman which called for "national peace government" and led observers to discern bid to replace Begin (NEW YORK TIMES, March 25, 1978, P1)

SADAT, WEIZMAN MEET

Israel Defense Minister Ezer Weizman meets with Egyptian President Anwar el-Sadat to discuss possibility of resuming peace negotiations between the 2 countries; Cairo meeting is first since talks on military aspects of Israeli settlements were suspended 8 weeks ago; Egyptians had hoped that visit would bring modification in Israel's bargaining position, but a presidential spokesman reported that no progress was made and that situation remained unchanged; Weizman reassured Sadat of Israel's intention to withdraw from southern Lebanon after UN peace-keeping force takes up position. (NEW YORK TIMES, March 31, 1978, P3)

EGYPT SCORES BEGIN

Egyptian officials conclude that no real progress in peace negotiations can be achieved as long as Israeli Prime Minister Menachem Begin remains in office; Egyptian hostility toward Begin had been mounting over his justification of Israeli settlements on occupied Arab territory, and was exacerbated by Israel's invasion of southern Lebanon; recent foreign policy debate in Israel's Parliament is deadlocked because of Arab insistence on Israeli withdrawal from occupied territories and establishment of Palestinian state, demands which Egyptian President Anwar el-Sadat contends are essential for durable peace in Middle East; Begin contends that United Nations resolution 242, which calls for Israeli withdrawal from Arab lands occupied during 1967 war, does not necessarily apply to West Bank of Jordan River and refuses to concede that there is legitimate Palestinian entity (NEW YORK TIMES, April 3, 1978, P3)

EGYPT ASKS U.S. PARTICIPATION

Official Egyptian sources claim that President Anwar el-Sadat is waiting for President Carter to fulfill pledge made during Sadat-Carter talks at Camp David in February 1978 that US would step in with plan to move Middle East peace talks forward if Israel and Egypt could not break deadlock; contend that commitment resulted in Sadat keeping peace initiative alive despite Israel's invasion of Lebanon; point out that Sadat feels any American proposal would be compatible with Egypt's position; add that strain in US-Israeli relations and opposition within Israel toward Prime Minister Begin's hardline position have encouraged Sadat to continue his waiting game; Sadat in meeting with delegates to conference of educators and editors in Cairo avoids questions about commitment, but does admit that he believes Carter is no longer just mediator in Israeli-Egyptian talks (NEW YORK TIMES, April 7, 1978, P2)

REDEFINED POSITION ANALYZED

Commentator James Reston calls Israel's redefined position on Middle East "tactical move" designed to reopen peace negotiations by recognizing 3 different interpretations of UN Security Council resolution on Middle East; says Israel's new position recognizes right of Palestinians in West Bank and Gaza Strip to participate in determination of their future, but limits that right to framework of talks to be held among Egypt, Israel, Jordan and representatives of Palestinian Arabs; says position pointedly excludes Palestine Liberation Organization, and omits possibility of direct vote by Palestinians; comments that some US officials are irritated by Prime Minister Begin's diplomacy in setting forth new, unclear proposals, and at same time, embarking on transcontinental tour celebrating 30th anniversary of Israel's independence   (NEW YORK TIMES, April 23, 1978, S4 P19)

SADAT PROPOSES INTERIM STEPS

Egyptian President Anwar Sadat, speaking on eve of Israel's 30th anniversary, suggests that West Bank of Jordan River might be returned to Jordan and Gaza Strip returned to Egypt as interim steps toward peace in Middle East; leaves open questions on degree of control by Jordan and Egypt, speed of Israeli withdrawal from 2 occupied territories and role of Palestine citizens' council; proposals seen as attempts by Sadat to calm Israeli fears of Palestine state   (NEW YORK TIMES, May 11, 1978, P16)

ISRAEL REJECTS DEADLINE

Israeli officials tersely reject 2-month deadline for Middle East peace progress proposed by Egyptian President Sadat in May 31 in news conference statement; contend it is impossible to negotiate peace under pressure of a deadline; assert that there is no time limit on 1975 disengagement agreement with Egypt, under which Israelis pulled back forces in Sinai and surrendered Gulf of Suez oilfields; Sadat, at news conference, had threatened not to renew 1975 agreement, a threat that puzzled Israelis   (NEW YORK TIMES, June 1, 1978, P11)

SADAT DISCLOSES WEIZMAN OFFER

Egyptian President Sadat discloses that Israeli Defense Minister Ezer Weizman, during March 1978 visit to Cairo, offered to return all of Sinai to Egypt in exchange for separate peace agreement with Egypt; states he rejected offer because peace settlement without other Arab countries is impossible; Sadat has been visiting Egyptian military units along Suez Canal, forewarning soldiers that they may have to fight to regain Sinai if peace negotiations fail   (NEW YORK TIMES, June 8, 1978, P7)

SHARP REPLY TO SADAT

Anonymous top-ranking Israeli official rebuts Egyptian President Sadat's recent statement threatening further war if Israel fails to act upon his peace initiative, charging that statement will neither change Israel's position nor contribute to Middle East peace settlement; anonymity is requested to avoid further acrimonious statements, but rebuttal is given to Israeli press and repeated by Israeli Foreign Ministry officials   (NEW YORK TIMES, June 8, 1978, P7)

CARTER-SADAT MEETING RUMORED

Carter Administration officials deny that President Carter plans to meet with Egyptian President Anwar el-Sadat as reported in Cairo weekly magazine *Rose el-Youssef*; article, quoting US sources, holds meeting is likely to take place before July 23; also reports that US refused Israeli proposal to hold Washington meeting of Israeli, Egyptian and US leaders to resume stalled peace talks on grounds that Egypt would reject such meeting unless Israel first presented new proposals   (NEW YORK TIMES, June 13, 1978, P7)

ISRAELI CABINET BACKS BEGIN

Israeli Cabinet releases statement on occupied Arab territories, indicating that it will negotiate "the nature of future relations" after 5 years of limited Palestinian self-rule, apparently based on plan proposed by Prime Minister Begin in December 1977; statement avoids issue of permanent sovereignty of territories, which US was hoping for commitment on; appears to leave open possibility that Begin's plan for limited autonomy could be continued beyond 5 years; Cabinet decision is viewed as political victory for Begin; is immediately attacked by opposition Labor Party   (NEW YORK TIMES, June 19, 1978, P1)

CABINET STATEMENT DISAPPOINTS U.S.

Carter Administration declines, pending further discussions, to give public response to latest Israeli Cabinet statement on West Bank, Gaza Strip and Palestinian issues, a statement which included the declaration that it would negotiate "the nature of future relations" after 5 years of limited Palestinian self-rule; however, privately some officials have acknowledged that Israeli statement was disappointing and fell short of what Administration was hoping for; statement also appeared to limit Palestinian participation in future negotiations to those West Bank and Gaza representatives who would be elected under the self-rule plan   (NEW YORK TIMES, June 19, 1978, P1)

KNESSET APPROVES STATEMENT

Israeli Parliament, after intense debate, approves Cabinet's June 18 statement about Israel's future plans for occupied West Bank of Jordan and Gaza Strip; vote is 59 in favor of Cabinet plan, 37 against it and 10 abstentions, including Deputy Prime Minister Yigael Yadin and other members of Democratic Movement for Change; Foreign Minister Dayan seeks to calm concerns of members of Parliament by assuring them that Prime Minister Begin's plan for autonomy in occupied regions would be permanent and not a transitional phase to a separate Palestinian homeland, as some had interpreted from Cabinet's vaguely worded statement   (NEW YORK TIMES, June 20, 1978, P1)

EGYPT PLEDGES CONTINUED EFFORT

Egyptian Foreign Minister Mohammed Ibrahim Kamel asserts that intransigence shown by Israeli Cabinet would not deter Egypt's attempts to work with US to revive Middle East peace initiative; made remarks after meeting with US Ambassador Hermann Eilts; US sought to determine Israel's views on political self-expression for Palestinians and sovereignty for Jordan West Bank after 5 years; Israeli Cabinet's decision on matters effectively defers consideration of permanent status of Israeli-occupied territories until after 5-year period proposed by Israeli Prime Minister Menachem Begin in his peace plan (NEW YORK TIMES, June 20, 1978, P3)

FORMER AMBASSADOR ATTACKS SADAT

Egyptian Ambassador to Portugal Lieutenant General Saad Eddin al-Shazli makes strong attack on Egyptian President Anwar el-Sadat; asserts Sadat regime is no better than former dictatorships in Portugal and Spain; expects to be fired for statement; Middle East News Agency notes Egyptian Government suspended Shazli on June 19 and ordered him to stand trial in Cairo   (NEW YORK TIMES, June 20, 1978, P3)

AMBASSADOR PURSUES DICTATORSHIP CHARGE

Egypt's Ambassador to Portugal Lieutenant General Saad Eddin al-Shazli, in Lisbon, says he is ready to discuss with President Sadat before an "international or inter-Arab committee" his charge that the Sadat Government is a dictatorship; confirms that he has been ordered to return to Egypt, but says he will not do so without guarantees that he will not be arrested and will be able to state his case against Sadat   (NEW YORK TIMES, June 21, 1978, P3)

STONY REACTION BY CARTER

Commentator James Reston suggests that Carter Administration is so angry over Israel's 5-year plan for West Bank and Gaza Strip that it is maintaining an "ominous silence"; suggests US is now "leaving question of Mr. Begin and his policies to the Israeli people" (NEW YORK TIMES, June 21, 1978, P23)

EGYPT PREPARES PEACE PLAN

Egypt's Foreign Minister Mohammed Ibrahim Kamel says Egypt is preparing a detailed peace proposal focusing on return of West Bank to Jordan and Gaza Strip to Egypt on an interim basis; makes disclosure following Alexandria meeting of Egypt's President Sadat with US Ambassador Eilts; says he may meet with Israel's Foreign Minister Moshe Dayan in London in July   (NEW YORK TIMES, June 25, 1978, P11)

ISRAEL REJECTS EGYPTIAN PLAN

Israeli Cabinet rejects "unreservedly" latest peace proposal being prepared by Egypt without waiting for formal notification of terms of plan; Jordan, under proposal, reportedly would resume control of West Bank and Egypt of Gaza Strip while they helped work out security guarantees for Israel as well as some autonomy for Palestinian population; Israeli Cabinet Secretary Aryeh Naor says plan had been rejected because it set prior conditions for renewal of negotiations; US's role as intermediary and Vice President Walter Mondale's scheduled visit to Egypt and Israel noted   (NEW YORK TIMES, June 26, 1978, P1)

EGYPTIAN OPTIONS OUTLINED

Speaker of Egyptian Parliament Sayed Marei asserts, in interview, that if Israel should reject Egypt's latest peace proposals, Egypt will renew pressure on Israel in UN and other international forums; suggests that among other options, Egypt might convene an Arab summit meeting to close Arab ranks behind a single position for negotiating with Israel; says he expects US to propose a peace formula after Vice President Mondale ends his visit to Egypt and Israel; on question of President Sadat's

Hermann F. Eilts, United States Ambassador to Egypt.

Department of State/Robert H. McNeill

repression of critical journalists, feels that Egyptian democracy has not been threatened   (NEW YORK TIMES,   June 27, 1978,   P4)

KAMEL SCORES REJECTION

Egypt's Foreign Minister Mohammed Ibrahim Kamel issues statement expressing Egypt's astonishment that Israel has rejected its peace proposal while it is still in drafting stage; cites UN Security Council Resolution 242, which calls for Israeli withdrawal from occupied areas, as reason for believing Israel would yield to Egyptian plan; Egyptian Foreign Ministry source also indicates that one attractive aspect of new plan is that Israelis might not have to deal directly with the Palestinians or with PLO but with Egypt and Jordan   (NEW YORK TIMES,   June 27, 1978,   P3)

EGYPT FIRM ON PLAN

Egyptian Foreign Minister Mohammed Kamel asserts that resumption of direct talks with Israel hinges on Israel's formal reaction to peace plan that Egypt is preparing; Egyptians indicate plan involves temporary return of Jordan West Bank and Gaza Strip to Egypt while future of 1.1 million residents of areas is negotiated; Israeli Cabinet rejected this idea on June 25, but Israel later softened its position   (NEW YORK TIMES,   June 29, 1978,   S2   P2)

SADAT ACCEPTS U.S. INVITATION

Egyptian President Anwar el-Sadat formally accepts US invitation to send Foreign Minister Mohammed Ibrahim Kamel to London conference with Secretary of State Vance and Israeli Foreign Minister Moshe Dayan; provides Vice President Mondale with written version of new Egyptian proposal for interim agreement, with Mondale noting proposal will be transferred to Israelis in a few days; Mondale holds he is confident Israel will also attend conference, while officials accompanying Mondale reveal Egyptian proposal contains some new twists, but that most of proposal will find little favor in Jersualem   (NEW YORK TIMES,   July 4, 1978,   P1)

EGYPTIAN PEACE PLAN OUTLINED

Egyptian peace proposal, presented to Vice President Mondale by Egyptian President Anwar el-Sadat, will be formally submitted to Israel July 5, with Ambassador Samuel W. Lewis outlining plan to Israeli Foreign Minister Moshe Dayan; plan reportedly includes some common points with Israel's 26-point plan, such as concept of 5-year transition period, creation of local Palestinian councils to assume administrative functions, and participation of Israel, Egypt and Jordan in negotiations over final status of Israeli-occupied areas; calls for wtihdrawal of all Israeli forces from West Bank and Gaza Strip after transition period and envisions phased return of land to Egypt and Jordan, but does not include specific role for PLO or project creation of independent Palestinian state; US officials hope plan will provide basis for negotiation at London meeting of Israeli and Egyptian Foreign Ministers and Secretary of State Vance   (NEW YORK TIMES,   July 5, 1978,   P1)

POLICE CONFISCATE LEFTIST NEWSPAPER

Egyptian security police confiscate issue of leftist party newspaper *Al Ahaly*, which resumed publication to test President Sadat's suppression of dissent, but Egyptian Attorney General Ahmed Moussa overturns action; says police seized issue because they judged it "sensational"; lead article says President Sadat is expected to take over post of Prime Minister, and Prime Minister Mamdouh Salem will become speaker of Parliament; Government officials deny report   (NEW YORK TIMES,   July 13, 1978,   P9)

WEIZMAN AND SADAT CONFER

Israeli Defense Minister Ezer Weizman, in unexpected move, meets with Egyptian President Anwar el-Sadat in Fuschl, Austria, to discuss Middle East peace issues; holds talks were very useful, but refuses to offer details on 3-hour meeting before reporting to Prime Minister Begin; later meets separately, for 6th time in 8 months, with Egypt's War Minister General Mohammed Abdel-Ghany el-Gamasy   (NEW YORK TIMES,   July 14, 1978,   P2)

LONDON TALKS BEGIN

New Middle East talks have begun at Leeds Castle, 40 miles from London, with Secretary of State Vance and Israeli and Egyptian foreign ministers participating; after 2 rounds of talks, both sides agree wide gaps still exist between Israeli and Egyptian positions; meanwhile, President Sadat is reported to have said that unless Israel accepts Egypt's proposals or introduces more positive plan of its own, Egypt will cut off talks with Israel; Vance opened talks with review of similarities and differences in Egyptian and Israeli positions   (NEW YORK TIMES,   July 19,   P1)

VANCE REPORTS ON TALKS

Secretary of State Vance tells news conference that although 2-day Middle East talks held in England produced no progress, meeting helped US keep up momentum in Israeli-Arab negotiations; plans to fly to Middle East in about 2 weeks for more exchanges with 2 sides; says he was impressed by intensity of exchanges between Israeli Foreign Minister Dayan and Egyptian Foreign Minister Kamel; meanwhile Israelis say they saw talks as direct negotiations, while Egyptians maintain that direct negotiations would take place only when Israel took more positive line   (NEW YORK TIMES,   July 20, 1978,   P1)

EGYPT ASKS WIDER U.S. ROLE

Egyptian official Dr. Morsi Saadeddin holds that recent Israeli-Egyptian Middle East talks in Britain showed continued inflexibility of Israeli government of Prime Minister Menachem Begin; suggests US must submit proposal to which two sides can agree; related item notes Egyptian daily newspaper *Al Akhbar* published open letter to President Carter from staff correspondent urging sharp and decisive action on Middle East problem   (NEW YORK TIMES,   July 20,   P6)

U.S. PLANNING MAJOR EFFORT

Secretary of State Vance's aides report, before leaving Great Britain with Vance for US, that he is planning a major effort to break Middle East negotiating stalemate, at risk of causing new strains between US and Israel; suggest that diplomatic effort needs to be made now because Egypt's President Sadat appears to have become more conciliatory in his thinking; Vance plans to fly to Middle East in first week of August for new talks with Egyptian and Israeli officials at as yet undetermined site   (NEW YORK TIMES,   July 21, 1978,   P1)

U.S. STILL OPTIMISTIC

State Secretary Vance reportedly gives President Carter fairly optimistic report on London talks he had with Egyptian Foreign Minister Mohammed Kamel and Israeli Foreign Minister Moshe Dayan; Vance allegedly believes that new negotiations would take place between Egypt and Israel despite Egyptian President Anwar el-Sadat's statement that Israel must advance some new elements to justify new talks   (NEW YORK TIMES,   July 22, 1978,   P3)

SADAT ASKS PARTY ABOLITION

Egypt's President Sadat announces at Cairo political meeting that he has asked Parliament to abolish Arab Socialist Union; declares he will form an independent party   (NEW YORK TIMES,   July 23, 1978,   P1)

ISRAEL REFUSES SADAT REQUEST

Israeli Cabinet refuses Egyptian President Anwar el-Sadat's request that Israel return Sinai Desert town of El Arish and Mount Sinai to Egypt in conciliatory gesture; Israeli Prime Minister Menachem Begin contends such unilateral moves are not feasible; suggests Israel already made gesture toward Egypt in his own peace plan; plan suggested form of civil rule for Palestinian Arabs in Israeli-occupied Jordan West Bank and Gaza Strip, where Israel would retain military presence for security purposes; Begin emphasizes Israel is ready to enter into negotiations based on reciprocity   (NEW YORK TIMES,   July 24, 1978,   P1)

EGYPT URGES NEW INPUT

Egyptian Foreign Ministry declares that there will be no further talks with Israel unless Israelis present new ideas or agree to reconsider Egypt's peace plan; Egyptian officials assert privately that they are confident that peace talks will resume; Foreign Minister Mohammed Ibrahim Kamel points to US State Secretary Vance's August 4, 1978, visit and suggests that if Vance hints that Israel would take positive stance, this could trigger reopening of talks   (NEW YORK TIMES,   July 25, 1978,   P3)

EGYPT ORDERS ISRAELI MISSION WITHDRAWN

Israeli Prime Minister Begin reports that Egypt has ordered withdrawal of 10-member Israeli military and technical mission from Egypt, which had been there since January 1978 as a symbol of direct Egyptian-Israeli relations;

assails Egyptian President Sadat's Middle East proposals; nevertheless, terms prospects for peace "excellent"; Egypt, meanwhile, reports that the action against the Israeli mission reflects a decision to avoid further direct contacts until Israel adopts a new position on peace talks   (NEW YORK TIMES,   July 27, 1978,   P1)

SADAT DETERMINED ON INITIATIVE

Egyptian President Sadat, in speech carried on radio and TV, asserts he is determined to continue peace initiative; reiterates, however, that he will not cede Arab land to Israel; concedes Israel has right to security, permanent peace and good neighborly relations, but maintains Israel has no right to Arab land   (NEW YORK TIMES,   July 28, 1978,   P2)

EGYPT, U.S. DISCUSS PEACE PROSPECTS

US special Middle East envoy Alfred L. Atherton Jr. meets with Egyptian Foreign Minister Mohammed Ibrahim Kamel for over 4 hours, but is unable to persuade Kamel that new round of direct Israeli-Egyptian talks is warranted; Kamel concedes there are some common elements in Israel's peace position, but holds they are coincidental and totally irrelevant; claims another Israeli-Egyptian meeting is possible if US offers "good proposal," but stresses that proposal should not include territory or sovereignty   (NEW YORK TIMES,   July 30, 1978,   P8)

United States special Middle East envoy Alfred L. Atherton Jr.

Department of State

SADAT SCORES ISRAELI VIEWS

Egyptian President Anwar el-Sadat, after meeting with US envoy Alfred Atherton, announces at press conference that he does not favor renewal of face-to-face talks with Israel at present; criticizes Israel's latest ideas on Middle East settlement as negative and backward; is ready to discuss peace only if there is prior agreement excluding compromise on issues of Arab land and sovereignty; US State Secretary Vance has asserted that he wanted date fixed for next meeting with Israeli and Egyptian foreign ministers before he returned to Middle East during week beginning August 6   (NEW YORK TIMES,   July 31, 1978,   P3)

U.S. URGES MORE TALKS

US rebukes Egyptian President Anwar el-Sadat over his rejection of US-sponsored meeting with Israel at foreign ministers' level to revive peace talks; President Carter, however, directs State Secretary Vance to go to Middle East as planned on August 5; Carter is also concerned over "tough line" adopted by Israeli Prime Minister Begin and will direct Vance to convey frustration of US to both Sadat and Begin; Vance is scheduled to spend two days each in Jerusalem and Cairo   (NEW YORK TIMES,   August 1, 1978,   P1)

PEACE PROSPECTS BLEAK

Financial Times editorial says prospects for peace in the Middle East do not look very optimistic; points out that US Secretary of State Cyrus Vance does not believe that his current trip to the Middle East will lead to dramatic progress, while at the same time acknowledges that negotiations have reached a critical point; notes that President Sadat's personal dislike of Prime Minister Begin would probably keep him from accepting an invitation to meet with him in Washington   (FINANCIAL TIMES,   August 7,   P10)

The Arab World Responds

SAUDIS COOL TO PEACE INITIATIVE

Saudi Arabian officials say government will probably withhold support for Egyptian peace efforts despite arguments they expect President Carter to advance when he arrives; say Saudi leaders will press Carter for greater efforts to ease Israeli-Arab tensions   (NEW YORK TIMES,   January 3, 1978,   P3)

SAUDI COMMENTS ON PEACE EFFORTS

Saudi Crown Prince Fahd says differences remain between Saudi Arabia and US on Middle East question, although there is "general understanding" regarding just and equitable solution, in interview with Barbara Walters for ABC; Foreign Minister Prince Saud al-Faisal says King Khalid indicated to President Carter on January 3 Saudi belief that conditions of lasting peace are withdrawal of Israeli troops from territories occupied in 1967, including East Jerusalem, self-determination for Palestinians and their right to return home   (NEW YORK TIMES,   January 5, 1978,   P3)

ASSAD ASSAILS SADAT

Syrian President Assad says President Sadat's peace initiatives destroyed efforts for peace which were becoming fruitful and amounted to capitulation; calls Sadat's move "pure theatrics"; says peace cannot be achieved without Arab unity; says he will accept "anything agreed upon between Palestinians and Jordanians" (NEW YORK TIMES,   January 9, 1978,   P7)

MIDEAST INSTABILITY FEARED

Commentator Jonathan C. Randal observes Jordan's King Hussein, Saudi Crown Prince Fahd and former Egyptian Foreign Minister Ismail Fahmy have publicly warned that breakdown of Israeli-Egyptian negotiations or separate Israeli-Egyptian peace settlement could destabilize vulnerable Arab regimes; points out instability could result in escalation of assassination attempts on Arab leaders, revolution, coups and resurgence of Soviet influence in Arab world (WASHINGTON POST, January 13, 1978, P20)

REJECTIONISTS MOUNT OPPOSITION

Syrians, Iraqis and other Arabs opposed to President Anwar el-Sadat's peace moves deride decision to suspend political talks as mere maneuver but conservative Arabs such as Saudis welcome decision as opportunity for reconciliation in Arab world; Syrian press continues to urge Sadat's overthrow; Palestine Liberation Organization (PLO) official Yasir Abed Rabbouh predicts Sadat will soon resume talks with Israelis; leftists and Nasserites hold rally in Beirut, Lebanon, on anniversary of price riots in Cairo, Alexandria and other Egyptian cities; similar rallies are held in Syria; rallies are part of campaign conducted by anti-Sadat Arabs since he started peace initiatives (NEW YORK TIMES, January 20, 1978, P7)

JORDAN'S ROLE ASSESSED

Commentator David Hirst sees a crisis looming about the future of Jordan and the Middle East in the light of current Egyptian-Israeli peace negotiations; stresses that Jordan continues to insist on complete Israeli withdrawal from occupied territories and self-determination for Palestinians; says Jordanian officials have never trusted Egyptian Prime Minister Anwar el-Sadat; says King Hussein will not allow himself to be instrument of an imposed solution; expects that separate peace between Egypt and Israel would tip military balance of power against "confrontation" states headed by Syria; claims Jordan would be embroiled and Hussein would veer toward Syrian President Assad; claims that intransigence of Israeli Prime Minister Menachem Begin is eroding Sadat's position very fast (MANCHESTER GUARDIAN WEEKLY, January 22, 1978, P7)

SYRIA TO STRENGTHEN ARMY

Syria says it will give priority to strengthening of its armed forces to insure strategic balance with Israel; says move will go hand in hand with efforts to isolate Egyptian President Sadat for his peace initiative; announcement is made by Foreign Minister Abdel-Halim Khaddam, who charges Sadat's contacts with Israel had plunged Middle East into "swamp of capitulation" (NEW YORK TIMES, January 25, 1978, P8)

SAUDI ARABIA LISTENING QUIETLY

Saudi Arabia becomes "great listener" and diligent mediator in Middle East as Egyptian President Sadat's peace initiative limps along, dividing Arab nations and raising apprehension about its outcome; neither attacks President Sadat nor bends to praise him; hopes peace initiatives will succeed, yet remains darkly pessimistic and suspicious of Israeli intentions; strives to remain untarnished by strong connections with what it fears could be disastrous negotiations; wants to be in position to "pick

up pieces" if peace talks collapse; fears that US is being drawn into position where it could bear onus of failure, along with President Sadat, if peace talks fail; maintains lasting peace in Middle East depends on 2 basic principles, Israeli withdrawal from all territories occupied in 1967 war and reestablishment of Palestinian people's rights (WALL STREET JOURNAL, January 27, 1978, P1)

SYRIA INVITES GUERRILLAS BACK

Syria, in apparent effort to frustrate President Sadat's peace initiative, gives Palestinian guerrillas permission to re-open their bases and to establish radio station on its territory (NEW YORK TIMES, February 2, 1978, P3)

ANTI-SADAT SUMMIT CONCLUDES

Meeting of so-called hard-line Arab leaders in Algiers concludes; leaders fail to agree on joint plan to thwart President Sadat's peace negotiations but issue strong denunciation of Sadat (NEW YORK TIMES, February 5, 1978, P16)

SADAT'S OPPONENTS DIVIDED

Article on Arab states that have rallied against Egyptian President Sadat's peace initiative notes they have not been able to create credible anti-Egyptian front because of their radical politics; notes interests of state, ideological quarrels and several brushfire wars seem to have taken precedence over proclaimed common cause (NEW YORK TIMES, February 19, 1978, S4 P2)

SYRIAN POSITION ANALYZED

Syria is bitterly opposed to Egyptian President Anwar Sadat's peace initiative toward Israel, but still believes settlement is possible if made on Arab terms; Syria would like to see ouster of Sadat, whom it believes is seeking separate peace with Israel and has betrayed Arabs; Syria favors formation of powerful united front which would push for diplomatic settlement from position of strength, and be prepared for war if peace efforts fail; Syria's leaders believe that Egyptian people will eventually discover that Sadat is unable to deliver on his promises of peace and prosperity, and that he will be replaced by more radical regime which will side with Syria and disavow Sadat's peace overtures; assert US support is reason for Israel's refusal to make concessions; Syria remains determined to put as many barriers in front of Sadat's peace initiative as possible (WALL STREET JOURNAL, March 2, 1978, P44)

SAUDI MAY RECOGNIZE ISRAEL

Saudi Arabian Crown Prince Fahd announces Saudi Arabia may consider recognizing Israel if comprehensive Middle East settlement provides for creation of Palestinian homeland, and if Israel withdraws from all occupied Arab lands; announcement, published in Kuwait newspaper *Al Rai Al Am*, emphasizes that settlement requires agreement of all Arab states (NEW YORK TIMES, March 10, 1978, S2 P16)

HUSSEIN REJECTS NEGOTIATIONS

Jordanian King Hussein refuses to join Egyptian-Israeli peace negotiations, despite urging of US envoy Alfred Atherton; Amman spokesman states Hussein has affirmed to Atherton that Jordan's policy is aimed at reaching a just peace based on Israeli withdrawal from occupied Arab land and guarantees of Palestinian people's national rights, including self-determination   (NEW YORK TIMES,   March 5, 1978,   P8)

ARAB LEAGUE CONVENES MEETING

Arab League opens semiannual council meeting with members trying to reconcile differences arising from President Anwar el-Sadat's peace initiative with Israel; Syria, Libya, Iraq, Algeria and South Yemen boycott meeting, and only half of 22 members send customary representatives; subjects for discussion include measures for greater Arab unity, renewal of Arab peacekeeping force in Lebanon, security in Red Sea and Horn of Africa, contributions for Palestine Liberation Organization (PLO) guerrillas and reevaluation of Arab-US relations   (NEW YORK TIMES,   March 28, 1978,   P6)

UNITED FRONT ASKED

Arab League foreign ministers and other officials call for immediate meeting of Arab leaders in order to present a united front against Israel; ask Sudan President Gaafar al-Numeiry to head committee to persuade Arab states to settle their differences; announcement is viewed as result of lobbying efforts by Saudi Arabia and other wealthy Arab nations concerned about rift caused by President Anwar el-Sadat's peace initiative with Israel   (NEW YORK TIMES,   March 29, 1978,   P4)

DIPLOMATIC OPTIONS NOTED

Commentator Clayton Fritchey observes increased interest among Palestinians and other Arabs for revival of Geneva Conference on Middle East; points to Palestine Liberation Organization (PLO) leader Yasir Arafat's suggestion that search for peace should be undertaken within Geneva approach; notes media in Syria and Jordan are calling for renewed Geneva conference; points out Egyptian President Anwar Sadat may still agree to bilateral pact with Israel that could lead to other such agreements between Israel and other Arab nations   (WASHINGTON POST,   April 8, 1978,   P21)

LIBYA POSES THREAT TO SADAT

Commentator Smith Hempstone examines threat to Egypt by Libya's Colonel Muammar Qaddafi who is supported by large supply of Russian arms; comments that Qaddafi is dedicated to Israel's destruction and views himself as champion of Moslems and bitter foe of Western "imperialism"; adds that he has supplied training, guns, and financial support for Palestinian, Irish, African and Philippine guerrillas; claims Qaddafi has amassed $2 billion arms inventory since 1974; mentions theory that Libya's arsenal is strategic reserve for USSR for use in future African conflict or against Europe in event of conflict with Atlantic Alliance   (US NEWS AND WORLD REPORT,   April 10, 1978,   P39)

INTELLECTUALS OPPOSING PEACE INITIATIVE

Commentator Christopher Wren sees signs of growing trend of opposition to Egyptian President Sadat's peace initiative with Israel, begun by Egyptian intellectuals and recently given political voice by an outburst in Parliament; notes that there has been no vociferousness or violent protests by majority of Egyptians, who appear disposed to wait in hope that Israeli criticism of Prime Minister Begin's policies will soften Israeli position and break stalemate in peace talks; sees, however, off-chance that disenchantment with peace initiative and concern over Egypt's alienation from some other Arab states may force Sadat to relinquish his initiative; foresees that as long as Sadat retains support of military, his policy could survive, and observes it is unlikely that Sadat will voluntarily give up initiative in face of his nomination for 1978 Nobel peace prize   (NEW YORK TIMES,   April 30, 1978,   S4 P2)

SUDAN SUPPORTING SADAT

President Gaafar al-Numeiry of Sudan, accompanied by Arab League Secretary General Mahmoud Riad, visits Damascus in attempt to improve strained relations between Syria and Egypt; Numeiry arrived from Egypt, where he had held long talks with President Sadat; speculation is rife in Cairo that Sudanese President would seek to arrange meeting between Sadat and Syrian President Assad, though Numeiry denies such as intent; Syrian officials, however, have said that such a meeting cannot take place as long as Egypt maintains its peace initiative with Israel   (NEW YORK TIMES,   May 7, 1978,   P13)

CONCILIATION TOUR ENDS

Sudanese President Gaafar al-Numeiry, in statement after meeting with President Sadat of Egypt, reiterates belief in possibility of convening an Arab reconciliation meeting; gives no reason for optimism; returns home to Sudan after 6-nation Arab tour, which included stops in Syria, Iraq, Tunisia, Algeria and Morocco as well as Egypt   (NEW YORK TIMES, May 14, 1978,   P28)

HUSSEIN URGES ISRAELI CONCESSIONS

Jordan's King Hussein asserts that stalled Middle East peace talks can only be revived by Israeli concessions; believes entire area will be headed for "tremendous upheavals" if no progress is made; questions whether peace is possible while Israeli Premier Menachem Begin is in power; maintains that Arab nations have done all they can to bring about peace solution   (CHICAGO TRIBUNE,   May 29, 1978,   P1)

JORDANIAN ROLE QUESTIONED

Commentator Christopher Wren reports that Jordan appears unwilling to take on proposed role as guarantor of future of occupied West Bank and Gaza Strip; Jordanian officials say there is no point in discussing a Jordanian role so long as Israel refuses to work out some transition for self-determination for Palestinians; also note that Jordan surrendered its claim to speak for Palestinians at Arab League summit meeting in Morocco in 1974; Jordanian foreign policy strategist Sherif Abdul-Hamid el-Sharaf observes that Jordan is not ready to step in unless specifically asked to do so by Palestinians in occupied areas   (NEW YORK TIMES,   June 21, 1978,   P3)

IRAQ BACKS SADAT CRITICS

Union of Arab Journalists condemns Egyptian President Sadat for his moves to purge the Egyptian press of his critics; organization says that it has decided to move its headquarters from Cairo to Baghdad; announcement follows 2-day meeting in Beirut initiated by Riad Taha, president of the Lebanese Association of Newspaper Owners; Iraqi Minister of Information, Saad Hammoudi, head of Association of Iraqi Journalists, says government is ready to grant Iraq citizenship to any Egyptian journalist or writer who might be deprived of his Egyptian citizenship as result of Sadat crackdown   (NEW YORK TIMES,   June 22, 1978,   P11)

SAUDI VIEWS DISCUSSED

Commentator Amos Perlmutter examines Saudi Arabian role in Middle East peace negotiations; suggests Saudi Arabia has failed to support Egypt's peace efforts because it fears strong Egypt that would become stronger after peace with Israel; contends Saudi Arabia lacks inherent capability to alleviate, moderate or resolve Middle East conflict and its foreign and military policies contribute to region's destabilization   (NEW YORK TIMES,   June 29, 1978,   P25)

O.A.U. SCORES ISRAEL

Organization of African Unity (OAU) ministers meeting at Khartoum, Sudan, condemn what they call Israel's aggression against Lebanon and its intransigence toward Egypt's peace initiative; express support of Palestine Liberation Organization (PLO)   (NEW YORK TIMES,   July 13, 1978,   P2)

ASSAD DENOUNCES INITIATIVE

Commentators Rowland Evans and Robert Novak recount recent conversation with Syrian President Hafez al-Assad; note Assad contends Egyptian President Sadat's peace initiative has boomeranged, leaving Israel united and Arabs divided; report Assad warns separate Israeli-Egyptian peace formed by US under "guise" of comprehensive settlement would extend and deepen Arab split and doom any early Mideast settlement; note Assad charges Israel has been stirring up northern Lebanese Christians and inciting them to attack Syrian forces; report Assad intends to keep forces in Lebanon so long as Lebanese Government asks him to stay   (WASHINGTON POST, July 17, 1978,   P15)

ARAB LEAGUE SEEKS SOLIDARITY

Arab League nations, meeting at Belgrade conference of non-aligned nations, agree on proposal for special UN General Assembly session to discuss Palestine issue and adopt a unified Middle East declaration; meeting's aim was to end rift in Arab world over Egyptian President Sadat's Israeli initiative; Kuwaiti source notes, however, that "fundamental differences remain"; Cairo delegates doubt that Israeli-Egyptian meeting in Sinai Peninsula desired by US will take place   (NEW YORK TIMES,   July 28, 1978,   P1)

SAUDIS SEE INITIATIVE FAILING

Saudi Arabia reportedly has told US special Middle East envoy Alfred L. Atherton Jr. that as result of Israeli "intransigence," Egyptian President Sadat's efforts to negotiate with Israel stand no chance of success, and that it is now necessary to reunite the Arabs; Saudi position has led to speculation that Sadat's harder position has resulted from pressures from Saudi Arabia   (NEW YORK TIMES, August 3, 1978,   P6)

SADAT RECALLS PEACE DELEGATION, DEMANDS SHIFT IN BEGIN POSITION

CAIRO TALKS STILL ON

After a Carter Telephone Call, Egyptian Agrees to Let Military Group Resume

By CHRISTOPHER S. WREN

Special to The New York Times

CAIRO, Jan. 18—President Anwar el-Sadat today ordered his Foreign Minister to return home immediately from Israel, where talks on political aspects of a peace settlement started yesterday, and he informed President Carter that the talks would resume once Israel changed its position.

The summoning home of Mohammed Ibrahim Kamel with his entire delegation scuttled the Jerusalem talks, in which the United States was also taking part, and raised serious doubt about the future of the peace initiative undertaken by Mr. Sadat two months ago.

Later, the Cairo television reported, President Carter telephoned Mr. Sadat and urged him to reconsider his stand. [Page A9.] The Egyptian leader agreed—in appreciation for Mr. Carter's Middle East peace efforts—to allow talks on military aspects of a settlement to resume in Cairo on Saturday. [In Jerusalem, however, it was not clear whether the Israeli delegation would go to Cairo for the military talks.]

May Have Fresh Surprises

In view of today's developments, it is possible that Mr. Sadat may have some fresh surprises to spring at the Parliament. At the outset of his peace initiative, he promised that he would resign if his efforts failed. Word of his forthcoming Saturday speech prompted speculation that he might try to do so. But in view of the support that his peace policies have generated in Egypt, it is not likely that such an offer would be taken up.

In an indication of the sudden chill, the Egyptians had announced earlier this evening that the Egyptian-Israeli Military Committee session, which was to resume tomorrow, would not take place, despite the expected arrival of the Israeli Defense Minister, Ezer Weizman.

The talks convened last week and then recessed on Friday.

This evening, a statement delivered over Egyptian television and radio by the Minister of Culture and Information, Abdel Moneim el-Sawi, explained that Mr. Sadat had recalled Mr. Kamel after it had become clear that the Israelis "all aim at deadlocking the situation and submitting partial solutions" that would not lead to a durable Middle East peace settlement.

Mr. Sadat reportedly complained to Mr. Carter that Israel sought "land and not peace."

Mr. Sadat's exact intentions in breaking off the Political Committee talks were unlikely to become fully known until Saturday, when he is scheduled to address a special session of the Egyptian People's Assembly, or Parliament, on the issue.

It was in a speech to Parliament that Mr. Sadat first declared his willingness to go to Israel in search of peace.

His decision to hold off until Saturday was considered significant because Secretary of State Cyrus R. Vance, who is in Jerusalem, is scheduled to stop and see Mr. Sadat here on Friday. He may presumably be offered a chance to "rescue" the peace process by interceding with Israel before Mr. Sadat announces his plans on Saturday.

Egypt has been pressing the United States to play a larger role in the talks with Israel and Mr. Carter's fast phone call to Mr. Sadat today indicated the extent to which Washington was already involved.

Last weekend, Mr. Vance postponed his departure for Jerusalem until both sides had agreed on a compromise wording of a disputed agenda point dealing with the Palestinian issue.

Mr. Sadat's dramatic warning today seemed directed almost as much at the United States as at Israel. The Egyptian leader has contended on numerous occasions that the Americans hold "99 percent of the cards" in the Middle East because they are the only ones who can make the Israelis less intransigent.

His willingness to let the military talks resume suggest that Mr. Sadat did not intend to disrupt his peace initiative altogether. Nonetheless, his decision to pull his team out today came as a shock to diplomats in both Cairo and Jerusalem. He had been keeping a low profile this week, entrusting a committee headed by Vice President Hosni Mubarek to monitor the progress of the negotiations.

The Egyptian statement issued by Mr. Sawi today indicated that Mr. Sadat was upset by the latest tough statements of Mr. Begin and his Foreign Minister, Moshe Dayan.

At a formal dinner Mr. Begin delivered a strong lecture to Mr. Kamel and informed his guest that Israel could not afford to return to the borders that prevailed before the 1967 war. On Monday, Mr. Dayan had remarked that it was better to let the peace initiative slip away than to jeopardize Israel's existence.

Mr. Sadat said in a pessimistic magazine interview here last weekend that he had "absolutely no hope" that a declaration of principles would come out of the Jerusalem talks because the Israelis were too "stiff-necked."

He has accused them of intransigence on two points of friction—Jewish settlements in the Sinai Peninsula, which Egypt wants removed, and self-determination for the Palestinians, which Israel has resisted.

One Cairo-based Western diplomat speculated that Mr. Kamel discovered at today's negotiating session, which lasted only 15 minutes, that the Israeli positions had not been changed. He sent word back to Mr. Sadat, who instructed him to come home.

NEW YORK TIMES, January 19, 1978, P1

Peace Alone Won't Solve Egypt's Basic Economic Ills

By CHRISTOPHER S. WREN

CAIRO — A young blacksmith's apprentice explained last week why he supported his President, Anwar el-Sadat. "I don't want war, I want to eat bread," Hamdi el-Sayed said.

For most Egyptians, Mr. Sadat's tempestuous initiative with Israel has been translated into expectations of more food, more jobs and more money. Abroad, it has been assumed that Egypt's considerable economic difficulties were a major factor in Mr. Sadat's decision to pursue peace.

Yet peace alone is unlikely to solve the economic malaise. Egypt has already received considerable financial assistance from the Persian Gulf countries and the United States among others and, having been bailed out of bankruptcy, does not quite know how to absorb more funds. According to one Western estimate, Egypt has yet to tap at least $4 billion in additional offers of development assistance.

With Mr. Sadat preoccupied with foreign affairs, the Government has been slow to come up with a priority list for aid projects. And it has been unwilling to improve its own deficit budget by cutting back consumer subsidies, something it tried last year but rescinded in the face of consumer riots.

During a visit here last week, Robert S. McNamara, president of the World Bank, gave a cautious endorsement of Cairo's efforts to stabilize the economy, but noted the potential for crisis posed by Egypt's population, growing by well over a million every year. Concern has been expressed privately that a domestic backlash could develop if peace does not bring a better life soon enough to the country's 39 million people, most of whom scrape by on less than $250 a year.

Egypt's emergence as a developing country was retarded by three decades of belligerency with Israel. Four wars drained its finances, weakened its economic infrastructure and left its cities to rampant decay. But the country has also been the casualty of its own bureaucratic inefficiency and indecision, searching for a Western-type free market economy without really sloughing off the constraints of Nasser-style socialism.

The deterioration is evident enough in Cairo, where eight million people are crammed into a city meant for three million. The telephone system is so delapidated that reaching a number across town can take all day. From dawn to dusk, the streets are clogged with honking vehicles for lack of up-to-date traffic facilities and a decent mass transit system. Anyone walking to an appointment must pick a route over cratered sidewalks and mounds of rubble. Once elegant buildings downtown have turned into dank tenements and electrical blackouts hit the city with almost predictable regularity.

Cairo's predicament only hints at the ailments that plague the economy as a whole. The crucial textile industry has had production cut back by power failures. Other plants, lacking spare parts and machinery, run at a fraction of capacity.

Schools, hospitals and welfare services have all suffered as a third and more of the Egyptian budget was devoted to military spending.

Egyptians tend to blame their economic plight on the burden they shouldered in the Arab crusade against Israel. It cost them not only 100,000 lives but 40 billion Egyptian pounds, nearly $60 billion at the current devalued rate of exchange. Proud of their Pharaonic roots, they felt humiliated at having to ask for help from allies who grew rich while rooting from the sidelines. "They treat us like beggars," fumed one Cairo newspaper editor.

Yet Egypt is relatively solvent today because other Arabs gave so generously after Arab self-esteem was restored by Egypt's initial victories in the 1973 war. To organize the aid effort, four wealthy oil producers — Saudi Arabia, Kuwait, Qatar and the United Arab Emirates — formed a consortium in early 1976, the Gulf Organization for the Development of Egypt, and capitalized it at $2 billion. The figure disappointed the Egyptians, who wanted a credit line of $8 to $10 billion.

Though the consortium made long-term development projects its priority, at least $850 million was siphoned off to pay the interest on Egypt's debts, some of which were more than six months overdue. Last fall, the Gulf lenders balked at letting the balance be used to keep Egypt solvent and insisted that, at least, it be used for capital equipment and key raw material imports. Western experts estimate that $450 million has yet to be drawn.

The United States also launched a politically motivated assistance program that is now running at nearly $1 billion a year, making Cairo Washington's largest recipient of economic aid. Nearly two-thirds of the money was allocated last year for imports of food and commodities, such as spare parts, with the rest budgeted for capital projects and technical assistance. Other lenders in recent years have included the Western European nations, Iran and Japan.

But Egypt's needs, while critical enough, are so diffuse and poorly defined that donors have been stymied about how and where to lend. The American effort has been aimed at overhauling the economy's infrastructure to the point where it can handle modern projects. One study determined that it would cost $200 million over five years to give the city of Alexandria

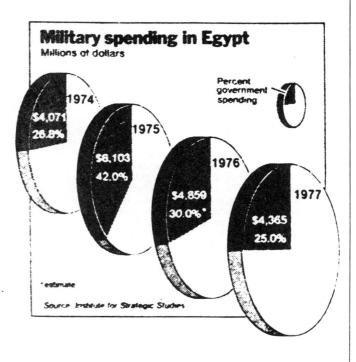

Military spending in Egypt
Millions of dollars

1974 — $4,071 — 26.8%
1975 — $6,103 — 42.0%
1976 — $4,859 — 30.0%*
1977 — $4,365 — 25.0%

Percent government spending

*estimate

Source: Institute for Strategic Studies

a satisfactory sewage system. "There are people out there waiting to spend money but they have to find out what the requirements are." said one Western economic specialist.

Part of the frustration comes from trying to slice through the swollen Egyptian bureaucracy, in which as many as four people hold a single post. One Western banker reported trying to telephone with the offer of a multimillion dollar loan and being unable to rouse anyone at the other end.

The Government has been counting on the fact that the domestic situation is improved from the riots of a year ago and officials expect the American and conservative Arab aid to keep flowing in as a hedge against political radicalization and consumer discontent. But other Egyptians wonder about the end result of the rising popular expectations. Said one Egyptian financial specialist. "What scares me is the reaction that could set in if peace doesn't bring all the answers."

NEW YORK TIMES, January 29, 1978, S4 P3

An Opposition Carefully Questions Sadat Policies

By CHRISTOPHER S. WREN

CAIRO — The former editor-in-chief of the influential newspaper, Al Ahram, caused a stir in Cairo recently with an interview that called upon Egypt to renounce the peace overtures of President Anwar el-Sadat.

"I urge the Egyptian Government to admit, even privately, the fact that the initiative has led us to nothing," Mohammed Heykal was quoted as telling the leftist weekly, Al Shali. "Months after the initiative, we have returned to where we were before this — hoping for American pressure on Israel."

Mr. Heykal, who lost his post on the semi-official newspaper four years ago because of policy differences with Mr. Sadat, was saying nothing that he had not already said in articles published abroad. But his decision to go on the record inside Egypt seemed based on a shrewd assessment of the current mood. His words found a ready hearing from more than a few educated Egyptians who have begun questioning how long Mr. Sadat's offer of peace with Israel should be left open.

The dissent runs counter to what has been happening inside Israel. The Israeli demonstrators who last week lined the road from Tel Aviv to Jerusalem urging "peace now" want Prime Minister Menachem Begin to be more flexible in the search for peace. Egyptian critics such as Mr. Heykal think Mr. Sadat has already been too conciliatory.

The disenchantment at home with Mr. Sadat's policy does not compare in size or intensity to the peace movement inside Israel. Except for a surprise outburst in the Egyptian Parliament two weeks ago, the grumbling has taken place largely in the drawing rooms of Cairo and not in the streets. The great majority of Egyptians cling to the hope that Mr. Sadat's peace efforts will somehow deliver a better life by freeing resources to cure the nation's economic ills. But intellectuals have become increasingly exasperated with the lack of progress and disturbed about the alienation from some other Arabs created by the Sadat initiative. The sympathetic chord that Mr. Heykal's remarks struck has suggested that the opposition, while still dimly perceived, could become significant.

The extent of impatience became evident two weeks ago in the People's Assembly, or Parliament, when the Deputy Foreign Minister, Boutros Ghali, testified before two dozen members of the foreign relations committee and was met with demands that the peace initiative be withdrawn. "Continuation of the direct talks is futile," the committee's head, Leila Takla, told Dr. Ghali. "The time has come for us to content ourselves with the mediation method and to close the door on direct negotiations."

Pleading for more time, Dr. Ghali reminded the deputies that barely 15 hours of formal negotiations with Israel had taken place and that "maybe after 50 hours of talks we can decide whether we succeeded or failed." Mahmoud el-Kadi, a prominent independent parliamentarian, retorted: "Not even after 2,000 hours and not even after the year 2000." Mr. el-Kadi contended that the direct dialogue had ended with the unsuccessful meeting between Mr. Sadat and Mr. Begin at Ismailia last December.

Disappointment with the stalemated initiative has not produced any vociferous or violent protests from among Egyptians. Last week the Government announced that it had broken up a terrorist ring linked to Palestinian extremist groups abroad and the Red Brigades in Italy. It alleged that the terrorists had plotted to sabotage the earlier peace talks in Cairo by attacking the site of the negotiations. Later, it was also reported that they had intended to assassinate Jordan's Prime Minister Modr Badran in Switzerland. But of two dozen suspects being detained, only one was Egyptian. Four were West European and the rest were Palestinians and other Arabs.

It is difficult to gauge how deeply the complaints about the peace initiative run among Egyptians, though casual remarks would indicate that malaise may be spreading. "All the educated people I know are saying that it has failed in realizing the goals of Sadat when he went to Jerusalem," one young woman said. "But it was a very good initiative. So why won't the Government admit that it has failed?"

The risk for Mr. Sadat is that such sentiments could become infectious, not just at home but also in other Arab countries that have refrained from criticizing his trip to Jerusalem. One barometer of Arab feeling has been Jordan's King Hussein, who called last week for a common Arab strategy to retrieve the Israeli-occupied Arab territories. "We have now come to a period during which there appears to be absolutely no chance of a just and durable peace because of Israel's arrogance and Arab weakness and disunity," the Jordanian monarch said. Such comments are bound to make Egyptians feel that they are fated to go it alone at a time when there is very little interest in a separate peace with Israel.

Opposition to Mr. Sadat's initiative has been minimized by recent events inside Israel like the small but growing peace movement and some criticism of Prime Minister Begin from within the Government coalition. This has made some Egyptians disposed to wait a little longer in hope that the Israeli position may soften.

So far, Mr. Sadat has ignored suggestions that he write off his initiative. In a recent interview with a local magazine, the Egyptian leader said, "I think it is my duty to be a little more patient [with Mr. Begin]." Mr. Sadat has been telling visitors that the Israelis were unprepared for his gesture and need more time to absorb its significance.

The armed forces, which constitute Egypt's only real power base, publicly continue to support Mr. Sadat, though an Egyptian source speculated that impatience with Israel may have reached the ranks of younger officers. As long as the President retains the backing of the military, his policy could survive.

But Mr. Sadat has hinted at deadline by noting pointedly that the mandate for the United Nations peacekeeping force in the Sinai peninsula comes up for renewal next October. If he lets it lapse, the cease-fire would not necessarily be scuttled but fresh tensions would be introduced between Egyptian and Israeli forces on opposite sides of the buffer zone.

It seems unlikely that Mr. Sadat would pack up his initiative before the Nobel peace prize, for which he has been nominated, is announced, also in October. But the dissatisfaction that is finding a voice at home raises the possibility, however remote, that his hand could be forced earlier.

NEW YORK TIMES, April 30, 1978, S4 P2

SADAT PLANS DRIVE ON POLITICAL CRITICS

Backed by Referendum, He Accuses Leaders of the Left and Right of Trying to Incite Class Conflict

By CHRISTOPHER S. WREN
Special to The New York Times

CAIRO, May 23—President Anwar el-Sadat indicated today that he would use the strong endorsement he received in Sunday's referendum to drive his main critics out of the country's leftist and conservative political parties.

Mr. Sadat accused his foes of trying to incite potentially bloody class conflicts and said that "now that the people have passed judgment, I shall not compromise under any circumstances and I shall accept nothing less than commitment" to what he called the Government's principles of social peace, national unity and socialist democracy.

But he contended that the mandate he had received to curb dissent did not mean he was turning Egypt away from "democracy," as his opponents have charged. "The democratic experiment is alive and I want it to succeed," Mr. Sadat said.

Outcome 'Support for Democracy'

He spoke at a news conference at his country residence north of Cairo, which he convened ostensibly to discuss the outcome of the referendum. Mr. Sadat said that his victory of 98.29 percent "is not support for me but it is support for democracy."

Under the referendum, Mr. Sadat received approval for his proposal to exclude Marxists from the press and public life and to forbid political activity by politicians who held office before the 1952 revolution or who formed the pro-Soviet faction that Mr. Sadat purged seven years ago.

Today, the President delivered a virtual monologue for about two hours, mainly in Arabic, to Egyptian editors and foreign correspondents. He pounded the table, shouted and gestured with pointed finger.

He devoted much of the time to denouncing the leftist Progressive Union Party and the rightist New Wafd Party. The two parties, which have been severely critical of Mr. Sadat's domestic policies, were the main targets of the referendum. Mr. Sadat said that he had no objection to either party's existence. "But I am against anyone," he declared, "who tries to exploit democracy for his own ends—be he on the left, on the right or in the center."

Purge of Leaders Expected

His often angry comments tended to confirm speculation here that he intended to use the referendum's results to purge the leadership of the two parties, notably the New Wafd chairman, Fuad Serag Eddin, and the leftist party leader, Khaled Mohieddin.

Mr. Serag Eddin was Minister of Interior before the 1952 revolution and was later convicted by a military court of corruption. He contends the charges were politically motivated. Mr. Mohieddin was with Gamal Abdel Nasser and Mr. Sadat in the Free Officers movement that deposed King Farouk in 1952. He was ousted from the military leadership formed by President Nasser for being too radical.

Today, the leftist party issued a statement urging steps to avoid a "futile confrontation" with the Government. The party also said that "we will continue our struggle wtihin the framework of human rights and the framework of the Constitution."

The referendum obligates the press to observe vague patriotic guidelines as defined by the Government. Mr. Sadat appeared to have a compliant press in mind when he said today that it should function as a "fourth authority," along with the executive, legislative and judicial branches.

The only newspaper that deviates substantially from the Government's line is the leftist weekly Al Ahaly, which Mr. Sadat condemned today as "full of anti-Government poison, hate and bitterness." Last week's issue was suppressed when it advocated that readers vote no in the referendum. Mr. Sadat is now expected to hobble the paper, if not close it altogether.

Some Egyptians Fear Repressions

The President admitted that his referendum had alarmed some Egyptians, who expect a "renunciation of democracy" with a return of detention camps and seizure of personal property for political reasons, as commonly occurred under the Nasser leadership. Mr. Sadat promised that this would not happen, "never, never."

In attacking the opposition, Mr. Sadat charged that the leftists wanted "to leap into power through bloodshed and sabotage," apparently an allusion to price riots in January 1977, which Mr. Sadat contends were instigated by Communists.

Mr. Sadat complained that the New Wafd Party, which is a reconstitution of the old Wafd Party that dominated politics under the monarchy, claims that "everything before the 1952 revolution was sweetness and light and everything afterward was a bitter pill."

In a remark that surprised some observers, he suggested that the two parties take a lesson in national unity from the Israelis, who, he said, rallied around Prime Minister Menachem Begin to resist American pressure to modify peace terms

NEW YORK TIMES, May 24, 1978, P11

Sadat, in Silencing Critics at Home, Provokes New Criticism Abroad

By CHRISTOPHER S. WREN
Special to The New York Times

CAIRO, June 11—President Anwar el-Sadat's domestic crackdown has rapidly muted formal political opposition, but it has left him visibly defensive about the implications both at home and abroad.

In the few weeks since a nationwide referendum gave Mr. Sadat a mandate to purge critics in politics and the press, one opposition party has dissolved in protest and the other has suspended political activity. A leftist newspaper that enraged Mr. Sadat with its muckraking has halted publication.

The same measures that strengthened the President's hand at home have eroded the image that he enjoyed abroad as a statesman above petty political battles. More than a few educated Egyptians say they have been antagonized by his contention that democracy remains unaffected. A Cairene commented, "Democracy has always been a one-man show in Egypt, but at least you didn't pretend that it was otherwise."

Some other Arabs seem unruffled by the latest developments, having usually found Egypt a little too liberal. Radical states such as Libya have joined the Soviet Union in deploring the situation for reasons of politics rather than of conscience.

Response Viewed as Excessive

Western diplomats here have generally expressed disappointment. Even some who believe that Mr. Sadat needed to rein in his critics suggest that his response was hasty, excessive and poorly executed.

Mr. Sadat has become sensitive about the kind of press exposure he is getting abroad, which differs markedly from the acclaim that followed his visit to Israel last November. After promising that there would be no reprisals, he has warned foreign correspondents that they may be expelled if they paint too dismal a picture of Egypt.

[President Sadat told a group of air force officers that Egypt would soon begin producing its own fighter-bombers, but did not give details.]

There has been more tough talk lately from the President, who commented several times that he should have cracked down on opponents a year ago, when he had the opportunity after the bloody riots over food prices in January 1977. If the leftists attempt any new anti-Government agitation, he said last week, "I will make their blood flow in the streets."

He has lashed out at university professors who asked him to reconsider his referendum, contending that they "could not be trusted to bring up our rising generations," and he has accused some Egyptian journalists of earning handsome fees for articles denigrating their country abroad. At least 60 journalists are being investigated for what they have published or broadcast.

The contentiousness has prompted speculation that internal difficulties could have accounted in part for Mr. Sadat's hints last week that Egypt might have to resort to war again if Israel spurned his peace initiative. But several diplomatic analysts here discount such a link though they agree that the lack of progress in his peace policy has left him frustrated.

The President's crackdown has focused on the opposition parties that emerged during his experiment with political pluralism. When their criticism became increasingly strident, he arranged a referendum that would bar leading activists from political affairs on various grounds of unfitness.

The conservative New Wafd Party, which resurrected the old Wafd movement that flourished before the overthrow of the monarchy in 1952, voted to disband rather than let the Government exclude its three top officials, who held various ministerial posts before 1952, from political activity. In doing so the party complained that the new measures had "swept away all the political freedom

gained by the people." Citing similar reasons, the leftist National Unionist Progressive Party suspended political activity indefinitely. It also concluded that continued publication of its controversial newspaper, Al Ahaly, was futile.

Parliament, the People's Assembly, is left with only the majority centrist party and a small sycophantic rightist party, both of which have backed Mr. Sadat. The Assembly has generally functioned as a rubber stamp for his foreign policy decisions, including his peace policy, and he is expected to encounter less resistance now on some domestic issues.

One reason that the two opposition parties, which had accounted between them for only two dozen of the 360 deputies, had inordinate impact was that Mr. Sadat had problems galvanizing the loyalist majority. He recently sent back a tax-reform bill on the ground that it did not go far enough in alleviating the disparity between rich and poor.

The bulk of the people, for whom life is a daily battle for subsistence, seem content to leave political matters to the President. He has insured their support by limning his critics as atheists, corrupt reactionaries or Soviet agents. While accusing the leftists of inciting class conflict, he has tried to discredit Mohammed Heykal, a prominent journalist now under investigation, by playing up his wealth and comfortable life style.

Sadat Says Egypt Will Make Planes

CAIRO, June 11 (UPI) — President Anwar el-Sadat said today that Egypt would manufacture its first fighter-bomber in 1980 and would also produce surface-to-air missiles and military jeeps.

Mr. Sadat made the announcement at a meeting with Egyptian Air Force officers at a Suez Canal military base.

Although Mr. Sadat did not go into detail, recent press reports have said Egypt was seeking a license from the French Dassault company to manufacture Mirage fighter-bombers in this country.

The reports said Egypt also was attempting to produce the French Crotale missile with French assistance and to manufacture military jeeps with the aid of the American Motors Company.

Egypt's efforts to establish a military industry are subsidized by a consortium of oil-producing Arab states.

NEW YORK TIMES, June 12, 1978, P1

Lenders to Get Egyptian Plan

$20 Billion Sought for Development

By YOUSSEF M. IBRAHIM

Egypt will present a detailed five-year development plan in Paris today to potential lenders from which it is seeking $20 billion in financing.

The presentation will be made at the second annual meeting of the Consultative Group on Egypt, a gathering of 13 nations under the auspices of the World Bank and several multinational aid groups. Egypt's top economic planners will outline their development needs between 1978 and 1982 and specific industrial and infrastructural projects started years ago but never completed because of lack of hard currency and the break in relations with the Soviet Union.

"I guess you can say this is something of a watershed meeting," Sherif Ghalib, Mideast economist for the Chase Manhattan Bank, said yesterday. "It will offer an indication of how creditors feel about the country by showing how much they are willing to put up in the way of help."

Members of Lending Group

The members of the Consultative Group are Britain, Canada, France, West Germany, Iran, Italy, Japan, Kuwait, the Netherlands, Qatar, Saudi Arabia, the United Arab Emirates and the United States.

At last year's meeting — the first of its kind for Egypt — it outlined its awesome economic problems. Egypt, it was disclosed, owed other nations $12 billion, plus several billions more in short-term obligations to commercial banks and suppliers of goods.

At the end of the 1977 meeting, Egypt obtained some $3.5 billion in aid, $2 billion of which came from the Gulf Organization for the Development of Egypt, a group made up of Saudi Arabia, Kuwait, Qatar and the United Arab Emirates. Another billion came from the United States and the rest from several other Western countries. Much of the money was used to pay arrears on debts and for food imports. None went toward development, and the $12 billion debt remained, although it was rescheduled for repayment over a longer term.

This year, Egypt hopes to obtain an additional $3 billion, which it is considered likely to get, but at far more demanding terms.

A Standby I.M.F. Credit

In their effort to persuade lenders, the Egyptians will be armed with a new three-year agreement with the International Monetary Fund granting a standby credit of $750 million. However, I.M.F. officials have said that the credits will be doled out on a yearly basis only after a review that assured the fund that Egypt was carrying out a program of economic reform.

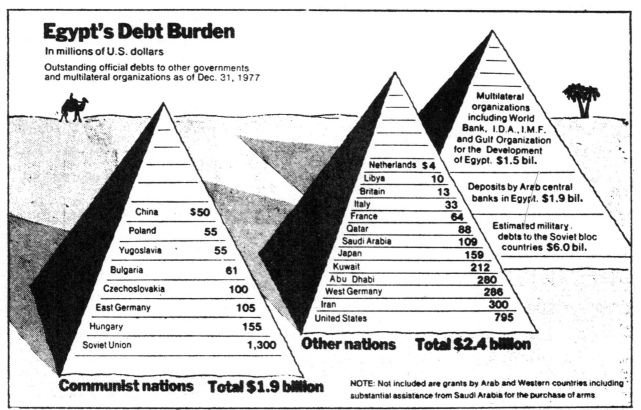

Egypt's Debt Burden

In millions of U.S. dollars

Outstanding official debts to other governments and multilateral organizations as of Dec. 31, 1977

Multilateral organizations including World Bank, I.D.A., I.M.F. and Gulf Organization for the Development of Egypt. $1.5 bil.

Deposits by Arab central banks in Egypt. $1.9 bil.

Estimated military debts to the Soviet bloc countries $6.0 bil.

Communist nations	
China	$50
Poland	55
Yugoslavia	55
Bulgaria	61
Czechoslovakia	100
East Germany	105
Hungary	155
Soviet Union	1,300

Communist nations   Total $1.9 billion

Other nations	
Netherlands	$4
Libya	10
Britain	13
Italy	33
France	64
Qatar	88
Saudi Arabia	109
Japan	159
Kuwait	212
Abu Dhabi	280
West Germany	286
Iran	300
United States	795

Other nations   Total $2.4 billion

NOTE: Not included are grants by Arab and Western countries including substantial assistance from Saudi Arabia for the purchase of arms.

The New York Times/June 14, 1978

Although fund officials would not discuss specifics, it is understood that part of the reform includes the removal of subsidies for more domestic industries; raising taxes and tariffs; reducing bank financing of the Government deficit while sustaining the 8 percent real growth in gross national product achieved last year. (Egypt's G.N.P. stands at $14 billion.) All of these measures would mean a continued rise in domestic prices, but with continued pressure for wage restraints.

Banking and State Department sources here are doubtful the Egyptians can maintain this kind of discipline. They point to the resignation of Abdel Moneim al-Kaissouni, Egypt's Deputy Prime Minister for economic affairs, two months ago because of what was viewed as President Anwar el-Sadat's disregard for Mr. al-Kaissouni's fiscal discipline. The Egyptian President, the sources said, chose to raise wages of public employees to dampen discontent over inflation.

In January 1977, when the Government suddenly lifted subsidies on essential foods, riots erupted, leaving 80 dead. President Sadat blamed Communists for the riots and initiated a crack-

down that is still in progress. But the measures have done little to quell mounting criticism of his economic policies.

Inflation, which has been running at over 20 percent a year since 1974, has alienated the poor and the middle class. And, according to the sources, the "open door" policy instituted in 1974 with great fanfare by President Sadat to attract foreign investors has yet to show what material benefits it has brought the Egyptian people, save for the gleaming Mercedes-Benz and Volvo cars driven by Egypt's new merchant class and the consumer goods piled up in downtown shops and sidewalk kiosks.

Nevertheless, Egypt will have some good news to offer at the Paris meeting. For one thing, its hard-currency revenues have improved substantially. In 1978, several bankers estimated, Egypt's revenues from tourism — a mushrooming industry — will reach $750 million, up from $100 million in 1973. Oil exports, which only started last year after the repossession of oil fields in the Sinai from the Israelis, are expected to bring in $330 million. The Suez Canal, in operation since 1975, will

generate $450 million. And, most importantly, remittances for the one million Egyptians working in Arab oil-producing countries such as Saudi Arabia, Kuwait and Libya are expected to send home $1.6 billion.

All of this, the bankers said, should go a long way toward easing Egypt's trade deficit, which informed sources say will be close to $3 billion in 1978.

The principal imports of the country continue to be food for the population of 39 million, increasing at an annual rate of 2.58 percent a year, according to the World Bank — another mouth to feed every 37 seconds.

The United States has been the largest single aid donor. Its assistance to Egypt has averaged $1 billion a year since 1975. The group of conservative Arab countries led by Saudi Arabia, however, has been the mainstay of financial assistance, and although the Arabs are demanding more order in the Egyptian economy as a condition for more aid, political observers feel they have no choice but to continue aiding Egypt.

NEW YORK TIMES, June 14, 1978, S4 P3

U.S. TO GIVE ISRAELIS A SADAT PEACE PLAN FOR OCCUPIED LANDS

BASIS FOR NEW TALKS SOUGHT

Proposals Submitted to Mondale by Egypt Call for an Interim 5-Year West Bank Rule

By TERENCE SMITH
Special to The New York Times

WASHINGTON, July 4 — An Egyptian Government peace proposal, calling for a five-year transitional period of rule in the Israeli-occupied West Bank of the Jordan and Gaza Strip and their eventual return to Jordanian and Egyptian administration, will be formally submitted to Israel tomorrow.

The plan, which reliable sources said contained specific security arrangements for Israel during the five years and the creation of local Palestinian councils

in the areas, will be outlined to Foreign Minister Moshe Dayan by Ambassador Samuel W. Lewis in Jerusalem.

Authoritative sources said that the Egyptian proposal, presented to Vice President Mondale by President Anwar el-Sadat in Alexandria yesterday, contained "some common points" with a 26-point plan put forward by Israel last December.

These include the concept of a five-year transitional period, the creation of local Palestinian councils to take over many of the administrative functions of the Israeli military government and the participation of Israel, Egypt and Jordan in negotiations over the final status of the areas.

Basis for Peace Talks Sought

American officials returning to Washington with Mr. Mondale early this morning said they hoped these common elements would provide the basis for negotiation at a meeting between the Israeli and Egyptian Foreign Ministers with Secretary of State Cyrus R. Vance in London later this month.

But the officials also stressed that there were major differences between the Israeli and Egyptian proposals.

The Egyptian plan, for example, calls for the eventual withdrawal of all Israeli forces from the two areas after the transitional period. It also envisions a phased return of the areas to Jordanian

and Egyptian administration, pending a final resolution of the Palestinian problem. It does not, however, include any specific role for the Palestine Liberation Organization. Nor does it specifically project the creation of an independent Palestinian state.

The Israeli proposal, on the other hand, would keep Israeli military forces in place indefinitely while granting the local Palestinians self-rule over administrative matters for a five-year period. Only after that would Israel be willing to discuss and agree upon the future status of the areas.

A Foundation for Negotiation

"Obviously neither plan is going to be acceptable to the other side in its entirety," a high American official told reporters aboard the Mondale plane while flying back to Washington. "But the basis for negotiation is there."

Ten days ago, there were press reports out of Cairo that the Egyptians had presented a proposal that would have required an Israeli withdrawal from the areas prior to negotiations.

Responding to the press reports, the Israeli Cabinet issued a statement denouncing the proposal as unacceptable. But American officials later explained that the press reports were incorrect and that no such proposal had been made by Egypt.

The Egyptian plan is contained in a

three-page, double-spaced document that Mr. Sadat gave to Mr. Mondale as they conferred on the lawn of an elegant beach house east of Alexandria. The details were relayed to President Carter at Camp David as the Mondale party flew home over the Atlantic.

Sources familiar with the Egyptian plan said it was a far more general document than the 26-point proposal Prime Minister Menachem Begin first put forward last December. One source said there was a "deliberate vagueness" to the Sadat plan that apparently had been built in for tactical negotiating purposes.

The timing of the Israeli withdrawal was not made clear in the document, for example, nor the sequence of the creation of the Palestianian councils and the resumption of Jordanian and Egyptian administration in the areas. American officials hope that these matters can be discussed at the London foreign ministers' conference, which is expected to open July 18 or 19.

The London meeting is expected to last for two or three days and lay the ground work for continuing negotiations. These may be conducted at the foreign ministers' or defense-ministers' level, either in London, or more probably, at some Middle Eastern site agreed to by both parties.

Three Documents for Discussion

Three documents will be on the table in London: the Israeli plan, the new Egyptian proposal and the draft "declaration of principles" that American officials tried unsuccessfully to negotiate between the two parties in January and February.

"We'll try to find the common ground in these documents and work out a mechanism for more negotiations," an American official aboard the Mondale plane said last night.

"No one means to gloss over the difficulties involved," the official continued. "The process is going to be long, controversial and hard. Both parties are going to begin from very different positions and we will have to see if they can close the gap."

American officials expect to hold intensive consultations with Israel and Egypt via diplomatic channels over the next 10 days to work out an agenda for the London meeting.

In addition, President Sadat is expected to meet this weekend or early next week in Vienna with Shimon Peres, the former Israeli Defense Minister and head of the opposition Labor Party. Presumably Mr. Sadat will use this meeting to try to build some support for his proposal in Israeli circles outside the Begin Government. It will be the second such meeting between the two men in Vienna in the last five months.

There also are tentative plans for a separate meeting between the Israeli and Egyptian Defense Ministers, Ezer Weizman and Gen. Mohammed Abdel Ghany el-Gamasy.

This meeting, which presumably would follow the London conference, could provide the forum for working out an agreement on the security provisions that would be part of any settlement. An American official said yesterday that a Weizman-Gamasy meeting could well prove to be "one of the most important aspects of the negotiating process."

Taken together, all these meetings represent the first significant movement in the stalled Israeli-Egyptian dialogue in the six months since the political talks between the two countries broke down in Jerusalem on Jan. 18.

NEW YORK TIMES, July 5, 1978, P1

An Egyptian Sadat Knows He Can Count On

Mohammed Ibrahim Kamel

By MARVINE HOWE
Special to The New York Times

CAIRO, July 18 — More than three decades ago, when Anwar el-Sadat spent six months in prison, he concluded that one of his fellow prisoners was a man he could count on in a tough spot. That man, Mohammed Ibrahim Kamel, now President Sadat's Foreign Minister, is representing Egypt at the Middle East talks in England.

Man in the News

"If the Israelis don't know yet that he can be tough, they will learn it this week," one of his aides remarked here as Mr. Kamel began the meeting at Leeds Castle outside London with Foreign Minister Moshe Dayan of Israel in the presence of Secretary of State Cyrus R. Vance.

As a negotiator, Egypt's Foreign Minister is said to be strong on principles. At 51 years of age, he has the well-tailored look of a banker. While he is generally informal and congenial, his aides say he is completely preoccupied by the problems of peace in the Middle East.

Unlike many high officials, he does not take off for weekends of relaxation by the sea in Alexandria. Instead, he stays here, often working over files. If he goes to Alexandria, it is for working sessions with President Sadat.

In his recent autobiography, Mr. Sadat described how he and Mr. Kamel were imprisoned in 1946 for six months on charges of complicity in the assassination of a pro-British Cabinet Minister. Someone was said to have made a confession, the President recalls, but he adds that he had been certain it could not have been the "dependable" Mr. Kamel.

Although long a professional diplomat, Mr. Kamel was little known here when he came into prominence late in December as the successor to Foreign Minister Ismail Fahmy, who resigned in protest against Mr. Sadat's dramatic decision to pay a visit to Israel.

Studied Law at Cairo University

According to an official biography, Mr. Kamel was born Jan. 6, 1927, graduated from Cairo University's law department in 1947, started his career as an official of the Council of State and joined the Foreign Ministry in 1955. He married Rashiqa Shaker, and they have two sons, both now at the university.

After serving in Egyptian missions to London, Mexico City and Ottawa, he was named an ambassador in 1964. He has been ambassador to several African countries, Sweden and West Germany, where he served for four years before becoming Foreign Minister.

To the Egyptian public, Mr. Kamel is still relatively unknown, being connected usually only to the peace initiative. His frequent travel abroad accounts in part for his lack of prominence at home. But in addition, he does not seek publicity and is brief in his statements to the press.

Come Call Him 'a Yes Man'

Most Egyptians who approve the Sadat peace moves approve of Mr. Kamel. Critics call him "a yes man" and praise former Foreign Minister Fahmy as a man who had the courage to express his views.

Some Egyptian journalists call Mr. Kamel the President's "hard-liner" in the peace talks and say his positions are much more rigid than those of Mr.

Sadat. It is generally agreed, however, that he has the President's confidence as a loyal career diplomat who can be relied upon to carry out Mr. Sadat's foreign-policy wishes.

When Mr. Fahmy resigned last December, a Foreign Ministry colleague quipped that the Foreign Minister "was only a cook in the kitchen and he thought that he was making the recipes."

Using a similar analogy, regarding Mr. Sadat as Egypt's foreign policy "chef," a lawyer here described Mr. Kamel as "the man in the street who can only express his ideas about the meal after it is cooked."

But this depiction was protested by a close associate, who said that Mr. Kamel "can give frank advice but is always polite, always a gentleman."

NEW YORK TIMES, July 19, 1978, P3

8

Israel at the Crossroads

United in face of 30 years of war and threats of war, Israel is divided over the new hope of peace. The journey of Sadat to Jerusalem in November of 1977 was the most convincing of several signs that Israel was no longer engaged in a struggle for her existence. Rather Israel would have to struggle to define what sort of existence the state should have, old questions which had been tabled in the 30 years of Israel's warfare with her Arab neighbors. Opening the old questions gave Israel a year of strife in 1978, of demonstrations and widely publicized splits in the cabinet. More significantly, the divisions in Israel were echoed in the world Zionist community and among Israel's oldest supporters, the Americans.

From 1948 to 1977 the labor unions' party, MAPAI, had provided fragile coalition governments with votes and a tradition of cabinet discipline. With opposition in the parliament ranging from two Marxist groups to religious fundamentalists, fiscal conservatives like Menachem Begin's Herut party to an international socialist bloc, the MAPAI managed to dominate Israeli politics, bringing the country through three wars against the Arabs.

A series of government crises, including Israel's setback against Egypt in 1973, double digit inflation, accusations of corruption which led to one minister's suicide and the resignation of Prime Minister Yitzhak Rabin, led to the government's fall and defeat in elections in 1977. At the root of MAPAI's defeat was the fact that the government had not won peace with the Arabs. Instead, in the decade since Israel's six day victory, the country had become diplomatically isolated, embargoed, censored—an international pariah. The voters wanted a change.

Ironically in turning to the conservative coalition called the Likud and headed by Herut leader Begin, the Israelis brought in a government which asked harder peace conditions then MAPAI had called for. The new Prime Minister Begin had resigned from a MAPAI coalition in 1970 over the government's decision to accept eventual return of the West Bank of the Jordan river, occupied since 1967, to the Arabs. Now, with peace in the offing, Begin insisted that Israel would never withdraw from the West Bank, but on the contrary would build Jewish settlements in the biblical homeland. "The Bible is our mandate," he explained.

Begin's stand on the West Bank provoked a controversy which reopened all the basic contradictions of Israeli society muted in the preceding three decades. If the Bible were the mandate for occupation of the West Bank, what of international law? Was Israel a nation-state bound and protected by international guarantees like other nation-states, or was it a special, religious entity? If it were a religious entity, would its laws specifically conform to the injunctions of the Bible, or the customs of religion in matters such as conscription of women, or performance of military duty on Sabbath?

Other matters raised by the West Bank issue were practical and economic. The hardliner agricultural minister argued that Israel had to retain the West Bank in order to meet the growing demand for food, while some Zionists felt that the original "return to the land" ideal of Zionism had been compromised by the heavy urbanization of Israel and that more land was required to preserve the farmer-soldier character of the Israelis.

The confrontation over these questions erupted in the new year when the Gush Emonim, a militant group of religious fundamentalists, planted trees at the opening of a new settlement at Shiloah on the West Bank. After the breakdown of peace talks between Israel and Egypt, 300 reserve officers of the Peace Now movement rallied some 40,000 supporters to demonstrate on April 7, 1978 against the government's stand on the occupied territories. Nine days later the Gush Emunim and other militant conservatives staged a counter rally, turning out in equal strength. MAPAI leaders Yitzhak Rabin, Abba Eban and Yigael Alon sharply criticized Prime Minister Begin for his position, while Likud coalition ministers like Sharon and Yadin toured the West Bank settlements and pledged their support to the settlers. Independent general Ezer Weizman, minister of defense for the government, publicly speculated on the wisdom of trying to hold on to the West Bank, giving rise to speculation that he might split with the government or try to replace Begin.

The world never had a better opportunity to observe the plurality and the occasional bitterness of Israeli politics. It seemed strange that a nation weary of war should have elected a leader apparently less willing than others to negotiate a peace. In one view, Begin's rise to the premiership can be seen as the working of a multiparty system which over-represents extreme-of-center groups. Other interpretations cite the nation's dissatisfaction with politicians, and a yearning for a figure of more prophetic stature, in the tradition of the nation's first premier, Ben Gurion. Begin, with his violent past, his ascetic way of life and his unyielding politics may draw closer to the aspirations of an increasingly Middle Eastern, introspective Israel.

That Menachem Begin has brought Israel closer to peace than 30 years of temperate MAPAI diplomacy is once again proof of the unpredictable nature of Middle East politics. Perhaps because of his impeccable integrity and his "credentials," both as a victim of concentration camps and as a terrorist, Begin emerged as an ideal spokesman for a frightened, threatened Israel. Only a leader with supreme confidence in his own judgment would agree to engage in one-to-one high-level diplomacy. It was a risk which stolid labor leaders might have balked at, but which Begin grasped eagerly.

Yet the career of Begin as Israel's Prime Minister has caused consternation for Israel's supporters in America. From the beginning American diplomats and Begin clashed over the interpretation of UN Resolution 242, which called, in the American view, for Israel to relinquish all the Arab lands occupied in 1967. In the Israeli view, only a partial return was called for. America held that the settling of Israelis in Sinai and on the West Bank was a violation of international law, while Begin argued security reasons and ideological necessity. American Jews, long-time observers of Israeli affairs, were themselves divided sharply between support for the state of Israel and a general agreement in principle with the American government's position. But when the USA decided to sell interceptor jets to Egypt and Saudi Arabia, linking them in a take-it-or-leave-it package with a plane sale to Israel, public opinion in America split over the justice and wisdom of the move. Jews and supporters of Israel worried that the Carter administration was preparing to abandon 30 years of commitment to Israeli security by the sale. The intensity of the debate probably helped focus the President's attention on the Middle East crisis, leading him to invite the two heads of state, Begin and Sadat, to a Camp David summit conference later in the year.

The Political Backdrop

CABINET SPLIT REPORTED

Israeli Cabinet is reportedly sharply split over Agriculture Minister Ariel Sharon's proposal to establish 4 new settlements and 20 outposts south of Gaza Strip within days; Sharon has threatened to campaign against peace proposals if plan is rejected; holds that unless Jewish population is greatly increased in West Bank and Gaza Strip, both will become havens for Palestinians who would proclaim independent state   (NEW YORK TIMES, January 8, 1978, P6)

EBAN ASSESSES BEGIN

Israeli Foreign Minister Abba Eban praises Prime Minister Menachem Begin's recognition of Egyptian sovereignty in Sinai, skill in setting up appropriate procedural machinery and willingness not to be too much tied to past slogans; Eban is most critical of Begin's lack of flexibility on Egyptian Israeli boundary and issue of settlements; holds that there are weaknesses in Begin's autonomy proposal for West Bank and Gaza; Eban says that essence of Begin's peace plan whether Begin realizes it or not is a peace treaty with Egypt and interim settlement with Palestinians; maintains that both Egypt and Israel look to US to extricate means by providing formulas which each can interpert in terms of their individual ideals   (TIMES OF LONDON, February 3, 1978, P14)

ISRAELIS SPLIT OVER TV FILM

Israeli Education and Cultural Affairs Minister Zevulun Hammer temporarily bans controversial television play; claims play, *The Tale of Hirbet Hiza*, which depicts Israeli soldiers treating Arabs harshly in war of 1948, would hurt negotiations with Egypt; liberal opinion in Israel assails Hammer's action as ill-disguised attempt at political censorship; *Jerusalem Post* asserts that banning of play did more to harm Israel's image than constant screening of film; Israeli television protests by going off air for 40 minutes   (WASHINGTON POST, February 9, 1978, P19)

WEST BANK SELF-RULE URGED

Israeli Foreign Minister Moshe Dayan urges Israel to grant self-rule to Arabs of West Bank and Gaza Strip, at meeting of his political supporters; proposes reducing military administration's authority to what is necessary to assure security   (NEW YORK TIMES, March 4, 1978, P5)

EZER WEIZMAN PROFILED

Biographic profile of Israeli Defense Minister Ezer Weizman, widely regarded as main contender to succeed Prime Minister Menachem Begin if Begin, who has serious heart condition, were to become disabled; mentions Weizman's autobiography *On Eagles' Wings*, which concentrates on vaguely cinematic career as pilot, but which byliner contends led Weizman to become founder of Israel's Air Force; profile highlights 1958–1966 leadership of Air Force, resignation over controversial right-wing political views, later accentuated by joining conservative Likud party, 7-month stint as Transport Minister in 1969 during Golda Meir Administration and role as campaign manager that brought Likud Party and Prime Minister Begin to power in 1977; mentions that Weizman's directness and impatience with minutiae have occasionally brought him into collisions with Begin (NEW YORK TIMES, March 5, 1978, S4 P6)

BEGIN RETAINS SUPPORT

Recent polls show that Israeli Prime Minister Menachem Begin is supported by 68% of his countrymen, yet he is widely criticized for handling of peace talks; Israelis reportedly feel that his opening offer of Egyptian sovereignty over all of Sinai was wrong   (TIME, March 6, 1978, P34)

ISRAEL FACING TOUGH QUESTIONS

Byliner William E. Farrell analyzes growing division in Israeli Cabinet over manner in which Israel should respond to Egyptian President Anwar el-Sadat's peace gestures; reports division centers on opposing views of 2 members, Agriculture Minister Ariel Sharon, considered leading "hawk," and Defense Minister Ezer Weizman, leading moderate, regarding issue of establishing settlements in occupied Arab lands; notes Weizman, who does not reject contention that settlements are necessary for defense but ordered freeze on settlement activity, was successful in having his order upheld by threatening to resign; holds controversy has lead to speculation on Prime Minister Begin's position, noting some believe he is biding his time, while others maintain Begin is losing his ability to control Cabinet; describes Weizman's political career, pointing out that Begin removed Weizman from leadership roles in 1972 when it appeared Weizman could pose leadership challenge, but that Weizman made comeback in 1977 when he managed Likud bloc's election victory   (NEW YORK TIMES, March 8, 1978, P1)

Ezer Weizman, Israel's Minister of Defense.

ALLON SCORES BEGIN STAND

Former Israeli Foreign Minister Yigal Allon holds Prime Minister Menachem Begin's controversial position on UN resolution calling for Israeli withdrawal from occupied Arab lands is hindering peace negotiations and damaging Israel's credibility; calls for full-scale Parliamentary debate on Begin's views, but challenge is rejected; dispute over interpretation of resolution has caused controversy within Begin's government, and is expected to be major topic at Begin's meeting with President Carter in US next week; in related action, Begin sharply responds to letter he received from over 300 army reservists expressing concern that his hard line on settlements is jeopardizing peace efforts; scores signers for making letter public before it was delivered to him, and holds government is making "supreme efforts" to prevent war and attain peace   (NEW YORK TIMES,   March 9, 1978,   P1)

BEGIN'S SUPPORT SLIPPING

Byliner William E. Farrell examines Israeli Prime Minister Menachem Begin's declining popularity at home; notes infighting within coalition government headed by right-wing Likud Party, intensified criticism from opposition Labor Party, and growing feeling that government has been too involved in peace negotiations while completely shunting aside problems such as wildcat strikes and runaway inflation; byliner also points to Begin's "glossing over" of frictions within Cabinet, composed of hawks, moderate conservatives, a few liberals and independents; reports that Labor Party, initially silent and enmeshed in internal squabbles and recriminations over ouster from power, has now started speaking more loudly in criticism of Begin's handling of Egyptian President Sadat's peace initiative; holds that while Begin is strong personality, he cannot act unilaterally, contrary to Sadat's perception while visiting Israel; sees consolidation of public opinion behind government after March 11, 1978, guerrilla raid on bus near Tel Aviv   (NEW YORK TIMES,   March 12, 1978,   S4   P2)

ISRAEL ANXIOUS ABOUT FUTURE

Commentator Arthur H. Samuelson outlines anticipated economic and social changes facing Israel if current peace initiative succeeds; notes many Israelis fear that peace would mean massive influx of cheap Arab labor into Israeli market and be detrimental to Israel's shipping industry; cites Israeli fear that Arab influx could undermine security and distinctive identity as Jewish state   (SATURDAY REVIEW,   March 18, 1978,   P7)

EBAN SCORES LIKUD INTRANSIGENCE

Former Israeli Foreign Minister Abba Eban warns Israeli Prime Minister Menachem Begin must either give up his Likud Party platform refusing any Israeli withdrawal from West Bank or give up his search for peace, in article excerpted from *Jerusalem Post*; points out Begin has refused to accept 1970 Israeli agreement that UN Security Council Resolution 242 meant Israel was committed to transfer of most of Judea, Samaria and Gaza territories to Jordan under peace agreement; maintains present government interpretation of Resolution 242, holding it does not apply to West Bank or Gaza, conflicts with established Israeli policy   (WASHINGTON POST,   March 24, 1978,   P21)

BEGIN'S STANCE ANALYZED

Washington Post editorial agrees with former Israeli Foreign Minister Abba Eban's assessment that obstacle to further Middle East peace talks is Israeli Prime Minister Menachem Begin's personal religious convictions against Israeli withdrawal from West Bank; notes Eban points out Begin resigned Cabinet post in 1970 when Israeli Government agreed that UN Resolution 242 applied to West Bank; contends Carter Administration initially failed to realize that religious foundation of Begin's West Bank position provided special problem and deviated from Israeli Government policy; points out Arabs have support of Resolution 242 and pre-Begin Israel in their push for some Arab sovereignty over West Bank   (WASHINGTON POST,   March 24, 1978,   P20)

PEACE MOVEMENT URGED

Israel's Defense Minister Ezer Weizman proposes formation of "national peace government," in newspaper *Maariv* interview; suggests such a party would include opposition Labor Party and present Carter Administration with a united front on Middle East issue; supports positions taken by Prime Minister Begin and Foreign Minister Dayan in talks with President Carter; maintains a national peace government would seek peace with Egypt without US participation; charges shuttle-diplomacy of Assistant Secretary of State Alfred L. Atherton Jr. may have obstructed peace process; suggests that meeting between Israeli and US leaders was not as disastrous as portrayed   (NEW YORK TIMES,   March 24, 1978,   P11)

SPLIT IN GOVERNMENT OBSERVED

London Times editorial holds that Israel Prime Minister Menachem Begin's "honeymoon" with Knesset is over and his authority is being undermined; says his meeting with President Carter has provoked debate over his competence as national leader instead of uniting country behind him   (TIMES OF LONDON,   March 25, 1978,   P15)

U.S. POLITICAL INTRIGUE RUMORED

Wall Street Journal editorial, commenting on rumors that US is conspiring to replace Israeli Prime Minister Menachem Begin, asserts question of who should be prime minister of Israel should be left strictly to Israelis; notes Carter Administration has officially denied reports of any US interference; points out that Israel has been known to dabble in US politics   (WALL STREET JOURNAL,   March 27, 1978,   P18)

ISRAELI VIEWS POLLED

Christian Science Monitor editorial says recent poll shows 70% of Israeli population prefers peace with secure and recognized borders over right to settle in the West Bank and Gaza; states Prime Minister Menachem Begin is in political trouble, with Defense Minister Ezer Weizman calling for "national peace government" representing all parties; urges Israeli people to make peace mandate clear to Begin or hand mandate to someone else   (CHRISTIAN SCIENCE MONITOR,   March 27, 1978,   P28)

INTERVENTION BRINGS BEGIN SUPPORT

Impact of Israeli invasion of southern Lebanon on popularity of government of Menachem Begin analyzed; degree to which support for Israeli government has diminished both in Israel and abroad, noted; rifts within Begin's own Cabinet are described as being so serious that Begin's Likud Party has presented an amendment to the Knesset that would empower the Prime Minister to dismiss an individual minister without the whole cabinet having to resign as is now the law; further examples of protests within Israel noted, and speculation made that failure to break the deadlock in peace negotiations will bring further pressure on Begin to step down
(FINANCIAL TIMES,   March 31, 1978,   P18)

DEMONSTRATORS URGE PEACE

April 1 demonstration in Tel Aviv by 25,000 to 45,000 persons against Prime Minister Menachem Begin's hard-line stand in talks with Egypt is largest protest since he took office; it is uncertain whether rally was one-time

affair or harbinger of grass-roots peace movement; rally was not inspired by any political faction, but came about after extensive publicity about letter to Begin by more than 300 reserve officers asking him to be more moderate; protesters are not calling for Begin's removal nor that he return all occupied territories, merely that he reconsider his position; Pzali Resheff, student who helped with rally, comments and states that there are plans for another rally in next few weeks; opposition of Finance Minister Simha Ehrlich to demonstration noted   (NEW YORK TIMES,   April 7, 1978,   P3)

BEGIN CABINET DYNAMICS OUTLINED

Israeli Prime Minister Menachem Begin is considered to be leader who is loner and tends to keep his own counsel; Begin, however, is reported to seek advice from Attorney General Aharon Barak and Eliahu Ben-Elissar, director of Prime Minister's office; Begin is said to counterbalance advice of Ariel Sharon, hawkish Agriculture Minister, with that of Ezer Weizman, more moderate Defense Minister; on internal Israeli policy Begin is said to consult with Finance Minister Simha Ehrlich, Minister of Interior and Police Dr. Yosef Burg, and Minister of Commerce and Industry Yigal Hurwitz; on informal level Begin will discuss ideas with Yehiel Kadishai and consults with Minister without Portfolio Haim Landau regarding matters, both domestic and foreign   (NEW YORK TIMES,   April 9, 1978,   P4)

ISRAELI DEBATE CHARACTERIZED

Israelis are increasingly attacking Prime Minister Menachem Begin's peace stance, but internal debate is thought to have a muted quality; the opposition, from army reserve officers, politicians and residents, questions government's hard-line proposals to retain control over all territories Israel has occupied on West Bank of Jordan River since 1967 war and size of invasion into Lebanon that followed Palestinian terrorist raid in Israel; critics also express concern over risks involved in giving up territory, uncertainties of negotiations and relations with US and Egypt; criticism from opposition party leader Shimon Peres, former Foreign Minister Abba Eban, Defense Minister Ezer Weizman, army reservists and civilians noted   (WALL STREET JOURNAL,   April 12, 1978,   P1)

BEGIN SUPPORTERS RALLY

Estimated 40,000 Israelis demonstrate in Tel Aviv in support of Prime Minister Menachem Begin's position in Israeli-Arab conflict; demonstration seeks to counter "Peace Now" demonstration by armed forces reservists 2 weeks earlier, including decorated war heroes, who had promoted greater Israeli concessions   (NEW YORK TIMES,   April 16, 1978,   P17)

DEBATE ON RESOLUTION 242

Israeli Cabinet issues statement reaffirming that UN Resolution 242 is basis for negotiations with neighboring Arab countries; statement is seen as attempt to resolve major source of friction with US, and to convey willingness to negotiate on all fronts; Israel's opposition Labor Party criticizes Likud coalition government's conciliatory move, asserting it is inadequate substitute for clear and credible policy; government spokesman contends statement does not indicate softening of official policy, and Cabinet Secretary Aryeh Naor points out government has not made new decision (NEW YORK TIMES, April 17, 1978, P1)

BEGIN'S POLICIES CHALLENGED

Two Israeli groups in Tel Aviv challenge Prime Minister Begin's policies, urging greater Israeli flexibility in seeking peace with Arabs; 1 group, composed of 360 professors and intellectuals, publishes signed petition in Tel Aviv newspaper, supporting so-called "Peace Now" campaign begun recently by 300 Israeli military reservists; 2nd group, 300 religious Israelis, writes protest letter to Prime Minster Begin stating that peace is more important than retaining occupied West Bank of Jordan River (NEW YORK TIMES, April 26, 1978, P8)

PEACE MOVEMENT GROWING

Summary of growing Israeli movement to urge Government of Prime Minister Begin to show more flexibility in search for peace notes movement does not yet pose political threat to Begin; holds, however, there have been rumors of lobbying for support from Democratic Movement for Change, most moderate faction of ruling coalition, which has 15 seats in 120-member Knesset; cites large turnout and support at several demonstrations and protests since Begin's unproductive visit to US in March (NEW YORK TIMES, April 30, 1978, S4 P2)

ISRAEL'S STATUS EVALUATED

London Times editorial evaluates the status of Israel on the occasion of its 30th anniversary; outlines Israel's many achievements, but notes that many of these achievements remain incomplete, and some are in danger of being vitiated entirely by the unsolved "Arab question"; says this is not so much a question of relations with neighboring Arab states, but the challenge posed by the problem of relations with the Arabs currently living under Israeli rule; notes that for the past 11 years Israeli society has been exposed to all the difficulties and dangers of an occupying power; warns that no viable solution is possible if Israel remains in occupation of the West Bank and Gaza Strip (TIMES OF LONDON, May 9, 1978, P19)

ISRAELI FRUSTRATIONS EXPRESSED

Commentator Anthony Lewis reports on sense of frustration felt by many Israelis who perceive their government is not acting in interest of peace; discusses about-face taken by General Yehoshafat Harkabi, who has long warned about Arab militarism; notes Harkabi recently signed Peace Now petition because he feels opportunity for peace is slipping away; reports Harkabi believes Arabs have moderated their views since 1967 and are willing to recognize Israeli in exchange for return of occupied land; comments many Israelis like Harkabi are discouraged that government has not seized current opportunity for peace (NEW YORK TIMES, May 22, 1978, P21)

NEW PARTY PROFILED

Profile of Israel's new moderate political party Democratic Movement for Change, headed by Deputy Prime Minister Yigael Yadin, holds party is currently troubled by internal quarreling, with some members urging that party leave Prime Minister Menachem Begin's coalition government; notes Yadin has come under increasing criticism for being too receptive to Begin's foreign policy, while Begin has been criticized for his hard line in refusing to make territorial concessions on occupied West Bank and Gaza Strip lands (NEW YORK TIMES, May 23, 1978, P2)

CABINET DEBATES, OPPOSITION MOUNTS

Israeli Cabinet begins major debate on questions posed by US on future of West Bank; a growing number of members of Democratic Movement for Change, new moderate political party headed by Deputy Prime Minister Yigal Yadin, are reportedly disturbed by Prime Minister Begin's firm opposition to territorial compromise on West Bank and Gaza; Israeli Labor Party urges Cabinet to consider both security of Israel and deterioration of close relationship between Israel and US; background details (NEW YORK TIMES, June 5, 1978, P1)

PLIGHT OF JEWISH REFUGEES STRESSED

Israeli Government and World Organization of Jews from Arab Countries (WOJAC) are dramatizing past plight of 1.5 million Jewish refugees from Arab countries, who are now Israeli citizens and comprise almost half of Israel's population; propaganda move is intended to counter widely-publicized cause of Palestinian refugees; WOJAC is trying to convince US to recognize cause of Arab Jews, and is attempting to get refugees to register claims for losses they suffered (LOS ANGELES TIMES, June 11, 1978, S4 P1)

CONSCRIPTION OF WOMEN DEBATED

Petition by women of high school age to Israeli Parliament to reject proposed new law that would exempt women from military service if they cited religious reasons causes political furor; move threatens government coalition because Agudat Israel Party threatens to quit coalition if legislation fails; Agudat argues that it is licentious for young women to mingle with young men without parental supervision (NEW YORK TIMES, July 4, 1978, P2)

BEGIN, PERES CLASH

Israeli Prime Minister Begin and opposition leader Shimon Peres clash in Parliament over Peres' meeting in Vienna with Egypt's President Sadat; Commerce Minister Yigal Hurwitz accuses Peres of wanting "to climb to power on Sadat's shoulders"; Peres declares he helped win friends for Israel; Peres reports that Sadat said he wanted all of Sinai returned and did not rule out border changes in West Bank, but that West Bank's future should be negotiated with Jordan, not Egypt (NEW YORK TIMES, July 20, 1978, P1)

BEGIN'S CONTROL QUESTIONED

Commentator William E. Farrell discusses Israeli Prime Minister Menachem Begin's dwindling control over discipline of his Cabinet and greater infighting on peace issues; focuses on recent personal initiatives by Defense Minister Ezer Weizman toward Egyptian President Anwar el-Sadat and contrasts their cool reception by hawkish Cabinet members; also summarizes frictions between Begin and Parliament, including conscription of women, captured territories and economic crisis   (NEW YORK TIMES,   July 23, 1978,   S4   P5)

CONSCRIPTION ISSUE SHAKES COALITION

Israel's Likud coalition government has been shaken by controversy over conscription into Army of Orthodox Jewish women; orthodox Agudat Israel Party's demands for exemption from draft for Orthodox women have been strongly resisted by Labor and Shelli Parties and Democratic Movement for Change; Agudat Israel threatened to quit Likud coalition if exemption did not pass; compromise bill exempts women who declare strict adherence to Sabbath and Jewish dietary regulations (TIME,   July 24, 1978,   P32)

LIKUD-LABOR CLASHES INCREASING

Political fight between Israeli Prime Minister Begin's governing Likud bloc and opposition Labor Party is becoming increasingly fractious and bitter, with Labor Party officials suggesting Begin is physically and mentally ill and questioning his ability to lead nation; Begin asserts it is "crude" to play politics with his health, while Cabinet issues statement condemning personal attacks on Begin   (NEW YORK TIMES,   July 24, 1978,   P3)

PEACE GROUP ERECTS MONUMENT

Five hundred supporters of Israel's "Peace Now" movement, started by several reserve army officers when Israel-Egypt peace talks stalemated, erect peace monument in Shiloh, Jewish settlement in occupied West Bank; hold Shiloh symbolizes minority of Israelis who oppose all moves leading to peace; group, which opposes policies Prime Minister Begin will take to September 5 Camp David summit, believes Begin government has secretly decided to set up 5 new Jewish settlements in West Bank; Begin refuses to comment on claim, but Parliament member denies charge, holding it is intended to embarrass government as Begin prepares for summit (NEW YORK TIMES,   August 12, 1978,   P49)

BEGIN'S COALITION DIMINISHES

Israeli Prime Minister Menachem Begin's coalition has lost 6-8 dovish members of Democratic Movement for Change in the Knesset, leaving Begin with comfortable majority of 20-24 votes instead of 36; members withdrew their support from the government because of Begin's refusal to make more territorial concessions to Egypt; pollsters report party has lost 75% of support it had in 1977 elections   (NEW YORK TIMES,   August 25, 1978,   P38)

BEDOUIN LIFE STYLE CHANGING

Commentator Laura Kayesh examines changing way of life for Bedouin population of Israel; notes Israeli government is attempting to force Bedouins to give up their nomadic life style and live in townships; reports many Bedouins who have moved into government settlements have abandoned shepherding, traditional means of livelihood, and have turned to other trades, such as farming and construction work   (SAN FRANCISCO CHRONICLE,   August 27, 1978,   P16)

BEGIN GAINS WIDE BACKING

Israeli Labor Party head Shimon Peres throws support behind peace plan Prime Minister Menachem Begin will bring to Middle East summit meeting at Camp David; Begin now enjoys backing of every major Israeli political party; only serious opposition to Begin plan comes from Peace Now movement, politically non-aligned group that scheduled September 2 parade and rally in Tel Aviv to

Two centuries-old water coming from recently discovered reservoirs beneath Israel's Negev Desert forms a new oasis for the Bedouin population.

Shown here is part of the usual Bedouin camp.

'Peace Now' demonstration in Jerusalem. Three hundred Israeli war veterans initiated this grass-roots peace movement in the aftermath of Egyptian President Anwar Sadat's visit to Jerusalem in November 1977.

urge that Israel show greater flexibility at summit; review of Begin's peace plan   (NEW YORK TIMES,   September 1,   P38)

'PEACE NOW' GROUP PROFILED

Profile of Israeli Peace Now organization, a grass-roots peace movement which was begun by 300 Israeli war veterans in aftermath of Egyptian President Sadat's visit to Jerusalem in November 1977; movement has become potential political force in past 6 months, criticizing Prime Minister Begin for being too inflexible in his dealings with Sadat; was responsible for demonstration involving 100,000 persons in Tel Aviv square prior to Begin's departure for Camp David summit talks with Sadat; Begin's supporters have accused Peace Now of undermining Government policy at a critical time   (NEW YORK TIMES,   September 12, 1978,   P58)

NEW ALIGNMENTS IN KNESSET REPORTED

Two splinter groups of shattered Democratic Movement for Change in Israeli Parliament have merged to organize new political party Shai as 7-member bloc opposed to Prime Minister Menachem Begin's Likud coalition; Meir Amit, who recently resigned as Minister of Transport and Communications in Likud Government, and law professor Amnon Rubenstein will lead new party; claim Shai will oppose Begin mostly on domestic issues, but also favors more flexibility in Arab-Israeli peace talks; Shai is expected to have liberal leanings   (LOS ANGELES TIMES,   September 15, 1978,   P14)

The Settlements Issue

SINAI SETTLERS EXPRESS OUTRAGE

Foreign Minister Moshe Dayan and Agriculture Minister Ariel Sharon fly to Yamit, Israeli-Occupied Sinai, to face angry crowd of about 2,000 Israeli settlers who fear Egypt will be given back all of Sinai Peninsula; Dayan says Israel has to make some concessions to Egypt and that Israel has never claimed right to rule northern Sinai; adds that if peace comes, some way may be worked out to keep settlers under protection of Israeli army but not under Israel's flag; Sharon urges settlers to remain   (NEW YORK TIMES,   January 2, 1978,   P3)

ISRAELIS POLLED ON SETTLEMENTS

Poll shows majority of Israelis oppose returning Israeli settlements in northern Sinai to Egyptian sovereignty even though they would remain under Israeli administration   (NEW YORK TIMES,   January 23, 1978,   P3)

SETTLERS EXPRESS DETERMINATION

Commentator Robert D. Kaplan reports residents of Elon Moreh in the heart of Israel's West Bank assert they intend to stay in Elon Moreh no matter what happens in Israeli-Arab conflict, because Elon Moreh is holy Jewish land; notes Elon Moreh was first of many "garinim," embryonic groups, to settle in West Bank after Yom Kippur War in attempt to thwart possible Israeli withdrawal from territories won in that war   (CHRISTIAN SCIENCE MONITOR, January 25, 1978,   P27)

SIGNIFICANCE OF SETTLEMENTS UNDERSCORED

News analysis of dispute between Israeli Prime Minister Begin and Egyptian President Sadat over Israel's settlements in Sinai observes President Carter and top aides failed to realize implications of issue and erroneously believed that any differences over Jewish settlements in Sinai could be resolved easily; says major factor in current dispute seems to be that from start of

Begin-Sadat exchanges attention focused on Palestinian question, with little attention paid to Sinai issue   (NEW YORK TIMES,   January 25, 1978,   P3)

CARTER CONCERNED OVER SETTLEMENT

President Carter sends message to Israeli Prime Minister Begin, delivered orally by Ambassador Samuel W. Lewis, in which he expresses concern over reports that a new civilian settlement is being established on West Bank of Jordan at Shiloh; message reminds Begin of personal commitment he made to Carter to prevent further Israeli settlement; State Department sources say report concerned settlement by Gush Emunim, but are not sure it was approved by Begin; suggest permission to excavate in Shiloh may have been obtained by subterfuge   (NEW YORK TIMES,   January 30, 1978,   P1)

NEW SETTLEMENTS REPORTED

Israeli newspaper *Maariv* reports Israel has set up 3 new military outposts in West Bank meant for civilian settlement starting next month, mostly by Gush Emunim; says settlements were approved by Begin government some time ago and will be built on schedule; notes new settlements will soon receive civilian status and will thus be eligible for financial aid and other forms of assistance from government; notes this will bring total settlements to 16 in West Bank, along with 23 in Jordan Valley; US State Department withholds comment awaiting further information; in US talks in 1977, Foreign Minister Moshe Dayan indicated additional settlers in West Bank would be limited to certain existing military installations   (NEW YORK TIMES,   February 1, 1978,   P1)

Israeli-occupied West Bank and Gaza Strip. At the end of November, a point of contention in peace negotiations between Israel and Egypt was Palestinian autonomy in these areas.

United Press International

DAYAN DEFENDS SETTLEMENTS

Israeli Foreign Minister Moshe Dayan denies American press reports that he promised President Carter Israel would desist from founding new West Bank settlements; maintains he merely told Carter that any new settlements made while peace talks were under way with Arabs would be in framework of military camps; Israeli Agriculture Minister Ariel Sharon reports Israeli government has not yet decided whether to establish settlement at Shiloh; notes approval has been given for archeological excavation at Shiloh involving students and Gush Emunim members   (NEW YORK TIMES,   February 2, 1978,   P1)

OPPOSITION CRITICAL ON SETTLEMENTS

Israel's opposition Labor Party criticizes Begin government for policy on settlements; says government's statements that Israelis camping at archeological site were only there to help dig could not "fool anybody" (NEW YORK TIMES,   February 3, 1978,   P4)

BEGIN'S SINCERITY CHALLENGED

Article on Israeli-Egyptian peace efforts notes sagacity and sincerity of Israeli Prime Minister Menachem Begin are being questioned as result of his apparent determination to continue Israel's controversial policy of creating settlements in occupied Arab lands; says main question is whether push for settlements will contribute to collapse of peace initiative   (NEW YORK TIMES,   February 5, 1978,   S4   P1)

SHILOH SETTLEMENT CRITICIZED

Israeli Cabinet Secretary Aryeh Naor defends government's decision to classify new community at ancient Shiloh on occupied West Bank as "archeological dig" rather than new Israeli settlement; Labor Party recently criticized Prime Minister Begin's policy on settlement in West Bank, and independent newspaper *Haaretz* warned that government's stand poses question of conduct of Israeli government and its credibility in eyes of Israel and world; settlers at Shiloh are members of nationalist Gush Emunim, who say that West Bank and Gaza Strip are open for settlement; planted trees on January 23 and laid cornerstone; said at time that talk of archeological dig was cover and that they planned permanent Israeli settlement   (NEW YORK TIMES,   February 6, 1978,   P8)

CABINET DEBATES SETTLEMENTS

Israeli Cabinet begins closed debate over settlements in occupied lands; Democratic Movement for Change party leader Yigael Yadin tells press he is pushing for freeze on new settlements; Agriculture Minister Ariel Sharon, charged with carrying out settlement policy, reportedly favors continued settlement; Defense Minister Ezer Weizman opposes establishing new settlements during negotiations with Egypt; Former Prime Minister Yitzhak Rabin maintains Israel's settlement policy undermines its credibility and calls Begin's handling of negotiations an "ill-conceived failure"; former government official Dr. Shlomo Avineri's article in the *Jerusalem Post* criticizes

Yigael Yadin, Deputy Prime Minister of Israel.

Begin; young Israelis' organization, Movement for Another Zionism, protests Shiloh settlement   (NEW YORK TIMES,   February 21, 1978,   P1)

MORE SETTLEMENTS PROPOSED

Proposal for creation of 31 new settlements in occupied Arab areas over next 4 years and for 24 new settlements within Israel is offered by World Zionist Organization and the Jewish Agency for Israel   (NEW YORK TIMES,   February 23, 1978,   P6)

CABINET UPHOLDS SETTLEMENT POLICY

Israeli Cabinet decides not to change its policy on settlements in occupied Arab lands, which involves expanding Jewish settlements in northern Sinai and creating 3 new ones on West Bank; decision follows 8 hours of debate and ends speculation that policy may be suspended because of increasing strain on US-Israeli relations and because of tense Egyptian-Israeli negotiations   (NEW YORK TIMES,   February 27, 1978,   P1)

NEW SETTLEMENT BARRED

Israeli Defense Minister Ezer Weizman has reportedly forbidden Israelis to move into new settlement site at Kadesh Barnea in occupied Sinai Peninsula   (NEW YORK TIMES,   March 2, 1978,   P4)

Chananya Herman/Zoom 77

New Gush Emunim settlement on the West Bank.

WEIZMAN, SHARON IN CLASH

Israeli Defense Minister Ezer Weizman warns Prime Minister Menachem Begin that he will cut short his visit to US and resign, if Agriculture Minister Ariel Sharon fails to comply with his orders not to begin work on new civilian settlement in West Bank; reports Begin agreed to cease plans for expansion of settlements until after Begin's meetings with President Carter, scheduled for week of March 13; dispute, primarily an Israeli domestic problem, strains US-Israeli relations, since US believes such settlements are illegal under international law; dispute has also overshadowed Weizman's mission in US, which involves Israel's request for over $10 billion in weapons in 1980's, and question of whether US will pay for costs of Israeli withdrawal from Sinai Peninsula   (NEW YORK TIMES, March 8, 1978, P1)

SETTLEMENTS POLICY OUTLINED

Commentator Ray Moseley comments on Israeli Prime Minister Menachem Begin's settlements policy; points out that Begin government holds that occupied territories are part of Israel's biblical land; believes government has resorted to using subterfuge in establishing some new settlements and adds that others have been disguised as military settlements; explains that political pressure for settlements has come mainly from right-wing religious and nationalistic factions in Israel which carry widespread influence; sees potential danger in biblical premise on which policy is based and warns that Israel could become expansionist state as result of this premise   (CHICAGO TRIBUNE, March 11, 1978, P10)

CABINET ENDORSES BEGIN'S PROPOSALS

Israeli Cabinet unanimously endorses Prime Minister Menachem Begin's peace proposals for Middle East that have placed him sharply at odds with views of President Carter; Begin's negative stands reportedly include: refusal to forbid new Israeli settlements in occupied lands; refusal to agree to withdraw from existing settlements in Sinai or allow them to be protected by anyone other then Israel; refusal to commit Israel to any withdrawal from West Bank or Gaza and refusal to agree that UN Resolution 242 requires such withdrawal; refusal to accept a US plan for Palestinian referendum 5 years after settlement; meanwhile, Shimon Peres, leader of opposition Labor Party, contends that Parliament would support compromise on Israeli-occupied lands that went beyond Begin's position, and chides Begin Administration for its conduct of foreign business; in separate development, Democratic Movement for Change, one of coalition parties with governing Likud Party, has been increasingly critical of Begin's refusal to relinquish any of Israeli settlements in West Bank or Gaza Strip   (NEW YORK TIMES, March 27, 1978, P1)

BEGIN PLEDGES SETTLEMENT SUPPORT

Israeli Prime Minister Menachem Begin tells Israelis living in occupied West Bank city of Hebron that they will be joined in coming years by hundreds of Jewish families; speaks at tenth anniversary celebration of Qiryat Arba, suburb known as power base for Gush Emunim nationalist group; spokesmen for Gush Emunim call on Israeli government to expropriate land around Qiryat Arba for growth, and for establishment of Jewish communities in Nablus and Jericho; Begin does not reply   (NEW YORK TIMES,   April 25, 1978,   P3)

MILITARY CHASTISED

Editorial welcomes stern disciplining by Israeli Defense Minister Ezer Weizman of Israeli officers in West Bank who either covered up or exceeded their authority in tear-gas bombing of school in Beit Jallah that left 12 students injured and many others panic-stricken; holds that there is no more important principle in present Middle East impasse than Israeli respect for rights of Arab population in occupied West Bank   (NEW YORK TIMES,   May 4, 1978,   P22)

WEIZMAN PROPOSES SETTLEMENTS PLAN

Israel's Defense Minister Ezer Weizman proposes expansion of 6 Israeli settlements in occupied West Bank into urban centers; calls for halt to more new colonies in area; plan conflicts with Agriculture Minister Ariel Sharon's concept of dotting West Bank with as many Jewish settlements as possible; Weizman's plan envisages settling 38,000 Israeli families in 6 localities; 4,500 Israeli civilians now live in nearly 3 dozen small communities; short-range Defense Ministry plan is to increase Jewish population to 10,000 in 3 years   (NEW YORK TIMES,   May 19, 1978,   P9)

ISRAELI CONFISCATION CHARGED

Bethlehem Mayor Elias Freij, an Arab, charges that Israeli government is planning to confiscate property owned by Arabs living abroad with aim of enlarging Jewish settlements; claims he was officially informed April 12 that about 80,000 acres around his town owned by Arabs in US, Canada and Latin American countries would be handed over to an Israeli "custodian of absentee property"; Israeli Defense Minister Ezer Weizman denies charge; some Israelis contend that Arab countries are quietly buying absentee-owned West Bank real estate to hamper Israeli seizure; Israeli lands authority maintains its aim is simply to tighten control to block fraudulent transactions; in related news, Arab students at Hebrew University in Jerusalem begin 3-day hunger strike to protest school's ban on organized Arab cultural and political activity   (NEW YORK TIMES,   May 24, 1978,   P12)

WEST BANK SETTLEMENT DESCRIBED

Commentator Anthony Lewis visits Nebi Salah in West Bank, new Israeli settlement consisting of 12 families who live in an old police station guarded by soldiers; reports that since land is unsuitable for farming, men commute to Tel Aviv to jobs; reports that residents claim good relations with Arab neighbors, but notes Israeli land settlement program is "recipe for conflict"; observes that concept behind Nebi Salah makes Middle East peace impossible   (NEW YORK TIMES,   May 29, 1978,   P13)

MILITANTS FOUND SETTLEMENT

Israeli Defense Minister Ezer Weizman acknowledges in Parliament that Israelis authorized to work on archeological dig at Shiloh in West Bank instead built homes; member of Parliament had produced pamphlet by militant Gush Emunim group showing plan for developing village there; in related news, Gush Emunim source says that about 60 of their people live at Shiloh site   (NEW YORK TIMES,   May 31, 1978,   P6)

GROUP DEMANDS LAND CONFISCATION

Israel's ultranationalist Gush Emunim movement demands confiscation of Arab land to make way for Jews to settle on West Bank of Jordan River; Moshe Shamir, prominent Gush Emunim supporter and right-wing member of Parliament, asserts that Arabs must be made to realize "that Israel has come here to stay" and that only by "obliterating" Arab hopes for Israeli withdrawal from West Bank will peace be achieved; movement is beginning campaign to persuade Israeli Prime Minister Begin's government to endorse more energetic settlement campaign   (NEW YORK TIMES,   June 8, 1978,   P9)

WEIZMAN, BEGIN CLASH

Israeli Defense Minister Ezer Weizman breaks his silence over dispute with Prime Minister Menachem Begin on policy in occupied Arab territories; indicates he would remain in Cabinet to fight for his beliefs; advocated declaration that Israel would negotiate permanent status of territories after five-year transition period; 14 of 19 Cabinet members approved vague statement suggesting that Begin's plan of limited self-rule by Palestinians in occupied areas could continue indefinitely after 5-year period   (NEW YORK TIMES,   June 24, 1978,   P3)

GOVERNMENT FREEZES SETTLEMENTS

Israeli Government suspends vote on plan to set up 5 new outpost settlements in Jordan Valley, until after Camp David summit starting September 5; Agriculture Minister Ariel Sharon reports that existing settlements will be expanded but that new settlements are definitely not being planned; agreement to freeze project reportedly was reached in phone conversations among Sharon, Prime Minister Begin and Foreign Minister Dayan   (NEW YORK TIMES,   August 15, 1978,   P20)

SETTLEMENTS SPURRING POLITICAL DIVISIONS

Commentator Flora Lewis sees issue of planned new Israeli settlements on West Bank as revealing painful political divisions facing Israel if peace negotiations advance; contrasts positions of Agriculture Minister Ariel Sharon, hardliner whose views mesh with those of biblical

Department of State

Samuel W. Lewis, U.S. Ambassador to Israel.

zealots and Deputy Premier Yigael Yadin, who opposes new settlements and whose party may quit government if settlements were to bar peace settlement; holds that all of Israel is aware that risky decision is near and this sensitivity is aggravating divisions   (NEW YORK TIMES, August 16, 1978, P23)

SETTLEMENT STATUS DISPUTED

Israel dedicates 2 settlements on West Bank of Jordan River, but Israeli officials and settlers go out of their way to contend that, because settlements had been approved by Israel in January, they are not new; disclaimers are seen as trying to avoid appearance of undercutting upcoming Camp David summit conference   (NEW YORK TIMES, August 18, 1978, P72)

ISRAELI SETTLEMENTS DISCUSSED

Commentator John K. Cooley details Israeli efforts to build settlements in occupied land on West Bank of Jordan River and Gaza Strip; cites Agriculture Minister Ariel Sharon who says Israel cannot stop settlement building during peace negotiations because negotiations may go on for years; discusses Israeli settlement establishment whose livelihood depends on settlement activity; says this establishment has members in almost all parts of political spectrum; tells of opposition to settlements by Peace Now and small group of army reservists; discusses increased settlement activity since Prime Minister Menachem Begin took office; details Palestinian protests to Israel's method of settlement and reimbursement for confiscated land (CHRISTIAN SCIENCE MONITOR, September 1, 1978, P12)

The American Alliance

BEGIN CONDEMNS ARMS SALES

Israeli Prime Minister Menachem Begin says US sale of weapons to Egypt, especially F-15 and F-16 warplanes, would heighten threat of war and have negative effect on peacemaking process; says sale of planes would fit into pattern of Egyptian pressure on Israel; is optimistic peace talks can resume; rejects notions that continuing development of settlements in occupied territories has eroded support for Israel in American public opinion; sees possibility for resumption of political talks   (NEW YORK TIMES,   February 9, 1978,   P3)

TOUGHER U.S. STANCE URGED

Financial Times editorial comments on Israeli government's rejection of US contention that Jewish settlements in occupied Arab territories are illegal; says fact that Begin has failed to lead his followers into accepting decisions about withdrawal and Palestinian homeland shows that US has yet to be fully decisive in its approach; concludes that US will have to show a far tougher face to Israel than it has dared until now, if outcome of Arab-Israeli question is not to affect related crisis like the fighting in Horn of Africa; says it is still not clear that Washington is aware of the consequences of failure   (FINANCIAL TIMES,   February 13, 1978,   P12)

U.S. AGAIN SCORES SETTLEMENTS

US again declares that it is opposed to Israeli settlements in occupied Arab territory, in statement by White House press secretary Jody Powell; Powell indicates statement is issued reluctantly and with no desire to prolong argument; reiterates that settlements established by Israel in occupied territory since 1967 are "obstacle to peace and contrary to international law"; meanwhile, Israeli Prime Minister Menachem Begin, in more conciliatory tone,

indicates that all issues, including settlements, are negotiable   (NEW YORK TIMES,   February 14, 1978,   P1)

SETTLEMENTS UNDERCUT U.S. SUPPORT

Commentator H.D.S. Greenway suggests rift between US and Israel over Israeli settlements may be major impediment to constructive peace talks; notes Israeli Prime Minister Menachem Begin's statement that US favors Egypt's position on matter, stating settlements are "essential" to Israel, widens rift between Israel and US; says renewed US insistence upon removal of settlements and self-determination for Palestinians causes further gap in relations   (WASHINGTON POST,   February 14, 1978,   P1)

U.S.-ISRAELI RELATIONS AT LOW

Relations between Israel and US are at lowest point in the 9 months since Prime Minister Menachem Begin took office; Israel is on defensive since US condemned Israeli settlements in Sinai and on West Bank of Jordan River; dispute over settlements may in fact be symptom of more profound change in US-Israeli relations; for first time an Arab statesman is accorded same respect as his Israeli counterpart in US public opinion; other factors influencing deterioration in relations is Israel's admission that it is

Israel's Prime Minister Menachem Begin.

supplying arms to Ethiopia and Israel's quest for closer trade and other ties with South Africa; officials in US government, including Vice President Mondale, are holding talks with US Jews to explain Administration's position; Foreign Minister Moshe Dayan has warned that Israel would not accept mediation efforts from US Jews because it is interpreted as move by Carter administration to make inroads with that group; US opinion reflects that for first time Israel may not be right   (FINANCIAL TIMES, February 14, 1978, P4)

PACKAGE DEAL FOR MIDDLE EAST

Secretary of State Cyrus Vance announces that US will sell $4.8 billion worth of advanced military airplanes to Egypt, Saudi Arabia and Israel; claims decision is designed to maintain existing military balance in Middle East; Saudi Arabia would be allowed to buy 60 F-15 planes and Israel 15, bringing Israel's total to 40; Israel would also be allowed to buy 75 General Dynamics F-16's; Egypt would be allowed to buy 50 Northrop Corporation F-5's, less sophisticated plane comparable to Soviet MIG-21's it already has; senior Administration officials concede they face sharp debate in Congress, which can disapprove sale by majority vote of both houses within 30 days of notification; Vance statement says official notification to Congress will be made early in April 1978; officials stress, however, that sales comprise a package, and if Congress rejects part of package Administration would have to reconsider other parts   (NEW YORK TIMES, February 15, 1978, P1)

U.S. ARMS SALES ANALYZED

Commentator Drew Middleton's analysis of potential impact of arms sales proposed by Carter Administration to Egypt and Saudi Arabia as well as Israel, based on assessments by military experts, contends that Israel's military dominance through quality and quantity of its weaponry is being eroded but is not likely to be destroyed; emphasizes that sophisticated US weaponry was once exclusively in Israeli hands, but will not be as result of new sales: Saudi Arabia's acquisition of F-15 airplanes from US, plus acquisition of sophisticated Soviet equipment by Syria, Iraq and Libya, including MIG-23 fighter-bombers by Iraq and Syria; Middleton reports military experts agree that Egypt's F-5 bombers may reinvigorate its Air Force, but are not comparable to Israel's F-15's as interceptors; cautions that introduction of modern weaponry into Middle East is undermining some of military claims of both sides; cites Syria's claim for Golan Heights is no longer militarily valid because Soviet 180-millimeter guns and missiles allow it to attack northern Israel or defend against invasion from positions as far east as Damascus area; suggests that Golan Heights is now important for agricultural reasons; counters Israeli objections to Saudi Arabia's F-15's by pointing out that it is air-to-air fighter and not bomber, hence defensive in nature, and that airplane is not easily transferable to other countries because of necessary sophisticated training of pilots required; reports consensus of military experts that Israel could still defeat any combination of Arab states even if "Eastern front" of Syria and Iraq is reinforced by Saudi Arabian, Libyan and Algerian forces   (NEW YORK TIMES, February 15, 1978, P1)

PLANE SALES TERMED LOGICAL

Financial Times editorial says that US decision to sell F-15 fighter aircraft to Israel, Saudi Arabia and Egypt is based on logic; says overall effect will be to buy time for US involvement in Israeli-Egyptian peace negotiations   (FINANCIAL TIMES, February 16, 1978, P1)

PLANE SALE DECISION SUPPORTED

Washington Post editorial supports President Carter's decision to sell military aircraft to Egypt, Saudi Arabia and Israel; asserts that unilateral sale to Israel without action on pending requests from Arab nations, would have been destabilizing; criticizes timing of sales; suggests they should have been delayed until Mideast peace negotiations were set more firmly on track   (WASHINGTON POST, February 16, 1978, P18)

ARMS SALE QUESTIONED

Miami Herald editorial questions if President Carter's arms proposal diminishes the likelihood of the Arab nations uniting against Israel if one Arab nation attacked Israel or if Israel attacked one of them; criticizes the approach that says the way to maintain the balance of power and preserve the peace is to arm both sides to the teeth with the most sophisticated means of destruction available; asks if increasing the armaments of both sides does not change the balance of power in the Middle East, then why do it   (MIAMI HERALD, February 16, 1978, P6)

BEGIN ASKS REAPPRAISAL

Israeli Prime Minister Menachem Begin calls on US to reappraise decision to supply military planes to Egypt and Saudi Arabia and announces he has accepted invitation by President Carter for 3-day visit in March 1978; holds that Saudi Arabian acquisition of F-15's, which he describes as "latest aircraft on earth," would make desert kingdom "confrontation state"; claims that Saudis have pledged to an Arab country that US planes would eventually be used against Israel; does not name country, but military source asserts it is Egypt   (NEW YORK TIMES, February 16, 1978, P1)

'MESSAGE TO BEGIN' SEEN

Commentator Karen Elliott House comments on President Carter's growing concern about stalled Middle East peace negotiations; sees Carter shifting from an "encouraging bystander" to a "blunt advocate"; sees Carter's decision to sell jet fighters to Egypt and Saudi Arabia as a message to Israeli Prime Minister Menachem Begin that Carter wants Begin to make some concessions on stalled peace talks; describes Carter as "angry" about new Israeli settlements in Israeli-occupied territories   (WALL STREET JOURNAL, February 17, 1978, P16)

ISRAEL RISKING U.S. SUPPORT

Commentator Carl Rowan notes Israel is risking support of US and rest of world by its policy of continued expansion of Israeli settlements in captured areas of the Sinai; also expresses dismay that Israeli Prime Minister Menachem Begin recently sent his finance minister to South Africa to "cement friendship" between the two countries, in the midst of worldwide furor over death of South African black leader Steve Biko; contends policies regarding the captured territories and South Africa only lead to greater isolation of Israel, rather than guaranteeing Israel's security   (ATLANTA CONSTITUTION, February 21, 1978, P4)

VANCE STRESSES 'PACKAGE' DEAL

Secretary of State Cyrus Vance warns that Carter Administration will withdraw its offer to provide Israel with 75 F-16 and 15 F-15 airplanes if Congress blocks sales of 60 F-15's to Saudi Arabia and 50 F-5E's to Egypt; holds sales are part of package and cannot be approved or rejected individually; Representative Clarence D. Long, chairman of House Appropriations subcommittee on foreign operations, criticizes $4.8 billion proposal, charging US with being "salesman of slaughter"; issue has reptedly caused controversy among Congressmen, many of whom fear Egypt and Saudi Arabia will use planes against Israel   (NEW YORK TIMES, February 25, 1978, P1)

U.S.-ISRAELI DIFFERENCES OUTLINED

Basic dimensions of US-Israeli differences over Israeli-occupied territories examined; real reason for Israel's anger over US Secretary of State Cyrus Vance's statement that Israeli settlements in occupied territories "should not exist" is reported as stemming from fact that US government discreetly cleared content of Egyptian President Anwar Sadat's speech to National Press Club, which was one of hardest-hitting and most skilful attacks made in US against policies of Menachem Begin; point is made that Vance was simply reiterating, in plainer words perhaps, what Carter has been saying since he entered the White House, specifically, that Israeli settlements in occupied territory are in violation of international law and constitute "an obstacle to peace"; US-Israeli relations said to be at lowest point since 1975   (MANCHESTER GUARDIAN WEEKLY, February 26, 1978, P13)

CARTER'S POLICIES TROUBLING U.S. JEWS

James M. Perry indicates President Carter may not realize how concerned American Jews are over his policies toward Israel; observes many Jews feel Carter is insensitive to plight of Israel and that his views concerning Israel have not been clearly defined, while other Jews believe Carter is yielding to Arab pressure and betraying Israel; sees Carter's approval of greater US arms sales to Egypt and Saudi Arabia and reduced arms sales to Israel as especially disturbing to US Jewish community; indicates that American Jews' affluence and relatively heavy political influence, and fact that most Jews live in urban areas on which elections can hinge, could prompt Carter to reevaluate his Middle East policy if Jewish disenchantment with him continues   (WALL STREET JOURNAL, March 2, 1978, P20)

WEIZMAN SEEKING U.S. ARMS

Israeli Defense Minister Ezer Weizman has met with Defense Secretary Harold Brown to discuss Israel's request for about $15 billion in American military equipment over next 10 years; Defense Department spokesman states that talk included issue of overall military balance in Middle East, status of peace negotiations and aspects of Israel's defense needs, such as planes and tanks; Weizman submitted Israeli case against sale of military aircraft to Saudi Arabia and its case for increasing number of aircraft to be sold to Israel; participants in talks state that no decisions have been made and no commitments made on Israeli arms requests   (NEW YORK TIMES, March 9, 1978, P14)

MEMORANDUM ON DEPLOYMENT ISSUED

State Department memorandum to House International Relations Committee directs attention to implementation of Carter Administration's proposed Middle East aircraft "package" deal, noting that Saudi Arabia plans to base US F-15 fighter planes at Dhahran and possibly Khamis Mushayt; memorandum is apparently intended to calm Israeli concern over possible deployment of F-15's at Tabuk, an airfield close to Israeli frontier; notes no commitments have yet been made on Administration's Middle East aircraft "package" deal; emphasizes extent of US technological support that both Egypt and Saudi Arabia would require before airplanes acquired from US could be operational   (NEW YORK TIMES, March 10, 1978, P7)

HOUSE COMMITTEE OPPOSES PACKAGE

Twenty-one of 37 members of House International Relations Committee send letter to President Carter stating their opposition to his decision linking sales of advanced fighter planes to Israel to similar sales to Saudi Arabia and Egypt; point out that under 1975 agreement, US pledged to supply planes to Israel without linkage to other sales, that sale to Saudi Arabia will have "destabilizing impact" in Middle East, and that under law, each arms sale should be considered separately; action by House committee preceded Carter's meeting with Israeli Defense Minister Ezer Weizman, who has also been urging reconsideration of package approach; Weizman notes issue was not discussed during meeting, and appears pleased with outcome of talks, revealing Carter reiterated US commitment to Israel's security; gives impression that he is not disturbed by recent US-Israeli differences, such as controversy over Israeli settlements in occupied Arab lands and interpretation of UN Security Council Resolution 242   (NEW YORK TIMES, March 11, 1978, P1)

PRESSURE ON BEGIN URGED

Commentator Tom Wicker argues that US Jewish community should greet Israeli Prime Minister Menachem Begin in his upcoming visit to US with the message that Egyptian President Sadat's peace initiative in 1977 created high hopes among Americans for settlement and that, despite admittedly important response by Israel,

Americans are disappointed that situation has deteriorated since then; deplores resignation of Presidential aide Mark Siegel as liaison with US Jewish community and also deplores statement by Conference of Presidents of Major American Jewish Organizations chairman Rabbi Alexander M. Schindler that Israel is not getting "square deal" from Administration; criticizes Schindler's demand for giving Begin impression that Israel may have anything it wants from US; points out that even in Israel there is widespread debate on wisdom of settlements in occupied lands and on interpretation of UN Resolution 242; holds that US has never concealed its differences with Begin Administration on settlement and withdrawal issues; defends President Carter's arms sales package of military planes to Saudi Arabia and Egypt, as well as Israel, as preserving Israeli aerial superiority while carefully weighing and preserving US interests; warns that President Carter's view is generally supported by American public opinion   (NEW YORK TIMES,   March 12, 1978,   S4   P19)

ARMS SALE IMPACT WEIGHED

Confidential Senate Foreign Relations Committee report on Carter Administration's proposed sale of 60 F-15 fighter planes to Saudi Arabia points out that approval of sale could upset Middle East negotiations, while rejection of sale could make Saudis less willing to increase oil production to meet Western needs in early 1980's; also holds sale will damage credibility of President Carter's policy of reducing arms exports, but does not recommend course of action regarding proposal, which is part of package that includes sale of 90 fighter planes to Israel and 50 less advanced planes to Egypt   (NEW YORK TIMES,   March 23, 1978,   P13)

U.S., ISRAEL AT IMPASSE

Washington Post editorial discusses US-Israeli relations; asserts that Carter Administration has given up hope that Israeli Prime Minister Menachem Begin will negotiate withdrawal from West Bank settlements; indicates Carter feels he has reached diplomatic end with Begin; states that Israeli officials are wrong in assuming that Carter's position on negotiations has changed since his December 1977 support of Begin's Sinai plan; observes that it is "tortuous time" for Israel and US   (WASHINGTON POST,   March 23, 1978,   P24)

U.S.-ISRAEL DISCORD ANALYZED

New York Times editorial examines troubled relationship between US and Israel; notes deep disagreements which surfaced at recent meeting between Prime Minister Begin and President Carter, including Begin's refusal to give up occupied Sinai, unwillingness to give back part of West Bank of Jordan River and refusal to give Palestinians say in their future, even if choices are limited to Israeli, Jordanian or international control; states that meeting provoked deep reactions in Israel, such as Defense Minister Ezer Weizman's calling for national peace government representing unified stand of all parties, Labor Party's attack of Begin policies and calling for new

election, and other papers urging Israel to rethink its position toward peace   (NEW YORK TIMES,   March 26, 1978,   S4   P1)

BALL QUESTIONS AID TO ISRAEL

Commentator George W. Ball says United States must consider long-term consequences in its decisions on aiding Israel; asserts that President Carter should make clear to Israel that it must take reasonable steps toward peace; says this is not "pressuring" Israel but is telling Israel that how US spends its money is "an attribute of sovereignty" and that to be faithful to larger world interests US cannot support policies that will lead to disastrous war through radicalization of Arab world; suggests Israel promise residents of its occupied territories a choice in who rules them at some point in future   (MIAMI HERALD,   March 26, 1978,   S5   P1)

RABIN COMMENTS ON RELATIONS

Former Israeli Prime Minister Yitzhak Rabin says in Boston news conference that Israel has made mistakes recently which have damaged relations with US but US support remains solid; Rabin calls for US to stop imposing conditions on Israeli pursuit of peace; doubts coalition government proposed by Defense Minister Ezer Weizman will be formed; does not comment on division among Israeli people on peace question   (CHRISTIAN SCIENCE MONITOR,   March 28,   P26)

CONGRESS DEBATES PACKAGE SALE

Carter Administration proposal to sell 200 fighter aircraft to Israel, Egypt and Saudi Arabia provokes fierce debate in Congress; debate revolves around whether and how the $4.8-billion package will affect Israel's future military security, the course of diplomatic efforts to achieve Middle East peace settlement and credibility of Carter's leadership in foreign affairs; deal provides 15 F-15's and 75 F-16's to Israel, 60 F-15's to Saudi Arabia and 50 F-5E's to Egypt; is controversial because it provides Israel with only half of planes requested, represents first US delivery of lethal military equipment to Arab participant in 1973 Middle East war and would make Saudi Arabia a direct military threat to Israel; Administration feels deal will help Middle East peace efforts and will not affect region's military balance; critics feel proposal will give Arabs military superiority and make Israel vulnerable to direct attack from Saudi bases   (NEW YORK TIMES,   March 31, 1978,   P2)

SAUDI ARMS RESTRICTION HINTED

White House officials hint President Carter may agree to restrict Saudi Arabia's use of military aircraft it would obtain in proposed Middle East arms sale to avoid time-consuming fight over controversial package, which involves Egypt, Saudi Arabia and Israel; note agreement may include prohibiting sale of equipment which transforms F-15 interceptor plane into fighter bomber, and prohibiting Saudis from stationing aircraft near Israeli border; stress, however, that Carter will not accept agreement to exclude Egypt or Saudi Arabia from sale or agreement which alters numbers or types of airplanes to be sold   (NEW YORK TIMES, April 25, 1978, P3)

DAYAN DOWNPLAYS U.S.-ISRAEL RIFT

Israeli Foreign Minister Moshe Dayan, in interview after 2 days of discussions with State Secretary Vance, comments that despite substantive differences, relations between Israel and US "are not bad"; expresses satisfaction with how things went in meeting with Vance; says discussions focused primarily on West Bank, Gaza Strip and future of Palestinians there; expresses wish to see talks with Egypt started again; voices sharp opposition to Carter Administration proposal to sell jet planes to Egypt and Saudia Arabia and concept of Israeli-Arab "package"   (NEW YORK TIMES, April 28, 1978, P7)

ARAB LOBBY PROFILED

Commentator Steven V. Roberts describes and assesses emerging Arab lobby in Washington, DC, characterizing its message as soft-spoken but tough; US cannot refuse to sell Saudi Arabia planes because it is heavily dependent on Saudi oil and Saudi dollars; defines lobby as loose array of Arab embassies, US companies and high-priced

Moshe Dayan, Minister for Foreign Affairs.

consultants; consultants include former Congressmen, former CIA operatives, politically connected lawyers, Congressmen's relatives, friends of the President; activities include publications, investments, university endowments, social parties and advertising   (NEW YORK TIMES, April 30, 1978, S4 P4)

CARTER'S CONTENTIONS QUESTIONED

Commentator William Safire refutes President Carter's justifications for arms sales to Saudi Arabia, particularly contention that he is simply carrying out commitment made by Ford Administration; criticizes Ford for secretly accepting State Department's recommendation to favorably consider Saudi bid for advanced aircraft, but points out Ford reserved right to veto plan; maintains Carter has taken what was an agreement-in-principle and made it specific commitment without veto right; asserts Carter took actual, written commitment, giving planes to Israel if they withdraw from Sinai, and made it conditional on fighter sales to Saudis; holds US could easily guarantee Saudis protection from invasion without also giving them means to destroy Israel   (NEW YORK TIMES, May 1, 1978, P21)

CARTER REAFFIRMS STANCE

President Carter reaffirms that he opposes formation of an independent Palestinian state on Jordan West Bank and that Israel should not have to withdraw completely from all occupied territories as part of overall settlement, in interview with Trude B. Feldman, writer for English-language Jewish newspapers; also repeats that Israeli Prime Minister Begin's self-rule plan for West Bank could be basis for a settlement   (NEW YORK TIMES, May 1, 1978, S2 P5)

CARTER CELEBRATES ISRAEL'S ANNIVERSARY

President Carter stages White House celebration of Israel's 30th anniversary attended by Israeli Prime Minister Begin and some 800 invited guests, including several hundred rabbis and other Jewish leaders; Carter and Begin affirm US-Israeli friendship in atmosphere of warm cordiality; Carter cites Jews' past suffering at hands of Nazis and announces he will appoint commission to report to him on a suitable memorial in US to insure that Americans "never forget"; Bronx, NY, Rabbi Avraham Weiss distributes copy of letter to Carter he said was signed by 150 rabbis criticizing sale of planes to Saudi Arabia and Egypt; in conversations with guests, national security adviser Zbigniew Brzezinski defends sale of planes by saying it is in Israel's interest to have better relations between US and moderate Arab states; suggests that peace could enable Israel to become "Switzerland of the Middle East," providing technical experts for its neighbors   (NEW YORK TIMES, May 2, 1978, P1)

SAUDI CITES COMMUNIST THREAT

State Department makes public a letter from Saudi Arabian King Khalid to President Carter in which Khalid declares that Saudi Arabia is seeking to buy F-15 fighter planes from US in order to thwart "Communist expansion in the area"; letter also declares that planes are being acquired for defensive purposes; State Department's disclosure of letter seen as an effort to lessen Congressional opposition to Carter Administration's proposed package deal to sell jet fighters to Saudi Arabia, Israel and Egypt   (NEW YORK TIMES, May 4, 1978, P1)

SAUDIS AGREE TO RESTRICTIONS

Defense Secretary Brown reports that Saudi Arabia has agreed to restrictions on use of US F-15 planes; in letter to Senate Foreign Relations Committee, reports that Saudi government has given assurance that it will not transfer F-15 aircraft to any other country or allow them to be used for training of nationals of any other country without US authorization; reports F-15's will not be equipped with special auxiliary fuel tanks or multiple bomb ejection racks and that Saudis have assured they do not intend to acquire combat aircraft from other countries while preparing for and receiving US F-15's; claims F-15 fighter would be "relatively ineffective in an offensive mode"; Senate opponents of plane sale suggest F-15 can be used to fly cover for Arabs attacking Israel; in related developments, Senator Frank Church decides to oppose proposed sale of all planes, while Senator Muriel Humphrey announces her support for Carter Administration plan   (NEW YORK TIMES, May 11, 1978, P1)

SENATE COMMITTEE VOTES

Senate Foreign Relations Committee, by vote of 8 to 8, blocks resolution to disapprove President Carter's proposed sale of military aircraft to Israel, Egypt and Saudi Arabia; unanimously decides, in unusual move, to send package to floor of Senate without recommendation for or against sale; move blocking disapproval measure is seen as victory for Carter Administration but decision to send package to Senate shocks Administration and Senate leaders who were hoping to avoid floor fight and full Senate vote on controversial package   (NEW YORK TIMES, May 12, 1978, P1)

SENATE APPROVES ARMS PACKAGE

Senate backs President Carter's proposed sale of advanced fighter planes to Israel, Egypt and Saudi Arabia by voting 54 to 44 against move to block sale; Carter holds he is "deeply gratified" by vote and maintains action reaffirms US commitment to Israel's security while also strengthening ties with Arab nations; Israeli Embassy issues statement asserting it is deeply concerned over supply of advanced weapons to countries maintaining state of war with Israel; vote follows day-long debate over Senator Joseph R. Biden Jr.'s proposal to block sale of controversial package, and is seen as "muted" triumph for Carter   (NEW YORK TIMES, May 16, 1978, P1)

VOTE SEEN AS CARTER TRIUMPH

Commentator Hedrick Smith analyzes Senate's decision to reluctantly support President Carter's proposed "package" sale of military planes to Israel, Egypt and Saudi Arabia; holds significance of action goes beyond issue of jet sales to more delicate issue of how far US should go in combining its commitment to Israel with new and expanding support for Arab moderates; notes White House believes Senate vote is vote of confidence for President Carter's Middle East strategy and maintains US now has genuine political base to work for "a moderate Middle East"; asserts, however, that many Senators, including Jacob Javits and Henry Jackson, fear sale will damage US-Israeli relations, with Javits predicting Arabs will harden their position and Israelis will suffer lower morale; maintains vote is victory for Carter Administration since even opponents are crediting White House and State Department with shrewdly combining toughness and flexibility at crucial moments to gain Senate majority   (NEW YORK TIMES, May 16, 1978, P1)

SENATE VOTE ANALYZED

Commentator Tom Wicker analyzes Senate decision to approve Mideast arms package, noting Senate was faced with determining whether rejection or approval of package offered best chance of peace; holds rejection would have been interpreted as acceptance of Israeli policy rather than Carter Administration policy, could have caused Arab world to conclude there is no real possibility of "even-handed" US policy, would have rebuffed Saudi Arabia, and could have encouraged Israeli Prime Minister Begin to continue his resistance to Israeli withdrawal from West Bank; also asserts Saudis would have turned to France for planes, and would have received them without restrictions on usage   (NEW YORK TIMES, May 16, 1978, P35)

ISRAEL REACTS TO VOTE

Byliner William E. Farrell reports reactions of Israeli politicians and press to "package" sale of US jet fighter planes; reports political opponents are charging Prime Minister Begin with mishandling opposition to the deal; notes that some members of coalition government have called for a revision of Begin's peace proposal to return Sinai to Egypt because sale of planes to Saudi Arabia puts it in confrontation with Israel; notes that editorials in Hebrew-language press uniformly speak of a further decline in relations with US, new strategic considerations, decline of pro-Israel lobby in Washington and emergence there of a powerful Arab lobby; notes that Foreign Minister Moshe Dayan and Defense Minister Ezer Weizman have tended to play down overall impact of plane package while Begin has tended to respond more emotionally   (NEW YORK TIMES, May 21, 1978, P4)

Israel's Turn to Rugged Capitalism

By WILLIAM E. FARRELL

JERUSALEM

Lost in all the fanfare of the visit of President Anwar el-Sadat of Egypt and the peace efforts has been Israel's enactment of far-reaching and radical economic measures. Israel has done no less than shift from its historic semi-Socialist style to an economy aimed at free-market capitalism in an effort to improve its sorry financial situation.

The sweeping economic measures announced in October by the right-of-center Government of Prime Minister Menachem Begin ended currency-control regulations that were in effect before Israel became a state in 1948. The mapecka kalkalit—economic uprooting—freed the Israeli pound from controls, eliminated export incentives and levies on imports and reduced Government subsidies on basic commodities, a move that directly affected every Israeli consumer.

Last July the American economist Milton Friedman visited Israel and acted as a consultant to the Begin Government. He praised Finance Minister Simha Ehrlich's new economic policy as showing boldness and vision. But many here, at least in the short run, are not so optimistic. The average Israeli citizen—who already pays some of the highest taxes—grapples with soaring food prices and writhes through the cloudy mists of inflation that currently envelop this nation of 3.6 million people.

While some, such as Professor Friedman, are urging patience, saying the policy will eventually result in an economic "miracle" similar to West Germany's postwar recovery, others are grimly surveying their immediate impact.

A recent cartoon in an English-language newspaper, The Jerusalem Post, reflected some of the country's anxieties. One Israeli tries to explain the meaning of it all to another. "It's simple," the first Israeli says. "We let the Israeli pound fall in value, allow free exchange of dollars, Israeli exports become dirt cheap and in the long run the economy is strengthened."

"And in the short run?" asks the second.

"We starve," declares the first.

The immediate impact of Israel's move to a free-market economy was a sharp drop in the value of the Israeli pound against the United States dollar—to 15 pounds to the dollar from 10, where it still hovers. The cost of living, according to the Israeli consumer price index, jumped 11.8 percent in November—the steepest monthly rise in the nation's economic history. Overall for 1977, prices went up by 41 percent while the gross national product showed a meager 1 percent increase.

The new economic policy is predicated on successfully curbing Israel's inflation rate, which has run about 38 percent for each of the last few years.

Recently Mr. Ehrlich told a gathering of businessmen in Tel Aviv that the abolition of currency controls had led to an improvement in the country's balance-of-payments deficit. Mr. Ehrlich forecasts for 1978 a deficit of $2.8 billion, some $500 million less than was previously forecast. In the new budget debt service is a larger item than defense for the first time. A total of 32 percent of the budget is earmarked for defense while 33 percent is set aside for debt service.

Crucial to the success of the Begin Government's economic boldness—and there are few who will defend the old system patched over by myriad regulations, gimmicks and placebos—is how the people respond.

The new policy triggered a spate of wildcat strikes and protests from Israel's volatile labor unions, for it seems to place the burden of stemming inflation on wage earners, professionals and small-business men. Israelis with foreign assets have been given a boon.

The big questions are: Will most of the people accept a lowering of the living standard in the hope of stabilizing the economy? Will the new system work or will it, as The Jerusalem Post's economic editor, Meir Merhav, asked, result in "a government of the poor, by the rich and for the rich?" □

NEW YORK TIMES, February 5, 1978, S12 P71

Israel's Eroding Might

Changes in the quality and quantity of Arab weaponry appear to be eroding Israel's military dominance in the Middle East, but not destroying it, according to qualified sources in Washington and in other Atlantic alliance capitals.

Military Analysis Israeli air power, expressed in the quality of planes and pilot training, was decisive in victories over the Arabs in the wars of 1967 and 1973. That advantage has been reduced but not eliminated, the sources said, by the announcement of

prospective United States aircraft deliveries to both sides in the Middle East.

Saudi Arabia will acquire 60 F-15's and Egypt will get 50 F-5E's. Israel will get 15 F-15's and 75 F-16's. The F-16's are not yet deployed by the United States Air Force or the other four NATO air forces that are buying them.

Israel's weapons situation has worsened on balance in one important respect. Until now, Israel had been the sole recipient in the Middle East of advanced American weaponry.

The announcement yesterday said that

60 F-15 fighters had been added to the advanced weapons already scheduled for delivery to Saudi Arabia.

These include 400 Maverick air-to-surface missiles, six batteries of Hawk surface-to-air missiles and 2,000 Sidewinder air-to-air missiles.

Syria, Iraq and Libya are receiving sophisticated Soviet equipment so that the balance at the end is tilting against Israel's dominance in the field of advanced weaponry.

One of Israel's continuing strategic concerns, which has not been dissipated by the groping toward Egyptian-Israeli peace negotiations, is the conviction among Israeli military leaders that Egypt could not stay out of another Arab-Israeli war. In early January, an Israeli general remarked that he was convinced that the twin forces of Arab nationalism and religious unity would overcome any tendencies in Cairo toward neutrality in a new war, even though the two governments might have concluded an agreement.

A combination of new Soviet arms shipments to Iraq, Syria and Libya and American sales to Egypt and Saudi Arabia are elements in the military change in the Middle East.

MIG-23's for Iraq and Syria

Since President Sadat opened his "peace offensive" by visiting Israel in November, the Soviet Union has rewarded the countries that opposed his policy with shipments of modern arms including additional MIG-23 fighter-bombers to Iraq and Syria.

Mr. Sadat, during his recent visit to the United States, pressed the Administration for 120 Northrop F-5E's to bolster his air force, whose effectiveness has been severely reduced by Moscow's refusal to send spare parts for Soviet-built planes.

Egypt got 50 F-5E's instead of the 120 Mr. Sadat had requested. These planes and the 44 French Mirage F-1's Egypt has ordered—scheduled for delivery in 18 months—will create training and maintenance problems for the Egyptian Air Force. Its combat strength of 365 planes has been exclusively of Soviet manufacture.

Should Congress approve the sale of the F-5E's, which would be paid for by Saudi Arabia, military analysts believe that the Egyptian Air Force would be reinvigorated. The F-5E, however, is not comparable to Israel's F-15 as an interceptor, they emphasized.

Sadat Stressed Defense Role

Mr. Sadat, according to defense officials, stressed to President Carter that he needed the aircraft not for operations against Israel but rather for defense and possibly for intervention in Somalia if

that country was invaded by Ethiopia.

In addition to being worried about the new arms shipments to the Arabs, Israeli military sources are concerned about any arrangement that would give Egypt military control of the so-called Rafah approaches commanding the major invasion route from Egypt to Israel.

The Rafah approaches are regarded by Israeli planners as a vital strategic area in which the Government has established a number of villages. The area is small, less than 2 percent of the Sinai Peninsula. It is bounded on the west by the town of El Arish and on the east by the town of Rafah. To the south are the sandy wastes of the northern Sinai, to the north the Mediterranean Sea.

The Israelis stress the military importance of the area. Control of the Rafah approaches, they say, means control of the Palestinian-inhabited Gaza Strip to the northeast on the coast and bars any drive into Israel's coastal plain.

The introduction of modern weaponry to the Middle East appears to some military analysts to have undermined some of the military claims on both sides.

For example, Syria's demand that the Golan Heights be returned no longer has a substantial military basis, according to Western officials. The Syrians, they point out, have weapons—Soviet-supplied 180-millimeter guns and missiles—that would enable them to attack northern Israel or defend against invasion from positions well east of the Golan Heights, in some cases as far east as the Damascus area. The Golan Heights area is important to Syria for agricultural reasons and from the standpoint of national esteem, but its military importance to Syria has been reduced.

Acquisition of F-15 fighters by Saudi Arabia has caused concern in Israeli military circles. The attitude among American officials is that this concern is exaggerated. The F-15, they insist, is an air to-air fighter not a fighter-bomber. Its use by the Saudis would be defensive not offensive, they contend.

The military effectiveness of the 60 F-15's for Saudi Arabia depends, qualified sources said, on the training procedures to be followed and their eventual deployment in Saudi Arabia.

Should they be deployed at Tabuk in Saudi Arabia near the Gulf of Aqaba, they would consititute a threat to Israeli air patrols and attack missions over the gulf and the Red Sea.

If the American deal with Saudi Arabia includes the training of Saudi pilots on F-15's in the United States, analysts speculated that the planes might be ready by the end of 1979. Training in Saudi Arabia with American instructors would take longer, they said.

Easy Transfer Is Doubted

American and NATO analysts are not prepared to accept the Israeli view that the F-15 could swiftly be transferred to another Arab country in the event of a general Middle East war.

The Saudis, they say, would not be likely to give away their best defensive aircraft in a war situation. Moreover, the transfer of the aircraft to an Arab air force that has had no training on this extremely sophisticated plane would not be easy. Finally, the command and control procedures and machinery for air combat by the F-15 would not be easily transferable.

Possibly the most unbalancing element in the current situation has been the transfer of advanced Soviet weapons to Iraq and Syria.

The weapons include additional MIG-23's, T-62 tanks, armored personnel carriers and surface-to-surface and surface-to-air missiles. The conclusion among qualified analysts is that both the quality and the quantity of Syrian and Iraqi weaponry have been improved.

However, they insist, this does not seriously weaken Israel's military position. The consensus among American and European analysts remains that Israel is strong enough to defeat any combination of Arab states even if the so-called "eastern front" of Syria and Iraq were reinforced by Saudi Arabian, Libyan and Algerian forces.

Yet there also is general agreement that military and political events in the Middle East have reduced Israel's advantage.

NEW YORK TIMES, February 15, 1978, P1

Settlements Debate Opened by Israelis; Cabinet Is Divided

Special to The New York Times

JERUSALEM, Feb. 20—Amid signs of divisions within the Israeli Government, the Cabinet began a debate today on the controversial policy concerning Jewish settlement in occupied Arab lands.

The extraordinary five-hour Cabinet session, called by Prime Minister Menachem Begin, was convened as a "ministe-

rial committee for security affairs." This is a device that makes it a criminal offense for anyone to reveal details of the proceedings.

Mr. Begin told reporters after the meeting that not every minister had had his say and that the subject would be resumed in a regular Cabinet meeting next Sunday. When asked whether there had been divisions among his ministers, he said differences of opinion were natural in an open society.

Policy a Source of Friction

The Israeli settlements in the West Bank, the Gaza Strip and Sinai have become an impediment to progress in the Israeli-Egyptian peace effort, a source of

friction with the United States, and a subject of domestic criticism from Israelis eager to maintain the momentum of the peace talks.

Yigael Yadin, the archeologist who is head of a party called the Democratic Movement for Change, told reporters that he was pushing for a freeze on new settlements. His party is a moderate member of Mr. Begin's coalition government, which also contains right-wing elements favoring continued Jewish settling of the Arab lands.

Chief among these advocates is Ariel Sharon, a former general who, as Minister of Agriculture, is charged with carrying out the settlement policy. There have been reports that he differs with Defense Minister Ezer Weizman, who opposes the setting up of new settlements at a time when talks with Egypt are in a fragile state.

Mr. Weizman has headed the Israeli delegation to military committee talks in Cairo. Recently, he ordered a halt of the expansion of settlements in northern Sinai, which technically falls under his department because it is under military occupation.

The work had been undertaken by Mr. Sharon on the ground that he was acting within his powers. This conflict of jurisdictions spawned reports that the two officials are engaged in a "ducal war," as the Labor Party newspaper Davar put it.

The situation has also led to speculation about the extent of Mr. Begin's control over his Government.

"The Cabinet is seesawing between the fear of establishing settlements and the fear of not establishing them," said a Davar editorial.

In the last few weeks, settlement work has been given a variety of labels in an apparent attempt to disguise its true nature. A group of settlers at the site of ancient Shiloh on the West Bank, who had been described as members of an archeological excavation, told reporters that they belonged to Gush Emunim, a nationalist group, and intended to establish a permanent community on the site.

Mr. Begin's dealings with Egypt were attacked over the weekend by Labor Party leaders attending a party symposium. Former Prime Minister Yitzhak Rabin said Mr. Begin's handling of the negotiations was "an ill-conceived failure." The settlement policy undermines Israel's credibilty, Mr. Rabin said. "What would happen if the other side tried to do such things?" he added. "How would Israel react? How can one respect a government which carries out settlements whether under an archeological cover or under a security cover?"

Dr. Shlomo Avineri, a former Foreign Ministry official and now professor of political science at Hebrew University,

said in an article in The Jerusalem Post that the Begin Government was "behaving as if we were trying to outwit the British mandatory authorities rather than behaving as an independent nation." This was an allusion to Mr. Begin's role as an underground leader in the struggle against Britain's mandate before Israel's independence.

Over the weekend a group of young Israelis, called Movement for Another Zionism, protested against the Shiloh settlement. Amos Arzieli, a medical student who leads the group, said, "We intend to show that there are groups in Israel who regard false exercises in settlement as undermining the foundation of peace and Israeli credibility in the world."

NEW YORK TIMES, February 21, 1978, P1

ISRAEL TO CONTINUE POLICY OF EXPANDING SINAI SETTLEMENTS

A FREEZE HAD BEEN EXPECTED

Action by Cabinet Also Approves 3 New West Bank Camps— U.S. Withholds Comment

---

By WILLIAM E. FARRELL
Special to The New York Times

JERUSALEM, Feb. 26—The Israeli Cabinet decided today not to change its policy on settlements in occupied Arab lands. The action approved the Begin Government's plan to expand Jewish settlements in northern Sinai and establish three new ones on the West Bank of the Jordan River.

The Cabinet's decision was announced after an eight-hour debate that began at a special session on Monday and continued at the regular weekly session today.

In the days between, there was speculation here that Prime Minister Menachem Begin's Government would freeze

or alter its settlement policy to ease the growing strain that the issue has caused between Israel and the United States.

Tense State of Negotiations

It was also expected that the policy would be suspended because of the tense state of negotiations between Egypt and Israel. President Anwar el-Sadat of Egypt has mentioned the northern Sinai settlements with regard to Israel's sincerity in responding to his peace initiative.

[State Department officials in Washington had no formal comment on the Israeli Cabinet's decision, but they said they had not expected any major policy changes before Mr. Begin's visit to the United States next month.]

Today Aryeh Naor, Israel's Cabinet Secretary, read a brief statement to reporters, written by Mr. Begin, that said the Cabinet had decided there was no need at this time for any new decision regarding the settlements in the occupied territories or with respect to the current political situation.

Mr. Naor refused to say whether the decision was unanimous, but there were strong indications that it was not. The Democratic Movement for Change, a member of Mr. Begin's coalition Government, said a few days ago that it favored a freeze on the settlements.

Technique to Stem Leaks

Like the Monday session, today's Cabinet meeting was convened as the Ministerial Committee for Security Affairs, a procedural device that makes disclosure of its proceedings illegal. Mr. Begin's

government has been using this technique increasingly to stem Cabinet leaks.

The three planned West Bank settlements are near Israeli military camps. One, Tel Kharis, in the western part of the territory, has already made the transition to a civilian settlement. The other two—Tapuach, about six miles from the Arab town of Nablus, and Silt-a-Dahar, north of Nablus—are scheduled to become civilian communities by the end of March.

Israel's settlement policy on Arab lands has long been criticized by the United States as illegal and as posing an "obstacle to peace." In recent weeks, the Carter Administration has been increasingly critical of the Begin Government on the settlements, calling some of them "duplicitous," such as the one at the site of ancient Shiloh, which Israel termed an archeological dig.

The issue has caused friction within Mr. Begin's coalition, which is led by the Likud bloc.

On one side, Defense Minister Ezer Weizman is said to have called for a cessation of settlement activity at a time of delicate negotiations with the Egyptians. On the other side, Agriculture Minister Ariel Sharon, who is responsible for carrying out the settlements policy, is pressing for major new developments.

Today's decision was viewed by some as an attempt to compromise these two opposing views. A few weeks ago, Mr. Weizman, who as Defense Minister is in charge of the occupied lands, ordered a halt in settlement expansion work in northern Sinai. Today's Cabinet move does not negate that order, but neither does it withdraw the Cabinet's previously espoused commitment to expand existing settlements on Egyptian land south of the Gaza Strip.

Negotiations in Virtual Suspension

The Cabinet debate was called in an atmosphere of American criticism of the settlements and at a time when the negotiations with Egypt are in virtual suspension. The decision to reaffirm existing policy came at a time when the special American envoy, Alfred L. Atherton Jr. is shuttling between Cairo and Jerusalem in an effort to establish a mutually agreeable declaration of principles between Israel and Egypt for achieving Middle East peace.

Mr. Atherton returned from Cairo Friday night with an Egyptian counterproposal for such a declaration, apparently in response to an Israeli draft that he took with him to Cairo after a visit here last week. There were reports here that the Egyptian plan represented a toughening of Mr. Sadat's views. The major obstacles to a declaration have focused on how to phrase the section dealing with the Palestinians, and on Mr. Sadat's insistence that Israel express a willingness to withdraw from all the territories seized during the 1967 war.

Hussein's Participation Crucial

Over the weekend, Foreign Minister Moshe Dayan told a radio interviewer that the Egyptian stance was hardening because Mr. Sadat had been unable thus far to induce King Hussein of Jordan to attend the negotiations. The King's participation is believed here to be crucial to discussion of the fate of the West bank and Gaza Palestinians.

Mr. Atherton met with Mr. Dayan last night, and the Foreign Minister has not revised his previous remarks, adding to the conviction that the Egyptian line has hardened.

Mr. Atherton is scheduled to meet with Mr. Begin tomorrow on the latest moves to get the Egyptian-Israeli talks going again.

One prominent critic of the Israeli settlements is Dr. David Owen, Britain's Foreign Secretary, who arrived here today for a state visit. Dr. Owen also stressed the importance of Jordanian involvement if the peace effort is to be revived.

NEW YORK TIMES, February 27, 1978, P1

U.S.-ISRAEL DISPUTE ERUPTS OVER YIELDING WEST BANK AND GAZA

U.N. RESOLUTION 242 AT ISSUE

Begin, Due for Washington Talks Soon, Denies Document Compels Pullback in 2 Key Regions

---

By BERNARD GWERTZMAN
Special to The New York Times

WASHINGTON, March 4—The Israeli Government of Prime Minister Menachem Begin has informed the United States that it does not accept the American view that a key United Nations Security Council resolution obligates Israel to withdraw occupation forces from at least part of the West Bank of the Jordan and the Gaza Strip.

This turn of events has produced a major behind-the-scenes dispute between the two countries, American and Israeli officials said today.

Because Prime Minister Begin and Foreign Minister Moshe Dayan are due in Washington in a little more than a week and Defense Minister Ezer Weizman is scheduled to arrive in a few days—all coming for talks with President Carter and other officials—the Administration has avoided a public airing of the latest disagreement. But Mr. Carter alluded to it Thursday in replies to questions at the National Press Club.

Officials Talking in Private

The outline of the conflict over how to interpret Resolution 242 has appeared in the Israeli press, and Administration officials are freely talking in private about the dispute.

The ostensible cause of it appears to involve semantics, but Administration officials stress that unless it is resolved it could upset any hopes for an overall Middle East peace settlement.

In the Administration view, as expressed in private conversations, the Begin Government has in effect turned its back on the single United Nations Security Council resolution that has been the basis for most Middle East diplomatic efforts in the last 11 years.

The Israelis insist that they still accept Resolution 242, but they acknowledge that their interpretation of it is different now, under the Begin Government, from what it was under the preceding Labor Party Government.

Political Issue in Israel

The matter has also become a domestic political issue in Israel. Last night at a meeting of Labor Party leaders, former Prime Ministers Golda Meir and Yitzhak Rabin said that Israel had been committed under their governments to an interpretation of Resolution 242 that included withdrawal from the West Bank.

In private conversation, Israeli officials bitterly accuse the Carter Administration of creating a new issue as a means of blaming Israel for Washington's inability to put pressure on Egypt and other Arabs to achieve progress in negotiations.

The latest dispute adds to a strain in relations. In recent weeks, Israel and the United States have exchanged accusations over Israel's policy of civilian settlements in the occupied areas and over American moves to link sales of advanced fighter planes to Israel to Congressional approval of similar sales to Egypt and Saudi Arabia.

Today, Senator Robert C. Byrd of West Virginia, the majority leader, told reporters that because of expected opposition to the plane sales he had asked the Administration to delay formal notification of Congress about them until after action on the Panama Canal treaties.

The dispute boils down to United States insistence that Israel is obligated under Resolution 242 to withdraw forces to some extent from all fronts, including the West Bank and Gaza. The Begin Government refuses to agree that it has such a commitment.

Without such a commitment, the United States believes Jordan would not enter the negotiations and Egypt would lose interest, in effect dooming the peace effort.

As a result of the 1967 war, Israel conquered the entire Sinai Peninsula from Egypt, the Golan Heights from Syria and the West Bank, including East Jerusalem, from Jordan, which had controlled the area since 1948. In addition, the Gaza Strip along the Mediterranean, administered by Egypt, was occupied by Israel.

Charging Israel as the aggressor, the Arabs, backed by Communist countries, demanded that the Israelis withdraw completely from these occupied areas but Israel insisted on insuring that its security never again be endangered.

A Compromise Resolution

As the result of protracted talks, a compromise document, Resolution 242, was agreed to on Nov. 22, 1967, by the Security Council. The key and controversial sections of that resolution stated:

"Fulfillment of Charter principles requires the establishment of a just and lasting peace in the Middle East which should include the application of both the following principles:

"(i) Withdrawal of Israeli armed forces from territories occupied in the recent conflict;

"(ii) Termination of all claims or states of belligerency and respect for and acknowledgement of the sovereignty, territorial integrity and political independence of every state in the area and their right to live in peace within secure and recognized boundaries free from threats or acts of force."

To this date, the Arabs have interpreted that resolution to mean that Israel must withdraw from "all" occupied land. The United States and Israel—until the Begin Government—had interpreted it to mean withdrawal from unspecified amounts of territory on all three fronts—Sinai, Golan and West Bank—with the exact borders to be negotiated.

Mr. Begin quit the Israeli Government in 1970 over the issue of withdrawal. He felt that because the ancient Jewish lands of Judea and Samaria were situated on what is now called the West Bank, Israel had not "occupied" that territory but rather had "liberated" it.

His Likud bloc campaigned for office in last year's elections on the program that the Gaza Strip and the West Bank were historically part of the land of Israel. This was a view challenged by the Labor Party, which had made proposals

for returning at least part of the land on each front to the Arabs in return for peace.

U.S. Affirmed View on Resolution

Because of concern over Mr. Begin's past views, the Carter Administration, last June, before Mr. Begin's first meeting with Mr. Carter, issued a strong statement reminding Israel that, in the American view, Resolution 242 "means withdrawal from all three fronts in the Middle East dispute."

Mr. Begin's Government issued a reply that it stood by Resolution 242 and that it was willing to discuss any of the territories. But the Israelis contended that Resolution 242 obligated them only to withdraw from some occupied land, not stating specifically that the West Bank and Gaza were among those lands to be evacuated.

The issue was dormant most of last year because the stress was on reconvening the Geneva conference on a Middle East settlement. But more recently, as the United States sought a draft agreeable to both Israel and Egypt on the principles to guide an overall settlement, the Egyptians raised questions whether the Israelis would ever agree, in fact, to withdraw troops from the West Bank and Gaza.

This is considered important, because otherwise the Egyptians would not agree

to the declaration of principles and it would be impossible to persuade King Hussein of Jordan to enter peace talks, Administration officials said.

When President Anwar el-Sadat of Egypt was here last month, a final statement on his talks with Mr. Carter said that Mr. Carter had affirmed that Resolution 242 was "applicable to all fronts of the conflict."

In recent weeks, Alfred L. Atherton Jr., the special American envoy in the Middle East, has been unable to persuade the Israelis to subscribe to that statement.

When Mr. Carter was asked after his press club speech Thursday what he hoped to achieve with Mr. Begin during their coming talks he refrained from going into much detail. But without explanation, he said that a "crucial element" for progress was adherence to the commitment to Resolution 242 as "a basis for continued negotiations and a solution."

"The abandonment of that would put us back many months or years," Mr. Carter said.

Officials said the President was referring to the problem that had arisen with

NEW YORK TIMES, March 5, 1978, P1

ISRAEL DEFENSE CHIEF THREATENS TO RESIGN IN SETTLEMENTS RIFT

BEGIN BLOCKS A NEW PROJECT

Weizman, in U.S., Reports Accord to Halt Activity in Arab Lands During Negotiation Effort

By BERNARD GWERTZMAN
Special to The New York Times

WASHINGTON, March 7—Ezer Weizman, Israel's Defense Minister, told Prime Minister Menachem Begin by telephone yesterday that he would cut short his official visit to the United States, return to Israel and resign if work was started—in defiance of his orders—on a new civilian settlement in the occupied West Bank of the Jordan River.

Aides of Mr. Weizman disclosed the

latest Israeli feud shortly before the former Air Force Chief of Staff arrived here this afternoon for talks with President Carter, Defense Secretary Harold Brown, Secretary of State Cyrus R. Vance and others.

According to the aides, Mr. Weizman's stormy conversation with Mr. Begin from his room in New York's Regency Hotel succeeded in blocking an effort by Agricultural Minister Ariel Sharon to bypass Mr. Weizman's orders, which were issued before he left for the United States Sunday.

Mr. Weizman told reporters at Andrews Air Force Base outside Washington that he spoke again today with Mr. Begin, and that it was agreed all expansion of settlements in Arab lands would cease until after talks next week between Prime Minister Begin and President Carter.

Both Agree on Issue

"We did have talk about how I look at things and how he looks at things," Mr. Weizman said. "We both look at things in the same way now. I sincerely hope we will solve this intricate and delicate problem."

Although high United States officials said the dispute over work on civilian settlements was primarily a domestic po-

litical matter for the Israelis, these officials paid close attention because the issue has become one of the main causes of strain in American-Israeli relations.

Mr. Weizman, who ranks second in the Herut Party headed by Mr. Begin, has become known as a relative moderate on most issues since the direct talks between Israel and Egypt began last November. He has been most often pitted against Mr. Sharon, a war hero, like Mr. Weizman, who has been pushing for as many new settlements as possible in the occupied lands.

The United States position has been that such settlements in occupied lands are illegal under international law and, in Mr. Vance's words, "should not exist."

President Anwar el-Sadat of Egypt has been particularly incensed over Israeli efforts to retain settlements in Sinai after a complete return of the peninsula to Egypt, as proposed in Mr. Begin's peace plan last December.

As Defense Minister, Mr. Weizman has authority over the occupied territories. Before he left for the United States he ordered a halt in preparations for a new civilian settlement at Nabi Salah, near Nablus. But Mr. Weizman, according to his aides, received word while in New York yesterday that Mr. Sharon had given the Gush Emunim, the nationalist-religious group that has been establishing settlements on the West Bank, permission to go ahead with the previously planned settlement at Nabi Salah.

The aides said that Mr. Weizman was so infuriated that he told Prime Minister Begin in the telephone conversation that he would return home at once and quit if Mr. Sharon persisted. Mr. Begin, who is due in Washington March 13 with Foreign Minister Moshe Dayan, reportedly assured Mr. Weizman that no work would take place on the settlements.

Furor Encourages Americans

The furor encouraged American officials who see in Mr. Weizman a force for moderation in Israel.

The dispute overshadowed for the moment Mr. Weizman's mission here for the discussion of a range of political and military matters.

On defense issues, according to Israeli sources, Mr. Weizman wants to discuss long-range request for weapon deliveries, into the 1980's, reportedly at a cost of more than $10 billion.

Mr. Weizman, who has headed the Israeli delegation in preliminary talks in Cairo on a possible accord, also wants to raise the question of whether the United States will pay for the costs involved in an Israeli withdrawal from Sinai.

Israeli officials have said it would cost about $1 billion to build four new air bases in Israel to replace the ones that would have to be given up in Sinai and to erect new defense lines at whatever borders are established.

Mr. Weizman also is expected to make Israel's case against the Administration's proposed package for the sale of advanced military aircraft to Egypt and Saudi Arabia as well as to Israel. The Israelis oppose the plan to sell 60 F-15's to Saudi Arabia, while their own request for 150 F-16's was cut to 75 and their request for 25 F-15's was reduced to 15.

Three Issues of Contention

The Carter Administration and Israel are at odds primarily over three issues:

the continuation of civilian settlements in occupied lands, the plane sales and varying interpretations of United Nations Security Council Resolution 242 of 1967.

On the Resolution 242 question, the United States has been concerned that the Begin Government was abandoning Israel's long-standing commitment to making at least some withdrawals from all the fronts in the 1967 war.

The Begin Government has argued that it was not obligated to withdraw from the West Bank and Gaza Strip and the United States has felt that without such an agreement it would not be possible to involve Jordan in the negotiations for a Middle East peace, or to get Egypt to agree to a declaration of principles.

NEW YORK TIMES, March 8, 1978, P1

A Tel Aviv Rally Protests Begin's Policy

By WILLIAM E. FARRELL
Special to The New York Times

JERUSALEM, April 6—"Suddenly we found ourselves leading a kind of movement," said Pzali Resheff, a law student. "We didn't really organize it well—it means people in Israel feel that people have got to do something."

Mr. Resheff, interviewed in his apartment here yesterday, was referring to a large rally in Tel Aviv last Saturday night at which thousands of Israelis urged Prime Minister Menachem Begin to review his tenacious stand that all of the occupied West Bank of the Jordan River and the Gaza Strip are historically part of Israel.

The rally—estimates of the attendance ranged from 25,000 to 45,000—was the largest protest against Mr. Begin's policies since he took office last June.

As far as can be determined, the rally was not inspired by any political faction but came about to a large extent spontaneously after extensive publicity about a letter to the Prime Minister last month by more than 300 reserve officers.

Momentum of Peace Effort Fading

The letter expressed concern that the peace campaign started by President Anwar el-Sadat of Egypt in mid-November was slipping away and that Mr. Begin should be more forthcoming on the issue of returning Arab lands captured by Israel during the 1967 war.

The Tel Aviv rally, which attracted mostly young members of the middle class, seems to have been a genuine show of concern that Mr. Begin's firm line against a West Bank and Gaza compromise, as well as his commitment to keeping Israeli settlements on

the Arab lands, would doom the already sputtering chance for Middle East peace.

It is uncertain whether the rally was a onetime affair or the harbinger of a grass-roots peace movement in Israel. The fairly moderate tone of the reserve officers' letter to Mr. Begin was reflected at the rally. Mr. Begin was asked not to resign but to modify his views.

There was no demand that he agree to return all of the West Bank and Gaza to the Arabs. Rather, he was urged to rethink, in the interest of a peace accord, his long-held conviction that Israel is sovereign over these lands because of their biblical associations with the Jews.

Restraint, Order and Respect

The mood of the rally was restrained and orderly.

"We have great respect for you, Mr. Begin," one speaker said. "We know that nobody is more concerned with achieving peace than you. All we ask is that you heed our voice, the voice of the hitherto silent majority and that you not be the captive of an extremist minority."

Mr. Resheff said the original intention of the letter signers to make a point of their military links was to thwart any attempts by Mr. Begin's supporters to say the letter was merely a predictable clamor from the left.

But that label also caught the eye of many Israeli reporters and editors and the letter was given a good deal of publicity. The letter, which received a brusque reply from Mr. Begin a few weeks ago, went out of its way to state that the signers in no way threat-

ened to refuse to serve in the armed forces if mobilized.

According to Mr. Resheff, the protest started when a few reserve officers talked about their feeling that Mr. Begin must soften his views if the peace effort was to have a chance.

Support Rallied by Telephone

Contacts were made by telephone with kibbutz members and with student and professionals. Some funds were donated, enough to pay for newspaper advertisements announcing the rally. One that appeared last Friday in the English-language Jerusalem Post said in part:

"We, the initiators of the reserve officers' letter, call on every Israeli citizen who is anxious that the prospects for peace should not be ruined to come to a mass rally."

The advertisements called on Israelis "to say they prefer peace to a greater Israel." The sponsors also held a news conference to publicize the rally.

Expressing surprise that peace sentiment had suddenly coalesced into "a kind of movement," Mr. Resheff said he knew of supporters from across the country's political spectrum, including some who voted for Mr. Begin and his Likud bloc.

"We don't have any political ambitions," Mr. Resheff said. "Our aim is to change the present policy. If tomorrow Mr. Begin said he would give up areas of the West Bank for the peace process then we can give up our struggle."

He said that he and other volunteers who helped organize the rally had been surprised by the turnout, with people coming from Jerusalem, Haifa, Tel Aviv and from kibbutzim throughout the country.

The rally was denounced by Mr. Begin's Finance Minister, Simha Ehrlich, who said it "smells of a putsch." The remarks provoked a demand from some of the rally organizers that Mr. Ehrlich apologize. But he refused.

Mr. Ehrlich heads the Liberal Party faction of Mr. Begin's right-of-center Likud group. That faction issued a statement saying that the "Peace now" slogan of the rally was one of appeasement and was "all too reminiscent of the slogan used by Neville Chamberlain after his agreement with Hitler, which, rather than ushering in an immediate era of peace, resulted in the most bloody war the world has known."

Mr. Resheff said that plans were being made for another rally in the next few weeks and that he hoped Mr. Begin would meet with a delegation of the people urging a policy change.

"We hope it will be a big peace movement, but now we don't know," he said. "People have gathered by their own initiative. It's difficult to say what will come of it."

Mr. Resheff stressed that Mr. Begin was not being asked to surrender all the occupied Arab lands, since some territory might have to be retained for security reasons.

"We don't ask him to say he is going back to the lines of the 4th of June, 1967," the law student continued, referring to the day before the war with the Arabs that led to Israel's conquest of Sinai, the West Bank, Gaza and the Golan Heights.

"We want him to say peace is more important than the territories we occupied in the 1967 war" and that "he is willing to give back territories when we're ready to sign for peace."

NEW YORK TIMES, April 7, 1978, P3

On 30th Year, Israel Honors Past, Ponders Present, Charts Future

By WILLIAM E. FARRELL
Special to The New York Times

JERUSALEM, May 10—After a day of intense mourning for its thousands of war dead, Israel tonight began celebrating its 30 tumultuous years as an independent nation.

Exactly 24 hours after the chilling wail of air raid sirens pierced every city and hamlet in the country to signal the onset of Memorial Day, Israel's main squares and town centers were flooded with lights and music.

It was a startling emotional shift on a day that began with mourning in military cemeteries, carpeted with brilliant spring flowers, and ended with singing, dancing and speeches to commemorate the start of Israel's fourth decade as a sovereign state.

Parades, Picnics and Concerts

Tomorrow, the festivities will get into full swing with parades and picnics, concerts and dances, religious services and revelry.

The linking of Memorial Day with Independence Day is a deliberate, although wrenching, annual reminder of the price this country of 3.6 million people has paid—four wars, nearly 13,000 dead—to fly the blue and white flag of the Israeli state.

Today, the country's colors beribboned public buildings, fluttered from lampposts and flew from terraces and roofs as Israel—still enmeshed in the coils of Arab enmity, still obsessed with ambivalences and ambiguities as it was in 1948—proclaimed its endurance.

The observances will end tomorrow with a military parade and an air force review.

The authorities have mobilized 10,000 police, border guards and soldiers, backed by helicopters and spotter planes to safeguard the anniversary events against terrorist attack.

For years the phrase "tiny Israel" was commonplace. Today the word "powerful" must be added, for it is a country that has become the major military power in the Middle East, equipped with the most sophisticated of weaponry and with the manpower trained to use the complex arms perfected by the technology of its chief ally, the United States, and in some instances by Israel itself.

For years the country has talked of peace with its Arab neighbors even as it has built its military establishment, has rebuffed assaults, has attacked and been attacked. And always peace has been outside the grasp of Israel and those neighbors—Jordan, Syria, Egypt and Lebanon.

Danger Helps to Unite People

The common threat of destruction has periodically served to bind up the deep divisions that exist among the Israelis. Israeli society is far from a cohesive homogeneous grouping of Jews.

Its citizens come from Europe, from North Africa, from Iraq, from the United States, from South Africa, from the Soviet Union, from Yemen, from Argentina, from Egypt, from India and from scores of other places labeled "the Diaspora."

The so-called "Oriental Jews," those from North Africa, Yemen, and Iraq, are at the bottom of the social and economic ladder. A majority of the population, they are underrepresented in the echelons of power and they are increasingly vocal about it.

The "Orientals" were instrumental in ousting the European-dominated Labor Party from power last May, although the group they helped put in power, Prime Minister Menachem Begin's Likud bloc, is also dominated by Jews of Russian, Polish and German background.

The disparities between these two segments of Israeli society are deep and troublesome. The education gap, the economic gulf, the cultural differences all remain to be bridged if these diverse elements—welded together only by their common Jewish heritage—are to blend into a common Israeli identity.

Fusing of Disparate Groups

The problem of fusing these disparate Jewish groups is also compounded by the fact that 15 percent of the country's citizens—roughly 500,000 people, are Arabs who stayed when Israel became a state in 1948. Technically and legally, they are Israeli citizens. But their status is not on a par with the Jews.

Citizens of Israel face some of the most rigorous demands anywhere—a third year of double-digit inflation that last year neared a rate of 40 percent, the military commitments demanded of them, heavy taxation, and a high level of tension caused by hostile neighbors and by close living conditions that are, in part, caused by security demands.

The cost of military might is exorbitant—approximately a third of the gross national product of about $12 billion—not to mention the tremendous burdens it imposes on a citizenry where women are subject to conscription and where men serve in the military reserves until they are 54.

Total Force of 400,000

Israeli military officials prefer not to use numbers when discussing Israel's defenses. But, according to The Military Balance, 1976-1977, an annual publication of the International Institute for Strategic Studies, Israel has a total armed force of 158,500, with mobilization to a total of 400,000 possible within 72 hours. The institute, a London-based independent center, engages in research on problems of international security.

Some inkling of the country's military power came in mid-March when Israel invaded southern Lebanon by land, sea and air after a Palestinian terrorist attack on Israeli civilians in which 36 persons and 9 attackers died.

Israelis are urbanites—about 80 percent

live in urban clusters—in contrast with the old Zionist ethos about the sanctity of working the soil.

The toiler on the rural kibbutz, or commune, is well known to the world and many of the older kibbutzim are very well-off, self-contained units. But the members represent only 3 percent of the country's population.

Less is known in the outside world about the urban slums, the illiteracy, the tensions between religious and secular Jews, juvenile delinquency, substandard housing and the whole host of urban ills of the kind that plague American cities.

Israel's demonstrated scientific genius in making barren land arable and profitable is also well known, less well known, except to Israelis, is the stultifying bureaucracy. A veritable army of pencil pushers is bound by regulations and rules that inflame the citizen and can torment the most erudite Talmudist.

Yesterday, at the Department of Motor Vehicles, a young Israeli turned to a foreigner spending his fourth morning in line to purchase a car and said, "Tomatoes we grow in the Negev with hardly any water, and this!" A gesture took in the warren of clerk's cages and jostling customers fighting off the idea of forming a queue.

"This," he went on angrily, "we inherited and perfected from the Ottomans."

There are few societies that analyze themselves so relentlessly as does Israel. Abetted by a free press, Israelis constantly are fighting it out in print. They fight over settlement policy, over Arab relations, over religious observances, over politics — a perennial favorite — over whether so-and-so is really a good artist, over anything remotely controversial. And, in Israel, everything is controversial.

The country thrives on its anomalies. The collective etiquette in such places as bus stops or stores is brusque, even rude. Yet the individual Israeli, more often than not, is considerate and a generous host.

The days to come will see the newspapers and magazines filled with looks back and looks ahead as the country, saddled as ever with problems, moves into its next decade.

Emigration is a Major Problem

A major problem is emigration, coupled with a fear that the character of Israel as a Jewish state will be imperiled in coming years unless many more Jews come here to settle.

There are jokes about Israeli visitors to New York trying to find a taxi driver who is not an Israeli. But the problem of Israeli-born Jews leaving, for reasons that range from the tension of living here to a desire to "make it" in a more affluent country, is a real one. It is real enough for the Government to have printed glossy posters with a postcard overlaid on a gorgeous view of the Galilee in spring that says, "Dear son, come back home." It is signed, "Israel."

Like so many things here, the prospect of the move by President Anwar el-Sadat for peace is greeted by many with ambivalence after so many years of war and violence, of oratorical posturing and shelved proposals for an accord, of the grim reality of relatives and loved ones perishing in battle.

Some sense of that ambivalence, or suspicion, was conveyed by Israel's Defense Minister, Ezer Weizman, in a recent interview with the Hebrew newspaper Yediot Ahronot. Mr. Weizman, who has visited Mr. Sadat in Cairo several times since the Egyptian President's trip to Jerusalem, said he understood the profound inability of some Israelis to believe in Mr. Sadat's sincerity after so many years of animosity.

"My feeling is, even after the talks with Sadat, that Egypt wants to arrive at a settlement," the Defense Minister said. "But I definitely understand Israelis who think I was 'worked on' in Egypt.

"They say, 'It can't be. After 30 years of war one of our ministers goes to Cairo and finds pleasant relations—there's something wrong, something must be wrong.'"

NEW YORK TIMES, May 11, 1978, P1

9

Camp David Summit

Yasir Arafat, one of the actors in the Middle East drama with a great deal at stake, predicted that the September Camp David summit would produce a face-saving, partial accord for America, Egypt and Israel. He pointed accurately to the fact that none of the three participants in the summit could afford to come away empty-handed. At the same time, neither side was expected to come forward with any major concessions. The risk of convening the summit was therefore very great for all three sides.

For Sadat, success at Camp David might put an end to his perilous, year long isolation in the Arab world. While backed by a war-weary public, Sadat faced threats of attack from radical Palestinian groups, and Pan-Arab Nationalists headed by his own former foreign minister Ismail Fahmi were calling for formation of a Palestinian government in exile to oppose Sadat's peace initiative. Failure at Camp David would weaken Sadat's position both at home and abroad, while the initiative for peace—so vital to Egypt domestically—would drift into the hands of other Arab states with less pressing reasons to make peace. Sadat's performance at Camp David would determine the future of Saudi Arabia's support for the flagging Egyptian economy. A perceived sellout of the Arab world might result in cutting off the lifeblood of foreign currency which the Saudis supply to stave off Egypt's bankruptcy. With the existence of his nation at stake, Sadat could not afford to come away from Camp David empty-handed.

Prime Minister Begin came to Camp David after a summer of the darkest period of US-Israel relations. Openly criticized by the US government for his insistence on retaining settlements in Sinai and on the West Bank, Begin had to demonstrate some flexibility and realism at the summit in order to restore US confidence in his government. Editorials appeared in the United States to the effect that though America shouldn't interfere in the domestic politics of a foreign country, America might "get rid" of Begin. Even American Jewish leaders were hoping to see a change in government. But with a deep conviction in the justice and the necessity of Israel's West Bank settlements, Begin had precious little room to move.

Nevertheless, with peace-fever sweeping Israel and America, he could not afford to leave Camp David empty-handed.

For President Carter a favorable outcome of the Camp David meetings would mean a great deal domestically. The President had campaigned on a promise of achieving peace in the Middle East, and since taking office had tied the prestige of the administration to the success of Sadat's peace efforts. Recent actions of the adminstration, including the planes sale to Saudi Arabia and Carter's call to recognize the "legitimate rights of the Palestinian People" had angered long-standing American friends of Israel and raised questions about the strengtn of America's commitment to its allies.

Equally important for Carter would be the impact of the summit on US foreign policy in the Middle East. Since 1973 when the Soviet Union and the United States jointly mediated a conclusion to the October War at a six-nation parley in Geneva, the USSR has been calling for a resumption of those talks. Because the Geneva meetings had become deadlocked over the issue of inviting the PLO to participate (a move the Israelis firmly rejected) both the USA and Israel have sought bilateral negotiations between Israel and individual Arab states rather than the USSR's multilateral approach. The US and Israel have similarly shied away from the UN forum, feeling that the Arab-led bloc of non-aligned nations was too hostile to Israel to mediate the conflict. A success at Camp David would enable the US to close the Soviet Union out of participation, interference or a gaining of credit in any peace settlement, while a failure might allow the Soviet Union and the non-aligned bloc to engineer an unfavorable settlement in the future. At the same time, America's credibility as a friend of both the Arabs and the Israelis would either be supported or damaged by the results of the summit.

Well aware that success at the Camp David summit would be crucial for the prestige of American foreign policy, Sadat warned President Carter not to play an "honest broker" role, passively mediating the talks, but to actively put forward a plan of his own. Israel, which had always rejected the idea of a settlement "imposed" by a third party, resisted this idea. Nevertheless, with the stakes as high as they were, Carter could not remain an "honest broker" in the talks. Rumors of American treaties to guarantee Israel navigation rights to the Suez Canal, of US aid for Egypt, of Hussein of Jordan's entry into the talks all suggested the imaginative steps the American participants were considering to keep the talks going.

Carter's negotiating strategy was to define the issues which Egypt and Israel could agree on, while avoiding a search for definite agreement on all points. It was a strategy suited to the nature of the Arab-Israeli conflict, which involves disputes over land, water, refugees, transit rights and reparations. By pressing both sides to disclose their immediate aims, and their minimal concessions, American negotiators and Carter were able to calibrate a degree of concurrence between the two sides' demands and willingness to concede on a few issues, including return of the Sinai to Egypt, removal of Israeli settlements from the Sinai and navigation rights for Israel of the Suez Canal.

The talks began on September 1, in strict secrecy, enabling the participants to put forward tentative, small concessions. When the momentum of small concessions got rolling, Carter presented Sadat and Begin with a general framework for settlement, not an independent American "secret plan" but a dovetailing draft of Israeli and Egyptian demands prepared by American diplomats. The two Middle Easterners accepted the draft, the most far-reaching settlement ever signed by the Israelis and the Arabs in 30 years of war. The draft called for Israel to withdraw partially from the Sinai within nine months, at the end of which period full diplomatic relations would be established. Israeli navigation of the Suez Canal would be guaranteed, and provision would be made for Israel to compensate Egypt for oil extracted from the occupied Sinai. A full peace treaty was to be signed in approximately three months, with December 17 as a target date.

The Camp David meeting broke up on September 18. Three days later Secretary of State Cyrus Vance toured Morocco, Jordan, Syria and Saudi Arabia to try to obtain backing for the peace plan. While Morocco and Saudi Arabia were "open" to further developments, Syria and Jordan nailed the plan for its major omission, its lack of a timetable for ending Israeli occupation of the West Bank. On this point, the delicate fabric of the plan's concessions and compromises began to unravel. Following their joint appearance before the US Congress with promises of peace, Begin and Sadat began to publicly trade accusations about shortcomings in the plan, while each claimed that the other was distorting key provisions. The United States meanwhile had hoped that the Israelis would suspend the expansion of settlements on the West Bank indefinitely, while instead Begin announced immediate expansion.

The growing rift sparked a new crisis on October 18 when Israeli and Egyptian diplomats met separately with "shuttle service" by Vance, but these meetings did not prevent Sadat from returning the draft of the treaty for further American revision on October 24. Begin, whose parliament had already approved the present draft on September 28, refused to consider any alteration. With Israeli and Egyptian diplomats continuing to discuss different versions of the treaty in the end of 1978, the cynical prognostication of Yasir Arafat seems to have been borne out. The settlement at Camp David was partial. Key issues such as the fate of the Israeli administered West Bank and the rights of the Palestinian refugees to reparations or repatriation were deferred by the very nature of the treaty. All three participants at the talks probably underestimated the desire of the other Middle East states for a comprehensive settlement, rejecting the step-by-step methods of Camp David. But while diplomats from all sides missed the December 17 deadline for concluding a treaty in their search to draft wording acceptable to both Begin and Sadat, Israeli and Egyptian commercial agents had already signed far-reaching cooperative agreements. Answering Hassan of Morocco's optimistic hope that Arab oil revenue and Israeli development technology will make the Middle East a "garden of Eden," war-weary publics in Israel and Egypt wait for the "Spirit of Camp David" to become a diplomatic reality.

PEACE PROCESS CONTINUING

William E. Farrell reviews Egyptian-Israeli Middle East peace efforts in 8 months since Egyptian President Sadat visited Jerusalem; holds average citizen in Cairo and Jerusalem responded to latest meeting between Foreign Ministers Moshe Dayan and Mohammed Ibrahim Kamel and Secretary of State Vance in Britain with little interest, feeling peace effort is back in hands of diplomats, international lawyers and technicians who meet behind closed doors; notes some dim hope that the 2 sides will achieve progress still flickers, but it has become clear that 3 decades of hatred and warfare cannot be quickly overcome   (NEW YORK TIMES, August 6, 1978, S6 P23)

PEACE PROSPECTS EXAMINED

Commentator Flora Lewis discusses controversy over reasons for failure of Middle East peace initiative, noting both sides have reverted to trying to persuade US to put pressure on other; holds, however, that exchanges have provided awareness of precisely what Israel and Egypt mean by "concessions," and have evidenced certain common interest in moving toward peace; sees dispute as involving rival claims to live on same land, as well as conflict of temperament between Egyptian President Sadat and Israeli Prime Minister Begin   (NEW YORK TIMES, August 6, 1978, S4 P2)

VANCE AND BEGIN HOLD TALKS

Secretary of State Vance and Israeli Prime Minister Begin meet for over 4 hours in Jerusalem, holding talks were serious, good and useful; Begin, who appears pleased that Egyptian President Sadat is being perceived as responsible for breakdown in Middle East negotiations, reveals Vance did not ask him to change his position; asserts Israel is willing to participate in meeting of foreign ministers, which was cancelled by Sadat, but adds no Israeli government could agree to Sadat's precondition that Israel withdraw from all occupied Arab lands before direct talks take place; Vance reports he shares Begin's hope that talks can be resumed, but does not agree that everything hinges on Sadat's reply   (NEW YORK TIMES, August 7, 1978, P1)

VANCE PLEASED WITH EGYPTIAN TALKS

State Secretary Vance starts talks with Egypt's President Sadat at Sadat's villa at Mamura, Egypt, in effort to persuade him to continue negotiations with Israel; State Department spokesman Hodding Carter 3d reports Vance feels "very good" about initial meeting; agrees with an Egyptian's assessment that there is no atmosphere of crisis   (NEW YORK TIMES, August 8, 1978, P1)

MIDDLE EAST SUMMIT ANNOUNCED

Egypt's President Sadat and Israel's Prime Minister Begin agree to meet at Camp David, Maryland, September 5 in response to invitation from President Carter; Sadat says he agreed because US promised to be "full partner" in peace negotiations; Begin says meeting was arranged without Israeli acceptance of earlier Egyptian preconditions for resumption of talks; Carter Administration sources stress that President Carter does not expect meeting itself to produce a settlement; suggest US fears deadlock might result in renewed Middle East fighting; prior to announcement of meeting, Carter met with bipartisan group of Congressional leaders; reported that Begin and Sadat wished to discuss sending US peacekeeping troops to Middle East; State Department spokesman comments that US is concerned that continued fighting in Lebanon will obstruct Israeli-Egypt talks; notes concern that Israel may be resupplying Christian forces in Lebanon with more arms   (NEW YORK TIMES, August 9, 1978, P1)

RISK FOR CARTER SEEN

Commentator Barry Schweid discusses upcoming Camp David summit meeting between Israel and Egypt and US role in search for Middle East settlement; suggests President Carter's image will improve if Egyptian President Anwar Sadat and Israeli Prime Minister Menachem Begin clear path to peace under his direction; emphasizes Carter could slip even further in public esteem if Israeli-Egyptian deadlock is not broken; notes Carter is acceding to Sadat request by assuming role of full partner in stalled negotiations   (NEW YORK TIMES, August 11, 1978, P48)

OIL THREAT RAISED

Arab and London oil tanker sources report that Arab oil producers may be considering another oil embargo against US in October if planned September 5 meeting between Israeli Prime Minister Begin, Egyptian President Sadat and President Carter does not lead to significant progress toward Middle East peace agreement; threat of embargo could be the reason behind recent major surge in international tanker freight markets   (JOURNAL OF COMMERCE, August 11, 1978, P1)

ATHERTON ARRIVES IN JORDAN

US special envoy to Mideast Alfred L. Atherton arrives in Jordan, where he will meet with King Hussein to discuss recent talks between Secretary of State Vance, Israeli Prime Minister Begin and Egyptian President Sadat; Jordan, which has remained neutral in inter-Arab dispute over direct peace contacts between Israel and Egypt, claims it will not participate in peace talks until Israel agrees to return all occupied Arab lands and allows independent Palestinian state   (NEW YORK TIMES, August 12, 1978, P82)

RABIN ASKS LIMIT TO U.S. ROLE

Former Israeli Prime Minister Yitzhak Rabin asserts that US, Israel and Egypt must change negotiating positions to ensure success of Camp David Middle East summit talks; advises President Carter must avoid presenting own specific plan in effort to ensure meeting's success because US should act strictly as mediator; contends Israel should seek limited, separate agreement with Egypt if full peace treaties are not achieved; maintains Egypt should not ask for full Israeli withdrawal from Jordan River

West Bank, Gaza Strip and Sinai Peninsula (NEW YORK TIMES, August 13, 1978, P82)

U.S. PREPARES FOR SUMMIT

Carter Administration planners say privately that their preparations include provisions for heightened role for President Carter at Camp David summit with Egypt and Israel; meanwhile, conflict of statements is arising from disclosure by Senator Charles Percy that Jordan's King Hussein may be called to discussions if Prime Minister Menachem Begin and President Anwar el-Sadat agree on framework for negotiations; Percy's disclosure follows meeting with State Secretary Cyrus Vance; planners continue to deny that Hussein would join talks at Camp David (NEW YORK TIMES, August 16, 1978, P16)

ARAB OPINION SURVEYED

Commentator James M. Markham surveys Arab opinion on upcoming Camp David US-Israel-Egypt summit in interviews conducted in Lebanon, Syria and Jordan and sees consensus that conference will fail; view is that US wants thinly disguised separate Egypt-Israel peace, but Israel will not make necessary concessions on West Bank; respondents cite US impotence in getting Israel to allow token Lebanese army into southern Lebanon, a less complex diplomatic task; Saudi Arabia endorsement of conference is seen as means to shift burden of expected failure from Egyptian President Sadat to Israeli Prime Minister Begin and President Carter, allowing Sadat to save face in Arab world (NEW YORK TIMES, August 18, 1978, P146)

ASSAD ASSAILS TALKS

Syrian President Hafez Assad says upcoming Camp David summit conference of Egypt, Israel and the US is a "new ambush for the Arab cause"; maintains any results of conference can only be against Arab interests; does not rule out a chance of future settlement between Arab countries and Israel under proper conditions and climate (NEW YORK TIMES, August 19, 1978, P162)

BEGIN ANNOUNCES SUMMIT PLANS

Israeli Prime Minister Menachem Begin says on August 27 that he will carry to Camp David summit meeting substantially same peace plan he submitted to Egyptian President Sadat at Ismaliya meeting of December, 1977; says Israeli mission will consider counterproposals, such as territorial compromise, but his own proposals will be consistent with cabinet decisions; decisions reached on August 27 were that Israeli delegation will endeavor to reach an agreement between parties, will submit plan for conclusion of peace treaties and will act to ensure continuation of negotiations between parties; Begin will be accompanied by Foreign Minister Moshe Dayan and Defense Minister Ezer Weizman (NEW YORK TIMES, August 28, 1978, P41)

CAMP DAVID PROSPECTS EXAMINED

Commentator Karen Elliott House discusses upcoming Camp David summit and personalities of men involved; contends that not only are Israeli Prime Minister Menachem Begin and Egyptian President Anwar Sadat far apart on issues, but there is basic conflict in their personal styles that will compound President Carter's job of bringing them to agreement; claims that what Carter hopes for, at best, is Camp David agreement for further talks (WALL STREET JOURNAL, September 1, 1978, P8)

MIDEAST SUMMIT SEEN AS SHIFT

Commentator Jim Hoagland asserts that President Carter's bid for Middle East summit at Camp David signals fundamental change in assessments and tactics; indicates that Israeli Prime Minister Menachem Begin's rising standing in Israel and abroad has forced Carter and Egyptian President Anwar Sadat to accept Begin's permanency in Israeli politics; asserts that Carter is stressing that Begin and Sadat compromise on West Bank issue; indicates that Carter will try to move Sadat towards public position of allowing some Israeli troops on West Bank for indefinite period; cites that Sadat has agreed to issue in private; cites that Begin's primary goal at summit is to boost his rising popularity at home; contends Sadat will try to raise his standing in Arab world by showing he is closer to Carter than Begin is (WASHINGTON POST, September 3, 1978, P1)

P.L.O. FORECASTS 'PARTIAL SUCCESS'

Palestine Liberation Organization (PLO) expects Camp David summit to achieve "partial success" in order to ensure continuation of direct peace talks and encourage moderate Arabs; PLO leader Yasir Arafat predicts that the tripartite conference will at most produce some vague declaration of principles aimed at "saving face" but will bypass the Palestinian problem (NEW YORK TIMES, September 6, 1978, P108)

CONFLICTING ASPIRATIONS HIGHLIGHTED

Israeli Prime Minister Menachem Begin and Egyptian President Anwar el-Sadat betray their differing personalities and aspirations in separate statements on Camp David summit; both leaders hint at their contradictory strategies and intimate their opposing views on role they hope President Carter will have at the summit; Sadat, in his statement, conveys a grander vision and greater sense of urgency; Begin puts emphasis on Israeli desire for peace (NEW YORK TIMES, September 6, 1978, P101)

CAMP DAVID SUMMIT BEGINS

President Carter, Israeli Prime Minister Menachem Begin and Egyptian President Anwar Sadat meet together for first time at Camp David in attempt to regain momentum towards settlement of Israeli-Arab conflict; three leaders issue joint statement asking world to pray for their success; almost no real news about substance of initial

Camp David meetings is revealed   (NEW YORK TIMES,   September 7, 1978,   P31)

ARAB-SOVIET PACT PROPOSED

Beirut, Lebanon, newspapers report Syrian Foreign Minister Abdel Halim Khaddam is proposing to hard-line Arab countries that they enter into defense pacts with USSR if US signs mutual defense treaty with Israel; Khaddam, who was in Moscow to discuss Camp David talks with USSR government, is reportedly coordinating Arab efforts to thwart any agreement that may be reached at summit, and has scheduled September 20 meeting with Libya, Algeria, South Yemen and PLO to map out strategy   (NEW YORK TIMES,   September 8, 1978,   P55)

PROGRESS INDICATED AT CAMP DAVID

President Carter, Israeli Prime Minister Begin and Egyptian President Sadat meet for more than 3 hours at Camp David September 7, indicating they are willing to prolong their efforts to achieve some progress toward Middle East settlement; press secretary Jody Powell continues to avoid disclosing character of talks, but denies US is contemplating any US presence in Middle East, speculation that arose from Defense Secretary Harold Brown's participation in talks   (NEW YORK TIMES,   September 8, 1978,   P23)

U.S. INVOLVEMENT FORESEEN IN MIDEAST

Commentator Stephen S. Rosenfeld observes any success achieved at Camp David summit on Middle East will serve to expand and deepen US permanent involvement in Middle East; believes US readiness to play larger continuing role as overseer or guarantor of any settlement reached will affect prospects of settlement as well as conditions of agreement; maintains American assurances offer likeliest way to bridge gaps between Israeli and Egyptian demands   (WASHINGTON POST, September 8, 1978,   P13)

SEPARATE MEETINGS AT CAMP DAVID

President Carter meets separately September 8 with Israeli Prime Minister Menachem Begin and Egyptian President Anwar el-Sadat at Camp David for new approaches to Middle East settlement; key advisers to three governments begin exploring details, with main focus considered to be future of Jordan West Bank; White House spokesman Jody Powell declines to give details of talks   (NEW YORK TIMES,   September 9, 1978,   P19)

SADAT'S POSITION ANALYZED

Commentator Jim Hoagland asserts Egyptian President Anwar Sadat would prefer failure to half-way measures; comments Sadat needs more than cosmetic proposals to improve his position in Arab world; claims failure would be acceptable tactical goal for Sadat; comments Egypt's

Egyptian President Anwar Sadat, President Carter and Israeli Prime Minister Menachem Begin meet together for the first time on September 6 at Camp David in an attempt to regain momentum toward settlement of the Arab-Israeli conflict.

Consulate General of Israel

Consulate General of Israel

Begin and Sadat greet one another during an informal meeting at Camp David.

desire for clear-cut success or failure was disclosed by Egyptian Minister Butros Ghali in interview with French newspaper *Le Monde*; asserts war is not credible option for Sadat in near future   (WASHINGTON POST,   September 9, 1978,   P1)

CAIRENES ANTICIPATING DISAPPOINTMENT

Commentator Christopher Wren reports from Cairo that Egyptian public tends to feel that outcome of Camp David summit will be less than what it wants; finds broad support for Sadat's refusal to resume formal negotiations with Israelis without prior concessions; finds Egyptians fear another war if summit meeting fails; notes that news blackout has dampened public's interest   (NEW YORK TIMES,   September 9, 1978,   P110)

SYRIAN PRESIDENT PREDICTS SUMMIT FAILURE

Syrian President Hafez Assad predicts Camp David peace summit will fail; holds that any agreement made will not last long because Arabs cannot accept territorial compromises   (NEW YORK TIMES,   September 11, 1978,   P36)

SUMMIT PARTICIPANTS VISIT GETTYSBURG

President Carter tours Gettysburg, Pennsylvania, Civil War battlefield September 10 with Israeli Prime Minister Menachem Begin and Egyptian President Anwar Sadat during recess in Camp David summit conference on Middle East   (NEW YORK TIMES,   September 11, 1978,   P34)

CAMP DAVID OUTLOOK BLEAK

Middle East summit conference at Camp David enters its 7th day September 11, with little indication that any progress has been made; White House press secretary Jody Powell tells press briefing he feels "there may have been an excessive air of optimism" among journalists covering meeting; President Carter, Prime Minister Begin and President Sadat have not met as a group for 4 days, although there have been daily bilateral meeting between Carter and other 2 leaders   (NEW YORK TIMES,   September 12, 1978,   P117)

ROLE FOR JORDAN ENVISAGED

Arab diplomats suggest that Jordanian King Hussein might join Egyptian President Sadat and Israeli Prime Minister

Begin in peace conference if Israel agrees to withdraw from Arab territories and if Israel recognizes right of Palestinians to self-determination; such conditions seem contrary to Begin's stated policies, but there have been rumors that Begin is going to Camp David summit conference ready to compromise after reaching "limited understandings" in secret meetings with Jordanian and moderate Palestinian representatives; Arab diplomats claim key "understanding" is that there would be no role for Palestine Liberation Organization (PLO) in any agreement involving occupied territories; in related developments, White House spokesman asserts there are no plans for King Hussein to join summit meeting; meanwhile, Syrian President Assad travels to West Germany for talks with President Walter Scheel; in another Mideast development, Scotland Yard reports that package bomb delivered to Iraqi Embassy in London September 11 was detected and safely defused   (NEW YORK TIMES, September 12, 1978, P75)

Begin and Sadat embrace as President Carter looks on after Carter announced on American TV that Egypt and Israel had concluded two agreements designed to be precursors of a peace treaty.

EGYPTIAN PRESS GLOOMY

Commentator Thomas W. Lippman observes deep gloom and pessimism are pervading Egyptian news reports about Camp David summit on Middle East; suggests news media is attempting to prepare Egyptian public for anticipated failure of summit; points out meeting was billed in advanced as "last chance" to achieve peace that President Anwar Sadat has promised Egyptian people; notes Cairo newspapers are stressing theme that President Carter has worked very hard for summit success, but has been unable to make Israelis be reasonable   (WASHINGTON POST, September 14, 1978, P2)

CAMP DAVID RESULTS ANNOUNCED

Jubilant President Carter announces on television that Egypt and Israel have concluded 2 agreements designed to lead to signing of peace treaty within 3 months and to provide for withdrawal of Israel's military government from West Bank of Jordan River and Gaza Strip; concedes that ultimate sovereignty over West Bank and Gaza, major issue, remains to be ironed out, but notes that local inhabitants of 2 areas are granted guaranteed voice on ultimate status of region, as well as pledge of "full autonomy and self-government" during 5-year transition period; Jordan is invited to join negotiations; Israel agrees not to create any new settlements on West Bank during 5-year period and negotiation of area's future; status of Jerusalem is not resolved; Sadat calls President Carter's role that of "full partner" and "indispensable" to future negotiations; ebullient Begin offers lavish praise for Sadat and Carter   (NEW YORK TIMES, September 18, 1978, P6)

CAMP DAVID ACCORDS ANALYZED

Commentator Charles Mohr claims both Egypt and Israel gave up or modified some of their orthodox political doctrines to reach Camp David accords, but holds some of most important features are implied rather than explicitly stated, leaving major questions unanswered; points out there is "touchy" political relationship between 2

frameworks for peace, although agreements are not formally dependent on each other; also contends US commitment and future role in peace process is unclear, questioning whether US will use its influence to gain Arab support for accords   (NEW YORK TIMES, September 19, 1978, P21)

SUMMIT'S POLITICAL EFFECTS CITED

Commentator Hedrick Smith examines political effects of Camp David summit on its participants; holds President Carter has emerged as political winner by gaining respect for his personal diplomacy and by strengthening his Presidency with such daring exercise; maintains summit has become unexpected breakthrough for Israeli Prime Minister Begin, who risked domestic furor by overturning long-held positions, while Egyptian President Sadat seems to have conceded most, with angry Arab reaction and Foreign Minister Kamel's resignation signalling perils of course he has taken   (NEW YORK TIMES, September 19, 1978, P17)

U.N. CAUTIOUS ON MIDEAST ACCORD

Announcement of Camp David agreements between Israel and Egypt results in mood of cautious reserve at UN; many delegates hold failure to deal with Palestinian problem may doom agreements; Secretary Kurt Waldheim, through spokesman, issues brief statement neither endorsing nor criticizing agreement; holds that while summit was unique and reflected enormous effort, many difficult problems remain and much depends on attitude of other parties concerned   (NEW YORK TIMES, September 19, 1978, P60)

CONGRESS BRIEFED ON MIDEAST ACCORDS

President Carter addresses special joint session of Congress, attended by both Egyptian President Sadat and Israeli Prime Minister Begin, to provide brief sketch of agreements reached at Camp David summit; holds agreements have changed impossible dream of Middle East peace into realistic expectation, and hails summit as bright moment in human history; announces he is sending Secretary of State Vance to Jordan and Saudi Arabia to explain and seek support for agreements, and praises Sadat and Begin for taking personal political risks in reaching agreements (NEW YORK TIMES, September 19, 1978, P13)

BEGIN ADDRESSES ISRAELI PUBLIC

Israeli Prime Minister Begin, in Israeli television broadcast, announces he expects domestic criticism of his Camp David actions, but strongly believes he "followed the right way"; declines to comment on how he will vote in Knesset on question of dismantling Israeli settlements in Sinai, one of conditions to peace treaty with Egypt, but US diplomats think he will seek Cabinet support for measure; stresses there will be no Palestinian state on West Bank, and maintains no secret agreements were made, with all documents to be made public (NEW YORK TIMES, September 19, 1978, P34)

SADAT ANNOUNCES 'JUST PEACE'

Egyptian President Sadat, in television broadcast from Washington, D.C., informs Egyptian people that "just peace" was achieved at Camp David summit; mood in Cairo is initially optimistic, but many Egyptians have adopted "wait-and-see" attitude; Sadat also confirms, in interview with ABC radio, that Foreign Minister Mohammed Ibrahim Kamel has submitted his resignation because of a difference of opinion, but refuses to provide details (NEW YORK TIMES, September 19, 1978, P11)

ARABS CONDEMN PEACE ACCORDS

PLO and Syria condemn Camp David peace accords as betrayal of Arab cause and insist Egyptian President Sadat had no right to speak for Arabs; moderate Arab states of Jordan, Kuwait and Saudi Arabia react to summit with formal silence, but private expressions of concern that accords will worsen inter-Arab divisions, aggravate Arab radicalism and provoke new unrest; Lebanese, in particular, express deep foreboding, predicting escalation of violence in Lebanon, focal point of Middle East tensions (NEW YORK TIMES, September 19, 1978, P7)

BEGIN'S ACTION ANALYZED

Commentator Flora Lewis maintains that while both Egyptian President Sadat and Israeli Prime Minister Begin made important compromises at Camp David summit, Begin was under intense psychological strain during talks; explains that Begin was forced to choose between his life-long convictions and loyalty to late Zionist leader Jabotinsky, and his chance to establish himself in history as man who brought peace to Israel; believes Begin struggled as much in making his Camp David decisions as Sadat must have struggled in making his decision to visit Jerusalem (NEW YORK TIMES, September 19, 1978, P65)

SADAT SEEKS BACKING

Egyptian President Anwar el-Sadat now turns to task of trying to convince other Arab leaders to support Egyptian-Israeli agreements reached at Camp David summit meeting; will leave Washington, DC, for Morocco where he may meet ranking Saudi Arabian official Prince Abdullah ibn Abdulaziz and discuss accords; Egyptian cabinet calls special session to endorse Sadat and Camp David achievements; Sadat must choose new foreign minister to replace Mohammed Ibrahim Kamel, who resigned before end of summit; no more resignations by Egyptian government officials are expected (NEW YORK TIMES, September 20, 1978, P24)

ARABS WARY OF ACCORD

Jordan announces it is neither legally nor morally bound by obligations over issues discussed at Camp David summit, which it did not attend; statement is clear sign that State Secretary Vance would not have easy time persuading Jordan's King Hussein to join peace talks at present; Jordan denounces separate action by any Arab party and calls for collective Arab responsibility for comprehensive settlement; Lebanese leadership is deeply concerned about repercussions of Camp David accords; Syria, Algeria, Libya and Palestine Liberation Organization (PLO) have already denounced Camp David accords as capitulation by Sadat, and will soon meet in Damascus to chart strategy to isolate Sadat and foil his unilateral initiative (NEW YORK TIMES, September 20, 1978, P19)

ISRAELIS FACED WITH CHOICE

Israeli Foreign Minister Moshe Dayan and Defense Minister Ezer Weizman assert that Israeli people must decide between retaining Israeli settlements in Sinai desert and signing peace treaty with Egypt; Egyptian President Anwar el-Sadat demanded at Camp David summit conference that Israel agree to abolish settlements in Sinai before peace pact could be signed; Israeli Prime Minister Menachem Begin left decision to Israeli parliament; Weizman emphasizes Camp David accords offer Israel chance for real peace agreement and normalization of relations (NEW YORK TIMES, September 20, 1978, P29)

CARTER GAINS NEW POPULARITY

Discussion of President Carter's new popularity as result of Egyptian-Israeli peace accords signed at Camp David summit meeting; CBS news poll released September 19 shows Carter's popularity jumped dramatically after summit; former Carter critics in and out of Democratic Party praise his effectiveness in bringing parties to agreement; former State Secretary Kissinger terms agreement a major achievement; Presidential aides suggest summit provided opportunity for Carter to demonstrate that his ability at Presidential leadership had been misjudged; Jewish leaders had been turning against Carter Presidency before summit, but now praise him for his role in securing peace agreement; political experts contend it is too early to tell what effect summit accord might have on mid-term elections   (NEW YORK TIMES, September 20, 1978, P14)

HUSSEIN'S REACTION DISAPPOINTS SADAT

Egyptian President Anwar el-Sadat is disappointed over Jordanian King Hussein's initial reaction to Camp David accords; declares he would bargain with Israel on future of Jordan West Bank and Gaza Strip, even if Hussein does not join negotiations; emphasizes President Carter's personal intervention stopped him from walking out September 15 from Camp David summit without any agreements; indicates he does not seek separate agreement with Israel, but wants comprehensive Middle East accord   (NEW YORK TIMES, September 20, 1978, P4)

ARAB POTENTIALS EXAMINED

Commentator Anthony Lewis examines potential gains for Arab side in Camp David peace accords for Middle East; concedes that there would have been no agreement if settlement depended on Israeli withdrawal from West Bank and Gaza; points to Prime Minister Begin's agreement to creation of "self-governing authority" for occupied Gaza and West Bank and retreat on his earlier demands that such self-government come only after final peace agreement and that it be permanent arrangement for area; argues that agreement opens way for renewal of political life in occupied areas and almost certain election of advocates of independent Palestinian state to self-governing authority   (NEW YORK TIMES, September 21, 1978, P71)

JORDANIAN POSITION SLATED

Jordan's King Hussein tells US State Secretary Cyrus Vance in Amman that Jordan still refuses to join US-backed Middle East peace negotiations in absence of firm guarantees of Israeli withdrawal from occupied Arab lands, including West Bank, Gaza, Golan Heights and East Jerusalem, and Palestinian's right to self-determination; does not shut door entirely to current process but declares that framework is not acceptable in present form; senior Jordanian officials criticize Egyptian President Sadat on 2 main points: disassociating Sinai problem from comprehensive settlement and agreeing to less than total Israeli withdrawal and Palestinian self-determination (NEW YORK TIMES, September 21, 1978, P20)

BEGIN REASSERTS ISRAELI CLAIMS

Israeli Prime Minister Menachem Begin declares unequivocally that Israeli troops will remain on West Bank of Jordan River and Gaza Strip after 5-year period specified in recently concluded Camp David agreements; assails PLO and its supporters; reasserts Israel's historic claims over West Bank saying "Bible is our mandate"; meanwhile, US negotiators concede that Israel had committed itself to restrict new settlements only during negotiating period leading to creation of autonomous, self-governing Palestinian council in occupied areas; express hopes that Israel will voluntarily restrict new settlements during 5-year period   (NEW YORK TIMES, September 21, 1978, P18)

SADAT SEEN AS WINNER

Commentator Joseph Kraft speculates that Egyptian President Anwar Sadat achieved greatest long-term gains at Camp David summit on Middle East; points out Sadat yielded nothing that was important to Egypt while securing return of entire Sinai desert to Egyptian sovereignty, obtaining airfields Israel wished to hold and most likely erasing Jewish settlements on West Bank   (WASHINGTON POST, September 21, 1978, P25)

SUMMIT STRATEGY ANALYZED

Commentator James M. Markham interprets results of Camp David summit as embodying step-by-step philosophy originated by former State Secretary Henry Kissinger; maintains that Kissinger's approach theorizes that sheer military/political weight of Egypt, quietly allied to Saudi Arabia, is enough to drag bulk of Arab world into settlement; argues that first Jordan and then Syria will be asked to move away from endorsement of Palestine Liberation Organization (PLO) as legitimate voice of all Palestinians; contends that angry rejection of Camp David by Syria and Jordan are mostly for public consumption, and not wholly privately embraced   (NEW YORK TIMES, September 21, 1978, P83)

SUMMIT SUCCESS ANALYZED

Commentator Stephen S. Rosenfeld applauds Camp David summit agreements; contends genius of agreements lies in distinguishing between issues that can be settled now and issues which must be delayed; points out that West Bank problem can not be solved now because of political and diplomatic hazards surrounding it; asserts that both Israeli Prime Minister Menachem Begin and Egyptian President Anwar Sadat are relying on passage of time to induce compromise on certain settlement points   (WASHINGTON POST, September 22, 1978, P17)

VANCE TO TALK WITH SAUDIS

State Secretary Vance flies to Saudi Arabia September 21 without winning Jordan's support for Camp David summit decisions but with assurances for continuing dialogue; Jordanian sources indicate Jordan asked US for more guarantees, more clarification and more time to consult other Arabs, namely Saudi Arabia and Syria; Vance hopes to persuade Saudis to endorse summit results, or at least get Jordanians to enter negotiations at early phase; is not expected to attempt to get Syria into peace talks, but merely urge it to give process a chance and exert restraining influence on PLO; Jordan holds that Arab summit conference, including Egypt if possible, is necessary now to secure effective and lasting Arab consensus   (NEW YORK TIMES, September 22, 1978, P23)

SADAT TALKS WITH HASSAN

Egyptian President Anwar el-Sadat resumes secret talks with Morocco's King Hassan II in apparent effort to solicit king's endorsement of Camp David summit conference agreements; Egyptian officials contend Sadat is anxious to obtain Hassan's public approval to avoid impression that agreements isolated Sadat in Arab world; Hassan is in constant touch with Saudi Arabia's King Khalid and Jordan's King Hussein, whose support is regarded as crucial to success of agreements (NEW YORK TIMES, September 22, 1978, P12)

CARTER LETTER TO SADAT REPORTED

Egyptian newspaper *Al Ahram* reports President Carter sent letter to Egyptian President Anwar el-Sadat saying that Arab sector of Jerusalem is indivisible part of Jordan West Bank; notes letter asserted US would consider as illegal any population change in Jerusalem's Arab sector; Israel agreed to eventual withdrawal from Jordan West Bank as part of Camp David summit conference peace framework (NEW YORK TIMES, September 22, 1978, P11)

ILLEGAL ISRAELI SQUATTERS ROUTED

Israeli soldiers rout about 150 Jewish Gush Emunim members who established illegal settlement on Israeli-occupied Arab Jordan West Bank; troops remove Nablus-area squatters, but another group of Gush Emunim members unsuccessfully attempts to set up second settlement south of Nablus; Gush Emunim pledges to try to set up new nucleus of community each night in West Bank until Prime Minister Menachem Begin recants on pledge made at Camp David summit that new Israeli settlements would not be set up on West Bank during next three months of peace negotiations with Egypt (NEW YORK TIMES, September 22, 1978, P1)

CAMP DAVID SUMMIT REVIEWED

Commentator Terence Smith offers detailed account of 13-day Camp David summit conference among Egypt, Israel and US, pieced together from public statements and private interviews with members of all 3 delegations; highlights: Egypt's adamant stand of no agreement without total Israeli withdrawal from Egyptian land, including crucial 18 settlements in Sinai; deadlocks, ultimatums and threats by both Egypt and Israel to walk out; crucial position of US, beginning on September 9, as arbitrator and author of 23 major drafts of accord, with innumerable revisions; contrasts in personalities of Egypt's President Sadat, Israel's Prime Minister Begin and President Carter; important assisting role of Vice President Mondale and aides Zbigniew Brzezinski and Hamilton Jordan; byliner sees Israel-Egypt separate peace as most significant accomplishment, defusing greatly possibilities of another major war (NEW YORK TIMES, September 23, 1978, P60)

ARAB SUMMIT INTERRUPTED

Summit conference in Damascus, Syria, of hardline Arab nations opposed to Camp David peace framework for Middle East is interrupted as Libyan leader Colonel Muammar el-Qaddafi and PLO leader Yasir Arafat fly to Jordan to try to persuade King Hussein not to join US-backed peace process; Syria asks US State Secretary Cyris Vance to postpone visit by one day because of interruption; US side is said to harbor no illusions of

persuading Syria to join peace formula, but it considers President Hafez al-Assad leader of hardliners and open to reason; leaders of various Palestinian guerrilla factions denounce Arafat for going to Jordan without consulting Palestinian delegation; summit conference discussions have centered on greater economic, military and political coordination among participants, closer ties with USSR and possible sanctions against Egypt (NEW YORK TIMES, September 23, 1978, P68)

VANCE FAILS WITH SAUDIS

State Secretary Cyrus Vance fails to obtain backing of Camp David peace accords on Middle East from Saudi Arabia in Riyadh meetings with seriously ill King Khalid and with Prince Fahd; Saudis cite same reasons as Jordanians: accords fail to guarantee ultimate Israeli withdrawal from occupied territories on West Bank of Jordan River and Gaza Strip, and fail to deal with occupied Arab Jerusalem, special concern to Saudis because of Isalmic holy places there (NEW YORK TIMES, September 23, 1978, P32)

MILITANTS DEFY BEGIN

First strident opposition to Israeli Prime Minister Menachem Begin's Camp David concessions involves defiant illegal settlement atop hill near militant Palestinian town of Nablus (West Bank of Jordan River) by members of Gush Emunim conservative religious bloc on evening of September 18; Israeli troops evict protesters on September 21; protesters oppose pledge not to erect new settlements in Gaza Strip or West Bank while peace negotiations are in progress (NEW YORK TIMES, September 23, 1978, P89)

THREE ISSUES IN DISPUTE

White House releases text of letters on 3 disputed issues which are being exchanged between Egypt, Israel and US as adjuncts to recently concluded Camp David summit peace framework for Middle East, but spokesman says there is indefinite delay on question of whether Israel had agreed to indefinite moratorium on new settlements on West Bank of Jordan River, as President Carter had understood, or 3-month moratorium, as Prime Minister Begin had understood; 9 letters released deal with Israeli settlements on Sinai Peninsula, status of city of Jerusalem and definitions of Palestinians and their representation in future peace talks (NEW YORK TIMES, September 23, 1978, P51)

EGYPTIANS CHEER SADAT

Thousands of Egyptians welcome President Anwar el-Sadat on his return from Camp David summit conference; cheering Egyptians line the streets from Cairo's airport to Presidential residence on the Nile; hand-painted Arabic banners hail Sadat as "Hero" and "Champion of Peace" (NEW YORK TIMES, September 24, 1978, P18)

NEW ARAB UNITY SEEN

Commentator Marvine Howe assesses Arab reception to Camp David agreements based on tour of key Arab states and talks with radical and moderate leaders; holds that, contrary to expectations, Camp David agreements seem to have helped Arab unity, with most of the Arabs unifying in opposition to prospect of separate Egypt-Israeli peace; reports that accords are widely viewed by other Arabs as "good deal for Egypt" but serious blow to Arab cause; notes that opposition has come, not only from nations such as Libya, Algeria, Syria, South Yemen, as well as PLO, but also from moderates such as senior Jordanian officials, who claim privately that Egyptian President Anwar el-Sadat has deceived them   (NEW YORK TIMES, September 26, 1978,   P14)

ARAB OPPOSITION DECLARED INEFFECTIVE

Commentator Joseph Kraft asserts that Arab world remains too divided to block Camp David summit accords signed by Egyptian President Anwar Sadat; outlines divisions among Arab states which crystallized after Sadat's trip to Jerusalem; points out attempts by Libyan leader Colonel Muammar Qaddafi and PLO leader Yasir Arafat to influence Jordan's King Hussein to oppose agreements have failed; asserts Sadat can be strengthened by support of Japanese, Europeans and Chinese; notes US can increase pressure for accords by sending up new defense or foreign-aid requests to benefit Israel, Egypt and possibly Jordan   (WASHINGTON POST,   September 26, 1978,   P15)

KNESSET DEBATES ACCORDS, SINAI

Israeli Prime Minister Menachem Begin opens parliamentary debate on securing peace treaty with Egypt and bluntly tells legislators that peace effort will collapse if Jewish settlements in Sinai desert are not withdrawn; opposition Labor Party leader Shimon Peres urges colleagues to accept Camp David agreements, but makes partisan attack on Begin's handling of peace effort and asserts that unduly high price is being paid for Israel-Egypt peace; former Begin ally Geula Cohen is ejected by parliamentary vote for heckling Begin   (NEW YORK TIMES,   September 26, 1978,   P17)

VANCE TOUR CONCLUDES

State Secretary Cyrus Vance returns from 5-day trip to Jordan, Saudi Arabia and Syria, conceding that no apparent progress had been made in President Carter's bid to gain Arab support for Camp David peace initiative for Middle East; senior US official is quoted as saying that Vance failed to change Syrian President Hafez al-Assad's views during Vance's last stop on September 24; privately, US officials now say that key individual is Jordan's King Hussein, who is undecided about Camp David accords   (NEW YORK TIMES,   September 26, 1978,   P13)

EGYPT LAUNCHES DIPLOMATIC CAMPAIGN

Egypt launches diplomatic campaign to win Arab backing for Camp David agreement with Israel; Egyptian Acting Foreign Minister Butros Ghali tells Arab ambassadors in Cairo that accords are only step toward comprehensive Middle East settlement; reportedly explains that negotiations for Jerusalem fall within arrangements pertaining to Jordan West Bank, which is included in 1 of 2 Camp David accords; sources at meeting note Ghali also pointed out that Egypt would carry out commitments for West Bank even if Jordan does not participate in negotiations   (NEW YORK TIMES,   September 27, 1978,   P58)

U.S.-ISRAELI DIFFERENCES NOTED

Carter Administration officials concede there is some disagreement between US and Israel on extent of commitments made by Prime Minister Begin at Camp David summit regarding Israeli settlements on West Bank; also acknowledge Israel may jeopardize one or both agreements if it insists on constructing new West Bank settlements during 5-year transition period; hold, however, that US will delay confrontation over settlements to avoid disrupting speedy implementation of agreements; note top officials insist settlements issue is relatively minor and will be overcome in near future   (NEW YORK TIMES,   September 27, 1978,   P36)

WEST BANK AUTONOMY EXAMINED

Commentator William E. Farrell maintains crucial next step in implementing Camp David agreements is establishment of transitional self-governing authority on Arab West Bank and Gaza Strip to replace 11-year-old Israeli military occupation; holds key question is whether Arab leaders will cooperate, noting agreement calls for Israel, Egypt and Jordan to create such self-governing mechanism, but Jordan has shown no inclination to take part in peace effort; also cites controversy over which leaders will act as elected representatives, and role of Palestine Liberation Organization (PLO) in transition government   (September 27, 1978,   P16)

ISRAELI PARLIAMENT APPROVES ACCORDS

Israeli Parliament approves Camp David summit accords after marathon debate and agrees to withdraw Israeli settlements from Sinai Peninsula if Egypt-Israel peace treaty is concluded; vote is 85–19, with 16 abstentions; Prime Minister Menachem Begin declares that Israel now has chance to end hostilities begun in 1948; extensive details of parliamentary debate given; outside parliament building about 800 protesters, including Gush Emunim members and residents of Sinai settlements, demonstrated and chanted disapproval of Camp David accords   (NEW YORK TIMES,   September 28, 1978,   P24)

U.S. GUARANTEES DISCUSSED

Commentator James Reston points out that although President Carter has expressed confidence that Egypt and Israel will sign peace agreement, he has not disclosed what he would do to guarantee such treaty; holds US has vaguely considered underwriting any general settlement in Middle East, but notes this would raise several questions, such as type of guarantee, whether guarantee would be contained in treaty ratified by Senate or by executive order, and whether commitment would cover both Egypt and Israel or only Israel   (NEW YORK TIMES, September 29, 1978, P67)

THREATS TO PEACE FORETOLD

Commentator Anthony Lewis takes note of jubilation with which Israeli populace has embraced risk of peace and prospect of ending its isolation from its neighbors, but offers arguments why Israel-Egypt separate peace is doomed in long run unless there is progress on West Bank and Gaza strip negotiations; warns of gravity of issue of new Israeli settlements after peace is completed, pointing out that rush of right-wing Israelis to settle would alienate West Bank moderates and King Hussein and make Egyptian President Sadat's position in Arab world increasingly untenable   (NEW YORK TIMES, September 29, 1978, P35)

AMBIVALENCE ON ACCORDS NOTED

Commentator Stephen Rosenfield discusses Bethlehem Mayor Elias Freij's ambivalence toward Camp David accords between Egypt and Israel; notes Freij first supported accords then expressed misgivings; suggests Freij is wobbling between hope and doubt; asserts Freij represents those on West Bank who would give accords a chance; asserts they want end of occupation within context that must be acceptable to their neighbors; notes Freij stated no solution is possible without approval of Palestine Liberation Organization   (WASHINGTON POST, September 29, 1978, P17)

VANCE ASSURES PALESTINIANS

State Secretary Cyrus Vance assures world community that Palestinians have gained "solid start" toward dignity and freedom from Camp David summit agreements, speech before UN General Assembly; calls for economic support in developing West Bank of Jordan River and Gaza Strip, where over one million Palestinians are to develop self-rule, and in resettling others there   (NEW YORK TIMES, September 30, 1978, P55)

P.L.O. LOSS FORESEEN

Commentator Clayton Fritchey predicts separate Egyptian-Israeli peace agreement could signal beginning of end for Palestine Liberation Organization (PLO); doubts that all Arab nations hostile to Camp David summit agreements will continue to back PLO indefinitely with money, arms and staging areas for terrorist operations; points out many Arabs are fed up with PLO which has caused havoc and dissention in nearly every country where guerrillas have been harbored; believes dissolution of PLO would not be detrimental to Palestinian people who have much to gain from Camp David agreements   (WASHINGTON POST, September 30, 1978, P15)

P.L.O. PARTICIPATION ASKED

Nine Palestinian leaders from Israeli-occupied West Bank tell US mediator Alfred L. Atherton they want Palestine Liberation Organization (PLO) participation in Middle East peace talks set up by Camp David accords and an end to Jewish settlement activity; attend meeting held at East Jerusalem home of US consular officer Donald Kruze; 14 other West Bank and Gaza leaders refuse to attend meeting, stating that Atherton should negotiate directly with PLO; Atherton says PLO cannot join in negotiations unless it will accept UN Security Council's resolution 242 which guarantees Israel's security   (NEW YORK TIMES, October 1, 1978, P36)

PALESTINIANS REJECT ACCORD

Discussion of Lebanese Palestinian reaction to Camp David accord; majority feel they were forgotten at Camp David, and among ordinary Palestinians there is overwhelming mood of disappointment because they had believed that any kind of framework for a comprehensive Middle East peace would have to include them; conversations with a broad cross-section of Lebanon's 400,000 Palestinians reveals a general rejection of Egyptian President Anwar el-Sadat as their spokesman and deep disillusionment in what is seen as his willingness "to sacrifice Palestinian rights for the sands of Sinai"   (NEW YORK TIMES, October 1, 1978, P87)

PALESTINIAN DISAPPOINTMENT REPORTED

Majority of Lebanese Palestinians feel they were forgotten at Camp David, and among ordinary Palestinians there is overwhelming mood of disappointment because they had believed that any kind of framework for a comprehensive Middle East peace would have to include them; conversations with a broad cross-section of Lebanon's 400,000 Palestinians reveal a general rejection of Egyptian President Anwar el-Sadat as their spokesman and deep disillusionment in what is seen as his willingness "to sacrifice Palestinian rights for the sands of Sinai"   (NEW YORK TIMES, October 1, 1978, P87)

BEGIN DEFENDS WEST BANK SETTLEMENTS

Israeli Prime Minister Menachem Begin says Camp David notes will prove he agreed to in effect suspend Israeli settlement in West Bank for only 3 months, in contrast to US statement that he consented to 5-year suspension; indicates he agreed to suspension of settlement during negotiations of Israeli-Egyptian peace treaty, which he expects will take about 3 months; declines to speculate on Knesset vote on settlement issue   (NEWSWEEK, October 2, 1978, P33)

BEGIN DISCUSSES CAMP DAVID ACCORDS

Israeli Prime Minister Menachem Begin asserts Israel did not compromise any basic principles in Camp David agreement; reiterates Israeli claim to Judea, Samaria and Gaza Strip; denies agreement commits Israel to prohibit new settlements in occupied lands during 5-year transition period; maintains Camp David agreement will succeed even if Jordanian King Hussein does not endorse it; says that peace treaty between just Israel and Egypt, even if condemned by other Arab governments, will ensure at least "de facto" peace in Middle East   (TIME, October 2, 1978, P21)

HUSSEIN SCORES MIDEAST ACCORDS

Jordanian King Hussein criticizes Camp David framework for peace in Middle East; says it deviates from UN Resolution 242, which had previously been US position; stresses pact will have to be revised before it will be acceptable to Jordan and other Arab nations; states Arab demands for total Israeli withdrawal from occupied lands and Arab sovereignty over Jerusalem are not negotiable; says he has support of PLO Leader Yasir Arafat and Libyan leader Muammar Qaddafi in seeking Palestinian solution; characterizes Camp David agreement as "pure sugarcoating" for Israeli Prime Minister Menachem Begin's goals   (NEWSWEEK, October 2, 1978, P33)

CARTER'S NEW POPULARITY EXAMINED

Newsweek cover story "Born Again!" examines President Carter's dramatic rise in popularity following success of his Camp David summit with Israeli Prime Minister Menachem Begin and Egyptian President Anwar Sadat; spirit of Camp David has restored to Carter an aura of public faith and goodwill not seen since his first days in office, and has eliminated popular perception of him as a well-meaning amateur unable to cope with demands of Presidency; has also dampened speculation about easy challenges to Carter in 1980 Democratic primaries; Carter's surge in popularity polls almost matches that won by President Nixon after January 1973 Vietnam accords, and betters that achieved by President Kennedy in October 1962 Cuban crisis; observers believe Carter must seek "encores" in SALT treaty and effective inflation plan if he is to maintain his new popular standing
(NEWSWEEK, October 2, 1978, P24)

IRAQ PROPOSES WAR FUND

Iraq proposes to send troops to Golan Heights Israeli-Syrian front; also proposes collective fund with $9 billion annual budget, drawn largely from conservative Arab oil states, to help finance Arab war effort against Israel for next 10 years, allowing $5 billion for Egypt to help it cope with economic burdens resulting from its withdrawal from peace initiative; Syria is officially silent on proposals   (NEW YORK TIMES, October 3, 1978, P25)

SADAT URGES BROADER PARTICIPATION

Egyptian President Sadat, in televised speech to Parliament on Camp David summit meeting, issues public invitation to President Carter to visit Egypt for signing of peace treaty with Israel after peace talks are concluded; urges Jordan and Syria to take advantage of Camp David formula to negotiate with Israel, hinting that terms are best they can hope to get; criticizes hard-line Arab countries who have opposed Camp David accords; after speech,

announcement is made that US-educated engineer Mustafa Khalil has been asked to form new government, succeeding present Prime Minister Mamdouh Salem
(NEW YORK TIMES, October 3, 1978, P20)

RISE IN TERRORISM SEEN

CIA report on international terrorism foresees rise in terrorist activities originating with Palestinian extremists; sees "Haddad Wing" of Popular Front for the Liberation of Palestine as source of most of terrorist activity; notes movement to unseat PLO leader Yasir Arafat and replace him with more aggressive leader who would endorse campaign of international terrorism; notes likelihood that even more moderate Palestinian groups might become involved in terrorism; notes coordination between Palestinian and west German terrorist groups   (NEW YORK TIMES, October 4, 1978, P51)

EGYPTIAN MILITARY CHANGE FORESEEN

Commentator Thomas W. Lippman speculates new role is being envisioned for Egyptian military in future; describes Egypt's recent annual display of military power showing Egypt remains most powerful military machine in Arab world while indicating changes in way forces are being equipped; points out Egypt's newest military acquisitions would be more useful in context of war in Africa than in war with Israel   (WASHINGTON POST, October 7, 1978, P16)

EGYPT'S ECONOMIC FUTURE PREDICTED

Egyptian officials and economists expect no sudden prosperity to emerge from eventual Egyptian-Israeli peace settlement; fear unrealistic expectations of prosperity by Egypt's 36 million poor could lead to violence; Planning Minister Esmat Abdel Meguid says Egypt may have some short-term benefits in form of increased availability of food; hopes that US aid will increase to $1.3 billion in 1979, including substantial increase in wheat shipments; discusses Egypt's future plans for development in Sinai, exploiting oil and mineral resources; forecasts million-barrel-per-day oil output from Sinai in 1980, which will increase net oil revenues to more than $1 billion per year   (LOS ANGELES TIMES, October 8, 1978, P1)

ANTI-CAMP DAVID SUMMIT PLANNED

Syrian President Hafez Assad accepts invitation by Iraqi President Ahmed Hassan el-Bakr to attend anti-Camp David summit in Baghdad November 1; action is seen as indication relations between Syria and Iraq, which have deteriorated since 1973, may be improving; Saudi Arabia, Jordan, Kuwait and most radical Arab states have stated they will attend, as has PLO leader Yasir Arafat, indicating possible reconciliation between Iraq and PLO; meeting will reportedly focus on plan to lure Egyptian President Sadat away from Camp David accords   (NEW YORK TIMES, October 9, 1978, P7)

MIDEAST BUSINESS BENEFITS FORESEEN

Egyptian-Israeli peace accord could produce additional benefit of mutually profitable business relationship between two countries; most immediate concern for Israel is possibility of exploiting Sinai oil resources jointly with Egypt; working visits by Israeli agricultural technicians seem promising; tourism between two countries could result from accords; other economic possibilities include investment by American and Jewish-owned companies in Egypt   (BUSINESS WEEK, October 9, 1978, P48)

PALESTINIANS OPPOSING ACCORDS

Palestinians living in West Bank and Gaza Strip are vehemently opposed to framework for Mideast peace worked out at Camp David, fearing self-rule with continued Israeli military presence will kill hopes for independence; position surprises many Israelis, who thought Palestinians would approve end to 11 years of Israeli military government and establishment of local administration; Israelis fear autonomy plan may lead to future independent Palestinian state, and are puzzled that Palestinians do not foresee same result   (NEW YORK TIMES, October 9, 1978, P1)

SINAI OIL EXPLORATION POSSIBLE

Amoco Egypt Oil Company expects to immediately start exploration work in eastern part of offshore Ramadan oil field now under Israeli control, if Egypt and Israel sign final peace agreement returning occupied Sinai to Egypt; Gulf of Suez Petroleum Company, joint venture of Amoco and Egypt, wants to develop Alma offshore oil field where Israelis struck oil in 1977, but Amoco officials say such development would require extensive negotiation; Amoco spokesman reports company assumes Egypt will take over these areas, but is uncertain about conditions of the takeover   (JOURNAL OF COMMERCE, October 10, 1978, P1)

ISRAEL PLANNING BORDER TOWNS

Israel discloses that it plans to invest over $2 billion in 20 new towns and development projects in Negev desert near Kerem Shalom, along Israeli-Egyptian border; new communities will be home to approximately 4,000 Israelis now living in controversial Jewish settlements in Sinai Peninsula, which is to revert to Egypt during next 3 years following signing of an Israeli-Egyptian peace treaty; spokesman for the Jewish Agency, country's semi-governmental authority for Jewish immigration and settlement, notes that cost of moving families is estimated at about $50,000 each; plans are also being made for highways between Negev and Sinai and an international airport at Beersheba at estimated cost of $500 million (NEW YORK TIMES, October 11, 1978, P37)

SADAT SCORES OTHER ARABS

Egyptian President Sadat angrily declares he has done enough for other Arabs by concluding Camp David accords, and asserts he will now concentrate on achieving peace with Israel; seems particularly upset by verbal attacks he has suffered from Syria and PLO; implies he will no longer work on behalf of Palestinians and other Arabs who refuse to participate in details of framework for peace, asserting their ingratitude and obscenities have gone

beyond all limits; comments made shortly after Egyptian delegation left for US to attend peace talks   (NEW YORK TIMES, October 11, 1978, P25)

CARTER DISCUSSES MIDEAST AGREEMENT

President Carter, at nationally-televised news conference, maintains that two parts of Camp David peace agreement are not legally interconnected; holds, however, that in his mind, and in minds of Egyptian President Sadat and Israeli Prime Minister Begin, they are interrelated; statement seems carefully aimed at displeasing neither Sadat nor Begin, who disagree on question; Egypt claims Israel cannot have peace in Sinai without progress on talks involving West Bank and Gaza Strip, while Israel contends issues are entirely separate   (NEW YORK TIMES, October 11, 1978, P3)

POST-CAMP DAVID TALKS BEGIN

Ministerial-level conference in Washington, D.C., between Israel and Egypt begins October 12 to conclude separate peace accord; some US officials see possibility of agreement within 2-3 weeks; principal Israeli negotiators are Foreign Minister Moshe Dayan and Defense Minister Ezer Weizman; Egypt is represented by new Defense Minister Kamal Hassan Ali and Acting Foreign Minister Boutros Ghali; US will see State Secretary Cyrus Vance leading US negotiators on first day, and will thereafter be replaced by Middle East envoy Alfred Atherton; President Carter is not expected to be involved in day-to-day talks or at working level; questions to be discussed include exact timetable for withdrawal of Israeli troops to El Arish-Ras Muhammad line, location of UN forces on Egyptian side and UN observers on Israeli side, freedom of navigation of Israeli shipping in Suez Canal and possible Egyptian claims for compensation for oil extracted by Israel from Sinai in recent years   (NEW YORK TIMES, October 12, 1978, P15)

ECONOMIC RESULTS OF TREATY EXAMINED

Israel expects peace treaty with Egypt to be inflationary and expensive to implement in short run; must step up rather than cut defense spending to finance ongoing war in north with Syria and along Jordan River; needs special assistance to evacuate forces from Sinai, construct new military airfields to replace Sinai bases and resettle and compensate Israelis who were evacuated from Sinai; economists warn that massive expenditures may worsen balance of payments deficit, which reached $7.56 billion in 1977, and cause further drain of manpower from industry; however, expect agreement to cause surge in foreign Egyptian-Israeli trade in long run   (FINANCIAL TIMES, October 13, 1978, P4)

CARTER URGES BROADER SOLUTION

President Carter opens Egyptian-Israeli peace talks October 12 by saying accord between 2 nations should lead to broader Middle East peace and to solution of Palestinian question; urges that Jordan and Palestinian Arabs living in Jordan West Bank and Gaza Strip areas and other Arab states join search for negotiated peace; does not plan to directly participate in Washington, DC, talks on daily basis; Carter's remarks seem designed to strike balance between Israeli and Egyptian views   (NEW YORK TIMES, October 13, 1978, P32)

NEW DIFFICULTIES ENCOUNTERED

President Carter meets separately with Israeli and Egyptian delegations, tactic he used during Camp David summit when talks drifted apart, but insists there is no crisis in current round of Mideast peace talks; Israeli Foreign Minister Moshe Dayan reveals, however, that negotiations have encountered some difficulties, and notes Carter told delegates to turn to him if talks reached impasse; refuses to disclose nature of problems, but statement is first public indication talks are not going smoothly   (NEW YORK TIMES, October 18, 1978, P3)

MIDDLE EAST TALKS INTERRUPTED

Middle East peace talks are interrupted October 20 as Israeli delegation returns to Jerusalem for consultation on difficult issues; Israeli Foreign Minister Moshe Dayan says that he and Defense Minister Ezer Weizman were told to return home by the cabinet for about 3 days of meetings; shortly after Israeli announcement, both sides were summoned to White House for separate talks with President Carter and Egyptian chief negotiator said afterwards that he too would leave for consultations with Cairo   (NEW YORK TIMES, October 21, 1978, P12)

SYRIA, IRAQ SETTLING DIFFERENCES

Syrian officials report President Hafez al-Assad plans to visit Iraq to discuss dangers of Camp David agreements; sources reveal Assad and Iraqi President Ahmed Hassan al-Bakr also hope to reconcile differences between their rival Baathist Party regimes; note meeting represents first summit between Syria and Iraq in 15 years, and signifies most concrete move thus far to end bitter political feud between countries   (NEW YORK TIMES, October 22, 1978, P24)

SADAT REQUESTS FURTHER STUDY

Egyptian President Anwar el-Sadat's press secretary Zaghloul Nassar announces that Sadat has sent back final draft of proposed Egypt-Israel peace treaty to his delegation in Washington, D.C., for further study; spokesman does not identify problems; sources disclose that Sadat wants more precise wording on issue of "linkage" between Egypt's normalization of relations with Israel and progress toward Palestinian self-rule in West Bank of Jordan River and Gaza Strip   (NEW YORK TIMES, October 24, 1978, P20)

U.S. CRITICIZES ISRAELI ACTION

US rebukes Israel for announcing its intention to increase population in its existing settlements on West Bank of Jordan River, first through diplomatic channels, later in unusual public statement by State Secretary Cyrus Vance; US officials see new Israeli action as endangering Israel-

Egypt peace treaty; State Department spokesman Hodding Carter 3d concedes at press briefing that there had been no exchange of letters by US, Egypt or Israel on settlements, a lapse which he attributes to "fallibility of man"; Israeli diplomats say Prime Minister Menachem Begin had been disturbed over reports that Assistant US State Secretary Harold Saunders had promised Jordan's King Hussein US support for Jordanian claims on West Bank   (NEW YORK TIMES, October 27, 1978, P9)

NEW WEST BANK SETTLEMENTS ANNOUNCED

Prime Minister Begin announces that Israel will go ahead with expansion of settlements on West Bank; discloses no plans; however, one radio report indicates that plans include new factories in Jordan Valley, estimated 500 new apartments on West Bank and new roads linking settlements; Israel Radio quotes Agriculture Minister Ariel Sharon as saying expansion plans kept some cabinet members from voting against amended Israel-Egypt peace treaty   (NEW YORK TIMES, October 27, 1978, P16)

NOBEL PEACE PRIZE AWARDED

Egyptian President Sadat and Israeli Prime Minister Begin were awarded the 1978 Nobel Peace Prize for their efforts in trying to attain Mideast peace settlement; Norwegian Nobel Committee also lauded President Carter for role he played in bringing Sadat and Begin together   (NEW YORK TIMES, October 28, 1978, P4)

EGYPT TO CONTINUE NEGOTIATING

Personal intercession of President Carter has apparently led Egypt to retreat from its threat to recall its top delegates from Washington peace talks with Israel for consultations; President Sadat says Nobel Peace Prize, which he shares with Israeli Prime Minister Menachem Begin, is meant to honor entire Egyptian people; plans to donate his half of $165,000 prize money to his delta village of Mit Abul Kom, which is already receiving some royalties from his autobiography   (NEW YORK TIMES, October 29, 1978, P7)

SYRIAN-IRAQI RECONCILIATION DISCUSSED

Commentator Drew Middleton on rapprochement of Iraq and Syria in face of Camp David agreement between Israel and Egypt; Soviet military shipments to both Commentator Drew Middleton on rapprochement of Iraq believed to have been made conditional on cooperation between them; creation of combined Syrian-Iraqi military command, envisaged by joint committee established to promote cooperation, is expected to strengthen PLO, which would have in it a patron as powerful as Egypt and clearly more belligerent toward Israel; consensus among objective military and diplomatic sources in US and Europe is that overall situation in Middle East has deteriorated seriously since Camp David accords and opening of peace talks   (NEW YORK TIMES, October 29, 1978, P52)

SOURCE OF ISRAEL'S ANGER CITED

Columnists Rowland Evans and Robert Novak report that Israel's recent display of anger at President Carter results from top-secret US answers to questions by King Hussein of Jordan about future of Jewish settlements on West Bank; note answers indicate that Carter expects Israeli inhabitants of settlements to begin leaving Arab territory at end of five-year transitional period; note Israeli Prime Minister Begin is also infuriated by statement that US would support proposal to permit Arab inhabitants of East Jerusalem who are not Israeli residents to vote in election leading to self-rule; contends conflict between Carter and Begin threatens to delay Israeli-Egyptian peace negotiations and risks future US economic retaliation against Israel   (WASHINGTON POST,   October 30, 1978,   P23)

BEGIN DEFENDS SETTLEMENTS

Israeli Prime Minister Begin, with approval of his cabinet, responds to President Carter's sharp criticism of Israeli expansion of existing Jewish settlements on occupied West Bank; contents and tone of reply are not disclosed, but reports indicate it was sharply worded and contained points made by Begin during political rally October 26; at rally, Begin pledged to reaffirm right of Jewish people to settle any part of Israel; expansion announcement caused furor in US, where Israeli-Egyptian peace negotiations are stalemated, and its timing has been criticized in Israel and abroad   (NEW YORK TIMES,   October 30, 1978,   P6)

CARTER INTERVENES IN TALKS

Egyptian President Sadat complies with President Carter's urgent requests to cancel recall of Egyptian negotiators, and orders them to remain at treaty talks in Washington; action avoids another extended delay and gives lift to negotiations, which have been complicated by Israeli decision to enlarge West Bank settlements; also dramatizes Carter's personal involvement in talks (NEW YORK TIMES,   October 30, 1978,   P12)

ARAB LEAGUE STATES ITS POSITION

Arab League summit meeting ends in Baghdad, Iraq, with declaration calling on Egypt to renounce its peace accord with Israel and not to sign peace treaty; mentions no sanctions against Egypt or criticism of President Anwar Sadat; text of declaration reportedly indicates victory for conservative states, led by Saudi Arabia, which have been urging moderation in demands for punitive measures; final declaration states that conference regards Camp David accord as infringement of the rights of the Palestinian people and the Arab nation; reaffirms right of Palestinians to return to their homeland and PLO's role as their sole legitimate representative   (NEW YORK TIMES,   November 6, 1978,   P3)

FORMER C/S EXPRESSES DOUBTS

Former Israeli Army Chief of staff Mordechai Gur, in interview, expresses doubts about Israeli-Egyptian Camp David peace accords; believes Israel is lying to itself in seeking peace via Camp David framework; feels chance of another war with Egypt has not totally disappeared; maintains Israel should build up its military power, so that any future territorial adjustments will be based on Israel's strength at that time   (NEWSWEEK,   November 6, 1978,   P68)

PROGRESS REPORTED IN MIDEAST ACCORDS

Secretary of State Vance and Egyptian and Israeli negotiators in Washington have reportedly moved close to completing political and economic parts of Egyptian-Israeli peace accords and made progress on concluding military section; diplomats report, however, that earlier hopes of signing treaty by mid-week seem to have faded; reveal some compromises gained by Vance are being sharply questioned in Egypt and Israel so additional negotiations may be needed on issues that were thought to be resolved; key unresolved problem remains method of linking accord to movement by Israel toward settlement with its other Arab neighbors   (NEW YORK TIMES,   November 6, 1978,   P1)

ISRAEL REJECTS TREATY LANGUAGE

Israel's chief peace negotiators Foreign Minister Moshe Dayan and Defense Minister Ezer Weizman tell US State Secretary Vance that their government has rejected compromise language aimed at resolving crucial political issue delaying Egyptian-Israeli peace treaty; note Israeli Cabinet told them to seek elimination from treaty's preamble of linkage between document and subsequent steps toward overall Arab-Israeli peace settlement; Egyptian President Anwar Sadat considers linkage between treaty and other peace steps crucial factor in overall peace efforts   (NEW YORK TIMES,   November 9, 1978,   P4)

MODERATE ARABS CONFUSED

West Bank Palestinian Arabs are reported divided and bewildered in aftermath of Camp David peace accords; moderate Arabs have ceased to publicly give serious consideration to offer of self-rule in accords as various pro-PLO mayors, only visible Arab political entities, have denounced accords and lack of recognition in accords for PLO; mayors include Hassam Shakaa of Nablus, Karim Khalaf of Ramallah and Hassan Milhem of Halhoul; silence by Jordan's King Hussein is complicating moderates' dilemma as many are still on Hussein payroll   (NEW YORK TIMES,   November 11, 1978,   P2)

EGYPT ASKS FOR TIMETABLE

Egypt has reportedly asked Israel to agree in advance to detailed timetable on relinquishing military rule in West Bank and Gaza Strip and transferring control to Palestinian council; Israeli Foreign Minister Dayan, speaking to reporters in Washington before flying to Toronto to brief Prime Minister Begin on peace negotiations, asserts that President Sadat's demands would firmly link Egyptian-Israel peace treaty to a solution of Palestinian question and that Israel does not desire such linkage; sources report that Carter Administration is troubled about delays in negotiation   (NEW YORK TIMES, November 11, 1978, P1)

MAYORS DIVIDED ON ACCORDS

West Bank Palestinian Arabs are reported divided and bewildered in aftermath of Camp David peace accords; moderate Arabs have ceased to publicly give serious consideration to offer of self-rule in accords as various pro-Palestine Liberation Organization (PLO) mayors, only visible Arab political entities, have denounced accords and lack of recognition in accords for PLO; mayors include Hassam Shakaa of Nablus, Karim Khalat of Ramallah and Hassan Milhem of Halhoul; silence by Jordan's King Hussein is complicating moderates' dilemma as many are still on Hussein payroll   (NEW YORK TIMES, November 11, 1978, P2)

ISRAELI CABINET REJECTS TIMETABLE

Israeli Cabinet rejects Egypt's demands to link Egyptian-Israeli peace treaty to timetable for a civil-autonomy plan for West Bank and Gaza Strip; asserts demands violate agreements reached at Camp David summit talks and are therefore unacceptable; Prime Minister Begin will return to Israel November 13 after 2-week visit to US and Canada, and is expected to preside over special Cabinet session on peace talks November 14   (NEW YORK TIMES, November 13, 1978, P5)

SECRET COMMITMENTS TO EGYPT DENIED

Carter Administration officials maintain President Carter did not offer Egyptian President Sadat any secret commitments or guarantees regarding future of West Bank, Gaza Strip and East Jerusalem; statement follows report by Moroccan King Hassan II asserting Sadat had told him of receiving such assurances from Carter; officials report only US commitment beyond text of two Israeli-Egyptian accords, involving pledge to help Israel build airfields, was publicly disclosed shortly after Camp David conference ended   (NEW YORK TIMES, November 13, 1978, P16)

NEW LINKAGE FORMULA PROPOSED

Secretary of State Vance and Israeli Foreign Minister Moshe Dayan reach tentative agreement on new linkage formula to end deadlock in Egyptian-Israeli peace treaty negotiations, but formula must still be approved by Israeli and Egyptian governments; Vance and Dayan meet with Israeli Prime Minister Begin in New York City, but meeting is apparently inconclusive, with Begin noting unspecified problems remain; delays and deadlocks have been caused by fact that negotiators from Egypt and Israel have been able to reach agreements, but their governments at home have sought changes   (NEW YORK TIMES, November 13, 1978, P1)

MILITARY ACCORD MADE PUBLIC

Israeli television broadcast reveals details of military accord for Israeli withdrawal from Sinai, which is part of Egyptian-Israeli peace treaty; reports that although negotiators agreed fully on withdrawal plan, accord cannot be concluded because of disagreement over Egypt's demand that 9-month withdrawal be executed in stages; maintains Egypt wants to take over parts of Sinai earlier so it can demonstrate accomplishments before 9 months are up   (NEW YORK TIMES, November 13, 1978, P5)

CARTER URGES FLEXIBILITY

Israeli-Egyptian peace talks slow as Israeli Prime Minister Begin and Egyptian President Sadat prepare to meet with their negotiators to discuss latest US proposal on critical "linkage question," tying Egyptian-Israeli peace accord to settlement of other Middle East questions; President Carter urges both sides to be flexible and continue working to reach agreement; thinks it would be "horrible" if peace agreement fails and asserts that tiny technicalities and legalisms have no historical significance compared with advantages of peace; refuses to state which side is being more stubborn, maintaining both have demanded assurances far above those reached at Camp David   (NEW YORK TIMES, November 14, 1978, P1)

ISRAEL APPROVES TREATY DRAFT

Israeli Cabinet approves US-sponsored draft of Israeli-Egyptian peace treaty, but rejects Egypt's demands that treaty be linked to timetable for Palestinian autonomy on West Bank of Jordan River and in Gaza Strip; vote is 15-2; draft includes matter of "linkage" in generalized terms in preamble; Cabinet declares, in move to defuse linkage controversy, that Israel is ready to begin talks on Palestinian question after completion of treaty formalities with Egypt; Prime Minister Menachem Begin, announcing decision, declares that Israel is ready to sign as long as Egypt reciprocates   (NEW YORK TIMES, November 22, 1978, P1)

DAYAN SEEKS TO CLOSE DEBATE

Israeli Foreign Minister Moshe Dayan tells senior Israeli Foreign Ministry officials that draft peace treaty Israel approved November 21 should not be opened for amendment and that Egypt should "take it or leave it"; makes remarks in closed Foreign Ministry meeting; Foreign Ministry's spokesman emphasizes that "take it or leave it" remark applies equally to Israeli Cabinet (NEW YORK TIMES, November 23, 1978, P5)

EGYPTIAN PRESS PUBLISHES TREATY

Egyptian newspaper *Al Ahram* publishes what it describes as text of projected Egyptian-Israeli peace treaty; action surprises US officials, who view publication of text and controversial preamble as deliberate decision; State Department reports it is unclear whether Egypt is attempting to pressure Israel or US, or trying to undermine negotiations; text makes no direct mention of crucial linkage issue, while preamble deals with issue in general terms (NEW YORK TIMES, November 24, 1978, P1)

VANCE UPHOLDS FURTHER NEGOTIATIONS

Secretary of State Vance holds Israeli acceptance of draft text of peace treaty with Egypt is insufficient to permit conclusion of negotiations; disagrees with Israeli Foreign Minister Moshe Dayan, who stated there was no longer need for further negotiations and that Egypt should accept treaty text on "take it or leave it" basis; points out draft text fails to meet Egypt's demand for timetable on Palestinian autonomy in West Bank and Gaza Strip; hopes both sides will eventually agree to US compromise proposal committing Egypt and Israel to make effort to hold elections for autonomy by end of 1979 (NEW YORK TIMES, November 25, 1978, P1)

TREATY PUBLICATION EXAMINED

Cairo analysts believe surprise publication of Israeli-Egyptian peace treaty text in *Al Ahram* newspaper was designed to demonstrate to Arab critics that Egypt is not negotiating separate peace; draft, identified as US-proposed compromise treaty approved by Israeli Cabinet, was obtained in Washington several days ago, leading to speculation there were consultations on decision to print text (NEW YORK TIMES, November 25, 1978, P4)

SADAT DISAPPOINTED AT DELAY

Egyptian President Anwar Sadat expresses disappointment in delay in reaching Israeli-Egyptian peace treaty; says it is certain elements in Israeli political parties, not Israeli people, who are responsible for obstruction; stresses key point of difficulty is linkage between Israeli-Egyptian treaty and autonomy on Gaza and West Bank; says he would like to meet again with President Carter and Israeli Prime Minister Menachem Begin; fears Saudi Arabia may be drifting toward "hardline" Arab nations; indicates he is not counting on receiving more arms from US (NEWSWEEK, November 27, 1978, P46)

JORDAN, P.L.O. IN PARLEY

Jordan and Palestine Liberation Organization (PLO) leaders agree on policy of noninterference in each other's internal affairs, after 3 days of talks in Jordan; meeting is expected to involve other political issues, such as possible joint stand against Israel and against autonomy plan for West Bank and Gaza Strip (NEW YORK TIMES, November 28, 1978, S2 P20)

BEGIN, STAFF CONSULT

Israel's Prime Minister Begin reportedly is consulting with aides about whether Israel should reopen stalled peace negotiations; meanwhile, Israeli Army engineering corps reports that it has started preparing ground for alternate military bases behind future "new borders" with Egypt; move is noted as indicating expectations for eventual treaty agreement with Egypt (NEW YORK TIMES, December 2, 1978, P4)

MIDEAST NEGOTIATIONS TO RESUME

State Secretary Vance reports that both Egypt and Israel have indicated that peace treaty negotiations will be resumed at unspecified date; US officials note that purpose of extended negotiations with Egypt's Prime Minister Mustafa Khalil is to persuade Egypt to drop its request for changes in Article 6 of draft treaty which states that treaty should have precedence over any other document signed by Egypt in past; in related development, Representative Paul Findley discloses statement by PLO leader Yasir Arafat during Damascus interview; reports that Arafat pledged that PLO would renounce violent means to enlarge an independent Palestinian state in West Bank and Gaza Strip, give de facto recognition to Israel and "live at peace" with Israelis (NEW YORK TIMES, December 2, 1978, P1)

BEGIN SUGGESTS INTERPRETATIVE LETTERS

Israeli Prime Minister Begin sends message to Egypt's President Sadat reportedly stating Israel would be willing, not to renegotiate peace treaty draft, but to discuss letters which would interpret treaty; has reportedly again rejected Egypt's demand for a timetable for autonomy of occupied lands; Israeli officials comment that self-governing machinery must necessarily precede such a timetable; meanwhile, Gaza Mayor Rashad Shawa contends that if Israelis really supported self-determination they would not build new settlements or maintain control over land ownership (NEW YORK TIMES, December 5, 1978, P1)

ARABS DEMONSTRATE ON WEST BANK

Arabs demonstrate in Ramallah on West Bank of Jordan to protest demolition of home of alleged Palestinian terrorist Abdul-Rahman Abdul-Fatah; Egyptian Foreign Ministry asserts that razing of West Bank houses by Israeli Army represents a threat to peace and security in Middle East; Fatah claims 800 soldiers attacked his house, but his wife claims they numbered 2,000 (NEW YORK TIMES, December 7, 1978, P7)

NOBEL PEACE PRIZE ACCEPTED

Israeli Prime Minister Begin and Egyptian President Sadat's personal representative Sayed Marei accept Nobel Peace Prize in Oslo, Norway, for leaders' work in trying to end Middle East wars; speeches of both leaders pledge to continue peace efforts, and both describe differences blocking peace treaty; Sadat's speech emphasizes rights of Palestinians and need for comprehensive peace settlement, while Begin reiterates his satisfaction with peace treaty draft document   (NEW YORK TIMES,   December 11, 1978,   P1)

PRO-ARAB BIAS SUSPECTED

Leaks of Assistant Secretary of State Harold Saunders' official US replies to Jordanian King Hussein's 14 questions on Camp David accords have fueled Israeli suspicion that US State Department and possibly White House have anti-Israel or at least pro-Arab bias; *Time* magazine, which has obtained complete text of answers, reports that many of questions and answers were not controversial or provocative   (TIME,   December 11, 1978,   P57)

VANCE REPORTS TREATY DEADLOCK

Israel rejects new proposals for peace treaty offered by State Secretary Vance and Egypt's President Sadat; Vance telephones President Carter from Israel to report that major differences remain, not only between Israel and Egypt, but also between Israel and US; Carter agrees that Vance should return to US December 15 after a final meeting with Israelis December 14 and overnight stop in Cairo; second summit meeting between Sadat, Begin and Carter to conclude treaty seen as possibility   (NEW YORK TIMES,   December 14, 1978,   P1)

CARTER PRESSURES ISRAELI CABINET

Carter Administration spokesman reports that US will suspend its mediating efforts if Israeli Cabinet rejects latest US proposals for Egyptian-Israeli treaty; stresses that US is not withdrawing entirely; President Carter comments that treaty acceptance is now up to Israel and rules out early reconvening of Camp David summit conference; Carter declares that he does not believe Israel's interests are threatened by terms holding up treaty; Administration sources suggest that main purpose of State Secretary Vance's recall from Middle East is to jolt Israel into serious consideration of proposals; American Jewish Committee assails Administration for unfairly criticizing Israel before it has had chance to explain itself; Israeli sources report that 2 new elements introduced by President Sadat are exchange of ambassadors linked to establishment of Arab self-government in occupied areas and proposed letter containing US interpretation of controversial part of Article 6 of draft treaty   (NEW YORK TIMES,   December 15, 1978,   P1)

ISRAEL REJECTS EGYPTIAN PROPOSALS

Israeli Cabinet rejects new peace proposals by Egypt; proposals, brought to Israel by US State Secretary Vance,

include call for delay in exchanging ambassadors until after Palestinian autonomy has been set up, target date of December 1979 for such autonomy in West Bank and Gaza Strip, review of security arrangements in Sinai after 5 years and recognition of Egypt's inter-Arab obligations in interpretive note; Prime Minister Begin declares that talks will continue but is unable to give date for such talks; says he would be willing to attend another summit conference called by US on matter if needed   (NEW YORK TIMES,   December 16, 1978,   P1)

ISRAELI CABINET STATEMENT SCORED

Carter Administration, irked by Israeli Cabinet's rejection of new peace proposals advanced by Egypt, accuses Israel of distorting nature of those proposals; reporters on plane carrying State Secretary Vance back to Washington are told that Cabinet statement is intemperate, poorly timed and partly contradicts Prime Minister Begin's statements to Vance during visit; examples of Israeli "distortions": Israel's claim that call for review of security arrangements in Sinai after 5 years is "basic change" of Camp David accords, although Israel's leaders agree that Article 4 needs clarification; Israel's claim that interpretive note on Article 6 "negates" its contents; Israel's complaint on delay in exchange of ambassadors, which, US says, is not required at all by Camp David accords   (NEW YORK TIMES,   December 16, 1978,   P1)

DISORDERS IN WEST BANK TOWN

Young Palestinians throw stones at Israeli patrols in Bethlehem, and youths from Halhoul block highway with 2 burning trucks to protest recent takeover of Arab land by Israeli military; Israeli soldiers disperse demonstrators and restore order after imposing curfew on Halhoul; Bethlehem Mayor Elias Freij asserts protestors were "kids" and that incident was not really confrontation with Israeli forces, but warns there is anger and unrest on West Bank over

Cyrus R. Vance, U.S. Secretary of State, flanks Sadat, Carter and Begin on national television as the three sign agreements generated by the Camp David summit.

Israel's plans for new settlements in occupied lands   (NEW YORK TIMES,   December 17, 1978,   P3)

P.L.O. COMPROMISE RELATED

Palestine Liberation Organization (PLO) French representative Ibrahim Souss, speaking to American Club in Paris, asserts PLO is prepared to cease hostile acts against Israel and to give Israel de facto recognition if Palestinian state is created on West Bank and Gaza Strip; reports proposal was outlined to Representative Paul Findley by PLO leader Yasir Arafat, and is considered major concession that has not been matched by any concession from Israel   (NEW YORK TIMES,   December 20, 1978,   P6)

P.L.O. ATTACK KILLS ONE

Palestinian rockets strike apartment building in Qiryat Shemona, Israel, killing 1 and wounding 9; many residents reportedly escaped injury because they were in artillery-resistant rooms built because of frequent shellings; USSR-supplied rockets, which have range of 15 miles, allow Palestinians to fire on northern Israeli towns from sites north of Litani River in Lebanon   (NEW YORK TIMES, December 22, 1978,   P15)

A Cautious Gathering At the Summit

By HEDRICK SMITH

WASHINGTON — The differences were hidden in the nuances and the delicate turns of diplomatic phrases, because both President Anwar el-Sadat of Egypt and Prime Minister Menachem Begin of Israel made their pilgrimage to Camp David in the common cause of peace, but the differences were there.

As if sworn to silence on the substance, they spoke in brief generalities at the welcoming ceremonies. Even so, they betrayed their differing personalities and aspirations, hinted at their contradictory strategies, and intimated their opposing views on the role they hope President Carter would play in the following crucial week.

Mr. Sadat, the tall, elegant Arab visionary given to the bold and unpredictable gesture, spoke in sweeping terms. Mr. Begin, the prim, proper, practical parliamentarian with a lawyer's eye for detail, was more modest, more precise.

The Israeli leader called this "the most momentous" of his five meetings with Mr. Carter and his three with Mr. Sadat, but quickly sought to deflate exaggerated expectations by treating the summit as one of a series on the long road toward an ultimate middle East settlement, not at all a make-it-or-break-it get-together as the Egyptians have portrayed it.

"We will make all endeavors possible so that the peace process can continue," Mr. Begin said cautiously, squinting through rimless spectacles into a warm afternoon sun.

Just two hours before, Mr. Sadat had conveyed a grander vision and a greater sense of urgency, "we cannot afford to fail the hopes of nations around the world," he declared, underscoring his own political need for some tangible breakthrough to justify to his fellow Arabs the peace initiative that he launched in Jerusalem last November. "This is no time for maneuvers in wornout ideas," he went on, obviously inviting some new proposals from Begin. "It is a time for magnanimity and reason."

Mr. Begin put his emphasis on the aching Israeli desire for peace. Mr. Sadat made it "peace with justice," a term that Arabs have long used to signify their demand for the return of occupied land and the right of return for Arab refugees from Palestine.

And finally, it was the Egyptian leader, flanked by Vice President Mondale and Secretary of State Cyrus R. Vance, who appealed openly for President Carter to intervene forcefully in the negotiating ahead.

The United States, he declared, is the nation "most qualified to be a full partner in the peace process" rather than merely the more hesitant "honest broker" that Mr. Begin would prefer. And then in closing, the Egyptian added lavishly that Mr. Carter had embarked on "a brave and gallant act of statesmanship" in merely convening what Mr. Sadat chose to dignify as "this conference."

Already, Mr. Carter has signified his intention to play the kind of activist role that the Egyptians prefer. This plus his talk of mandatory compromises has seemed to put Mr. Begin and his colleagues a bit on guard as they journeyed to the President's Maryland mountain retreat last Tuesday.

But even if Mr. Carter and his diplomatic experts believe that Mr. Begin may be asked to make the most painful concessions, they have shown a keen sense of the delicacy of the moment and the need for public even-handedness.

As the two visitors arrived at Andrews Air Force Base outside Washington for their formal welcome, Mr. Mondale struck a careful balance.

He welcomed Sadat with expressions of American respect for his "wisdom, courage, statesmanship." To the Israeli Prime Minister, he spoke admiringly of his leadership — "its genius, its passion, its strength" — and above all of his "commitment to peace."

If anything, the special warmth for Mr. Begin reflects the Administration's assessment that the confrontation between Mr. Carter and the Israeli leader last March, which nearly broke into the open, was a costly mistake, not to be repeated at this sensitive juncture.

Washington has worked hard to bring Mr. Begin back to the center of the peace diplomacy after Mr. Sadat tried to negotiate over his head with the Israeli Defense Minister, Ezer Weizman, and with the opposition leader, Shimon Peres. The American view is that this was a serious miscalculation that enabled Begin to rally public support.

Now, Mr. Carter evidently hopes that with gentle cajolery he can probe Mr. Begin's position for private flexibility in the hope that the Israeli leader, as well as Mr. Sadat, will be more committed to the cause of peace than he is wedded to retention of control over all of the occupied Arab lands on the west Bank and in Gaza.

The talks began gently and modestly, behind a veil of near total secrecy because of the President's conviction that both sides were more likely to compromise if they didn't have to worry about how they would look in the press until the entire round of negotiations was completed.

On Tuesday evening, Mr. Carter held a three-and-a-half hour exploratory session with Prime Minister Begin, presumably to sound him out on any new ideas or changes in the 26-point plan for limited local rule on the West Bank that the Israeli Premier had surfaced last December. Then, Wednesday morning, the American leader held a similar session with President Sadat before bringing the two adversaries together Wednesday afternoon for their first try at negotiating.

The American expectation is that the talks will stretch on for possibly as much as ten days, assuming that the first couple of days were needed by both sides to let off steam, restate some of their familiar positions and to establish some of the rapport and optimism that they felt last November during Mr. Sadat's spectacular visit to Jerusalem.

If little omens matter, the first harbingers were mildly favorable. President Sadat and Prime Minister Begin bumped into each other when they were out for a midday stroll Wednesday on the 134-acre Presidential retreat. At this first encounter, it was later disclosed, they exchanged brief pleasantries and each remarked to the other: "You look good and healthy." Then, they joined Mr. Carter in issuing a prayer for "peace and justice."

NYT Weekly Review, September 10, 1978, P1

Old Issues Bedevil A New Forum

By CHARLES MOHR

THURMONT, Maryland — The participants in the Camp David summit conference on the Middle East discovered, as have so many others on the same search before, that there is no quick road to peace in that troubled area.

The news from the meeting was deliberately kept to a minimum but reporters were able to get the general drift of where the discussions were heading. At one stage for example, it was learned that President Carter apparently had been trying to get some concessions from Israel — without much success.

"Getting Israel to move was the problem all along, even before the summit began," said one official. And he remained ambivalent about the chances for success.

"It's too early to make a judgment either way," he said at that stage.

The talks among President Carter, President Anwar el-Sadat of Egypt and Prime Minister Menachem Begin of Israel, as expected, focussed on the issues of the Israeli-occupied West Bank of the Jordan River and the future of the Palestinian Arabs. According to Mr. Carter's press secretay, Jody Powell, it was on those questions that the President made an "intense effort."

When the leaders and their principal advisers took several hours off to tour the Civil War battlefield at nearby Gettysburg, Pennsylvania, an Egyptian journalist asked Israel's defense minister Ezer Weizman how things looked.

"We need another two or three days more for things to crystalize," said the tall and grizzled Mr. Weizman in the Arabic language, which he speaks. Then he added, in the same language, "Not yet."

The so-called Camp David summit conference, which began in earnest the previous week at Mr. Carter's official mountaintop retreat near here, proceeded at a patient and deliberate pace. After the battlefield tour, Mr. Carter, Prime Minister Begin and their advisers met for a bilateral meeting.

All three leaders did spend considerable amount of time together in Mr. Carter's limousine going to, making and coming from the battlefield tour. Meanwhile, it was also learned that defense Minister Weizman last week met alone with President Sadat, with whom he has established good personal rapport. It was the second such meeting between the Egyptian president and the Israeli defense minister since the talks began.

The conference is unusual in several ways. In most cases summit conferences are called only to ratify agreements reached in painstaking lower-level diplomacy. But decades of diplomacy, no matter how painstaking, have not resolved the Middle East problem, and Mr. Carter convened this meeting to try top-level negotiation.

Thus, both the character and the length of the summit have been unusual.

Since the summit was convened, Mr. Carter has kept his guests tightly isolated in Camp David and has imposed a lid of secrecy to prevent the Egyptians and Israelis from competitive and selective "leaks" of news meant to make the other side look bad.

Thus, considerable efforts were made to prevent the battlefield tour from turning into a running press conference, and those efforts succeeded for practical purposes.

The three leaders and such advisers as Mr. Weizman, Israeli Foreign Minister Moshe Dayan and Egyptian Foreign Minister Muhammed Kamil, all of them wearing the blue jackets with a "Camp David" breast patch given to such guests at the camp, made their first stop at the Virginia Monument, which is surrounded by a statue of Robert E. Lee on horseback.

From this point, the group could view

the mile of undulating terrain across which, on the afternoon of July 3, 1863, General Lee had launched a charge by almost 13,000 Southern infantry men on the Union lines on Cemetery Ridge.

When a reporter did manage to ask Mr. Carter a question, it was whether the South could have won the battle.

"Yes, with. tanks," said the American President. Then he said that the Confederacy could have used such military men as President Sadat, Mr. Dayan and Mr. Weizman.

Asked how the talks were going, Mr. Begin said with a smile, "It is going well, as you can see."

Although a National Park service historian was along to explain the intricacies of the Gettysburgs battle, Mr. Carter also did a good deal of explaining to Mr. Sadat, who was dressed in a camel-hair sportsjacket and black turtleneck shirt, and Mr. Begin who wore a vested suit and tie.

As the leaders gathered to inspect tarnished old 19th century cannon and discuss the details of such antiquated ordinance, Mr. Carter was heard at one point to say that while a smooth bore cannon had a range of a mile and a rifled artillery piece a range of 3½ miles "The C.B.U. only ranged 300 to 400 yards."

The entire group of leaders broke into laughter. The remark may have seen enigmatic. It appeared to be a reference to the use of "cannister" charges by the Union artillery that shattered the Confederate charge of July 3. Cannister consisted of a container of steel pellets shot from the muzzle of such 19th century cannon.

C.B.U. stands for Cluster Bomb Unit, an aerial bomb weapon that shatters hundreds of steel balls in a lethal pattern. The United States used such weapons in Vietnam, and later furnished them to Israel which has used them in combat against Arab states. The militarily sophisticated group of negotiators, most of them former military officers, seem to have no difficulty in understanding Mr. Carter's remark.

The group also visited the place where President Lincoln delivered the Gettysburg Address as well as other major battlefield landmarks.

Mr. Begin also found another diversion. He played several games of chess with Zbignien Brzezinski, Mr. Carter's national security adviser.

NYT Weekly Review, September 17, 1978, P1

A Surprising Summit, But So Far Peace is Partial

By HEDRICK SMITH

WASHINGTON — The Camp David summit marked a spectacular success for the personal diplomacy of President Carter, an unexpectedly solid breakthrough for Prime Minister Menachem Begin of Israel, and a calculated out parlous gamble for President Anwar el - Sadat of Egypt.

In spite of the euphoria of the moment, the participants themselves conceded that a multitude of pitfalls and obstacles could upset the fragile agreements and, indeed, snags appeared almost at once.

Yet whatever ultimately happens, Mr. Carter emerged an indisputable political winner. He strengthened his Presidency by having dared to undertake such a risky exercise in peacemaking, and by having engineered not only more progress than any previous American President — in his own words, "far more substance than anyone dreamed."

From the first reactions in Israel, it was apparent that Prime Minister Begin risked a domestic political furor by overturning several cherished Israeli positions. But, as his ebullience at the signing ceremonies suggested, he sensed that he had permanently altered the political landscape of the Middle East by bringing within reach a separate Egyptian-Israeli peace treaty. That alone, if it comes to pass as the Camp David agreements envision, will transform the political dynamics of the Middle East and radically reduce the risk of war.

It was President Sadat of Egypt, having accommodated the prime Israeli urge for a peace treaty, who seemed to have conceded the most and risked compounding his political isolation in the Arab world. Not only the angry reaction from some Arab capitals but the resignation of his own foreign minister signaled the perils of the course he has taken.

For he came to Camp David saying he would rather accept failure than compromise on Arab principles and left having settled for less — no pledge of ultimate Israeli withdrawal from the West Bank and Gaza Strip, considerably less than unfettered Palestinian self-determination, and no more than a vague expression of intent on the right of return for 1.2 million Palestinian refugees.

Mr. Sadat won a good deal but still gambled heavily. He gambled that he would win a ringing support at home for achieving for Egypt what no one thought he could — Israel's promise to give up all the Egyptian territory she has captured since 1948 — and that he gained enough of an opening wedge on the West Bank and Gaza Strip to pass the burden of those negotiations essentially to King Hussein of Jordan and moderate Palestinians themselves.

Far more than Mr. Begin, Mr. Sadat gambled on the process of history. He made his bet that the Israeli withdrawal, now to begin, and the process of turning over fragments of power to the Arabs on the West Bank and Gaza Strip, would prove irreversible, and that in time even Israelis would see benefit in carrying it further.

Even more fundamentally, he gambled that President Carter would feel so deeply committed personally to see the Camp David accords fulfilled that he would not let the process stop.

Yet even though Mr. Carter thrust himself front and center, even going so far as to break the deadlock by offering an American peace formula, he did so without involving the United States in policing the ultimate agreement. So far, Washington's only promise is to build two airfields for Israel in the Negev to replace those she is giving up on Sinai. Although the full intricacies of the negotiations have yet to be revealed, it is clear that Prime Minister Begin's tactic was to trade away major concessions on the Sinai front and minor ones elsewhere in order to keep vital controls and security protection on the West Bank and Gaza.

He was throwing his most touchy political issue, Egypt's demand that Israel dismantle its settlements on Sinai, to the Israeli Knesset. Yet, in spite of quick opposition, he was evidently confident that Israelis would see this worth the price of peace itself.

But he himself acknowledged for the first time "the legitimate rights of the Palestinians," agreed to have Palestinians from the West Bank and Gaza take part in negotiations on the future of those areas and ultimately to ratify or reject the final agreement. He promised a temporary freeze on Israeli settlements on the West Bank, pledged to reduce Israeli security forces from roughly 11,000 to 6,000 in that region, and accepted "full autonomy" for a local governing authority of Palestinians with its own police force.

But as the Israeli Prime Minster pointed out in a radio interview, he did all that without promising to pull out totally from the West Bank and Gaza Strip. When someone asked if Israeli troops might still be there in ten-fifteen years, he replied: "Why not?"

He also kept Israeli veto power over the establishment of an independent Palestinian state as well as a veto over participation in negotiations by leaders of the Palestine Liberation Organization, whom Israel considers objectionable. And he shrewdly set aside the explosive question of the ultimate sovereignty over the West Bank and Gaza.

The Americans have made a point of separating the Egyptian-Israeli peace negotiations from the broader framework of negotiations in the West Bank and other areas. But as one official conceded, "Legally they are not linked, but you have to face the political realities. Lack of progress on the West Bank is certainly going to affect Sadat's attitude on his own peace treaty. So is reaction in the rest of the Arab world." Washington expected such Arab radicals as the Soviet Union, to denounce the Camp David accords. What is critical in the next few days is the reaction of moderate Arabs in Jordan and Saudi Arabia.

If Mr. Sadat can gain King Hussein's collaboration and at least tacit support from Saudi Arabia, despite initial negative reactions from both, the Camp David agreements will stand a chance of practical fulfillment. With that response, one American negotiator remarked, "Much will depend on the good will and good faith" of the Egyptians and Israelis in the next three months.

NYT Weekly Review, September 24, 1978, P1

Among the Arabs, The Old Dilemmas Now Get Sharper

By JAMES M. MARKHAM

MADRID — The strategy and content of the Camp David agreements are unspoken, posthumous triumphs for the step-by-step diplomacy fathered by Secretary of State Henry Kissinger in the two years after the 1973 Middle East war — a method criticized by Jimmy Carter as he first reached the presidency.

The Kissinger approach was that the sheer military and political weight of Egypt, in quiet alliance with Saudi Arabia, was sufficient to drag the bulk of the Arab world in its wake. The second Israeli-Egyptian Sinai disengagement agreement of September 1975 was bitterly attacked by Mr. Sadat's Arab enemies, but it held. Camp David amounts to the third accord, and possibly more.

With an Israeli evacuation from the Egyptian Sinai in sight, the next "step" is, logically, Jordan, which is now placed in the painful position of watching Egypt drift off into a separate peace with Israel or making a decision to itself join the process started at Camp David. If King

Hussein chooses the second option, he will surely be buffeted by verbal blasts from next-door Syria—not to speak of the bitter hostility of the Palestine Liberation Organization, which has a moral claim on many of his own Palestinian subjects.

Jordan and also Saudi Arabia, which in the American strategy must be the Arab anchor of any Middle East settlement, issued statements criticizing and distancing themselves from the Camp David conclusions. But each statement left a loophole: The Saudis say they have no right to prevent "any Arab country" from regaining conquered territory and the Jordanians entered the ambiguous caveat that the Hashemite kingdom "will not hesitate to exercise its responsibilities and role toward the cause of peace in the area and in safeguarding and defending the rights of the Palestinian people."

"I would see them as holding positions," said a well-placed Western diplomat in Amman who, like others, thought the negative tone of the Saudi and Jordanian declarations were aimed at Arab popular consumption. "It's very wait-and-see. People here were surprised how much

UPI

King Hussein

detail there was in the Camp David agreements.''

What the Saudis and the Jordanians undoubtedly wanted to know from Secretary of State Cyrus R. Vance as he visited their capitals was what guarantees the United States could provide that after the five-year transitional period envisaged in the Camp David accord the Israelis will relinquish their hold on the West Bank and the Gaza Strip. Moreover, they would ask what assurances the Americans could give that some Arab access or control over East Jerusalem, seized by Israel in 1967, will one day be restored.

As the man being asked to step next into the negotiations, King Hussein is dammed if he does and damned if he doesn't, and will now have to choose between risking Arab or American displeasure. His kingdom is heavily subsidized by the United States — and by the Saudis — and by joining the Camp David momentum he can rescue Mr. Carter's argument that a "framework" for peace in the Middle East has been negotiated, not just an Egyptian-Israeli deal.

The King is being asked, in effect, to jettison, as was Mr. Sadat, the 1974 Rabat Arab resolution that declared the P.L.O. "the sole legitimate representative of the Palestinian people," and move into a kind of joint occupation of the West Bank with the Israelis. But so far, he has no guarantee that the West Bank will finally be linked with the East Bank of his kingdom; nor have the Israelis shown any sign of giving the Hashemite monarch a share of Jerusalem.

The King is known to be eager to recover the West Bank, even though many of his advisers are opposed to policing an area whose Palestinian inhabitants have angry memories of harsh Hashemite rule prior to Israel's 1967 conquest. The diplomatic problem will be to find a formula that makes King Hussein look like the vehicle for fulfilling Palestinian aspirations — not a dictator called in by Washington to snuff them out. Absorption of the West Bank will make Jordan overwhelmingly Palestinian in population, a long-term worry for the King.

One of King Hussein's main calculations as he makes, or sidesteps, the next step Washington has in mind will be his judgment of Anwar el-Sadat's staying power in Egypt. This, in turn, will pivot importantly on what the Saudis, who keep Mr. Sadat's regime financially afloat, tell the King privately. With Arab opinion being stirred by radios in Damascus, Baghdad and Tripoli against Camp David, public statements may for some time be a bad guide to the true comportment of Arab regimes.

This is perhaps nowhere more true than in Syria, which sharply attacked the Camp David accords -- which themselves

Associated Press

President Sadat (left), Mrs. Rosalyn Carter and Prime Minister Begin.

conspicuously failed to mention the Israeli-occupied Golan Heights. But President Hafez al-Assad has been in close touch with King Hussein, and agreed to receive Mr. Vance in Damascus.

Syria's predicament reveals the tough, realpolitik assumptions of Henry Kissinger — and now, it seems, Jimmy Carter — on the Middle East. Bereft of a military ally in Cairo, Damascus cannot contemplate a war with Israel; Mr. Assad knows the thin, bottom-line value of the support of the Arab "steadfastness" states that gathered in his capital last week. If King Hussein falls into place, Hafez al-Assad may ultimately have no choice but to follow suit, protesting all the way to the conference table.

"Assad will do nothing, absolutely nothing, for my reasons," Henry Kissinger once complained. "For me to want something is nothing for Assad. It's what he wants — that's what counts. He's very intelligent."

What President Assad wants today, probably even more than getting the Israelis off the Golan Heights, is a free

hand in Lebanon, where 35,000 Syrian soldiers are mired in a bloody slugging match with 10,000 entrenched Maronite Christian irregulars, armed and openly supported by Israel. Israel's backing of the Maronites gives it a lever over Syrian behavior, not only in Lebanon but on the broader Middle East front. In a similar manner, so does the United States influence over Israel's behavior in Lebanon.

As far as Syria is concerned, the beginnings of an eventual peace, or war, could take shape in Lebanon, at the expense of armed Lebanese and Palestinian bands that over the last three years have been converted into little more than proxies for Arab and Israeli interests. Baldly put, what Mr. Assad has to offer the United States (and Israel) is his army's ability to pacify all of Lebanon, including the Palestinian guerrillas, allies of the moment; the price could be acknowledgement that Syria is the paramount power in Lebanon and Israel's abandonment of its newfound Christian allies there.

Should Jordan, and then Syria, be hauled

in Egypt's wake into the Camp David momentum, the big losers, of course, would be the Beirut-based leadership of the Palestine Liberation Organization. The Camp David documents, with their provisions for a Palestinian police force, elections and local government institutions, were clearly crafted to split the Palestinian community between the several million living in exile and the 1.1 million living under Israeli occupation.

So far, there is little sign that such a schism has started, and P.L.O. strength is great on the West Bank and Gaza. But if West Bank Palestinians saw an op-

portunity of ridding themselves of the Israeli occupation, even if it meant falling under Hashemite rule again, there seems little doubt that some would come forward and collaborate with the semi-autonomous bodies limned in the Camp David documents.

A scenario of Jordan and then Syria falling into place, step-by-step, probably rests, however, on an American ability to wrest from the Israelis firmer commitments that the lands they occupied in 1967 will, in large measure, become Arab again. Sinai has always been the easiest chunk of captured territory for the Israelis to think about letting go, but even there

Mr. Begin has felt he must saddle the Knesset with the decision to abandon the Sinai settlements, which are useful to the Israeli Air Force.

There is no mention in the Camp David accords of the future of the West Bank settlements, which, like the question of Jewish land purchases, are irritants to Arab pride and perceptions of sovereignty. Leaving the West Bank will be far harder for the Israelis to swallow than leaving Sinai — not to speak of perhaps one day "Vaticanizing" East Jerusalem or pulling down off Syria's Golan Heights.

NYT Weekly Review, September 24, 1978, P3

Arab League Appeals to Egyptians To Renounce Accord With Israelis

BAGHDAD, Iraq, Nov. 5 (Reuters) — The Arab League summit meeting ended tonight with an unexpectedly mild declaration calling on Egypt to renounce its peace accord with Israel and not to sign a peace treaty, but with no mention of sanctions against Egypt or direct criticism of President Anwar el-Sadat.

Conference sources said there might have been some secret agreement on action to frustrate Egyptian and Israeli peace plans. But even if the 21 leaders meeting here — representing all the Arab League nations except Egypt — have decided to impose a political or economic boycott against Cairo, the text of the declaration indicated a victory for conservative states, led by Saudi Arabia, which have been urging moderation in the face of demands for harsh punitive measures.

The mild action came as a surprise in a conference marked by major steps toward unity of radical forces. Just today, Iraq and the Palestine Liberation Organization, opponents in a bloody underground war earlier this year, agreed to patch up their differences. A similar reconciliation came yesterday between two former enemies, King Hussein of Jordan and the P.L.O.'s leader, Yasir Arafat.

After presenting the final announcement, Foreign Minister Saadun Hamadi of Iraq indicated there were secret decisions when he said: "I cannot disclose the

specific resolutions." He confirmed that the group had discussed imposing a boycott on Egypt, but he would not elaborate.

Opinion on Camp David Accord

The final declaration, read by Mr. Hammadi, said the conference regarded the Camp David accord as an infringement of the rights of the Palestinian people and the Arab nation.

The Arab leaders said the accord contradicted resolutions of previous Arab summit meetings and would not lead to a just peace in the Middle East. They reaffirmed their "non-approval" of the peace plan and their refusal to accept its consequences.

The summit meeting stressed the need for Arab unity in order to deal with the "strategic defect" caused by Egypt's withdrawal from the conflict with Israel.

The declaration reaffirmed the Palestinians' right to return to their homeland and the P.L.O.'s role as their sole legitimate representative. It called on all Arab states to give the P.L.O. their maximum support.

President Ahmed Hassan al-Bakr of Iraq said the meeting had succeeded in preserving the unity of Arab ranks and had proved the Arabs' determination to uphold the principles of freedom, dignity and justice.

Status of Jerusalem

King Hussein promised to stand fast in

defense of Arab rights in the occupied territories, especially the restoration of Jerusalem to the Arabs. Sources said the King delayed a state visit to West Germany to stay for the entire conference.

Crown Prince Fahd of Saudi Arabia, pledging to work for the liberation of Jerusalem from Israeli rule, said he hoped the next Arab summit conference would be held in the holy city. He also said the Arabs hoped "sisterly Egypt" would rejoin the Arab society.

Earlier today, the conferees had seemed certain to announce measures against Egypt, especially after President Sadat yesterday bluntly rejected an offer of $50 billion over 10 years to abandon his unilateral peace initiative.

Well-informed sources at the meeting, however, said the conservative states, led by Saudi Arabia, were still trying to exert a moderating influence, and they apparently succeeded to some extent.

The sources said the conferees considered several measures against Egypt if Mr. Sadat signs a definitive peace treaty, including cutting all political and diplomatic ties, cutting off aid, boycotting Egyptian companies which dealt with Israel, and expelling Egypt from the Arab League and moving the organization's headquarters from Cairo to another Arab capital.

NEW YORK TIMES, November 6, 1978, P3

Text of Draft Treaty Published in Cairo

CAIRO, Nov. 23 (UPI) — Following is an unofficial translation from the Arabic of what the Cairo newspaper Al Ahram said was the draft text of a proposed peace treaty between Israel and Egypt:.

The Governments of the Arab Republic of Egypt and the State of Israel:

Preamble:

Convinced of the urgent necessity of

establishing a just, overall and durable peace in the Middle East, in accordance with the U.N. Security Council Resolutions 242 and 338;

Affirming the commitment of the two Governments to the peace framework

agreed at Camp David on Sept. 17, 1978;

Noting that the above-mentioned framework is a suitable framework intended to constitute a basis for peace, not only between Egypt and Israel, but also between Israel and each of her other Arab neighbors that are ready to negotiate peace with her on this basis;

Wishing to end the state of war between them and establish peace that would allow all states of the region to live in security;

Convinced that the conclusion of a peace treaty between Egypt and Israel constitutes an important step toward an overall peace in the region and toward a sttlement of the Arab-Israeli conflict in all its aspects;

Urging the other Arab parties involved in this dispute to join the peace-making process with Israel, a process guided by the principles of the above-mentioned framework and based on these principles;

Wishing to promote cordial relations and cooperation between them, on the basis of the U.N. Charter and the principles of international law...the two Governments approve the following articles, in a free exercise of sovereignty and in implementation of the framework for the conclusion of a peace treaty between Egypt and Israel:

Article I

1. The state of war between the two parties will be terminated and peace will be established between them immediately on the exchange of the instruments of ratification of this treaty.

2. Israel will withdraw all its armed forces and civilians from Sinai behind the international boundary line between Egypt and Palestine (under mandate), as explained in the attached protocol (No. 1), and Egypt will resume the exercise of its full sovereignty over Sinai.

3. After the interim withdrawal, explained in annex No. 1., is completed, the two parties will establish normal and cordial relations, as explained in Article III.

Article II

The permanent borders between Egypt and Israel are the international and recognized boundary lines between Egypt and the territory of Palestine, which was formerly under mandate, as explained on the map (annex No. 2), without this affecting the question of the status of the Gaza Strip. The two parties declare that these borders are inviolable and that each will respect the territorial integrity of the other, including territorial waters and air space.

Article III

1. The two parties will remain committed to the provisions of the U.N. Charter and the principles of international law governing relations between States in the time of peace, and in particular:

A. The two parties recognize and respect each other's sovereignty, territorial integrity and political independence.

B. They recognize and respect each other's right to live in peace within their secure and recognized boundaries.

C. They will refrain from the use of force, or the threat to use force, either directly or indirectly, against each other, and will settle all disputes between them by peaceful methods.

2. Each of the two parties is committed to guarantee that hostile military action, violence and threats do not stem from its territory and are not launched from there, either by troops under its control or any other troops stationed on its territory against the population or property of the other side.

Each of the two parties is also committed to refrain from organizing any military aggression, act of sabotage or violence against the other side anywhere, and from inciting, abetting, assisting or participating in such actions. Each side is committed to putting the perpetrators of such actions on trial.

3. The two parties agree that the normal relations which will be established between them will include full recognition, diplomatic, economic and cultural relations, the termination of economic boycott and barriers impeding the free movement of persons and commodities. They guarantee that their citizens, in a reciprocal manner, will have the necessary legal rights.

The process of establishing these relations, in a parallel manner with the implementation of other articles of this treaty, are outlined in annex No. 3.

Article IV

1. In order to insure a maximm of security for the two parties, in an equal and reciprocal manner, agreed arrangements of security will be made, including the establishment of zones of limited forces on the lands of Egypt and Israel and the presence of U.N. Troops and observers. The nature and timing of these arrangements are described in detail in annex No. 1.

2. The two parties agree to the stationing of U.N. Personnel in the area defined in annex No. 1. The two parties agree not to request the withdrawal of the U.N. Personnel and that these personnel will not leave unless their departure is approved by the U.N. Security Council, including its five permanent members...

3. A joint committee will be established to supervise the implementation of this treaty, in accordance with annex No. 1.

4. Either party is entitled to request a reconsideration of the security arrangements outlined in paragraphs 1 and 2 of this article, and amendments can be made by mutual agreement.

Article V

1. The vessels of Israel and sea cargo heading to it or coming from it will have the right of free passage through the Suez Canal and its openings in the Suez Gulf and the Mediterranean on the basis of the treaty of 1888, which is applicable to all states.

Israeli citizens, vessels and cargo heading to Israel or coming from there will not be discriminated against in all matters related to the use of the Canal.

2. The two sides consider the Straits of Tiran and Aqaba Gulf free international waterways, open to all states for free maritime passage and overflights, without any barriers. The two sides will respect each other's right to navigation and flights to either of the two countries through the Straits of Tiran and the Aqaba Gulf.

Article VI

1. This treaty does not affect and cannot be interpreted to affect in any way the rights and obligations of the two parties under the U.N. Charter.

2. The two parties are committed to honor, with good will, their commitments under this treaty regardless of the actions or reactions of any other party, and independently of any pretext that is not mentioned in this treaty.

3. Moreover, they are committed to take all the necessary measures to apply it in their relations with the articles of the multilateral treaties of which they are members, including the presentation of appropriate notification to the U.N. Secretary General and the other quarters with which these treaties are lodged.

4. The two parties are committed not to undertake any commitments in violation of this treaty.

5. In accordance with article 103 of the U.N. Charter, and in case of a contradiction between the commitments of the parties under this treaty and any of their other commitments, their commitments under this treaty will be binding and will be implemented.

Article VII

1. Disputes concerning the application or interpretation of this treaty will be settled by means of negotiations.

2. Any disputes of this kind which cannot be settled through negotiations will be settled either by mutual consent or will be referred to an arbitration committee.

Article VIII

The two parties agree to set up a conciliation committee to settle all mutual claims of financial compensation.

Article IX

1. This treaty will be effective once the instruments of its ratification are exchanged.

2. This treaty replaces the agreement concluded between Egypt and Israel in September 1975.

3. All protocols, annexes and maps attached to this treaty should be considered as basic parts of it.

4. This treaty will be communicated to the U.N. Secretary General in accordance with Article 102 of the U.N. Charter.

NEW YORK TIMES, November 24, 1978, P14

Text of Annex of Peace Treaty

Special to The New York Times

TEL AVIV, Nov. 25 — Following is the text of the draft of Annex III of the Treaty of Peace between the Arab Republic of Egypt and the State of Israel, as published today by the Israeli Foreign Ministry;

Article 1
DIPLOMATIC AND CONSULAR RELATIONS

The parties agree to establish diplomatic and consular relations and to exchange ambassadors upon completion of the interim withdrawal.

Article 2
.ECONOMIC AND TRADE RELATIONS

1. The parties agree to remove all discriminatory barriers to normal economic relations and to terminate economic boycotts of each other upon completion of the interim withdrawal.

2. As soon as possible, and not later than six months after the completion of the interim withdrawal the parties will enter negotiations with a view to concluding an agreement on trade and commerce for the purpose of promoting beneficial economic relations.

Article 3
CULTURAL RELATIONS

1. The parties agree to establish normal cultural relations following completion of the interim withdrawal.

2. They agree on the desirability of cultural exchanges in all fields and shall, as soon as possible and not later than six months after completion of the interim withdrawal, enter into negotiations with a view to concluding a cultural agreement for this purpose.

Article 4
FREEDOM OF MOVEMENT

1. Upon completion of the interim withdrawal, each party will permit the free movement of the nationals and vehicles of the other into and within its territory according to the general rules applicable to nationals and vehicles of other states. Neither party will impose discriminatory restriction on the free movement of persons and vehicles from its territory to the territory of the other.

2. Neutral unimpeded access to places of religious and historical significance will be provided on a nondiscriminatory basis.

Article 5
COOPERATION FOR DEVELOPMENT AND GOOD NEIGHBORLY RELATIONS

1. The parties recognize a mutuality of interest in good neighborly relations and agree to consider means to promote such relations.

2. The parties will cooperate in promoting peace, stability and development in their region. Each agrees to consider proposals the other may wish to make to this end.

3. The parties shall seek to foster mutual understanding and tolerance and will, accordingly, abstain from hostile propaganda against each other.

Article 6
TRANSPORTATION AND TELECOMMUNICATIONS

1. The parties recognize as applicable to each other the rights, privileges and obligations provided for the aviation agreements to which they are both party, particularly by the Convention on International Civil Aviation, 1944 (the Chicago Convention) and the International Air Services Transit Agreement, 1944.

2. Upon completion of the interim withdrawal any declaration of national emergency by a party under Article 39 of the Chicago Convention will not be applied to the other party on a discriminatory basis.

3. Egypt agrees that the use of oilfields left by Israel near El Arish, Rafah, Ras el Nagb and Sharm el Sheik shall be for civilian purposes only, including possible commercial use by all nations.

4. As soon as possible and not later than six months after the completion of the interim withdrawal the parties shall enter into negotiations for the purpose of concluding a civil aviation agreement.

5. The parties will reopen and maintain roads and railways between their countries and will consider further road and rail links. The parties further agree that a highway will be constructed and maintained between Egypt, Israel and Jordan near Eilat with guaranteed free and peaceful passage of persons, vehicles and goods between Egypt and Jordan, without prejudice to the sovereignty over that part of the highway which falls within their respective territory.

6. Upon completion of the interim withdrawal, normal postal, telephone, telex, data mail, wireless and cable communications and television relay service by cable, radio and satellite shall be established between the two parties in accordance with all relevant international conventions and regulations.

7. Upon completion of the interim withdrawall, each party shall grant normal access to its ports for vessels and cargoes of the other as well as vessels and cargoes destined for or coming from the other. Such access shall be granted on the same conditions generally applicable to vessels and cargoes of other nations. Article 5 of the Treaty of Peace will be implemented upon the exchange of instruments of ratification of the aforementioned treaty.

Article 7
ENJOYMENT OF HUMAN RIGHTS

The parties affirm their commitment to respect and observe human rights and fundamental freedoms for all, and they will promote these rights and freedoms in accordance with the United Nations Charter.

Article 8
TERRITORIAL SEAS

Without prejudice to the provisions of Article 5 of the Treaty of Peace each party recognizes the right of the vessels of the other party to innocent passage through its territorial sea in accordance with the rules of international law.

NEW YORK TIMES, November 26, 1978, P11

10
The Strategic Balance

The great powers' concern with the Middle East is evidenced by the constantly contested balance of power in the region. 1978 saw the United States cementing relations with Iran, Egypt and Saudi Arabia through arms sales, wooing Iraq and Syria with the promise of aid, and even striking a rapprochement with radical South Yemen. USSR moves provoked US counter moves, while brushfire wars along the periphery of the Middle East in Spanish Sahara, Chad, Somalia, Eritrea, Oman, in addition to coups in Afghanistan and Yemen all readjusted the balance of power in 1978. Each event affected the powers' ability to maintain a foothold, whether these be naval facilities, listening posts, or simply fly-over rights.

Before trying to weigh up the gains and losses of the powers in the year's events, a brief survey of the ebb and flow of great power influences is first necessary to put such gains and losses into perspective. The Middle East has gained a reputation as one of the most unstable regions in the global strategic balance. Perhaps the only stable factor in its history has been the increasing importance of oil. Since the British admiralty's 1913 decision to refit the fleet from coal-burning to oil, Middle Eastern oil has been the object of strategic rivalries among the powers. Before World War I, Britain, Russia and Germany struggled to gain key oil concessions in Iran and Mesopotamia, but the advent of war and revolution left Britain in a commanding position. Military bases in Egypt, naval bases in Aden, air bases at Habaniye in Iraq, plus exclusive control of Anglo-Iraq and Anglo-Persian oil—these were the cornerstones of what seemed to be England's stable Middle Eastern empire.

Britain's high profile in the Middle East proved to be a liability. Its military presence rubbed raw nationalist sensibilities, while the unwillingness of the imperial authorities to interfere progressively in the domestic affairs of the region provoked disappointment among Middle East liberals. Nationalists began to play a spoiler role in imperial affairs, a role they would continue to play when other powers replaced the British. During World War II, pro-Nazi coups d'etat took place in Syria and Iraq, while the Arabs of Palestine, restive at the British policy of allowing Jewish immigration, sought help from Nazi agents to resist Britain. Turkey, independent but long friendly to Britain, seemed to tilt to the Nazis. Independent Iran, too, drew close to the Nazis, and, to safeguard its oil interests in that country, Britain joined the Soviet Union in a forcible occupation of Iran. The stability of Britain's influence in the region had proved to be fleeting. Bases and troops did not safeguard British interests in the Middle East, but undermined them.

With the outbreak of the Cold War rivalry with the Soviet Union, Britain, having missed the lessons of the war, tried to "stabilize" its influence in the region by forming defense pacts with Egypt, Turkey, Iraq and Iran, directed against the threat of Soviet aggression. The "Northern Tier," Turkey, Iraq and Iran, had already been victimized by Soviet territorial demands, and so joined the Western bloc's Baghdad Pact in 1955. Egypt, however, virulently anti-British in the wake of the "Palestinian affair," saw the Soviet Union as the lesser, or at least the more remote of the two evils, and called for Britain to evacuate the country. In the same year as the Baghdad Pact President Gamal Abdul Nasser of Egypt surprised the Arab world by accepting arms from the Soviet Union; he was the first Arab leader to do so. At the same time he sought American financing for the high dam at Aswan, establishing a pattern of exploiting the East-West rivalry by playing the two sides off one another. Nasser's lesson that Middle Eastern leaders could avoid dependence on the imperial powers by turning to their rivals was quickly applied throughout the Middle East. The pro-British monarchy of Iraq was overthrown with the new government relying heavily on the Communists. By 1956 the Soviet Bloc replaced Britain as the Middle East's largest trading partner.

During the Cold War period the United States became involved in the Middle East just as the Soviet Union did. With its limited involvement in the region, the US was welcomed by Middle Eastern regimes to counterbalance the influence of the British and the Soviets which was on the rise. America was as eager to supplant North Atlantic Treaty Organization (NATO) ally Britain's influence there as it was the Soviet's. When the premier of Afghanistan sought to reduce dependence on Soviet aid he received a promise from President Dwight D. Eisenhower: "a dollar for every ruble." When Nasser nationalized the Suez Canal and had to dislodge an Anglo-French military force from the canal zone, he received diplomatic support from Eisenhower's Secretary of State John Foster Dulles. When Britain announced her final withdrawal from the Middle East in 1971, Egypt and the Soviet Union signed a defense pact, and the United States began to train and arm the Iranian army. In the 1973 Arab-Israeli war, simultaneous arms lifts by the Russians and the Americans brought the powers' rivalry in the Middle East into sharp relief.

The two-way rivalry of the US and the USSR has shown a stable pattern, but has left the region anything but stable. The Middle East continues to play one off against the other, giving rise to rapid and unexpected realignments. These realignments in turn cause mutual recriminations between the US and the USSR that each is pursuing a policy of "adventurism." The US cites Russia's spoiler role in many issues, such as not voting for Israel's admission to the UN in 1948 and condemning

Zionism in the same forum in 1976, for supplying arms now to the Kurds of Kurdistan, now to Baghdad, Iraq for supporting Somalia in 1977 and rival Ethiopia in 1978. The US, for its part, also backed the Kurds on behalf of ally Iran, and withdrew support when Iran and Iraq became reconciled, a betrayal that lead to the disastrous collapse of Kurdish independence. Though critical of the Soviets supplying arms to mutual antagonists in a conflict, the US sells arms to Morocco and Algeria, Egypt and Israel. The spoiler role is forced on the powers by circumstances as they seek steady alignments in the region.

The strategic balance at the end of 1978? Morocco, Egypt and Saudi Arabia had moved closer to the United States. Algeria may move more rapidly towards the West as it emerges from the socialist regime of Boumedienne. Iraq and Syria had sought closer contacts with the West in order to counter Soviet influence earlier in the year, but fearful of America's influence should the US-sponsored Egyptian-Israeli peace initiative succeed, both countries have retreated into cooperation with the Soviet Union. South Yemen and Afghanistan, already close to the Soviets, have strengthened these ties in wake of leftist coups. The Soviet successes in both Ethiopia and Somalia have reanchored their influence on that periphery of the region. At the same time, because of internal difficulties, Iran, Pakistan and Turkey are reassessing their commitment to the Central Treaty Organization (CENTO). The pendulum seems to be swinging toward the Soviets, a fact that has caused American policymakers major concern over the region. They may take solace from the fact that the pendulum swings both ways. As Soviet influence becomes too visible, regimes may turn back towards the United States. Or they may recall the visit of Chinese Foreign Minister Hua through the Middle East this year, and welcome a new counterweight to Soviet or American power in the region.

STRATEGIC BALANCE WEIGHED

Interagency study, *Military Strategy and Force Posture Review,* completed in June 1977 and issued by Defense Department, assesses US ability to withstand Soviet attack in various parts of globe; warns that USSR could threaten Western oil supplies by stopping tankers at sea or by directly attacking Arab oil-producing nations; however, foresees US would have advantage in Middle East war and that Israeli presence could deter attack; maintains US would be able to introduce more and better ground and naval forces, but warns of possible USSR attack against US Sixth Fleet in Mediterranean; concludes that US would prevail in conflict with USSR in Africa   (NEW YORK TIMES,   January 6, 1978,   P1)

U.S.S.R. AIRLIFT CAPACITY TESTED

USSR airlift of arms to Ethiopia appears to have been part of large exercise designed to test USSR Air Force's ability to move supplies and troops to northeast Africa and Middle East; transfer of weapons and technicians by air and sea to Ethiopia also demonstrates high priority USSR accords establishment of permanent base in strategically important Ethiopia   (NEW YORK TIMES,   January 8, 1978,   P8)

SAUDI DEFENSE CAPABILITY UPGRADED

Saudi Arabia is reported modernizing and expanding its army in the north, near Iraq, Jordan and Israel, and is spending several billion dollars a year on its military establishment; Arab and Western sources say military role is purely defensive, since army consists of only 35,000 men and national guard of 26,000; much of military spending is for construction of military installations; purchases of US military equipment and role of US in retraining Saudi army troops noted; military forces are under the command of Defense Minister Prince Sultan while Prince Abdullah commands the national guard   (NEW YORK TIMES,   January 9, 1978,   P6)

SOVIET AIRLIFT WORRIES MONARCHS

Saudi Arabian sources forecast that the Shah of Iran's meetings with Saudi Arabian King Khalid and other Saudi leaders will focus on the current massive Soviet airlifts of weapons and personnel to the Horn of Africa and the Middle East; Iran and Saudi Arabia both equip their armed forces mainly from the US, have strongly anticommunist leaders and view with concern any Soviet backing of radical regimes geographically close to them   (CHRISTIAN SCIENCE MONITOR,   January 11, 1978,   P1)

CARTER WARNED ON SOVIETS

Commentators Rowland Evans and Robert Novak reveal Shah of Iran, French President Valery Giscard d'Estaing and Saudi Arabian King Khalid warned President Carter during recent world tour that US must apply "countervailing pressure" to deepening Soviet intrusion in Ethiopia; report leaders urged Carter to halt SALT talks indefinitely to compel USSR to halt military operations in Ethiopia; observe USSR refused to halt Ethiopian operations following US protest by Under Secretary of State Philip Habib in December 1978   (WASHINGTON POST,   January 12, 1978,   P27)

SOVIET AIRLIFT EXAMINED

Commentator James Buxton looks at airlift of Soviet arms to Ethiopia; notes that western intelligence sources believe Ethiopia may have received $1 billion worth of tanks, aircraft and other equipment since April 1977; suggests that US and its allies are worried that USSR intends to help country's revolutionary government defeat secessionists campaigning within borders and establish permanent military presence; discusses strategic trade location of Ethiopia; remarks that Saudi Arabia and Iran are pressuring US to take action   (FINANCIAL TIMES,   January 19, 1978,   P22)

MORE SOVIET ARMS TO SYRIA

Joint communique issued after Syrian President Hafez al-Assad conferred with USSR leader Brezhnev in Moscow indicates USSR will increase arms aid   (NEW YORK TIMES,   February 2, 1978,   P4)

U.S. NOT TO FURNISH ARMS

Secretary Vance says US is adhering to policy of not providing arms to either side in Ethiopian-Somali conflict; denies US is permitting Iran and Saudi Arabia to transfer US weapons   (NEW YORK TIMES,   February 15, 1978,   P9)

POWER BLOCS OUTLINED

Commentator David Hirst examines emergence of pro-US and pro-Soviet Arab groupings; observes Egypt and Iran lead nations allied with US, which also include Sudan and Morocco, while Syria, Algeria, Libya, South Yemen, and the Palestinians have, each for its own reasons, aligned with USSR; notes misgivings in pro-Soviet camp; suggests oil-producing Gulf states, Jordan and Saudi Arabia form 3d grouping which fears strong Egyptian-Iranian alliance; holds divided Iraqi leadership may hold key to region's power balance if it can overcome its present paralysis   (MANCHESTER GUARDIAN,   February 19, 1978,   P7)

U.S. INTERVENTION SPECULATED

Commentator Stephen S. Rosenfeld speculates on US military intervention in Persian Gulf; reports Defense Secretary Harold Brown has been implying some sort of action beyond diplomacy; notes Brown is concerned about impact of Soviet presence on NATO and oil supplies; suggests US would use military force not against oil producers but with their consent and in their behalf   (WASHINGTON POST,   February 24, 1978,   P21)

SOVIET-EGYPTIAN RELATIONS ANALYZED

Commentator Clayton Fritchey asserts that Israeli-feared Egyptian rapprochement with USSR is unlikely as long as Anwar Sadat remains President; suggests that Sadat may feel compelled to step aside if current Mideast peace negotiations fail; notes Sadat has stressed that US holds 99% of cards in success of negotiations; discusses possibility that Sadat would attempt last-minute reconciliation with USSR; reveals that Sadat maintains secret diplomatic relations with Soviets; points to reports showing that USSR has continued arms shipments to Egypt despite Sadat's repeated denials (WASHINGTON POST, February 25, 1978, P15)

GULF RULER VOICES CONCERN

Sultan Qabus ibn Said of Oman is increasingly concerned about Soviet and Cuban intervention in Horn of Africa; Qabus has been trying to warn other Persian Gulf rulers including Saudi Arabian king and Shah of Iran that Soviet intervention is threatening stability and oil of Middle East and security of its sea lanes; Qabus has also expressed concern about the amount of Soviet military weaponry and Cuban troops in bordering South Yemen; US officials apparently regard Oman's concern with degree of detachment; some area rulers feel that US may not be reliable or credible military protector despite its dependence on Arab oil (WASHINGTON POST, March 5, 1978, P12)

ISRAEL EXPLAINS DEFENSE NEEDS

Israeli Defense Minister Ezer Weizman has met with Defense Secretary Harold Brown to discuss Israel's request for about $15 billion in American military equipment over next 10 years; Defense Department spokesman states that talk included issue of overall military balance in Middle East, status of peace negotiations and aspects of Israel's defense needs, such as planes and tanks; Weizman submitted Israeli case against sale of military aircraft to Saudi Arabia and its case for increasing number of aircraft to be sold to Israel; participants in talks state that no decisions have been made and no commitments made on Israeli arms requests (NEW YORK TIMES, March 9, 1978, P14)

U.S. PREPARATIONS UNDER WAY

Commentator Richard Burt assesses superpower tensions around Horn of Africa and on Indian Ocean; concludes that arms control no longer fits in with thinking of either US or USSR around Horn; notes that Defense Department is assembling 100,000-man "quick reaction force" to deploy along Persian Gulf in event of Soviet intervention there; USSR has lost important naval base in Somalia and thus is

American naval forces in the Indian Ocean.

Naval Photographic Center, Washington, D.C.

seen as not wishing to be confined to current status quo; Burt also mentions that conservative oil producing states like Saudi Arabia and Iran are very worried over permanent Soviet bridgehead in region   (NEW YORK TIMES, March 12, 1978, S4 P3)

SUEZ 'NOT STRATEGIC'

Commentator James Burnham suggests that Carter Administration may have good reasons for its passive policy toward Ethiopian-Somalian situation in Africa; maintains control over entrance to Red Sea and thus passage to and from Suez Canal is no longer militarily and economically important; claims other African nations would oppose US intervention on Somalia's side while Somalia was still fighting for annexation of areas beyond its borders; urges US to keep low profile at this time while letting friendly Mideast countries know that US has no objection to their aiding Somalia militarily; counsels applying diplomatic and psychological pressure on USSR   (NATIONAL REVIEW, March 17, 1978, P331)

ISRAEL MONITORING SOVIET MOVES

Israeli Air Force bases at Etzion, Eytam and Ofira in Sinai Peninsula seen as crucial factor for long-range surveillance over Red Sea, Gulf of Aden and western areas of Indian Ocean in anticipation of successful Soviet penetration of Ethiopia; US Admiral Robert J. Hanks reported recently that Soviet warships were using facilities at Umm Qasr and Basra in Iraq, at Aden in South Yemen and at Indian ports; Soviet Navy represents prime military force in Indian Ocean, with usual squadron made up of missile-armed cruiser, 2 destroyers, landing ship, oceanographic research vessel and several submarines; should remain powerful military influence in area with continued access to Aden and anchorages off island of Socotra in Gulf of Aden, and with possible future hold on Ethiopian port of Massawa on Red Sea; military planners insist that US retain operational rights at Etzion, continue to develop military base at Diego Garcia and reinforce Middle East naval force   (NEW YORK TIMES, March 26, 1978, P10)

SOVIET SUPPLIES CAUSING CONCERN

Israelis fear impact of agreement between PLO leader Yasir Arafat and USSR, in which PLO promised to continue attacks against Israel in return for delivery of light weapons and expanded training facilities in East Europe and Middle East; are also concerned over Soviet promise to equip Syria with number of heavy weapons; US discounts impact of Soviet arms aid, insisting that Israel is powerful enough to deal with any combination of Arab forces   (NEW YORK TIMES, March 27, 1978, P3)

GUARANTEES FOR ISRAEL PROBED

Commentator James Reston discusses issue of US treaty guarantees for Israel; contends US would be in a better position to prevent outbreak of war under a treaty obligation with bases than it is now; observes that US military presence has been argued as needed to discourage military adventures, noting that both Israel and Arab states have a common interest in discouraging Communist influence in Middle East and Africa; reports that some Washington officials are beginning to believe US should not wait until Israel and Arab states negotiate a comprehensive settlement before facing question of US guarantees   (NEW YORK TIMES, April 9, 1978, S4 P19)

SOVIET WEAPONS DISPLAYED

Israel releases inventory of weapons captured from Palestinians in southern Lebanon; notes presence of Soviet weapons of type not previously seen in Middle East, including 73-millimeter recoilless gun and Strela-7 anti-aircraft missile; other captured weapons: 6 Lebanese Chariot tanks, 2 older Sherman tanks, 19 antitank guns, recoilless guns and 40 of latest Soviet grenade launchers; also large number of Katyusha rocket launchers and miscellaneous ammunition   (NEW YORK TIMES, April 13, 1978, P3)

ISRAELI ARMS USE LIMITED

Carter Administration has begun talks with Israel to insure that US-supplied anti-personnel cluster bombs are not again used against civilian targets in Middle East, according to State Department spokesman Tom Reston; bombs break apart and scatter smaller bombs containing pellets across wide areas, and were supplied to Israel after 1973 Middle East war; Administration seeks greater assurances from Israel that would compel Israeli military commanders to seek civilian approval before cluster bombs are used   (NEW YORK TIMES, April 14, 1978, P8)

SOVIETS ENTRENCHED IN ETHIOPIA

Commentator Joseph Kraft asserts that USSR has acquired vast local power in Ethiopia; notes that Soviets have delivered about $1 billion in military and economic aid to that African nation in past year alone; contends that Soviets have not made same kind of mistakes which caused them to get expelled from Egypt, the Sudan, Somalia and Syria; notes Russians themselves have not been in evidence in Ethiopia but have let more genial Cubans become visible; reports that USSR has wholeheartedly supported military objectives of Ethiopian leader Lieutenant Colonel Mengistu Haile Mariam; concludes that US, with no real assets in area, must wait for Soviets to make errors   (WASHINGTON POST, April 25, 1978, P17)

TURKEY'S 'BUFFER' EXAMINED

Turkish Prime Minister Bulent Ecevit, in interview, comments on pursuit of stronger trilateral economic agreements involving Turkey, USSR and either Syria or Iraq; charges that NATO countries are indifferent or helpless in dealing with Turkey's growing economic and military needs; Turkey's strategic role as buffer in Mideast is attracting growing interest; US fears that any further movement by Turkey toward USSR could have damaging implications for policy in Mideast and on Western defense alliances   (WALL STREET JOURNAL, May 3, 1978, P11)

AFGHANISTAN COUP RESPONSE CRITICIZED

Commentators Rowland Evans and Robert Novak criticize President Carter's failure to issue tough warning to USSR against Soviet support for communist takeover in previously neutral Afghanistan; charge Administration's silence in response to warnings of Afghan coup is example of Administration's inertia in meeting current Soviet worldwide offensive; observe installation of pro-Soviet Afghan government has already compelled Iran to reinforce its eastern frontiers with Afghanistan (WASHINGTON POST, May 8, 1978, P23)

U.S.-LIBYAN DEALS REVEALED

Commentator Jack Anderson scores growing US-Libyan ties; asserts that Libyan leader Muammar Qaddafi is one of world's most dangerous and irresponsible leaders; cites that Commerce Department is close to approving sale of 400 heavy duty trucks to Libya; notes Federal Aviation Administration has agreed to train 18 Libyans as navigational aides at its Oklahoma City training academy; reports that State Department has approved sale of executive jetliner to Qaddafi; outlines controversy associated with Qaddafi's gift of $750,000 to Georgetown University's foreign service school (WASHINGTON POST, May 18, 1978, P10)

PAKISTAN REVIEWS FOREIGN POLICY

Shake-up in Pakistan's foreign policy is under way after leftist coup in neighboring Afghanistan in April; contrary to expectations that Pakistan would now depend more on the Central Treaty Organization (CENTO), Pakistan's military regime is now canvassing the advantages of leaving CENTO and moving instead to a well-armed non-alignment; fresh thinking reflects disillusionment with the 2 non-regional CENTO members, US and Britain (TIMES OF LONDON, May 20, 1978, P5)

PAKISTAN OUTLOOK EXPLAINED

High ranking Pakistan official, insisting on anonymity, says Pakistan is deeply concerned over what it regards as pro-Moscow government in Afghanistan established in April following coup; says US must realize that historic readjustment has taken place in this part of world, and act accordingly; Pakistanis believe settlement of Afghan-Pakistan border issues affecting Pathan tribesmen is now remote; hope US will look more favorably on military aid for Pakistan now that pro-Soviet government has emerged in Afghanistan (NEW YORK TIMES, May 20, 1978, P4)

KISSINGER COMMENTS ON U.S.S.R. MOVES

Commentator William F. Buckley discusses Henry Kissinger's analysis of Communist presence in Africa in remarks to International Radio and Television Society; notes that Kissinger claimed USSR is trying to outflank Middle East and to demonstrate that US cannot protect its allies; criticizes President Carter for not having developed effective policy to counter Soviet and Cuban advances (NATIONAL REVIEW, May 26, 1978, P673)

SOVIET ACTIONS TROUBLE SHAH

Commentator Clayton Kirkpatrick reports that Shah of Iran sees great possibility cold war will expand; explains that leftist-inspired revolution in Afghanistan, Soviet and Cuban aggression in Ethiopia and Somalia, threat of Soviet intervention in Eritrea, and Cuban mercenaries in South Yemen have raised fears in Arab states around Gulf; adds that Shah has long predicted that Soviets would seek warm weather port which would give them access to Indian Ocean (CHICAGO TRIBUNE, May 26, 1978, S5 P2)

SAUDIS, FRENCH MEET ON AFRICA

King Khalid of Saudi Arabia ends 3-day state visit to France, visit which officials see as evidence that France and Saudi Arabia share anxieties on situations in Africa and Middle East; Saudi Arabian Foreign Minister Prince Saud al-Faisal, at news conference, denounces "foreign intervention in Africa and elsewhere," and does not rule out possibility that Saudis will help finance inter-African security force that is being considered to "stabilize" instability in Zaire (NEW YORK TIMES, June 1, 1978, P7)

CARTER URGES EMBARGO REPEAL

President Carter announces the repeal of arms embargo on Turkey is his highest priority foreign policy issue; gives memorandum outlining his 3-week drive to achieve repeal to 14 selected House of Representatives members, all of whom are known to favor repeal; memorandum projects Congressional testimony by military and civilian leaders, solicits canvassing of uncommitted Congressional members by 14 Representatives, and details efforts to rally grass-roots support by working with veterans' organizations; Carter, in his appeal to House members, holds embargo is negative act that has strained relations

On May 17 Ethiopian troops backed by Cuban troops and Soviet advisers broke out of their encircled enclave of Asmara, smashing a siege by Eritrean rebels.

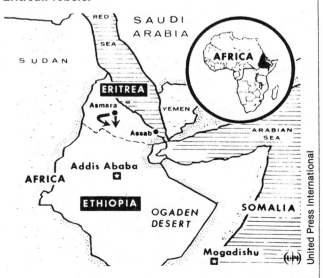

between US and Turkey, between Turkey and Greece, and between US and Greece; also maintains embargo has disrupted cohesiveness of NATO, stalemated progress on Cyprus and failed to promote peace in Middle East or Europe; repeal effort faces resistance from Congressional members who are sympathetic to Greece, and Greek Prime Minister Constantine Caramanlis has warned Carter that repeal will damage US-Greek relations and set back Cyprus negotiations   (NEW YORK TIMES, June 2, 1978, P1)

U.S. WEAKNESS SCORED

Thomas Moorer, retired admiral and former chairman of Joint Chiefs of Staff, contrasts Soviet military and political global objectives with "general erosion" in US commitment to fundamental national security objectives; proposes measures to prevent Soviet Union from creating environment in Middle East, Persian Gulf and Horn of Africa that could result in denial of oil to US, NATO and Japan, and measures to deter Soviets from overt action against either Iran or Saudi Arabia   (NEW YORK TIMES, June 8, 1978, P27)

MOROCCO'S WAR DEBTS NOTED

Morocco's King Hassan begins disclosing cost of nation's defense commitments as moderate, pro-Western power in Africa and supporter of Arab causes in Middle East; Hassan admits kingdom has been living beyond its means; involvements include sending troops to aid Zaire regime of President Mobutu twice in one year   (NEW YORK TIMES, June 9, 1978, P26)

EGYPT CONCERNED OVER AFRICA

Egypt's War Minister General Mohammed Abdel-Ghany el-Ghamasy expresses concern that if Soviet and Cuban activities in Ethiopia are directed against Sudan they will become "an indirect threat to Egypt"; expresses anxiety about flow of sophisticated Soviet arms to Libya, commenting that Libyans could not operate these weapons themselves; claims Egyptian army is in good condition despite cut-off of spare parts from USSR; however, concedes need for modernized equipment; confirms that Egypt is sending artillery and military advisers to Zaire   (NEW YORK TIMES, June 11, 1978, P5)

SHAH ASKS REGIONAL PACT

Shah of Iran renews plea for mutual security pact among Persian Gulf states, including Saudi Arabia, Iraq and the smaller Gulf states; Iran had made original proposal on pact 3 years earlier but no agreement has heretofore developed; new plea is believed spurred by recent assassination of Yemen's president, coup in Afghanistan and Soviet intervention in Ethiopia   (NEW YORK TIMES, July 3, 1978, P3)

IRAQI CAUTIONS ON U.S.S.R.

Iraqi President Saddam Hussein, in interview, cautions against Soviet military actions in Africa and Persian Gulf; claims USSR will not be satisfied until entire world is under Communist control; fears that Iraq will be enmeshed in East-West battlefield; asserts that recent execution of Communist officers in Iraqi military was not intended as warning to USSR; says officers were executed because they were subversives; related article discusses Iraqi leaders' growing disenchantment with their former patron, USSR; notes Hussein has been buying weapons from Western Europe to limit Iraq's dependence on Soviet arms   (NEWSWEEK, July 17, 1978, P50)

LONG-TERM U.S. GOALS ASSESSED

Cornell University Professor Emeritus Edward Whiting Fox criticizes US arms sales and other overtures to Saudi Arabia; argues that permanent Middle East security would be better served if US, fully backing "our one strong, dependable" Middle Eastern ally Israel, sets up naval bases on Mediterranean and Red Sea Israeli coasts and air base between the 2; warns against considering Saudi Arabia superpower   (NEW YORK TIMES, July 23, 1978, S4 P18)

SOVIET INFLUENCE WEIGHED

US and Western European intelligence analysts see strategic gains of global significance in USSR's growing influence and control in Southern Yemen and in Afghanistan; gains here and in Ethiopia are said to have greater strategic significance than USSR involvement in Egypt a decade earlier; in South Yemen, Soviet bases at Socotra island, in Aden and at Al Makulla are significant; 20 USSR-Afghanistan aid agreements have been signed since President N. M. Taraki came to power in April   (NEW YORK TIMES, July 31, 1978, P2)

AID FOR SYRIA REQUESTED

State Department urges Congress to restore $90 million in economic aid to Syria, cut by House of Representatives earlier in week from foreign aid bill; spokesman Hodding Carter 3d says that Administration will apply to Senate to restore funds for Syria later in August   (NEW YORK TIMES, August 8, 1978, P7)

AID FOR SAUDIS ASKED

Defense Department sends to Congress for approval two military aid packages for Saudi Arabia; one package charges Saudi Arabia $1.3 billion for 3-year extension of US training, maintenance, construction and support services related to its previous purchase of 114 F-5 fighter planes; other proposal provides $220 million in training and equipment for a logistics battalion and support for 4 other battalions in Saudi national guard   (NEW YORK TIMES, August 19, 1978, P138)

SHAH AND CHINESE LEADER MEET

Chinese leader Hua Kuo-feng begins summit discussions with Shah of Iran in Teheran; security concerns and common suspicions about USSR are said to be elements of the talks   (NEW YORK TIMES, August 31, 1978, P1)

SOMALIA, LACKING AID, TROUBLED

Somalia's expulsion of Russian experts last autumn and abrupt discontinuation of all Soviet aid pose serious problems for backward Somalian economy; Somalia has followed strategy of developing arable areas, gradually resettling nomad groups and improving quality of rangeland; had mixed feelings over Soviet aid, and complaints over slow shipments, lack of spare parts and inefficient and impractical schemes were common; is relying on stepped-up aid from UN, Arab world and European Economic Community countries to compensate for Russian effort; Chinese are assisting in various projects and are expected to provide spare parts for Russian equipment   (NEW YORK TIMES,   September 1, 1978,   P10)

JOINT BASE CONSTRUCTION WEIGHED

Pentagon spokesman Thomas B. Ross discloses that US and Israel may collaborate on construction of 2 military air bases in Negev Desert; notes that construction costs would range between $300 million and $1 billion; adds that project would take form of a grant   (NEW YORK TIMES, September 20, 1978,   P32)

SENATE APPROVES AID

Senate clears way for appropriating $1.7 billion in economic support aid to Egypt, Israel, Jordan and Syria as State Secretary Vance continues Middle East peace mission; attempt to eliminate $90 million aid fund for Syria was abandoned at Carter Administration request; House of Representatives cut Syrian aid fund out of foreign aid bill in retaliation for Syrian occupation troops' shelling of Christian residential area in Lebanon; matter will be considered again when bill comes before Senate-House conference committee   (NEW YORK TIMES,   September 22, 1978,   P10)

U.S. INFLUENCE GROWING

Commentator Jim Hoagland asserts that President Carter's part in Camp David summit has greatly expanded US role in Middle East and effectively shut door on USSR; reveals that details now emerging from talks indicate that Carter, Israeli Prime Minister Menachem Begin and Egyptian President Anwar Sadat were in accord on menace of growing Soviet and Cuban threat in Africa and Red Sea region; asserts that Saudi Arabia and other Arab nations must now decide whether they fear Soviets more than they dislike Camp David accords   (WASHINGTON POST,   September 24, 1978,   P19)

BASE PROPOSALS LACK SUPPORT

Administration sources disclose that American, Israeli and Egyptian leaders are all "distinctly cool" to idea of basing any US military forces in Middle East; Congressional sources reveal that Administration floated idea among key Senators and met stiff opposition; other ideas similarly opposed include building US naval base at Haifa port and stationing US troops in West Bank for peacekeeping purposes   (NEW YORK TIMES,   September 28, 1978,   P39)

SYRIAN AID APPROVED

House-Senate conference committee gives conditional approval to $90 million foreign aid fund for Syria if President Carter certifies it will help Middle East peace process; approval came after efforts of Vice President Mondale and National Security Chief Brzezinski and after reported insistence by President Carter that full amount be approved; House originally had removed entire amount from foreign aid bill and House conferees voted to restore only $60 million of it   (NEW YORK TIMES, September 29, 1978,   P10)

EMBARGO OF TURKEY ENDS

President Carter formally ends 3-year embargo on arms shipments to Turkey, declaring Turkey is acting in good faith to achieve peaceful settlement of Cyprus problem; asserts action enables US to resume full military cooperation with Turkey and begin new chapter in US-Turkey relations; declaration coincides with White House announcement that Carter signed into law $2.8 billion foreign military aid authorization act that empowered him to lift embargo   (NEW YORK TIMES,   October 4, 1978,   P8)

TURKEY REOPENING U.S. BASES

Pentagon sources disclose that Turkey has agreed to reopen 4 military bases used by the US for gathering intelligence information from USSR until they were closed down in 1975; Turkish government shut down bases in retaliation for US arms embargo imposed against Turkey after Turkey invaded Cyprus in 1974; a 5th US base at Karamursel is being turned over to Turkish government   (NEW YORK TIMES,   October 4, 1978,   P13)

NEW MIDEAST POLICY SOUGHT

Senator Frank Church calls on US to create new Middle East policy which offers massive aid as incentive to permanent peace in Middle East; holds policy should concentrate first on Egypt and Israel for their role as initial peacemakers, and that Jordan and Syria should be offered same measure of support if and when they participate in peace efforts; adds policy should also clearly indicate that aid would be withdrawn from countries that fail to cooperate   (NEW YORK TIMES,   October 6, 1978,   P32)

MOROCCAN KING SEEKS AID

Commentator Ronald Koven discusses Moroccan King Hassan II's upcoming visit to US; observes one of main goals of Hassan's visit is to try to unblock US Congressional restrictions against selling Morocco more F-5 combat support jets for use in Western Sahara war; reports Hassan is said to believe strongly that West owes him gratitude for supplying troops against rebels in Zaire's Shaba Province and for backing Egypt's peace efforts with Israel   (WASHINGTON POST,   November 16, 1978,   P29)

AIRLIFT TO ETHIOPIA SEEN AS SOVIET TEST

Aid Far Exceeded Requirements but Showed Ability of Russians to Transport It to Africa

By DREW MIDDLETON

The Soviet airlift of arms to Ethiopia appears to have been part of a large exercise designed to test the Soviet Air Force's ability to move supplies and troops to northeast Africa and the Middle East, according to United States and Atlantic alliance analysts.

The transfer of weapons and technicians by air and sea to Ethiopia also demonstrated, the sources said, the high priority Moscow accords the establishment of a permanent base in this strategically important area.

But all together, the air supply operations that began Nov. 26 far exceeded Ethiopia's immediate requirements. Estimates are that 225 transport aircraft, or about 12 percent of the transport fleet, were flown to Addis Ababa, Aden and Maputo in Mozambique.

There are reports that some of the aircraft were empty. This supports the basic assumption that the operation was a test of transport capabilities for which the supply of the Ethiopian forces provided an excuse.

The Resources Russians Used

During the same period of late November and early December, the Russians sent many merchant ships from bases in the Black Sea to Ethiopia. There are also reports that some Soviet rail lines were closed to regular traffic so that war supplies could be transported to ports as part of the exercise.

At the height of the operation, the Russians launched Cosmos 964, a military reconnaissance satellite, which may have played a role in the command and control of the overall exercise.

The majority of the planes in the first phase were Antonov 22's, the workhorse of the Soviet transport fleet.

However, some European reports say that Tupelov 76's, the civil aviation version of the Tu-VG bomber, known in the West by the code name Backfire, also were employed in flights from Soviet Central Asia to Aden and Maputo.

Speculations on the Reasons

Documentation of the Soviet operation by American satellites, surveillance ships of the Navy in the Mediterranean and the Indian Ocean and by radar sites along the routes taken by the Soviet aircraft is now fairly complete.

But why the Russians mounted so extensive an operation remains a mystery.

One theory held by American analysts is that after being ousted from Egypt in 1972 and from Somalia in 1977, the Soviet high command believed it necessary to demonstrate to allies and potential enemies in the area that it could sustain a friendly government, in this case Ethiopia.

There is general agreement, however, that the Russians count on building a new center of political and military power in Ethiopia because the Government there, having broken with Washington, has no place to turn.

Influence in the Area

Firmly established in Ethiopian air bases, the Russians would be in a position to influence events in the states bordering on the Red Sea and the Gulf of Aden.

Ethiopia has no coast bordering the Indian Ocean, and to that extent is a less desirable power base than Somalia. But Russian presence there creates the possibility of political or military interference in the former French territory of Djibouti on the western side of the Bab el Mandeb strait leading from the Gulf of Aden into the Red Sea.

Sources in the North Atlantic Treaty Organization also pointed out that a strong, pro-Soviet Ethiopia, dependent on the Soviet Union for arms, technical aid and economic assistance, would be seen in Moscow as a balance to growing United States influence in Saudi Arabia and Egypt.

Present estimates are that there are 500 Soviet advisers and technicians and 1,500 Cubans, perhaps 1,000 of them military personnel, in Ethiopia.

Russian influence in Ethiopia also figures significantly in Moscow's rivalry with Peking over the leadership of third-world countries in Africa.

More Than Promises

Peking, with more limited resources, has sought support on the grounds that it and not "the socialist imperialists" in Moscow is the legitimate political and ideological mentor of developing countries.

But in Ethiopia, as in Vietnam, Angola, and Mozambique, the Russians have delivered mor than propaganda and promises.

The air supply operation entailed certain political risks for the Russians. The flights were recorded in Yugoslavia, Pakistan, Iran, Turkey, Greece, Israel, Egypt, the Sudan and Libya. Of these countries, only Libya can be counted a Soviet ally. Early last year, Yugoslavia protested the violation of its air space by Russian transports flying to the Middle East.

Protests from these states is not expected to stop future exercises. To Western military planners, the operation was necessary to display the Soviet ability to project military power over great distances to achieve political ends.

Most consider it an expansion of the operation in Angola in 1975, which evoked no serious diplomatic or military reaction in the West. The expectation of one senior officer is that the Soviet high command now believes it has "a license and the ability to intervene by air at increasingly great distances."

NEW YORK TIMES, January 8, 1978, P9

U.S. PLANS FIRST JET SALE TO CAIRO, REDUCES ISRAELI ORDER FOR CRAFT; SAUDIS GET 60; DEBATE IS EXPECTED

Vance Says Advanced Planes for Arabs Help Promote 'Course of Moderation'

By GRAHAM HOVEY
Special to The New York Times

WASHINGTON, Feb. 14—The Carter Administration announced today that it would approve the sale of $4.8 billion worth of advanced military planes to Egypt, Saudi Arabia and Israel.

It said the decision was designed to maintain the existing military balance and to advance the cause of peace in the Middle East.

Senior officials conceded that they would face a tough debate in Congress over the decisions to sell fighter aircraft to Egypt—the first time by the United

States—to provide Saudi Arabia with the most advanced of American military planes and to give Israel far less in new weaponry than it had requested.

Offered as a Package

The officials emphasized, however, that the decisions represented a package and said that if Congress rejected parts of the package the Administration would have to reconsider the other parts, keeping in mind the military balance between Israel and the Arab nations.

The officials break down the $4.8 billion package into components of $2.5 billion for Saudi Arabia, $1.9 billion for Israel and $400 million for Egypt.

Under law, Congress can block any arms transactions of this scale by majority vote in both the House and Senate within 30 days after it has been formally notified of the Administration's intent.

In a statement announcing the decisions, Secretary of State Cyrus R. Vance said the Administration would begin informing Congress and consulting with it next week and would submit its formal notification after Congress returned from its Easter recess early in April.

Under the program, Saudi Arabia would be allowed to acquire 60 of the F-15's and Israel would get 15 of the fighters, made by the McDonnell Douglas Corporation and described as the most advanced plane in the United States Air Force.

Israel has already bought 25 of the F-15's and thus would have a force of 40 by late 1981, when deliveries would be carried out under the decisions announced today.

Israel, under the new program, could also buy 75 of the less sophisticated F-16 fighters, made by General Dynamics, with delivery scheduled for the last quarter of 1981.

Administration officials said earlier that Israel had asked for 25 more F-15's and 150 F-16's.

Senior officials said today that Israel's request for authorization to produce the F-16 was a matter that would "have to await further discussions" before a decision could be expected.

Egypt would acquire 50 of the F-5 fighters, made by the Northrop Corporation, a far less-sophisticated plane than the F-15 or the F-16 and a plane not used by the United States Air Force.

The United States has 10 F-5's on hand, so deliveries to Egypt would start in the third quarter of this year.

High officials, who asked that their names not be divulged, said the first sale of combat aircraft to Egypt by the United States would not represent a qualitative improvement in Egyptian air-combat capability.

They said the F-5's were comparable with MIG-21's that Egypt obtained in the past from the Soviet Union, but for which it has been unable to obtain regular supplies of spare parts since President Sadat moved after the 1973 war to seek United

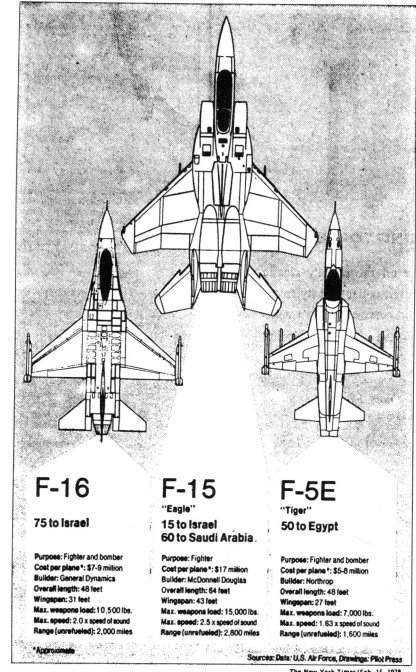

States help in achieving disengagement agreements with Israel.

In his statement, Secretary of State Vance appeared to be trying to blunt expected opposition from various quarters. He emphasized the Administration's intention for full consultation with Congress, said the projected sales would be consistent with President Carter's goal of restraining global arms transfers and declared:

"Our commitment to Israel's security has been and remains firm. Israel must

have full confidence in its ability to assure its own defense."

But Mr. Vance insisted:

"Egypt, too, must have reasonable assurance of its ability to defend itself if it is to continue the peace negotiations with confidence.

"We believe we have a basic interest in responding to Egypt's legitimate needs."

"Saudi Arabia," the Secretary of State added, "is of immense importance in promoting a course of moderation in the

Middle East, with respect to peacemaking and other regional initiatives and more broadly in world affairs, as in petroleum and financial policy."

"The Saudi Government has a legitimate requirement to modernize its very limited air defenses," he said. "We believe their request is reasonable and in our interest to fulfill."

The senior officials, in a joint background briefing, said the F-5's for Egypt could not be used effectively against Israel's more sophisticated aircraft but could counter threats from Libya, with which Egypt fought a brief border war last year.

They added that the Saudis needed the F-15's to be able to counter a rapid build-up of military strength in the air and on the ground in Iraq, which obtains its planes and equipment from the Soviet Union.

Early reactions from Capitol Hill and elsewhere indicated, however, that the Administration's position on sales to Egypt and Saudi Arabia would face powerful opposition, especially at a time of already embittered relations between the United States and Israel over the issue of Israeli settlements in Sinai.

Senator Jacob K. Javits, Republican of New York, said he would be "interested particularly in finding out whether there is a connection respecting the timing of these sales in view of the stalemate in the Egypt-Israeli negotiations and the U.S. position on Israeli settlements."

Without waiting for Prime Minister Menachem Begin's expected comment in Parliament tomorrow, Israeli officials in Washington issued a statement criticizing the projected sales to Egypt and Saudi Arabia.

The Israeli officials said the sale to Egypt would affect the balance of power in the Middle East and "may have a negative effect on Egypt's willingness to compromise and moderate its position" in the peace negotiations.

They said the Saudis would be unable to operate the F-15 aircraft and thus in a crisis with Israel would transfer the planes to "confrontation states engaged in active fighting with Israel" or employ mercenaries, probably Americans, to fly the planes.

Some of the Israeli contentions were echoed in Congress.

Senator Daniel P. Moynihan, Democrat of New York, said he was confident that Congress would disapprove the sale of the F-15's to Saudi Arabia and indicated a belief that the sale to Egypt would disrupt the military balance in the Middle East.

"It certainly seems to be an ill-timed intrusion into the peacemaking process," Mr. Moynihan said of the projected sale to Egypt,

In a letter to President Carter, written before the sales announcement, Clarence D. Long, chairman of the House Appropriations subcommittee on foreign operations, said he would "make every effort to deny these proposals to send military equipment to Egypt."

"I would be surprised if the Congress were not supportive of this denial," said Mr. Long, a Maryland Democrat. He urged the President to drop any proposals for selling aircraft to Egypt and Saudi Arabia "once and for all," and said later today that he would also favor dropping the projected sales to Israel at this time.

Dayan Critical of Sale to Egypt

LOS ANGELES, Feb. 14 (Reuters)—Foreign Minister Moshe Dayan of Israel said here today the Carter Administration's intention to sell advanced fighters to Egypt was premature and would have a bad effect on the security of Israel.

Mr. Dayan said at a news conference that Israel felt the United States should not begin to provide arms to Egypt until a peace agreement had been reached between Cairo and the Israelis.

Mr. Dayan declined to speculate as to whether the arms sales decision and State Department criticism of Israel settlements in Sinai meant a shift of United States support away from Israel.

Israelis Deplore U. S. Decision

JERUSALEM, Feb. 14 (AP)—Israeli officials today attacked President Carter's decision today to sell military planes to Egypt and Saudi Arabia, claiming it could increase the risk of a new Mideast war.

Defense Minister Ezer Weizman said he would make no statement until tomorrow after Parliament has discussed the matter.

Haim Landau, a minister without portfolio, said the sale of advanced planes to Egypt and Saudi Arabia heightened the danger of war.

NEW YORK TIMES, February 15, 1978, P1

If War in the Horn Is Over, Superpower Tension Is Not

By RICHARD BURT

WASHINGTON — Somalia's decision last week to withdraw its forces from Ethiopia and seek a negotiated settlement over the disputed Ogaden region has raised hopes in the Carter Administration that the Soviet Union's military involvement in the Horn of Africa might soon be brought to an end. It has also opened the way for reviving President Carter's proposal for a superpower understanding over military forces in the Indian Ocean, first proposed in April last year when the idea did seem to have a plausible ring.

For a start, while both the United States and the Soviet Union had slowly built up their naval presence in the region, it was hard to argue that an arms race was under way. Since the late 1940's, the United States Navy had maintained a three-ship force based at the island sheikdom of Bahrein, and following the 1973 Middle East war, it had started to sail aircraft carriers in and out of the area periodically. The Soviet navy entered the Indian Ocean in 1968 and gradually increased its permanent presence to 20 vessels, 10 of them warships, by 1973. After that, Soviet naval activity in the region leveled. Mr. Carter's call for a military understanding in the Indian Ocean thus came when the naval balance appeared stable.

In fact, France, and not either of the two superpowers, normally keeps the largest naval force in the region, using facilities in newly independent Djibouti. Britain and Australia regularly exercise their naval muscle in the region as do the growing navies of India and Iran. Moreover, as Mr. Carter's security advisers pointed out, the prospects for regional conflict among nations circling the Indian Ocean had declined. After Vietnam, the United States had pulled its bases out of Thailand, India and Pakistan were getting along and renewed conflict in the Middle East seemed unlikely.

Yet by early this year it was clear that the Administration's scheme for demilitarization had gone by the boards. Soviet involvement in the Horn of Africa, together with growing American concern over the security of oil supplies, had made the Indian Ocean a new focal point of superpower tensions. These developments have yet to significantly alter patterns of Soviet and American naval deployment in the region. But Moscow's activities in the Horn pose new threats.

At present, these are limited to the northwest quadrant of the Indian Ocean, where on the Horn, 10,000 Cuban forces and 1,000 Soviet military advisers helped Ethiopia repel invading Somali forces in the Ogaden province. But straddling the strategic waters of the Red Sea and the Gulf of Aden, the Horn has a strategic value far beyond its resources and population.

While officials continue to argue over what the final outcome of Soviet involvement in the area will be, even a slim possibility that Moscow might be able to exploit the conflict to establish a permanent bridge-head in the region has stirred

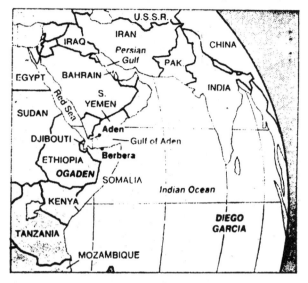

widespread fears among conservative, oil-producing states such as Iran and Saudi Arabia as well as consumer nations in Western Europe. The proximity of the Ethiopian-Somali conflict to oil production areas and shipment routes has also not been ignored by the Defense Department which has been assembling contingency plans for rapidly responding to possible threats to Western oil supplies.

But even if the Somali withdrawal does end the Russian and Cuban presence in the Horn, troubling questions over the possibility of future Communist involvement elsewhere in Africa remain. The most likely is that Prime Minister Ian D. Smith's so-called internal settlement in Rhodesia might lead Mozambique and others to ask for increased Soviet and Cuban support to aid nationalist groups not in the arrangement.

Ironically, in view of these concerns, the record of the Administration's effort shows that Indian Ocean arms control has been complicated as much by Soviet losses in the region

as by gains. Despite Mr. Carter's talk of demilitarization, when negotiators met for the first time last spring to discuss a formula for the region, American officials unveiled a proposal for "stabilizing" the presence of bases, ships and aircraft. In effect, the United States wanted to freeze the military status quo. That would have meant that both sides could continue to maintain their existing fleets and patterns of operation. In particular, it meant that the United States Navy would be able to hold on to its base at Diego Garcia, recently expanded to accomodate a carrier task force and long-range patrol aircraft. In return, the Soviet navy was to be allowed to continue to use facilities at the Somali port of Berbera, which included an air base, floating dry dock and a missile storage site.

Not surprisingly, Moscow disagreed with aspects of the stabilization idea, particularly the fact that it would not limit Washington's ability to send nuclear-armed submarines and carrier-based aircraft into the region. But officials report that at a second round of talks last fall, Moscow appeared ready to accept several elements of the freeze proposal.

Moscow's decision, however, to step up its support for Ethiopia in the conflict on the Horn led Somali President Siad Barre in mid-November to throw the Russian navy out of Berbera. Although the Soviet leadeship may have judged this to be an acceptable cost in view of the political benefits of cementing ties with the larger and more populous Ethiopia, the loss of Berbera introduced a snag into the Indian Ocean talks.

The trouble was that having just lost its primary base in the area, Moscow was little interested in an arrangement that froze the existing situation. "To get an agreement, the Russians basically told us that we would have to help them find another base," explained one official.

But while Moscow may be getting another naval port, this time at Aden in South Yemen, continuing Soviet involvement in the Horn has led the Administration to give up Indian Ocean arms control for the time being. And while Paul Warnke, the director of the Arms Control and Disarmament Agency, led a delegation to Berne, Switzerland last month for more talks, his main mission was to tell Moscow that progress in negotiations would be linked to Soviet actions in the Horn.

With the arms talks on ice, the Pentagon is putting together a 100,000-strong "quick reaction" force of Army and Marine units — not for the Horn — but for possible deployment to the Persian Gulf in the event of Soviet intervention there. For the present, arms control no longer fits in with either Soviet or American thinking about the region.

NEW YORK TIMES, March 12, 1978, S4 P3

U.S. Is Concerned About Future Of 3 Israeli Air Bases in Sinai

By DREW MIDDLETON

One of the most important military problems facing Israel, and to a considerable measure the United States, is the future of three Israeli Air Force bases in the Sinai peninsula.

From the American standpoint the most important of these is the base at Etzion, situated about 15 miles southwest of the Israeli town of Eilat just over the frontier into Sinai.

According to qualified allied sources, the United States Air Force has been using the base for long-range surveillance flights over the Red Sea, the Gulf of Aden and the western areas of the Indian Ocean.

These are areas of mounting strategic interest to the United States. The successful Soviet political and military penetration of Ethiopia, intelligence analysts say, will lead to the establishment of Soviet air bases there.

New African Strategy

What Pentagon experts call Moscow's new African strategy has focused American military attention on the shipborne traffic in the area, including oil moving out of the Persian Gulf past the Horn of Africa on its way to the United States and Europe.

A United States "window" opening on this increasingly important area is regarded as vital by strategic planners. Consequently the future of Etzion in the event of any Israeli agreement with Egypt to abandon Sinai has become a military problem with global implications.

Early this decade, Israeli-built air bases at Eytam near El Arish on Sinai's Mediterranean coast and at Ofira near Sharm el Sheik at the southern tip of the peninsula. The third base, Etzion, was the most expensive—it cost more than $4 billion—

and the most sophisticated, able to handle high-performance reconnaissance and combat aircraft.

Aircraft at these three Israeli bases can range over the entire Red Sea area and protect oil and other materials reaching Eilat from Iran and Africa.

President Anwar el-Sadat of Egypt in last winter's abortive peace negtiations wanted the bases handed over as part of a settlement. The Israelis refused, although the Carter Administration seemed to support the Egyptian request.

Sharp differences exist in the Administration over the importance of the bases, particularly Etzion, to American defense policy.

A group of Navy and Air Force officers at the Pentagon insists that the expansion of Soviet naval and air power in the Indian Ocean and probable Soviet acquisition of new bases in Ethiopia increase the value of Etzion.

Rear Adm. Robert J. Hanks, now retired, pointed out in a recent article that Soviet warships use the facilities at Umm Qasr and Basra in Iraq, at Aden in South Yemen and at Indian ports.

Soviet Calls at Mauritius

Admiral Hanks, who commanded the Navy's Middle East Force based on Bahrain from 1972 to 1975, also reported that the Soviet Navy now makes routine calls at Port Louis in Mauritius in the southern Indian Ocean.

The Soviet Navy is the prime military force in the Indian Ocean. Squadrons from the Soviet Pacific Fleet, whose headquarters are at Vladivostok, operate regularly in the ocean. The usual squadron is made up of a missile-armed cruiser, two destroyers, a landing ship, an oceanographic research vessel and two or more submarines.

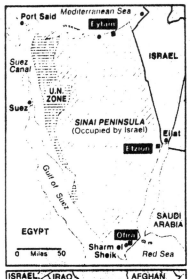

The New York Times/March 26, 1978

Israeli air bases are situated at Etzion, Eytam and Ofira, in Sinai.

The Soviet maritime penetration is not limited to warships, military sources emphasize. Since the late 1960's, the number of Soviet merchantmen, fishing vessels

and scientific ships in the Indian Ocean has increased. All of these, these sources said, can be considered ancillary to the main military force.

Soviet merchant shipping also carries much of the arms trade across the Indian Ocean. The South Africans and Rhodesians report that Soviet transports and freighters have delivered more than 200 heavy tanks and 35 crated MIG-21 fighters to Mozambique.

The Russian naval position in the area has not been drastically damaged by the recent loss of the use of Berbera in Somalia. Military sources insist that as long as the naval squadron has continued access to Aden, anchorages off the island of Socotra in the Gulf of Aden, and, possibly in the future, the Ethiopian port of Massawa on the Red Sea, the Soviet Union will exercise a powerful military influence in the waters around the Horn of Africa.

Soviet air and sea deployments in the area and the ability to fly in troops and equipment have convinced experienced officers in Washington and at NATO headquarters in Brussels that by establishing naval and air supremacy over the Red Sea, the Gulf of Aden, the Persian Gulf and the western reaches of the Indian Ocean, the Russians are in position to "cut NATO's throat."

Contemplating this deployment of Soviet power, planners insist that the United States must retain operational rights at Etzion, whether the base is under Israeli or Egyptian control; must continue to develop the naval and air base at Diego Garcia, and must reinforce the Middle East naval force beyond its present strength of two destroyers and one old command ship.

NEW YORK TIMES, March 26, 1978, P10

NEW AFGHAN REGIME WORRIES PAKISTANIS

They Regard Northern Neighbor as Pro-Soviet, and Fear U.S. Will Not Respond With Aid

By WILLIAM BORDERS
Special to The New York Times

ISLAMABAD, Pakistan, May 19—Pakistan is deeply concerned about what it regards as a pro-Moscow Government established last month in Afghanistan after a violent coup.

"For all practical purposes, the Soviet Union now has a border with Pakistan," said a high-ranking official, insisting on

anonymity, because "whoever they are, we have to live with them."

"The United States must realize that there has been a historic readjustment in this part of the world and act accordingly," he said, expressing a view that seems widespread here in Pakistan's capital, a sleek, newly built city in the gray-brown Himalayan foothills.

The Pakistanis, besides facing what they see as a more acute Soviet threat with the emergence of the new Afghan regime, now also expect a renewal of their old dispute with Afghanistan over the tribal territory known on the other side of the border as Pushtunistan. The disputed territory, along the legendary Khyber Pass, is inhabited by fierce Pathan warriors in floppy white turbans and billowy pajama suits who wander back and forth across the disputed border as they please, paying little heed to the governments on either side.

Daud Was Willing to Accept Border

The Pakistanis say that Afghanistan's former President, Mohammad Daud, who paid a friendly visit early this year, had

been about to agree to the border along the so-called Durand Line, drawn by the British in the 19th century.

But now President Daud is dead, brought down by machine-gun fire during the coup in Kabul on April 28, and the Government of Prime Minister Noor Mohammad Taraki has shown no eagerness to negotiate on the issue. In fact, shortly after the coup, the Kabul radio broadcast messages of congratulations from the leaders of Pathan tribes on this side of the border, indicating that it did not regard the region as part of Pakistan.

If the Soviet Union is to exercise increased influence on Afghanistan's Government, as diplomats and other knowledgeable people here and in Kabul believe, a settlement of the border dispute now seems remote.

One person with long experience in Afghanistan, where Western countries and the Soviet Union have spent years struggling for control of the trackless deserts and mountains, said, "The Soviets would rather hold that issue in reserve, even if they put no immediate pressure on it."

More U.S. Aid Is Doubted

Pakistani officials hope that the emergence of an Afghan Government regarded as pro-Communist might encourage the United States to increase its military sales or aid to its beleaguered ally here. In private conversations, however, they concede that the mood in Washington does not seem to augur well for such a decision.

Last year, the Carter Administration stopped the sale of 100 A-7 fighter airplanes, for which Pakistan would have paid in cash. Pakistanis said at the time, and are repeating bitterly now, that the Americans are willing to arm Iran, which is also on Afghanistan's border, but not Pakistan, because this country has no oil to sell.

Iran and Pakistan, together with Britain and Turkey, are allied with the United States in the Central Treaty Organiza-tion, a regional pact established in 1955 during the cold war. But people here are increasingly questioning its value. Agha Shahi, the Foreign Secretary said, "The feeling here is that CENTO has not been meaningful in this new situation."

NEW YORK TIMES, May 20, 1978, P4

Countering Soviet Global Aims

M. Apisman.

By Thomas H. Moore

WASHINGTON—A general erosion in our commitment to fundamental national-security objectives has been brought about in part by the perception that the competition between the Soviet Union and the United States for dominance in world affairs is over.

While the United States has in recent years backed away from such competition, there is no evidence that the Russians have departed from their plan to attain dominance.

Many see détente as Soviet willingness to retreat, but Moscow openly describes it simply as one more approach in its plan.

While the United States seems lacking in resolve, the Soviet Union remains committed to its national strategies, which include the following: avoidance of a major confrontation, or nuclear conflict, with the West until the outcome favors the Soviet Union; development of the capability to win an Atlantic alliance-Warsaw Pact conflict; and creation of an environment in third-world countries conducive to Soviet orientation and alignment; exploitation of wars of liberation and "anticolonialism" against "capitalist" nations; development of the means to isolate the United States through denying sea lines of communication; creation of an environment of debilitating competition among Western nations, fostering dissension among them.

The Soviet Union underwrites its objectives militarily and politically by doing the following: accelerating its development of intercontinental ballistic missiles and submarine-launched ballistic missiles; maintaining a massive military force in Europe opposing the North Atlantic Treaty Organization; developing naval forces for projection of power and acquisition of base rights in the Indian Ocean, the Mediterranean and the Caribbean; supporting uprisings, most recently in Angola, Afghanistan and the Horn of Africa; deploying a Navy capable of threatening our access to sea lines of communication in a crisis; and creating an environment of increased competition for scarce resources in the West, particularly with Middle East oil.

If we are to counter these Soviet objectives, we must be visibly committed to our own. Objectives critical to our national security must be underwritten with explicit strategies. To underwrite those objectives, our political statements and commitments must be orchestrated with the deployment and posture of our forces.

We must strive to insure that no situation becomes critical — that each area of concern remains stable. Our emphasis must be on decisive actions to deter events that might lead to a crisis rather than reacting after the situation is out of hand.

In recent years, we have supported the following four national objectives:

We deter an attack by the Russians on our cities by the threat of reprisal attacks against theirs. Military forces in the form of the nuclear triad — submarines, land-based missiles and airplanes — are maintained to underwrite this strategy.

We deter a nuclear attack on our forces by threat of reprisal, and by basing our forces and targeting them against the Russians' nuclear and conventional forces so that the Russians perceive no net advantage in an initial attack.

We deter aggression against NATO by an overall military conventional and nuclear capability to contain such attacks, coupled with a firm commitment that any attack on our allies involves the United States. This objective is underwritten by the deployment of our Army and Air Force units in allied territory, by the presence of our Navy units on the southern and northern flanks of NATO, and by the maintenance of United States Navy forces worldwide to protect the sea lanes to Europe.

We maintain a military presence in the Western Pacific to keep Japan and South Korea aligned with us, and to prevent the Russians from coercing the People's Republic of China into an alignment against us. Also, China's present alignment draws Soviet divisions from the European front.

Recent events underscore what should be a fifth national objective equally critical to our national security, and a major component of a viable global strategy:

Preventing the Soviet Union from creating an environment in the Middle East, the Persian Gulf, and the Horn of Africa that could result in denial of oil to the United States, NATO and Japan, and deterring the Russians from any overt action against either Iran or Saudi Arabia.

There is a consensus that an uninterrupted flow of oil from the Persian Gulf is essential to the well-being of most Western nations. Such an interruption, if prolonged, would have a debilitating effect during peacetime, a devastating effect during wartime. Oil from the Gulf could be denied to the West as a result of destruction of the oil fields or through a takeover of the producing countries. However, it is far more likely that the flow of oil would be disrupted as a result of Soviet coercion.

Through actions such as those in Ethiopia and Afghanistan the Russians can create the perception that the United States is impotent to respond and unreliable as an ally. In the presence of this environment, Saudi Arabia and Iran (long enjoying a special relationship with the United States) may be forced to decide that their national interests are best served by making substantial concessions to the Russians.

The United States must proceed now to develop a clearly understood and fully supported strategy — both political and military — that underwrites the fifth objective. Admonitions and verbal commitments will not suffice. Neither is it appropriate to adopt the attitude that we should wait and see what happens, that the situation is "not critical yet." Both Saudi Arabia and Iran are deeply concerned by the gathering storm and are distressed by our seeming lack of concern and commitment.

In particular, I would urge that we do the following:

Insure that the President is under no constraint that would prevent him from exercising his authority to counter Soviet initiatives promptly and decisively.

Make arrangements with the Governments of Iran and Saudi Arabia for the intermittent deployment of two carrier forces to the Eastern African littoral and Arabian Sea, conducting selected exercises inside the Persian Gulf on a random basis. Since we lack land bases of any kind in that region, the carriers would provide a visible presence and timely manifestation of United States resolve.

Revitalize the bilateral security agreement of 1959 with Iran and explore the possibility of similar bilateral arrangements with Saudi Arabia.

Explore with our allies (NATO and Japan) joint guarantees and military pacts that adequately reflect our common responsibility for maintaining stability in the region and for the security of the sea routes to oil-producing nations.

Exempt Saudi Arabia and Iran from quota restrictions on the transfer of military equipment, explicitly recognizing that they are as important to our national security as the other nations that enjoy this privilege.

Formally arrange for the periodic conduct of joint United States-allied-Saudi-Iranian exercises involving all branches of the armed services — directed at possible external threats — in the Persian Gulf region.

■

Stability in the Persian Gulf is critical to the United States, NATO and Japan. Our security is threatened if any of these three power centers does not remain strong. The Russians are engaging in actions that give a clear message about their aspirations. The Saudis and Iranians are very concerned; they cannot avoid questioning our commitment, our reliability, and the wisdom of maintaining their alignment with the United States.

We must demonstrate our commitment by following an explicit political and military strategy. We must do this now lest we be faced very soon with a fatal and unsolvable problem.

Thomas H. Moorer, a retired Admiral, was chairman of the Joint Chiefs of Staff from July 1970 to July 1974.

Soviet Position in Aden and Kabul Seen Improving

By DREW MIDDLETON

Western European and United States intelligence analysts say the Soviet Union is solidifying its hold on three military bases on Southern Yemen's territory and is consolidating an already influential military and political position in Afghanistan.

The expansion of Soviet influence in the two countries, and continued Soviet activity in Ethiopia in support of that country's campaign to bring Eritrean secessionists under control, should more than compensate the Russians for the loss of bases in Somalia, according to experts on the area. The Somalis forced them to leave because of their aid to Ethiopia in the conflict over Ethiopia's arid Ogaden region.

Soviet policies in the three areas are said to have resulted in the achievement of a strategic position of greater global significance than that enjoyed a decade ago, when the Russians made a heavy military and political investment in Egypt. In the present strategic situation, it was said, the establishment of naval and air bases on or near the principal oil routes is a more important factor in the global balance than military support for client states.

Three Bases in Southern Yemen

The pattern of activity in Southern Yemen reflects Moscow's interest in the area. The Russians control three important bases: the island of Socotra, in the Arabian Sea 150 miles east of the tip of the Horn of Africa; and bases at Aden and Al Mukulla, about 80 miles east of Aden on the Arabian Sea.

Most analysts consider Socotra the most important. According to European reports, the Soviet Union is building electronic-surveillance stations and a communications center in the mountain range that bisects the island, which is 72 miles long. There are also reports, as yet unconfirmed, that they are building surface-to-surface missile bases. Anchorages for Soviet surface ships have been established along the northern coast.

The base in Aden serves as headquarters for Soviet military activity in the Horn of Africa and the Persian Gulf area. One European estimate is that 1,000 to 1,500 military personnel, including communications technicians and intelligence specialists, are stationed in Aden. The Russians also control a section of Aden's main airport, which in the last six months has been a stop on the main supply route from the Soviet Union to Ethiopia.

Air Base Under Construction

The Russians are also constructing an air base near the international airport at Khormaksar, adjacent to Aden. When completed, it will be able to support 60 jet fighters and will feature storage depots for artillery ammunition, torpedoes and missiles. Soviet Army units equipped with surface-to-air missiles will be in charge of its security.

Al Mukulla's importance is geographical. It lies astride the road from Aden to Oman, the northern coast of which is on the Gulf of Oman across from Iran. Its northern coast lies near the Strait of Hormuz, through which oil tankers from the Persian Gulf pass en route to the United States, Western Europe and Japan. The Russians have taken over Al Mukulla's port and airport.

As for Afghanistan, consolidation of the Soviet position is said to have been rapid since President Noor Mohammad Taraki assumed power in Kabul in April. More then 20 aid agreements have been signed, there has been an influx of Soviet advisers and technicians, and Soviet transport aircraft are bringing in arms and equipment to replace that destroyed in the fighting during the coup.

Western diplomats in Kabul believe that the Soviet Union also seeks a friendship treaty, including mutual security clauses. The Iranian and Pakistani Governments are concerned over such a possibility, fearing that Afghan forces armed with Soviet weapons and directed by Soviet officers would inject a new military element into a troubled region.

NEW YORK TIMES, July 31, 1978, P2

Bibliography

This list provides full bibliographic information on the articles abstracted in The Middle East *and other articles and books pertinent to Middle East topics. It includes approximately 2,500 entries that derive from the newspapers and magazines contributing to The Information Bank. A list of these sources is found on page xii of this book.*

The bibliography, arranged by chapter and chapter subdivision, gives in alphabetical order the names of newspapers and magazines. Below each newspaper and magazine are entries giving titles of books and captions (headlines) of articles. Books (mentioned in the newspaper and/or magazine) are listed first, in alphabetical order, followed by articles, in chronological order. Each entry concludes with the date, section (S) number (when applicable) and page (P) number of source material (for example, Oct 23, 1978, S3 P8). Those articles abstracted in The Middle East *and all full-text articles reprinted in* The Middle East *have an asterisk to the left of the entry.*

Some newspapers are divided into sections, each of which starts with page 1. To identify which page 1 an abstract refers to, section numbers are included (when applicable) in the bibliographic citations. These section numbers correspond to the numbers or letters assigned to sections by the newspapers; S4, then, denotes either Section 4 or Section D, depending on the system a newspaper uses. If an article appears in the first section, no section reference appears in the bibliographic citation. Similarly, no section is noted if a newspaper contains only one section. Sections 11, 21, 22 and 23 of the New York Times *are regional supplements included only in Sunday editions distributed to limited parts of the New York metropolitan area. All four supplements are included in the* New York Times *on microfilm. Page numbers for* New York Times *articles refer to the Final Late City Edition, which is the edition used for the* Times *on microfilm.*

Key to Acronyms

This list contains acronyms that appear in the bibliography.

AMF	Arab Monetary Fund
AOI	Arab Organization Industrialization
AWACS	Airborne Warning and Control Systems

GATT	General Agreement on Tariffs and Trade
IMF	International Monetary Fund
NUS	National Union of Students
QECD	Economic Cooperation and Development
OPEC	Organization of Petroleum Exporting Countries
SABIC	Saudi Basic Industries Corporation
SPA	Saudi Port Authority
UAE	United Arab Emirates
WMI	Waste Management, Inc.

1. THE IMPACT OF OIL

The Changing Face of the Middle East

AVIATION WEEK AND SPACE TECHNOLOGY
* Arabs develop arms industry. May 15, 1978, P14

BUSINESS WEEK
* West finds welcome in Algeria. Mar 27, 1978, P36

CHICAGO TRIBUNE
Focus on Shah's industrial development. Jan 8, 1978, P1
Focus on Iranian military. Jan 9, 1978, P1

CHRISTIAN SCIENCE MONITOR
* Oil money develops Sudan. Feb 24, 1978, P13
Israeli-occupied Lebanon described. May 10, 1978, P4

EDMONTON JOURNAL
Canada-Arabia compared on solar research. Aug 10, 1978, S8, P1

FAR EASTERN ECONOMIC REVIEW
Pakistan woos Arab support. Jan 6, 1978, P53
S. Korean trade with Mideast examined. Jan 6, 1978, P47
Sri Lanka and Mideast relations examined. Jan 6, 1978, P54

FINANCIAL TIMES
* Europeans seeking Algerian contracts. Jan 12, 1978, P2
* Insurance risks in Mideast noted. Jan 19, 1978, P9
* Saudi G.N.P. rising. Jan 24, 1978, P6
* Arabs back Sudan farming. Jan 26. 1978, P4
Iran to aid India. Feb 6, 1978, P3
Saudi's request for F-15's affects relations. Feb 10, 1978, P17
* Sudan development reviewed. Feb 16, 1978, P3
Kuwait profiled. Feb 27, 1978, P13
Desalination expansion in Mideast. Mar 6, 1978, P3
* Saudi economic development profiled. Mar 20, 1978, P13
* French jets to Mideast. Mar 23, 1978, P6
* Bahrain's economy profiled. Apr 3, 1978, P15
* Gulf states diversify industry. Apr 17, 1978, P14
* Saudi economic development surveyed. Apr 17, 1978, P15
* British-Iranian arms complex planned. May 11, 1978, P1
Slower Gulf industrialization seen. Aug 7, 1978, P5
* Gulf states aid Egypt. Aug 15, 1978, P3
Algeria examines past, future plans. Aug 31, 1978, P4
* Yemeni boom tied to oil. Sept 25, 1978, P3
* Mideast construction declines. Sept 27, 1978, P29
Saudis push for heavy industry. Oct 27, 1978, P4
Arab tourism examined. Nov 1, 1978, P17

FOREIGN POLICY
Rationale for arms sales to Iran. July, 1978, P56

FORTUNE
Saudi industry assessed. July 31, 1978, P110
* Saudis seek social balance. July 31, 1978, P114

HOUSTON CHRONICLE
Saudi's seek no oil growth. Apr 25, 1978, P17

JOURNAL OF COMMERCE
* Syria seeks diversification from oil. Sept 29, 1978, P9
Saudi's development of ports examined. Oct 18, 1978, P1
Saudi's Dammam port examined. Oct 19, 1978, P1

LOS ANGELES TIMES
* Mideast food crisis foreseen. Nov 26, 1978, S5, P8

NATIONAL JOURNAL
Saudi's emerging power affects U.S. Mar 4, 1978, P336

NEWSWEEK
* New architecture in Mideast. June 5, 1978, P65

NEW YORK TIMES
U.S. arm sales abroad surveyed. Jan 8, 1978, P34
Saudi army expanding near Iraq. Jan 9, 1978, P6
Goals for modernization of Jidda. Jan 12, 1978, P4
* Petrodollars aid Egypt's economy. Jan 29, 1978, S4, P3
Survey of Gulf slowdown noted. Feb 5, 1978, S12, P70
* Saudi growth continues. Feb 11, 1978, P27
* Jubail complex detailed. Feb 13, 1978, S4, P1
* Saudis building industrial site. Feb 13, 1978, S4, P3
* Saudi weapons facility planned. Feb 18, 1978, P1
* Mideast facing development setbacks. Feb 20, 1978, S4, P1
French support Mideast arms. Mar 15, 1978, P7
$796.1 million contract for Iranian ships. Mar 24, 1978, S4, P3
$1.5 billion dam project in Iran. June 7, 1978, P4
Saudis pay $24 million for arms. June 12, 1978, S4, P15
* Saudis tap natural gas. June 13, 1978, P25
$600 million arm sale to Iran approved. July 16, 1978, P26
* Petrodollars support Egypt's debt. June 17, 1978, P28
* Koreans build in Mideast. June 19, 1978, S4, P5
A.M.F.'s aims, principles reported. June 20, 1978, S4, P3
Sophisticated arms to Iran considered. July 30, 1978, P11
Sale of planes to Iran modified. Aug 17, 1978, P3
Carter rejects Iran's request for bombers. Aug 18, 1978, P48
Military aid proposals for Arabia to Congress. Aug 19, 1978, P138
$1.2 billion sale in arms to Saudis. Aug 22, 1978, P41
* Concern voiced on Mideast arms. Sept 6, 1978, P114
Question of Iran's buying planes from A.M.S.T. Sept 15, 1978, P64

TIME
Saudi Arabia profiled. May 22, 1978, P34

TIMES OF LONDON
Sudan profiled. Jan 10, 1978, P7
Britain aids Mideast arms technology. Jan 13, 1978, P6
Officials guilty of corruption in Iran sales. Jan 19, 1978, P2
Iran's purchase of tanks clarified. Jan 21, 1978, P15
Political, economic, social aspects of U.A.E. Apr 24, 1978, S2, P1
U.A.E. political, social, economic aspects profiled. Apr 24, 1978, S2, P1
Survey of Kuwait development. June 12, 1978, S2, P1

TORONTO STAR
Newfoundland's Come-by-Chance profiled. June 24, 1978, P6

WALL STREET JOURNAL
Value of helicopters to Iran doubles. Mar 14, 1978, P20
Germany to supply arms to Iran. Mar 15, 1978, P19

Northrop Corp. to provide aid to Saudis. June 22, 1978, P4
$80 million Kuwaitian "Disneyland" planned. June 26, 1978, P1
* Egyptian sugar project launched. July 18, 1978, P37
$263.5 million sale to Iran planned. Aug 14, 1978, P4
Gun sale to Iran planned. Aug 15, 1978, P3
$1.15 billion arms sale to Saudis planned. Aug 22, 1978, P6

WASHINGTON POST

* Iraqi atom sale disclosed. Jan 12, 1978, P7
* Middle East development slowing. Jan 15, 1978, S8, P2
Saudi's conflicting culture described. Jan 15, 1978, S2 P1
* Saudi facing cultural conflict. Jan 15, 1978, S2, P1
A.W.A.C.S. secrets slipped to U.S.S.R. Feb 2, 1978, P9
Iraq's emergence as power examined. Aug 6, 1978, P1
Iraq's self-determination evaluated. Aug 8, 1978, P1
Mideast to produce arms. Sept 9, 1978, P11
Employment in Arab states grows. Sept 17, 1978, P1
* Egypt copes with Aswan problems. Nov 12, 1978, S2, P2
* Arab development projects profiled. Nov 23, 1978, S5, P10

The Middle East in World Economy

AMERICAN BANKER

* O.P.E.C. investments termed modest. May 12, 1978, P4

ATLANTA CONSTITUTION

Arab investors seek investment advice. Mar 30, 1978, S4, P13
Rumors of Arab takeover of S.W. Georgia examined. Apr 2, 1978, P16

BUSINESS WEEK

Chemical companies negotiate with S.A.B.I.C. Mar 13, 1978, P43
* Saudis debate corporate takeovers. July 30, 1978, P38
* Riyal shuns reserve currency role. Sept 11, 1978, P126
* Montedison gets petrodollar investment. Oct 2, 1978, P48

CHRISTIAN SCIENCE MONITOR

* Arab aid studied. June 15, 1978, P1

FAR EASTERN ECONOMIC REVIEW

Conferences held for trilateral economic plan. Mar 31, 1978, P36

FINANCIAL TIMES

British corporation to build Egyptian boats. Jan 13, 1978, P32
Britain to repay commission payments. Jan 20, 1978, P6
* Bahrain's banking hits $15 billion. Feb 9, 1978, P27
Japan to build power plant in Iran. Mar 10, 1978, P6
Saudi's investments with France, U.S. Mar 15, 1978, P2
Saudi's economic plans detailed. Apr 17, 1978, P15
Algerian oil company's investment plan. May 5, 1978, P32
* Saudi buys French bank. May 6, 1978, P25
Saudi-French talks focus on economic cooperation. May 31, 1978, P2
U.A.E. political, economic conditions examined. June 26, 1978, P11
Thompson-C.S.F. subsidize Arab company. July 25, 1978, P22
* Kuwait slows spending. Aug 3, 1978, P3

HOUSTON CHRONICLE

$120 million Arab investment in Houston. May 18, 1978, S2, P1
Arab-backed corporation invests in Houston. Aug 23, 1978, P24

JOURNAL OF COMMERCE

* Greek-Arab bank formed. June 29, 1978, P1
Syria seeks partners for oil exploration. Sept 28, 1978, P10
U.S. businessmen face challenge in Syrian markets. Oct 5, 1978, P3

MIDDLE EAST

* Arab aid criticized. Jan 1978, P66

NEWSWEEK

Khayl affirms Saudi support of U.S. dollar. Oct 9, 1978, P82

NEW YORK TIMES

Syria-Libya sign economic pact. Jan 23, 1978, P5
Miller questioned about Textron deal. Jan 25, 1978, S4, P1
Iranians, Saudis buy California property. Feb 5, 1978, P17

Investigation of Miller's Textron deal planned. Feb 10, 1978, S2, P1
Evidence of Textron payments heard. Feb 14, 1978, P49
Investigation of Textron. Feb 15, 1978, S4, P1
Textron memo casts doubt on testimony. Feb 27, 1978, S4, P1
Rolls-Royce to supply Mideast with engines. Mar 3, 1978, S4, P5
Bell Helicopter profiled. Mar 4, 1978, P27
Iran's carpet industry declines. Mar 12, 1978, P23
* Arab investment group formed. Mar 20, 1978, S4, P1
* Arab aid projects grow. Apr 10, 1978, S4, P1
* Petrodollars recycled in U.S. Apr 29, 1978, P29
Mideast investors pay $50 million for hotels. May 5, 1978, P1
Loews Corp. buys N.Y.C. hotels. June 1, 1978, P1
* Arabs are investing cautiously. June 15, 1978, S4, P1
* Petrodollars favor U.S. banks. June 15, 1978, S4, P4
* Drooping dollar draws Arab investors. Aug 22, 1978, P18
* O.P.E.C. shows payments deficit. Sept 13, 1978, P31

SAN FRANCISCO CHRONICLE

Mideast investors eye U.S. real estate. Aug 11, 1978, P2

TIMES OF LONDON

* Petrodollars in London markets. Mar 7, 1978, S2, P1
* Arab banking reviewed. Apr 10, 1978, S2, P1

WALL STREET JOURNAL

$120 million construction for copper in Oman. Jan 24, 1978, P12
Textron subsidy sales to Iran reviewed. Jan 25, 1978, P3
* World economy worries Saudis. Feb 1, 1978, P16
* O.P.E.C. debt grows. Feb 9, 1978, P16
Procedure of Textron's Iranian deal. Feb 22, 1978, P1
Litton receives $501.1 million contract. May 24, 1978, P5
* Investor for the Arabs. May 9, 1978, P1
Arab investors buy oil stock. July 28, 1978, P12

WASHINGTON POST

Impact of Saudi's $142 billion 5-year plan. Jan 10, 1978, P12
Mideast economic developments surveyed. Jan 15, 1978, S8, P2
Petrodollars fuel U.S. economy. Feb 21, 1978, P1
* Saudis seeking influence in U.S. July 23, 1978, S3, P7

2.   A DURABLE OPEC

BUSINESS WEEK

O.P.E.C. to set floor price for natural gas. Jan 9, 1978, P72
* O.P.E.C. cohesion assessed. June 12, 1978, P60
* Future of O.P.E.C. considered. July 10, 1978, P27
* O.P.E.C. president Sabah interviewed. July 24, 1978, P136
* Oil demand on rise. Oct 9, 1978, P46
Economics of oil pricing interpreted. Nov 6, 1978, P100

CHICAGO TRIBUNE

O.P.E.C.'s decision on oil prices interpreted. Jan 3, 1978, S3, P2.

CHRISTIAN SCIENCE MONITOR

West Management, Inc. profiled. Mar 22, 1978, P11

ECONOMIST

* O.P.E.C. pricing scored. Apr 1, 1978, P65

ECONOMIST OF LONDON

Less rich O.P.E.C. countries affected by dollar. Feb 4, 1978, P87

FAR EASTERN ECONOMIC REVIEW

Analysis of Arabia's relation with Asia. Jan 6, 1978, P27
O.P.E.C. develops trilateral economic plan. Mar 31, 1978, P36

FINANCIAL TIMES

* Basket pricing urged. Jan 16, 1978, P8
O.P.E.C.'s outlook on oil supplies analyzed. July 7, 1978, P31
* O.P.E.C. decision assessed. June 21, 1978, P18

FOREIGN POLICY

* Oil weapon pondered. Apr 1978, P53
* Stable oil prices foreseen. Apr 1978, P36

HOUSTON CHRONICLE

Saudis say no to another oil embargo. Oct 17, 1978, P15

JOURNAL OF COMMERCE

* O.P.E.C. caution analyzed. June 23, 1978, P4
* Oil pricing discussed. July 31, 1978, P4
  Threat of oil embargo depends on Mideast peace. Aug 11, 1978, P1

LATIN AMERICAN ECONOMIC REVIEW

Ronald Muller interviewed. Jan 6, 1978, P5

NEWSWEEK

* Saudis cite trade figures. May 8, 1978, P77

NEW YORK TIMES

* Report urges hard line. Jan 4, 1978, S4, P1
* Kuwait adjusts heavy crude. Jan 18, 1978, S4, P2
* O.P.E.C. ponders dollar slide. Feb 2, 1978, S4, P10
  Acronyms defined. Feb 5, 1978, S12, P9
  Oil supply-and-demands's effects on O.P.E.C. Feb 5, 1978, S12, P10
* O.P.E.C.-U.S. cooperation sought. Mar 2, 1978, S4, P13
* Dollar slide threatens O.P.E.C. rift. Mar 7, 1978, P53
* Meeting on dollar slide. Mar 9, 1978, S4, P7
* Oil pricing changes considered. Mar 17, 1978, S4, P2
  O.P.E.C. discusses dollar devaluation. Mar 23, 1978, S4, P3
  O.P.E.C.'s Geneva meeting postponed. Mar 29, 1978, S4, P9
* Oil price increase looms. Apr 7, 1978, P1
  Saudis oppose O.P.E.C. price increase. Apr 23, 1978, P7
* Monetary system revisions scored. Apr 28, 1978, P1
  Venezuela supports O.P.E.C.'s price hike. May 6, 1978, P33
* O.P.E.C. seeks stable economy. May 7, 1978, P6
* Oil hike splits ministers. May 8, 1978, S4, P1
* Saudi oil exports slip. May 11, 1978, S4, P9
* Oil glut cools price rise. May 23, 1978, S4, P11
  Oil shortage by 2000 unlikely. June 6, 1978, S4, P15
* Saudi shores sinking dollar. June 20, 1978, S4, P1
* O.P.E.C. split foreseen. June 18, 1978, S5, P1
* Deadlock over oil prices. June 19, 1978, S4, P1
  A.M.F. president Hashim interviewed. June 20, 1978, P3
* O.P.E.C. to maintain prices. June 20, 1978, P1
  O.P.E.C.'s financial reserves increased. June 22, 1978, S4, P6
  Saudi's Yamani supports small increases. June 27, 1978, S4, P12
* Iranian warns of price rise. June 30, 1978, S4, P1
  Economic problems caused by oil prices evaluated. July 2, 1978, S3, P12
* O.P.E.C. discusses dollar. July 18, 1978, S4, P1
* Dollar slides in renomination fears. July 22, 1978, P32
  O.P.E.C.'s recommendation for computing prices. July 22, 1978, P26
  Inflation, dollar decline raise oil price. Aug 10, 1978, P27
  Oil price-rise devalues dollar. Aug 10, 1978, P108
* Price rise rumors noted. Aug 12, 1978, P24
  O.P.E.C.'s oil pricing analyzed. Aug 24, 1978, P120
* O.P.E.C. financial need cited. Sept 30, 1978, P54
* O.P.E.C. chief sees substantial rise. Oct 10, 1978, P6
* Downstream expansion sought. Oct 10, 1978, P1
* Oil industry diversification sought. Oct 12, 1978, P4
* Split in O.P.E.C. threatened. Oct 16, 1978, P24
* Saudis will seek freeze. Nov 20, 1978, P1
  A break in O.P.E.C.'s price freeze seen. Nov 24, 1978, Pa
  Sharp price increase affects economy. Nov 26, 1978, S3, P1
  Impact of price increases on U.S. economy. Dec 15, 1978, S4, P1
  O.P.E.C. to end freeze on prices. Dec 15, 1978, P1
  Yamani supports gradual increases. Dec 16, 1978, P29
* U.S. deplores hike. Dec 18, 1978, P1
* 14.5% hike, highest in 5 years. Dec 19, 1978, P1

TIMES OF LONDON

* Yamani emphasizes independent posture. Jan 3, 1978, S2, P1

WALL STREET JOURNAL

* Production levels disputed. May 18, 1978, P29
  O.P.E.C. to discuss oil price at meeting. June 16, 1978, P1
* End of oil glut predicted. July 13, 1978, P12

3. A FRAGILE MOSAIC

Politics in Transition

CHRISTIAN SCIENCE MONITOR

* Baluchi insurgency foreseen. June 9, 1978, P4
* Kurdish unrest continues. June 13, 1978, P4
  Sudan's Dinka tribe profiled. June 30, 1978, P12

FAR EASTERN ECONOMIC REVIEW

Asia and Arabs analyzed. Jan 6, 1978, P27

FINANCIAL TIMES

* Algeria, France clash on Polisario. Jan 11, 1978, P1
  French-Algerian relations decline. Jan 11, 1978, P3
  Saudi's policy on contracts described. Jan 18, 1978, P5
* Pakistan tribes favor separatism. Feb 11, 1978, P10
* Sudan seeks reconciliation. Mar 21, 1978, P4
  Sudan's Nimeiry speech summarized. May 26, 1978, P4
  Politics, economy in Sudan examined. July 13, 1978, P19
* Foreigners under constraint in Arabia. July 25, 1978, P16

FOREIGN POLICY

* Trilateral order observed. Jan 1978, P90
* Pakistan insurgency reviewed. Oct 1978, P136

LOS ANGELES TIMES

* Western Sahara fighting continues. May 8, 1978, P1

MANCHESTER GUARDIAN WEEKLY

Release of French hostages analyzed. Jan 1, 1978, P1
France's involvement in Sahara noted. Jan 8, 1978, P11
* Sudan is following moderate course. Feb 26, 1978, P11
History of Mauritania. Mar 5, 1978, P12

MIDDLE EAST

* Polisario front profiled. Jan 1978, P31

NEW YORK TIMES

Conflict in Western Sahara described. Jan 22, 1978, S4, P4
* Sudan achieves reconciliation. Apr 13, 1978, P6
  Sudan's Nimeiry visits Damascus. May 7, 1978, P13
  Nimeiry's tour through Mideast analyzed. May 9, 1978, P20
  Sudan's Nimeiry's visits described. May 11, 1978, S4, P14
* Political violence disrupting Turkey. May 17, 1978, S4, P6
* Iran fears separatist threat. May 20, 1978, S4, P3
  African conflict source for world war. May 21, 1978, S4, P1
* Numeiri returns exiles. June 2, 1978, P4
* Libyan attack reported. June 24, 1978, P4
  Mauritanian government intentions scored. July 12, 1978, P18
* Polisario in cease-fire. July 13, 1978, P2
  Nimeiry reorganizes Cabinet. July 30, 1978, P6
* Saudi insecurity described. July 30, 1978, S4, P23
  Lafghdaf interviewed on peace prospects. Aug 20, 1978, P120
* Morocco and Algeria clash. Oct 3, 1978, P56
  Iraq cancels Arab meeting. Oct 16, 1978, P15
* Syria, Iraq reconciling differences. Oct 22, 1978, P24
  Boumedienne's U.S.S.R. visit reported. Nov 15, 1978, P4
* Religious upheaval threatens region. Nov 19, 1978, S4, P19
  Boumedienne cancels U.S.S.R. trip. Nov 20, 1978, P6
  Boumedienne's health status reported. Nov 23, 1978, P13
* Uncertainty in Algeria. Nov 24, 1978, P5
* Religious minorities imperiled in Iran. Dec 10, 1978, P1
  U.S. rejects contract to import Algerian gas. Dec 20, 1978, S4, P1
* Ethnic strife in Turkey. Dec 26, 1978, P1
* Boumedienne's death announced. Dec 27, 1978, P1

TIME

* Greek community is embattled. Apr 3, 1978, P44
  Saudi Arabia profiled. May 22, 1978, P34

TIMES OF LONDON

  Imprisonment of Sudan poet Sharif described. Jan 16, 1978, P6
  Case for Saharans' independence made. Mar 6, 1978, P19
* Kurds and Iraqis in conflict. Apr 24, 1978, P6
* Qaddafi supports Polisario. June 5, 1978, P7

US NEWS AND WORLD REPORT

* Libyan arms threat cited. Apr 10, 1978, P39

WASHINGTON POST

  Mideast economic developments reviewed. Jan 15, 1978, S8, P2
* Confessional rivalry plagues Syria. Apr 7, 1978, P20
  Sudan's refusal to devalue currency analyzed. May 7, 1978, S6, P2
  Barzani's heavy security described. July 23, 1978, P11

Afghanistan

FINANCIAL TIMES

  Work problems delay canal's construction. Apr 12, 1978, P4
* Five-year plan adopted. Oct 31, 1978, P31
* French firm wins contract. Dec 18, 1978, P3

LOS ANGELES TIMES

* Population "apathetic" to takeover. Nov 4, 1978, P1

NEW YORK TIMES

  Hafez al-Assad re-elected. Feb 10, 1978, P8
  Afghanistan profiled. Apr 28, 1978, P6
* Afghan regime overthrown. Apr 28, 1978, P1
* Fighting in Kabul continues. Apr 29, 1978, P3
  Afghani coup reviewed. Apr 30, 1978, S4, P2
* Afghan radio details killings. Apr 30, 1978, P10
* New Afghan leader emerges. May 1, 1978, P1
* New regime in firm seat. May 2, 1978, P5
* U.S. taken by surprise. May 2, 1978, P4
* Khalq party described. May 3, 1978, P1
* New regime lists policies. May 4, 1978, P11
  Taraki's views of Afghan government. May 5, 1978, P5
  Afghani's new regime profiled. May 6, 1978, P5
  Prime minister outlines diplomacy. May 7, 1978, P1
  Afghani's new regime begins purge. May 9, 1978, P13
  Japan recognizes Afghan government. May 10, 1978, P2
  Atrocities against Afghani scholars condemned. May 12, 1978, P6
  New Afghani regime analyzed. May 20, 1978, P18
  New Afghan government profiled. June 4, 1978, S6, P28
  Afghan government strips King's citizenship. June 15, 1978, P7
* Afghan-Soviet ties strengthened. June 16, 1978, P1
  Soviet influence in Afghanistan analyzed. June 24, 1978, P5
* Civil war in Afghanistan seen. July 1, 1978, P4
  Abdullah Saleh elected president. July 18, 1978, P4
* U.S.-Afghan ties discussed. Aug 14, 1978, P4
* Counter-coup quashed. Aug 19, 1978, P161
* India to help Afghanistan. Sept 22, 1978, P113
* Afghan radicals cautious. Sept 24, 1978, P14
* Afghanistan slowly moves left. Sept 24, 1978, P14
* Afghanistan in Soviet orbit. Nov 18, 1978, P1
* Treaty signed with U.S.S.R. Dec 6, 1978, P1

TIMES OF LONDON

* New regime profiled. May 9, 1978, P18
* Regime's programs analyzed. May 30, 1978, P15

US NEWS AND WORLD REPORT

* Moslems oppose new regime. Dec 11, 1978, P55

WASHINGTON POST

* Afghans to seek non-alignment. May 8, 1978, P16
* Soviet role in Afghanistan examined. May 29, 1978, P12
* West supports new government. Nov 2, 1978, P30
* Government faces opposition. Nov 7, 1978, P17

Yemen

CHICAGO TRIBUNE

* Two Yemens skirmish. July 4, 1978, P10

MIDDLE EAST

  Yemen's development plan described. Jan 1978, P28
* North Yemen development profiled. Jan 1978, P30

NEW YORK TIMES

* Ghashmi assassinated. June 15, 1978, P1
  S. Yemen-Yemen tensions reviewed. June 25, 1978, P4
* Southern Yemen denies involvement. June 26, 1978, P5
* Robayya Ali ousted. June 27, 1978, P1
* U.S. mission thwarted. June 27, 1978, P2
  South Yemen profiled. June 27, 1978, P6
* Marxists seize power. June 28, 1978, P7
  Aden radio recognizes deaths in fighting. June 29, 1978, P14
  S. Yemen responsible for Hussein's death. June 30, 1978, P7
* South Yemen moderates purged. June 30, 1978, P7
* South Yemen complicity charged. July 2, 1978, P8
  S. Yemen-Yemen border war foreseen. July 4, 1978, P2
  Recent coups analyzed. July 12, 1978, P18
  Final battle of coup in Aden described. July 16, 1978, P11
  Southern Yemen announces election. July 31, 1978, P3
* U.S. drops diplomatic exchange. Aug 6, 1978, P11
* Political opponents executed. Nov 6, 1978, P25
* China to build conference hall. Dec 22, 1978, P7
* Leftist president elected. Dec 29, 1978, P7

TIMES OF LONDON

* North Yemen leader profiled. May 10, 1978, P18
* Yemen: feud reviewed. June 27, 1978, P17

WALL STREET JOURNAL

* Yemenis nationalize British interest. Mar 27, 1978, P7

WASHINGTON POST

  U.S.-S. Yemen relations supported. June 28, 1978, P14
* U.S. Yemen policy scored. July 7, 1978, P19
  Conditions in Yemen after Ismail. Aug 15, 1978, P8
* Aden suffers economic decline. Aug 15, 1978, P8
* U.S. interests seen endangered. Dec 20, 1978, P19

4. ANARCHY IN LEBANON

Israel Crosses the Border

CHRISTIAN SCIENCE MONITOR

* Israeli policy scored. Mar 17, 1978, P28
* Lebanese factions described. Jan 6, 1978, P16

EDMONTON JOURNAL

* Problems for U.N. force foreseen. Mar 21, 1978, P15

FINANCIAL TIMES

* Retaliatory raid appraised. Mar 16, 1978, P20

LOS ANGELES TIMES

* Israeli aims analyzed. Mar 26, 1978, S6, P2

MIDDLE EAST

* Housing problems reviewed. Jan 1978, P74

NEW YORK TIMES

  Clash of forces in South Lebanon. Jan 5, 1978, P7
  Sarkis opposes Mideast agreement. Jan 7, 1978, P7
  Splits in Lebanese society analyzed. Jan 16, 1978, P2
* P.L.O. buildup worries rightists. Jan 26, 1978, P10
* Anti-Palestinian feeling rising. Feb 6, 1978, P8
* Syrians and Lebanese clash. Feb 8, 1978, P9
* Right-wing militia attacked. Feb 9, 1978, P5

* Syrian aims analyzed. Feb 12, 1978, P3
* Sarkis and Syria in accord. Feb 13, 1978, P4
* Palestinians, rightists clash. Feb 14, 1978, P11
* Military tribunal established. Feb 15, 1978, P3
* Israeli collusion charged. Feb 19, 1978, P14
* Lebanese Moslems flee Israelis. Feb 26, 1978, P11
* New outbreak of fighting reported. Mar 4, 1978, P3
* Terrorists attack Israelis. Mar 12, 1978, P1
* Raid coincides with Begin's visit. Mar 13, 1978, P10
* Begin hints reprisal. Mar 13, 1978, P1
* Israel crosses into Lebanon. Mar 15, 1978, P1
* P.L.O. reports invasion. Mar 15, 1978, P1
* King Khalid appeals for Israeli ceasefire. Mar 16, 1978, P17
* P.L.O. refugees move north. Mar 16, 1978, P1
* P.L.O. asks Red Cross to aid civilians. Mar 16, 1978, P16
* History of civil war in Lebanon reviewed. Mar 16, 1978, P17
* Political tensions rise from bomb blasts. Mar 16, 1978, P17
* Tueni protests Israel's "naked aggression." Mar 16, 1978, P17
* Israeli aims analyzed. Mar 16, 1978, P17
* Israeli line advances. Mar 16, 1978, P1
* Diplomatic impact of Israeli invasion assessed. Mar 17, 1978, P10
* Events in Lebanon described. Mar 17, 1978, P1
* Hafez al-Assad counters Israeli invasion. Mar 17, 1978, P11
* Israeli planes bomb refugee camps. Mar 17, 1978, P10
* U.S. role in Mideast affairs reviewed. Mar 17, 1978, P1
* U.S. statement on Mideast conflict summarized. Mar 17, 1978, P10
* Lebanese battlefield analyzed. Mar 17, 1978, P10
* Lebanese score incursion. Mar 17, 1978, P10
* Hussein calls summit to deal with fighting. Mar 18, 1978, P6
* Pope accuses Israel of random bombing. Mar 18, 1978, P6
* Lebanese demand withdrawal. Mar 18, 1978, P6
* Refugees flood Beirut. Mar 18, 1978, P1
* Israel seeks security zone. Mar 18, 1978, P6
* Observers skeptical on U.S. plan. Mar 18, 1978, P6
* Syria encourages military response. Mar 19, 1978, P10
* War in Lebanon continues. Mar 19, 1978, P10
* Israelis launch offensive. Mar 19, 1978, P10
* Israelis to probe deeper into Lebanon. Mar 19, 1978, P10
* Young proposes Israeli withdrawal. Mar 19, 1978, P1
* Refugees, casualties swell. Mar 19, 1978, P1
* U.N. calls for withdrawal. Mar 20, 1978, P1
* Israeli forces begin drive to Tyre. Mar 20, 1978, P15
* Refugees face "life of exile." Mar 20, 1978, P14
* U.S. resolution on Israeli occupation summarized. Mar 20, 1978, P10
* Israel consolidates position. Mar 20, 1978, P1
* Israeli occupations in Lebanon described. Mar 21, 1978, P16
* Israeli attack on south Lebanon analyzed. Mar 21, 1978, P17
* Plans for U.N. peacekeeping described. Mar 21, 1978, P16
* Israeli tactics assessed. Mar 21, 1978, P16
* Israel considers resolution. Mar 21, 1978, P1
* Israel orders cease-fire. Mar 22, 1978, P1
* Israel to withdraw eagerly from Lebanon. Mar 23, 1978, P14
* U.N. peacekeeping force in Lebanon described. Mar 23, 1978, P1
* French peacekeeping force criticized. Mar 23, 1978, P16
* U.N. troops arrive. Mar 23, 1978, P16
* Lebanon appeals for aid for refugees. Mar 24, 1978, P1
* U.N. peacekeeping force enters Lebanon. Mar 24, 1978, P10
* People's fear, desolation described. Mar 25, 1978, P1
* P.L.O. refuses to leave Tyre. Mar 25, 1978, P3
* Fighting abates. Mar 25, 1978, P1
* Accusation of shelling reviewed. Mar 26, 1978, P10
* Thankless role of U.N. force described. Mar 26, 1978, S4, P2
* Syria's Lebanon role reviewed. Mar 26, 1978, S4, P2
* Israel's invasion of Lebanon assessed. Mar 27, 1978, P3
* P.L.O. charged with firing on U.N. forces. Mar 27, 1978, P3
* U.N. forces in middle of crossfire. Mar 27, 1978, P3
* Arab League meeting reviewed. Mar 28, 1978, P6
* P.L.O., Israel continue battle. Mar 28, 1978, P3
* Weizman tours N. Israel. Mar 28, 1978, P5
* Arafat accepts cease-fire. Mar 29, 1978, P3
* Arafat accepts cease-fire. Mar 29, 1978, P3
* P.L.O.-Israeli clash on Khardali Bridge. Mar 29, 1978, P3
* Cease-fire doubted as blast kills 1. Mar 30, 1978, P10
* Al-Fatah to hold fire. Mar 30, 1978, P11
* Peace returns to Lebanon. Mar 31, 1978, P3
* P.L.O. observes cease-fire. Apr 1, 1978, P3
* Arafat pledges to continue cease-fire. Apr 2, 1978, P3
* Residents adjust lives to Beirut fighting. Apr 2, 1978, P3
* Combatants, U.N. forces fortify positions. Apr 3, 1978, P4
* P.L.O., Israel in deadlock. Apr 5, 1978, P10
* Israeli withdrawal planned. Apr 7, 1978, P1

* Israeli operation in Lebanon summarized. Apr 8, 1978, P4
* Appeal for Israeli withdrawal made. Apr 9, 1978, P4
* Plans for return of refugees made. Apr 10, 1978, P3
* Gunfire injures 4. Apr 12, 1978, P3
* Israel begins withdrawal. Apr 12, 1978, P1
* Israeli's second phase of withdrawal. Apr 15, 1978, P6
* Charge Israelis have not vacated area. Apr 16, 1978, P8
* Agreement on Israeli withdrawal reached. Apr 19, 1978, P3
* Arafat pledges cease-fire on Israel. Apr 19, 1978, P3
* Arafat's diplomacy described. Apr 25, 1978, P3
* Israelis in Tyre. Apr 27, 1978, P3
* P.L.O. charges Israelis with attack. Apr 28, 1978, P6
* Hoss to form new government. Apr 29, 1978, P6
* Third phase of Israeli withdrawal begins. May 1, 1978, P3
* U.N., P.L.O. in parley. May 6, 1978, P3
* Arafat rejects cease-fire. May 12, 1978, P7
* P.L.O. moves into U.N. territory. May 18, 1978, P15
* P.L.O. pledges cooperation. May 26, 1978, P4
* P.L.O. to restrain guerrillas. May 28, 1978, P3
* P.L.O. asserts rights in Lebanon. May 29, 1978, P7
* Impact of U.N. forces described. May 30, 1978, P2
* Sarkis, Assad in parley. June 2, 1978, P6
* Arafat-U.N.'s Erskine discuss violence. June 3, 1978, P5
* Al-Fatah's views on Israeli raid. June 4, 1978, P9
* Israelis attack Dahr Burja base. June 9, 1978, P3
* Israeli attack on P.L.O. summarized. June 10, 1978, P1
* Progress in Israeli withdrawal described. June 10, 1978, P4
* Erskine's views on Israeli withdrawal. June 11, 1978, P11
* Israel's withdrawal criticized by Lebanese. June 12, 1978, P3
* U.N. forces caught in middle of opposition. June 12, 1978, P3
* Israeli evacuation under way. June 13, 1978, P3
* U.N.'s efforts in Lebanon interpreted. June 21, 1978, P3
* Israeli forces complete withdrawal. June 14, 1978, P1

TIMES OF LONDON

* Syrian position examined. Apr 14, 1978, P14
* U.N.-P.L.O. clashes termed inevitable. May 17, 1978, P6

WALL STREET JOURNAL

* Refugees flee to Beirut. May 10, 1978, P1

WASHINGTON POST

* Syrian dilemma noted. Mar 16, 1978, P14
* Arab inaction observed. Mar 17, 1978, P21

Armies and Factions

FINANCIAL TIMES

* Traditional violence reviewed. July 5, 1978, P16

NEW YORK TIMES

* Clashes break out in Beirut. Apr 13, 1978, P3
* Beirut cease-fire announced. Apr 14, 1978, P9
* Syria shells Christians. Apr 18, 1978, P5
* Muslims, Christians parley. Apr 21, 1978, P9
* Christian-Moslem leaders reach agreement. Apr 24, 1978, P8
* P.L.O. to retain role. Apr 26, 1978, P8
* Ban on militias sought. Apr 28, 1978, P6
* Tension in Tyre sees 3 dead. May 3, 1978, P16
* Guerrillas fire on U.N. forces. May 10, 1978, P6
* 3 dead in Lebanese fighting. May 13, 1978, P7
* U.N. resumes patrol in Tyre. May 15, 1978, S2, P4
* Sarkis calls on technocrats. May 16, 1978, P8
* Guerrillas leave Maarake, ending confrontation. May 16, 1978, P3
* Lebanon to redeploy army. June 6, 1978, P12
* Crime on rise in Lebanon. June 7, 1978, P3
* Protection of Christians' enclaves asked. June 7, 1978, P3
* P.L.O. disarmament sought. June 8, 1978, P9
* Son of ex-president killed. June 14, 1978, P12
* Franjieh vows vengeance. June 15, 1978, P14
* Christian extremists hamper U.N. efforts. June 17, 1978, P4
* Rival Christian factions's clash interpreted. June 18, 1978, S4, P2
* Split in Christian factions described. June 18, 1978, P7
* Syria calls Haddad "outlaw." June 18, 1978, P7
* Haddad, Shidiak arrested for interference. June 20, 1978, P3
* Traditional violence haunts Lebanon. June 26, 1978, P8

* Franjieh vendetta continues. June 29, 1978, P7
* Sarkis struggles with feuds. June 30, 1978, P7
* Syrians, Christians in combat. July 2, 1978, P1
  Lebanon's internal conflict reviewed. July 2, 1978, S4, P4
  New fighting in Lebanon described. July 3, 1978, P3
* Christian divisions analyzed. July 4, 1978, P2
  100 dead in Syrian attack. July 4, 1978, P3
  Butros, Hafez plan halt to hostilities. July 5, 1978, P3
* Israel warns Syria. July 7, 1978, P1
  Israeli stand on Lebanon conflict. July 7, 1978, P3
  Fighting in Lebanon ebbs. July 9, 1978, P3
  Syrian military role in Lebanon summarized. July 9, 1978, S4, P1
* Sarkis resigns. July 10, 1978, P5
  People flee Beirut as fighting resumes. July 11, 1978, P3
* Syrian-Christian break analyzed. July 12, 1978, P6
  Assad-Halabi schedule talks. July 12, 1978, P6
  Sarkis' resignation scored. July 13, 1978, P9
* Sarkis to stay. July 16, 1978, P4
  Beirut fighting stops. July 17, 1978, P4
  Karam assails Syria's peacekeeping efforts. July 17, 1978, P16
  Report of battle in Lebanon since truce. July 23, 1978, P8
  Fighting in Lebanon described. July 24, 1978, P3
  Syria shells Christians at Al Hadath. July 26, 1978, P7
  Lebanon decides to assist U.N. July 29, 1978, P5
* Realignment of factions seen. July 30, 1978, S4, P2
  Lebanon to move army to South. July 31, 1978, P4
  Lebanese army moves into S. Lebanon. Aug 1, 1978, P3
  Christians attack U.N. force. Aug 2, 1978, P3
  Israel accused of disrupting deployment. Aug 2, 1978, P3
  Israel fires upon U.N. forces. Aug 3, 1978, P5
  Syria to support Lebanon in deployment. Aug 4, 1978, P3
  Haddad orders cease-fire at Lebanese forces. Aug 5, 1978, P5
  Opposing sides reach agreement. Aug 7, 1978, P3
* Proxy war seen. Aug 8, 1978, P3
* Syrians fire on Christians. Aug 12, 1978, P111
  Syria blasts Christians in E. Beirut. Aug 13, 1978, P61
  Battalion re-deployed into S. Lebanon. Aug 16, 1978, P136
* Syrian withdrawal urged. Aug 17, 1978, P45
  U.N.-Lebanese Army leaders meet. Aug 17, 1978, P21
  Mortar rounds fired into seaport areas. Aug 19, 1978, P204
  Shuttle diplomacy fails to break impasse. Aug 23, 1978, P120
  U.N. forces asked to move to Israeli border. Aug 26, 1978, P142
  Syrian-Christian battle described. Aug 27, 1978, P85
  Syrian forces break fighting lull. Sept 1, 1978, P138
  Normalcy in Lebanon achievement for U.N. Sept 2, 1978, P152
  Christians in alliance with Israel. Sept 7, 1978, P93
* Kidnappings on the rise. Sept 8, 1978, P105
  Syrian shelling intensified. Sept 9, 1978, P101
  4 die in Syrian attack on Christians. Sept 10, 1978, P11
  Syrians attack Christians. Sept 11, 1978, P43
  Beirut fighting described. Oct 1, 1978, P64
* Sarkis seeks solution. Oct 3, 1978, P14
* Beirut suffers urban breakdown. Oct 5, 1978, P10
  Syrian-Christian forces in "war of attrition." Oct 6, 1978, P1
  U.N. tries to stop bloodshed. Oct 6, 1978, P26
  Lebanon events to be international. Oct 7, 1978, P5
  Cease-fire on Lebanese fronts ordered. Oct 8, 1978, P17
* Cease-fire holding. Oct 9, 1978, P10
  Dayan's purpose, goals for Israel in Lebanon. Oct 9, 1978, P41
  Sarkis seeks support for plan. Oct 10, 1978, P19
  Developments may cause renewed offensive. Oct 11, 1978, P18
  Lebanon's losses assessed. Oct 11, 1978, P20
  Truce used for re-grouping. Oct 12, 1978, P29
* Arab summit on Lebanon. Oct 15, 1978, P54
* French minister scores Israel. Oct 17, 1978, P21
* Arabs end Lebanon summit. Oct 18, 1978, P8
* Syrian troops to withdraw. Oct 19, 1978, P50
* Security plan implemented. Oct 20, 1978, P13
* Syrian troops begin withdrawal. Oct 21, 1978, P14
* Haddad and Shidiak on trial. Oct 23, 1978, P31
* New plan to end conflict. Oct 26, 1978, P23
* Palestinians offer truce. Nov 14, 1978, P2
* Armenians suffer casualties. Nov 14, 1978, P2
* Security plan thwarted. Nov 16, 1978, P6
* Lebanon devastated by war. Dec 6, 1978, P2

WASHINGTON POST

* Truce for Beirut sought. Aug 10, 1978, P31
* Maronite strategy reviewed. Oct 8, 1978, P23

5. IRAN IN REVOLUTION

BUSINESS WEEK

* Oil barter compounds trade difficulties. Feb 20, 1978, P40
  Iran's economic development hurt by unrest. Nov 27, 1978, P42

CHICAGO TRIBUNE

  Shah's plan for industrial development. Jan 8, 1978, P1
* Iran's military profiled. Jan 9, 1978, P1
* Iran relaxes repression. Jan 10, 1978, P1
  U.S. advisors in Iran spotlighted. Jan 11, 1978, P1
* Iran's economic inequities. Jan 11, 1978, P1
  Charge of U.S.-Iran cooperation in suppression. May 14, 1978, P8

CHRISTIAN SCIENCE MONITOR

* Iranian society "opening up." Sept 15, 1978, P27
* Shah's goals outlined. June 6, 1978, P7
* Empress lauds women's advance. Feb 8, 1978, P22
* Role of press outlined. May 30, 1978, P5

ECONOMIST OF LONDON

* Shah reported loosening grip. Mar 4, 1978, P59

FINANCIAL TIMES

* Appointment discussed. Aug 30, 1978, P14
* Foreign exchange outflow up. Sept 25, 1978, P42
* Strikes hit government, business. Mar 14, 1978, P2
* Iran's transformation profiled. Mar 15, 1978, P4
* Balance of trade worsens. Apr 14, 1978, P3
* Shah's problems analyzed. May 15, 1978, P23
  Iran profiled. Sept 12, 1978, P17

JOURNAL OF COMMERCE

* Oil strike takes toll. Nov 1, 1978, P1

MIAMI HERALD

  Crown Prince Reza profiled. Aug 15, 1978, S6, P1

NEWSWEEK

* Shah charges communist interference. July 24, 1978, P56

NEW YORK TIMES

  Carter's visit to Iran protested. Jan 1, 1978, P12
  20 killed by police in Qom. Jan 11, 1978, P6
* Scandal taints arms sales. Jan 11, 1978, S4, P1
  Demonstrations on Farah's New York visit. Jan 12, 1978, S2, P3
* Empress describes Iran's turmoil. Jan 13, 1978, S2, P3
  Author granted passport. Jan 30, 1978, P8
  6 dead, 125 hurt in anti-Shah riot. Feb 20, 1978, P6
  Tabriz patroled by police. Feb 21, 1978, P9
* Demonstrations in Tabriz. Feb 22, 1978, P9
  Troops withdraw from Tabriz. Feb 24, 1978, P10
  Shah's problems reviewed. Feb 26, 1978, S4, P1
* Legal proceedings scored. Mar 1, 1978, P20
  Police commander reported dead. Mar 2, 1978, S6, P6
* Widespread discontent reported. Mar 5, 1978, P7
  Iranian students plead not guilty to trespass. Mar 14, 1978, P22
* Savak rebuked over Tabriz. Mar 16, 1978, P14
* Use of force protested. Mar 17, 1978, P2
* Political opposition continues. Apr 2, 1978, S4, P5
  Banks, public buildings attacked. Apr 3, 1978, P6
  65 youth arrested for anti-Shah activity. Apr 23, 1978, P7
  23 students in Bobol arrested. May 7, 1978, P25
* Religious dissidents in clash. May 10, 1978, P6
* Rioting in Qom. May 11, 1978, P11
* Shah takes precautions. May 12, 1978, P4
  Iran's civil unrest reviewed. May 14, 1978, S4, P2
* Government issues warning. May 14, 1978, P12
  Students-police clash in Iran. May 17, 1978, P14
* Shah's opposition profiled. May 18, 1978, P1
  Bomb rocks Qom. May 23, 1978, P12
* Troops patrol Teheran streets. May 26, 1978, P2
  Teheran students riot over coeducation. June 1, 1978, P7
  Teheran student riots reviewed. June 4, 1978, S4, P2
* Opposition's grievances analyzed. June 4, 1978, P1

* Teheran university closed. June 4, 1978, P10
Iranian students march on White House. June 6, 1978, P7
Savak head demoted. June 7, 1978, P2
* New security chief named. June 8, 1978, P22
* Author criticizes regime. June 18, 1978, P28
* Protests peaceful across Iran. June 18, 1978, P8
* Conduct code promulgated. July 4, 1978, P1
* U.S. military ties strong. July 9, 1978, P1
Dr. Hosseim visits New York City. July 16, 1978, S7, P31
* Violence in Mashhad. July 26, 1978, P7
Scores hurt, arrested in week's rioting. Aug 2, 1978, P6
Clashes in Shiraz reported. Aug 13, 1978, P63
1 killed, 45 hurt in bomb blast. Aug 15, 1978, P56
Results of restaurant bombing described. Aug 16, 1978, P48
* Shah promises free elections. Aug 16, 1978, P5
* Theater burns in Abadan. Aug 21, 1978, P20
* Crackdown in fire aftermath. Aug 22, 1978, P45
* Fire investigation continues. Aug 23, 1978, P79
* "White Revolution" reforms analyzed. Aug 23, 1978, P15
* Demonstrators protest arson. Aug 24, 1978, P77
* Sharif-Emami named prime minister. Aug 28, 1978, P9
* Opposition leaders released. Sept 1, 1978, P28
* Shah's quandary explored. Sept 5, 1978, P37
* Mass protest in capital. Sept 9, 1978, P14
* Crown prince profiled. Sept 10, 1978, P127
* Tanks are called out. Sept 10, 1978, P82
* Shah outlines strategy. Sept 12, 1978, P97
* Molla suspected kidnapped. Sept 13, 1978, P78
* New crackdown, arrests reported. Sept 13, 1978, P108
* Noncooperation vowed. Sept 16, 1978, P66
* Emami seeks legislative backing. Sept 17, 1978, P10
* "Paper" reforms scored. Sept 17, 1978, P18
* Youths demonstrate against Shah. Sept 29, 1978, P90
* Khomeini in Paris. Oct 7, 1978, P44
* Women's rights threatened. Oct 7, 1978, P24
Iran's religious leaders call for shutdown. Oct 16, 1978, P26
* Prime minister Sharif-Emani resigns. Nov 6, 1978, P1
* Opposition leaders denounce Shah. Nov 6, 1978, P18
* Iran's strategic importance noted. Nov 6, 1978, P18
* Military rule declared. Nov 7, 1978, P1
* Students and merchants unite. Nov 7, 1978, P15
* Khomeini calls for dethronement. Nov 7, 1978, P1
* Anti-Shah positions examined. Nov 8, 1978, P14
* Uncertain future seen for Iran. Nov 8, 1978, P26
* Iranian government cracks down. Nov 8, 1978, P1
* Former prime minister arrested. Nov 9, 1978, P1
* Opposition party urges strikes. Nov 10, 1978, P11
* Foreigners leaving Iran. Nov 11, 1978, P1
* National Front leader arrested. Nov 12, 1978, P1
* Strikers returning to work. Nov 14, 1978, P1
* Oil industry struck. Nov 15, 1978, P1
* Religious fundamentalism assessed. Nov 15, 1978, P29
* U.S.-Iran ties assessed. Nov 15, 1978, P3
* Rural-urban shift cited. Nov 16, 1978, P11
* Lack of support noted. Nov 18, 1978, P1
Iran celebrates army with parade. Nov 18, 1978, P5
* Shah declares determination. Nov 19, 1978, P1
* Political prisoners freed. Nov 20, 1978, P1
* Azhari receives confidence vote. Nov 23, 1978, P2
Versions of Iranian rioting described. Nov 25, 1978, P3
Strike harms Iran's business. Nov 27, 1978, P7
* Economy in paralysis. Nov 28, 1978, S4, P1
* Ayatollah calls strike. December 1, 1978, P6
7 killed in Iran demonstration. Dec 2, 1978, P4
Moharram holiday results in riot. Dec 3, 1978, P1
* Teheran reported quieter. Dec 4, 1978, P1
French warn Khomeini to halt violence. Dec 5, 1978, P10
Iran's civil unrest reviewed. Dec 5, 1978, P1
* Shah allows parades. Dec 9, 1978, P1
* Foreigners leave Iran. Dec 10, 1978, P1
* Asshura protest draws thousands. Dec 11, 1978, P1
* Opposition to Shah grows. Dec 12, 1978, P1
Rioting in Isfahan described. Dec 13, 1978, P1
U.S. sends experts to aid Shah. Dec 14, 1978, P1
Description of pro-Shah demonstration. Dec 14, 1978, P1
* Shah meets with opposition. Dec 15, 1978, P1
* Iran army under stress. Dec 19, 1978, P1
* U.S. intelligence criticized. Dec 21, 1978, P1
* Crisis causes economic upheaval. Dec 22, 1978, P1
* U.S. navy on alert. Dec 30, 1978, P1

* New government conflict. Dec 30, 1978, P1
* Oil shortage affects country. Dec 31, 1978, P1

TIME

* Conflict with clergy traced. June 15, 1978, P39
Iranian political unrest examined. Sept 18, 1978, P32

TIMES OF LONDON

N.U.S.'s allegations denied. Jan 31, 1978, P5
Shah's views on Manian. Apr 28, 1978, P17
* Economic lag cited. May 16, 1978, P15
* Prison conditions scored. May 19, 1978, P8
* Iran's course debated. May 20, 1978, P15
* Root of discontent traced. May 26, 1978, P18

US NEWS AND WORLD REPORT

* Shah presents views. June 26, 1978, P37

WALL STREET JOURNAL

Textron's helicopter sale summarized. Feb 22, 1978, P1
* Drastic rent laws imposed. July 25, 1978, P8
* Conservatives grow militant. Aug 15, 1978, P1
* Opposition to liberalization broad. Aug 3, 1978, P12

WASHINGTON POST

* Clashes in holy city. Jan 20, 1978, P31
11 injured in Washington riot file suit. Apr 15, 1978, S2, P3
* Causes of Qom violence traced. May 26, 1978, P23
* Uneasiness about future discerned. May 29, 1978, P23
* Curfew imposed in Isfahan. Aug 12, 1978, P15
U.S. involvement in Iran protested. Aug 19, 1978, P4
* Economy darkens celebrations. Aug 20, 1978, P29
* "Frantic" modernization scored. Aug 29, 1978, P15
* Unfulfilled expectations pervasive. Sept 9, 1978, P14
Iran's political situation analyzed. Sept 15, 1978, P18
Gholam-Hossein Sa'edi freedom supported. Oct 10, 1978, P19
Khomeini profiled. Nov 15, 1978, S4, P1
* Shah's behavior assessed. Nov 17, 1978, S1, P22
* Shah's acumen doubted. Nov 19, 1978, S3, P6
L.A.'s Persian community split over Shah. Nov 24, 1978, P21
* Anguish for moderates. Nov 26, 1978, P25
Shareatmodary interviewed. Nov 28, 1978, P20

6. THE PALESTINIANS

The Homeland Issue

CHRISTIAN SCIENCE MONITOR

* West bank Arabs dissatisfied. June 8, 1978, P20

FINANCIAL TIMES

Egyptian-U.S. relations "cool" after Carter comment. Jan 3, 1978, P10

MIDDLE EAST

Sadat's Israel visit analyzed. Jan, 1978, P14

NEWSWEEK

Begin, Assad interviewed. Jan 16, 1978, P40

NEW YORK TIMES

Sadat optimistic about solutions to problems. Jan 2, 1978, P3
Plans for peace interpreted. Jan 2, 1978, P20
* Saudis support Palestinian state. Jan 2, 1978, P3
Israel to subscribe to Carter's peace terms. Jan 5, 1978, P16
Sadat's views surveyed. Jan 5, 1978, P1
Sarkis opposes settlement. Jan 7, 1978, P4
* Carter discloses referendum plan. Jan 8, 1978, P1
* Sadat calls for transition. Jan 9, 1978, P7
U.S.'s plan for agreement summarized. Jan 14, 1978, P1

*   Self-determination plan proposed. Jan 22, 1978, S4, P19
    Israel to probe reports of torture. Jan 28, 1978, P5
*   Palestine summit sought. Feb 4, 1978, P3
    Convicted spy hanged. Feb 14, 1978, P38
    Medoune Fall's request analyzed. Feb 17, 1978, P26
*   Kuwait is home to Palestinians. Feb 19, 1978, P16
*   Palestinians divided on aims. Feb 19, 1978, P1
*   Problems of "Homeland" examined. Feb 20, 1978, P1
    Egyptian rescue mission reported. Feb 21, 1978, P1
    Assault on hijacked plane explained. Feb 22, 1978, P1
    Kyprianou-Sadat to rebuild ties. Feb 22, 1978, P7
    Kyprianou defends Cyprus' actions. Feb 23, 1978, P3
*   Palestinian aims analyzed. Feb 23, 1978, P21
    Decision to free hostages lauded. Feb 24, 1978, P6
    Israeli oranges "cleared" for sale. Feb 25, 1978, P6
    Egypt-Cyprus severed relations explained. Feb 24, 1978, P6
    Raid at Larnaca reviewed. Feb 26, 1978, S4, P1
    Shah leaves Cyprus. Feb 27, 1978, P6
*   Egypt's new mood analyzed. Feb 28, 1978, P3
    Khadar-Ahmed al-Ali hearing noted. Feb 28, 1978, P9
    Al Ahram murder trial reported. Mar 1, 1978, P8
    Find safe solutions to Mideast problems. Mar 1, 1978, P26
*   P.L.O. scores Egyptian actions. Mar 1, 1978, P12
    Nuseibeh letter criticizes Herzog. Mar 6, 1978, P20
    Mideast events reviewed. Mar 12, 1978, S4, P1
    Impact of bus bombing on Israel. Mar 13, 1978, P10
    Israeli-Arab refugees contrasted. Mar 13, 1978, P20
    Call for United Arab stand against terrorism. Mar 14, 1978, P34
*   Syrian comments on U.S. stance. Mar 17, 1978, P29
    Raid on Israel highway described. Mar 20, 1978, P14
    Atmosphere in Israeli towns described. Mar 21, 1978, P14
    Israel upholds proposals made to Egypt. Apr 24, 1978, P7
    Ansari sentenced for hijacking. Apr 27, 1978, P9
*   Arafat stresses guarantees. May 2, 1978, P1
    Plans for Mideast settlement criticized. May 2, 1978, P11
*   Palestinian outlook profiled. May 4, 1978, P22
    Esmail's terrorism analyzed. June 2, 1978, P23
    Israeli bus firebombed. June 7, 1978, P19
    Esmail convicted for terrorism. June 8, 1978, P4
    Release of Esmail desired. June 11, 1978, S4, P20
    Esmail sentenced to 15 months in prison. June 13, 1978, P4
*   Jordanian role examined. June 21, 1978, P3
*   Bethlehem mayor asks aid. July 20, 1978, P8
    Arrest 29 suspected of sabotage. July 25, 1978, S2, P9
*   West Bank resentment noted. July 25, 1978, P2
    France expels Iraqi aides. Aug 3, 1978, P7
    Iraqi consulate raided. Aug 3, 1978, P7
    Vance to spur peace talks. Aug 5, 1978, P1
    Security at Islambad tightened. Aug 7, 1978, P3
    Beirut building bombed. Aug 13, 1978, P172
*   Zionist proposes Palestinian state. Aug 26, 1978, P97
*   Dayan assesses West Bank. Sept 2, 1978, P7
*   West Bank Arabs protest. Sept 15, 1978, P135
    Film *Terror in the Promised Land* reviewed. Oct 29, 1978, P65
*   P.L.O.'s diplomatic gains noted. Dec 25, 1978, P8

WALL STREET JOURNAL

*   Homeland establishment seen essential. Jan 13, 1978, P12
*   Divergent views noted. Jan 25, 1978, P1

WASHINGTON POST

*   Terrorist impact questioned. Feb 21, 1978, P16
    Cyprus killings interpreted. Feb 24, 1978, P20
*   Homeland plans reviewed. Apr 26, 1978, P27
*   Eight professors barred. June 24, 1978, P2
    Felicia Langer interviewed. July 31, 1978, S3, P1
    Occupation's hardships told. Oct 19, 1978, P1

The PLO

CHRISTIAN SCIENCE MONITOR

    Begin's feelings toward Palestinians interpreted. Mar 13, 1978, P32
*   Arafat strengthens Soviet ties. Mar 31, 1978, P27

LOS ANGELES TIMES

    Arafat hunts for P.L.O. splinter group. May 5, 1978, P1

MANCHESTER GUARDIAN

    P.L.O.-Egyptian government link reported. Jan 1, 1978, P11
*   Arafat affirms P.L.O.'s primacy. Jan 8, 1978, P1
    Said Hammami profiled. Jan 15, 1978, P4

NEW YORK TIMES

    Accuse Carter of halting P.L.O. cause. Jan 1, 1978, P8
*   Palestinians rally for P.L.O. Jan 2, 1978, P3
*   P.L.O. warns Carter. Jan 2, 1978, P3
    Hussein interview excerpted. Jan 3, 1978, P4
*   Palestinian solution sought. Jan 3, 1978, P1
    Carter's comments about Palestine explained. Jan 5, 1978, P5
*   P.L.O. representative killed. Jan 5, 1978, P3
    Arab-Palestinian conflicts noted. Jan 8, 1978, S4, P18
    Carter's views on Palestinian referendum. Jan 8, 1978, P1
    P.L.O.'s participation in talks supported. Jan 12, 1978, P19
    Palestinians, American Indians paralleled. Feb 14, 1978, P34
*   Sadat aide assassinated. Feb 19, 1978, P1
*   Egypt defends raid. Feb 20, 1978, P1
*   Egyptian commandos storm jetliner. Feb 20, 1978, P1
    Palestinians in Israel described. Feb 20, 1978, P10
*   Cyprus, Egypt withdraw missions. Feb 21, 1978, P1
    Palestinian's attitude toward violence described. Feb 21, 1978, P14
*   Arafat scores Cyprus attack. Feb 22, 1978, P7
*   Egypt breaks Cyprus ties. Feb 23, 1978, P3
*   Egypt rescinds Palestinian privileges. Feb 28, 1978, P1
*   Improved Jordan ties sought. Mar 3, 1978, P3
    Hussein refused to join talks. Mar 5, 1978, P8
    Arafat-Soviet meeting reported. Mar 8, 1978, S4, P17
*   Terrorists attack bus. Mar 12, 1978, P14
    P.L.O. attack on Israel interpreted. Mar 13, 1978, P21
*   Terrorist raid detailed. Mar 13, 1978, P10
*   Saudis critical of raid. Mar 15, 1978, P10
*   Aim of raid explained. Mar 17, 1978, P7
    P.L.O. raid mars peace efforts. Mar 19, 1978, S4, P1
    Jordanian envoy states position. Mar 20, 1978, P20
    P.L.O. representation issue linked to terrorism. Mar 22, 1978, P12
    El-Wade Haddad is buried. Apr 4, 1978, P36
    2 Palestinians face death sentence. Apr 9, 1978, S4, P4
*   Egypt hunts terrorists. Apr 12, 1978, P13
*   Senator scores P.L.O. Apr 14, 1978, P7
*   Attack preparations alleged. Apr 27, 1978, P3
    W. German youths killed in P.L.O. raid. Apr 27, 1978, P4
*   Terrorist targets alleged. Apr 30, 1978, P40
    Carter opposes Palestinian state. May 1, 1978. S2. P5
    P.L.O.'s Washington, D.C. office opens. May 2, 1978, P12
    P.L.O.'s efforts to halt attacks on U.N. noted. May 5, 1978, P8
    P.L.O. attack on Jerusalem reported. May 8, 1978, P3
    Impact of P.L.O. raid on Egypt. May 13, 1978, P10
    Peace talks hampered by P.L.O. raids. Mar 13, 1978, P1
    French forces praised for foiling P.L.O. raid. May 22, 1978, P12
*   Splits in P.L.O. reported. May 25, 1978, P14
*   Terrorists bomb bus. June 3, 1978, P2
    Arafat peace efforts noted. June 5, 1978, P10
*   Jordan Valley settlement raided. June 13, 1978, P3
    Creation of Palestinian state argued. June 15, 1978, P23
*   "Moderate" Palestinian killed. June 16, 1978, P4
*   P.L.O. gain in Lebanon seen. June 25, 1978, P10
*   U.S. stance on P.L.O. assailed. June 28, 1978, P23
*   Bomb rocks Jerusalem market. June 30, 1978, P4
*   Fatah, Iraq in clash. July 18, 1978, P2
*   Iraqi mission hit. Aug 2, 1978, P3
*   P.L.O.-Iraq feud continues. Aug 4, 1978, P1
*   Iraqi ties reported. Aug 5, 1978, P24
*   Funeral for P.L.O. official. Aug 6, 1978, P10
*   Iraqis-P.L.O. fighting summarized. Aug 6, 1978, S4, P1
*   P.L.O. policy change foreseen. Aug 6, 1978, S4, P1
*   Iraq condemns feuding. Aug 7, 1978, P3
*   Feud results in 80 deaths. Aug 14, 1978, P69
*   Council to mediate. Aug 18, 1978, P11
    Arafat admits bombing. Aug 19, 1978, P211
    P.L.O. views Camp David. Sept 6, 1978, P108
    Hussein predicts Israeli aggression. Sept 9, 1978, P99
    P.L.O.'s right to free speech defended. Sept 24, 1978, P24

TIMES OF LONDON

    Israeli view of Palestinians analyzed. July 31, 1978, P12
    Palestinian issue reviewed. Aug 10, 1978, P12

WASHINGTON POST

Cyprus' support of P.L.O. denied. Feb 26, 1978, S4, P6
* Arafat's stand on terror. Mar 24, 1978, S2, P17
Idi Amin-Arafat relationship examined. June 29, 1978, P9
Peace agreement could weaken P.L.O. Sept 30, 1978, P15
Karim Khalaf-Abu-Gazaleh interviewed. Oct 5, 1978, S2, P1
Campaign to promote P.L.O. rights reported. Oct 7, 1978, P1
Nafez Nazzal profiled. Oct 7, 1978, S7, P1

7. EGYPT ON ITS OWN COURSE

The Political Backdrop

CHRISTIAN SCIENCE MONITOR

Egypt cultivates desert. July 27, 1978, P6

FINANCIAL TIMES

* Sadat faces hardships. May 13, 1978, P2
Pyramids Oasis Project seen as failure. May 31, 1978, P6
Egypt profiled. July 31, 1978, P11

HOUSTON CHRONICLE

* U.S. crucial to Sadat. Feb 26, 1978, S3, P27

JOURNAL OF COMMERCE

* Free port described. Mar 27, 1978, P1
* U.S. investment may increase. Mar 29, 1978, P1
* Spending program outlined. May 1, 1978, P10
* Suez planning for boom. May 8, 1978, P1
Egyptian airlines, airports discussed. Aug 22, 1978, P1

MANCHESTER GUARDIAN

Egypt's family planning scored. Jan 8, 1978, P9
* Egypt's development portrayed. Jan 15, 1978, P13
* Egypt's future termed bleak. Jan 22, 1978, P13
Wafd party examined. Feb 5, 1978, P11

NATIONAL JOURNAL

* Increased U.S. role seen. Apr 8, 1978, P564

NEW YORK TIMES

* World Bank hopeful. Jan 30, 1978, P6
* Wafd party revived. Feb 5, 1978, P13
* Wafd leader chosen. Feb 18, 1978, P4
* Port Said booming. Apr 19, 1978, P3
* Sadat tightens grip. May 3, 1978, P16
* Cabinet shuffle purges economist. May 10, 1978, P4
* Sadat calls for referendum. May 15, 1978, P1
Al Ahali ordered to cease publication. May 18, 1978, P8
* Clampdown accompanies referendum. May 19, 1978, P7
Egyptian referendum analyzed. May 21, 1978, P7
* Referendum's aim analyzed. May 22, 1978, P6
* Sadat reviews endorsement. May 23, 1978, P2
* Sadat denounces opposition. May 24, 1978, P11
* Sadat clashes with critics. May 25, 1978, P7
Egyptian journalists investigated. May 27, 1978, P2
* Crackdown points up uncertainty. May 29, 1978, P2
* Press hit in crackdown. May 29, 1978, P2
Egyptian editor interrogated. May 30, 1978, P2
* I.M.F. vote of confidence. June 2, 1978, S4, P9
* Wafd disbands in protest. June 3, 1978, P1
* Leftists suspend activity. June 6, 1978, P3
* Court upholds leftists. June 8, 1978, P10
Writers critical of Egypt expelled. June 8, 1978, P22
Sadat's "crackdown" criticized. June 9, 1978, P26
Novelist Durrell's impressions of Egypt. June 11, 1978, S6, P42
* Sadat's image damaged. June 12, 1978, P1
Egypt details economic plan. June 14, 1978, S4, P3
Al Abram's editor questioned. June 15, 1978, P7
Egypt ambassador scores Sadat. June 20, 1978, P3
Egypt's ambassador interviewed. June 21, 1978, P3
Sadat to start independent party. July 23, 1978, P1
Police confiscate newspaper. July 13, 1978, P9

Egypt prohibits athletes from competition. July 25, 1978, P4
Egypt surveyed. July 31, 1978, P11
Soft-drink business in Egypt reported. Aug 1, 1978, S4, P1
* Tight strings on I.M.F. loan. Aug 1, 1978, P4
* Egyptian parties merge. Aug 14, 1978, P61
Sadat launches new party. Aug 15, 1978, P94
Premier journalist suspended. Aug 20, 1978, P83
* Salem resigns. Sept 2, 1978, P32
Al Ahali's problems detailed. Sept 7, 1978, P37
* Demobilization difficulties analyzed. Sept 29, 1978, P96
* New cabinet formed. Oct 5, 1978, P14

TIMES OF LONDON

* Goals of Neo-Wafd noted. Apr 20, 1978, P18

WALL STREET JOURNAL

Invest $23 billion in Egypt's sugar beet crop. July 18, 1978, P37
I.M.F. to lend Egypt $750 million. Aug 1, 1978, P4

WASHINGTON POST

* Wafdist profiled. May 6, 1978, P14
Overpopulation in Egypt analyzed. May 23, 1978, P17
* New Egyptian army in making. Oct 7, 1978, P16
Causes for high Egyptian birth rates. Oct 20, 1978, P15

Diplomacy after Jerusalem

CHRISTIAN SCIENCE MONITOR

Peace talks stalled. Feb 24, 1978, P26

FINANCIAL TIMES

Resumption of peace talks termed "dangerous." July 6, 1978, P18
* Peace prospects bleak. Aug 7, 1978, P10

MANCHESTER GUARDIAN

Impact of peace talks analyzed. Feb 5, 1978, P6

NEW YORK TIMES

* Hussein rejects current negotiations. Jan 2, 1978, P3
* Sadat to take "flexible" stand. Jan 4, 1978, P1
* Begin rejects self-determination. Jan 5, 1978, P3
* Carter, Sadat meet at Aswan. Jan 5, 1978, P1
* U.S. advances peace plan. Jan 14, 1978, P1
* Sadat discouraged. Jan 15, 1978, P6
* Vance delays visit. Jan 15, 1978, P1
* Kamel, Dayan and Vance confer. Jan 18, 1978, P1
* Foreign minister Kamel recalled. Jan 19, 1978, P1
* Egyptian-Israeli convergence seen. Jan 22, 1978, P1
* Sadat explains position. Jan 22, 1978, P1
* Egypt solicits support for peace. Jan 24, 1978, P3
* Israel continues talks. Jan 30, 1978, P1
* Sadat and Carter meet. Feb 5, 1978, P1
* Summit meeting concludes. Feb 6, 1978, P1
* Sadat scores Begin. Feb 7, 1978, P1
* Sadat, Carter conclude talks. Feb 9, 1978, P1
* Conflict on U.N. resolution. Mar 5, 1978, P1
* Begin, Sadat exchange notes. Mar 6, 1978, P1
* Egyptian, Israeli positions analyzed. Mar 7, 1978, P34
* Begin's perspective examined. Mar 10, 1978, P29
* Carter, Begin talks wind up. Mar 23, 1978, P1
* Begin appeals for support. Mar 24, 1978, P1
* Begin describes talks with Carter. Mar 25, 1978, P1
* Sadat, Weizman meet. Mar 31, 1978, P3
* Egypt scores Begin. Apr 3, 1978, P3
* Egypt asks U.S. participation. Apr 7, 1978, P2
* Redefined position analyzed. Apr 23, 1978, S4, P19
Kamel's statement on peace analyzed. May 2, 1978, P11
* Sadat proposes interim steps. May 11, 1978, P16
* Israel rejects deadline. June 1, 1978, P11
* Sadat discloses Weizman offer. June 8, 1978, P7
* Sharp reply to Sadat. June 8, 1978, P7
* Carter-Sadat meeting rumored. June 13, 1978, P7
* Cabinet statement disappoints U.S. June 19, 1978, P1
* Israeli cabinet backs Begin. June 19, 1978, P1
* Egypt pledges continued effort. June 20, 1978, P3
* Former ambassador attacks Sadat. June 20, 1978, P3

* Knesset approves statement. June 20, 1978, P1
* Ambassador pursues dictatorship charge. June 21, 1978, P3
* Stony reaction by Carter. June 21, 1978, P23
* Egypt prepares peace plan. June 25, 1978, P11
* Israel rejects Egyptian plan. June 26, 1978, P1
* Egyptian options outlined. June 27, 1978, P4
* Kamel scores rejection. June 27, 1978, P3
* Egypt firm on plan. June 29, 1978, S2, P2
* Sadat accepts U.S.invitation. July 4, 1978, P1
* Egyptian peace plan outlined. July 5, 1978, P1
* Egypt peace plan summarized. July 9, 1978, S4, P12
  Israeli-Egypt talks analyzed. July 13, 1978, P21
* Police confiscate leftist newspaper. July 13, 1978, P19
* Weizman and Sadat confer. July 14, 1978, P2
  Egypt's Kamel profiled. July 19, 1978, P3
* London talks begin. July 19, 1978, P1
* Egypt asks wider U.S. role. July 20, 1978, P6
* Vance reports on talks. July 20, 1978, P6
* U.S. planning major effort. July 21, 1978, P1
  Kamel says break-through necessary. July 22, 1978, P3
* U.S. still optimistic. July 22, 1978, P3
* Sadat asks party abolition. July 23, 1978, P1
* Israel refuses Sadat request. July 24, 1978, P1
* Egypt urges new input. July 25, 1978, P3
* Egypt orders Israeli mission withdrawn. July 27, 1978, P1
* Sadat determined on initiative. July 28, 1978, P2
* Egypt, U.S. discuss peace prospects. July 30, 1978, P8
* Sadat scores Israeli views. July 31, 1978, P3
  U.S. urges more talks. Aug 1, 1978, P1

TIMES OF LONDON

  Sadat's actions criticized. May 29, 1978, P9

WALL STREET JOURNAL

* Effect of incursion analyzed. Mar 23, 1978, P20
  Sadat's problems analyzed. May 25, 1978, P24

WASHINGTON POST

* Talks break-off analyzed. Jan 19, 1978, P20
* U.S. role seen pivotal. Feb 3, 1978, P21
  Sadat's criticism of peace analyzed. Feb 7, 1978, P16
  Carter to support Sadat. Feb 9, 1978, P25
* Egypt's mood analyzed. Mar 9, 1978, P1
  Sadat-Begin's motives reviewed. Apr 1, 1978, P13
  Egypt's strategy analyzed. May 26, 1978, P21

The Arab World Responds

CHICAGO TRIBUNE

* Hussein urges Israeli concessions. May 29, 1978, P1

MANCHESTER GUARDIAN

* Jordan's role assessed. Jan 22, 1978, P7

NEW YORK REVIEW

  Suzy Eban's impressions of Semailia. Mar 6, 1978, P70

NEW YORK TIMES

* Saudis cool to peace initiative. Jan 3, 1978, P3
* Saudi comments on peace efforts. Jan 5, 1978, P3
* Assad assails Sadat. Jan 9, 1978, P7
* Rejectionists mount oppression. Jan 20, 1978, P7
* Syria to strengthen army. Jan 25, 1978, P8
  Arab leaders' react to Egypt. Feb 1, 1978, P9
  Arab leaders plan strategy. Feb 4, 1978, P3
* Anti-Sadat summit concludes. Feb 5, 1978, P16
* Sadat's opponents divided. Feb 19, 1978, S4, P2
* Hussein rejects negotiations. Mar 5, 1978, P8
* Saudi may recognize Israel. Mar 10, 1978, S2, P16
  Syrian-Iraqi alliance seen. Mar 19, 1978, P10
* Arab League convenes meeting. Mar 28, 1978, P6
* United front asked. Mar 29, 1978, P4
* Intellectuals opposing peace initiative. Apr 30, 1978, S4, P2
* Sudan supporting Sadat. May 7, 1978, P13
* Conciliation tour ends. May 14, 1978, P28
  Decision to prosecute Sadat made. July 17, 1978, P10
  Jordan hits Israeli stance. June 20, 1978, P17

* Jordanian role questioned. June 21, 1978, P3
* Iraq backs Sadat critics. June 22, 1978, P11.
  Israel to participate in conference. July 3, 1978, P1
  Sadat-Peres split on issues. July 10, 1978, P1
  Lament Israel's rejection of peace proposal. July 11, 1978, P3
* O.A.U. scores Israel. July 13, 1978, P2
  U.S. responds to Egypt's decision. July 28, 1978, P2
* Saudi views discussed. June 29, 1978, P25
  O.A.U. scores Israel. July 13, 1978, P2
* Arab League seeks solidarity. July 28, 1978, P1
* Saudis see initiative failing. Aug 3, 1978, P6
  Arabs discuss views. Aug 28, 1978, P1

US NEWS AND WORLD REPORT

* Libya poses threat to Sadat. Apr 10, 1978, P39

WALL STREET JOURNAL

* Saudi Arabia listening quietly. Jan 27, 1978, P1
* Syrian position analyzed. Mar 2, 1978, P44

WASHINGTON POST

* Mideast instability feared. Jan 13, 1978, P20
* Diplomatic options noted. Apr 8, 1978, P21
  U.S. pressure on Israel crucial to peace. July 7, 1978, P19
* Assad denounces initiative. July 17, 1978, P15

8. ISRAEL AT THE CROSSROADS

The Political Backdrop

CHRISTIAN SCIENCE MONITOR

  Begin's decision on peace policy analyzed. Apr 5, 1978, P23
* Israeli views polled. Mar 27, 1978, P28
  Economic, social examination of Israel. July 19, 1978, S2, P1

FINANCIAL TIMES

  Break in Egyptian-Israeli talks interpreted. Jan 24, 1978, P22
  Israel's Ezer Weizman profiled. Mar 18, 1978, P28
* Intervention brings Begin support. Mar 31, 1978, P18

LOS ANGELES TIMES

* Plight of Jewish refugees stressed. June 11, 1978, S4, P1
* New alignments in Knesset reported. Sept 15, 1978, P14

NEW YORK TIMES

  Sinai settlers express outrage. Jan 2, 1978, P3
  Shmuel Katz campaigns against Begin. Jan 6, 1978, P5
* Cabinet split reported. Jan 8, 1978, P6
  Israel's Ariel Sharon's plan spurs debate. Jan 8, 1978, P6
  Dayan's role in negotiations discussed. Jan 15, 1978, S4, P3
  Hussein criticizes Israeli leaders. Jan 24, 1978, P2
  Israel's Labor Party criticizes Begin. Feb 3, 1978, P4
  Sadat's speech to Press Club reviewed. Feb 7, 1978, P1
  Dayan's interpretation of Mideast reviewed. Feb 9, 1978, P4
  Impact of Hussein's refusal to participate in talks. Feb 14, 1978, P7
* West Bank self-rule urged. Mar 4, 1978, P5
* Ezer Weizman profiled. Mar 5, 1978, P6
* Israel facing tough questions. Mar 8, 1978, P1
* Allon scores Begin stand. Mar 9, 1978, P1
* Begin's support slipping. Mar 12, 1978, P7
  Ezer Weizman profiled. Mar 16, 1978, P16
* Peace movement urged. Mar 24, 1978, P15
  Begin calls talks in U.S. "difficult." Mar 25, 1978, P1
* Demonstrators urge peace. Apr 7, 1978, P3
* Begin cabinet dynamics outlined. Apr 9, 1978, P4
* Begin supporters rally. Apr 16, 1978, P17
* Debate on resolution 242. Apr 17, 1978, P1
* Begin's policies challenged. Apr 26, 1978, P8
* 2 Israeli groups urge peace. Apr 26, 1978, P8
* Peace movement growing. Apr 30, 1978, S4, P2
  Egypt's peace gestures questioned. May 13, 1978, P3
  Eytan's views on Arabs noted. May 15, 1978, P4

Weizman's expansion plan explained. May 19, 1978, P9
* New party profiled. May 23, 1978, P2
  Begin's proposals for peace described. May 27, 1978, P1
* Cabinet debates, opposition mounts. June 5, 1978, P1
* Conscription of women debated. July 4, 1978, P2
  In-fighting in Israeli Cabinet summarized. July 18, 1978, S4, P2
* Begin, Peres clash. July 20, 1978, P1
  Moshe Dayan profiled. July 20, 1978, P8
  Labor Party questions Begin's abilities. July 22, 1978, P3
* Begin's control questioned. July 23, 1978, S4, P5
* Likud-Labor clashes increasing. July 24, 1978, P3
  Begin resistance of criticism examined. July 25, 1978, P4
* Peace group erects monument. Aug 12, 1978, P49
  D.M.C. reduces Begins strength in Parliament. Aug 24, 1978, P79
* Begin's coalition diminishes. Aug 25, 1978, P38
* Begin gains wide backing. Sept 1, 1978, P38
* "Peace Now" group profiled. Sept 12, 1978, P58
  Gush Emunim members relocate. Sept 22, 1978, P1

SAN FRANCISCO CHRONICLE

* Bedouin life style changing. Aug 27, 1978, P16

SATURDAY REVIEW

* Israel anxious about future. Mar 18, 1978, P7

TIME

* Begin retains support. Mar 6, 1978, P34
* Conscription issue shakes coalition. July 24, 1978, P32

TIMES OF LONDON

* Eban assesses Begin. Feb 3, 1978, P14
  Impact of unrest on Israeli economy. Feb 7, 1978, S2, P1
* Split in government observed. Mar 25, 1978, P15
* Israel's status evaluated. May 9, 1978, P19
* Israeli frustrations expressed. May 22, 1978, P21
  Diaspora Jewry a trend in Israeli affairs. June 8, 1978, P16
  Weizman's remarks on West Bank examined. June 20, 1978, P17

WALL STREET JOURNAL

* U.S. political intrigue rumored. Mar 27, 1978, P18
* Israeli debate characterized. Apr 12, 1978, P1
  Begin controls policies despite criticism. Aug 3, 1978, P1
  Israelis attack Begin's peace stance. Apr 12, 1978, P1

WASHINGTON POST

* Concern of Yamit citizens described. Jan 11, 1978, P1
  Begin's position in peace talks criticized. Jan 20, 1978, P17
  Sadat's criticism of Israeli proposals lauded. Feb 7, 1978, P16
* Israelis split over TV film. Feb 9, 1978, P19
  Weizman's popularity analyzed. Feb 10, 1978, P20
  Stalled negotiations in Mideast analyzed. Mar 6, 1978, P1
* Begin's stance analyzed. Mar 24, 1978, P20
* Eban scores Likud intrasigence. Mar 24, 1978, P21
  Begin's control of government supported. Apr 11, 1978, P19
  Sadat's gains at Camp David described. Sept 21, 1978, P25
  Zionist Geula Cohen profiled. Oct 11, 1978, S2, P1
  Lova Eliav profiled. Oct 12, 1978, S4, P1

The Settlements Issue

ATLANTA CONSTITUTION

Arms sale an issue in U.S.-Israel relations. Apr 28, 1978, P4

BUSINESS WEEK

U.S. foreign arms sales increase. Feb 13, 1978, P31

CHICAGO TRIBUNE

* Settlements policy outlined. Mar 11, 1978, P10

CHRISTIAN SCIENCE MONITOR

* Settlers express determination. Jan 25, 1978, P27
  New settlements on West Bank scored. Feb 2, 1978, P24
  Israel jeopardizes U.S. support. Mar 16, 1978, P35
  Israel-U.S. friendship depends on arms sale. May 15, 1978, P28
* Israeli settlements discussed. Sept 1, 1978, P12

NEW YORK TIMES

* Sinai settlers express outrage. Jan 2, 1978, P3
  Impact of peace settlement on Begin. Jan 14, 1978, P3
* Israelis polled on settlements. Jan 23, 1978, P3
* Significance of settlements underscored. Jan 25, 1978, P3
* Carter concerned over settlement. Jan 30, 1978, P1
  Approval for new settlement cited. Feb 1, 1978, P1
* New settlements reported. Feb 1, 1978, P1
* Dayan defends settlements. Feb 2, 1978, P1
* Opposition critical on settlements. Feb 3, 1978, P4
* Begin's sincerity challenged. Feb 5, 1978, S4, P1
* Shiloh settlement criticized. Feb 6, 1978, P8
  Israel to sacrifice Sinai for peace. Feb 11, 1978, P1
* U.S. Support of Israeli settlements denied. Feb 13, 1978, P1
  New settlements in Sinai halted. Feb 14, 1978, P8
* U.S. opposes Israeli settlements. Feb 14, 1978, P1
  Legality of settlements in Arab lands debated. Feb 17, 1978, P2
* Cabinet debates settlements. Feb 21, 1978, P1
* More settlements proposed. Feb 23, 1978, P6
  Unsure future in Sinai settlements. Feb 24, 1978, P2
  Israel's debate over occupied lands reviewed. Feb 26, 1978, S4, P3
* Cabinet upholds settlement policy. Feb 27, 1978, P1
* New settlement barred. Mar 2, 1978, P4
  Israelis are not to move into Kadesa Barnea. Mar 2, 1978, P4
* Weizman, Sharon in clash. Mar 8, 1978, P1
* Cabinet endorses Begin's proposals. Mar 27, 1978, P1
  Israel's return of land to Arabs lauded. Apr 2, 1978, P3
  Work on settlement Nebi Salah resumes. Apr 18, 1978, P5
* Begin pledges settlement support. Apr 25, 1978, P3
* Military chastised. May 4, 1978, P22
* Weizman proposes settlements plan. May 19, 1978, P9
* Israeli confiscation charged. May 24, 1978, P12
* West Bank settlement described. May 29, 1978, P13
* Militants found settlement. May 31, 1978, P6
  Israel's concern with occupied lands analyzed. June 1, 1978, P21
* Group demands land confiscation. June 8, 1978, P9
* Weizman, Begin clash. June 24, 1978, P3
* Government freezes settlements. Aug 15, 1978, P20
  Israel's decision to delay settlements praised. Aug 15, 1978, P167
  Impact of West Bank settlements on Israel. Aug 16, 1978, P23
* Settlements spurring political divisions. Aug 16, 1978, P23
* Settlement status disputed. Aug 18, 1978, P72
  2 West Bank settlements dedicated. Aug 19, 1978, P159
  Refusal to dismantle settlements means war. Sept 20, 1978, P59
  Opposition to West Bank removal described. Sept 23, 1978, P89
  Settlers protest removal from Sinai. Sept 26, 1978, P25

TIMES OF LONDON

Prefer peace at price of settlements. May 12, 1978, P17
Weizman criticizes Israel's West Bank policy. June 20, 1978, P17

WASHINGTON POST

Concern of Yamit citizens described. Jan 11, 1978, P1
Begin's plan to add settlements scored. Feb 2, 1978, P18
West Bank profiled. Feb 19, 1978, P4
Israel's withdraw from West Bank interpreted. Apr 18, 1978, P13
Life on West Bank described. Sept 2, 1978, P1
Removal from Diklia described. Sept 29, 1978, S4, P1
Settler's lives on Sinai described. Sept 30, 1978, S4, P1

The American Alliance

ATLANTA CONSTITUTION

* Israel risking U.S. support. Feb 21, 1978, P4

CHRISTIAN SCIENCE MONITOR

* Rabin comments on relations. Mar 28, 1978, P26

FINANCIAL TIMES

* Tougher U.S. stance urged. Feb 13, 1978, P12
  U.S.'s role in Arab-Israeli question analyzed. Feb 13, 1978, P12

* U.S.-Israeli relations at low. Feb 14, 1978, P4
* Plane sales termed logical. Feb 16, 1978, P1
  Arms sale interpreted. Feb 16, 1978, P20
  Israel's concern over jet sale. May 3, 1978, P16

LOS ANGELES TIMES

Carter's Mideast sale interpreted. Feb 23, 1978, S2, P7

MANCHESTER GUARDIAN WEEKLY

* U.S.-Israeli differences outlined. Feb 26, 1978, P13

MIAMI HERALD

* Arms sale questioned. Feb 16, 1978, P6
  Impact of arms sale interpreted. Feb 16, 1978, S1, P6
  U.S., Israel relations interpreted. Mar 26, 1978, S5, P1
* Ball questions aid to Israel. Mar 26, 1978, S5, P1
  Senate's approval of arms sale interpreted. May 15, 1978, P6

NEW YORK TIMES

* Begin condemns arms sales. Feb 9, 1978, P3
* U.S. again scores settlements. Feb 14, 1978, P1
* Package deal for Middle East. Feb 15, 1978, P1
* U.S. arms sales analyzed. Feb 15, 1978, P1
  Arms sale may trigger war. Feb 15, 1978, P10
  Dayan's view of arms sale. Feb 15, 1978, P10
* Begin asks reappraisal. Feb 16, 1978, P1
* Vance stresses "package" deal. Feb 25, 1978, P1
  All or nothing for sale. Feb 25, 1978, P1
* Weizman seeking U.S. arms. Mar 9, 1978, P14
* Memorandum on deployment issued. Mar 10, 1978, P7
* House committee opposes package. Mar 11, 1978, P1
* Pressure on Begin urged. Mar 12, 1978, S4, P19
  Begin, Dayan arrive in U.S. Mar 20, 1978, P1
* Arms sale impact weighed. Mar 23, 1978, P13
* U.S.-Israel discord analyzed. Mar 26, 1978, S4, P1
  American Jewish groups criticized. Mar 27, 1978, P19
* Congress debates package sale. Mar 31, 1978, P2
  Urge Carter to abandon sale. Apr 23, 1978, P7
* Saudi arms restriction hinted. Apr 25, 1978, P3
* Dayan downplays U.S.-Israel rift. Apr 28, 1978, P7
  U.S.-Israeli relations "not bad." Apr 28, 1978, P7
  Mideast sale may be abandoned. Apr 29, 1978, P1
* Arab lobby profiled. Apr 30, 1978, S4, P4
* Carter's contentions questioned. May 1, 1978, P21
* Carter reaffirms stance. May 1, 1978, S2, P5
* Carter celebrates Israel's anniversary. May 2, 1978, P1
* Saudi cites communist threat. May 4, 1978, P1
  Arms sales supported in Senate. May 7, 1978, P4
  Begin's U.S. visit summarized. May 7, 1978, S4, P4
  Carter's Mideast sale assessed. May 11, 1978, P22
* Saudis agree to restrictions. May 11, 1978, P1
* Senate committee votes. May 12, 1978, P1
* Senate approves arms package. May 16, 1978, P1
* Senate vote analyzed. May 16, 1978, P35
* Vote seen as Carter triumph. May 16, 1978, P1
  Senate's decision on arms sale analyzed. May 16, 1978, P1
  Wicker's analysis of arms sale. May 16, 1978, P35
  Arms sale interpreted. May 17, 1978, P23
  Impact of jet sale on McDonnell Corp. May 17, 1978, S4, P2
  U.S.'s Mideast jet sale deplored. May 17, 1978, P3
  Arms sale debate in Senate reviewed. May 21, 1978, S4, P2
  Arms sale interpreted. May 21, 1978, S4, P2
* Israel reacts to vote. May 21, 1978, P4
  U.S.-Israel arrange future of West Bank. Sept 21, 1978, P5
  U.S. suggests ways to reach peace. Oct 26, 1978, P34

WALL STREET JOURNAL

* "Message to Begin" seen. Feb 25, 1978, P1
* Carter's policies troubling U.S. Jews. Mar 2, 1978, P20
  Support for Mideast sale analyzed. May 4, 1978, P20
  Senate debate on arms sale summarized. May 12, 1978, P20
  Senate's approval of arms sale lauded. May 17, 1978, P22
  U.S.'s Mideast sale seen "damaging." May 19, 1978, P16

WASHINGTON POST

Urge U.S. to reconsider arms sale. Jan 28, 1978, P16
U.S.-Arab governments relations tenuous. Feb 3, 1978, P21
U.S.-Israeli rift hampers Mideast peace. Feb 14, 1978, P1

* Settlements undercut U.S. support. Feb 14, 1978, P1
* Plane sale decision supported. Feb 16, 1978, P18
  Impact of arms sale on peace efforts. Feb 23, 1978, P19
  Israel-U.S. relations erode. Mar 22, 1978, P16
* U.S., Israel at impasse. Mar 23, 1978, P24
  Urge Carter to defer Mideast sale. Apr 26, 1978, P26
  Arms sale supported. Apr 28, 1978, P18

9.   THE CAMP DAVID SUMMIT

AMERICAN SCHOLAR

Israeli military force overhauled. Sept 1978, P13

BUSINESS WEEK

Israel's economy analyzed. Oct 9, 1978, P60
* Mideast business benefits foreseen. Oct 9, 1978, P48

CHICAGO TRIBUNE

Pearson, Anthony. *Conspiracy of Silence: the Attack on the USS Liberty.* New York: Quarter Books, 1978. 179pp (cited in article of Aug 29, 1978, P6)

FINANCIAL TIMES

Pessimistic outlook for peace predicted. Aug 7, 1978, P10
Importance of Camp David described. Aug 10, 1978, P14
Begin's weakness told. Sept 25, 1978, P17
* Economic results of treaty examined. Oct 13, 1978, P4

JOURNAL OF COMMERCE

* Oil threat raised. Aug 11, 1978, P1
  Peace frameworks lauded. Sept 27, 1978, P4
  Oil exploration depends on peace treaty. Oct 10, 1978, P1
* Sinai oil exploration possible. Oct 10, 1978, P1
  Oil exploration on Sinai reported. Oct 20, 1978, P1

LOS ANGELES TIMES

* Egypt's economic future predicted. Oct 8, 1978, P1

NEWSWEEK

Begin interviewed. Aug 20, 1978, P34
Begin comments on Camp David. Aug 28, 1978, P34
* Carter's new popularity examined. Oct 2, 1978, P24

NEW YORK TIMES

* Peace process continuing. Aug 6, 1978, S6, P23
* Peace prospects examined. Aug 6, 1978, S4, P2
  Vance's activities in Jerusalem summarized. Aug 6, 1978, P1
* Vance and Begin hold talks. Aug 7, 1978, P1
* Vance pleased with Egyptian talks. Aug 8, 1978, P1
  Vance, Sadat hold talks. Aug 8, 1978, P1
  Begin's view of Camp David. Aug 9, 1978, P3
  Carter's meeting with Sadat, Begin interpreted. Aug 9, 1978, P1
  Egypt tells new U.S. role. Aug 9, 1978, P3
* Middle East summit announced. Aug 9, 1978, P1
  Sadat, Begin call "truce" before summit begins. Aug 10, 1978, P44
  Summit viewed as "triumph" for Sadat. Aug 10, 1978, P35
  Camp David seen as hopeful. Aug 11, 1978, P20
* Risk for Carter seen. Aug 11, 1978, P48
* Atherton arrives in Jordan. Aug 12, 1978, P82
* Rabin asks limit to U.S. role. Aug 13, 1978, P82
  New settlements on West Bank planned. Aug 14, 1978, P2
  Carter interviewed on summit. Aug 14, 1978, P36
  Envoy Atherton returns to U.S. Aug 14, 1978, P50
  Warning from Egypt to U.S. told. Aug 14, 1978, P38
  Carter to participate fully in summit. Aug 15, 1978, P152
  Delay settlements on West Bank lauded. Aug 15, 1978, P167
* US prepares for summit. Aug 16, 1978, P16
* Arab opinion surveyed. Aug 18, 1978, P146
  Arabs pessimistic over summit. Aug 18, 1978, P146

* Assad assails talks. Aug 19, 1978, P162
  Ideas to end deadlock offered. Aug 19, 1978, P51
  Dayan, Rabin comment on summit. Aug 20, 1978, P72
  Begin offers plan for agreement. Aug 21, 1978, P52
  Sadat, Begin announce intentions. Aug 23, 1978, P93
  Sadat refuses Begin's plan. Aug 24, 1978, P37
  Begin's coalition loses dovish members. Aug 25, 1978, P38
  Political implications from summit analyzed. Aug 26, 1978, P155
* Begin announces summit plans. Aug 28, 1978, P41
  Egypt-Austria talk about nuclear waste. Aug 30, 1978, P103
  May use U.S. troops for peace. Aug 31, 1978, P51
  Use of U.S. troops for peace scored. Sept 1, 1978, P163
  Begin addresses Sadat to pledge "no more wars." Sept 3, 1978, P28
  Hussein doubtful on talks. Sept 3, 1978, P76
  Begin an "obstacle" to peace, says Sadat. Sept 4, 1978, P20
  Camp David interpreted. Sept 4, 1978, P56
* Conflicting aspirations highlighted. Sept 6, 1978, P101
* P.L.O. forecasts "partial success." Sept 6, 1978, P108
* Camp David summit begins. Sept 7, 1978, P31
  Pope Paul I prays for Mideast peace. Sept 7, 1978, P38
* Arab-Soviet pact proposed. Sept 8, 1978, P23
* Progress indicated at Camp David. Sept 8, 1978, P55
* Cairenes anticipating disappointment. Sept 9, 1978, P110
  New approaches to settlement discussed. Sept 9, 1978, P19
* Separate meetings at Camp David. Sept 9, 1978, P19
  Assad's interview in *Der Spiegel* reported. Sept 11, 1978, P76
  Camp David's progress reported. Sept 11, 1978, P17
* Summit participants visit Gettysburg. Sept 11, 1978, P34
* Syrian president predicts summit failure. Sept 11, 1978, P36
* Camp David outlook bleak. Sept 12, 1978, P117
* Role for Jordan envisaged. Sept 12, 1978, P75
* Camp David results announced. Sept 18, 1978, P6
* Arabs condemn peace accords. Sept 19, 1978, P11
* Begin's action analyzed. Sept 19, 1978, P65
* Begin addresses Israeli public. Sept 19, 1978, P34
* Camp David accords analyzed. Sept 19, 1978, P21
  Camp David agreement seen as "cautious." Sept 19, 1978, P60
* Congress briefed on Mideast accords. Sept 19, 1978, P13
  Egypt, Israel compromise to reach accord. Sept 19, 1978, P21
  P.L.O., Syria hit accord. Sept 19, 1978, P7
* Sadat announces "just peace." Sept 19, 1978, P11
* Summit's political effects cited. Sept 19, 1978, P17
* U.N. cautious on Mideast accord. Sept 19, 1978, P60
* Arabs wary of accord. Sept 20, 1978, P19
  Camp David's impact on Israel. Sept 20, 1978, P55
* Carter gains new popularity. Sept 20, 1978, P14
  Israelis faced with choice. Sept 20, 1978, P29
  Failure to dismantle Sinai settlements told. Sept 20, 1978, P59
* Hussein's reaction disappoints Sadat. Sept 20, 1978, P4
  Jordanians stay aloof from accord. Sept 20, 1978, P60
  Peace accord analyzed. Sept 20, 1978, P25
* Arab potentials examined. Sept 21, 1978, P71
* Jordanian position slated. September 21, 1978, P20
* Begin reasserts Israeli claims. Sept 21, 1978, P18
  Controversy over Sinai seen in State Dept. Sept 21, 1978, P5
  Summit strategy analyzed. Sept 21, 1978, P83
* Jordanian position slated. September 21, 1978, P20
  Camp David's success examined. Sept 22, 1978, P88
  Carter-Begin dispute discussed. Sept 22, 1978, P7
* Carter letter to Sadat reported. Sept 22, 1978, P11
* Illegal Israeli squatters routed. Sept 22, 1978, P1
  $1.7 billion in Mideast aid. Sept 22, 1978, P10
* Sadat talks with Hassan. Sept 22, 1978, P12
* Vance to talk with Saudis. Sept 22, 1978, P23
  Anti-accord summit analyzed. Sept 23, 1978, P68
  Arab nations oppose Camp David. Sept 23, 1978, P68
* Arab summit interrupted. Sept 23, 1978, P68
  Camp David's impact on Arab countries. Sept 23, 1978, P53
* Camp David summit reviewed. Sept 23, 1978, P60
* Militants defy Begin. Sept 23, 1978, P89
* Three issues in dispute. Sept 23, 1978, P51
* U.S. aid to Arabs upheld. Sept 23, 1978, P18
* Vance fails with Saudis. Sept 23, 1978, P32
  Anti-Sadat conference ends. Sept 24, 1978, P20
  Egyptians cheer Sadat. Sept 24, 1978, P18
  Kissinger's comments on Camp David analyzed. Sept 24, 1978, P41
  Peace prospects assessed. Sept 24, 1978, S3, P1
  Two frameworks for peace signed. Sept 25, 1978, P10
  Vance tour concludes. Sept 25, 1978, P7
* Knesset debates accords, Sinai. Sept 26, 1978, P17
* New Arab unity seen. Sept 26, 1978, P14

* Vance tour concludes. Sept 26, 1978, P13
* Egypt launches diplomatic campaign. Sept 27, 1978, P58
* Israeli settlers demonstrate. Sept 27, 1978, P19
  Israeli troops evacuate settlement. Sept 27, 1978, P1
* U.S. Israeli differences noted. Sept 27, 1978, P36
* West Bank autonomy examined. September 27, 1978, P16
* Israeli parliament approves accords. Sept 28, 1978, P24
  U.S. forces in Mideast analyzed. Sept 28, 1978, P39
  Acceptance of accords signals peace. Sept 29, 1978, P21
  Israeli delegation to discuss peace. Sept 29, 1978, P19
* Threats to peace foretold. Sept 29, 1978, P35
* U.S. guarantees discussed. Sept 29, 1978, P67
  Begin discussion on resumption of talks. Sept 30, 1978, P17
  Carter's confidence in accord expressed. Sept 30, 1978, P3
  Egypt-Israel reach understanding on Gaza. Sept 30, 1978, P23
  Egypt's Ghali interviewed. Sept 30, 1978, P18
  Israel's Hurwitz resigns. Sept 30, 1978, 32.
* Vance assures Palestinians. Sept 30, 1978, P55
* Palestinian disappointment reported. Oct 1, 1978, P87
* Palestinians reject accord. Oct 1, 1978, P87
* P.L.O. participation asked. Oct 1, 1978, P36
  Sadat sees no barriers to talks. Oct 1, 1978, P10
  U.S. confers with Palestinians. Oct 1, 1978, P36
* Begin defends West Bank settlements. Oct 2, 1978, P33
* Hussein scores Mideast accords. Oct 2, 1978, P33
* Iraq proposes war fund. Oct 3, 1978, P25
  Offer to convene peace talks in Washington. Oct 3, 1978, P12
  Sadat urges broader participation. Oct 3, 1978, P20
* Rise in terrorism seen. Oct 4, 1978, P51
  Camp David accord interpreted. Oct 5, 1978, P52
  Fifth anniversary of Mideast War observed. Oct 7, 1978, P28
  Treaty discussion in Washington. Oct 8, 1978, P14
* Anti-Camp David summit planned. Oct 9, 1978, P7
  Egyptians see early peace. Oct 9, 1978, P16
  Iraqi President joins anti-summit meeting. Oct 9, 1978, P7
  Israeli Cabinet to discuss treaty at Washington meeting. Oct 9, 1978, P8
  Palestinians opposing accords. Oct 9, 1978, P1
  Ford's participation in summit reported. Oct 10, 1978, P34
  Sarkis seeks support from Saudis. Oct 10, 1978, P19
  Weizman's comments on peace talks reported. Oct 10, 1978, P22
* Carter discusses Mideast agreement. Oct 11, 1978, P3
* Israel planning border towns. Oct 11, 1978, P37
* Sadat scores other Arabs. Oct 11, 1978, P25
* Post-Camp David talks begin. Oct 12, 1978, P15
  Carter urges broader solution. Oct 13, 1978, P32
  U.S. offers new compromise. Oct 14, 1978, P1
  Israel's Barak's role in Camp David talks. Oct 16, 1978, P14
  New difficulties encountered. Oct 18, 1978, P3
  Peace soldiers enter Lebanon. Oct 19, 1978, P50
* Middle East talks interrupted. Oct 21, 1978, P12
* Syria, Iraq settling differences. Oct 22, 1978, P24
  Dayan presents treaty to Begin's cabinet. Oct 23, 1978, P6
  Syria reopens trade with Iraq. Oct 23, 1978, P26
  Deliberations on peace treaty reported. Oct 24, 1978, P60
* Sadat requests further study. Oct 24, 1978, P20
* New West Bank settlements announced. Oct 27, 1978, P16
* U.S. criticizes Israeli action. Oct 27, 1978, P9
* Nobel Peace Prize awarded. Oct 28, 1978, P4
* Egypt to continue negotiating. Oct 29, 1978, P7
* Syrian-Iraqi reconciliation discussed. Oct 29, 1978, P52
  Arabs to block accords. Oct 30, 1978, P10
* Begin defends settlements. Oct 30, 1978, P6
* Carter's criticism of Israeli expansion scored. Oct 30, 1978, P6
* Carter intervenes in talks. Oct 30, 1978, P12
  Alma oilfield's impact on Israel's economy. Nov 6, 1978, P77
* Arab League states its position. Nov 6, 1978, P3
* Progress reported in Mideast accords. Nov 6, 1978, P1
* Israel rejects treaty language. Nov 9, 1978, P4
* Egypt asks for timetable. Nov 11, 1978, P1
* Mayors divided on accords. Nov 11, 1978, P2
* Moderate Arabs confused. Nov 11, 1978, P2
* Israeli cabinet rejects timetable. Nov 13, 1978, P5
* Military accord made public. Nov 13, 1978, P5
  New linkage formula proposed. Nov 13, 1978, P1
* Secret commitments to Egypt denied. Nov 13, 1978, P16
  U.S. commitments to Arabs told. Nov 13, 1978, P1
  Vance-Dayan end treaty deadlock. Nov 13, 1978, P1
* Carter urges flexibility. Nov 14, 1978, P1
  Peace talk's effect on Palestinians. Nov 14, 1978, P2
  Egyptians' "flexibility" told. Nov 17, 1978, P1
  Egypt agrees to U.S. timetable. Nov 18, 1978, P6

Vance's views on treaty reported. Nov 18, 1978, P1
Weizman hopeful about peace accord. Nov 18, 1978, P6
* Israel approves treaty draft. Nov 22, 1978, P1
* Dayan seeks to close debate. Nov 23, 1978, P5
* Egyptian press publishes treaty. Nov 24, 1978, P1
* Treaty publication examined. Nov 25, 1978, P4
* Vance upholds further negotiations. Nov 25, 1978, P1
* Sadat disappointed at delay. Nov 27, 1978, P46
* Jordan, P.L.O. in parley. Nov 28, 1978, S2, P20
* Begin, staff consult. Dec 2, 1978, P4
* Mideast negotiations to resume. Dec 2, 1978, P1
* Begin suggests interpretative letters. Dec 5, 1978, P1
* Arabs demonstrate on West Bank. Dec 7, 1978, P7
* Nobel Peace Prize accepted. Dec 11, 1978, P1
* Vance reports treaty deadlock. Dec 14, 1978, P1
* Carter presses Israeli cabinet. Dec 15, 1978, P1
* Israeli cabinet statement scored. Dec 16, 1978, P1
* Israel rejects Egyptian proposals. Dec 16, 1978, P1
Egypt adopts "wait and see" attitude. Dec 17, 1978, P1
* Disorders in West Bank town. Dec 17, 1978, P3
* P.L.O. compromise related. Dec 20, 1978, P6
* P.L.O. attack kills one. Dec 22, 1978, P15

TIME

* Begin discusses Camp David accords. Oct 2, 1978, P21
* Pro-Arab bias suspected. Dec 11, 1978, P57

TIMES OF LONDON

Begin, Menachem. *White Nights: The Story of a Prisoner in Russia.*
    Katie Kaplan, trans. New York: Harper, 1979, 240pp (cited in article
    of Jan 28, 1979, P12)
Camp David interpreted. Aug 10, 1978, P13

WALL STREET JOURNAL

Summit's impact seen as doubtful. Aug 11, 1978, P10
* Camp David prospects examined. Sept 1, 1978, P8
Comprehensive accord signed. Sept 19, 1978, P1

WASHINGTON POST

Shift in emphasis at summit seen. Aug 10, 1978, P1
Pledges to stop verbal attacks received. Aug 11, 1978, P1
Rami Khouri analyzes summit. Aug 22, 1978, P22
* Mideast summit seen as shift. Sept 3, 1978, P1
* U.S. involvement foreseen in Mideast. Sept 8, 1978, P13
* Egyptian press gloomy. Sept 14, 1978, P2
Knesset braces for vote. Sept 20, 1978, P10
* Summit success analyzed. Sept 22, 1978, P17
Peace linked to U.S. policy gains. Sept 24, 1978, P19
* Arab opposition declared ineffective. Sept 26, 1978, P15
Criticism of Sadat, Begin analyzed. Sept 27, 1978, P20
* Ambivalence on accords noted. Sept 29, 1978, P17
* P.L.O. loss foreseen. Sept 30, 1978, P15
Carter's policy for peace analyzed. Oct 2, 1978, P23
Carter's success at summit recognized. Oct 7, 1978, P19
* Egyptian military change foreseen. Oct 7, 1978, P16
Arabian Moslems allowed to travel to Mecca. Oct 26, 1978, P21
* Source of Israel's anger cited. Oct 30, 1978, P23

10. THE STRATEGIC BALANCE

ATLANTA CONSTITUTION

U.S. image in Third World criticized. June 4, 1978, S3, P3

CHICAGO TRIBUNE

Shah's views of Mideast reported. May 26, 1978, S5, P2
* Soviet actions trouble Shah. May 26, 1978, S5, P2

CHRISTIAN SCIENCE MONITOR

* Soviet airlift worries monarchs. Jan 11, 1978, P1
Soviet moves assessed. Jan 30, 1978, P1
No arms to Turkey aids Soviet. May 19, 1978, P28
U.S.-Israel relationship outlined. May 25, 1978, P27
Soviet threat to oil told. Aug 14, 1978, P26

FINANCIAL TIMES

* Soviet airlift examined. Jan 19, 1978, P22

JOURNAL OF COMMERCE

Iran seen as cornerstone. Nov 7, 1978, P14

LOS ANGELES TIMES

CENTO's problems detailed. May 26, 1978, P1
Events effect Iranian oil routes. May 27, 1978, P24

MANCHESTER GUARDIAN

Soviet-U.S. relations reviewed. Jan 1, 1978, P7
U.S. pressure on Soviets urged. Jan 29, 1978, P10
* Power blocs outlined. Feb 19, 1978, P7

MIAMI HERALD

Aid to Mideast interpreted. Oct 23, 1978, P6

NATIONAL REVIEW

* Suez "not strategic." Mar 17, 1978, P33
* Kissinger comments on U.S.S.R. moves. May 26, 1978, P673
Soviet drive to Indian Ocean seen. May 26, 1978, P634
Soviet's expansion in Mideast analyzed. Aug 18, 1978, P1005

NEWSWEEK

Soviet campaign in Africa analyzed. Mar 13, 1978, P36
* Iraqi cautions over U.S.S.R. July 17, 1978, P50

NEW YORK TIMES

France-U.S. policies in Mideast reviewed. Jan 5, 1978, P6
* U.S.S.R. airlift capacity tested. Jan 8, 1978, P8
* Saudi defense capability upgraded. Jan 9, 1978, P6
U.S.S.R.'s military aid in Syria told. Jan 12, 1978, P10
U.S.-Soviet relations reviewed. Jan 15, 1978, S4, P21
* More Soviet arms to Syria. Feb 2, 1978, P4
Sadat sees conflict with Soviets. Feb 2, 1978, P7
Kremlin discusses Horn. Feb 8, 1978, P5
U.S. policy on Somali conflict reported. Feb 8, 1978, P1
U.S. rejects arms to Somalis. Feb 8, 1978, P4
Human rights in countries termed "bleak." Feb 10, 1978, P1
Human rights in U.S.-aided countries evaluated. Feb 10, 1978, P14
U.S. aid to Somalis urged. Feb 14, 1978, P1
Moroccan jet sale shelved. Feb 28, 1978, P6
* U.S. not to furnish arms. Feb 15, 1978, P9
Tass scores Carter on arms sale. Feb 16, 1978, P4
Tito and U.S. confer on Mideast. Mar 8, 1978, P3
* Israel explains defense needs. Mar 9, 1978, P14
* U.S. preparations under way. Mar 12, 1978, S4, P3
* Israel monitoring Soviet moves. Mar 26, 1978, P10
* Soviet supplies causing concern. Mar 27, 1978, P3
* Guarantees for Israel probed. Apr 9, 1978, S4, P19
* Soviet weapons displayed. Apr 13, 1978, P3
* Israeli arms use limited. Apr 14, 1978, P8
Carter's efforts in Africa analyzed. May 19, 1978, P27
* Pakistan outlook explained. May 20, 1978, P4
Role for West examined. June 1, 1978, P3
* Saudis, French meet on Africa. June 1, 1978, P7
* Carter urges embargo repeal. June 2, 1978, P1
Saudi Arabia ready for African role. June 2, 1978, P1
* U.S. weakness scored. June 8, 1978, P27
* Morocco's war debts noted. June 9, 1978, P26
* Egypt concerned over Africa. June 11, 1978, P5
U.S. advisor sees Islamic unity in Horn. June 16, 1978, P27
* Shah asks regional pact. July 3, 1978, P3
* U.S.S.R. threat to Horn told. July 3, 1978, P3
Soviet gain in S. Yemen, Afghanistan. July 9, 1978, S4, P3
U.S.S.R.'s influence rises. July 9, 1978, S4, P3
* Long-term U.S. goals assessed. July 23, 1978, S4, P18
* Soviet influence weighed. July 31, 1978, P3
House rejects $7.4 billion foreign aid. Aug 4, 1978, P26
* Aid for Syria requested. Aug 8, 1978, P7
China's Hua tours E. Europe. Aug 26, 1978, P127
Plans to bury nuclear waste in Egypt. Aug 30, 1978, P103
* Aid for Saudis asked. Aug 31, 1978, P1
* Shah and Chinese leader meet. Aug 31, 1978, P1
* Somalia, lacking aid, troubled. Sept 1, 1978, P10

Arabs react to U.S.-Israeli treaty. Sept 8, 1978, P55
* Joint base construction weighed. Sept 20, 1978, P32
* Senate approves aid. Sept 22, 1978, P10
Syrian aid debated. Sept 23, 1978, P18
* Base proposals lack support. Sept 28, 1978, P39
* Syrian aid approved. Sept 29, 1978, P10
* Embargo of Turkey ends. Oct 4, 1978, P8
* Turkey reopening U.S. base. Oct 4, 1978, P13
* New Mideast policy sought. Oct 6, 1978, P32
Brezhnev warning on Iran. Nov 20, 1978, P5
U.S. responds to Brezhnev's warning. Nov 20, 1978, P1

TIMES OF LONDON

* Pakistan reviews foreign policy. May 20, 1978, P5

US NEW AND WORLD REPORT

U.S. foreign policy analyzed. Jan 16, 1978, P80
Brzezinski interviewed. Feb 13, 1978, P28

WALL STREET JOURNAL

$326 million loans to countries reported. Mar 28, 1978, P35
Turkey's strategic importance analyzed. Apr 7, 1978, P16

Soviet influence in world examined. July 12, 1978, P20
U.S.S.R.-Cuba's involvement in Africa analyzed. May 2, 1978, P22
* Turkey's "buffer" examined. May 3, 1978, P11
W. Germans to aid Egypt. July 3, 1978, P2

WASHINGTON POST

* Carter warned on Soviets. Jan 12, 1978, P27
Conflict in arms policy discussed. Feb 18, 1978, P17
* U.S. intervention speculated. Feb 24, 1978, P21
* Soviet-Egyptian relations analyzed. Feb 25, 1978, P15
* Gulf ruler voices concern. Mar 5, 1978, P12
Propose U.S. to make base on Sinai. Mar 12, 1978, S3, P8
South Yemen threat toid. Mar 20, 1978, P21
Soviet aid to S. Yemen analyzed. Mar 20, 1978, P21
Somali sours on Saudi aid. Apr 18, 1978, P18
* Soviets entrenched in Ethiopia. Apr 25, 1978, P17
* Afghanistan coup response criticized. May 8, 1978, P23
* U.S.-Libyan deals revealed. May 18, 1978, P10
Arms sale not used politically. June 5, 1978, P23
International problems face U.S.S.R. Aug 25, 1978, P19
* U.S. influence growing. Sept 24, 1978, P19
Israeli weaponry reported. Sept 20, 1978, P10
* Moroccan king seeks aid. Nov 16, 1978, P29

Index